BUSINESS AND PROFESSIONAL COMMUNICATION:

Managing Information In An Information Age

Wallace V. Schmidt
Rollins College

Greg H. Gardner
Rollins College

SOUTH-WESTERN College Publishing

An International Thomson Publishing Company

Sponsoring Editor: Randy G. Haubner
Production Editor: Holly Terry
Production House: UpperCase Publication Services
Cover Design: Michael H. Stratton
Cover Illustration: Michael H. Stratton
Internal Design: Ellen Pettengell
Marketing Manager: Stephen E. Momper

I(T)P

International Thomson Publishing
South-Western College Publishing is an ITP Company. The trademark ITP is used under license.

1 2 3 4 5 MT 9 8 7 6 5
Printed in the United States of America

Library of Congress Cataloging-in-Publication Data:

Schmidt, Wallace V.
    Business and professional communication : managing information in an
information age / Wallace V. Schmidt, Greg H. Gardner.
        p. cm.
    Includes bibliographical references and indexes.
    ISBN 0-538-83250-9
    1. Business communication.   2. Communication in organizations.
I. Gardner, Greg.   II. Title.
HF5718.S298   1995
658.4'5—dc20   94-38520
                                                            CIP

Dedicated to

*My parents Clarence and Sylvia Schmidt
my brother Roger, my wife Susan
and my son Matt*

and

*My parents Glen and Edith Gardner
my wife Laurie and my daughter Janae
for they have taught me
what real communication is all about*

About the Authors

Wallace V. Schmidt is professor of organizational communication at Rollins College/Hamilton Holt School,Winter Park, Florida, teaching courses in communication theory, organizational communication, interviewing, conflict resolution, and intercultural communication. Previously, he has taught at Hofstra University, Texas Tech University, and The University of Texas at Tyler. He holds an M.A. from the University of Nebraska and a Ph.D. in Communications from New York University. Wally is an active member of the International Communication Association, Speech Communication Association, Association for Business Communication, Southern Speech Communication Association, Florida Communication Association, and the American Society for Training and Development. He has presented professional papers at international, national, regional, and state conferences and conducted business workshops in the areas of managerial leadership, teambuilding, interviewing, creative problem solving, presentational power, and corporate cultures and diversity in the workplace. His articles have been published in the *Australian Communication Journal, AIB Proceedings, ABC-SE Proceedings, ABC-SW Proceedings, HBO People and Communication Skills, Southern Speech Communication Journal, Texas Speech Communication Journal* and *Training.* He is co-author of *The Public Forum* and is currently writing *Contemporary Interviewing: Principles, Practices, and Procedures.* He is a nationally certified arbitrator for the Better Business Bureau and currently serves on the Board of Governors of the International and American Associations of Clinical Nutritionists. In 1992, he received the Walter E. Barden Distinguished Teaching award from Rollins College.

   Greg H. Gardner is chair and professor of organizational communication at Rollins College/Hamilton Holt School, Winter Park, Florida. He teaches courses in interpersonal communication, and public and managerial speaking, and senior seminars in organizational communication. Previously, he has taught at McKendree College, Winona State University, University of North Dakota, Northern Michigan University, Humboldt State University, and Northern Arizona University. He holds an M.A. and Ph.D. in Rhetoric and Communication Theory from Bowling Green State University. Greg is an active member of the Speech Communication Association, Association for Business Communication, Southern Speech Communication Association, Public Relations Society of America, and American Society for Training and Development. He has presented professional papers at national, regional, and state conferences, served as consultant to business and industry, and been involved in freelance speechwriting. Workshops and seminars have been conducted for business in interpersonal communication, presentational power, and effective listening. His publications include *Speaking Effectively in Public Settings, The Role of the Affirmative in Academic Debate,* and articles in the *Australian Communication Journal, Proceedings on National Issues in Higher Education, Proceedings on Non-Traditional and Interdisciplinary Programs* and *Trial Diplomacy Journal.*

They believe that the study of communication is one in which we're all practitioners. Essential to this is the recognition that the field of communication is changing rapidly and that in contemporary society there are multiple forms of discourse that require personal skill and responsibility.

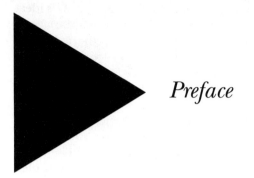

Preface

Business and Professional Communication: Managing Information in an Information Age is a practical and positive book for anyone who wants to better understand the dynamic and perplexing nature of human-to-human communication in the business and professional arena. It is for those who want to understand the basic principles and practices of communication used in the modern organization and who are ready to apply those principles and practices.

Forty years ago, P.E. Lull founded the Communication Research Center at Purdue University. Activities at this center awakened among many an interest in organizational communication and influenced its growth in departments of speech and communication throughout the country. The extensive and rapid growth and development of courses in this field of study, occurring particularly in the last few years, have resulted in a demand for texts to meet varying populations. For the most part, these textbooks are either theoretical or practical—a mutual exclusivity that isn't necessary. In this book, we integrate theoretical principles in the area of organizational communication with the practices used in myriad organizational arenas. Our purpose is to address both perspectives, and an undergraduate/professional population. We believe it offers a fresh approach.

Business and Professional Communication is written to meet special needs:

▶ It provides an awareness and understanding of organizational communication—a vital, unique, and dynamic process involving people. The factors affecting the speaker, message, channel, and audience are intimately fused with the nature or exigencies of the organizational setting. Emphasis is shifted from a simple listing of communication principles or mere reporting of theoretical data to an examination of a business arena filled with activity.

▶ It integrates recent research findings with real-life situations and practical applications. A variety of conceptual models and theoretical data are compared and placed in the organizational arena as they actually exist and change.

▶ It supplies tools for insight, understanding, and change, and develops necessary communication skills. Tools and skills fundamental to functioning effectively within organizations are introduced. When put to use, they will result in positive personal growth.

We've made a deliberate effort to write a readable text that presents its ideas coherently and lucidly. The ideas are tied together to maintain a consistent focus on the importance of effective communication. The book begins by developing a framework for organizational communication, exploring the communication process. The communication variables are then applied to the organizational context, for it is how they are uniquely influenced by the organization that constitutes the study of organizational communication. Attention is constantly placed on the human element of the organization, and this leads naturally to the specific skills required of the organizational communicator and the actual management of information. Finally, we examine change, innovation, and the overriding ethics of business. Throughout the text, articles and stories illustrate the ongoing dynamics of the business and professional arena.

We *do not* necessarily provide answers. We provide a framework that can alter the way you think about issues, help you define things in ways that are more understandable and acceptable to others, and begin a development process that can lead to new skills. We supply insight based on research and application, and offer challenging questions that prompt you to make the choices. Our purpose is to logically address and actively reach out and discover what seems to us to be a very important subject—organizational communication—the management of information in an information age.

▶ ACKNOWLEDGMENTS

Business and Professional Communication could not have been possible without the encouragement, generous support, and participation of a number of people. For their acceptance of our ideas and candid, timely suggestions for improving the text, we thank those anonymous reviewers who read early and late editions of the manuscript.

We particularly thank William J. Jordan at North Carolina State University, William J. McKeough and Charles Fleischman at Hofstra University, and Oliver L. Niehouse, president of Niehouse and Associates, for their significant contributions to selected portions of the text. Their insights and reflective thinking gave direction to the sections on interviewing, business writing, and flexible leadership.

For their camaraderie and moral support, we thank Donald Rogers, Marvin Newman, and Kim White-Mills, our colleagues in the Department of Organizational Communication at Rollins College. We further express a debt of gratitude to those who initially ignited and fanned our curiosity in communication—Professors Raymond Yeager and Tom Rickey at Bowling Green State University, and the faculties at Midland Lutheran College, the University of Nebraska, and New York University. Thanks is also expressed to Julian Kaufman, a mentor and friend.

We must also thank the many students who've enrolled in our courses over the years, particularly those at Rollins College and the Hamilton Holt School, whose personal experiences and corporate stories served as windows to the world of work. Moreover, appreciation is extended to those who participated in the three Speech Communication Association short courses we conducted in Teaching Business and Professional Communication; the interests and concerns they shared are reflected in the structure of this text.

At South-Western College Publishing Company, we thank Holly Terry and the production experts whose efforts transformed an exciting idea into a book. Where we carelessly dropped examples, stretched sentences, split infinitives, and dangled participles, Christine Cotting took a kinder, gentler approach and kept us on schedule. For their confidence in this flagship venture, we gratefully acknowledge Jeanne Busemeyer who initiated the project, general manager Mike Needham, and sponsoring editor Randy Haubner for their continued faith and encouragement.

Most importantly, we appreciate the support of our families who both encouraged us and tolerated us during the weekends and late nights of writing, with only an occasional suggestion that perhaps we should be doing something else.

W. V. S.

G. H. G.

Brief Table of Contents

Table of Contents

We live in an organized society. We are born in organizations, educated by them, and spend most of our lives working for them. An organization may be a manufacturing firm, insurance company, governmental agency, hospital, university, labor union, ski resort, public school system, church, or airline. It may be small or large, simple or complex. Effective communication is the key to entering the organizational arena. Most of us are more Don Quixote than Horatio Alger, and the modern organization is our windmill.

UNIT ONE

Communication in a Technological Society

▶ 1 Describes our emerging "information age" and defines the need for effective communication in business and the professions.

▶ 2 Presents a composite model of the communication process and discusses the salient variables.

▶ 3 Applies the communication process to the organization, examining the nature of organizations and selected managerial philosophies and theories.

▶ 4 Explores the communication climate, managerial styles, organizational structure, networks, and message flow.

CHAPTER ONE

1

Introduction to Business and Professional Communication

LEARNING OBJECTIVES:

To describe the new "information age" and discuss emerging trends

To define organizational communication and identify its major dimensions

To identify important communication competencies recognized by employers, and needed in business and the professions

To examine and illustrate the impact of new technology on changing corporate cultures

M arshall McLuhan observes in *Understanding Media* that "the effects of technology do not occur at the level of opinions or concepts, but alter 'sense ratios' or patterns of perception steadily and without resistance."[1] The emerging "information age" is steadily reshaping our perception of society and our ideas about management, organization, education, and work itself. Previous "sense ratios" are yielding to a restructuring of relationships which prompts Alvin Toffler to predict that "like the sifting and grinding of tectonic plates in advance of an earthquake, will come one of the rarest events in human history: a revolution in the very nature of power."[2] At the center of this upheaval of activity is an increasing need for information, the management of information, and the ability to communicate ideas effectively. This chapter examines our information society, focusing on the need for effective communication and the impact of technology on changing corporate cultures.

The age of "information shock" is upon us, with the amount of available information doubling every two-and-a-half years. This means 90 percent of the information accessible to workers in 2007 will have been created after 1987. A weekday edition of the *New York Times* contains more information than the average person was likely to come across in a lifetime in seventeenth-century England.[3] Marshall McLuhan has said, "We live in an electronic age in which information travels at the speed of light."[4] This explosion of information in society, the ability to access electronically nearly everything being written about anything, the rapid and continuing diffusion of computers throughout homes and offices, is literally a *revolution* in progress. Futurologist Alvin Toffler refers to this revolution as the "Third Wave of human change—the start of the new, post-smokestack civilization."[5]

As we advance into the terra incognita of tomorrow, it is important that we survey the changing landscape with its emphasis on "wholeness," cooperation, and the mutual dependence of mind, matter, and spirit. The changes currently underway will significantly impact how we manage communication in a technological society. This chapter examines our information society, the need for effective communication in business and the professions, the impact of technology and changing corporate cultures, and the scope of organizational communication. It serves as a framework for the theoretical discussion and skill development to follow.

▶ OUR INFORMATION SOCIETY

Our technological society has truly become the information society. *Forbes* magazine's latest list of the ten richest Americans, all billionaires, includes seven whose fortunes were based on media, communications, or computers—software and services rather than hardware and manufacturing. They reflect what some call the new "softnomics." Labor in this advanced economy no longer consists of working on "things," writes historian Mark Poster of the University of California–Irvine, but of "men and women acting on other men and women, or . . . people acting on information and information acting on people."[6] One out of every two Americans now works in some aspect of information processing, and no matter what the field, everyone is affected by information processing—by more machines, better systems, more trained personnel to remain more competitive.

Workers today can be more usefully grouped by the amount of information processing or "mind-work" they do as part of their jobs than by the label they wear or whether they happen to work in a store, truck, factory, hospital, or office. At the top end of what Toffler calls the "mind-work spectrum" we have the research scientist, the financial analyst, the computer programmer, and the secretary, or for that matter, the file clerk. Their individual functions differ and they work at vastly different levels of abstraction, but they move information around or generate more information. In the middle of the mind-work spectrum is a broad range of "mixed" jobs— tasks requiring the worker to perform physical labor, and to handle information. For example, the Federal Express or United Parcel Service driver handles boxes and packages, but also operates a computer at his or her side. Auto mechanics at Ford dealerships may still have greasy hands but they also use a computer system designed by Hewlett-Packard to help them in troubleshooting problems. And, although the hotel clerk, the nurse, and many others deal with people, they also spend a considerable amount of their time generating, getting, or giving out information. It is the purely manual jobs at the bottom end of the spectrum that are disappearing. As this information society unfolds, with fewer manual jobs in the economy, the "proletariat" is becoming a minority and being increasingly replaced by a "cognitariate."[7]

Brainpower has always been an essential asset, but it has never before been so important for business. Every company depends increasingly on knowledge—patents, processes, management skills, technologies, information about customers and suppliers, and old-fashioned experience. Information has become a vital asset:

▶ Corporate planners need information about scientific and technological developments; economic, political, and social trends; shifts in consumer behavior; population densities; raw materials supply data worldwide.

▶ Financial officers need information about earnings reports; public disclosure requirements; industry group capital investment patterns; merger, acquisition, and consolidation data; accounting standards and regulations; economic forecasts.

▶ Marketing executives need information about new product developments; competition; demographic profiles and social forces; consumer spending patterns.

▶ General counsels need information about status of litigation related to companies, products, and services in their field; trends in trademark, copyright and patent laws; liability and damage claims; regulatory commission activities; "privacy" legislation.

▶ Public affairs officers need information about the company's position as seen by the media, the financial press, and public interest groups; environmental activity related to the company; corporate social responsibility; shareholder relations; the public's attitudes on private enterprise.[8]

Added together, this information or knowledge is intellectual capital. Hugh Mac-Donald of ICL, the British computer maker, calls it "knowledge that exists in an organization that can be used to create differential advantage."[9] In other words, it's the sum of everything everybody in your company knows that gives you a competitive edge in the marketplace.

Knowledge has become the ultimate resource of business. To describe this change to an information age Jeffrey Hallett compares the changes in basic characteristics from agriculture- to industry- to information-based societies and economies[10] as follows:

	Agriculture	*Manufacturing*	*Information*
Dominant technology	plow	machine	computer
Science	civil engineering	mechanical engineering	bioengineering
Goal	survival	material wealth	personal growth
Output	food	goods	information
Strategic resource	land	capital	knowledge
Organizational form	family	corporation	network
Energy source	animal	fossil fuel	mind
Primary work	farmer	laborer	entrepreneur
Nature of production	self	mass	individualized

Successful organizations today are those adapting their behavior to the realities of the current environment—an environment of constant, unyielding change. As we increasingly engage in mind-work, forecasters project the following long-term societal trends in the labor force, work, and management for the twenty-first century:

Rise of knowledge industries and a knowledge-dependent society:

▶ About half of all service workers will be involved in collecting, analyzing, synthesizing, structuring, storing, or retrieving information as a basis of knowledge by the year 2000. Half of these people will be working at home.

▶ By 1995, 80% of all managers will be knowledge workers.

▶ There will continue to be vast opportunities within the computer industry for developers of hardware and software.

▶ Computer "expert systems" will issue reports and recommend actions based on data gathered electronically—all without human intervention.

▶ Computers will provide access to all the card catalogs of the world's libraries by the late 1990's. Readers will be able to call up millions of volumes from distant libraries on a PC screen. Videodiscs will enhance books by providing visual and audio information, even recording smells, tastes, and feels.

Growth of information industries, movement toward an information society:

▶ Computer competence will approach 100% in U.S. urban areas by the year 2000.

▶ Seventy percent of U.S. homes will have computers in 2001, compared with 18% today; more than three-fourths will be equipped to permit communication via network.

▶ Computers in the home means that we will have vast new powers over information and services. These increased powers will affect education, work, health care, shopping, banking and finance, etc.

▶ Personal computers will be used for voting, filing income tax returns, applying for auto license plates, and taking tests such as college entrance exams and professional accreditation.

▶ Five of the 10 fastest growing careers between now and 2001 will be computer-related, with the demand for programmers and systems analysts growing by 70%.

▶ The Integrated Services Digital Network (ISDN), an internationally agreed standard means of linking public and private networks, will change the economics of data transmission and acquisition by allowing data to be transmitted in its digital form without the expense of signal processing done by modems. This will bring data capability to the relatively small user by 2001. . . .

The typical large business will be information-based, composed of specialists who guide themselves based on information from colleagues, customers, and headquarters:

▶ Decision processes, management structure, and modes of work are being transformed as businesses take the first steps from using data to using information (data that has been analyzed and diagnosed). The advent of data-processing capability has allowed this transformation of data into information.

▶ Information-based organizations require more specialists who will be found in operations, not at corporate headquarters.

▶ Upper management will clearly state performance expectations for the organization, its parts, and its specialists, and managers will supply the feedback necessary to determine if results have met expectations.[11]

Managing information, then, may well be the single-greatest challenge facing the modern organization in the twenty-first century.

A number of commonly held myths contribute to difficulties in effectively managing information.[12] The first myth is that information is a commodity. Information can be bought and sold in the marketplace, but it cannot be "transferred" as such; rather, it is "transmitted." Once it is sold, a seller no longer possesses a commodity; not so with information—both the sender and receiver possess it.

A second commonly held myth is that information is power. Although information usually offers a greater potential for power, the critical concern for business should be how the information is used. A misguided belief that information *is* power can lead to rigidly controlling the dissemination of information and secretly stockpiling information to the detriment of the organization. The focus becomes "who knows what" rather than "how can what they know help achieve organizational goals." Sharing is a must for innovation and economic growth. Tom Peters notes that "information hoarding . . . commonplace throughout American industry, service and manufacturing alike . . . . will be an impossible millstone around the neck of tomorrow's organization."[13]

Many believe that more information is better—a third myth. There is a fundamental error in this kind of thinking. Information can never provide a 100 percent guarantee of what the future holds. No amount of information can ever provide a complete picture. And some evidence suggests that, although extra information may increase the decision maker's confidence, the net result may be that "decision makers arrive at poorer decisions but are more confident in their choices."[14]

A fourth frequently accepted myth is that information is value-free. All information is value-laden. It is always gathered for certain reasons, from different perspectives, and reported in particular contexts which alter the nature and meaning of the information. Assumptions underlie all observations and failure to recognize this can lead to uninformed decisions, premature closures of discussions, and the stifling of innovative ideas.

Finally, a fifth myth is that information is knowledge. Information does not always translate into understanding. Information is unconnected facts or data that have been fitted into categories and classification schemes or other patterns. Knowledge goes beyond the facts; it connects and explains them. Knowledge further refines information and seeks to reconcile seemingly disparate findings. Plans, theories, and models need to be set forth to organize the information until the data begin to "make sense," to have meaning. In sum, then, producing information is important, but even more important is producing knowledge and communicating it.

▶ NEED FOR EFFECTIVE COMMUNICATION IN BUSINESS AND PROFESSIONS

Communication is the life blood of an organization. The importance of effective communication to an organization's successful operation is well recognized. Almost without exception, every theory written about organizations and management has identified effective communication as a fundamental prerequisite for attaining high levels of organizational effectiveness. This is even more important as we enter an information society and management becomes increasingly aware of its responsibility for understanding, developing, and coordinating large groups of people engaged in varied activities. Mike Woodcock and Dave Francis suggest that a manager has "the power to create a nurturing, creative climate for employees, or one that leads to sterility, conformity, hostility, and rebellion."[15] Lee O. Thayer similarly notes that insofar as the administration of any organization is almost totally dependent upon communication for its execution, the effectiveness of an organization's communication system is "the best measure of the effectiveness of its administration."[16] Paul Pigors, Charles Myers, and F. T. Malm concur and further observe that "administrators of the future to do their jobs effectively, will have to develop a common language structure which represents accurately the interdependent realities of the phenomena with which they deal—technical, economic, social, and human."[17]

How, then, can effective communication systems be established and communication improved within the modern organization? Certainly an initial step is creating an awareness of the significance of effective communication for all who occupy or hope to occupy positions within organizations. Equally important is developing the requisite skills for effective communication. Vincent DiSalvo identifies those skills most frequently cited for meeting specific communication demands as: (1) listening, (2) written communication (letters, memos, written reports, proposals and requests for information), (3) oral reporting (usually one-on-one or in small groups within the organization), (4) motivating/persuading (to get people to do their jobs, to sell one's ideas to others in the organization), (5) interpersonal skills (being able to get along with people and with one's work group, to deal with people problems), (6) informational interviewing, and (7) small-group problem solving.[18]

June Smith similarly reports seven skills needed by those seeking employment in business and the professions: (1) public speaking skills, (2) knowledge of communication theory and the flow of messages through organizations, (3) interviewing skills, (4) small-group meeting skills, (5) dyadic communication skills, (6) listening skills, and (7) leadership.[19]

The results of a more recent study by Dan Curtis, Jerry Winsor, and Ronald Stephens further confirm that the skills most valued in the contemporary job-entry market are communication skills. The skills of oral communication (both interpersonal and public), listening, written communication, and the trait of enthusiasm seem most important.[20]

Dennis Dunne, Director of Communications for the Office of the Assessor in Cook County, Illinois, observed during the 1972 Summer Conference of the Speech Communication Association that "organizations need well-rounded, mature people who can relate to others."[21] Employers are increasingly recognizing the importance of communication in everyday activities.[22] They include communication, writing, interpersonal communication, problem solving, and listening as requisite skills for success in the organizational arena. Surveys of major employers reveal that the quality most sought in job applicants is proficiency in oral and written communication. Technical expertise, grade-point average, even recommendations from professors are not nearly as important as high ratings in speaking and writing ability. In 1985, the Business Forum, made up of 42 university presidents and 52 corporate chief executives, presented a report that further expanded the essential role played by communication in organizations.[23] And 12 of the most successful graduates of Virginia Polytechnic Institute's College of Engineering were asked what advice they would give incoming freshmen concerning activities and coursework, beyond science and engineering requirements, to help prepare them for their careers. Ten of the 12 specifically cited the need for training in oral communication.[24]

▶ ORGANIZATIONAL COMMUNICATION DEFINED

Communication is an interactional process in which meaning is stimulated through the sending and receiving of verbal and nonverbal messages. An organization is a social grouping that establishes task and/or interpersonal patterns of relationships for the attainment of specific objectives. Thus, our working definition of organizational communication will be the study of the flow and impact of messages within a network of interactional relationships.

T. Tortoriello, S. Blatt, and S. DeWine, 1978

Organizational communication may be defined as the display and interpretation of messages among units who are part of a particular organization. An organization is comprised of communication units in hierarchical relations to each other and functioning in an environment.

R. W. Pace, 1983

Organizational communication is an evolutionary, culturally dependent process of sharing information and creating relationships in environments designed for manageable, cooperative, goal-oriented behavior.

G. Wilson, H. Goodall, and C. Waagen, 1986

Organizational communication is the process of creating and exchanging messages within a network of inter-dependent relationships to cope with environmental uncertainty.

G. Goldhaber, 1991

Sources: T. Tortoriello, S. Blatt, and S. DeWine, *Communication in the Organization: An Applied Approach* (New York: McGraw-Hill, 1978); R. W. Pace, *Organizational Communication: Foundations for Human Resource Development* (Englewood Cliffs, NJ: Prentice Hall, 1983); G. Wilson, H. Goodall, and C. Waagen, *Organizational Communication* (New York: Harper and Row, 1986); G. Goldhaber, *Organizational Communication*, 5th ed. (Dubuque, IA: Wm. C. Brown, 1991).

Employers stress the need for both functional skills (communication and persuasion, organizational management, research and investigation, human services, information management, and design and planning) and adaptive skills (aptitude, attitude, self-management, and work habits). They further report that good verbal and written communication skills are qualities that many job applicants lack. Therefore, employers suggest among other things that educators help students to develop or improve their nontechnical skills, to develop their awareness of the demands of the workplace, and to take advantage of opportunities to apply their skills through internships or work experience.[25]

It is little wonder, then, that courses and training programs in organizational communication and business and professional speaking are considered valuable by organizations and represent the fastest growing areas within the communication discipline, if not within most academic institutions. A survey by Cal Downs and Michael Larimer cites a number of reasons for the importance of such courses:

▶ Organizational communication is a legitimate area for theoretical consideration because an organization has its unique traits which impinge on the communication process, and represents an environment in which a significant portion of communication takes place. It provides an excellent environment for the bridging of theory and practice.

- ▶ Organizational communication is significant because it represents an area for action research.
- ▶ Organizational communication is simply in demand by students.[26]

There is a widespread need for organizational communication, and all indications are that it will remain a growing area of significant interest—but what *is* organizational communication?

It is both similar to and distinct from other types of communication. Certainly the communication skills that make you an effective communicator in everyday life will assist you in being an effective communicator in the workplace. Yet, organizational communication is distinct because of the context or environment in which it occurs. It is more than the daily interactions of individuals within organizations; rather "it is the process through which organizations create and shape events."[27]

As a process, organizational communication can best be understood as an interdependent system that includes internal, external, and personal communication dimensions. *Internal dimensions* include communicating organizational objectives; expressing managerial philosophy; leadership style; decision making and problem solving; organizational structure; upward, downward, and horizontal messages; formal and informal communication flow within the organization; technology; reward system; employee motivation; organizational culture; communication climate; and all of the activities necessary to coordinate and transform personal and organizational energy into a product or service characteristic of the system. *External dimensions* include societal cultural influences, economic influences, legal and regulatory constraints, communication with customers and vendors, public relations, sales, advertising, and all of the activities necessary in exporting a product or service into the environment. (These two dimensions will be more fully examined later in Unit One.) Finally, the *personal communication dimension* includes the skills necessary for communicating in business and the professions—listening, interpersonal communication, interviewing, small-group participation, conferences, public speaking, persuading, and such writing competencies as reports, letters, memos, bulletins, and proposals. (The oral competencies of this dimension will be more fully developed in Unit Two of the text.) Taken together, then, organizational communication represents the study of a complex, dynamic, open social system through which energy flows to and from the environment via the interaction of people and messages within the system.

As we enter the information age and the perplexities involved in managing and disseminating information increase, there will be greater pressure to better understand the nature and function of organizational communication and to communicate ideas effectively. The emerging technology in computers and telecommunications will significantly influence new as well as existing organizations, affecting how we communicate and manage information. This new age will prompt changes in corporate cultures that will affect you and your work.

▶ IMPACT OF TECHNOLOGY AND CHANGING CORPORATE CULTURES

Samuel F. B. Morse sent his historic telegram—"What hath God wrought!"—opening the age of telecommunications, and starting a powerful process that is still unfolding. The latest product of this process is the computer. Today, nothing is more fun-

▶ INFORMATION SKILLS BACK IN DEMAND

By Carol Kleiman

CHICAGO—Just a decade ago, top employers looked for workers with good technical skills and stressed the importance of being expert at number crunching.

Today, that's not enough. The plethora of information that must be communicated makes the old arts of writing, speaking and listening work necessities.

These attributes are referred to by human resource managers as "good communication skills," and the phrase has become an employment buzzword of the job market of the 1990s, as necessary for engineers as for sales personnel, as essential for support staff as for supervisors and managers.

Take a look at the classified ads and you will see the change. Employers want people with "good communication skills" in jobs that range from clerical workers to hospital administrators. They want people who can read well, write clearly and speak effectively.

"With the increasing problems of public education and the high rate of illiteracy in the nation, employers more and more are asking for people with good communication skills," said Leon A. Farley, managing partner of the senior-level executive search firm in San Francisco that bears his name. "My thesis is, if you can't speak well, it means you can't think well. You need to have a clear image of what you want to say."

Lack of communication skills affects the bottom line, corporations are finding.

"Companies are finally saying it's costing us billions of dollars a year in productivity losses because employees don't know how to write or stand up and give speeches," said Roger E. Flax, president and chief executive officer of Motivational Systems, a West Orange, N.J., management and sales training firm that trains some 50,000 people a year in communication skills. "Today, it's not what you say but how you say it. It's not what you write but how you write it."

His recent survey of 200 corporate vice presidents shows they spend more than 20 percent of their time writing business communications.

Nan Kilkeary, head of Kilkeary Communications in Chicago, who helps corporations solve communication problems, says the major stumbling block is "an inability to shape information that has relevance and is sharply focused."

Some clues that you don't have good communication skills, Kilkeary said, are: "Your boss asks you to explain what you just said; no one gets your directions right; nobody comes to your presentations; and people ask you to keep your speeches short—before you give them."

"You have to practice writing and speaking because they often don't come naturally," said Judy E. Lease, assistant professor of communications at the University of Utah's college of business in Salt Lake City. "You have to start with the basics, with confidence and good interpersonal skills. If you can't communicate one on one, it's difficult to speak or write effectively."

Lease, formerly director of the management communication center of Tulane University's school of business in New Orleans, said she gives her classes assignments to make a 30-second statement and to be prepared to answer questions about it. She also assigns a media interview with a student as the person being interviewed on some major event, such as the Exxon Valdez oil spill.

"Trying to get your ideas across as clearly and concisely as possible and understanding and targeting your audience is the essence of good communication skills," Lease said.

When employers say they want good communicators, they're not looking for people who know how to joke with colleagues at the water fountain, said Paul E. Nelson, dean of the college of communication at Ohio University Athens. "They're looking for what I call high-fidelity transmitting—meaning the ability to get information from one mind to another with as little distortion as possible."

"You can learn these skills in college and in seminars. Try to learn the things you've previously shunned. People go through life saying they can't write or do public speaking and avoid them. That keeps you from learning. You won't get better unless you practice."

Source: Carol Kleiman, "Information Skills Back in Demand," *The Orlando Sentinel,* September 30, 1990, D-3. Reprinted by permission: Tribune Media Services.

damental to the future of work and careers than the computer. Jeffrey Hallett observes that "like the printing press, electric motor, internal combustion engine and the telegraph, the computer is causing a basic redefinition of society."[28] Barrie Sherman sim-

▶ PCs MAY MAKE MANAGERS MORE TYPIST THAN MANAGER

By Dennis Eskow

Increasing use of PCs and decreasing support staffs are conspiring to rob middle managers of management time, a Georgia Institute of Technology economist's analysis indicates.

Peter Sassone, an economist at Georgia Tech's Ivan Allen College of Management in Atlanta, analyzed 17 studies conducted over the past five years of managers' use of time. He said the unpublished report, compiled at the request of a client, suggests that corporations may have to redefine specialties to get the most out of managers.

"We found an increasing number of senior managers doing the work of junior professionals and even support staff," Sassone said. "It isn't just the time wasted in typing letters that should have been handled by a support person. It's the time spent in doing such non-management tasks as scheduling meetings and following up memos. This is work that can be done by junior-level people."

But the study notes that staff levels are being reduced as businesses struggle to cope with an increasingly difficult economy.

Sassone said there is a point at which the money saved by removing junior or support staffers is eaten up by the loss of management efficiency.

"Good PC planning strives to avoid forcing the manager into non-management tasks," said Darryl Stewart, senior systems consultant at MacMillan Publishing Co. in New York. "But that in itself can be difficult to control. You put the PC in the hands of the manager, and you are counting on him or her to protect their own schedules" by not getting overwhelmed with non-management chores.

But Sassone's study found that managers don't always protect their own time. Sassone said that a study of 184 managers' workdays revealed that, on average, they spent less than 27 percent of their time attending to management-level responsibilities.

Stewart said, "In the future, the best way to control the manager's use of PC time is going to be through the Executive Information System [EIS].

"By placing the PC in the manager's office and telling him or her to use the EIS, you are providing strong guidance. You are saying, 'This is a management tool.' If the EIS is the main reason for a manager to have a PC, they will be less likely to wander off into non-management areas."

Sassone agreed that keeping managers from doing non-management tasks has to be stressed by upper management. "It really boils down to corporate culture," Sassone said. "If the corporation gives a manager a computer and pulls out support staff, it is saying one thing. If it maintains support staff levels, then middle managers can delegate responsibility."

If given a choice, Sassone said, middle managers will generally allow themselves to slip into other roles, losing effectiveness as managers.

Warren Winter, systems coordinator for Pfizer Hospital Products Group Inc. in New York, said, "We have talked about what managers should be doing with computers, and we have concluded that in our company they don't give up much management time to perform clerical duties."

Sassone said, "There are a lot of progressive companies where the management role is clearly defined and managers create business plans, do personnel functions—hiring and firing—and they represent the company outside.

"But the majority of corporations today are letting the senior manager do work that an entry-level manager can do, or letting a middle manager stand in line for the photocopier or having the manager set up a meeting.

"In the future," he said, "somebody is going to have to define positions that handle the non-management functions. You don't want to settle for managers who manage 30 percent of the time."

Source: Dennis Eskow, "PCs May Make Managers More Typist Than Manager," *PC Week* (October 29, 1990): 185, 187. Reprinted from *PC Week,* copyright © 1990, Ziff-Davis Publishing Company, L.P.

ilarly notes that "it has the right to stand alongside gun powder, the steam engine, and the aeroplane as a truly major society changer."[29]

Admittedly the computer is simply a tool, an invention that enables people to accomplish tasks more efficiently and effectively than was possible before. All prior tools likewise contributed to human progress by easing and simplifying tasks. They allowed extraordinary increases in the ability to cut, stamp, roll, pound, move, press, and otherwise beat materials into submission, creating products that helped raise the standard of living. These tools and the engines that drove them were the essence of the industrial era, shaping our ideas about work and about society in general. However, the computer is unlike the tools of the past. It stimulates, assists, and expands the creative process rather than performing a specific physical chore, although applications in the area of robotics reduce the demand for manual labor. Computers have been labeled the first "meta-medium" because their programming allows us unlimited simulation possibilities.[30] They can be used to design cars, planes, and buildings, to simulate space flights, and to develop problem-solution scenarios. All of this occurs before actual construction, or the placing of people in jeopardy or personal commitment. In sum, computers are a "general, all purpose communications device."[31]

The phenomenon of computers and computer-related technologies is affecting the workplace and society in general. It is stimulating and supporting a revolution because it democratizes access to, and control over, information. Existing arrangements and rules about who can or should have access to information are not simply mechanisms of information management but rather reflect power relationships within organizations and the marketplace. Changing the rules of access to information changes the organization itself. It means that those at lower levels suddenly have the same information as those at higher levels. The power of knowing something that others do not is disappearing and is being replaced by the power of being able to do something creative, innovative, or useful with the information. IDS' Harvey Golub adds that "there's something about the culture—not just the knowledge but the way it gets applied—that gives the organization skills beyond the talent of the people."[32]

The need for more sophisticated information has contributed to increased attention being given to information analysis, presentation methods, and quality. The traditional office has given way to the network concept and to electronic office systems that use computer technology to enable information workers to simplify and streamline office work. These systems include word processing, electronic mail, voice mail, facsimile, teleconferencing, videoconferencing, desktop publishing, and telecommuting. Such tools allow office workers to effectively perform otherwise complex tasks that might not be attempted without computer support.[33] As a result, a whole new set of relationships is evolving, with the secretarial function, for example, becoming more of a professional information management occupation than that of a personal attendant. Moreover, a broad spectrum of information jobs is emerging, from chief information officer to specialist in internal or external databases, computer graphics expert, and desktop publishing editor.

Word Processing: the most widely adapted use of computers in offices is for word processing, with an estimated 75 percent of the companies in the U.S. employing some form of it today. Word processing provides a mechanism for preparing text, correcting errors or revising without retyping, and saving information for future reference without a thick paper trail. It is estimated that a secretary's productivity can be increased from 25 to 200 percent by using word processing.[34]

Electronic Mail: this transmission of messages at high speeds through such telecommunications channels as telephone lines permits a caller to leave a message in the recipient's electronic mailbox. The receiving party reviews the accumulated messages that can be called up on the computer monitor and takes appropriate action when time permits. Because 70 percent of all business phone calls are not completed, electronic mail is particularly attractive to long-distance callers with offices located throughout the U.S. and in foreign countries.[35]

Voice Mail: an alternative to electronic mail, voice mail digitizes speech dictation, stores the message on a disk, and can forward the voice output to other ones as requested. Both electronic and voice mail allow messages to be stamped for time and date of origin.

Facsimile: facsimile (FAX) is used to transmit and receive nonelectronic documents electronically. FAX machines resemble copiers in the way they work except that the copy is transmitted through existing telephone lines. Businesses are increasingly finding the need to quickly exchange images of documents between distant locations with this technology.

Tele/Videoconferencing: teleconferencing is an audioconference or updated conference call; videoconferencing includes anything from a freeze-frame or slow-scan black-and-white or color picture to full-motion black-and-white or color video. Tele/videoconferencing permits people at one location to talk to and be seen by people gathered in as many as 100 locations. Some firms have this equipment at their corporate headquarters with receiving locations at divisions scattered around the country. Satellite technology even enables corporations with offices in different countries to take advantage of tele/videoconferencing. Firms use these systems mainly for problem-solving meetings, screening interviews, formal presentations to a number of locations, and training sessions. As the technology improves and its advantages become clear, tele/videoconferencing will be used more often. But not even the most ardent advocates of the office of the future claim that electronic meetings will replace face-to-face meetings for all purposes.[36]

Desktop Publishing: desktop publishing is the design and production of stylized documents that combine text and graphics using a personal computer and laser printer. Typical desktop publishing applications include newsletters, business correspondence, reports, invoices, forms, marketing brochures, management presentations, and instructional material. Desktop publishing enables the office worker to create a high-quality document with a small amount of investment and equipment.

Telecommuting: telecommuting allows people to work at home using private data networks or information utilities, and as more and more of the tasks to be performed are information processing tasks, as the world becomes increasingly integrated, as technology allows electronic transfers of information to occur more smoothly and efficiently, it will become a technological alternative to actual commuting. The value of assembling masses of people in one place at the same time makes less and less sense. It has been estimated that the annual cost of providing office space for a single employee is between $4,000 and $6,000. In cities such as New York, Tokyo, and London, it is far greater than that. Predictions are that 10 to 30 percent of the workforce will be off-site in the year 2000. Many organizations already support some level of telecommuting, but there is general resistance because it suggests a major violation of the rules of organization and management. If people are performing their tasks at home, they can't be seen. Who knows or can control what they're doing? Moreover, managers experience a lack of purpose by not having employees reporting daily. Consequently, a powerful sense of security is still associated with the ability to see employees at their desks or workstations. But with growing pressure for any cost reductions that can make our firms and our economy more competitive, the mental resistance to telecommuting may be overcome and "electronic cottages" will be more widespread.[37]

:) Standard	:] Gleep	: l) Laughing	:-(Sad
:-[Vampire	:-Q Smoking	:-% Banker	0:-) Angel
C=:-) Chef	=!:-)= Uncle Sam	*<:-) Wearing Santa Hat	
+-:-) Pope	0-) Cyclops	7:-) Reagan	:-o) Clown
>-) Asian Smiling Face	B-) Wearing Glasses	X-(Dead	

:-)</////> Corporate-Type Guy (see the necktie?)

C=)>;*{)) A drunk, devilish chef with a toupee in an updraft, a mustache, and a double chin

Source: Bernard Blackman and Theodore Clevenger, Jr., "Use of Computer Symbols as Nonverbal Communication in Computer Bulletin Boards" (paper presented at a meeting of the Florida Communication Association, Tallahassee, FL, 1990).

"Ergonomics," the science of adapting machines and the work environment to suit workers' needs, is only now beginning to address the psychological problems of isolation, stress, and overwork. A special problem created by computers and communication with the computer is a depersonalization or "technological isolation." Human communication networks can yield to communication machines, with the user losing a vital quality of face-to-face interactions. Interestingly enough, some computer users have developed pictographs called "emoticons" or "smilies" that express personal feelings or emotions, and substitute for the otherwise missing nonverbal cues (see Exhibit 1-1). James Bach defines an emoticon as "a figure created with the symbols on a key board that is read with the head tilted to the left and used to convey the spirit in which a line of text was typed."[38] For example, :-) represents happiness, :-(is sadness, and :-0 may symbolize yawning and boredom. It seems a smile, so wondrous and complex off-line, has multiple meanings even on-line. The automation of traditional offices has also generated concerns about exposure to radiation from terminals; physical problems stemming from fatigue, eye strain, and lower back pain; and stress from overwork.

As information systems are implemented in businesses, managers face the new challenges of integrating technology and personnel to achieve the highest possible degree of productivity. But the real challenge to potential gains in productivity resides in the human and organizational element of the process, not in the technology. A major study sponsored by the National Academy of Science, National Research Council, and the Manufacturing Studies Board reached precisely the same conclusion in 1986. The report stated that the successful implementation of technology requires:

- ► a highly skilled, flexible, problem-solving, interacting and committed work force;
- ► a flexible, human and innovative management organization with fewer levels and fewer job classifications;
- ► a high retention rate of well-trained workers;
- ► a strong partnership between management and labor unions, where labor unions represent the work force;

► TRENDS OF THE TIMES: TODAY'S CITIZEN HAS 'POWER OF A POTENTATE'
By Adele Malott

John Naisbitt is the world's No. 1 hitchhiker on what he calls "the global information highway" that leads from his mountain aerie in Colorado through this decade of the 1990s, and around the world to the millennium.

Naisbitt's trend forecasts, which have been cataloged in three books—most recently in Megatrends 2000, written with his partner and wife, Patricia Aburdene—are not the stuff of Buck Rogers' science fiction. Naisbitt lives what he writes.

Although his company is headquartered in Washington, D.C., he has not been in his office for four years. He works from what he calls his "control center" in Telluride, Colo., with mountains encircling his windowed cockpit.

From this town of 1,250, Naisbitt reaches into many countries each day to pluck information and monitor global trends, telephoning Japan or Brazil and reading publications like London's *Financial Times* as easily as he calls friends next door and reads the local weekly. Using the technology of computers, cellular phones, television video, and fax machines, Naisbitt draws daily on the data in worldwide print and electronic media to find the trends people have adopted and will use to get to 2000, the thousand-year millennial gateway.

The information at his fingertips gives Citizen Naisbitt the kind of knowledge and power once accorded only kings and khans, prime ministers and potentates. And that information, Naisbitt says, gives ordinary people "a very powerful resource . . . to leverage what they're doing, and to create and communicate."

The results of that communication and creation on a global scale, he says, are apparent in our everyday lives:

► Americans eat pizza one evening and sushi the next.

► While Muscovites munch Big Macs in Moscow, Parisians reject paté for TexMex tacos.

► Residents of Ocobana, Peru, a village of 400, watch the world on battery-powered television sets even before their village has running water or electricity.

► Americans choose Benetton designs and flowing caftans, while Minnie Mouse dresses in a kimono for the opening of the all-American Disneyland in Japan.

It is this information now available about other countries and cultures that gives individuals the power of choice. And, Naisbitt says, "The number of options is how you can tell if a person or country is growing—if the options are increasing."

"Being a global citizen," Naisbitt says, "is very important as we move closer to a single-economy world in which we are not conducting trade among 160 countries, but are operating in a single marketplace."

As an example, Naisbitt points to the year 1992, when the dozen countries of the European Community drop their border requirements—for everything from customs and passports to competition for jobs and business—to create something economically like the United States in Europe.

Individual's Power Grows

Domestically, Naisbitt says, the growing power of the individual has resulted in an inverted political structure, with citizens wielding petitions and referenda, and candidates running on their own merits, leaving political parties tagging along behind to endorse the candidates who win. Naisbitt explains, "But even as we move toward a single-market world where we're so economically dependent on one another, we'll do the very human thing, and that is to assert our distinctiveness. And what distinguishes us is our language, history and our arts." It's a composite that Naisbitt calls "cultural nationalism" and is our way of treasuring our traditions and roots. It explains a burgeoning renaissance in the arts at the expense of sports—with business becoming the primary arts patron—and a growing religious reaffirmation as the millennium nears.

Age of the Entrepreneur

With the individual in charge, the entrepreneur becomes a vital factor in the changing face of the world, Naisbitt says. He points to Great Britain's former Prime Minister Margaret Thatcher and her role in returning state-controlled enterprises to the private sector through individual ownership.

Privatization, Naisbitt says, is spreading throughout the world. Although he acknowledges that the United States does not have as many opportunities for privatization as other nations, he says there are some tempting targets, such as converting Social Security to private insurance and pensions, and finding alternatives to the monopolistic U.S. Postal Service.

One new area for privatization particularly intriguing for Naisbitt is America's education system, which he describes as one created for yesterday's era, for the industrial economy, instead of one designed for the global information economy. "And the best way," he says, "to find schools that fit that new need is in free, open competition, where entrepreneurs can put forth their ideas and open a school."

To emphasize his point, Naisbitt cites surveys that show how poorly our knowledge keeps pace with the facts. He says a recent Gallup Poll, as well as many similar pools, reveals that 58 percent of Americans believe Japan has an economy larger than the United States. In truth our economy is 2 1/2 times bigger than Japan's.

Naisbitt says the present educational system is "the one dark cloud on an otherwise bright horizon because it is not customer driven . . . is not innovative . . . and it will take something like taking it private, so all schools will compete to do a better job for students." He says he is surprised at the increasing talk about privatizing of schools and is even more surprised at the positive reaction his audiences give to private entrepreneurial schools.

"One of our great educational strengths," Naisbitt says, "is our decentralization, with 15,000 to 20,000 school districts operating independently." He believes the increasing interest in educational choice means that in the very near future some district "will divide up the money spent on education and give it to the parents to spend." The result, he says, will be a district that may be "a model instructing and inspiring the rest of us."

Another great strength of the United States, Naisbitt says, is the way we "rejuvenate and enrich our talent pool." He points out that every year since 1970, the United States has allowed more legal immigration than the rest of the world combined, giving our population more youth and energy. In contrast, Naisbitt says, Japan—with its restrictive immigration policies—is getting older faster. By the end of the 1990s, he expects that the United States will have the youngest population of all the major industrial countries.

The persistently upbeat Naisbitt believes that Americans "have not even begun to experience the real potential of their fantastic human resource mix," which he promises will be their competitive edge in the global economy "as we move toward the millennium."

An Extraordinary Time

Naisbitt, who is looking forward to having fun throughout all of these changes ("Otherwise," he says, "it wouldn't be worth it") closes his latest book, *Megatrends 2000*, with this promise: "The 1990s will be an extraordinary time. The countdown—1992, 1993, 1994—is just about to begin. Get ready. You possess a front-row seat to the most challenging yet most exciting decade in the history of civilization."

Source: Adele Malott, "Trends of the Times: Today's Citizen Has 'Power of a Potentate,'" *Friendly Exchange* (Fall 1991): 31–33. Reprinted by permission of *Friendly Exchange,* the magazine of Farmers Insurance Group of Companies © 1991.

▶ unprecedented efforts to communicate thoroughly to employees the competitive realities of the business, the conditions requiring advanced manufacturing technology, and the plans for implementing it;

▶ employee participation in the implementation activities;

▶ broad training that begins before assignment to the project.[39]

Robert Kurtz, a former GE officer and chairman of the Manufacturing Studies Board, further stated in the introduction to the report that ". . . without changes in corporate culture, organizational structures and human resource management, new technologies will not produce the results needed for competitive manufacturing."[40] In other words, it's the people that make the difference—now and in the future. The challenges created by this information age are far more difficult than plugging in a new machine—they require creative thinking, new attitudes, and a willingness to embrace change.

► SUMMARY

The new information environment affects all forms of work. Certainly the most life-threatening disease facing management is the lack of the right information. Consequently, establishing an effective communication system and developing effective communication skills are essentials rather than luxuries. Gerald Goldhaber, after concluding an eight-year study of the public and private sectors, places organizations in one of four categories, depending on the stability of the environment and the effectiveness of their communication system:

1. Is the organization in a state of *proactive relaxation,* in which the environment is relatively stable and the communication system is very effective? Is it experiencing a "honeymoon period" in which it may be lulled into complacency? As with most marriages, wait until the honeymoon ends!
2. Is the organization in a state of *proactive coping,* in which the environment is highly uncertain? Conditions within and outside the organization are changing rapidly and the effects of the changes are felt directly on the organization and its communication system. However, the organization is equipped with a highly effective communication system and can cope with these changes, just as a good marriage is equipped to handle the instability of living.
3. Is the organization in a state of *reactive hibernation,* in which the environment is stable, but the communication system is ill suited to cope with any sudden and dramatic changes? Similar to a time bomb ticking away, organizations in hibernation are about to explode the moment the environment changes.
4. Finally, is the organization in a state of *reactive stress,* in which the environment becomes highly unstable and the communication system is unable to cope? The explosion has occurred and collapse is inevitable.[41]

The turbulence and uncertainty of this new age demand that organizations hoping to achieve their objectives engage in proactive coping. And, it is the strategies and techniques of proactive coping that have begun to shape the study of organizational communication.

The dramatic changes we are experiencing point to the importance of an educated workforce. Once jobs could be filled by anyone willing to do the physical work associated with them. In the future, there will be precious few of those opportunities. To varying degrees, all activities will employ the new potentials represented by computers and other aspects of information handling. Effective oral and written communication competencies will be premium qualities possessed by those engaged in this mind-work.

Because this is a new age, we cannot expect to understand it fully or to project with high degrees of certainty. What must be embraced, however, is a real willingness to change, to learn, and to accept uncertainty as the norm. How do you read the following line?

OPPORTUNITYISNOWHERE

Some may see it as "opportunity is no where." We suggest that it be read as "opportunity is now here." Unbelievable opportunities lie ahead for those with a positive perspective and there is much to look forward to. The curtain is just now beginning to rise on a marvelous future.

► QUESTIONS FOR DISCUSSION AND SKILL DEVELOPMENT

1. Think of an organization for which you've worked and with which you are quite familiar. List the differing roles and functions that people assume and perform within the organization. For each role, what types of information are processed daily? By what means? How are communication, technology and job design related? What critical functions does communication serve within the organization? In your view, which is most important for the maintenance and growth of the organization?

2. How would you define "organizational communication"? What communication skills do you consider to be most important to business and the professions? Select three people from the following categories: a friend; a corporate officer, manager/supervisor, or professional; and a communication specialist from consulting, training, or teaching. How does each define the term "organizational communication"? What communication skills does each consider to be most important? How are their responses similar/different from one another's as well as yours? Explain.

3. List all technological improvements which have become part of the modern organizational structure. What are the advantages and disadvantages of each? What implications do your observations have for managers in organizations?

4. What future trends do you foresee?

▶ NOTES

1. Marshall McLuhan, *Understanding Media* (New York: Signet Books, 1964): 35.
2. Alvin Toffler, *Powershift* (New York: Bantam Books, 1990): 4.
3. R. S. Wurman, *Information Anxiety* (New York: Doubleday, 1989).
4. Marshall McLuhan, *The Gutenberg Galaxy* (New York: Signet Books, 1962): 43
5. Toffler, *Powershift*, xx.
6. Ibid., 9.
7. Ibid., 75.
8. Gerald M. Goldhaber, "Communication Strategies: Pathways to Corporate Power" (Address delivered to the PRSA Institute, Arden House, Harriman, NY, September 24, 1981).
9. Thomas A. Stewart, "Brainpower," *Fortune* (June 3, 1991): 44–60.
10. Jeffrey J. Hallett, *Worklife Visions* (Alexandria, VA: American Society for Personnel Administration, 1987): 23.
11. Marvin J. Cetron, Wanda Rocha, and Rebecca Luchins, "Into the 21st Century: Long-Term Trends Affecting the United States," *The Futurist* (July-August 1988): 29–40. Courtesy of *The Futurist*, World Future Society, 7910 Woodmont Ave., Suite 450, Bethesda, MD 20897.
12. Phillip G. Clampitt, *Communicating for Managerial Effectiveness* (Newbury Park, CA: Sage, 1991): 75–78.
13. Tom Peters, *Thriving on Chaos* (New York: Harper and Row, 1987): 610.
14. C. A. O'Reilly, J. A. Chatman, and J. C. Anderson, "Message Flow and Decision Making," in: F. M. Jablin, L. L. Putnam, K. H. Roberts, and L. W. Porter, eds., *Handbook of Organizational Communication* (Newbury Park, CA: Sage, 1987): 600–623.
15. Mike Woodcock and Dave Francis, *Unlocking Your Organization* (Lafolla, CA: University Associates, 1978): 53.
16. Lee O. Thayer, *Administrative Communication* (Homewood, IL: Richard D. Irwin, 1961): 3.
17. Paul Pigors, Charles Myers, and F. T. Malm, *Management of Human Resources: Readings in Personnel Administration*, 3rd ed. (New York: McGraw-Hill, 1975): 128.
18. Vincent DiSalvo, "A Summary of Current Research Identifying Communication Skills in Various Organizational Contexts," *Communication Education* 29 (1980): 283–290.
19. June Smith, *An Examination of the Status of Organizational Communication Programs in Texas Colleges and Universities* (Houston, TX: Texas Speech Communication Association, 1982).
20. Dan B. Curtis, Jerry L. Winsor, and Ronald D. Stephens, "National Preferences in Business and Communication Education," *Communication Education* 38 (1989): 6–14.
21. Dennis Dunne, "Careers in Communication" (Paper presented at the Speech Communication Association Summer Conference, Chicago, IL, 1972).
22. L. Barker, J. Edwards, C. Gains, K. Gladney, and F. Holley, "An Investigation of Proportional Time Spent in Various Communication Activities by College Students," *Journal of Applied Communication Research* 8 (1980): 101–109.

23. "Business Forum," *USA Today,* May 20, 1985, B-1.

24. L. Nystrom, *Engineering Now* (Blackburg, VA: College of Engineering, Virginia Polytechnic Institute and State University, 1983).

25. C. Murphy and L. Jenks, *Getting a Job—What Skills Are Needed?* (San Francisco: Far West Lab for Educational Research and Development, 1982).

26. Cal Downs and Michael W. Larimer, "The Status of Organizational Communication in Speech Departments," *Speech Teacher* 23 (1974): 325–329.

27. Pamela Shockley-Zalabak, *Fundamentals of Organizational Communication,* 2nd ed. (New York: Longman Publishing, 1991): 31.

28. Hallett, *Worklife Visions,* 63.

29. Barrie Sherman, *The New Revolution* (Chichester, NY: John Wiley & Sons, 1985): 21.

30. Donald E. Williams, "Rhetorically Acculturating the Computer as a Given of Society," *American Behavioral Scientist* 32 (1988): 208–222.

31. Werner J. Severin, *Communication Theories* (New York: Longman Publishing, 1988).

32. Stewart, "Brainpower," 60.

33. Thomas H. Athey and Robert W. Zmud, *Computer and Information Systems,* 2nd ed. (Glenview, IL: Scott, Foresman, 1988).

34. Thomas V. Dock and James C. Wetherbe, *Computer Information Systems for Business* (St. Paul, MN: West Publishing, 1988).

35. John J. Cornell, "Managing Human Factors in the Automated Office," *Modern Office Procedures* 27 (1982): 51–64.

36. Dock and Wetherbe, *Computer Information Systems.*

37. R. A. Hirschheim, *Office Automation: A Social and Organizational Perspective* (New York: John Wiley & Sons, 1985.

38. Bernard Blackman and Theodore Clevenger, Jr., "Use of Computer Symbols as Nonverbal Communication in Computer Bulletin Boards" (Paper presented at a meeting of the Florida Communication Association, Tallahassee, FL, 1990).

39. *Toward a New Era in Manufacturing* (Washington, D.C.: National Academy Press, 1986).

40. Ibid.

41. Goldhaber, "Communication Strategies."

C H A P T E R   T W O

2

The Process of Communication

LEARNING OBJECTIVES:

To define communication

To discuss selected communication models and increase understanding of the communication process

To distinguish between meaning and the symbols that stimulate meaning, recognizing that meaning exists only in people

To discuss how our nonverbal behaviors influence the communication process

To identify and select appropriate channels of communication

To use feedback as a self-monitoring instrument in communication

ommunication is perhaps the most complex structure we engage in. A knowledge of basic communication principles is necessary to understand how communication functions within business and professional settings. This chapter provides a fundamental framework within which to consider the dynamics involved when communicating with others.

Communication has emerged as a necessary object of attention in the twentieth century, not because it is new but because the advent of modern technology has rendered certain types of communication unwieldy or virtually obsolete. Primitive human existence was dependent upon oral–aural skills. Tribal men and women lived in essentially a speaking and listening culture with survival dependent upon the exercising of these skills. With the invention of the printing process, Western civilization and its communication were radically altered. The eye became dominant, with reading and writing the principal communication forms. Today we are returning to an oral–aural culture because of developments in electronic technology and a growing sense that written communication is inefficient and ineffective. The visual communication skills developed by the civilized world are now in conflict with the emerging trend toward oral–aural processes. Marshall McLuhan observes that civilization gave "the barbarian or tribal man an eye for an ear"[1] which is not at odds with our increasingly electronic world where communication is rapid. Previous communication barriers are being broken down and a "global village" is being created. Space satellites, the ability to conduct conference calls anywhere in the world, and our emerging computer technology all make international communication more accessible and contribute to our changing communication processes.

Studies estimate that executives, managers, and supervisors spend at least 75 percent of their time at work communicating. Thirty hours of every 40-hour week are spent writing and speaking, reading and listening. The remaining ten hours are spent carrying out activities based on this communication. These studies further indicate that 90 percent of all communication is oral and each time there is oral communication at least one listener and often more are present.[2] There is an increasing trend to rely more upon human-to-human communication.

▶ COMMUNICATION DEFINED

What do we mean by communication? Some might consider it to be the sending of ideas from one person to another. Others might say that it is people sending messages for particular purposes in particular settings. Each of these definitions calls attention to important variables, but communication is a more complex process: more than people interacting, more than message sending. It is also more than a natural ability, knack, or easily acquired behavior. It is an activity we regularly engage in and which requires careful attention. Communicating effectively is a lifelong learning process.

Here we define communication as essentially the sharing of ideas and self with others in a particular setting. This definition is in keeping with the *Oxford English Dictionary* which notes that the Latin root of communication means "to make common to many, share."[3] According to this definition, when people communicate effectively they express their ideas and feelings in a way that is understandable to each of them. Each has a direct effect on the other and on subsequent communication. Therefore, communication is an interactive process of mutual influence. Viewing communication as a process suggests that it is a planned behavior and makes clear that intentions are a necessary element. The notion of communication plans defines when human behavior represents communication and when it does not. A plan is a set of behaviors that accomplish a particular purpose. The plans we form are controlled by our beliefs, attitudes, and values.[4]

Accepting communication as being planned helps us recognize that human communication is *transactional*. By this we mean communication involves people sending each other messages which reflect the motivations of the participants. We expect people to react to our messages and we, in turn, respond to theirs. When we communicate, we try to affect our environment and we understand that others also communicate to exert such influence. We anticipate a give-and-take in communication—an interaction of human motivations. Human-to-human communication, then, represents a complex, dynamic process in which a variety of elements and variables interact to produce effects. Unfortunately, many people mistakenly view human communication as an elementary operation which can be taken for granted, a perception that frequently leads to costly misunderstandings and communication breakdowns. We forget that human communication is a major means of identification with others and a principle skill we possess for adapting to our world and influencing the world around us. Communication is also extremely important in enabling people to coordinate their efforts and to produce a variety of goods and services that would not be produced if people worked independently.

▶ BASIC MODELS OF HUMAN COMMUNICATION

Just as there are numerous definitions of communication, there is no single comprehensive model of the communication process. Here, we will look at representative models that permit at least a peek at the overall communication process and can contribute to the development of a composite model and a discussion of the basic components included in most communication models.

Shannon-Weaver Model

The Shannon-Weaver model (Exhibit 2-1) represents a contemporary linear view which has done much to advance the *information theory* approach to communication. They describe information theory as "exceedingly general in its scope, fundamental in the problems it treats, and of classic simplicity and power in the results it reaches."[5] "Information," in the information theory sense of the word, should not be confused with "information" as it is usually understood. Conventionally, information is thought of as what we know; we think of information in terms of meaning. Information theorists define information as "a measure of one's freedom of choice when one selects a message," so information "refers not to the content contained in a message but to all possible messages that could be transmitted."[6] Information, then, is equated with uncertainty and its reduction. Through information theory, concepts such as channel (the communication medium) and noise (interference) are introduced as part and parcel of the communication process.

Shannon and Weaver describe what happens to the information in a message from the time it is transmitted by a source until it is received at a destination. This model presents a system in which a *transmitter* acts upon information from a *source* to put it into a *channel* in the form of a *signal*. This signal, together with additional stimuli called *noise*, is picked up by the receiver at a *destination*.

The source is the originator of a message—it may be you, your supervisor, or an employee. The message may consist of spoken or written words, music, pictures, or anything else. The transmitter converts the message to a signal suitable for the chan-

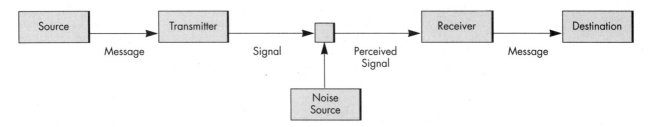

nel to be used. The channel is the medium that transmits the signal from the transmitter to the receiver. It may be air and sound waves, as in speech communication; print, as in memos and letters; or air, light, and electronic impulses, as in computers or television. Within any channel there are potentially interfering obstacles to communication that are generally referred to as noise. Noise may be any type of interference. It may be the physical disturbance created by machinery or telephones ringing, or the psychological distractions resulting from established beliefs, prior attitudes, personal prejudices or biases. The receiver performs the inverse operation of the transmitter by reconstructing the message from the signal. The destination is the person for whom the message is intended. Although a receiver shares a number of characteristics with the source, at the same time the receiver is an individual with unique experiences, beliefs, attitudes, values, and desires. Consequently, the message or idea received cannot be identical but only similar to that sent.

The Shannon-Weaver model contributes to our understanding of several important concepts. It gives a precise meaning to the term information and the notion of a message composed of entropy and redundancy and the necessary balance between them for efficient communication. *Entropy* is the degree of randomness, lack of organization, disorder or uncertainty in a situation. The more entropy in a system, the less predictability. The less predictability, the greater the potential information, because you need more messages to predict the outcome of a complex situation than of a simple one. *Redundancy* reduces the relative entropy of the message through consistency and repetition. When talking with someone in a noisy environment or explaining a complicated idea, you probably find it necessary to repeat and rephrase key portions of the message to ensure reception. Using redundancy to overcome the noise in the channel reduces the amount of information that can be transmitted in a given time.

Information theory also introduced a word to our vocabulary that is being heard with greater frequency today—"bit." A bit is a measure of the actual amount of information in a message. Bit comes from condensing the term "binary digit." Computers make use of this binary code. The information theory approach to communication is especially useful for theorizing about message transmission using computers and the electronic media.

Critics of this approach to communication argue that it has limited utility when applied to human communication. It does not deal with meaning in a conventional sense, and meaning is most important in the context of human communication. Information theory is essentially a mathematical approach, concentrating on the transfer of electronic signals. Feedback and the notion of communication being a two-way process is not addressed. Yet, the Shannon-Weaver model has provided us with a rich set of concepts and propositions to draw upon.

Berlo Model

Berlo synthesizes the major components of the earlier linear approaches in developing the Source-Message-Channel-Receiver (S-M-C-R) model of communication (Exhibit 2-2).[7] His might be considered a "hi-fidelic" model because it sets forth the major variables involved and describes the overlying structure of the communication process without suggesting specific relationships among the variables.

According to Berlo's model, the main responsibility for creating the message lies with the source. The source may be an individual or an entire organization, although

S	**M**	**C**	**R**
Source	Message	Channel	Receiver
Communication Skills	Content	Seeing	Communication Skills
Attitudes	Treatment	Hearing	Attitudes
Knowledge	Code	Touching	Knowledge
Social System		Smelling	Social System
Culture		Tasting	Culture

the traditional focus has been on the individual. The communicator who originates the message possesses communication skills, needs, attitudes, and knowledge within a particular social-cultural system. The second major communication variable is the message. Messages are stimuli transmitted by sources. They are transmitted both verbally and nonverbally, intentionally and unintentionally, and they often involve the transmission of attitudes as well as ideas. The channel, the means by which messages travel from source to receiver, is the third variable considered in Berlo's model. Each of us uses a variety of channels when sending and receiving messages. You might choose a written channel (memo), a face-to-face encounter (conference), or an electronic medium (telephone). Our primary senses of sight, hearing, touch, taste, and smell also represent channels of communication. Within any channel exist potentially interfering variables referred to as noise. Finally, the model focuses on the receiver. The message conveyed via a channel is received by a receiver who also possesses certain communication skills, needs, attitudes, knowledge, and social-economic-cultural perspectives.

Berlo does a great deal more than simply synthesize current theoretical concepts He advances the notion of communication as a process. This approach has dramatically influenced the study of communication for the past three decades. Communication definitions that describe it as the process of exchanging symbols or a process in which many interrelated variables influence each other reflect Berlo's influence.

A process orientation to communication focuses on the interdependence of variables. This approach suggests that events and relationships are dynamic, continuous, and constantly changing. All of the factors involved in a process are in continuous interaction with each other simultaneously; all of the variables affect and influence each other. In this context, communication is without a distinct beginning, an end, or a set of boundaries.

Composite Model

The communication models examined thus far have been linear in nature or have presented human-to-human communication as a circular response. Frank E. X. Dance makes an astute observation regarding such models:

> The linear model does well in directing our attention to the forward direction of communication and to the fact that a word once uttered cannot be recalled. The changing aspect of communication is also implied in a linear model. However, the linear image betrays reality in not providing for a modification of communicative behavior in the future based upon communicative success or shortcomings in the past.

The circular communication image does an excellent job of making the point that what and how one communicates has an effect that may alter future communication. The main shortcoming of this circular model is that, if accurately understood, it also suggests that communication comes back full-circle, to exactly the same point from which it started.[18]

Dance succinctly places the previous models in perspective and suggests there is probably little hope for developing a completely isomorphic geometric model of something as complex as human communication. Although not perfect, the following composite model (Exhibit 2-3) can help us better visualize the communication process.[9] It integrates previously discussed variables with additional factors that influence human-to-human communication.

This model presents communication as a progression of interactions between two *semantic reactors* or people occupying a world of symbols. When communicating, we react at many levels. The momentum of our accumulated past, the drawing power of our anticipated future, and the influence of an immediate present all affect our message(s). Communication is not simply an exchange of information, but the encounter of two or more people "psycho-logically." Needs, attitudes, and feelings are transmitted as signals through a channel or medium. Noise within the channel can disrupt and distort the message(s) received. This necessitates *feedback* as a means of evaluating and shaping further messages. Communication consists, therefore, of mutually selecting, arranging, and transmitting meaningful symbols. These *transactional* exchanges of symbols bring the participants together in an integral relationship that is constantly being redefined.

The *helix* suggests that no two interactions can ever repeat themselves as exact duplicates. It gives "geometric testimony to the concept that communication, while moving forward, is at the same moment coming back upon itself and being affected by its past behavior."[10] Human communication viewed in a helical fashion is always progressing upward because of increased sensitivities, even as it turns upon itself and is affected by its own past conformations. As communication continues, the helix grows larger in circumference, symbolizing increasing understanding, awareness, trust, and competency.

▶ **EXHIBIT 2-3**
Composite Model

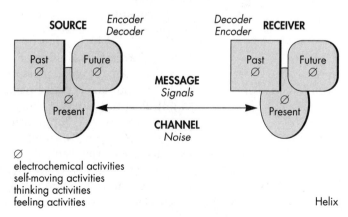

This composite model represents a cumulative image of communication. It reflects the following principles which we believe characterize the communication process:

1. Communication is a complex and dynamic process.
2. Communication is a bidirectional and helical exchange of symbols.
3. Communication is a purposeful transaction between people.
4. Communication is a multidimensional progression.
5. Communication is a continuous and irreversible series of actions.

In the remainder of the chapter, we will explore these principles further and take a closer look at the factors and processes presented.

▶ COMPONENTS OF THE COMMUNICATION PROCESS

Communication competency requires "the ability and willingness of an individual to participate responsibly in a transaction in such a way as to maximize the outcomes of shared meanings."[11] In other words, it involves a personal commitment to mutually sharing/understanding meaning(s) with others. Regardless of whether you are communicating with only one person, a small group, or many people, the basic process of communication with its potential problems and misunderstandings remains the same. Communication competency can be improved and problems and misunderstandings minimized by an awareness of the essential factors involved when communicating with others and by understanding the dynamics of the communication event. The basic integrating elements of communication include: source factors, message factors, channel factors, receiver factors, and environmental factors.

Source Factors

Communication includes all of the factors that are brought into play upon and by a person as he or she attempts to establish relationships with others. A communication relationship represents a unique reciprocal bond with another person, a bond shaped by those participating and, at the same time, revealing the participants. The limits of communication are mutually established and, during the course of communicating, personal intentions, attitudes, and values are disclosed. There are several source elements affecting the communication process which deserve attention: electrochemical activities, self-moving activities, thinking activities, feeling activities, the present environment, the past, and the future.

Electrochemical Activities. Electrochemical activities—which include the physiological elements of blood pressure, pulse, blood sugar, hemoglobin levels, and amino acid concentrations—and circadian or life rhythms affect our moods and our communication with others. These activities represent an intrapersonal communication system whereby we communicate with ourselves; we are both message creator and message consumer. This internal communication system can be measured by physicians using electroencephalograms, isotope tracing, and other such techniques. Scientists have suggested that we all can become more attuned to inner body rhythms that affect our daily behavior,[12] and such knowledge can help us lessen tensions and relieve stress when dealing with others or deliberating decisions.

Self-Moving Activities. Self-moving activities refer to the functioning of vital organs as well as the bodily mechanisms used to produce sound, written symbols, facial expressions, gestures, and physical movement. Included also are the activities we engage in daily in adjusting to our environment. How you express yourself through speech or writing and the use of gestures and physical movement affects your message and influences others.

Thinking Activities. Thinking activities involve our abilities to reason, conceptualize, solve problems, and reach decisions. They affect the entire communication process, influencing our speaking, listening, reading, and writing skills. You are judged to be intelligent or unintelligent, reasonable or unreasonable, capable or incapable, based upon your thinking abilities as communicated to others. Your thinking abilities determine your mental proficiency.

Feeling Activities. Feeling activities represent those individual psychological elements that motivate and give direction to our behavior. We all possess personal drives and instincts, needs, attitudes, and values. These affect our purposes, ambitions, desires, and reactions. Our feeling activities comprise love and hate, joy and sorrow, commitment and indifference, trust and contempt, and the many levels of aspiration, satisfaction, and frustration. Your internal emotions expressed externally affect your messages to and responses from others.

Present Environment. We all occupy a place in a world of symbols which represents our immediate environment. This environmental setting is fundamental to the communication process because, as David Berlo observes, "social and cultural systems partly determine the word choices which people make, the purposes they have for communication, the meanings they attach to certain words, their choice of receivers, the channels they use for this or that kind of message."[13] This environment has many aspects: physical, psychological, social, cultural, professional, racial, and national. Your environment influences what, to whom, how, and why you communicate.

The Past. We may share an immediate setting with others, but we also possess individual images and personal experiences—a past. Your past influences your perceptions. For example, if you enjoyed working with a fellow student or coworker on a project, you might look forward to working with that person again; or, if the experience was less than positive, your next meeting probably will be characterized by hesitancy, reluctance, and apprehension. Although the present is the center of communication activity, the past as it was and as you imagined it significantly affects your communication behavior. For example, how and where you were raised determines to a large measure what you consider to be "normal." Or, what you grew up without may influence what you value. *Perception* is the process by which you select some things from your environment, organize those selections into a pattern, and then interpret that pattern or give meaning to what you have seen. Past experiences influence how you pattern and interpret current events. Similarly, your past influences your values, attitudes, beliefs, language–nonlanguage, codes of behavior, response behavior, initiative behavior, roles, and expectations.

The Future. Finally, we are all influenced by an anticipated future. Immediate and long-range goals shape our communication with others. Whether in a family set-

▶ WHILE BODY RESTS, DREAMS GO TO WORK

By Linda Shrieves

You awaken, sweaty and nervous, the victim of a terrible dream.

Your boss, the company tyrant, was shoving a boulder onto your shoulders and demanding that you carry this monstrosity up five flights of stairs. In the background stand your co-workers, laughing and pointing at you, the office pack mule.

Before you make your last halting steps toward the stairs, your back straining and your knees threatening to buckle, the boss adds one final threat: Fail to make it to the top and you"re fired.

Welcome to the dream world of work, brought to you regularly, if not nightly, by your brainstem. Cognizant of your memories, fears and anxieties, the brain draws on everyday behavior, emotions and settings to produce those elaborate plays each night.

And, as many people well know, work is the stuff dreams are made of.

People dream about conflicts with co-workers, about the project that has so far stumped them, about bizarre scenarios that hold some meaning or ideas about work.

Robert Louis Stevenson said he got the idea for Dr. Jekyll and Mr. Hyde from a dream. Elias Howe, who was struggling to invent a sewing machine, dreamed that he was captured by savages carrying spears with holes in their tips—the idea that inspired him to thread the needle at its end, not the middle.

And, though this sounds weird, dream researchers say all those work dreams are not at all strange.

"What you tend to dream about are those activities that preoccupy you and, because most of us are involved in the world of work, it occupies many of our dreams," says Dr. Milton Kramer, director of the Sleep Disorders Center of Greater Cincinnati. If you take large samples of dreams what you find is that they reflect the day-to-day activity of the dreamer

"Most of us dream about going to work and being late, about being left out of meetings," Kramer said. "In one study, researchers decided to collect the dreams of college kids. Well, what they reflected were the lives of college kids."

Not nearly as exotic as you would like to think.

Still, even work dreams tend toward the fantastic—because the brain sometimes expresses hidden feelings in metaphors that aren't always clear.

Take, for instance, the college professor who was in the process of creating a women's studies department. Deep down, she felt ambivalent about the university's male-dominated hierarchy and its dedication to a women's studies department.

In a dream this female professor saw herself building a beauty salon and teaching students how to become beauticians. Hidden behind the metaphors, said dream researchers, was her feeling that the university's administrators privately ridiculed the formation of a women's studies department.

Metaphors, such as the beauty shop, frequently appear in dreams. "A dream about the workplace could be metaphorical or an actual scenario," Kramer said. "The work situation can become a metaphor for a number of other situations. But clearly if I'm up for a raise and I dream about a work situation, it's probably a straightforward dream.

"On the other hand, I've seen some Vietnam veterans who dream about Vietnam some 10 or 20 years after. Vietnam for them has become a metaphor for their feelings about current life situations. Or there are baseball metaphors that we employ when we think of work, such as 'I hope I don't strike out.'"

Theories abound about why people dream and what dreams mean, but for centuries scientists only had theories. In 1953, however, scientists made a groundbreaking discovery: that dreams occur during "rapid eye movement," or REM, sleep, when bodies actually undergo physical changes. During that sleep a person's eyes dart around, limbs are paralyzed and respiration and heartbeat are irregular.

REM sleep occurs about every 90 minutes, so during a night when you sleep about seven hours you average four to five dreams. As the night wears on, the dreams become progressively longer and more complex. The dream a person is likely to remember is the final one of the night.

Scientists speculate that humans were dreaming even as hunters and gatherers. In fact, birds dream and so do mammals of almost all types. Reptiles don't dream, however, leading researchers to speculate that dreaming evolved about 130 million years ago, after reptiles branched off from a common ancestor.

Today, certain dreams are common. Flying, falling or finding yourself naked in public seem to be the products of everyday human fears and aspirations. Likewise, it's natural that anxieties about work—fear that you're not doing a good job, stress or insecurity—manifest themselves in dreams in which you're locked out of a meeting, you're shouldering a burden too big to carry or you're being strangled by the boss.

Feelings of insecurity crop up frequently in dreams. For instance, one Orlando public relations professional confessed that every time she is under a lot of stress at work she dreams that she's back at Disney World waiting tables—one of her college jobs.

"It's terrible. I keep mixing up the orders. I can't keep up," she said. "And the ultimate irony is that the uniform doesn't fit. I'm too big for it."

Why some people dream about work more than others is probably a matter of perspective, said Dr. Shauna Laughna, a staff psychologist at Florida Hospital's Sleep Disorder Center in Orlando.

"If your work has become such a part of your life that you have lunch and picnics with your workers, with no boundary between your home life and work life, you probably won't experience a disturbing work dream," said Laughna, who usually discusses dreams with patients if they have recurring or very disturbing dreams. "Your co-workers will probably just drift in and out of your dreams."

The most common disturbing work dream, Laughna said, involves problems at work.

"Sometimes in your dream, you will simply replay the problem at work, or you will try to solve it," Laughna said. "More often what you'll get instead is a feeling state that reflects what's going on at work. For instance, you might have the feeling of being trapped or the feeling that a large weight is on you. And that your boss is pushing this weight down on you."

But if there is such a thing as a happy work-related dream, how come no one seems to recall them?

"The dreams you're most likely to remember are the ones that have strong emotional pull, which is going to be something either very, very pleasant or very, very unpleasant. And, frankly, most of us aren't greeted at our workplace with a silver platter and a massage therapist," Laughna said.

Allison Miller's work dreams would probably make her the envy of her peers. Shortly after Miller started a new job last December, she began to dream that she could fly—an experience that left her feeling terrific after each of the dreams.

As public relations liaison for an Orlando interior design firm, Miller said she felt an immediate acceptance and warmth when she started the job.

In her first flying dream, she was at a party with the rest of the staff. Standing beside one co-worker, she confided that she could fly, but she didn't want him to say anything to the others. After she gave her speech to her colleagues, they applauded and warmly congratulated her. She returned to the side of the room. When the meeting broke up and everyone began socializing, her confidant said, "Oh, go ahead. You're among friends." So Miller got a running start, flapped her arms and took off—much to the delight of her colleagues.

"You wake up in the morning and you feel warm and fuzzy all over," said Miller, who has vivid dreams. "The feeling lasted all day long. It was an amazing morale booster. But I have to attribute it to the environment here at work. It's not so much the stuff I'm doing at work, but the people. I feel very comfortable, I wish I could have those dreams whenever I want.

"In fact, I wish other people could have those dreams. They're really wonderful."

Source: Linda Shrieves, "While Body Rests, Dreams Go to Work," *The Orlando Sentinel*, May 15, 1990, E1–E2.

ting, social setting, or work setting, who you communicate with and for what purpose is shaped by your goals. Purposes for communication are influenced by what you expect or anticipate in the future. For example, your graduating from college, or getting a particular job, or being admitted to certain social circles, or marrying, or preparing a future for your children all represent goals—some immediate and others distant.

All of these source factors set you apart, make you one of a kind, and shape your very being. They can be discussed as individual components of the communication process, but, in reality, they are mutually influencing and, taken together, constitute your *frame of reference*. Each person's frame of reference is uniquely different. Think of your frame of reference as an invisible picture frame, and through it everything you sense and experience is interpreted. Some people may have a large frame permitting a broad view of what is going on, or a small frame limiting observation. The glass in some frames may be thin and clear, allowing for accurate viewing, or thick and tinted, distorting images and creating a false sense of reality. Consequently, your frame of reference significantly influences your communication with others. Certainly, differences in frames of reference account for some of our communication difficulties.

Message Factors

Communication involves the sending of messages that convey information requests, thoughts, and emotions. José Aranguren, a Spanish philosopher and student of communication has defined communication as any transmission of information by (a) the emission, (b) the conduction, and (c) the reception of (d) a message.[14] So, when we communicate with someone, we do so with one purpose: to create in his or her mind the idea residing in ours. Typically, we use words to stimulate thoughts in others. Used correctly, they can stimulate ideas similar to our own; used incorrectly, they may stimulate ideas completely different from what we had intended. And, as if this were not problem enough, the gestures, postures, and environments that accompany these words often serve to modify their meanings, making accurate interpretation even more difficult. Here we will examine the verbal and nonverbal elements of communication in order to better understand these often-confusing message codes. This understanding can help you become more effective message senders and more tolerant message receivers.

Verbal Messages. Verbal messages involve the use of language (words), that linguistic structure into which we are all born, to influence others. Steven Beebe and John Masterson explain that "words are the tools with which we make sense of the world and share that sense with others." Because we are able to represent our world through symbols, we have the ability to "foresee events, to reflect on past experiences, to plan, to make decisions, and to consciously control our own behavior."[15] Words, then, provide us with verbal vehicles for transmitting information and creating messages. However, language can be problematic. The problem is that of meaning—the same word often means different things to different people. Consider that there are currently about 600,000 words in the English language, with educated adults using about 2,000 words in daily conversation, and for the 500 most frequently used words there are some 14,000 dictionary meanings.

Language may be fragile, dulled by wrong usage, and often not readily at hand, but it is a principal medium by which we can make ourselves understood by other people. When you are aware of how words stimulate meanings in the mind, you can improve your language behavior so that you and others are sharing meaning rather than just exchanging words.

Language and Verbal Systems. The real world is a world of facts, objects, situations, and events. The verbal symbolic world is one of words that allow you to describe the real world. The word "snow," for instance, conjures up different images for people living in Anchorage, Boston, Denver, Dallas, and Los Angeles. For some it is a matter-of-fact occurrence, for others a rude inconvenience, and for still others an unusual phenomenon. Also, it may be several inches in depth or a light dusting, heavy and wet, a soft powder, or an icy slush.

Alfred Korzybski, the founder of general semantics, used the analogy of distinguishing between a map and the territory to clarify the importance of differentiating between verbal symbols and structural reality. He put forth three propositions whereby we, as *semantic reactors,* might consider this relationship: (1) the map is not the territory (the symbol is not the thing symbolized); (2) the map does not represent all the territory (symbols cannot say all there is to be said about a thing); and (3) the ideal map would have to include a map of itself (symbols are self-reflective).[16] So, when you encounter a word, you are seeing a type of map, not the actual territory it represents. Words are not things; maps are not territories.

Language and Meaning. The symbols used to create language are both arbitrary and ambiguous. Yet, communication is a process of exchanging mutually understood symbols to stimulate meaning in another person. Indeed, human language exists to allow us to share meaning. If symbols themselves do not contain meaning, how then is meaning created out of symbols? Meaning is a human creation accomplished when human beings interpret symbols. Words don't mean; people mean. The meaning of symbols is supplied by people and their culture. Symbols themselves carry no innate meaning; they may mean one thing to one person and something different to someone else.

Charles Ogden and I. A. Richards in their book, *The Meaning of Meaning,* developed a "triangle of meaning" that illustrates the interrelationships among referents, thoughts, and symbols (Exhibit 2-4).[17]

Communication begins with a *thought.* You think of an *object* and then select what you consider to be an appropriate *symbol* to represent this object. The thought, object, and symbol form the points of the triangle. The important relationships are these: a direct relationship exists between thought and object, and between thought and symbol; an inferred relationship exists between object and symbol. In other words, the object(s) of communication can be precise and the symbol(s) of communication can be specifically selected, but we can only hope that others will perceive a similar relationship between object(s) and symbol(s) and come to a similar understanding of the thought(s) being conveyed. For example, the word "rock" can mean a hard substance found in quarries, a type of contemporary music, or a valuable stone set in a ring. Or, you see a narrow body of water but is it a "creek," "stream," or "river"?

► **EXHIBIT 2-4**
Triangle of Meaning

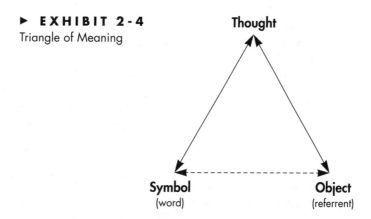

Thought

Symbol
(word)

Object
(referent)

Each of these verbal symbols conveys a different image. So, although the meaning of a given symbol can appear quite clear, no two people hold exactly the same meaning for the symbol. Thus, we only stir up meaning within receivers.

If people do not share the same meaning for symbols, how is communication possible? To answer this, we must distinguish between two types of meaning, *denotative* and *connotative*. Denotative refers to the actual or agreed upon meaning or meanings of a word. These are essentially rational relationships established between an object and a word. This meaning is frequently referred to as the literal or "dictionary" meaning. Connotative meaning refers to subjective associations—the personal and emotional attachments that people associate with a word or symbol. This meaning contains all of the judgments and evaluations that people have for a word or symbol. The word "college," as an example, has both denotative and connotative meanings. Its denotative meaning is "an institution of higher learning offering courses of instruction in a number of disciplines usually leading to a bachelor's degree." Or, it might be referring to a specific college such as Boston, Lee, Monmouth, or Spoon River. Its connotative meaning might be "a place to party for four years." Other connotative meanings for college are "an institution that will prepare me to get a job," and "the place where I learned to think and reason and accept responsibility."

Communication could not occur if people did not operate with some denotative meanings. Dictionaries are created to provide us with the "correct" or "accepted" definitions of words, but one's personal, private meanings ultimately determine any response to certain symbols. And although we try to explain our feelings to others, thus to some degree sharing them, the feelings still are ours and ours alone.

Language and Abstraction. *Abstraction* is a process of selecting some details and omitting others. Any use of language involves some abstraction, and, indeed, abstraction is one of the most useful features of language. It allows us to think in categories, to generalize. Much human knowledge is intimately bound up in the process of categorizing or classifying. We classify foods, modes of transportation, types of business, occupations, geographical areas as well as ideas and concepts. Abstraction is a useful characteristic of words, but it is also one that can lead to problems, particularly if you are not aware of abstractions.[18]

All words involve some abstraction or leaving out of details, but some words are more abstract than others. For example, words having a physical correspondence, such as the word "book," are less abstract than words like "truth" or "freedom" which represent ideas or concepts in the mind and do not necessarily have a physical basis. And as words become more and more abstract, their correspondence to reality becomes less and less direct. S. I. Hayakawa has developed a useful diagram, called an "abstraction ladder," to illustrate how words can have differing degrees of abstraction.[18]

Exhibit 2-5 presents an abstraction ladder that takes a particular object, an automobile belonging to one of the authors of this text, and shows how it can be referred to at different levels of abstraction. The lowest level of abstraction, at which no details are omitted, is the process level, the level at which scientists using instruments can observe the car. The second level is the car as an object that we can experience with our senses. Notice that even at this level—the level of everyday observation—some details are being left out. This is partly a result of sensory limitations and partly because we can only observe from one point at a time. The third level is the first verbal level, the first level involving the use of words. At this level the words being used refer to

Verbal Levels	
8	Transportation
7	Land transportation
6	Motor vehicle
5	Car
4	Datsun
3	Gardner's Datsun 200SX
Nonverbal Levels	
2 (object level)	The red Datsun with sunroof, black pinstriping, and black interior
1 (process level)	The car as a combination of molecules and atomic particles

one particular object—"Gardner's Datsun 210 SX." At the fourth level, we can use the word "Datsun" to refer to the same object. We have now assigned the object to a category, the category of all Datsuns. We have left out the detail which would distinguish this particular Datsun from all other Datsuns. At the next level, that of the word "car," more distinguishing details are omitted and our Datsun is included with Mazda, Volvos, Fords, and all other makes of cars. At the sixth level, we could refer to the car as a "motor vehicle," putting it into a category that also includes trucks, buses, and jeeps and leaves out still more detail. At the seventh level, we could use the term "land transportation," categorizing the car with railroad trains, horse-and-buggy outfits, and snowmobiles. And at the eighth level, we could refer to the car as "transportation," placing it in a category which would also include airplanes and ships. Notice that at each level more detail is left out until at the eighth level we come to the very abstract word "transportation." This is one of the characteristics of abstract words: they do not suggest a clear picture of something in reality, and people often have very different meanings in mind for them.

Because our language is limited and because we abstract and categorize, communication is not easy. The use of high-level abstractions can lead to ambiguities and vagueness that creates confusion in the interpretation of messages. High-level abstractions are words like "justice," democracy," "mankind," "peace," and "law and order." When words like these are used in a message that does not also contain words at lower levels of abstraction, it is difficult to know what the message is saying. Highly abstract words that are not accompanied by more concrete words have been referred to as "words cut loose from their moorings."[19] They are not anchored to lower levels of abstraction. Remember, you have something specific to say and this requires that careful attention be given to word choice. The value of being precise and the need for clarification is obvious in the following example:

> A plumber wrote the U.S. Bureau of Standards about using hydrochloric acid to clear drainpipes. . . .
>
> Several days later he received this reply, "The efficacy of hydrochloric acid is indisputable, but the corrosive residue is incompatible with metallic permanence."

Confused, he wrote again and asked if the acid "is okay to use or not."

A second letter advised him, "We cannot assume responsibility for the production of toxic and noxious residue, and suggest that you use an alternative procedure."

Still baffled, he wrote, "Do you mean it's okay to use hydrochloric acid?"

A final letter resolved the question. "Don't use hydrochloric acid. It eats the hell out of pipes."[20]

Nothing can be more problematic than faltering and fumbling, or wandering off into vague profundities. Using more precise language can help you clarify your own thoughts, which in turn will make you a better communicator.

Meta-messages represent a special kind of communication problem. *Meta-messages* are the deeper, below-the-surface messages being conveyed. They illustrate the multidimensional nature of language. Gerard I. Nierenberg and Henry H. Calero suggest that talk exists on at least three levels of meaning: (1) what the speaker says; (2) what the speaker thinks is said; and (3) what the listener thinks the speaker said.[21] In their book, *Meta-Talk,* these authors explore the subliminal significance or hidden meaning of more than 350 phrases used everyday. They explain the deliberate use of false modesty, softness, foreboders, continuers, convincers, strokes, and pleaders.

Language provides us with a way of interpreting reality and verbal messages provide a way of conveying that interpretation. The intent of language is to convey a message, not merely symbols. Lewis Carroll expressed an awareness of this in his children's story, *Alice In Wonderland*:

"Then you should say what you mean," the March Hare went on.

"I do," Alice hastily replied, "at least—I mean what I say—that's the same thing, you know."

"Not the same thing a bit!" said the Hatter. "Why, you might as well say that 'I see what I eat' is the same thing as 'I eat what I see'!"

Or, as former president of the United States Richard Nixon once said: "I know you believe you understand what you think I said. But I am not sure you realize that what you heard is not what I meant."

Language and Perception. Language influences the way a linguistic system develops and is transmitted. As a set of signs, symbols, and signals, language has a grammar associated with it. All languages have their own unique organizational patterns. Communication becomes possible when people share a system of order and grammar. Edward Sapir and Benjamin Lee Whorf observe:

Human beings do not live in the objective world alone, nor alone in the world of social activity as ordinarily understood, but are very much at the mercy of the particular language which has become the medium of expression for their society. . . . The fact of the matter is that the "real world" is to a large extent unconsciously built upon the language habits of the group.[22]

So, they conclude that "the background linguistic system of each language is not merely a reproducing instrument for voicing ideas but rather is itself the shaper of ideas, the program and guide for the individual's mental activity, for his analysis of impressions, for his synthesis of his mental stock in trade."[23] The Sapir-Whorf hypothesis suggests that language functions not simply as a device for reporting experience but, more significantly, as a way of defining experience for its users. The language system we learn from our culture has a profound influence on how we interpret the world. The Eskimo language is an example of how languages develop, in part, in response to environmental conditions. Eskimos have many different words for snow and are more likely to notice and think about differences in snowfalls than are native speakers of English who have only a single term for snow. English leads us to lump all types of snow together and to ignore differences that the Eskimo highlights. A less dramatic example occurred when a move from the midwest to New York City forced one of the authors of this text to make certain adjustments in his world of meaning. "Sacks" were now made of cloth and "bags" were made of paper, "regular" coffee included cream and sugar instead of being black, and a breakfast roll had become a piece of "Danish."

The Sapir-Whorf hypothesis is important because it suggests that there is a connection between one's language and behavior. If language shapes perception and perception shapes behavior, then language can strongly influence one's actual behavior. To be an effective communicator, you must be aware of the relationship between language and culture. You have to learn about the culture of the person with whom you are communicating and acquire an understanding of her or his interests, concerns, and needs so as to better realize how language represents them.

Language and Function. Words are tools and become important only when they are used, so we must ask, "How are words used? What functions do messages serve?"

The various functions of language have been described in several lists or typologies. Whatmough identifies four basic functions of language: (1) the informative or referential function, concerned with communicating facts; (2) the dynamic function, concerned with shaping or changing attitudes and opinions; (3) the emotive function, devoted to directing the behavior of others; and (4) the aesthetic function, concerned with giving the form of a message a certain artistic impact or aesthetic distinctiveness.[24] Lavidge and Steiner list three functions or dimensions of messages: (1) cognitive, or messages that provide information and facts; (2) affective, or messages that change attitudes and feelings; and (3) conative, or messages that stimulate or direct desires.[25]

W. Charles Redding suggests three general functions of messages within the organizational arena: (1) task messages, which relate to products, services, and activities of specific concern to the organization, such as improving sales, quality of products, and customer service; (2) maintenance messages, which help the organization to remain alive and perpetuate itself, such as policy and regulation messages; and (3) human messages, which are directed at people within the organization and affect their attitudes, morale, satisfaction, and self-fulfillment.[26] To this list, Gerald Goldhaber adds innovative messages, or those messages which enable an organization to innovate and adapt to its changing environment.[27]

Finally, Harold Lasswell notes three functions of messages and the mass media: (1) surveillance, or the providing of information essential to the economy, the public, and society; (2) correlation, or the selection and interpretation of information about the environment through commentaries and editorials; and (3) transmission of culture, or the communication of values from one generation to another or from the members of a society to newcomers.[28] To these three functions Charles Wright adds a fourth, entertainment or those messages designed to fill our leisure time and provide private respite.[29]

These lists are intended to sensitize you to the role words play in communication and the multiple functions language serves in the sending and receiving of messages. By viewing words as symbolic tools and focusing on the functions language performs, you can become better message senders/receivers.

Nonverbal Messages. Nonverbal messages are those silent messages expressed by other than linguistic means and include those behavioral cues that are not part of our language code, but are transmitted by people and the environment in communication situations. Verbal symbols are undeniably important, forming the basic unit of our communication with others. But of at least equal importance is the myriad of unspoken, nonverbal cues that accompany spoken messages. Indeed, some would argue that these cues are even more important than words. Dean C. Barnlund's review of the literature on nonverbal communication led him to conclude:

> Many, and sometimes most, of the critical meanings generated in human encounters are elicited by touch, glance, vocal nuance, gesture, or facial expression with or without the aid of words. From the moment of separation, people observe each other with all their senses; hearing, pause, and intonation, attending to dress and carriage, observing glance and facial tension, as well as noting word choice and syntax. Every harmony or disharmony of signals guides the interpretation of passing mood or enduring attribute. Out of the evaluations of kinetic, vocal, and verbal cues decisions are made to argue or agree, to laugh or blush, to relax or resist, to continue or cut off conversation.[30]

Barnlund describes well the broad dimensions of nonverbal messages and their impact on our communication with others. His observations take on greater impact when we consider Ray Birdwhistell's claim that during face-to-face communication only 35 percent of the meaning comes from words, and 65 percent comes from the nonverbal messages.[31] Albert Mehrabian, a psychologist working in the area of nonverbal behavior, contends further that 93 percent of the emotional impact of a message comes from a nonverbal source, and only 7 percent is verbal.[32] So, when combined with the verbal message, nonverbal cues are quite effective in conveying feelings. And, in some interactions our voices and our actions speak so loudly that our words are often unheard or are not considered important. It is vital, then, to examine the functions nonverbal messages play in our interactions with people and to consider the vast array of nonverbal cues that influence our communication with others.

Functions of Nonverbal Messages. Each of us is born with the capacity to communicate nonverbally and it seems that our culture dictates our nonverbal behavior. As children, we learn the appropriate postures, gestures, and facial expressions and are also taught what many of these mean. Like verbal communication, our nonverbal behaviors are acquired through cultural conditioning, and they perform many important functions in the total communication process. These behaviors are particularly important relationally because many of the decisions we make about whether we like a person or about their status or responsiveness to us are based on these cues. We express emotions and convey attitudes nonverbally; we present ourselves and regulate our communication with others nonverbally.

Expressing Emotion. Nonverbal behavior is particularly effective in communicating affect—indicating our emotional state. Our facial expressions or the way we sit at a given moment can reflect our moods more adequately than words. Emotions can also be expressed in other bodily ways. Hand gestures can be used to express such emotions as anger, terror, love, and hate. The way we dress can express compliance or defiance. The gait with which we walk can express happiness, sadness, urgency, or despair. These emotions, expressed bodily, tend to repeat, complement, and accent what is verbally communicated, thereby making them more recognizable.

Certain primary emotions are commonly expressed facially by all people: love, happiness, sadness, surprise, fear, anger, and disgust.[33] Other emotions, however, are much more difficult to express (e.g., loneliness and trust), and we are culture-bound and our acculturation influences our interpretations of nonverbal cues. For example, in our culture we cry when we're happy and we cry when we're sad. In some middle-eastern countries, blowing smoke in a young woman's face indicates a personal interest.

Conveying Attitudes. Our attitudes can also be expressed nonverbally. For instance, we convey our attitudes with our eyes, hands, physical movement, voice, and even silence. The eyes reveal much about our attitudes toward others, indicating interest or disinterest, concern or lack of it. They can encourage us to engage in conversation or discontinue it.[34] Hands and physical movement also indicate our attitudes. A clenched fist, wagging finger, and erect posture all suggest an authoritarian attitude. Other gestures and movements suggest less forceful attitudes and feelings—for example, when we approach another person with an outstretched hand and grasp it and shake it in greeting or friendship. Again, these nonverbal cues are culture-bound and tend to repeat, complement, and reinforce what is verbally communicated.

Presenting Ourselves. Nonverbal communication serves as an important means of self-presentation. Others come to know us by the nonverbal messages we send. Whether in casual conversation, business settings, or informal socials, our nonverbal behavior is a telling part of self-presentation. The wringing of hands might indicate nervousness, drumming on the table may suggest boredom. The way we carry ourselves can communicate to others our sense of confidence and control or our lack of it. Walking with head drooped, shoulders sagging; slamming your fist on a table during an argument; wearing expensive clothing; arriving late for an appointment—all revealing cues. Our various moods and their degrees of emphasis are communicated nonverbally, and how we send and receive these signals is an important aspect of self-presentation.

Regulating Communication. Finally, nonverbal behaviors serve a regulatory function in our communication with others. They can repeat, contradict, substitute, complement, underline or accent, and direct our verbal messages.[35] A warm hand on the shoulder, a nod of the head, an erect posture, a pointing finger, a loud voice, short intermittent gazes, or a hostile glare are only some of the unspoken cues that influence the meaning of words exchanged when communicating with others. And often our actions speak louder than words. Mehrabian notes that "when any nonverbal behavior contradicts speech, it is more likely to determine the total impact of the message . . . touching, position, postures, gestures, as well as facial and vocal expressions can all outweigh words and determine the feelings conveyed by a message."[36] So, when contradictions occur, it will probably be the nonverbal behavior that is believed.

Nonverbal behavior can direct communication by controlling the interaction. As a regulator, it operates in terms of initiating interaction, clarifying relationships, directing turn-taking, guiding emotional expression, and initiating leave-taking. In other words, through nonverbal messages people discover such things as whether they are to communicate or not, what is appropriate to say, who speaks first, and when to end a conversation. The appropriateness of communication, conversational rules, and situational norms are conveyed nonverbally.[37]

Types of Nonverbal Messages. We send and receive several types of nonverbal messages during the process of communication. We have learned to symbolize in many ways other than words. Yet, it is not easy to dissect human interaction and make one interpretation based solely on verbal behavior and another on only nonverbal behavior. The verbal and nonverbal dimensions are integrally related. Still, nonverbal cues have been categorized and the classification scheme used here reflects what is generally subsumable under the label "nonverbal": (1) signs and emblems; (2) body motion; (3) objects, artifacts, surroundings; (4) space and territory; (5) touch; (6) time; and (7) paralanguage.

Signs and Emblems. Signs and emblems include all of those gestures which supplant words, numbers, and punctuation marks. They may vary from the monosyllabic gesture of the hitchhiker to such complex systems as the American Sign Language for the deaf. These nonverbal signals have a direct verbal translation of a word or two, or a phrase.

Signs and emblems are often culture specific. The gesture used to represent "A-Okay" or the hitchhiker's prominent thumb are common emblems for a large part of our culture. However, elsewhere they would be interpreted the same as a middle-finger gesture we use to display frustration and anger. And, although most emblems are produced with the hands, such signals can be communicated in other ways. A nose-wrinkle may say, "I'm disgusted" or "Phew! It stinks!" A shrug of the shoulders may communicate helplessness or uncertainty. The number of signs and emblems used within a given culture may vary considerable—from less than 100 (American) to more than 250 (Israeli).[38]

Body Motion. Body motion, or *kinesics,* includes gestures, facial expressions, eye behavior, posture, and movements of the body—the limbs, hands, head, and legs. Ray Birdwhistell has estimated that there are over 700,000 possible physical signs (head movements, facial expressions) that can be transmitted via body movement.[39] Where signs or emblems represent intentionally communicated messages, body motion or "language" is principally an unconscious, intuitive activity directly tied to or accompanying speech. We use the language of our body to communicate feelings and attitudes. Expressions such as, "if looks could kill," "it's all over your face," or "a picture is worth a thousand words" call attention to the significance of body motion.

We use gestures not only in a broad, expansive manner but also in subtle, less animated ways. The effect of gestures upon our communication is something of a mystery, but tentative findings indicate that frequent gestural activity is associated with one's effort to exert influence over others.[40] A more discrete use of gestures can also provide clues to unspoken feelings. For example, fidgeting, clenched hands, and other restless movements can be signs of nervousness. Whitened knuckles and clenched fists can signal anger. And, the absence of gestures can also be revealing, suggesting that the speaker is unenthusiastic about the subject being discussed. Failing to accompany appropriate gestures with words seems to signal boredom, discomfort, or fatigue.

Facial Expression. The face is a tremendously complicated channel of expression to interpret but one to which we give immediate attention. We like a face or we don't. We think it is animated or expressionless. But what do we see that makes us judge someone to be sad or happy or frightened or angry? Isolating which facial cues specify which emotions is more difficult than simply judging a face. The size of a person's nose, the distance between the eyes, the fullness of the lips and eyebrows, and the wearing of glasses are among the many facial characteristics that serve as emotional/personality indicators. Research indicates that happiness is shown most by the lower face and eyes; sadness is seen primarily in the eyes; surprise is indicated by the eyes and lower face; anger is revealed in the lower face, brows, and forehead; and fear is shown most clearly in the eyes.[41]

Ekman and Friesen have developed a useful classification system for various styles of facial expression. They label the people using these styles as: (1) the Withholder—there is little facial movement and actual feeling states are inhibited; (2) the Revealer—the face leaves little doubt how the person feels and emotions are continually being transmitted; (3) the Unwitting Expressor—a limited number of expressions are unconsciously sent and received; (4) the Blank Expressor—the person believes emotions are being portrayed, but others see only a blank face; (5) the Substitute Expressor—the facial expression shows an emotion other than the one the person thinks is being displayed; (6) the Frozen-Affect Expressor—a person born with facial configurations that result in a constant emotional display even when in a relaxed, neutral state; (7) the Ever-Ready Expressor—a person prone to displaying a given emotion, as an initial response, to almost any stimulus; and (8) the Flooded-Affect Expressor—a person involved in intense life crisis is often overwhelmed by a single emotion (fear) which colors all other emotional states.[42]

The face has considerable communicative potential, mirroring both our intentions and our feelings. It is capable of making hundreds of distinct movements and communicating many emotional states with incredible speed. The feelings most easily identified are surprise, fear, anger, disgust, happiness, and sadness.

Eye Contact. Eyes and eye movement, or *oculesics,* convey attitudes and communicate much information. Psychologists have found that the eyes are a very telling communication channel and that we are remarkably accurate in judging the message(s) being sent. Direct eye contact, particularly in Western cultures, is interpreted positively and is a signal of trust and mutual attention and interest. For example, most personal interactions are initiated by a short period during which two people look directly at one another. If one becomes enamored of the other, he or she may spend more time staring at the person than listening to what is being said. Gazes during conversations also serve a regulatory function, indicating turn-taking. Even the pupils of the eyes can communicate excitement, interest, and surprise. In large metropolitan areas, however, where people are crowded together with others they neither know nor care about, some develop a deliberate strategy of avoiding eye contact—a practice that can cause outsiders to view the city as a hostile and unfriendly place. Observing eye contact can be an "eye-opening" experience revealing interest, concern, surprise, tension, anxiety, and status.

Action Language. Our actions also communicate nonverbally, conveying interest or boredom, agreement or disagreement as well as the basic emotions of happiness, sadness, calm, and urgency. When interacting with others, for example, our head movements can encourage or discourage communication. The vertical or horizontal movement of the head, consciously or unconsciously, during a conversation can indicate interest and agreement or disinterest and lack of consent. Or, the way we walk and the tempo of our movement convey meaning. Consider the slow, somber movements of a funeral march compared with the free, uninhibited movements of dancing. Just think about the many ways we describe how people move—"she's jumping with joy," "they're dragging their heels," "he's shuffling about." We all have our own pace, tempo, and rhythm, and those who know us can tell how we feel by how we move.

Posture, too, is an important nonverbal communication channel. Research reveals over a thousand different postures which may provide information about such things as attitude, status, emotion, and warmth.[43] For example, leaning back in a chair, looking around the room, and unresponsive head and facial displays are all relationally implicit messages conveyed by posture.

Objects, Artifacts, and Surroundings. Our physical appearance, the clothing we wear, and the furnishings that surround us communicate something to others. Citations and diplomas on the wall, a wooden desk and leather chair, and a pinstriped suit complemented by an appropriate tie tell a lot about a person. Characteristics such as intelligence, sociability, trustworthiness, and success are initially determined by physical appearance. Status and prestige are also communicated by dress and appearance.[44] And, although these may be imprecise and unclear measures, they are important factors influencing our self-images and our relationships with others. Consider, for instance, the successful Chicago attorney trying a case in southern Illinois who drives down in a pickup truck, wearing rumpled clothing. Or, the New York City attorney, making in excess of $300,000 a year, who removes his jacket, rolls up his sleeves, and wears the most conservative tie he owns when working in upstate farming areas. Both of these attorneys understand the persuasive and manipulative power of physical appearance and dress, and they understand that rural juries react negatively to lawyers who "put on airs."

Our surroundings also say something about who we are and where we are. We encounter others in a limitless number of places—buses, homes, apartments, elevators, restaurants, offices, parks, hotels, sports arenas, factories, libraries, movie theaters, classrooms, and so on. We evaluate these environments along similar dimensions, and we are influenced by and likewise influence our environments.

One familiar dimension along which environments can be classified is a formal/informal continuum. Our determination of each may be based on the people present, the functions performed, or the objects in the room—wall hangings, light fixtures, drapes, paneling, carpeting, and furniture. In business, for example, the chair is a familiar but telling piece of furniture. Executive offices are furnished with expansive wooden desks and high-backed leather chairs; mid-level managers and supervisors have metal desks and standard plastic and chrome chairs; secretaries are usually issued those uncomfortably small, semicircular-backed chairs on rollers. Here, the assigned chair designates status, prestige, job function, and potential power.

Environments can also be judged as being private or public. Private environments are more enclosed, reduce distance, and encourage intimacy. Messages are less constrained, encouraging close, personal communication with others. Public environments may or may not be more distant. We may be seated on the other side of a room or the other side of a desk, in an interlocking chair in an airport, or standing in an elevator—all are public environments. Communication in these instances is impersonal, hesitant, guarded, and oftentimes superficial. Environments can encourage encounters and contribute to communication or prove countercommunicative.

Our environments are also filled with people who affect our behavior. These people may be perceived as active or passive participants, depending on the degree to which they are perceived as being involved. When others are perceived to be active ingredients in the environment, they may either facilitate or inhibit communication. We notice the gender, relate to the familiarity, and respond to the status of others in our surroundings. Their presence may increase our motivation to "look good" in what we say and do, or cause us to be cautious. What we say, how we say it, and who we say it to are influenced by the others in our environment(s).

Space and Territory. Anthropologist Edward Hall observes that "spatial changes give a tone to a communication, accent it, and at times even override the spoken word."[45] *Proxemics* is the study of how we use the space around us and the messages conveyed by distance. Each of us carries around a sort of invisible bubble of personal space wherever we go. The elevator door opens and you and the rest of an impatient horde of people crowd into the tiny cubicle. With everyone jammed together, you pull your arms close to your sides, communicating that you don't mean to intentionally invade someone else's space. You accept a luncheon invitation and when you're seated at the restaurant you unconsciously divide the table in half—one side is yours, one side is his. You enter your supervisor's office, glance around the room, and she motions you to a chair opposite her desk. Each of these is an example of how you establish and regulate territory or personal space.

Distance defines our relationships and determines the nature and function of our communication with others. Hall has identified four distances ranging from public to intimate that affect our communication with others.[46] *Public distance* (6–20 ft.) involves large groups of people and the messages sent are intended for such groups. *Social distance* (20 in.–6 ft.) is closer, involves few people, and is suitable for business discussions and conversations at social gatherings. Messages are more directed but still not personal. *Personal distance* (12–20 in.) is a "moving in" representing something more than casual conversation. Still, someone is kept at arm's length. Messages are increasingly more personal but less so than if we we were to stand closer. *Intimate distance* (3–12 in.) is very reserved, close, and private, and is used when the people we are communicating with are emotionally and relationally close to us. Self-defenses are lowered and messages are personally confidential. These four spatial zones may expand or contract according to factors in the situation and one's cultural background. People from different cultures have different expectations about the distance one should keep during a conversation. Still, each of us regulates our space in certain ways influencing our communication with others and affecting our personal orientations and experiences.

Touch. Touch, or *haptics,* is a potent nonverbal message code that stimulates meanings in some interesting and significant ways. It may be our most basic or primitive code. Deprived of physical contact—signs of love and affection—young children are physically retarded and psychologically impaired. To develop into happy, well-adjusted adults, children need the warmth, tenderness, and security that only touching provides.[47]

On a recent trip to Japan, American Businessman Bruce Neff unwittingly broke a key cultural rule. The Data General manager abruptly chopped an order he had placed with a Japanese firm by one-third. "It was an ordinary procedure that in the U.S. would have taken 15 minutes," he recalled. But the Japanese were shocked and threatened by the unexpected cutback, and launched into negotiations with Neff that dragged on for three days.

As the Japanese invest abroad, more and more U.S. businessmen will find themselves doing deals with them. The corporate style that works for Americans at home may not go over with their new colleagues or competitors. Neff and many other Boston-area executives are turning to Ikuko Atsumi, 43, a Japanese poet and feminist who has lived in the U.S. since 1981. She is president of the New England Japanese Center, which teaches often bewildered Americans how to do business with her countrymen. Says Atsumi: "To succeed in Japan, the fastest shortcut is to learn Japanese culture."

The heart of the center's program is a series of eight afternoon seminars with titles like "The Samurai Spirit in Business Strategy" and "The Concentration Power of Zen in Business." For $60 a session, executives learn everything from how to drink green tea (slowly, unlike sake, which is downed in a gulp) to where to sit during a conference (not in the first seats offered) and when and where to take off one's shoes. The students are taught *go*, a traditional Japanese board game, and are introduced to the psychology behind sumo wrestling.

The sessions, which combine lectures and role playing, have been a hit with many managers. Firms that have sent executives to the courses include Digital Equipment, Polaroid and Data General. Edward Colbert, chairman of Data Instruments, a maker of electronic sensors that does $1 million in annual business with Japan, was delighted with a seminar on the Japanese use of silence. Confused by the pauses that cropped up when he traveled with Japanese associates, Colbert learned that what strikes an American as an awkward halt in conversation may be a refreshing respite to a Japanese. Said Colbert: "Now I wonder, what did they think of all my jabbering?"

Atsumi, the former publisher of the Japanese magazine *The Feminist: Asian Women,* went to the U.S. after she was awarded a fellowship to Radcliffe. When she later sought work at the electronics companies around Boston, she was startled to find how little many American executives seemed to know about Japan. Says she: "They know they have a lot to learn, but because they're so busy, they want some kind of instant pill to learn it."

Her response was the New England Japanese Center, which she runs out of her home in Stow, Mass. Along with the seminars, the center offers services ranging from translation and language instruction to private lessons in Japanese manners, which Atsumi gives in a den outfitted as a traditional Japanese sitting room. Clients who prefer to let someone else do the deal making can also turn to Atsumi for help. For a fee ranging from $100 an hour to 10% commission, she will negotiate contracts with Japanese companies herself.

America, however, is basically a nontactile society. For example, people who live in San Juan, Puerto Rico, touch an average of one hundred-eighty times per conversation, but people from Gainesville, Florida, touch an average of two times per conversation.[48] Still, touching plays a vital role in selected situations. Heslin and Alper suggest five functions that touch serves in nonverbal communication.[49] *Functional-professional touch* is impersonal, and evidenced by the many professional/client relationships—doctor/patient, nurse/patient, hair stylist/client. *Social-polite touch* is part of the greeting behaviors in a culture and includes handshaking, hugging, and kissing. *Friendship-warmth touch* involves maintaining and reinforcing the bond of friendship between people and may be expressed by hugging and holding. *Love-intimacy touch* also is reinforcing but the relationship is deep and personal, requiring gentle touches and caresses to communicate mutual "soft" feelings. *Sexual-arousal touch* is highly intimate and functions to satisfy sexual needs.

Touch is also particularly effective as a message code in communicating specialized emotional meanings, power, and status.[50] If we want to comfort and reassure someone who has had an unfortunate experience, nonverbal messages such as a compassionate look and a comforting tone of voice are helpful. But holding the person or putting an arm around his or her shoulders is particularly effective in conveying warmth and sympathy. Another emotional meaning that can be communicated clearly by touch is hostility. Shoving, hitting, slapping, grabbing, or shaking creates a vivid feeling of hostility. Power and status are also communicated effectively by touch. Frequent touching is associated with greater power and status, so supervisors are more likely to touch their subordinates than subordinates are to touch their bosses.

It seems, then, that touching influences the development of our psyches, communicates emotions, and helps shape our relationships. Although we need to be held, caressed, and embraced, only certain people are permitted close enough to stroke us intimately.

Time. Time, or *chronemics,* is a particularly important dimension of nonverbal communication. We are constantly reminded of its importance by such everyday expressions as "time flies," "don't waste time," "it's about time," "time is money," "I can give you some time," and "I can find time." Most Americans are serious, if not neurotic, about time and are quick to attribute messages and attitudes to "time" behavior. For example, a call at 3 A.M. is usually thought of as being important and urgent, but it could just be a prank call or wrong number. Being on time for a business appointment communicates interest and responsibility, but you want to be "fashionably late" to an informal social gathering.

Time also reflects status and power. Higher-status people act in ways that control the time of others. Superiors, for instance, typically establish the agenda for meetings and determine the amount of time spent in committees, conferences, and other business situations.[51] Greater status may also excuse the abuse of time while still expecting rigid adherence by others.

Cultural expectations and personality influence how time is perceived. Punctuality is interpreted differently in Latin American countries, and Hispanic and Greek cultures are much more relaxed in their daily use of time. Many Westerners find the slow Japanese business style to be incomprehensible, time consuming, and frustrating, and the Japanese find us to be rude and wonder about our "strange hurry."

Personality, too, can determine how time functions for different people. Researchers have identified four basic personality types and each experiences time in unique ways that affect their communication behaviors.[52] The *thinking type* perceives time as flowing from the past to the future with the present as a time for assessing where an idea, for instance, has been and where it is probably headed. Thinking types enjoy being logical, plotting issues out through time, discovering principles and processes for a problem—planning. This type sees time as linear. The *feeling type* is "trapped in the remembrance of things past." For them, the present is shaped by past experiences. This extreme association with the past makes change difficult. The *sensation type* perceives time mainly in terms of the present; where they have been or where they are going are relatively unimportant. Sensation types are realists who cannot tolerate delay and are more action oriented. They are particularly competent in dealing with crises and making immediate decisions. Finally, the *intuitive type* views time primarily in terms of the future. This type is preoccupied with what is possible. Life is spent looking ahead,

▶ SOME PEOPLE SEE WRISTWATCHES AS MENTAL HANDCUFFS

By Loraine O'Connell

In today's frantic world, time is of the essence. Most of us lead far more hectic lives than a mere 24-hour day can accommodate. What with jobs, kids, chores, errands, social obligations and a few hours of sleep each night, most people feel pressed for—and by—time.

But not everybody really knows what time it is. Not everybody really cares. There are among us some defiant souls who not only don't have time on their hands—they don't have it on their wrists either. They refuse to wear a watch, and their reasons range from the common-sensical to the cosmic.

Gerry Lingelback, owner of a Union Park pizza parlor, simply doesn't like wearing jewelry.

"I don't wear bracelets, don't wear rings or any of that stuff," said Lingelbach, 32.

Besides, jewelry can be a hazard in his line of work. Lingelbach tells of a former business partner who was tossing pizza dough around one day when his wristwatch sailed off into a bowl of cheese. Talk about time flying. . . .

Like most people who eschew watches, Lingelbach doesn't feel that he's missing anything.

"I'm not in a job and never have been in a job where I've needed to know what time it was," he said. "But I'd be constantly looking at a watch if I wore it."

By not wearing a watch, Lingelbach frees himself from that need to know what time it is—and more power to him, says Bob Ziller, a social psychologist at the University of Florida.

Ziller, who wears a watch every day, theorizes that the devices are a kind of chain binding us to society's pressures.

"Some people don't like being chained to this kind of societal demand. So by not wearing one, they're in control, not a clock or watch."

Hank McDaniel, 36, co-owner of a Winter Park ad agency, is a prime example of that theory.

"If you don't wear a watch, you are cognizant of time second by second," he said. "You truly feel time and feel that you can control it. You don't feel it controls you."

McDaniel is so into controlling time, in fact, that he plays beat-the-clock every morning.

"It's like a challenge for me. The closer I can wake up to that alarm clock ringing, the better I feel. I've gotten now to where I can open my eyes and in 10 seconds the clock goes off."

He has an uncanny awareness of time despite his disdain for watches. He never misses a deadline and is late for appointments "only when I want to be."

"He's remarkable," says his partner, Lon Winter. "If I ask him what time it is, he's usually within five minutes of being right."

McDaniel attributes this knack to a well-developed "bioclock," which he discovered in adolescence and has been perfecting ever since.

"If I have to get up at 4 in the morning, I'll set myself to get up at 4. I think it all started when I was about 12. Someone asked me one time what time it was and I said 3:30. I didn't have a watch on. And the person said, "How did you do that?"

Although lots of people have given him watches, which he neatly tucks away in their original boxes, it's clear that McDaniel was destined never to wear one.

"If it's an electric watch, it burns up; if it's a waterproof watch, it sucks water; if it's a self-winding watch, it overwinds and breaks. I'm talking $500 watches. I even had one that started running backward."

The only concession McDaniel makes to time is a small clock that sits behind his chair so that he never has to look at it. It's strictly for visitors.

"It keeps people from having to look at their own watches, which annoys me. What's more important? What we're talking about or what time it is?"

Some Type A personalities—those hard-charging, time-driven folks—would have trouble answering that question. In fact, personality may be another factor separating watch-wearers from non-wearers.

A watch "is a kind of mental straitjacket we wear," said Ziller, the UF psychologist. "In a sense we're bound by time. It may be that people who don't wear watches are less anxious, more laid-back people."

That description certainly fits John Citrone, 22, of Orlando. A recent UCF graduate in journalism, Citrone is a free spirit, a drummer in a rock band who marches to his own rather unique beat. Just ask him why he never wears a watch—then sit back and listen as the words tumble out. It's obvious he has spent some time thinking about . . . time.

"What is time? I don't understand the concept. Why can't there be 13 months? Why not make noon when the sun comes up and 12 midnight when the sun goes down? We have a weekend when nobody works. Why don't we work all those weekends and then have a five-week vacation in the summer?"

OK, OK, John. . . .

"And I don't understand people who wear watches but set them 15 minutes ahead. My car clock is off by about 45 minutes, but I don't want to have to reset it. It's a pain, but it's been that way forever. If it falls off the dashboard, I'll leave it on the floor."

But, John, what about. . . ?

"This military time gets me too. They have to do everything differently. . . ."

Of course, Citrone does some things a bit differently too.

Like McDaniel, he relies on his biological clock to tell him when to get up and when to go to sleep.

"I sleep maybe four hours. I'm up 'till 3 or 4 o'clock in the morning," Citrone said. I don't see any point in sleeping if you don't have to. Just because the sun goes down doesn't mean you have to sleep."

Mary Richard is another free spirit. Like Lingelbach,

McDaniel and Citrone, she has been given watches over the years but doesn't see any reason to wear one.

"If I absolutely have to know what time it is, I ask someone, and there are always clocks around."

Wearing a watch is right up there with balancing her checkbook on her list of meaningless activities. Richard is not given to planning ahead and admits to being fashionably late to just about everything.

"If I have some place to go, I wouldn't say I'll kill myself trying to get there on time," she said. "I will make some effort because other people are more in tune with time and more worried about it. I'm more concerned with other things—you know, the manatees, the loss of the rain forest, world hunger."

Source: Loraine O'Connell, "Some People See Wristwatches as Mental Handcuffs," *The Orlando Sentinel*, May 30, 1990, E1–E3.

trying to see around the next bend in the road—a road which is never straight because one bend always leads to another. Intuitives feel they must change the world to realize their visions of the future. This sense of mission, when combined with a vision of what could be, is perhaps their most outstanding talent.

Time, serving a variety of functions in communication and influencing the way messages are formed and received, communicates in many clear and forceful ways.

Paralanguage. Paralanguage, or *paralinguistics,* refers to something beyond or in addition to language itself. Such variables as tone, volume, breathiness, nasality, and pitch offer a lot of information about a speaker's personality, attitude, status, and feelings. With information from the voice it is possible to predict physical characteristics, aptitudes and interests, personality traits, and overall personality.[53] Listeners can correctly identify a speaker's ethnic group, education, and dialectal region.[54] There is evidence, too, that social status can be determined in large part by the signals we receive from the voice alone.[55] And, we make judgments about the drawl, the rate, and the clipping of sounds.

Listeners can also identify certain emotions from vocal cues. Affection, anger, boredom, disgust, fear, joy, and sadness can be clearly expressed.[56] Voice is a predictor and an initial indicator, and we react to it.

Verbal and nonverbal messages convey content and define relationships. Through the use of verbal symbols, words and language, we relay information, opinions, and attitudes in an effort to influence the behavior of others. Language, however, is a complex and at times troublesome vehicle affecting both the cultures and the people involved in meaningful exchange. Especially bothersome is the arbitrary and often abstract relationship among words, objects, and thoughts.

Nonverbal messages are outside of spoken and written languages, but they transmit a great deal of meaning. Where words usually convey ideas, nonverbal cues express emotions, attitudes, and self, and serve certain regulatory functions. Nonverbally, we communicate through signs and emblems, our body motion, the objects and artifacts that are our surroundings, space and territory, touch, time, and our voice and vocalizations. The quantity of nonverbal stimuli that exists indicates how important it is to the total process of communication. However, although a large portion of the meaning of our message(s) is carried nonverbally, these codes are culturally influenced and overreactions to nonverbal cues can create many misunderstandings.

Given our discussion of message factors, particularly nonverbal cues, we can see that we cannot *not* behave and consequently we cannot *not* communicate. No matter what we do, we send out messages that say something about ourselves. In effect, each of us is a kind of transmitter that cannot be shut off.

Channel Factors

A message achieves physical reality after passing through a given channel of communication. A channel is the medium selected to carry the message—air and light waves; air, light, and sound waves; or electrical impulses. Channels of communication, then, include such oral, face-to-face activities as conversations, business presentations, meetings, interviews, and discussions, and such written activities as letters, memos, news bulletins, reports, proposals, policies, and manuals. They also include such technological processes as the telephone, teletype, word-processing machines, microfilm, radio, television, videotape, and computers. The channel selected determines whether the messages will be communicated to a narrow internal group of others or to a large, external portion of the public.

The channel is basic to any study of communication and the channel chosen significantly influences the nature of the message received. In many instances, the success of your message depends on the channel you select. For example, during the 1960 presidential debates, John Kennedy was more effective using the medium of television than was Richard Nixon, whose bushy eyebrows and gaunt appearance projected a less dynamic and less credible public image. Or consider the fireside chats delivered by Franklin Roosevelt and Jimmy Carter: Roosevelt sat behind his desk in the oval office and broadcast his messages over the radio; Carter used television and was therefore compelled to sit casually dressed in front of a fireplace complete with crackling wood fire. So, mediums of communication each have characteristics that define their limitations; determine degrees of formality, closeness and distance, and personal concern; and create certain receiver expectations. Marshall McLuhan, a media pioneer, observes:

> . . . the medium is the message. . . . the personal and social consequences of any medium—that is, of any extension of ourselves—result from the new scale that is introduced into our affairs by each extension of ourselves, or by any new technology. . . . This fact, characteristic of all media, means that the "content" of any medium is always another medium. The content of writing is speech, just as the written word is the content of print, and print is the content of the telegraph. . . . For the "message" of any medium or technology is the change of scale or pace or pattern that it introduced into human affairs.[57]

In other words, McLuhan is saying the medium shapes the message and influences the event that forms the basis of the message. Therefore, the channel of communication becomes an integral part of the total communication process.

Politicians have long realized the importance of the available channels of communication. Their effective use of oratory and the skills of the public platform are well documented in the many anthologies of great speakers. Certainly Abraham Lincoln was aware of the impact of the print media and newspapers when he released his brief but carefully composed Gettysburg Address. Teddy Roosevelt, Rough Rider, explorer, and man of action, was in large measure a packaged person.[58] And Ronald Reagan has been labeled by many as the "Great Communicator" largely because of the media acumen that enabled him to project a confident, credible, trustworthy image well grounded in frontier values.[59] Media decisions and the effective use of current channels are playing an increasingly important role in political campaigning and in the total political arena.

Business is also aware of the importance of the varying communication channels and the functions they can serve. Hiebert, Unguarit, and Bohn, writing about the economics of mass communication, note that annually "business spends a sum that is approximately 2 percent of the gross national product (GNP) in order to sell their goods and services to American consumers." They add that in "1973 business spent nearly $8 billion on newspaper ads; $1.5 billion on magazine space; $1.6 billion on radio time; $4.6 billion on television advertising; for a total of approximately $25 billion."[60] This reflects the amount spent in a single year on only one aspect of external communication—advertising. It doesn't include public relations and sales efforts, or such scanning and information-gathering activities as client surveys, market research, industrial intelligence, wage and salary surveys, and economic forecasts. Additionally, there are the many internal communication activities such as orientation sessions, departmental meetings, policy sessions, reports, focus groups, quality circles, and correspondence. In every instance an appropriate channel of communication must be selected.

Organizations process information through many channels and each of these channels can influence messages differently. This has lead Daft and Lengel to introduce the concept of "media richness," where richness is "the medium's capacity to change understanding," and to develop a "richness hierarchy."[61] According to this perspective, face-to-face interactions are the richest medium, followed in descending order by videophone and videoconferencing, telephone, electronic mail, personally addressed documents such as memos and letters, and formal, unaddressed documents such as bulletins and flyers. Face-to-face interactions are considered the richest medium because they allow for immediate feedback so that understanding can be checked and multiple cues provided to convey information beyond the spoken word, thus enhancing the understanding of the message. Face-to-face communications also use a more personal, natural language, and the messages are tailored to the receiver. Written communications are typically lower in richness than oral communications because feedback is limited, certain auditory and visual cues are filtered out, and the tone of the message is considerably less personal, conforming to a standard format. This suggests, then, that each medium is a complex information-conveying channel unique in terms of feedback, cues, and language variety which, in turn, significantly affect message content and reception.

These findings assume applicability if we consider what happened to the Pierce-Arrow. The Pierce-Arrow was a stylish automobile successfully manufactured in Buffalo, New York. However, by the 1950s Pierce-Arrow sales had dramatically declined and the corporation's catastrophic financial difficulties had brought it to the brink of foreclosure. In an attempt to avoid closing its doors, management personally met with the employees and discussed their desperate situation. The employees agreed to work for a month without pay to carry the company through the crisis and avoid otherwise-impending disaster, but three weeks later Pierce-Arrow publicly announced its close. Although the employees were paid for work performed, despite their previous agreement, they were extremely resentful of the company's not personally informing them of the shutdown. Here a rich medium was successfully used to initially persuade the employees, and a less-rich medium was later used to inform them of the close. The final outcome probably could not have been avoided, but it could have been more effectively communicated to employees. Lee Iacocca and Chrysler had a similar situation with a more positive result in the mid-1970s. Iacocca was able to personally persuade employees to forego salary increases to stabilize Chrysler financially with the help of a sizable government loan that he also personally orchestrated. Using the rich medium of face-to-face discussions he was able to avoid closing and to save Chrysler.

Channels of communication are receiving considerably more attention today than they did in the past. McLuhan, in *The Medium Is the Message,* suggests why when he writes:

> The medium, or process of our time—electric technology—is reshaping and restructuring patterns of social interdependence and every aspect of our personal life. It is forcing us to reconsider and re-evaluate practically every thought, every action, and every institution formerly taken for granted. Everything is changing . . . changing dramatically.[62]

Modern technology has made available a variety of new mediums of communication—voice messaging, faxing, electronic mail, teleconferencing, and computer conferencing—which exert a profound influence on us and our environments.[63] These new electronic mediums with their unique properties present both challenges and opportunities.

Computers have also revolutionized the way we manage information. They competently manage voluminous data, codifying, storing, processing information as it relentlessly increases in quantum leaps. "It can collect *and never forget* facts, numbers, symbols, statements; it can hold statistics and compute trends; it can find connections between items in different files, connections that may have escaped the human operators."[64] Computers, claims Raymond K. Neff, biostatistician, "can do all that a library can do. . . . Computers can do even more." In being able to rearrange and edit text, and to synthesize diverse information from many sources, "the computer can make information dynamic, whereas the library can only make it available."[65]

Remarkable in its appeal, the computer, its applications, and its effects appear to be ubiquitous. At the University of Utah, Kristin M. McBride and Ann M. B. Austin experimentally discovered that approximately 91 percent of young children chose the computer as their preferred activity channel in a play situation during classroom activities.[66] Wayne Danielson reports that, at the University of Wisconsin, forest management is taught by using a computer simulator to show growth patterns of trees and the effects of different harvesting policies.[67] And, in Harvard University's prestigious graduate program in business administration, students explore management problems through the use of computer simulations. Moreover, physicians, engineers and lawyers are using three-dimensional, computer-generated visualization to depict anatomical features and structural processes, and to demonstrate courtroom evidence.[68] Still, given these advances, development plans for computers now blue-printed exceed expectations thought grandiose when first introduced. Laser disk storage technology will make possible unequalled capacity; on one side of a single disk the contents of an entire set of an encyclopedia can be stored, with ample space remaining for the filing of annual updating editions. Any item of encyclopedic information so recorded can be accessed in mere fractions of a second. Even more spectacular are predictions for the computers of the next century. These machines will register input of voice, graphics, and handwriting; they will be able to recognize people, their voices, and their general characteristics. Simultaneous input functioning, in contrast to current serial input, will characterize these advanced computers because multiple processing will stem from multiple inputs. Endowed with this ability, these computers will have a unique mode of prioritizing, reasoning, and thinking.[69]

Despite this ongoing explosion in compute technology, L. M. Branscomb of IBM observes that computers serve only as a problem-solving mechanism, as a "powerful servant," not as a "powerful god."[70] Joseph Weizenbaum, professor of computer science at M.I.T., further declares that no nonhuman organism, such as a computer, can "confront genuine human problems in human terms." These systems permit "the asking of only certain kinds of questions," and accept "only certain kinds of data."[71] He insistently maintains that various human concerns are not amenable to computer processing and that there are indeed human objectives and human inquiries that are inappropriate for machines. As a computer scientist, he counsels us about the dangers of theorizing "that life is what is computable and only that."[72] For example, in Toronto, Harvey A. Skinner and Barbara A. Allen found that people with alcohol-related problems who voluntarily sought help at a counseling clinic answered personal questions consistently whether asked in a computerized interview, a face-to-face interview, or a self-report questionnaire. But clients generally found the computerized interview "more interesting and relaxing" than the other two modes of information gathering, suggesting "favorable acceptance of the computer." However, the Canadian researchers contrasted this finding with the observation that "face-to-face assessment formats have the advantage of allowing clinicians to probe and obtain more in-depth knowledge of a client, which may result in better treatment planning and outcome," indicating a significant limitation of computer usage in diagnostic efforts by behavioral therapists.[73] Human beings and computers, therefore, exist and operate in a shared sphere, but are distinctive from each other.

Jean-Louis Gassee, who formerly managed a subsidiary of the Apple Computer Corporation in France and who now serves as vice president for product development in the Macintosh Division, observes that "the computer is only a tool, a mediator; if the data it has been given are wrong, the output will be meaningless. . . . Discernment remains an essential virtue that no tool . . . can replace."[74] Proceeding from this premise, Gassee refers to computers as being designed for a "subordinate place" and declares that they are an "instrument that allows the mind to take flight. What counts is for progress in technology to give priority to compatibility with the desires of human beings and with their intelligence."[75] Unable to make decisions for us, computers save time and free the mind by making several complicated calculations at once. Supplied with data, human beings can proceed to make decisions from among options. Samuel Turkle points out that "computers are not good or bad, they are powerful," and advises that there be allowance for a "continuity between the psychologies of machines and people."[76] Augmenting this advice, Donald E. Williams, professor of communication at the University of Florida, notes that the computer "should be understood and respected in terms of its operating dynamics, its performance, dependent on commands by a human being."[77] Certainly, then, our selecting an appropriate channel of communication will continue to be an important and influential factor.

Noise, as noted earlier in the chapter, is any distracting stimulus present in a channel that is picked up by the receiver; it exists in all channels of communication. This interference can be either a physical or a semantic discordance. The former includes those aspects frequently labeled as "noise" such as loud sounds, bright lights, and room temperature. The latter refers to "message noise"—divergent backgrounds, held prejudices, and message interests. Both can distort and block communication, thus significantly influencing the potential of communication effectiveness.

These hindrances or barriers change the message, and these changes are referred to by communication scholars as *entropy*. As used in the field of communication, entropy refers to a loss of information, shift of emphasis, or addition of new symbols, all contributing to possible misinterpretations. It might be considered a measure of message disorder.

Channels of communication influence the message and its reception, and within any channel there is an element of noise or interference. This interference can be either physical or psychological in nature. The study of noise is a study of entropy, and it can be useful as a means of identifying disorders and overcoming communication barriers.

Receiver Factors

Receivers are typically thought of as people who receive messages from other people and the environment. However, as receivers, we are continuously transacting with our environment and thereby also sending messages. Receivers share with senders of messages the basic source factors, feelings, past experiences, and physiological processes.

Two specific receiver dimensions deserve attention. Receivers assess the credibility of sources and messages, deciding whether to trust and believe or to reject the communication. They also provide feedback which binds the communication process together.

Credibility, or perceived trustworthiness, dynamism, competency, and dependability, has long been recognized as a definitive variable in the communication process. Some 2,300 years ago, Aristotle observed, "We believe good men more fully and more readily than others; this is true generally whatever the question is, and absolutely true where exact certainty is impossible and opinions are divided . . . his character may almost be called the most effective means of persuasion he possesses."[78] How we present ourselves and how we are perceived affects our impact on others. Yale researchers Hovland and Mandell noted in 1952 that speakers perceived as having admirable motives tend to be more credible, and those seen as having selfish or self-serving motives are considered less credible.[79]

Perception is central to establishing credibility. How we perceive others determines their trustworthiness. Saying "trust me" does not establish a trusting relationship; it must be experienced. Paul Watzlawick and his associates describe the very interesting way in which trusting relationships are established between trainers and bottlenosed porpoises. A trainer places a hand into the mouth of the porpoise, which has jaws and teeth capable of biting the hand off cleanly. The porpoise, seemingly aware of the vulnerability of the human hand, next moves to reciprocate by placing the forward ventral portion of its body (the most vulnerable part, corresponding to the human throat) upon the trainer's hand. Thus, messages of trust are exchanged and credibility achieved.[80] Human-to-human relationships require similar risk-taking to establish trust but the process is not quite as simple. We are reticent to make ourselves vulnerable and tend to be cautious in our communication and self-disclosure. Similarly, we are doubtful and questioning of others until their veracity is proven. A study of 137 executives and purchasing directors from 70 metalworking companies found that decisions on awarding contracts were more than twice as likely to be based on the credibility of the suppliers than on any other factor. They felt that someone they could work well with, who was honest and dependable, was even more important than price.[81]

What influences credibility? Some of the influences include physical appearance, power, competence, trustworthiness, good will, idealism, and dynamism. The general attractiveness, style of dress, manners, age, and physical aspects of height–weight–muscle tone, and voice initially affect credibility. Power, whether legitimate, rewarding, or coercive, influences receivers. Competence refers to a source's expertise or qualifications that make one an authority. However, trustworthiness can ultimately be measured only by one's past performance. Past behaviors give evidence whether a person is trustworthy or honest, dependable, and consistent in behavior. Goodwill refers to a source's ability to understand the receiver's needs and to be aware of the respective/mutual needs. Idealism is the perceived ability to dream, to aspire to higher ideals, to be more virtuous. Finally, dynamism reveals a person who is energetic, totally involved, and committed.

These elements of credibility interact with each other and with all of the other communication variables that are operative during any particular communication event. Anything and everything can influence the receiver's perception of a source's credibility. That credibility is not a static factor, but rather a dynamic one that is ever-changing throughout the course of communication.

Feedback refers to the verbal and nonverbal responses to messages. Verbal feedback includes spoken or written responses; nonverbal feedback consists of vocal inflections, gestures, and even silence. It is impossible to have verbal feedback without some form of nonverbal feedback, but it is possible to have only nonverbal feedback such as applause, laughing, or yawns of boredom. Feedback provides us a way of determining whether messages sent are interpreted as intended and consequently can be a self-monitoring device, allowing us to modify our behaviors until the responses meet our expectations.

Feedback may be immediate or delayed, depending on the channel selected. Face-to-face interactions provide immediate feedback; print and selected electronic media necessarily provide more delayed feedback. And, despite its time-consuming features, feedback increases accuracy and understanding, and promotes participation and involvement. It is readily apparent that feedback is vital to the total communication process.

Environmental Factors

Communicators use their receptive senses to receive and their past conditioning to interpret the symbols that make up our environment. Edward Hall says, "Man's relationship to his environment is a function of his sensory apparatus plus how this apparatus is conditioned to respond."[82]

There are too many factors, combinations of factors, and combinations of responses to be able to predict with any certainty the precise influence of the physical environment on communication. What can be described are some selected aspects which affect the communication process. Among the aspects that might serve as a useful way of examining environmental influences are: symbol overload, visual components, and atmosphere.

Symbol overload is the giving and receiving of too much information. The number of symbols with potential information value making up our environment can be imposing and overwhelming. Such symbol density presents a formidable barrier to communication and can create confusion. However, because a large number of messages may overburden individuals and work groups, messages are reduced by two key processes—message routing and message summarizing.[83] *Message routing* causes a particular communication or message to be distributed to only an identified few, thus greatly reducing the information-processing load for the many having little or no use for the information. *Message summarizing* plays a similar role, reducing the size of the message and at the same time faithfully reproducing its meaning. For example, large sets of numbers are replaced by their average, and multipage reports are replaced by abstracts.

Visual components are also a part of the environment. Visually, we are concerned with objects, their function, their spatial relationships to each other, and their relationship to other elements of the communicative process. The design of buildings, the rooms in which communication takes place, and their furnishings influence messages.

The atmosphere is the resultant composite of all environmental stimuli. It may be formal or informal, depending upon the degree of ritual governing the communication situation. A White House press conference will be considerably more formal than a typical classroom discussion.

Key factors existing in our composite model and influencing the total communication process have been identified and described. Although our discussion treated each factor in isolation, each component actually functions in conjunction with the others. Communication with others is essentially "the encounter of two semantic reactors, of two human capsules in flight, each following its own orbit, with its mass, its momentum, its direction, and its capacity to withstand shocks."[84]

▶ SUMMARY

In this chapter, the process of communication has been the focus of attention. We examined human communication as a major means of identification with others and as a principle skill for adapting to our world and influencing the world around us.

Basic models describing the communication process were presented in an effort to better clarify this act we call human communication. These disparate views isolated the variables in the process, allowing us to better see the essential interaction. This revealed communication to be something more than the simple process we generally take for granted. Communication was revealed to be a complex, dynamic process in which a number of factors interact to produce effects.

Recognizing that no model has yet been developed to account for the very complex nature of communication, a composite model identifying primary factors was presented. This model provided a means to more fully define selected source factors, message factors, channel factors, receiver factors, and environmental factors. Analysis of these factors revealed core elements involved in the communication process—you and me, our ideas, our problems and decisions, our words and actions, a time, a place, and an immediate situation.

Communication permits us to make contact. Effective communication can unlock people to each other and reveal to them their world. Howard Martin and C. William Colburn observe that "we have to understand talk as thoroughly as we can, and we need the faith to believe that it can, in crucial ways, make us one people."[85]

In the following chapters, the factors affecting communication—source, message, channel, receiver, and environment—are overlaid onto the organizational setting. Emphasis is shifted from a general examination of communication principles to an examination of a business and professional arena filled with activity.

▶ QUESTIONS FOR DISCUSSION AND SKILL DEVELOPMENT

1. Why is it difficult to define communication in a way that is widely accepted? What is your personal definition of communication? Why have you chosen it?

2. What views of communication are provided by the selected models? What are the main foci in the Shannon-Weaver information theory model? What is communication like according to Berlo's process model? How does the composite model reflect each of these perspectives? How is it different? Draw a model describing your definition of communication. What elements are emphasized? Why?

3. Select a person with whom you have had several misunderstandings and/or disagreements. Make a detailed list of the person's likes, dislikes, background, abilities, and so on until you have a fairly good idea of his or her frame of reference. Then make a similar list for yourself. How do the two lists compare? Could frame-of-reference differences account for the misunderstandings and/or disagreements?

4. What are signs, symbols, and signals? How does language result in meaning? Distinguish between denotative and connotative meanings. What do words do? According to the Sapir-Whorf hypothesis, what is the relationship between language and our perceptions of reality? How do semantic principles relate to perceptual problems that often exist between managers and their subordinates? Select a profession or occupation and note the jargon or word usage unique to that field.

5. How do nonverbal and verbal messages relate to each other? Do verbal or nonverbal codes communicate cognitive messages more effectively? Affective messages? List three differences between verbal and nonverbal messages you have observed in business and professional settings. Give specific examples.

6. Watch the television newscasters on two or three stations. Do they dress differently? What impressions does each communicate? Look at pictures of high government and corporate officials. What kinds of clothing do they wear? What impressions does each communicate?

7. Daily we turn to various mediums to discover what has been happening. Rank-order the following news sources in terms of which you most frequently use and trust, and explain why: radio—newspapers—news magazines—television.

8. Write in a narrative form about a personal experience pertaining to a specific communication problem. What led to the problem? Why did you see it as a problem? Did others see it as a problem? How serious was the problem? What attempts were made to resolve the problem? What advice would you give others experiencing a similar problem? Identify the salient features and relate them to the communication variables and concerns discussed in class.

9. Prepare a "Personal Communication Log." For a single day, monitor the various communication activities you engage in and for what purpose(s). Who do you talk to? Why? What type(s) of communication do you engage in most frequently? Be specific. What about listening?

1. Marshall McLuhan, *The Gutenberg Galaxy* (New York: Signet Books, 1969): 43.
2. Ernest G. Bormann, William S. Howell, Ralph G. Nichols, and George L. Shapiro, *Interpersonal Communication in the Modern Organization* (Englewood Cliffs, NJ: Prentice Hall, 1969): 17.
3. *The Oxford English Dictionary,* 2nd ed., vol. II (Oxford: Clarendon, 1961): 699.
4. Gary Cronkhite, *Communication and Awareness* (Menlo Park, CA: Cummings, 1976).
5. Claude Shannon and Warren Weaver, *The Mathematical Theory of Communication* (Urbana, IL: University of Illinois Press, 1949): 114.
6. L. C. Hawes, *Pragmatics of Analogueing: Theory and Model Construction in Communication* (Reading, MA: Addison-Wesley, 1975): 87.
7. David K. Berlo, *The Process of Communication: An Introduction to Theory and Practice* (New York: Holt, Rinehart & Winston, 1960): 49. Copyright © 1960 by Holt, Rinehart & Winston, Inc., and renewed by David K. Berlo, reproduced by permission of the publisher.
8. Frank E.X. Dance, *Human Communication Theory* (New York: Holt, Rinehart & Winston, 1967): 294–295.
9. This composite model reflects a general semantics perspective. See Alfred Korzybski, *Science and Sanity,* 4th ed. (Lakerville, CT: Institute of General Semantics, 1958); Wendell Johnson, *People and Quandries* (New York: Harper and Row, 1946); and J. Samuel Bois, *The Art of Awareness* (Dubuque, IA: Wm. C. Brown, 1966).
10. Dance, *Human Communication Theory,* 296.
11. Stephen Littlejohn and David Jabusch, "Communication Competence: Model and Application," *Journal of Applied Communication Research* 10 (1982): 29–37.
12. Gay Gaer Luce, *Body Time* (New York: Bantam Books, 1971).
13. Berlo, *Process of Communication,* 49.
14. J. L. Aranguren, *Human Communication* (New York: McGraw-Hill, 1967): 11.
15. Steven Beebe and John Masterson, *Communicating in Small Groups* (Glenview, IL: Scott, Foresman, 1982): 27.
16. Korzybski, *Science and Sanity,* 58.
17. Charles Ogden and I. A. Richards, *The Meaning of Meaning* (New York: Harcourt, Brace and World, 1946): 11.
18. S. I. Hayakawa, *The Use and Misuse of Language* (Greenwich, CT: Fawcett, 1962): 179.
19. S. I. Hayakawa, *Language in Thought and Action,* 2nd ed. (Orlando, FL: Harcourt Brace Jovanovich, 1964): 189.
20. Stuart Chase, *The Power of Words* (New York: Harcourt Brace Jovanovich, 1953): 154.
21. Gerard I. Nierenberg and Henry H. Calero, *Meta-Talk* (New York: Pocket Books, 1974).
22. D. Mandelbaum, *Selected Writings of Edward Sapir in Language, Culture, and Personality* (Los Angeles: University of California Press, 1949): 16.
23. John B. Carroll, *Language, Thought, and Reality: Selected Writings of Benjamin Lee Whorf* (New York: John Wiley & Sons, 1956): 212–213.
24. J. Whatmough, *Language: A Modern Synthesis* (New York: New American Library, 1956).
25. R. Lavidge and G. Steiner, "A Model for Predictive Measurements of Advertising Effectiveness," *Journal of Marketing* 25 (1961): 59–62.
26. W. Charles Redding, *Communication Within the Organization* (New York: Industrial Communication Council, 1972).
27. Gerald Goldhaber, *Organizational Communication,* 5th ed. (Dubuque, IA: Wm. C. Brown, 1990).
28. Harold Lasswell, "The Structure and Function of Communication in Society," in: L. Bryson, ed. *The Communication of Ideas* (New York: Institute for Religious and Social Studies, 1948).
29. Charles Wright, *Mass Communication* (New York: Random House, 1959).
30. Dean Barnlund, *Interpersonal Communication: Survey and Studies* (New York: Houghton Mifflin, 1968): 535–536.
31. Ray Birdwhistell, "Background to Kinesics," *ETC* 13 (1955): 10–18.
32. Albert Mehrabian, "Communication Without Words," *Psychology Today* 2 (1968): 53.
33. Paul Ekman and Wallace Friesen, "The Repertoire of Nonverbal Behavior: Categories, Origins, Usage, and Coding," *Semiotica* 1 (1969): 49–98.
34. Mark L. Knapp, *Essentials of Nonverbal Communication* (New York: Holt, Rinehart & Winston, 1980).

35. Dale G. Leathers, *Successful Nonverbal Communication: Principles and Applications* (New York: Macmillan, 1986).

36. Albert Mehrabian, *Silent Messages* (Belmont, CA: Wadsworth, 1971).

37. J. K. Burgoon, D. B. Buller, J. L. Hale, and M. A. de Turk, "Relational Messages Associated with Nonverbal Behaviors," *Human Communication Research* 10 (1984): 351–378.

38. Randall Harrison, "Nonverbal Behavior: An Approach to Human Communication," in: R. Budd and B. Ruben, eds., *Approaches to Human Communication* (New York: Spartan Books, 1972).

39. Ray Birdwhistell, *Kinesics and Context* (New York: Ballantine Books, 1970).

40. See H. Rosenfeld, "Instrumental Affiliative Functions of Facial and Gestural Expressions," *Journal of Personality and Social Psychology* 4 (1966): 65–72; and Albert Mehrabian and M. Williams, "Nonverbal Concomitants of Perceived and Intended Persuasiveness," *Journal of Personality and Social Psychology* 13 (1969): 37–58.

41. Paul Ekman, Wallace Friesen, and P. Ellsworth, *The Face and Emotion* (New York: Pergamon Press, 1971).

42. Ekman and Friesen, "Repertoire of Nonverbal Behavior," *Semiotica*, 49–98.

43. Mark Knapp, *Nonverbal Communication in Human Interaction,* 2nd ed. (New York: Holt, Rinehart & Winston, 1978).

44. Martin Remland, "Developing Leadership Skills in Nonverbal Communication: A Situational Perspective," *Journal of Business Communication* 3 (1981): 17–29.

45. Edward T. Hall, *The Hidden Dimension* (New York: Doubleday, 1966).

46. Edward T. Hall, *The Silent Language* (Garden City, NY: Anchor Books, 1973): 60–96.

47. Knapp, *Essentials of Nonverbal Communication.*

48. Carole Wade and Carol Jarvis, *Psychology* (New York: Harper and Row, 1987): 338.

49. R. Heslin and T. Alper, "Touch: A Bonding Gesture," in: J. M. Wiemann and R. P. Harrison, eds., *Nonverbal Interaction* (Beverly Hills, CA: Sage, 1983): 47–75.

50. Leathers, *Successful Nonverbal Communication.*

51. Remland, "Developing Leadership Skills," *Journal of Business Communication.*

52. H. Mann, M. Siegler, and H. Osmond, "Four Types of Time and Four Ways of Perceiving Time," *Psychology Today* (December 1972): 76–84.

53. E. Kramer, "Judgment of Personal Characteristics and Emotions from Nonverbal Properties," *Psychology Bulletin* 60 (1963): 408–420.

54. G. P. Nerbonne, "The Identification of Speaker Characteristics on the Basis of Aural Cues" (Ph.D. diss., Michigan State University, 1967).

55. S. L. Harms, "Listener Judgments of Status Cues in Speech," *Quarterly Journal of Speech* 47 (1961): 164–168.

56. J. Davitz, *The Communication of Emotional Meaning* (New York: McGraw-Hill, 1964).

57. Marshall McLuhan, *Understanding Media* (New York: Signet Books, 1964): 23–24.

58. George N. Gordon, *Persuasion* (New York: Hastings House, 1971): 132–151.

59. Roderick P. Hart, *Verbal Style and the Presidency* (New York: Academic Press, 1984): 212–237; also see Craig Allen Smith, *Political Communication* (New York: Harcourt Brace Jovanovich, 1990).

60. Ray Hiebert, Donald Unguarit, and Thomas Bohn, *Mass Media* (New York: David McKay, 1974): 36.

61. R. L. Daft and R. H. Lengel, "Organizational Information Requirements, Media Richness, and Structural Design," *Management Science* 32 (1986): 554–571.

62. Marshall McLuhan, *The Medium Is the Message* (New York: Bantam Books, 1967): 5.

63. Mary J. Culnan and M. Lynne Markus, "Information Technologies," in: Fredric M. Jablin, Linda L. Putnam, Karlene H. Roberts, and Lyman W. Porter, eds., *Handbook of Organizational Communication* (Newbury Park, CA: Sage, 1987): 420–443.

64. G. Simons, *Silicon Shock: The Menace of the Computer Invasion* (Oxford: Basil Blackwell, 1985): 3.

65. Raymond K. Neff, "Computing in the University—the Implications of New Technologies," *Perspectives in Computing* 7 (1987): 15.

66. Kristin M. McBride and Ann M. B. Austin, "Computer Affect of Pre-School Children and Perceived Affect of Their Parents, Teachers, and Peers," *Journal of Genetic Psychology* 147 (1986): 497–506.

67. Wayne Danielson, "The Next Generation of Academic Microcomputer Software," *Perspectives in Computing* 7 (1987): 34–40.

68. G. Stix, "Seeing is Believing," *Scientific American* 265 (December 1991): 140–145.

69. B. Sherman, *The New Revolution: The Impact of Computers in Society* (Chichester, England: John Wiley & Sons, 1985).

70. L. M. Branscomb, "Information: The Ultimate Frontier," *Science* 203 (1979): 143–147.

71. Joseph Weizenbaum, *Computer Power and Human Reason: From Judgment to Calculation* (New York: W. H. Freeman, 1976): 222–223.

72. Ibid., 198–200.

73. Harvey A. Skinner and Barbara A. Allen, "Does the Computer Make a Difference? Computerized versus Face-to Face Versus Self-Report Assessment of Alcohol, Drug, and Tobacco Use," *Journal of Consulting and Clinical Psychology* 51 (1983): 267–275.

74. Jean-Louis Gassee, *The Third Apple: Personal Computers and the Cultural Revolution*. I. A. Leonard, trans. (San Diego, CA: Harcourt Brace Jovanovich, 1985): 31.

75. Ibid., 124–125.

76. Samuel Turkle, *The Second Self: Computers and the Human Spirit* (New York: Simon & Schuster, 1984): 272, 323.

77. Donald E. Williams, "Rhetorically Acculturating the Computer as a Given of Society," *American Behavioral Scientist* 32 (1985): 221.

78. Aristotle, *Rhetoric*.

79. Carl Hovland and H. Mandell, "An Experimental Comparison of Conclusion Drawing," *Journal of Abnormal and Social Psychology* 47 (1952): 581–588.

80. Paul Watzlawick, Janet Beavin, and Don Jackson, *Pragmatics of Human Communication* (New York: W. W. Norton, 1967): 103–104.

81. Roger P. Wilcox, *Communication at Work: Writing and Speaking* (Boston: Houghton Mifflin, 1977): 301–302.

82. Hall, *Hidden Dimension*, 51.

83. George P. Hubner and Richard L. Daft, "The Information Environments of Organizations," in: Fredric M. Jablin, Linda L. Putnam, Karlene H. Roberts, and Lyman W. Porter, eds., *Handbook of Organizational Communication* (Newbury Park, CA: Sage, 1987): 130–164.

84. J. Samuel Bois, *The Art of Awareness* (Dubuque, IA: Wm. C. Brown, 1966): 24.

85. Howard H. Martin and C. William Colburn, *Communication and Consensus* (New York: Harcourt Brace Jovanovich, 1972): 19.

CHAPTER THREE

3

The Nature of Organizations and Theoretical Perspectives

LEARNING OBJECTIVES:

To compare and contrast the functional and the meaning-centered approaches to organizational communication

To define and illustrate the term "organization"

To distinguish between open and closed systems

To identify and discuss external environmental factors influencing organizational communication

To identify and define critical internal factors affecting organizational communication

To define the influence of organizational culture on organizations

To understand and explain the basic theories of management that have evolved over the years

To view communication as the fundamental organizational process

We are all organization men and women, with organizations an accepted part of life. All organizations are significantly affected by and, in turn, affect the environment of which they are a part. Although numerous external environmental factors influence all organizations, the core culture and basic philosophy and assumptions of management have very significant effects on organizations. This chapter presents a model of organizational communication, and explores external and selected internal factors that influence organizational practices and, therefore, organizational communication and effectiveness.

It seems so far away, the manor house, an Italian Renaissance monument, shining like Gatsby's elusive green light through the mist of fiction.

It is called Villa Carola, or at least that is what it was called when the late Isaac Guggenheim had it built in 1918. Breathtaking, it stands majestically on a hill overlooking Hempstead Harbor, a perfect site for catching a fragrant breeze . . . or the yearning glances of those kept at a distance. Villa Carola is the whim of another time, surrounded by marble fountains and pampered gardens and lush glades. There are satellites of gatehouses, and beachouses and servants' quarters; the driveways are like great staircases, designed for impressive entrances by important people . . . all the splendors of unlimited wealth.[1]

But the Astors and Woolworths no longer have adjoining mansions, and the 40-room Villa Carola belongs to IBM, which uses it as an executive management training center. Villa Carola, or the Manor House, is reserved as an education center for only a few hundred of the company's top management personnel who are put through executive training courses for two or three weeks. It is regarded as an important indication of a splendid career trajectory when someone is chosen to go through the classes at the Manor House. Jim Parkel, director of management and development planning for IBM, explains the basic purpose of the school: "We try to give our people some life-planning instruction."[2] The intent is to provide information about management style, including courses in interpersonal relationships—communicating.

Since 1938, when Chester Barnard defined the main task of a manager or executive as that of communication,[3] it has been demonstrated continuously that the organization man and woman are communicating people. Effective communication is essential for career development and vital to the life of the modern organization. Executive leadership and management are so closely related to communication that they are almost synonymous.

There seems to be common agreement that communication is the key activity for keeping an organization integrated because it links the parts together. For example, industrial analysts observe that of the 4,500,000 companies in this country, the average length of life is seven years. About 450,000 will go broke this year and another 375,000 will become inactive. In 1986, 138 banks failed, the largest number in one year since the Great Depression of the 1930s. A major cause of problems contributing to this chaos and leading to the eventual collapse of firms rests with ineffective communication—uncertainty, lack of information, and failure to listen carefully.

A number of unique factors operating in the modern organization influence communication. Here, we will overlay the communication process discussed in the previous chapter onto the anatomy and physiology of organizations. The anatomy involves separating the parts of the organization and analyzing their positions, relations, structures, and functions. The physiology deals with the processes and dynamic interactions associated with the life of the organization, and relates to the ways in which the various segments are interdependent and work in cooperation with one another.

▶ FUNCTIONAL AND MEANING-CENTERED PERSPECTIVES

The process of organizational communication can be viewed from functional and/or meaning-centered perspectives.[4] Both of these perspectives address different questions about organizational communication. The *functional perspective* focuses on struc-

▶ IMPORTANCE OF COMMUNICATION AND MANAGEMENT

. . . [C]ommunication is not a secondary or derived aspect of organization—a "helper" of the other presumably more basic functions. It is rather the essence of organized activity and is a basic process out of which all other functions derive. It is entirely possible to view an organization as an elaborate system for gathering, evaluating, combining, and disseminating information.

A. Bavelos and D. Barret

The manager has a specific tool: information. He does not handle people; he motivates, guides, organizes people to do their own work. His tool—his only tool—to do all this is the spoken or written words or the language of numbers.

P. F. Drucker

What is the distinctive job of every manager or supervisor? What is the most important thing he has to do? None of the obvious answers gets to the heart of the manager's job. Nor does the usual breakdown into such activities as planning and assigning work, instructing subordinates, reviewing and appraising progress, establishing and maintaining controls. No matter how varied the activities or how special some of the skills involved, in the final analysis the job of every executive or supervisor is communication. Essentially, he must get work down through other people and to accomplish this he must communicate effectively with them.

American Management Association

Management is communication. . . . The one single thing that each and every manager depends on, that sorts the successes from the failures, is the ability to communicate with other people and to organize their communications among themselves. Your true manager is a catalyst; in his presence, work is achieved that otherwise wouldn't be, even if he himself does not contribute directly to it. *But he can only succeed in that catalytic role if he can inform, instruct, persuade, and motivate other people (and not only those subordinate to him). He can do none of these things unless he can effectively communicate, not merely information, but also attitudes, moods, emotions.* As well as being able to communicate himself, he needs to be receptive; he needs to be able to listen to others, to understand them, to pick up signals from them even if they are unconscious ones. This means being sensitive to all of the physical signs, the nervous habits, the gestures, and expressions with which people supplement their verbal communications. This is a skill that is indispensable to management. . . .

C. Duerr

Communication plays the central role in all administration. Administration is communication.

L. O. Thayer

Business isn't complicated. The complications arise when people are cut off from information they need.

J. F. Welch, Jr.

In every organization that I have come into contact with, communication is usually the number one problem, or it is at least associated with virtually every major problem which the organization faces. This ranges from basic problems of human misunderstanding, all the way to major financial, marketing, and production problems associated with the inability of people to properly communicate with one another.

R. Hilgert

Sources: Alex Bavelos and Dermot Barret, "An Experimental Approach to Organizational Communication," *Personnel* 12 (1951): 368; Peter F. Drucker, *The Practice of Management* (New York: Harper and Row, 1954): 346; Joseph M. Dooher and Viviane Marquist, *Effective Communication on the Job* (New York: American Management Association, 1956): 15; Carl Duerr, *Management Kinetics* (New York: McGraw-Hill, 1971): xiii; Lee O. Thayer, *Administrative Communication* (Homewood, IL: Richard D. Irwin, 1961): 76; N. Tichy and R. Chann, "Speed, Simplicity, Self-Confidence: An Interview with Jack Welch," *Harvard Business Review* 67 (1989): 112-121; and Paul R. Timm, *Managerial Communication: A Finger on the Pulse* (Englewood Cliffs, NJ: Prentice Hall, 1980): 20.

ture and asks what purpose communication serves within organizations and how messages move. The *meaning-centered perspective* focuses on the individual and asks if communication is the process through which organizing, decision making, problem solving, influence, and culture occur. The functional perspective describes organizational reality in such terms as tall/flat structures, chains of command, scale and scope, positions, roles, communication flow, and communication channels; the meaning-centered perspective identifies reality through human interaction and describes it in terms of communication rules and climate.

The functional perspective helps us understand organizational communication by describing what messages do and how they move through organizations. This perspective views communication as a complex organizational process that serves organizing, relationship, and change functions—information processing. The way messages move is described by examining communication networks, channels, message directions, communication load, and distortion. This perspective suggests that communication transmits rules, regulations, and information throughout the organization; that communication establishes and defines human relationships, helps people identify with goals and opportunities, and is the process by which the organization generates and manages change.

The meaning-centered perspective views communication as the dynamic interaction of human beings in organizational contexts and seeks to understand the construction of shared realities. As such, to understand the communication process there is a need to look beyond the technical function or the interpretations of messages. How messages facilitate social order, maintain structure, and set up patterns is of prime importance. The issue is how communication helps or hinders the process of coordination in an organization. From this perspective, influence style, decision making, problem solving, team building, communication climate, and organizational culture become critical variables. Specifically, the meaning-centered perspective suggests that organizations exist through human interaction; structure and technologies result from the information to which people react.

Functional and/or meaning-centered perspectives can serve as frameworks for examining organizational systems/subsystems as well as for analyzing specific organizational situations and problems. Each perspective assumes a unique focus, permitting us to identify important factors and necessary skills contributing to communication effectiveness and organizational success.

▶ORGANIZATIONS DEFINED

Organizations have existed for thousands of years; they are not unique to this highly technological age. The pharaohs of Egypt used organizations to build the Pyramids. The emperors of China used organizations to construct irrigation systems and the Great Wall of China. And the early popes fashioned a universal church. There were even early manuals which might loosely be viewed as guides to organizational behavior (see, for example, Machiavelli's *The Prince*). This century, however, has ushered in what A. G. Kefalas refers to as the "Age of Organizational Awareness." He observes that "historians will most likely describe this age as man's conscious attempt to devise a coherent set of general propositions which could be used as principles in explaining the most prevalent phenomenon of the time, namely the rise, the establishment, the growth and, at times, the disappearance of social organizations, such as business enterprises, educational institutions, and so on."[5] He is saying that understanding the modern organization and its transformation has become an active concern. Scholars in diverse fields of study are trying to define modern organizations and are searching for a theory of organizational behavior. The insights provided by economists, management analysts, sociologists, industrial psychologists, organizational consultants, and those in communication still exist as bits and pieces, somewhat like the pieces of a jigsaw puzzle before they are put into place, making a completed picture impossible. And complicating matters is the currently chaotic organizational environment that challenges everything we thought we knew and demands coping with uncertainty. Alvin Toffler observes that "the period beginning in the mid-1950s and ending approximately seventy-five years later, in 2025... can be called the hinge of history, the period in which smokestack civilization, having dominated the earth for centuries, is finally replaced by another, far different one following a period of world-shaking power struggles."[6] What this means is a period of redefinition.

J. G. March and H. A. Simon note that "it is easier, and probably more useful, to give examples of formal organizations than to define them."[7] Any examination of the listings in the New York Stock Exchange, or AMEX would serve as examples or illustrations of modern organizations, as would *Baron's* listing of colleges and universities or the many federal, county, and local governmental agencies. A simple but more descriptive definition, written in a journalistic style, comes from Porter, Lawler, and Hackman:

1. Who: composed of individuals and groups.
2. Why: in order to achieve certain goals and objectives.
3 & 4. How: by means of differentiated functions that are intended to be rationally coordinated and directed.
5. When: through time on a continuous basis.[8]

Perhaps the most complete and encompassing definition is provided by Amitai Etzioni:

Organizations are social units (or human groupings) deliberately constructed and reconstructed to seek specific goals. Corporations, armies, schools, hospitals, churches, and prisons are included; tribes, classes, ethnic groups, friendship groups, and families are excluded. Organizations are characterized by: (1) divisions of labor, power, and communication responsibilities, divisions which are not random or traditionally patterned, but deliberately planned to enhance the realization of specific goals; (2) the presence of one or more power centers which control the concerted efforts of the organization and direct them toward its goals; these power centers also must review continuously the organization's performance and re-pattern its structure, where necessary, to increase its efficiency; (3) substitution of personnel, i.e., unsatisfactory persons can be removed and others assigned their tasks. The organization can also recombine its personnel through transfer and promotion.... Hence, organizations are much more in control of their nature and destiny than any other social grouping.[9]

This classic definition brings together the key elements characterizing organizations both for today and tomorrow. They are deliberate entities evincing a division of labor and directing people toward particular goals. As this definition suggests, organizations represent a complex combination of activities and behaviors.

►ORGANIZATIONS AS SYSTEMS

Critical to an understanding of organizational communication from either a functional or a meaning-centered perspective is the realization that an organization is a system of individuals working for some common, explicit purpose or goal. H. G. Hicks observes that "an organization is a structural process in which persons interact for objectives."[10] This work is accomplished through an established hierarchical structure and a division of labor that relies on a formal/informal communication subsystem. This subsystem links external and internal environments and integrates all activity. Communication provides a means for making and executing decisions, obtaining feedback, and adjusting organizational objectives and procedures as the situation demands. The modern organization is essentially a communication-processing system.

A systems approach to organizations and organizational communication is indeed a holistic one where a change in the appropriate pattern and balance in any one part will affect the whole, initiating patterns of adjustment and readjustment capable of changing the whole. As Wilden expresses it, "causes cause causes to cause causes."[11] Put another way, "the organization is an open, sociotechnical system composed of a number of subsystems and in continuing interaction with its environmental suprasystem."[12] A systems perspective calls attention to the elements that compose the organization—its internally related parts—and its economic/societal cultural/environmental interface. This means that an organization is an open system and consequently its internal components continuously interact with its external environment. Open systems continually take in new information, transform that information, and give information back to the environment. Communication is an essential element in this open system, pervading all activities in the modern organization; it is the living fluid and brain waves of those making up today's organization. By contrast, closed systems are characterized by a lack of input communication, making it difficult to make good decisions and stay current with the environment. It is critical, then, that organizations not be closed, isolated, self-contained systems, for where there is no open exchange, be it internal or external, a system will stagnate and wither. This can be labeled entropy as opposed to a steady state where growth and development occur.

The modern organization, when considered as an open system, can be characterized as being:

1. diverse—a multiplicity of paths exist to obtain organizational goals.
2. self-regulating—the modern organization is flexible, capable of adjusting to adversity and unexpected difficulties.
3. self-corrective—feedback, whether positive or negative, serves to regulate both internal and external activities.
4. cyclical—just as we considered the communication process to be cyclical and constantly moving in a helical motion, so we can view the modern organization as being dynamic, changing, and moving through ever-more-complex cycles.
5. energetic—energy can be stored and used when most needed so that fresh approaches are introduced into the system and people are motivated.

Thus, in studying the modern organization it is most useful to concentrate on the processes linking the parts together—communication—rather than to microanalyze individual structural components. So, here, a systems model or framework will be advanced to make sense of organizational behavior.

▶ MODEL OF ORGANIZATIONAL COMMUNICATION

If a picture is worth a thousand words, a visual model can be helpful in conceptualizing the variables central to organizational communication (see Exhibit 3-1). The model outlined assumes a systems perspective. This approach places organizational

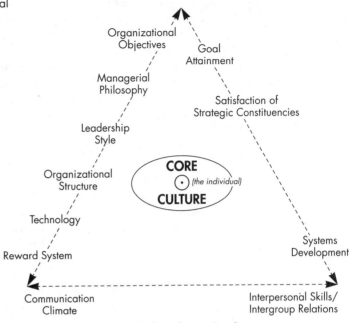

▶ **EXHIBIT 3-1**
Model of Organizational
Communication System

Changing External Environment

Organizational
Objectives

Goal
Attainment

Managerial
Philosophy

Satisfaction of
Strategic Constituencies

Leadership
Style

CORE ⊙ *(the individual)* **CULTURE**

Organizational
Structure

Technology

Systems
Development

Reward System

Communication
Climate

Interpersonal Skills/
Intergroup Relations

**Societal Culture/Values
Economic Conditions**

communication within the larger context of the organization by focusing on the dynamics displayed by the many interacting variables and elements.

The organization exists in a changing external environment comprising fluctuating economic conditions and a prevailing societal culture with its values. The permeable membrane composing the inner triangle suggests the open interface between the organization and its environment. It emphasizes the importance of organizations to be flexible, porous, and adaptive. The environment can be said to represent a set of constraints, opportunities, or threats to the organization. In negotiating with its external environment, the organization adopts a set of goals that, in turn, influence its internal climate.

One side of the triangle lists those elements making up the internal organization (organizational objectives, managerial philosophy, leadership style, organizational structure, technology, and reward system); the second side identifies those components contributing to organizational effectiveness (goal attainment, satisfaction of strategic constituencies, and systems development). Serving as a base and connecting the two sides is a communication system. Characterized by a climate of trust or distrust, supportiveness or defensiveness, and dependent upon interpersonal skills and intergroup relations, this communication system is vital to the continued maintenance and growth of the organization.

· The inner circle depicts the organizational center or core culture—the vision, mission, philosophy, and set of values. And the molecular figure represents the individual human element central to all organizational activity. Nothing happens in an organization until people take action. Any organization is made up of executives, managers, supervisors, secretaries, custodians, and many others who carry on the day-to-day activities. The art of administration is to accomplish goals *through* people, not around, behind, or without them. And the effectiveness of any communication system is dependent upon the awareness and skills of the people in the organization. In his book *Organizational Management Through Communication,* Richard K. Allen refers to an organizational sickness that he labels "communicatrophia," and defines as the "hysterical indifference to the communication problems going on around oneself."[13] This is an illness that plagues many organizations and directs attention to the importance of effective communicators in organizations.

The survival of any system is dependent upon its ability to evolve and adapt to changing circumstances. The connecting arrows in Exhibit 3-1 suggest the interdependence of elements and need for continuous feedback to make necessary adjustments. Organizations grow through modification and expansion of existing goals and the incorporation of new goals. Continued growth and development is dependent upon their communication systems to effectively integrate an existing and changing external environment with an internal environment.

The model used in this text presents a systems framework and thus views the modern organization as a dynamic order of parts and processes that interact and are interdependent. Let's discuss further the influence of the external environment and identify the significant variables or factors affecting the organization.

▶ EXTERNAL ENVIRONMENT

The external environment is all the factors (economic, educational, political, legal, technological, and cultural aspects) that directly influence the decision-making, problem-solving apparatus of the internal organizational system. Tosi and Hammer succinctly define the external environment as being "made up of those influences which are beyond the boundary of the organization, but which interact with it."[14]

Organizations do not exist in isolation; like people, they interact with their environment. More specifically, organizations are significantly influenced by the environment that surrounds them, and they, in turn, influence that environment. As a current example of an industry revolution, we have seen the introduction of home computers. A number of small computer companies recognized that they would have difficulty competing with IBM and Honeywell in the large-computer hardware market, so they developed less expensive retail models that could be sold to individuals for use in their homes or on office desktops. Every organization must remain alert to a changing external environment.

Societal Cultural Influences

Organizations develop and exist as part of a larger social system commonly referred to as society. One of the more important aspects of any society is its culture, and culture significantly influences organizations. Culture refers to a way of life, including such things as knowledge, beliefs, values, customs, practices, and socially prescribed roles. Cultures vary, and the particular culture surrounding any organization has definite effects on the internal makeup of the organization. It determines what technologies are available for use in the organization, what rewards are used, what leadership styles are acceptable, what specific objectives are sought, and, through defining roles, the way different groups in the organization interact.

Societal culture is the "collective mental programs of the people in an environment."[15] Hellriegel and Slocum define culture as a "society's attitudes, beliefs and values; as all those features characteristic of a society's stage of advancement; and as all of a society's social, political, educational, legal and economic characteristics."[16] The emphasis is on collective rather than individual phenomena, and essentially taps the collective values and beliefs of a nation or society.

Given the importance of societal cultural aspects, let's look at the concept in more detail. We can start by asking about the underlying dimensions. Sociologist Kingsley Davis has identified six general traits characteristic of U.S. culture. He says we are:

1. *democratic* in the sense of favoring equal opportunity to rise socially by merit rather than birth
2. *worldly* in emphasizing values such as the pursuit of a calling, accumulation of wealth, and achievement of status
3. *ascetic* in stressing physical abstinence and stern sobriety, thrift, industry, and prudence
4. *individualistic* in placing responsibility upon the individual himself for his economic, political, religious destiny, and in stressing personal ambition, self-reliance, private enterprise, and entrepreneurial ability
5. *rationalistic* and *empirical* in assuming a world order discoverable through sensory observation of nature
6. *utilitarian* in pursuing practical ends with the best available means and conceiving human welfare as attainable by human knowledge and action[17]

Others have focused on different characteristics. Margaret Mead, in her book *And Keep Your Powder Dry*, emphasizes our aggressiveness and calls attention to material success.[18] Wayne Minnick includes rejection of authority, rationality, sociality, and patriotism.[19] Sociologist Herbert Gans identifies what he calls "enduring values" that reflect the nation and society and are projected by the media. They include:

1. Ethnocentrism—valuing one's own race, nation, or culture above all others
2. Altruistic democracy—implications that politics should be based on the public interest and service
3. Responsible capitalism—an optimistic faith that businessmen and women will compete with each other but that they will refrain from unreasonable profits and gross exploitation of workers or customers
4. Small-town pastoralism—favoring small towns over other types of settlements including the desirability of nature and smallness
5. Individualism—preservation of the freedom of rugged individualism against the encroachments of nation and society
6. Moderation—discouragement of excess or extremism
7. Order—respect for authority and relevant enduring values, concern for social cohesion
8. Leadership—moral and otherwise competent leadership, honest and candid with vision, physical stamina, and courage[20]

The specific values of any culture are almost endless, but some values have greater effect on organizations than others. Farmer and Richman observe that the following values in any culture have significant impact on organizations in that culture:

1. Attitudes toward authority
2. Attitudes toward wealth and material things
3. Attitudes toward change and risk-taking
4. Attitudes toward freedom and independence
5. Attitudes toward achievement and work
6. Attitudes toward social status and prestige of particular types of occupations
7. Attitudes toward education in general and various types of education in particular
8. Attitudes toward property and ownership[21]

The specific forms that these attitudes take influence the elements composing the internal organizational environment.

George Hofstede has conducted cross-cultural research that reduces these attitudes to four cultural dimensions that have important linkings with organizational and managerial aspects—power distance, uncertainty avoidance, individualism versus collectivism, and masculinity versus femininity. *Power distance (PD)* is the extent to which a culture accepts the inequality of the distribution of power between people. In high-PD countries, power holders are entitled to privileges and it is expected that there will be clear and strong superior–subordinate relationships. In low-PD countries there is more power equality and sharing. *Uncertainty avoidance (UA)* reflects the degree to which people feel threatened by and try to avoid ambiguous and uncertain situations. High-UA cultures deal with uncertainty through rules and rituals; low-UA cultures are not as rule-bound. *Individualism versus collectivism (I–C)* refers to whether a society is loosely knit, with people primarily responsible for themselves and their immediate families, or tightly knit with a heavy group emphasis and a sharp differentiation between in-groups and out-groups. In the latter, group rather than individual action and initiative tend to be emphasized. Finally, the *masculinity versus femininity (M–F)* dimension relates to the socialization process. In high-M–F countries, the dominant values are masculine in terms of assertiveness and acquisition of tangible things. There is sharp sex-role differentiation in jobs and the like. Hofstede concludes that the U.S. is below average on power distance and uncertainty avoidance, well above average on masculinity versus femininity, and very high on individualism (in fact, it was the highest of the 40 countries sampled).[22]

Still another useful dimension for explaining cultural variability is Hall's construct of low- and high-context cultures. In a *low-context culture,* such as the U.S., information is abundant, procedures are fully explained, and expectations are discussed frequently. A culture, such as Japan, in which information about procedure is rarely communicated, is labeled a *high-context culture*—members are expected to know how to perform in various situations, but the rules of cultural performance remain implicit.[23] The intercultural communication breakdown that most frequently occurs, considering low- and high-context systems, is when one person assumes and operates out of a high-context mind-set while the other person expects explanation, looking for a low-context condition. These assumptions are rarely understood, much less discussed, among intercultural participants.

The previous discussion makes it abundantly clear that societal cultural values significantly influence how organizations develop and evolve. Important questions become, To what extent do people inside organizations reflect the values of society? To what extent do they share such values? and What are the implications of this sharing? These questions illustrate the relationship between a changing societal culture and the communication system that transmits social values and beliefs. A host culture comprises diverse groups that must be incorporated into the organization. These groups comprise both individuals who reflect their society to a greater or lesser degree and individuals who possess values, beliefs, and so forth separate from those emphasized by the general culture. The U.S. may more accurately be perceived as a "salad bowl" than a "melting pot" and organizations must be able to cope with this cultural diversity.

Moreover, a growing number of organizations are becoming involved in multinational activities. Internationally, then, modern organizations must be knowledgeable and equipped to encounter the varied communication systems of significantly different cultures. Walter Wriston, the former head of Citicorp, describes the reality of this interchange in *Risk and Other Four-Letter Words*:

> Natural gas owned by Indonesia's Pertamina, flows out of a well discovered by Royal Dutch Shell into a liquification plant designed by French engineers and built by a Korean construction company. The liquified gas is loaded onto U.S. flag tankers, built in U.S. yards after a Norwegian design. The ships shuttle to Japan and deliver the liquid gas to a Japanese public utility, which uses it to provide electricity that powers an electronics factory making television sets that are shipped aboard a Hong Kong-owned containership to California for sale to American farmers in Louisiana who grow rice that is sold to Indonesia and shipped there aboard Greek bulk carriers. All of the various facilities, ships, products, and services involved in the complex series of events are financed by U.S., European, and Japanese commercial banks, working in some cases with international and local government agencies. These facilities, ships, products, and services are insured and reinsured by U.S., European, and Japanese insurance companies. Investors in these facilities, ships, products, and services are located throughout the world. *This illustration is not only factual, it is typical of transactions that take place over and over again daily throughout the globe.*[24]

Organizations simultaneously function within an immediate culture and secondary cultures, and differences exist. Today, we need to recognize these differences and be aware of them. We need to value this diversity and learn to use it positively. As cultural participants, we need to respect each other, understand our differences, acquire the motivation to collaborate, and be willing to work together.

To increase cultural understanding, colleges and universities are beginning to develop intensive programs in "intercultural communication" or "cross-cultural communication" or "global management." They combine a study of the culture, the political system, religion, anthropology, and the language of a country or region with traditional business concerns.[25] Our foreign competitors are similarly engaged in this effort. In 1972 a Japanese enterprise established the Japan American Institute of Management Science in Hawaii. The students at the Institute are Japanese junior executives chosen to receive instruction in the English language, intercultural communication, comparative management systems in the U.S. and Japan, business law, and management application of computers. The major objectives of the Institute are to help students understand the American business subculture and to enable them to acquire practical interpersonal communication skills in various business-related situations. Kazuo Nishiyama expresses the essence of these efforts when he observes that the "challenge . . . is to find a means to facilitate the bringing together of persons whose economic and political needs demand interaction, but whose linguistic and cultural systems seem designed to confound that communication."[26]

Culture, to a large degree, determines the role played by organizations and their operations within society. The interaction between the organization and its cultural environment is crucial, and an organization's interface with its external cultural environment(s) cannot be discounted.

Economic Influences

All organizations operate within an economic system and are subject to the influence of whatever economic conditions prevail. Economic conditions influencing business organizations, both private and public, include the level of employment or unemployment, competition in the marketplace, salary levels, interest rates, tax structure, and the consumers themselves. Any organization must receive and seek out information relative to these economic influences to improve its own internal system.

The monitoring of economic trends can reveal a great deal to an organization with respect to future orders, realistic inventory levels, price changes, cost of new debt servicing, and new wage demands. An example of negative economic trends and their impacts occurred in the 1979–80 recession when interest rates soared and made the issuance of new mortgages extremely difficult, virtually shutting down the entire housing construction industry for a period of more than 18 months. Builders who foresaw this and planned accordingly stayed in business; those who did not failed financially.

Essentially there are two fundamental economic systems—capitalism and socialism—with other formulas existing on a continuum somewhere between those two poles. Each possesses certain characteristics that profoundly influence organizational development and growth. The foremost feature of a capitalistic system is free enterprise. Private ownership, profit incentive, and freedom from governmental regulation and control are all features of a capitalistic system. Socialism is characterized by government ownership and planning; individual, private incentive is discouraged. Most contemporary economic systems contain some capitalistic and some socialistic tendencies. At best, they lean more heavily in one direction than another. For example, the U.S. is probably more capitalistic than socialistic, but it evinces governmental influence in the form of regulation and controls. Similarly, consider the dismantled Soviet Union which typified a socialistic system—limited elements of free enterprise existed there and increased under perestroika. The new federations currently exploring capitalism will probably create a mixture of systems with the help of Western advisors.

Economic influences generally affect an organization's internal system favorably or unfavorably. These economic influences are themselves very much affected by the dominant culture as well as external cultures. For example, political affairs, domestic and international, can strongly dictate favorable or unfavorable economic influences. Currently within the U.S. and abroad the energy crisis is a strong economic influence affecting all organizations. This factor is also highly political and largely controlled by international interests.

Customer tastes also change and may leave you with a great product but no market. Ethyl Corporation made tetra-ethyl lead, the anti-knock compound in gasoline. In the late 1980s, the Environmental Protection Agency banned the product, drying up the market for Ethyl's only product. Ethyl fought the ban at public hearings and in the courts, buying time to diversify into new areas.[27] By contrast, when the Depository Institution's Deregulation Act of 1980 permitted both commercial banks and savings and loan associations to offer interest-bearing checking or NOW accounts savings and loan associations were forced to recruit and hire bank operations personnel familiar with checking accounts, and commercial banks were faced with paying interest on what were previously "free" core deposits. To both industries this new legislation was a very expensive and market-threatening experience.

Organizations exist within an external environment and are influenced by that environment. Cultural and economic influences represent critical aspects of any relevant environment and significantly affect the growth, development, and innovativeness of an organization's internal system. For instance, when the relevant external environment is rapidly changing, an organization is more likely to be innovative. Organizations actively seeking to control their environment rather than merely adjust to it are more innovative. Examples abound—universities vary curricula to meet changing demands of students, petroleum industries explore energy alternatives when OPEC demands higher prices for crude oil, and businesses of all kind focus on quality to meet increasing competition and the changing demands of customers. Many changes in an organization come about as a result of the influences exerted by a fluctuating external environment. Organizations are heavily influenced by their environment, especially by the two elements of culture and economic conditions.

▶ INTERNAL ORGANIZATIONAL ELEMENTS

External environmental influences on organizations are not independent; they are interrelated and determine the internal nature and characteristics of the organization. Different cultures and economic conditions are likely to result in organizations' being developed and operated differently. The most important internal elements of the organization that affect the communication system are: organizational objectives, managerial philosophy, leadership style, organizational structure, technology, and the reward system. Critical to these elements is the prevailing organizational culture and the people who make up the organization.

Organizational Objectives

All organizations have more or less specific objectives, usually presented as mission statements, which they try to achieve. An organization's specific objectives affect its communication system and greatly influence its formal design, climate, and effectiveness. They determine what specific decisions need to be made, when, and by whom. Moreover, the degree to which the objectives are known, understood, and accepted by organizational members has important influences people's attitudes and motivation. The communication system is intended to supply decision makers with appropriate information and employees with the necessary knowledge and understanding of the dominant mission.

▶ AUTOCRATIC LEADERS NOW OUT OF STEP

By Mindy Fetterman

In 1944, Warren Bennis was a 20-year-old U.S. Army captain—one of the youngest in the European theater of war. When he returned to the USA, he had a Purple Heart, a Bronze Star Medal and an interest in how leaders lead.

Now, 50 years after the bombing of Pearl Harbor sent the United States into World War II, Bennis sees one legacy of the war fading fast: the military-style manager.

For a generation of corporate executives, the leadership model they learned in the infantry, on the ships and in the air during World War II became a field guide for how to run a company. Bureaucracies were built on command and control. Orders came from the top. Grunts at the bottom followed them.

The CEO as Gen. George S. Patton.

"They believed in three words: control, order and predictability," says Bennis, author of 15 books on organizational psychology. "It was the Army pyramid. The hierarchy, line of command and division of labor. It was 'Rank has its privileges' and 'It's lonely at the top.'"

That hierarchical training carried over to corporate life. "I've always felt like I call the shots," says Allen Paulson, 67, CEO of Gulfstream Aerospace Corp. who served in the Air Force from 1943 to 1945. "It's the only way I know to run a company. I think of myself as benevolent dictator."

"We were a lot more autocratic than the current generation," says B. F. "Chip" Backlund, 67, president of Better Banks, a group of seven banks in Peoria, Ill. He was in the Iwo Jima and Okinawa campaigns with the Navy.

In the face of tough competition worldwide—especially, and ironically, from Japan—much of that military management style is disappearing. WWII-veteran CEOs are retiring, and younger CEOs with little or no war background are struggling to make companies less bureaucratic and more responsive. In the business world, the Japanese have proven the success of teamwork and small, quick-strike units.

Bulky bureaucracies can't compete. "The problem is, managing a war and managing a company are very different," says Charles Garfield, author of *Second to None*, a book on management. "In war, command and control make sense. Compliance of soldiers makes sense. It's a crisis. But companies aren't in crisis every day. You need a lot more input from the soldiers than the generals."

For all its faults, the military style of management was a key to the rapid growth and success of U.S. companies after the war.

"At the time, it was a good discipline for business. We were just emerging as a world force," says Tom Russell,

retired CEO of Federal-Mogul, an engine-parts company. He was an Army staff sergeant from 1943 to 1946. "Now, I think it's passe. We're encouraging people on the firing line to make decisions, not to be told what to do from above."

The military style worked because the workforce in the 1950s was less educated and needed more direct supervision, Russell says. "Today, people say, 'Well, have you thought of doing it this way?'"

Even the military is changing its management style to focus on "autonomy of units, a federation of units," says Bennis, who has made training videos for the Military Academy at West Point. "Ask a cadet today what's the most significant thing about leadership, and he'll say, 'Creating trust.'"

But old habits die hard. Despite all the talk about empowering workers, the military model is still copied. Companies still hire actors dressed as Patton for inspirational speeches. The 1949 movie *12 O'Clock High,* with Gregory Peck as a commander who whips a WWII bomber unit into shape through intimidation, is still a popular executive-training film.

And in times like these, when a recession squeezes a company, the military model comes roaring back. "You get *Business Week* writing a story about the toughest bosses in America and telling tales of General Patton-like managers who slice and cut, slashing and burning. We revere that," says Garfield. "Every time I hear about it, I cringe. People don't think about loyalty and what happens to the workers who remain. That's the long-term effect."

For the 15 million men in uniform, World War II was a "terrific laboratory of leadership," says Bennis, 66. "You could see right away the results in number of dead, wounded, even the number of people who got trench foot. It varied by leader."

The dictatorial commander wasn't always the most successful. "The best were all good listeners," says Bennis. "They got a lot of involvement from their people. They had a clear mission of what they were doing. And all had a strong protective quality toward their men. It wasn't macho. It was maestro."

WWII formed the management styles of CEOs in some not-so-obvious ways:

▶ *Take a hill a day.* Harold Burson, 70, chairman of public-relations company Burson-Marsteller, was a combat engineer in the Army.

"I learned to be content with consistent, small gains and to know what your objectives are. If you put all your resources against your objectives, you can be very successful."

▶ *You can do it.* Paulson was in pilot training at the end of the war but never flew. Later, he'd break around-the-world flying records in a Gulfstream corporate jet.

"One thing the Air Force gives you is confidence that you can accomplish something," he says.

▶ *Do the dirty work yourself.* During the war, Ken Dahlberg was a flying ace who twice shot down four German planes in one day. He used $1,500 in back pay accumulated while he was in a German POW camp, the famous Stalag 17 outside Munich, to start his own company. Minneapolis-based Dahlberg Inc. sells Miracle Ear hearing aids (1990 revenue: $75 million). "The hordes of young people coming out of the service were very pragmatic. They were realists," says Dahlberg, 74. "They understood how to work—everybody came up through the ranks—and they know how to take off their coats and roll up their sleeves."

His 38-year-old son, Jeffrey, now CEO of Dahlberg, has a totally different style, his father says. "He's much more relaxed than I ever was."

Source: Mindy Fetterman, "Autocratic Leaders Now Out of Step," *USA Today,* December 9, 1991, 1B, 2B. Copyright 1991, *USA Today.* Reprinted with permission.

Managerial Philosophy

Managerial philosophy and assumptions refer to basic values and beliefs about the nature of people, organizations, and managing. They are basic variables that shape the character of the other internal elements. That is, a managerial philosophy has a basic influence on the actions that determine how the organization operates. Philosophies differ and different philosophies result in different organizational objectives, organizational structures, leadership styles, technologies used, and reward systems.

Consider, for example, the differences in the way various classes are conducted. Some involve more lecture or more discussion or more homework than others. Certainly, part of these differences arise because different instructors have different ideas about students and the best way to help people learn. The implementation of a particular instructor's philosophy characterizes the nature of the course, the communication climate, and the conduct of students. Similarly, managerial philosophies and assumptions influence managerial and organizational communication and effectiveness.

Leadership Style

Individuals, not organizations, exercise leadership styles, but in most organizations a particular leadership style seems to be the most prevalent and characteristic style. The leadership style of the organization is a major factor affecting who makes what decisions and how such decisions are made. Leadership style also influences the use that is made of information, and it has significant effects on people's willingness to communicate. Leadership styles are roles, and such types of organizational roles are determined by sociocultural values and managerial philosophy and assumptions. Different cultures and philosophies produce different leadership styles.

Organizational Structure

Cultural attitudes toward the appropriate and legitimate use of authority and the acceptability and durability of various types of activity impose broad limits within which a managerial philosophy operates to structure the organization. The structural design of an organization defines the lines of authority, the flow of messages, the communication networks, and the relationships that make up a large part of its communication system. Structure influences organizational effectiveness and significantly affects the workplace, job content, individual's attitudes, and the communication climate that exists.

Technology

Different cultural conditions tend to determine what technologies are available for use, and differing economic conditions and managerial philosophies determine what technology is used and how specific jobs are structured. The type of technology used to achieve organizational objectives affects the way things are done and determines who communicates what to whom and how. The type of technology used by the organization is a major determinant of the way jobs are designed and of the nature of the job that any individual performs.

Reward System

Similar to the other elements of the organization, the nature of the reward system used by the organization also varies according to cultural and economic conditions and the philosophy of management. Certainly, the type of reward system used affects the type of information needed to reward people; so reward systems influence people's attitudes, motivation, and perceptions of job satisfaction. And, a diverse workforce demands a differing reward system. Thus, the design of the reward system is determined in part by the needs of the individuals involved as well as by the needs of the organization.

Core Culture

Organizations, like societies, have cultures. Values, myths, rituals, heroes, and devils are all part of corporate life. The core culture of an organization represents prevailing beliefs and values, and reflects the shared realities that encourage individual motivation and commitment, forming the basis for consensus and integration. An organization's culture is the unique sense of the place that an organization generates through ways of doing and ways of communicating about the organization. For example, Disney World has a legendary culture of customer service. Rick Johnson, who conducts seminars about the Disney culture, explains: "You can't force people to smile. Each guest at Disney World sees an average of 73 employees per visit, and we would have to supervise them continually. Of course, we can't do that, so instead we try to get employees to buy into the corporate culture."[28] Then employees are expected to behave according to those general principles as unique situations occur. This cultural approach offers a unique and expedient method of coordinating the activities within the organization.

Organizational culture, then, is the underlying belief and value structure of an organization collectively shared by the employees that is symbolically expressed in a variety of overt and subtle ways. The culture allows workers to be self-motivated and holds the organization together in the absence of threats and rewards. Note also that culture can be thought of as a process or a condition, for an organization's culture is simultaneously somewhat stable and constantly evolving as new challenges are encountered. Mike Paconowsky at the University of Colorado Communication Department and Nick O'Donnell-Trujillo at Southern Methodist University Communication Department make abundantly clear the significance of culture as an organizational element when they observe that "organizational culture is not just another piece of the puzzle; it is the puzzle. . . . culture is not something an organization has; a culture is something an organization *is*."[29]

The Individual

Organizations in their most basic sense are composed of individuals who process information and interrelate to perform the daily activities necessary to achieve the defined organizational objectives. Regardless of technology, it is humans using interpersonal and relational skills that account for the overall success or failure. This perspective has prompted Karl Weick, the Rensis Likert Professor of Organizational Behavior and Psychology at the University of Michigan, to propose that organizations as such do not exist, but rather are *in the process of existing* through ongoing human interaction. Weick focuses on the common process of organizing (verb) rather than the static structure of the organization (noun) and equates organizing with information processing. In other words, there is no such thing as an organization, only the ongoing interactions among human activities—interactions that continually create and shape events.[30] Tom Peters confirms the importance of an empowered workforce when he writes, "We don't want for evidence that the average worker is capable of moving mountains—if only we'll ask him or her to do so, and construct a supportive environment. . . . the chief reason for our failure in world-class competition is our failure to tap our work force's potential. . . . Truly involved people can do anything."[31]

In summary, a system made up of these elements within the organization results from environmental influences and produces an organizational communication system that operates with some degree of effectiveness and that has important influences on overall organizational effectiveness. Each of the factors tends to affect and be affected by the others. Because the core culture of an organization and its managerial philosophy and assumptions have a prevailing influence on the other elements and significantly impact all who work in an organizational environment, we will examine these two factors in more depth. Chapter 4 further examines the communication climate and the structural dimensions of organizations noting the human impact on the organizational communication system. Later chapters focus on the specific skills necessary to achieve organizational goals and explore the nature of change and innovation as they relate to organizational effectiveness

▶ORGANIZATIONAL CULTURE

Within the last decade or so, organizational culture has become one of the most active research areas within organizational studies. One impetus for the study of organizational culture came from a realization by a number of people that traditional organizational approaches were not as useful as they might be in leading to an understanding of observed disparities between organizational goals and outcomes or between strategy and implementation. This line of inquiry began to suggest that organizational models were incomplete without the inclusion of cultural aspects.

Previously we defined organizational culture as the core beliefs and values shared by organizational members and permeating the organization. Included in this definition were the shared realities, myths, mores, reminiscences, heroes, stories, rites and rituals that provide the members with unique, symbolic, common ground. Edgar Schein takes an organization's culture to be "the assumptions that underlie the values and determine not only behavior patterns, but also such visible artifacts as architecture, office layout, dress codes, and so on."[32] These assumptions over time become less and less open to discussion, determining the decisions made and shaping the entire atmosphere of the organization. Culture, then, is:

1. a pattern of shared basic assumptions,
2. invented, discovered, or developed by a given group,
3. as it learns to cope with its problems of external adaptation and internal integration,
4. that has worked well enough to be considered valid, and, therefore,
5. is to be taught to new members of the group as the
6. correct way to perceive, think, and feel in relation to those problems.[33]

Alan Kantrow further notes the controlling influence of culture when he observes that it "is the anchor about which an organization swings on a chain of varying length, nosing at one or another distance into different winds and different directions but always linked to a firm point of reference that tethers such explorations within bounds."[34] So, if one were to describe the different organizational habits they witnessed—those rather repetitive ways by which the organization's members seem to get things done—they would be describing the organization's culture.

Peeled-Onion Conception of Organizational Culture

James Hunt proposes a "peeled-onion" conception of organizational culture that consists of three layers. The outer first layer includes artifacts and patterns of behavior. Examples are written and spoken language and jargon, office layouts, organizational structure, dress codes, technology, and behavioral norms. Habits, rites, and rituals also are found here. The content of this layer is visible but often not decipherable without some consideration of the deeper levels. The second layer contains beliefs and values. This layer reveals how people are regarded in the organization, how they relate to one another, and how the organization deals with its external environment. It shows ways in which people communicate, explain, and rationalize or justify what is said and done as an organizational community. This layer also includes ethos, philosophies, ideologies, attitudes, and ethical/moral codes. The third layer encompasses the basic, unconscious assumptions and perceptions that are taken for granted and tend to be unconfrontable and nondebatable. Hunt refers to these as "automatic schemas" that subtly dictate to organizational members how to perceive and think and feel about things.[35]

This peeled-onion conceptualization helps tie together the wide range of different definitions and commonly identified dimensions of organizational culture. It is also consistent with the organization "is" rather than "has" concept of culture. All of the layers are linked together, with the outer, more visible layers easier to change than the deeper ones.

Communicating Organizational Culture

An organization's culture is communicated in many ways. The most important of these is through its informal interpersonal networks.[36] It is through interactions with longtime members that new recruits are encultured—they learn the language and appropriate behaviors of the group, hear its stories and legends, and observe the rites and rituals in which its members engage. This informal socialization teaches members what is appropriate dress, how to arrange one's office, and how much leeway they have in being on time for appointments and meeting deadlines. Awards ceremonies, recognition dinners, annual picnics, and all the daily routines symbolically convey what is important.[37] For example, during executive meetings at Sears there is an empty chair at the conference table with the words, "The Customer," emblazoned on it. Through this simple symbolic device the executives are forced to reckon with the customer's desires. The chair is a visual reminder of the need to satisfy the customer.[38]

Socialization starts with an emphasis on hiring right-type members initially because they will more easily identify with role models and adapt to the specific organizational culture. At best, however, formal training will be required to ensure that members internalize core values and assumptions.[39] Research indicates that the initial weeks of employment are a critical period to exert influence. Supervisors, to some extent, lose their power to shape the values, beliefs, and behaviors of employees after the first month or so. This makes the training procedures extremely important because they not only teach specific skills, but also convey the organization's philosophy. Detailed discussions of the organization's history, successes, and failures help to instill organizational values into employees. Some companies, like IBM, go through extensive discussions of organizational values—not just the "whats" but also the "whys" of policy. One IBM employee observes, "After you're done with their training, you know what they believe, why they believe it and you end up believing it."[40] Thorough explanations of an organization's philosophy during training helps embed the value system and shows that the organization takes its values seriously and expects the values to be lived out on a day-to-day basis.

An organization's culture is also passed along through formal and informal written communication—memos, house organs, annual reports, mission statements, and official policies. It may also be displayed on bulletin boards or in posters that present policy messages. Written channels underscore dominant themes like service, quality, and creativity, and they legitimize salient values. These recitations can act as a kind of organizational mantra in which repeating the words weaves a magic incantation. Written messages focus employee spirit and energize workers to act out core values.[41]

Every organization has a culture that shapes behavior. Sometimes the culture works to assist an organization through a crisis. Culture worked for Johnson & Johnson when it hit the tampered-with-Tylenol crises in 1982 and 1985. When news of the problem came in, managers used the company vision to make decisions. The company's vision states in part, "We believe our first responsibility is to the doctors, nurses, and patients, to mothers and all others who use our products and services. . . . We are responsible to the communities in which we live and work and to the world as

▶ COMMUNICATING A CULTURE: THE PIXIE DUST FORMULA

A prime example of a company with a strong corporate culture is the Walt Disney Company. The Disney culture is so strong that people who have never worked for the company possess a wealth of knowledge about it. Words like friendly, clean, helpful, and fun are only a few of the qualities the general public associates with the company.

The Disney philosophy is based on service through people. Walt Disney expressed this founding theme when he noted, "You can dream, create, design and build the most wonderful place on earth. . . but it requires people to make that dream a reality." Red Pope, a long-time Disney observer and writer, comments: "How Disney looks upon people, internally and externally, handles them, communicates with them, rewards them, is in my view the basic foundation upon which its five decades of success stand. . . ."

Disney's corporate culture is based on the company's past traditions, present operations, and vision for the future. Being mindful of the past keeps the traditions of the company alive—with so much growth and expansion, it is viewed by management as more important than ever not to lose sight of: who founded the company, why and when; where has the company been; what were its original purposes and philosophies; what are the operational standards and guidelines for making decisions; how has it grown and what has it accomplished? The company has as its basis, such traditions as quality, uniqueness, value and friendliness, concepts just as valid today as they were in 1955 when Disneyland opened. While looking back, the Walt Disney Company also has its feet very firmly planted in the present by placing emphasis on the current operation: what is happening now and why; how well is it being done; what is the guest response? Finally, a careful balance of traditions and present operations is tempered with a strong sense of commitment to the future: where will the company's vision take it; what are the plans for getting there; what is each cast member's role in the "Big Picture"?

To perpetuate such a culture, a special type of training was needed. The Disney University was founded in 1955 at Disneyland Park to help develop the kind of person who could make Walt's dream a reality. A whole new concept in guest service was begun which was so successful that today it remains unchallenged as the philosophical basis for Disney's entire "people operation."

Although the name Disney University implies training and education, its involvement extends well beyond that. At the Disney University, they do more than train. They have a responsibility to the whole person, to help employees achieve their personal goals as the company achieves its goals. The Disney University, at Walt Disney World Co., is comprised of seven distinct sub-departments that act as one to form the whole—Cast Development, Cast Communications, Cast Activities, Program Design and Quality Assurance, Office Resources, Seminar Productions, and the "I Have an Idea" Office. Their mission is employee education, development, motivation, morale, communications, and the total working experience.

Programs offered through the Disney University are designed to support the "Pixie Dust Formula"—*Training + Communication + Care = Pride.* It is believed that attention to every small detail of this formula contributes to the success of the company and ultimately results in the pride cast members have in the company's philosophy and goals.

Training

Before training as a cast member even begins, in fact, before a person even becomes a cast member, an applicant's experience at the Casting Center (Disney's employment office) provides an introduction to the Disney culture. The unique architectural design of the building says "Disney" before a potential cast member walks in the door—it is clear that this is not the employment center of just any ordinary company.

The Casting Center welcomes applicants seven days a week. Applicants discover the conditions of pay, availability, transportation requirements, and appearance guidelines through a unique 12-minute video presentation in a 100-seat theater. Then, all cast members go through an extensive two-day orientation class, or as Disney refers to it, "Traditions." The goal of Disney Traditions is to infuse new cast members with enthusiasm toward the new roles, and to instill great pride in being a part of the Disney organization.

Other classes reinforce the corporate culture throughout a cast member's tenure with the company. *Disney Way I: The Disney Difference* discusses what makes the Walt Disney World Resort successful. Participants explore the concepts of team work and synergy and discuss business strategies and the challenges of delivering a quality product to guests. *Disney Way II: Disney Dynamics* concentrates on the varied business components of the company, illustrating its future direction. Finally, *We've Come a Long Way, Mickey* serves as a day of reorientation to company traditions and philosophy for cast members with five or more years of service.

Communication

At the Walt Disney World Resort, the challenge is to communicate with cast members who work in many different job classifications. The company has three goals to accomplish through its communications with over 32,000 cast members: (1) To disseminate relevant information, (2) in an effective, appropriate medium, and (3) on a timely basis. Four mediums are utilized by Disney to communicate internally: personal contact, print, audio/visual, and environmental. Personal communication occurs through "management by walking around." Assistant supervisors are encouraged to spend approximately 70% of their time working in the area alongside their hourly cast members. This philosophy helps to break down some barriers of communication as these assistant supervisors are viewed by the hourly cast as "one of us, one who understands what it is like to be in the trenches." All cast members wear name tags bearing their first name only, regardless of their position within the organization. The only "Mr." at Disney is "Mr. Toad" of "Mr. Toad's Wild Ride." Cast members are encouraged to offer suggestions, challenge policies, and become an active member of the organization.

Eyes & Ears is the weekly newsletter developed to communicate and reinforce the Disney corporate culture by providing historical perspectives; stories on past achievements; current success stories; recent outstanding gains; and future plans through artists' renderings. In addition to Eyes & Ears is the Flash 4500 Bulletin which is used to quickly communicate information regarding any internal change of policy, or the company's position on a particularly "HOT" issue. Limiting the frequency of this publication heightens its awareness and importance.

Audio/visuals are used to support the training programs and serve as a means to update the cast. Examples are the award-winning film Making Magic, which is shown in the Traditions orientation classes, and the videos produced each year for the State of Our World Address Update to all cast members.

To build a positive and effective communications network for a company the size of Disney, it is important to listen to cast members and to learn from them. In order to encourage upward communication and participation within the company, the Walt Disney Company has developed the "I Have an Idea Program," whereby cast members can receive cash awards, resort stays, meals, and other merchandise for ideas that will help benefit the company. Moreover, every two years the company conducts what is called "The Cast Opinion Poll." Its intent is to elicit cast members'

views on the company and their work environment. The results of the survey are collected and analyzed by an outside, independent agency which reports back to the company's top manage-ment. Task forces are established to address each issue and offer improvements for the entire cast which are then conveyed through a special issue of Eyes & Ears.

Care

The last component of the Pixie Dust Formula is care. This encompasses a variety of activities, recognition, appreciation, and benefits provided by the company. The Distinguished Service Awards Banquet recognizes Disney cast members for more than ten years of quality service. It is an event that is sprinkled with "pixie dust," spectacular entertainment, good food, and friends, but most importantly, it is a night to honor the company's most valuable asset—its people. Another special evening for cast members and their families is the annual Christmas party, where the Magic Kingdom Park is briefly closed to the public. Moreover, there are special "cast days" and complimentary tickets provided to the company's theme parks. All this to create a sense of family and show employees how much they are appreciated.

Communicating a strong, positive, consistent corporate culture has contributed to Disney's success. Admittedly, such a strong culture has occasionally created problems. For example, before Michael Eisner and Frank Wells were appointed as the company's Chief Executive Officers, the company was suffering from a bad case of "What would Walt do?" And, in 1984, a takeover attempt which probably would have meant the splitting up and sale of company assets was barely avoided. Still, the company has grown from a shop set up in Walt's uncle's garage to a multi-billion dollar corporation with seven business segments—the Walt Disney Studios, Walt Disney Imagineering, Disney Consumer Products, Corporate Administration, Disney Development Company, and Hollywood Records. And with all this, as Walt Disney liked to say, "We're just getting started." In January 1991, Michael Eisner announced a "Disney Decade" of tremendous growth. So, as the Walt Disney Company faces its future, it draws on its heritage of creativity, innovation, quality, and teamwork, always remembering "it all started with a mouse."

Source: Student journal entry, Hamilton Holt School of Rollins College, Winter Park, FL, Fall 1991.

well." Using these statements as empowerers of their behavior, Johnson & Johnson managers recalled every package from every shelf in the world. Managers were applauded for taking responsibility and the dramatic short-term financial loss.[42]

The culture of an organization can also be communicated by sources external to the organization. Advertisements in the mass media, public relations campaigns, speeches by executive officers, and daily interactions with customers and suppliers project a public image of the organization to its members. In other words, as an organization communicates to the environment, it reveals its values and style to those outside the organization and to its own members. The external communication feeds back to affect its internal culture.

It is through communicating its culture that an organization's values move from objective truths to subjective realities; that is, employees transform rhetoric about values into personal commitments and experiences. Infused with a "passion," they act spontaneously and in accord with core cultural assumptions. Consider the case of the janitor who was the sole person on duty at a commissary of Domino's Pizza Distribution Company. He took an off-hours call from a franchisee about to run out of pepperoni. Knowing that having a franchisee run out of anything is the cardinal sin at Domino's Distribution, he located keys to a truck, loaded the vehicle with one small box of pepperoni, and drove hundred of miles to keep the franchisee from closing. All this on his own initiative, never thinking that the distributor would want him to do anything else. Or, how about the junior telecommunications expert at Federal Express who, following a blizzard in the California Sierras, rented a helicopter, was dropped onto a snowbound mountaintop, trudged three-quarters of a mile in chest-deep snow, and fixed a downed line to keep Fed Ex in business. These actions, although spontaneous, were hardly accidental.[43]

Cultures and Subcultures

Much of the literature treats organizational cultures as monolithic—there is one culture for a given organization. Small organizations like entrepreneurial firms may exhibit restricted organizational cultures, but as organizations grow they develop subcultures. This may result from organizational hierarchy, division of labor, geographic dispersion of work units, differential professional socialization, or environmental demands.[44] For example, General Motor's Chevrolet division is quite likely to have a different culture in many ways than the Cadillac division, even though both will tend to share common elements of the overall GM culture. Or, a particular type of job such as design engineer, or particular unit or department like marketing may reflect a characteristic culture. Also, in extreme cases, where there is a large proportion of nonbasic assumptions and these are counter to each other, there may exist "organizational countercultures."[45] These countercultures are groups or units that stand in opposition to the larger culture. This is usually expressed through dysfunctional competition. For instance, Paul Newman's role in the 1967 movie *Cool Hand Luke* illustrates a man's countercultural individualism and quest for freedom while doing service on a chain gang headed by a sadistic warden. It provides a classic example of communication that doesn't work. The core assumptions of chain-gang life are not fully transferred to Luke who then represents a potentially disruptive force. And when, just after using a blackjack to drive Luke to the ground, the warden declares, "What we've got here is a failure to communicate," the statement seems cruelly ironic—but true nonetheless.

So, the assumption of a single organizational culture can be risky. First, such assumptions may cause one to overlook possible diversity within the organization.

Second, important aspects detected in a subculture may not necessarily be determining forces in the overall culture of the organization. Finally, subcultures also influence organizational effectiveness.[46]

Consequences of Culture

The core culture influences an organization in a variety of ways. For instance, culture affects employee motivation. There can be no greater motivation for employees than their belief in what they're doing, what the organization does, and what the organization stands for. Excellent organizations are motivating because of their core culture. Deal and Kennedy researched 80 companies over six months and discovered that the consistently high performers were characterized as strong culture companies. They found that "a strong culture has almost always been the driving force behind continuing success in American business."[47] In their best-selling *In Search of Excellence*, Peters and Waterman identified cultural themes that most nearly characterized excellent, innovative companies. These themes focus on the individuals in the organization and suggest that "excellent companies were, above all, brilliant on the basics." The themes identified by Peters and Waterman[48] are as follows:

1. *A bias for action.* Excellent organizations make decisions and take action.
2. *Close to the customer.* Service, reliability, innovative products, and continual concern for customer needs are fundamental to excellent organizations. The close-to-the-customer value results in new product ideas and serves as the basis for innovation.
3. *Autonomy and entrepreneurship.* Excellent organizations want leaders in all types of organizational activity. They encourage risk taking and innovation and empower people to be creative.
4. *Productivity through people.* Workers at all organizational levels are the source of quality and the source of productivity. Excellent organizations fight against a we/they management/labor attitude.
5. *Hands-on, value driven.* The basic philosophy and values of the organization contribute to achievement and are considered the core of excellence.
6. *Stick to the knitting.* Excellent organizations stay in the businesses they know and grow by doing what they do extremely well.
7. *Simple form, lean staff.* Excellent organizations maintain lean, simple organizational structures with open channels of communication. None of the excellent companies are run with complicated organizational structures.
8. *Simultaneous loose–tight properties.* Excellent organizations are both centralized and decentralized with autonomy and entrepreneurship being encouraged at all levels within the organization. Decision making is often decentralized, yet core values are very centralized and rigidly supported.
9. *Clear, explicit philosophy.* Excellent organizations stand for something. A great deal of time and attention is given to shaping and fine-tuning values to conform to the economic and business environment of the organization and to communicating them to the organization. These values are known and shared by all the people who work for the organization.

Peters and Waterman conclude that "the dominance and coherence of culture proved to be an essential quality of the excellent companies. . . . the stronger the culture and the more it was directed toward the marketplace the less need was there for policy manuals, organization charts, or detailed procedures and rules. In these companies, people way down the line know what they are supposed to do in most situations because the handful of guiding values is crystal clear."

Culture also impacts the quantity and quality of innovations developed and influences how the organization will respond to change. It can provide the impetus for creative innovation and actively encourage quick and decisive change when conditions demand. One study of Toyota Motor Company revealed that they received an average of over 13 suggestions per employee per year. During the same time period, General Motors averaged less than one idea per employee despite incentives of up to $10,000. Over 90 percent of the suggestions at Toyota were implemented during the year of the study; less than 33 percent were used at GM.[49] Japanese car manufacturers routinely bring new cars to market in three years, but companies based in the U.S. typically take five years.[50] All of these consequences evolve from a commitment to the task and the organization and from a well-cultivated culture. Then the question becomes: Does the culture foster the necessary innovation and degree of change? The answer has critical consequences for an organization's long-term survival.

Finally, culture may negatively influence how an organization analyzes and solves problems. Paul Bates, a noted scholar from the University of Bath, England, writes in a thought-provoking article:

> People in organizations evolve in their daily interactions with one another a system of shared perspectives or "collectively held and sanctioned definitions of the situation" which make up the culture of these organizations. The culture, once established, prescribes for its creators and inheritors certain ways of believing, thinking and acting which in some circumstances can prevent meaningful interaction and induce a condition of "learned helplessness"—that is a psychological state in which people are unable to conceptualize their problems in such a way as to be able to resolve them. In short, attempts at problem-solving may become culture-bound.[51]

His research suggests that culture can, and in fact does, restrain organizational thought. Meaningful alternatives may not be explored because "that's not how things are done around here." Peters and Waterman also recognized this potential problem when they observed that "the excellent companies are marked by very strong cultures, so strong that you either buy into their norms or get out. There's no halfway house for most people. . . ."[52]

Briefly, an organization's culture is an irrefutable fact of life and clearly its core values have consequences. There is a wide range of symbolic cues revealing organizational values. Some are implicit, like symbols, graphic designs and newsletters, while others are more explicit, like corporate heroes and slogans. Nowhere, however, is an organization's cultural values made more abundantly clear than in its managerial philosophy and assumptions.

▶ MANAGERIAL PHILOSOPHIES AND ORGANIZATIONAL THEORIES

Managerial philosophies and organizational theories along with their assumptions reflect an organization's culture and influence organizational goals, practices, communication, efficiency, and the total effectiveness of the system. As used here, the *managerial philosophy* refers to the underlying beliefs, attitudes, values, and assumptions that shape human relationships within the organization and contribute to the organization as a whole. The way managers manage is significantly influenced by their philosophy of management. The famous social scientist Douglas McGregor put it this way: ". . . the assumptions management holds about controlling its human resources determine the whole character of the enterprise."[53] What McGregor seems to be saying is that behind all managerial behavior is a philosophy—a set of assumptions. *Organizational theory* refers to the emergence of differing managerial philosophies during varying historic periods. So, in focusing on managerial philosophies and organizational theories, we are concerning ourselves with management's conscious or unconscious view of people's abilities, initiative and motivations, and behavior in particular sets of circumstances.

Scientific Management School

The scientific management school or classical approach evolved during and dominated the period spanning the middle of the nineteenth century to World War I. This school was well described by Frederick Taylor in his classic work *Principles of Scientific Management* where he attempted to convince readers that the inefficiency in most organizations arises from a lack of systematic management and that "the best management is a true science, resting upon clearly defined laws, rules, and principles, as a foundation."[54] Taylor's approach to organizations was highly structured and mechanistic. His famed "time and motion" studies at the Bethlehem Steel plant attempted to break down each minute aspect of a given job and to match each worker with the task he could most efficiently perform. Management was held responsible for devising the scientific method of work and for teaching workers this scientific method for task performance.

Translated into practice, this classical approach emphasized organizational specialization, use of the physical and mental capabilities of workers, and motivation through monetary incentives. Specialization was necessary in achieving classical ends; all organizations must reveal a formal division of labor, authority, and responsibility, as well as a formal division of status and prestige. Moreover, as an organizational theory, it considered the working man or woman to be a rational economic being driven by the fear of hunger and a desire for profit. Thus, a central tenet of those accepting the classical approach was the pursuit of maximum prosperity for all involved with the organization. This required constant evaluation, analysis, and enforcement of work standards by management.

Two of the foremost writers who further contributed to this classical, scientific management tradition were Henri Fayol and Max Weber. Taken together, their writings centered almost exclusively on the structure of formal organizations. In his *General and Industrial Management,* Fayol proposed 14 principles of administration or management that he viewed as essential for effective organization. Among these recommended principles were division of work (specialization), authority and responsibility (power), discipline (obedience), unity of command (one boss), unity of direction (one plan), subordination of individual interest to the general interest (concern for the organization first), remuneration (fair pay), centralization (consolidation), scalar chain (chain of command), order (everyone has a unique position), equity (firm but fair), stability of tenure of personnel (low turnover), initiative (thinking out a plan), and esprit de corps (high morale).[55] Fayol was one of the few classicists to recognize that at least in crisis situations some structural flexibility should be permitted. He opined that people at the same level in the organizational hierarchy, although perhaps in different divisions, might be allowed to communicate directly to insure a speedy and efficient solution to any major problem. This early notion of horizontal communication has come to be labeled "Fayol's Bridge."

Max Weber, a German sociologist, concentrated on organizational authority and what he called "bureaucracy." In *The Theory of Social and Economic Organization*, he identified three types of authority: charismatic, traditional, and bureaucratic.[56] *Charismatic authority* is based on the personal attributes of the individual exerting authority. *Traditional authority* evolves from the customs of a group or society, and passes from individual to individual based on tradition rather than ability or task competence. *Bureaucracy* is considered a legitimate basis of authority and rests on the belief that rationality and predictability are desirable goals for both organizations and individuals. Thus, the bureaucratic system aims to maximize these qualities through careful structuring of the organization; the creation of specific and frequently consulted rights, duties, and procedures; and the encouragement of impersonality in interpersonal relations, with selection and promotion of personnel based solely on technical competence. According to Weber, a bureaucracy is an organization having the following characteristics:

1. formal rules, regulations, and procedures that standardize and direct the actions of organization members to ensure continuity
2. division of labor where workers in their areas of competence and specialization work toward specific goals under predetermined leaders
3. hierarchy of formal organizational authority and the legitimization of power roles which is based on the position held and individual competence
4. employment of qualified personnel solely on the basis of technical competence and the ability of perform the job
5. interchangeability of personnel enabling organizational activities and tasks to be accomplished by different people
6. impersonality and professionalism permeates interpersonal relationships with task performance having a high priority
7. written job descriptions outline the formal duties and responsibilities for all organizational members
8. rationality and predictability in organizational activities promotes order in the organization

Weber believed that, as a major form of organization, bureaucracy had been with us since the Middle Ages and would continue indefinitely. Although complaints against bureaucracy have been numerous, many contemporary writers agree with him that bureaucracy is simply inescapable.[57] The federal government is probably the best example of the omnipresence of bureaucracy in our lives.

The tenets of the scientific management school, emerging from the works of Taylor, Fayol, and Weber, were extremely influential in the early 1900s and continue today to influence how organizations are designed, how performance standards are established, and how work efficiency is measured. As a managerial philosophy and organizational theory, its purpose is clearly defined and its procedures are objectively selected to accomplish this purpose. Authority, as with all positions within the organization, is assigned to those with the ability to responsibly and effectively occupy an office or position. Demonstrated ability governs assignment of positions—line, functional, and staff. All positions and tasks are studied in an effort to achieve greatest efficiency. Purpose and maximum efficiency are the important internal organizational factors. It has been noted that "a full half of what organizational analysis is all about—namely, the formal organization—is covered by the Classical and Neo-Classical approach."[58]

However, it is the theory's assumptions about human nature that have drawn the sharpest criticism. As an intellectual product of the industrial revolution, scientific management was dominated by the image of the machine, with organizations being described as well-oiled, unemotional, goal-oriented, automatic mechanisms, and with those in the workforce regarded in the same mechanistic fashion. Amitai Etzioni observes:

> Although Taylor originally set out to study the interaction between human characteristics and the characteristics of the machine, the relationship between these two elements which make up the industrial work process, he ended up by focusing on a far more limited subject: The physical characteristics of the human body in routine jobs—e.g., shoveling coal or picking up loads. Eventually Taylor came to view human and machine resources not so much as mutually adaptable, but rather man functioning as an appendage to the industrial machine.[59]

It is this narrow and unvalidated view that has always operated against adoption of the classical approach to management. Communication, from the scientific management point of view, was to be a tool of management designed to facilitate task completion and, as such, was to operate as one of many organizational variables. Specifically, communication was required to train workers and provide daily instructions of job requirements. For the most part, communication was perceived as primarily a vertical phenomenon (top-down) and as a tool for supervisory command and control. The neglect to consider the motivating power of social and emotional factors, as well as the failure to deal with the critical role of communication in relating internal and external environments, leads proponents of this approach into a whole thicket of managerial problems.

Human Relations School

The human relations approach to management is generally attributed to Elton Mayo and his Harvard associates[60] who discovered that:

1. the amount of work carried out by a worker is not determined by his physical capacity but by his social "capacity."
2. noneconomic rewards play a central role in determining the motivation and happiness of the worker.
3. the highest specialization is by no means the most efficient form of division of labor.
4. workers do not react to management and its norms and rewards as individuals but as members of groups.

This approach emphasized the role of communication and documented through experiments and field studies its crucial influence on organizations and organizational behavior. The human relations movement focused on interpersonal relations and the influential nature of variables affecting informal communication systems—worker's attitudes, morale, participation, leadership, and social relations.

The series of studies conducted at the Western Electric Company's Hawthorne Works in Chicago from 1927 to 1932 provided the framework for the human relations movement.[61] From the outset there were some unexpected findings referred to as the "Hawthorne Effect." Mayo and his associates worked with factors such as lighting, noise, and heating to determine what combination of conditions would increase productivity. However, lighting intensity seemed to have limited effects on worker production; in fact, an interesting phenomenon occurred, even under conditions of poor lighting, longer work days, and fewer rest pauses: workers continued to increase their productivity. The Hawthorne studies clearly indicated that a worker's feelings, attitudes, and capabilities could not be ignored—"people-oriented" management was more effective than "production-oriented" management.

Mayo's Hawthorne studies revealed the salience of the informal work group as a source of motivation. Specifically, informal work groups were found to establish production standards and to enforce those norms, thus suggesting that a strong motivation to work rested within the dynamics of the small work groups to which individuals belonged and in which they discovered their most meaningful social relationships. Other valuable findings included the importance of participative decision making and democratic leadership within organizations. In general, workers were found to be more productive, more independent, and more satisfied with their work when they were allowed to participate in decisions that directly affected their work activities. Communication became much more than the mere conveyance of orders from superiors to subordinates; rather, it involved intergroup relations, the exchange of information between management and employees, and, in general, a recognition of the importance of informal communication and the dynamics of small-group interaction.

Where the scientific management approach stresses organization, structure, and the management of human beings, the human relations approach encourages employee input, participation, and decision making. Emphasis is given to the establishment of social and cooperative relationships. In assuming this approach, workers are treated as human beings with feelings and emotions who see the organization as something more than a workplace. The human relations movement, an employee-centered approach, actively involves workers with the internal organizational environment. In sum, this orientation relates work and the organizational structure to the social needs of the employees and in so doing obtains full cooperation and support for organizational objectives.

Critics of the human relations school perceive it as "warm feeling" training and label it a "country club" approach to management.[62] They question the claim that increased worker morale invariably leads to increased organizational efficiency. Others maintain that the movement was manipulative and insincere—that it feigned an interest in worker's needs and happiness while manipulating these as a means to increase productivity. These critics provide a hypothetical case that illustrates and spoofs the human relations approach to handling people and organizational problems:

> In a typical Human Relations training movie we see a happy factory in which the wheels hum steadily and the workers rhythmically serve the machines with smiles on their faces. A dark type with long sideburns who sweeps the floors in the factory

spreads a rumor that mass firing is imminent since the new machines will take over the work of many of the workers. The wheels turn slower, the workers are sad. In the evening they carry their gloom to their suburban homes. The next morning, the reassuring voice of their boss comes over the intercom. He tells them that the rumor is absolutely false; the machines are to be set up in a new wing and more workers will be hired since the factory is expanding its production. Everybody sighs in relief, smiles return, the machines hum speedily and steadily again. Only the dark floor sweeper is sad. Nobody will listen to his rumors anymore. The moral is clear: had management been careful to communicate its development plans to its workers, the crisis would have been averted. Once it occurred, increase in communication eliminated it like magic.[63]

The intent of the scenario is not to question the fact that genuine communication mediates or reduces communication-created problems within the organization, but to indicate that not all problems can simply be communicated away. What if workers were skeptical to accept management's explanation? What if the rumor were true?

Harold Rush summarizes the thinking and criticism of the human relations approach:

Here the emphasis was on creating a work force with high morale. It represented an attempt to break down formal or arbitrary boundaries that are part of the fabric of a stratified and bureaucratic organizational structure. Managers trained in human relations learned to be "friendly" toward their subordinates, to call them by their first names, and generally to try to keep people content as a part of "one big happy family." The attempt to democratize the organization found expression in company-sponsored recreational activities, and in increased emphasis on fringe benefits. The human relations movement . . . has been criticized widely as manipulative, insincere, and, most importantly, as ignoring the reality of economic variables. It is accused of equating high morale with high productivity. To some organization theorists, this represents a naive and simplistic view of the nature of man. They hold that, on the contrary, "there are a lot of happy but unproductive workers."[64]

To be sure, the human relations approach has provided management with new insights and has pointed to "people-oriented" ways for resolving organizational difficulties. Indeed, most contemporary organizations include much of the thinking generated by the human relations theorists.

Human Resources School

The human resources school emerged as a response to the earlier schools of managerial thinking and addresses both production and human organizational concerns. The human resources advocates recognize the inevitable external pressures and internal strains that influence organizational decision making. The organization is viewed as a system where all parts affect the whole and every action has repercussions throughout the entire organization. The systems approach emphasizes interaction with the larger environment, and, as Katz and Kahn suggest, "is basically concerned with problems of relationships, of structure, and of interdependence rather than the constant attributes of objects."[65] Internal organizational operations are then contingent or dependent upon external environmental needs and individual needs. Lawrence and

Lorsch identify three primary relationships that determine how organizations operate and respond to their environment. Specifically, organizations have what they call "interfaces" at the organization-to-environment, group-to-group, and individual-to-organization levels. They suggest that organizational design and operation should be based on these three interfaces that differ for all organizations.[66] So, an organization must adapt to changing circumstances and to the needs of individuals and the environment in which the organization operates.

The human resources orientation further suggests that considerable attention be given to the development and use of human resources. This managerial outlook is predicated upon "the development of a set of values that regards employees as important productive entities; the conscious utilization of these value judgments in making decisions affecting those individuals; and the acquisition of a pattern of thinking or rational analysis which attempts to achieve the most effective and satisfactory utilization of human talents."[67] All workers are seen as previously untapped resources of creative suggestions and ideas. Management's job is to discover how to reveal those talents and allow each individual to contribute to the organization in increasingly diversified ways. Managers accepting human resources ideas encourage subordinate participation in significant decision making and prompt workers to exercise self-control and self-direction whenever the organizational task permits. The human resources approach has dual goals—increased employee satisfaction and morale, and improved organizational decision making—both of which are viewed as intricate parts of the same process.

There is much disagreement as to the attributes needed by upper management. Perrin Stryker, an observer of U.S. industry, notes:

> The assumption that there is an executive type is widely accepted, either openly or implicitly. Yet any executive presumably knows that a company needs all kinds of managers for different levels of jobs. The qualities most needed by a shop superintendent are likely to be quite opposed to those needed by a coordinating vice president of manufacturing. The literature of executive development is loaded with efforts to define the qualities needed by executives, and by themselves these sound quite rational. Few, for instance, would dispute the fact that a top manager needs good judgment, the ability to make decisions, the ability to win respect of others, and all the other well-worn phrases any management man could mention. But one has only to look at the successful manager in any company to see how enormously their particular qualities vary from any ideal list of executive virtues.[68]

However, the human resources approach demands of managers a certain combination of technical, human, and conceptual skills not previously required.[69] Technical skills imply an understanding of and proficiency in a specific kind of activity or special function, i.e., an engineer, a buyer, or an accountant. The skill is familiar and concrete. Human skills involve the ability to work with people—to deal with superiors, equals, and subordinates. Attitudes, assumptions, and beliefs are communicated to others in their own contexts. Sensitivity to others in times of decision making and in day-to-day behavior, is adequately expressed. Conceptual skills involve the ability to see the organization as a whole and extend to visualizing the individual business in relationship to the industry, the community, and the political, social, and economic forces of the nation as a whole. This system's mindedness is paramount for those accepting this organizational theory.

Raymond Miles, in a landmark article, presents a human resources model that focuses on communication, decision making, and the multiple aspects involved in problem solving.[70] Miles does not regard the effects of communication as controlled or manipulated by any particular authority. He considers a climate conducive to improved decision making one that can meet changing organizational circumstances and that is essential to organizational growth and development. An efficient communication system, therefore, represents a powerful instrument for the adjustment of structure and processes, and the applicability of human resources.

In sum, the human resources school broadens the concerns of contemporary organizations to include: (1) both formal and informal elements of the organization and their articulation; (2) the scope of informal groups and the relations between such groups inside and outside the organization; (3) both lower and higher ranks; (4) both social and material rewards, and their effects on each other; and (5) the interaction between the organization and its environment. Critical to such a theory is an effective communication system and an ability to understand the differences in people.

Teamwork School

Much has been said and written about the success of the Japanese philosophy of management as compared with its U.S. counterparts. W. Edwards Deming, father of the Japanese quality revolution via statistical process control, significantly influenced and shaped the reconstruction of Japanese business following World War II. He was cognizant of, and sensitive to, the Japanese culture when designing an efficient managerial system, and his ideas largely contributed to the development of the teamwork school.

If we understand the economic and cultural differences between Japan and the U.S., then we can more easily understand some of their management "innovations." Since World War II and its obvious devastation of the Japanese economy, Japan has chosen to concentrate its industrial efforts primarily in three areas: steel, automobiles, and consumer electronics. The U.S. has a broad economy of industries and businesses which must compete at home and abroad. Japan is also a very homogeneous country with regard to race, religion, language, and culture and this promotes egalitarianism, harmony, and solidarity. The U.S. has a broad, diverse ethnic and cultural mix. An atmosphere of crisis management in Japan that rises from a heavy reliance upon foreign raw materials places a constant pressure on workers; high productivity and excellence are promoted as the way to build a more independent Japan. But the expansiveness of U.S. culture along with our management structure and labor union movement have encouraged tangible financial rewards as the main incentive to work. Moreover, Japanese respect for the individual and reverence for the elderly make it easier to use compensation systems that rely more upon recognition. Because of these economic and cultural factors, an atmosphere of mutual trust, caring, and support exists in most Japanese organizations and fosters effective teamwork. There is an inextricable link between Japanese productivity and the cultural values of the people. Japanese writer Kawesaki Ichir notes, "In Japan work is a ceremony. To the Western worker, the job is an instrument for the enrichment and satisfaction of the real part of life, which exists outside the place of work. For the Japanese worker, life and job are so closely interwoven that it cannot be said where one ends and the other begins."[71]

U.S. and Japanese organizations likewise exhibit different characteristics. U.S. organizations are typified by short-term employment, individual decision making and responsibility, rapid promotion, formal control, specialized career paths, and segmented concerns. On the other hand, Japanese organizations can be characterized by lifetime employment, consensual decision making, group or collective responsibility, slow advancement, informal control, generalized career paths, and holistic concerns. The Japanese rely more on style, superordinate goals, staff, and skills; the focus in the U.S. is more on strategy, structure, and systems.[72]

These economic, cultural, and organizational differences also affect communication within Japanese and U.S. organizations. Howard and Teramoto found a greater total volume of communication within Japanese than in U.S. corporations. They reported that this increased volume of communication helped the Japanese members know and trust each other when carrying out their jobs.[73] Further studies reveal that Japanese companies exhibit a significantly higher number of face-to-face contacts. This may be attributed to the difficulty of adapting word processing equipment to the Japanese language, thus making it more efficient for Japanese managers to use face-to-face communication. Still another reason for the heavy reliance upon such personal contact may be that the Japanese workspace in most companies is quite crowded, forcing close contact among many workers regardless of their hierarchical placement in the company's structure.[74] Richard Pascale and Anthony Athos contend that the Japanese reliance upon face-to-face communication, openness, lateral communication across functional areas, bottom-up information flow, and participative decision making results from their focus on people rather than on systems.[75]

Honda's office design exemplifies teamwork management principles and serves as an instructive contrast with Western managerial thinking and traditional office layouts. The executive suite is moved from the customary top floor to midbuilding and there are no separate offices on the executive floor—not even for the chief executive. He sits in a corner at a round desk with the other executives scattered about the room at round desks. Why round? So that anybody who wants can sit down for a discussion at will. The counterpart fortresses of Detroit reveal executives shut off behind solid wooden doors, protected by secretaries in outer offices, and reached via long, anonymous corridors.

Honda's office radicalism, in one of the world's toughest industries, has high symbolism. Taking the executive suite off the top floor signals that there is no exclusive, literally higher, authority. Putting the emphasis on easy access to the rest of the company signals that involvement figures high in the corporate values. Placing top executives in an open office signifies the intention to have an open style in which rank and status have no practical importance. The round tables indicate that decisions are only to be taken after full discussion among colleagues who are always on tap. The proximity of the desks establishes that lines of communication are to be short and easily opened.[76]

William Ouchi argues that U.S. culture is changing, requiring a rethinking of some of the elements of the traditional organization. He contends that a teamwork approach can more appropriately address the changing social needs of workers in ways that support important cultural values—such as individuality—while adjusting to the evolution of new values, beliefs, and needs. Ouchi proposes a Theory Z organization where Japanese strength in human resources, social cohesion, job security, and holistic concern for employees is merged with U.S. strength in speedy decision making, management innovations, risk-taking skills, and individual freedom. He identifies 13 steps necessary to achieve such an organizational perspective:

1. Initiate the development of trust by encouraging a candid discussion of Theory Z among managers and by personally displaying openness and integrity.
2. Work with managers to determine company objectives and strategies and identify inconsistencies in the theory and the practice of management philosophy.
3. Openly support the desired management philosophy.
4. Create work structures that promote cooperation.
5. Develop interpersonal skills by recognizing and improving patterns of group interaction and group leadership.
6. Monitor progress toward change by formally testing for changed behavior in individuals and by obtaining observations from outsiders.
7. Involve the union in change of plans and processes.
8. Stabilize employment by distributing the burden of bad times among shareholders, managers, and employees.
9. Emphasize the importance of long-term performance by slowing monetary promotions and increasing non-monetary evaluations.
10. Broaden career paths; promote understanding by de-emphasizing specialization.
11. Involve employees in the process of change *only after* visible results have been achieved from the above steps at the management level.
12. Solicit and implement suggestions from workers as a group.
13. Maintain open communication to promote continued growth of holistic attitudes.[77]

This synthesis retains individual achievement and advancement as a model but encourages collaboration and provides a continuing sense of organizational community. It seeks a sociotechnical integration or balance of human social-psychological needs with organizational goals.

Presently, some U.S. firms are beginning to commingle members of all key functions, assimilate each function's traditional feudal authority, and use teams. Cross-training, or the development of a variety of job skills, and participative management techniques such as teambuilding and quality circles are becoming increasingly popular. Among the traditional firms adopting a teamwork perspective is Ford Motor Company. Team Taurus created a car that won awards for design and quality and came in under the proposed product development budget by almost one-half billion dollars.

Traditionally, product development at Ford was sequential. Mary Walton describes it in *The Deming Management Method:*

> Designers designed a car on paper, then gave it to the engineers, who figured out how to make it. Their plans were passed along to the manufacturing and purchasing people, who respectively set up the lines and selected the suppliers on competitive bids. The next step in the process was the production plant. Then came marketing, the legal and dealer service departments, and then finally the customers. In each stage, if a major glitch developed, the car was bumped back to the design phase for changes. The farther along in the sequence, however, the more difficult it was to make changes. In manufacturing, for example, "We wouldn't see the plans until maybe a year before production started," Taurus project leader Lew Veraldi said. "We would go back to engineering and say can you do it this way. They'd say, 'Go peddle your papers. It's already tooled. I can't afford it.'"[78]

That changed, Walton reports, again quoting project leader Veraldi:

> With Taurus . . . we brought all disciplines together, and did the whole process simultaneously as well as sequentially. The manufacturing people worked right with the design people, engineering people, sales and purchasing, legal, service, and marketing.
>
> In sales and marketing we had dealers come in and tell us what they wanted in a car to make it more user-friendly, to make it adapt to a customer, based on problems they saw on the floor in selling.
>
> We had insurance companies—Allstate, State Farm, American Road . . . tell us how to design a car so when accidents occur it would minimize the customer's expense in fixing it after a collision. One of the problems mentioned by insurance companies was the difficulty in realigning a car that had suffered front-end damage. As a result, Taurus and Sable have cross marks engraved on a suspension tower under the hood to define the center of gravity as an aid in front-end alignment. Team Taurus included Ford's legal and safety advisers, who advised on forthcoming trends in the laws so we could design for them rather than patching later on.
>
> Manufacturing was brought into the act early. We went to all the stamping plants, assembly plants, and put layouts on the walls. We asked them how to make it easier to build. We talked to hourly people. Team Taurus collected thousands of suggestions and incorporated most of them. It's amazing the dedication and commitment you can get from people. . . . We will never go back to the old ways because we know so much about what they can bring to the party.[79]

Today, 3M, Hewlett-Packard, Frito-Lay, Union Carbide, Lockheed, Xerox, Westinghouse, Polaroid, and over 400 other major manufacturing and service industries are breaking down old organizational barriers and adopting similar teamwork programs.[80] It is a management trend that is rapidly gaining acceptance for its strong emphasis on worker participation and quality control.

The teamwork school represents a considerable theoretical and pragmatic departure from the simplistic notions of the classicists. It rests on several key assumptions:

▶ Employees want to participate in the decisions that affect them.
▶ Employees have valuable insights that can improve productivity.
▶ Employees express higher job satisfaction when they participate in job-related decisions.
▶ Employee expertise should be tapped by management to improve productivity and quality of work life.

The teamwork school recognizes that today's workers cannot be "driven" through the use of mandate, force, and coercion by the authority figures. Times have changed, and people's basic needs for survival are not so pressing. The approach recognizes that workers are not motivated solely by money and other economic advantages. Rather, workers can contribute much useful input to the decision-making process, are better motivated to carry out goals that they helped to formulate, and are more loyal to an organization if they feel that they have a part in running it.

Still, the teamwork school recognizes the responsibility of top administration to maintain control of the organization and to exercise leadership in setting and accomplishing goals. Indeed, workers may not always possess the training, knowledge, or expertise to make top-level decisions nor will they always make decisions that in the long-run are in the best interest of the total organization. Consequently,

► COMMUNICATION AND THE CHIEF EXECUTIVE IN A TOTAL QUALITY MANAGEMENT ORGANIZATION

By Jerry W. Koehler and Thom Dupper

Total Quality Management (TQM) is a transformational initiative which is reshaping American organizations in the 1990's. The goal of TQM is quality improvement. It involves several principles and strategies which must be embraced by every level and function within the organization. One key is a renewed effort to improve organizational communications. At the employee and supervisor level, TQM demands a much higher level of effective group interaction. On the organizational level, TQM requires a free-flowing communications system, devoid of the traditional blocking, filtering and gatekeeping roles of the past.

Simply stated, TQM will not deliver promised quality improvement unless the CEO and top management are willing to rethink their communication orientation and retool their inventory of existing communication methodologies.

It is no longer sufficient to cite an open door policy as proof of a viable upward communications channel. Open doors mean little if the CEO is unwilling to protect the source of the communication from lower organizational retribution. That is rather like telling the gladiator all he has to do is get past all the lions to make it through the open arena door.

The traditional "open door" also implies that the CEO spends much time in the friendly confines of the office. Organizational news, especially bad news, must somehow find its way into that open door. With a TQM culture, the CEO is flushed out of the executive suite and into the day-to-day world of the organization. The CEO seeks out and rewards news of all types—especially bad news, because the CEO understands that the ability to grow is directly tied to the ability to know.

Finally, with TQM, the CEO must live the new culture which demands mutual respect and genuine concern for all within the organization. The TQM CEO understands the value of being a visible part of every function within the organization, and of being thought of as a team member rather than the boss. This "management by walking around" becomes even more important as the TQM organization flattens out by eliminating unnecessary levels of management.

Generally, the organization reflects the values of the leader. Because TQM represents cultural change of major proportions, the CEO must assume the role of chief transformational agent within the organization. In the wake of so many fleeting, specialized organizational development gimmicks which have tended to gain widespread acceptance followed by quick rejection, TQM requires special handling and care so it doesn't appear to be "just another improvement program."

Most of that responsibility falls on the shoulders of the CEO. Top management must forge a vision of the future state and become the highly visible manifestation of the future executive. The TQM CEO must become the standard-bearer of the new culture by speaking openly and frequently to other employees; by joining and participating in routine team meetings; and by recognizing and rewarding quality work.

Top management must also act to ensure the quality of communications throughout the organization, starting with their own meetings, since TQM organizations spend so much time in meetings.

Customers, owners and employees form impressions about the organization from its communications. Newsletters, bulletins, brochures and exhibits play a critical role in developing organizational identity, and the CEO along with top management should be involved in the form and substance of these elements. Each of these communication facets should be as carefully crafted as any product that goes out the door.

Organizational communication plays a larger and more significant role in the TQM culture than in the typical hierarchal organization. To succeed as the chief transformational agent toward this new culture, the TQM CEO must become a proficient and visible master of effective interpersonal, small group and public communication.

Source: Jerry W. Koehler and Thom Dupper, "Communication and the Chief Executive in a Total Quality Management Organization," *The Bulletin of Organizational Communication* 2 (August 1990): 2.

the greatest challenge is to convince workers that their input is really desired and valuable, and that they really are in large part in control of the operations of the enterprise, while at the same time retaining final authority and control for top management.

The implications for communication are clear. Communicating trust, commitment, and respect becomes the critical dynamism behind this management theory; the workers' sense of these feelings sustains their work attitudes and performance. Therefore, a good flow of communication in all directions is essential. Further, if workers are to participate in the decision-making process, they must have the information readily available to them that is necessary for that participation. This requires active listening, and to listen is to validate others.

The teamwork school is not without criticism. Perhaps noted management consultant Edgar Schein expressed it best when he critiqued both Ouchi's and Pascale and Athos's books: "We cannot produce cultural change simply by pointing to another culture and saying that some of the things they do would be neat here."[81] It is important to remember that the teamwork school of thought developed in a particular economic and cultural milieu. If an organization simply imports this management philosophy and its techniques without the requisite understanding of the underlying values concerning human potential and long-term development of human resources, there can be little chance for lasting success.[82] However, when deliberately implemented with a full awareness of their implications, these management principles have had such far-reaching benefits as "better communication between supervisors and workers, improved motivation, and closer identification with organizational goals."[83]

In the society of 1900 when Taylorism flourished, the modern organization was still in its infancy. To appreciate the remarkable amount of change that has occurred since the turn of the century look at just three examples in three different areas. Then, there wasn't a university in the world with a student enrollment over 6,000. Today, a school of that size is considered small. The entire federal government in Washington, D.C., in the year 1900 could have been housed in only one of today's federal office buildings. The business giant of the day—Standard Oil—was dismembered into 14 separate companies in 1911. Each of the 14 grew to more than four times the size of the original company and today the largest of these—Exxon, Mobil, Standard Oil of California—regularly rank at the top on the *Fortune 500* list.

Our society and our organizations have changed considerably since 1900. Equally significant, and accompanying this change, are evolving managerial philosophies and organizational theories. Available literature does not suggest any one best way to organize and manage people. As Harvey Sherman points out, "It all depends."[84] Edgar Schein elaborates further when he writes: "Man can respond to many different kinds of managerial strategies, depending on his own motives and abilities and the nature of the task; in other words, there is no one correct managerial strategy that will work for all men at all times."[85]

▶ SUMMARY

This chapter proposed that an open-system framework is the most meaningful way of looking at organizations in general and communication systems in particular. By assuming a systems approach to organizations and organizational communication, emphasis is given to the total nature of the modern organization. Accordingly, a model recognizing the mutual impact of external and internal influences upon the organization and its communication processing system was developed.

Every organization exists within and is a part of an external environment. Among the predominant external influences are the prevailing societal culture and economic conditions. Moreover, all organizations create a certain internal environment or culture. The core culture of an organization significantly affects the other internal elements—organizational objectives, managerial philosophy, leadership style, organizational structure, technology, reward system, and individual employee behavior.

Prevailing managerial assumptions and organizational theories particularly reflect an organization's culture. Theories of management range from the mechanistic classical theories where management was regarded as directing, forcing, coercing, and employees were seen as motivated only by economic advantages; to contemporary humanistic theories which present varying viewpoints on how to enhance relationships that benefit both people and organizations. These viewpoints integrate organizational structure, technology, and people with the larger environments in which organizations exist.

In the next chapter, we will explore communication climate, organizational structure, networks, and message flow. We will focus particularly on how communication enters into the managerial process at all levels and in all functions, regardless of the kind of management theory to which the administration subscribes.

▶ QUESTIONS FOR DISCUSSION AND SKILL DEVELOPMENT

1. Describe the most important elements of societal culture, insofar as organizations are concerned. How does the current impetus to "go international" relate to the influence of societal cultures? What will organizations have to do to achieve a global advantage?

2. Explain what economics is. What does the concept "economic system" mean? How do economic systems affect organizations? What significant economic conditions exist at the present time in your area? How are these conditions affecting organizations?

3. The culture of an organization is encoded in the images, metaphors, artifacts, beliefs, values, myths, and other symbolic constructs that decorate and give form to the experience of everyday life. Think about an organization with which you are familiar. How would you describe its culture? What are the principal images or metaphors that people use to describe it? What physical impression does the organization and its artifacts create? What kinds of beliefs and values dominate it? What are the primary norms? What are the main ceremonies and rituals and what purposes do they serve? What language dominates everyday discourse? What are the dominant stories or legends that people tell? What messages are they trying to convey? What reward systems are in place? What messages do they send in terms of activities or accomplishments that are valued, and those that are not? What are the favorite topics of informal conversation? Think of three influential people in the organization. In what ways do they symbolize the character of the organization? Are there identifiable subcultures in the organization? How are they differentiated? Are they in conflict or in harmony? What effects do these subcultures have on the organization? What functions do these groupings serve for their members? Is their overall impact positive or negative? Would you classify this organization's culture as being strong or weak? Should efforts be made to change it?

4. Compare the older, classical management theory to the newer, humanistic theories of management. What impact do these theories have on job satisfaction as a means of achieving greater productivity? Can the group-oriented Japanese approach to management be made to work in this country? Think of an organization for which you have worked or with which you are quite familiar. Which organization theory seems to prevail within this organization? Cite specific examples to support your views.

5. Compare and contrast some managerial theories with communication models that logically should be subscribed to by organizational administrators.

1. Kenneth Gross, "IBM's School for Success," *LI Newsday's Magazine for Long Island* (July 13, 1975): 7.

2. Ibid.

3. Chester Barnard, *The Functions of the Executive* (Boston: Harvard University Press, 1968) (originally published in 1938).

4. Pamela Shockley-Zalabak, *Fundamentals of Organizational Communication,* 2nd ed. (New York: Longman Publishing, 1991).

5. A. G. Kefalas, "Organizational Communication: A Systems Viewpoint," in: Richard C. Huseman, Cal M. Logue, Dwight L. Freshly, eds., *Readings in Interpersonal and Organizational Communication* (Boston: Holbrook Press, 1977): 25.

6. Alvin Toffler, *Powershift* (New York: Bantam, 1990): xix.

7. J. G. March and H. A. Simon, *Organizations* (New York: John Wiley & Sons, 1958): 1.

8. L. W. Porter, E. F. Lawler, and J. R. Hackman, *Behavior in Organizations* (New York: McGraw-Hill, 1975): 89.

9. Amitai Etzioni, *Modern Organizations* (Englewood Cliffs, NJ: Prentice Hall, 1964): 3.

10. H. G. Hicks, *The Management of Organizations: A Systems and Human Approach* (New York: McGraw-Hill, 1972): 23.

11. A. Wilden, *System and Structure* (London: Tavistock, 1980): 39.

12. R. A. Johnson, *The Theory and Management of Systems,* 3rd ed. (New York: McGraw-Hill, 1973): 23.

13. R. K. Allen, *Organizational Management Through Communication* (New York: Harper and Row, 1977): 55.

14. H. L. Tosi and C. Hammer, *Organizational Behavior and Management: A Contingency Approach* (Chicago: St. Clair Press, 1974): 5.

15. G. Hofstede, *Culture's Consequences: International Differences in Work-Related Values* (Beverly Hills, CA: Sage, 1980): 25.

16. D. Hellriegel and J. Slocum, *Management: A Contingency Approach* (Reading, MA: Addison-Wesley, 1974): 17.

17. Kingsley Davis, "Mental Hygiene and the Class Structure," *Psychiatry* 1 (1938): 55–56.

18. Margaret Mead, *And Keep Your Powder Dry* (New York: W. Morrow and Co., 1942).

19. Wayne C. Minnick, *The Art of Persuasion* (Boston: Houghton Mifflin, 1968): 217–218.

20. Herbert J. Gans, "The Messages Behind the News," *Columbia Journalism Review* (January-February, 1979): 40–45.

21. R. N. Farmer and B. Richman, *Comparative Management and Economic Progress* (Homewood, IL: Richard D. Irwin, 1965).

22. Hofstede, *Culture's Consequences;* G. Hofstede, "Dimensions of National Cultures in Fifty Countries and Three Regions," in: J. Dergowski and R. Anuis, eds., *Explications in Cross-Cultural Psychology* (Liste, The Netherlands: Suets and Zeithnger, 1983): 335–355.

23. Edward T. Hall, *Beyond Culture* (Garden City, NY: Anchor Books, 1976).

24. Walter Wriston, *Risk and Other Four Letter Words* (New York: Harper and Row, 1986).

25. G. S. Hampshire, "The Pace Partnership: Business and Liberal Arts," *Lubin Letter* (May/June 1990): 5–6.

26. Kazuo Nishiyama, "Speech Training for Japanese Businessmen," *Speech Teacher* 24 (1975): 255.

27. Kerry Hannon, "Life After Lead," *Forbes* (May 5, 1987): 65.

28. D. C. McGill, "A 'Mickey Mouse' Class—For Real," *New York Times,* August 27, 1989, 4F.

29. Michael Paconowsky and Nick O'Donnell-Trujillo, "Organizational Communication as Cultural Performance," *Communication Monographs* 50 (1983): 146.

30. Karl Weick, *The Social Psychology of Organizing* (Reading, MA: Addison-Wesley, 1969).

31. Tom Peters, *Thriving On Chaos* (New York: Harper and Row, 1987): 344–345.

32. Edgar H. Schein, "The Role of the Founder in Creating Organizational Culture," *Organizational Dynamics* 12 (1983): 13–28.

33. Edgar H. Schein, "What Is Culture," in: Peter J. Frost, Larry F. Moore, Meryl R. Louis, Craig C. Lundberg, and Joanne Martin, eds., *Reframing Organizational Culture* (Newbury Park, CA: Sage, 1991): 247.

34. Alan Kantrow, *The Constraints of Corporate Tradition* (New York: Harper and Row, 1984): 75.

35. James Hunt, *Leadership, A New Synthesis* (Newbury Park, CA: Sage, 1991): 220–222.

36. E. Rogers and R. Agarwala-Rogers, *Communication in Organizations* (New York: Free Press, 1976).

37. Paconowsky and O'Donnell-Trujillo, "Organizational Communication," 126–147.

38. J. S. DeMott, "Sears' Sizzling New Vitality," *Time* (August 20, 1984): 82–90.

39. D. C. Feldman, *Managing Careers in Organizations* (Glenview, IL: Scott, Foresman, 1988); E. H. Schein, "Organizational Culture," *Psychologist* 45 (1990): 109–119.

40. Phillip Clampitt, *Communicating for Managerial Effectiveness* (Newbury Park, CA: Sage, 1991): 66.

41. H. Broms and H. Gahmberg, "Communication to Self in Organizations and Cultures," *Administrative Service Quarterly* 28 (1983): 482–495.

42. "At Johnson and Johnson a Mistake Can Be a Badge of Honor," *Business Week* (September 26, 1988): 126–128.

43. Peters, *Thriving on Chaos*, 351–352.

44. K. L. Gregory, "Native-view Paradigms—Multiple Cultures and Conflicts in Organizations," *Administrative Science Quarterly* 28 (1983): 359–376.

45. J. Martin and C. Siehl, "Organizational Culture and Counterculture: An Uneasy Symbiosis," *Organizational Dynamics* (Autumn 1983): 52–54.

46. M. R. Louis, "An Investigator's Guide to Workplace Culture" in P. J. Frost , L. F. Moore, M. R. Louis, C. C. Lundberg, and J. Martin, *Organizational Culture* (Newbury Park, CA: Sage, 1985).

47. Terrence Deal and Allen Kennedy, *Corporate Cultures: The Rites and Rituals of Corporate Life* (Reading, MA: Addison-Wesley): 5.

48. T. S. Peters and R. H. Waterman, *In Search of Excellence* (New York: Harper and Row, 1982): 75–76.

49. K. Nishiyama, "Japanese Quality Control Circles" (Paper presented at the Thirty-First Annual Conference of the International Communication Association, Minneapolis, MN, 1981).

50. R. Mitchell, "Nurturing Those Ideas," *Business Week* (December 1989): 106–108.

51. Paul Bates, "The Impact of Organizational Culture on Approaches to Organizational Problem-Solving," *Organizational Studies* 5 (1984): 43–66.

52. Peters and Waterman, *In Search of Excellence*, 77.

53. Douglas McGregor, *The Human Side of Enterprise* (New York: McGraw-Hill, 1960).

54. Frederick W. Taylor, *The Principles of Scientific Management* (New York: Harper and Row, 1913).

55. Henri Fayol, *General and Industrial Management,* Constance Stoors, trans. (London: Pitman and Sons, 1949).

56. Max Weber, *The Theory of Social and Economic Organization,* A. Henderson and T. Parsons, trans. (New York: Oxford University Press, 1948).

57. C. Perrow, *Complex Organizations: A Critical Essay* (Glenview, IL: Scott, Foresman, 1972).

58. Etzioni, *Modern Organizations*, 31.

59. Ibid., 21.

60. Elton Mayo, *The Social Problems of an Industrial Civilization* (Boston: School of Business Administration, Harvard University, 1945).

61. Fritz Roethlisberger and William Dickson, *Management and the Worker* (Cambridge, MA: Harvard University Press, 1939); and R. H. Franke and J. D. Kaul, "The Hawthorne Experiments: First Statistical Interpolation," *American Sociological Review* 43 (1978): 623–643.

62. Edgar Huse and James Bowditch, *Behavior in Organizations* (Reading, MA: Addison-Wesley, 1973).

63. Etzioni, *Modern Organizations*, 43.

64. Harold Rush, "The World of Work and the Behavioral Sciences: A Perspective and an Overview," in: Fred Luthans, ed., *Contemporary Readings in Organizational Behavior* (New York: McGraw-Hill, 1972): 58–69.

65. D. Katz and R. Kahn, *The Social Psychology of Organizations* (New York: John Wiley & Sons, 1966).

66. P. Lawrence and J. Lorsch, *Developing Organizations: Diagnosis and Action* (Reading, MA: Addison-Wesley, 1969).

67. Leon C. Meggenson, *Personnel, A Behavioral Approach to Administration* (Homewood, IL: Richard D. Irwin, 1972): 47.

68. Perrin Stryker, "The Growing Pains of Executive Development,"*Advanced Management* (August 1954): 15.

69. Robert L. Katz, "Skills of an Effective Administrator," *Harvard Business Review* (September-October 1974): 91.

70. Raymond Miles, "Keeping Informed—Human Relations or Human Resources?" *Harvard Business Review* (July-August 1965): 148–163.

71. Frank Gibney, *Japan: The Fragile Superpower* (New York: W. W. Norton, 1975): 180.

72. William G. Ouchi, *Theory Z: How American Business Can Meet the Japanese Challenge* (adapted from pages 97–129). Copyright © 1981 by Addison-Wesley Publishing Co., Inc. Reprinted by permission of the publisher.

73. N. Howard and Y. Teramoto, "The Really Important Differences Between Japanese and Western Management," *Management International Review* 3 (1981): 19–30.

74. Richard Pascale, "Communication and Decision-Making Across Cultures: Japanese and American Comparisons," *Administrative Science Quarterly* 23 (1978): 91–109.

75. Richard Pascale and Anthony Athos, *The Art of Japanese Management: Applications for American Management* (New York: Simon & Schuster, 1981).

76. Robert Heller, *The Decision Makers* (New York: Truman Talley Books/Plume, 1991).

77. Ouchi, *Theory Z.*

78. Mary Walton, *The Deming Management Method* (New York: Dodd, Mead and Company, 1986).

79. Ibid.

80. Joyce L. Poll and David L. Poll, "The Potential for Application of Quality Circles in the American Public Sector," *Public Productivity Review* 7 (1983): 103–126.

81. Edgar Schein, "Does Japanese Management Style Have a Message for American Managers?" *Sloan Management Review* 22 (1981): 55–68.

82. Chimezie Osigueh, *Organizational Science Abroad: Constraints and Perspectives* (New York: Plenum Press, 1989).

83. Stephen Bryant and Joseph Kearns, "Workers' Brains as Well as Their Bodies," *Public Administration Review* 42 (1982): 144–150.

84. Harvey Sherman, *It All Depends: A Pragmatic Approach to Organizations* (Tuscaloosa, AL: University of Alabama Press, 1966).

85. Edgar Schein, *Organization Psychology*, 2nd ed. (Englewood Cliffs, NJ: Prentice Hall, 1970).

Communication Climate, Organizational Structure, Networks, and Message Flow

LEARNING OBJECTIVES:

To describe organizational and communication climates, and compare/contrast them with organizational culture

To identify and describe the range of behavior styles that managers use to influence workers

To detail the assumptions of McGregor's Theory X and Theory Y management

To present and describe the key motivational assumptions of Likert, Maslow, and Herzberg

To distinguish among tall, flat, and matrix organizational structures

To identify formal and informal communication networks, and describe communication roles

To identify and describe downward, horizontal, and upward message flow

C ommunication in organizations is a vital aspect of their daily operations, of their planning and policy-making, and of their achieving the objectives for which they were formed. It is influenced by the internal climate and structure of the organization, and consists primarily of a downward flow, a horizontal flow, an upward flow, and the unofficial flow of information that knows no chain of command and is restricted to no level or area of the organization and goes by the name "grapevine." This chapter examines the dimensions of an organization's communication climate and describes the impact of organizational structure, networks, and message flow on the total organizational system.

The first systematic design of an organization took place during an expansion of the Soho Engineering Foundry in Great Britain in 1800.[1] Equipment purchases, factory layout, job design, and incentive systems all were based on carefully obtained information. One of the primary concerns of the designers of the Soho plant was effective formal communication, i.e., the exchange of particular kinds of information through formally established channels, for purposes the organization had defined and accepted. The designers realized that to succeed they would need to create the proper communication climate and information-processing system. Thus, as early as 1800, some managers understood that guiding and constraining employees' actions and coordination depended on effective communication.

▶ COMMUNICATION CLIMATE AND MANAGERIAL STYLE

The modern organization is a complex system both existing within an external environment and possessing an internal climate. A system's *climate* is the state of its internal nature as perceived by its members. Climate concerns whether people's expectations about what it should be like to work in an organization are being met. Kurt Lewin, one of the first to study organizational climate, describes the concept as follows:

> To characterize properly the psychological field, one has to take into account such specific items as particular goals, stimuli, needs, social relations, as well as more general characteristics of the field as the atmosphere (for instance the friendly, tense, or hostile atmosphere) or the amount of freedom. These characteristics of the field as a whole are as important in psychology as, for instance, the field of gravity for the explanation of events in classical physics. Psychological atmospheres are empirical realities and are scientifically describable facts.[2]

Lewin and his colleagues had little difficulty in demonstrating the "empirical reality" of psychological atmospheres or climates. In organizational communication research, climate is generally considered to be an index of an individual's psychological state in the context of the organization. This index is multidimensional, focusing on the members' perceptions of such factors as the supportiveness of the superior–subordinate relations, quality and accuracy of message flow, relational openness, communication satisfaction, and organizational commitment.[3]

Regardless of whether one focuses on only one dimension of climate or combines them to measure multidimensional attributes, there appears to be a number of common assumptions regarding this construct. Among the more important assumptions are:

▶ Organizational climate is a molar concept in the same sense that personality is a molar concept [the properties of each must be perceived as a whole].

▶ The climate of a particular organization, while certainly not unchanging, nevertheless has an air of permanence or at least some continuity over time.

▶ Phenomenologically, climate is external to the individual, yet cognitively, the climate is internal to the extent that it is affected by individual perceptions.

▶ Climate is reality-based and thus is capable of being shared in the sense that observers or participants may agree upon the climate of an organization or group, although this consensus may be constrained by individual differences in perceptions.

► The climate of an organization potentially impacts the behavior of people in the system.[4]

Although there is considerable consensus about the assumptions underlying the climate construct, there is still some validity in Guion's observation that "the concept of organizational climate is undoubtedly important, but it also seems to be one of the fuzziest concepts to come along in some time."[5] One fuzzy point is the distinction between organizational culture and organizational climate. How do culture and climate differ? Climate is only one aspect of culture—patterns of beliefs and expectations shared by the organization's members. Climate refers to whether or not expectations are being met, but culture is concerned with the nature of the expectations themselves. Thus, although culture is an emergent property of group interaction, climate may be taken to be individuals' psychological perceptions of the characteristics of an organization's practices and procedures. Moreover, climate is often short-term and may depend on the current management of an organization, but culture is usually long-term, rooted in deeply held values, and often very hard to change.[6]

The basic tenet of communication climate is that an individual's cognitive and affective perceptions of an organization influence that individual's behavior in the organization. The concept of communication climate might be thought of as the spirit or philosophy that dominates the organization and is responsible for the interpersonal relationships that exist among its people. These relationships may be friendly and produce positive effects on the growth of the organization and the mental well-being of the individuals, or they may be hostile and produce negative effects. Lytton Guimaraes defines "communication integration" or communication climate as "the degree to which the subsystems or individuals in a communication system are structurally interlinked."[7] Thus, the communication climate within an organization ranges on a continuum from supportive to defensive which can be measured by the degree to which members of an organization find formal and informal communication systems to be open or closed.

It is generally accepted that climate arises from, and is sustained by, organizational practices—the systematized and customary activities deemed important by the organization or its members. Before managers can expect much to happen—a flow of ideas, maximum effort, cooperation—they must create the right sort of atmosphere or climate and practice their vision. "I recall a district manager I had," says J. C. Penney chairman Donald Seibert. "When he came to look at my store, I knew he would be most interested in departments that were difficult to manage or had problems. If he was going to use his time effectively on a visit, he wanted to get into problem areas so he could contribute to a solution, not just look at everything that was working well. So instead of trying to think of every success story we had, I told him everything that was wrong in the store—where we had goofed or simply didn't have an answer." He continues, "Looking back I think what the district manager looked for was enough concern about the business to show that we were not afraid to be identified with problems as well as successes."[8] Or, consider the comments of Doyle Dane Bernbach, founder of a supertalent ad agency: "I'm amused when other agencies try to hire my people away. They'd have to 'hire' the whole environment. For a flower to blossom, you need the right soil as well as the right seed."[9]

In the performance of their duties, managers adopt certain principles characterizing a preferred management style. *Managerial style* refers to the pattern of com-

► THE TAKE OVER: A CHANGE IN COMMUNICATION CLIMATE

About seven years ago I made a career change and joined the company that I currently work for. This company seemed too good to be true. The employees were paid well, the benefit program was probably the best in the state, every employee was considered important, from the janitor to the CEO, and employees treated each other with respect. Moreover, management communicated to the employees on a regular basis. Communication was a key part of the management philosophy here and management worked very hard to maintain an open line of communication with its employees.

As part of the effort to keep communication flowing, every month we had a company-wide meeting in the auditorium which we called "Family Council." The meeting was always videotaped so that copies of the tape could be sent to all of the offices around the world. The purpose of the meeting was to share information about the company with all employees, such as sales, revenue, earnings before tax, new products, new clients, marketing strategies, and big projects that were in progress. We would also introduce and welcome new employees, talk about upcoming events and social functions. It was very relaxed and open. The management of the company took pride in the amount, frequency, and effectiveness of communication with employees. When I first joined the company I was amazed at the amount of information they shared with the employees, and the air of openness in which it was shared. This was something that was not done by any previous employer.

Two years ago the company was acquired by another company. As one might expect in an acquisition situation, the majority of the employees were more than a little concerned about such matters as whether or not they would still have a job or is the new parent company going to change anything. Immediately following the acquisition, a senior executive from the new parent company attended one of our "Family Council" meetings and assured everyone that no one was going to lose their job and that everything would continue to operate as it had in the past. He even said that one of the things that impressed them about our company was its unique management philosophy and open communication climate. They hoped to learn a lot from us.

This was reassuring to hear. We all knew how special our company was and we did not want anything to ruin it. For a while things operated as they had in the past, but it soon became apparent that things were going to change. Shortly thereafter about twelve people were laid off. This little surprise was not accepted well by the employees. We were offered no explanation by our new parent company.

Our management did, however, explain why the lay-offs had been necessary.

As our employees began communicating with their employees on a daily basis, it became clear that they were not used to our open and informal style. When a message is sent, the sender usually wants to make sure it was received and properly interpreted, otherwise how do you know that what was received is what was intended. These people know only one method of communicating, and that is to blurt out some message, usually in an abrupt and rude manner, and not ask or wait for any kind of response. They also do a lot of screaming and yelling at each other.

We were not accustomed to their methods of communicating and it was difficult to adjust to. Management from the new parent company was definitely losing its credibility fast. People were very nervous about their jobs. Morale around the company dropped to an all-time low. Rumors began floating around about what was going to happen next. What was left or our old management team tried their best to put things in proper perspective, but it was impossible to erase the messages we had already been exposed to.

It was announced that the CEO of our new parent company would be attending our upcoming "Family Council" and that if anyone had any questions they should write them down and forward them to the president of our company. As I understand it, there were about twenty-six different questions received from employees.

We assembled for "Family Council," eagerly anticipating the answers to the questions we had submitted. "Family Council" began with its usual formalities and then our new parent company CEO was given the floor. Before he began speaking, he asked that the videotape be shut off and that everyone who was not a full-time employee of the company leave the room. He began his speech by saying that he could not believe the questions that he had received. He had expected questions about the company strategy for the next couple of years and instead had received questions which dealt with current situations. Obviously, he could not understand that when people are so concerned about the present they certainly are not going to be thinking two years down the road. So the questions had been divided up into categories, one of which was "those that did not even deserve an answer."

As he spoke it was clear he was not happy about the questions we had asked him. He was so angry that at times his voice was shaky. He was very rigid and did not appear comfortable at all. Instead of trying to project empathy, he used sarcasm. He did not smile once. It was very confusing to be invited to ask questions only to discover that the invitation was not a sincere one.

We all left "Family Council" that day in shock. We had never been spoken to in that manner before. I know personally that our management team was extremely upset with the situation but there was nothing they could do about it. It is now very clear to me why the employees of our parent company are so abrupt and rude. They are following in the footsteps of their fearless leader/dictator.

Source: Student journal entry, Hamilton Holt School of Rollins College, Winter Park, FL, Fall 1991.

munication behavior that one person manifests to influence another person. Derived from the milieu of organizational literature, one's managerial style or, more generally, interpersonal influence style represents a personal modification and adaptation of established philosophies and theories to the particular culture, social system, and technological complex within which a manager operates. Thus, a preferred managerial style establishes the climate of communication and serves to define the parameters within which a manager tries to solve or resolve problems. Robert Schoenberg observes that it "is not only a matter of the boss's personal commitments being riveted by style. . . . style (especially if it is strong, clearly defined and emphatic) informs the doings and attitudes of the whole group."[10]

Social scientists have long sought to describe and classify the typical behavior of individuals in terms of phenomena called "style." Classifications of style have been widely discussed in psychology, business, and communication, with many different schema being developed. It seems that most of the style descriptions focus on the functions of leadership, but in different ways. One of the first and still most widely used style description continua was developed by Robert Tannenbaum and Warren Schmidt.[11] They identify a range of behavior styles that managers can and do use in their influence attempts (see Exhibit 4-1). The way in which authority is used is the main characteristic determining the general management leadership style. The use of authority varies from extreme usage on the left to minimal usage on the right. Stated another way, the use of authority on the left-hand side of the continuum is predominantly to coerce, entice, persuade, and reward people; the use of authority on the right is predominantly shared with the followers. The diagonal line moving from left to right indicates that less and less authority is used to manage as subordinates are allowed greater amounts of freedom and influence on decisions.

Perhaps the best-known of the management style theories of leadership is that developed by Robert Blake and Anne Adams McCanse. Their "Leadership Grid® Theory" hypothesizes that management styles or leadership approaches are based on two central dimensions: concern for relationships with people and concern for task production. The grid describes five leadership styles: impoverished, authority–compliance, country club, middle-of-the-road, and team (see Exhibit 4-2).[12]

Impoverished Management (1,1). The impoverished manager has little concern either for people or for production. The basic approach is almost an abdication of the real leadership function. The image is one of being present, but the response is one of absence when it involves the task of supervising or of efforts dedicated to production. This person might best be characterized as "both unfriendly and lazy, if he is having a good day, and gravely and obstinate on a bad day."[13]

Chapter 4   Communication Climate, Structure, Networks, and Message Flow   **4-6**

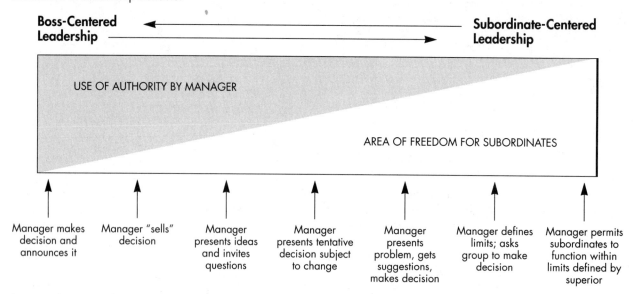

Source: Robert Tannenbaum and Warren H. Schmidt, "How to Choose a Leadership Pattern," *Harvard Business Review* 36 (March–April 1958), p. 96.

Authority–Compliance Management (9,1). The task-centered superior–subordinate relationship is based on the exercise of authority and obedience. This autocratic leadership approach is primarily concerned with goals or task achievement, and exhibits little concern for personal relationships. Simply stated, the task style is to decide what must be done, make sure people understand what must be done, and then be sure that they do what must be done for effective and efficient task accomplishment.

Country Club Management (1,9). The country club manager emphasizes interpersonal relationships at the expense of goal achievement. Because the general approach here is to keep people happy enough to accomplish the task, lots of effort is devoted to developing pleasant working conditions and an atmosphere of friendliness, informality, and lack of pressure. The manager is more the big brother or big sister than the boss. Work tempo is comfortable and employees are expected to perform because of loyalty and acceptance.

Middle-of-the-Road Management (5,5). This person exhibits a concern both for people and for production, but not to the extent that conflict becomes a danger. The idea behind this style is that people's satisfactions must be balanced against the organization's needs for production. The approach is one of persuasion coupled with "tactful prodding." Compromise is the key to balancing concerns for people and for production.

Team Management (9,9). The team manager is concerned with people and with production, and has a strong commitment to both. A primary identifying factor of this manager is the use of goal setting in stimulating and directing people toward the organization's achievement. The general approach is to involve people and give them a "stake" in the organizational achievements and to generate commitment by using their abilities to get the best possible results. This leadership style respects differing points of view, values diversity, shares decision making, and strives for problem solving designed to correct rather than postpone problems. The style is highly desirable, but team leaders must depend on team followers for this style of leadership to work.

Blake and McCanse also define two other leadership styles not depicted in the two-dimensional portion of their figure: paternalistic and opportunistic management. The former style—a "father knows best" approach—strives for high results and uses reward and punishment to gain compliance. Such leaders focus on a high level of concern for people to reward for compliance or punish for rejection.

The opportunist uses whatever Grid style is needed to obtain selfish interest and self-promotion. He or she adapts to situations to gain the maximum advantage. Performance occurs according to a system of exchanges and effort is given only for an equivalent measure of the same.

In defining managerial styles, William J. Reddin uses the same people and production dimensions, but suggests that the effectiveness of any particular style depends on the situation. The Reddin Management Style Survey is unique in that it provides a situational approach to management. It identifies four basic styles, each represented by more effective and less effective versions.[14] This construct is attractive because of the potential to describe the relationship between effective and ineffective manage-

▶ **EXHIBIT 4-2**
The Leadership Grid

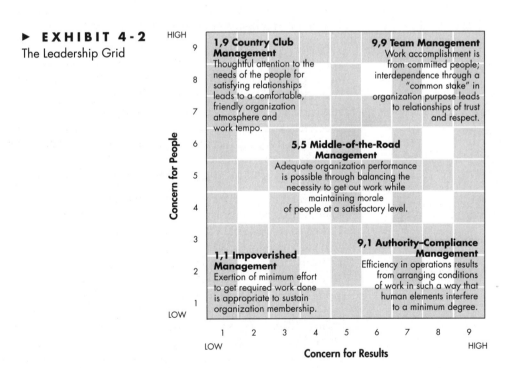

Source: *Leadership Dilemmas—Grid Solutions,* by Robert R. Blake and Anne Adams McCanse (formerly the Managerial Grid figure by Robert R. Blake and Jane S. Mouton) (Houston: Gulf Publishing Company), p. 29. Copyright 1991 by Scientific Methods, Inc. Reproduced by permission of the owners.

ment styles in terms of communication style dimensions. Reddin's classifications of management styles include:

Separated Style. The separated manager has an orientation toward procedures, methods, and systems, with emphasis on accuracy, conservation, prudence, and noninvolvement. The "bureaucrat" is the more effective version. This manager is perceived as conscientious and primarily interested in rules and procedures for their own sake, wanting to control the situation by their use. The "deserter" is the less effective version. This manager is uninvolved and passive or negative.

Related Style. The related manager is basically oriented to other people, creating a work atmosphere of security and acceptance, and using friendship and understanding to influence others. Related managers are more sensitive to the demands of the human system than to the demands of the technical system. The "developer" is the more effective version. This manager is perceived as having implicit trust in people and as being primarily concerned with developing them as individuals. The "missionary" is the less effective version. This manager is perceived as being primarily interested in harmony.

Dedicated Style. The dedicated manager basically directs the work of others, and is most useful when much must be done very quickly or when a profound change is needed. Dedicated managers seldom flounder and they make decisions quickly. The "benevolent autocrat" is the more effective version. This manager is perceived as knowing what he wants and how to get it without creating resentment. The "autocrat" is the less effective version. This manager is perceived as having no confidence in others, as unpleasant, and as interested only in the immediate task.

Integrated Style. An integrated manager wants to structure things so there is a highly cooperative approach toward the achievement of organizational goals. She or he works to integrate the needs of the individual with the needs of the organization and to align personal and organizational goals. The "executive" is the more effective version. This manager is seen as a positive motivating force who sets high standards, treats everyone fairly, and prefers team management. The "compromiser" is the less effective version. This manager is considered a poor decision maker, one who allows various pressures in a situation to exert considerable influence, and who avoids or minimizes immediate pressures and problems rather than maximizing long-term production.

Style is indeed a very useful way to categorize or label behaviors in order to understand which communicative behaviors are preferred by people and which ones are linked to managerial effectiveness. There is little agreement among researchers as to what precisely constitutes communication or management style, but the real value of studying behavior in this manner is that it enables us to focus on people's preferred ways of communicating or managing and how those ways may differ from the preferences of others. Dimensions of style provide a systematic way of focusing on how people communicate. John McGrath and Cal Downs found that there is a substantive link between communication style and management style. When respondents were grouped according to their dominant management style, they showed a clear preference for certain communication styles. Moreover, their study revealed that Reddin's effective "executive style" was more clearly related to positive communication style dimensions than was any other management style. This style clearly stood out as the one that possessed more positive communication attributes—conversational, convivial, unsecretive, frank, approachable, attentive, animated, dynamic, and precise. Although they stop short of claiming this to be the "one best style," they do observe that the "evidence suggests that it is the one that is best described in terms of positive communication attributes, which are often viewed as an important aspect in depicting managerial success."[15]

It is important for you to keep in mind how inappropriate it is to apply a single style to all situations and how this can lead to multiple problems. Rather, you need to recognize the importance of developing and using a repertoire of managerial styles applicable to particular situations, involving a specific person or groups of people at given periods of time and under given sets of circumstances. For example, a certain style of management may work well in the research and development department, but not well at all in the production department. Style in this context provides a relevant way to place the right people in the right jobs.

The above discussion on communication climate and style takes on more meaning when the underlying assumptions regarding human nature, work, and motivation are made explicit. These assumptions relate to the relationship between task and maintenance functions suggesting not only that these functions are independent of each other but also that they are complementary. Thus, the concept of communication climate and managerial styles acquires sharper definition by examining the works of Jack Gibb, Douglas McGregor, Rensis Likert, Abraham Maslow, and Frederick Herzberg.

Gibb's Supportive and Defensive Climates

Jack Gibb distinguishes between supportive and defensive communication climates and managerial styles.[16] A *supportive climate,* contributing to a supportive style, is characterized by:

1. *description* (nonjudgmental, asking questions for information, presenting feelings, events, perceptions or processes without calling for or implying change on the receivers)
2. *problem orientation* (defining mutual problems and seeking solutions without inhibiting the receiver's goals, decisions and progress)
3. *spontaneity* (free of deception, unhidden motives, honest and straightforward)
4. *equality* (mutual trust and respect, participative planning without influence of power, status, appearance)
5. *empathy* (respecting the worth of the listener, identifying, sharing and accepting problems, feelings and values)
6. *provisionalism* (willingness to experiment with one's own behavior, attitudes and ideas)

On the other hand, a *defensive climate,* contributing to a defensive style, is characterized by:

1. *evaluation* (passing judgment, blaming, praising, questioning standards, values and motives)
2. *control* (trying to do something to another, attempting to change an attitude or behavior of another)
3. *strategy* (manipulation and tricking others)
4. *neutrality* (expressing lack of concern for another's welfare)

5. *superiority* (an attitude of superiority in wealth, intellectual ability, physical characteristics)

6. *certainty* (dogmatic, needing to be right, wanting to win)

The importance of fostering a supportive rather than a defensive climate is underscored by W. Charles Redding when he says "the climate of the organization is more crucial than are communication skills or techniques (taken by themselves) in creating an effective organization."[17] The concern for establishing a climate where supportive relationships can thrive underlies much of today's research in organizational communication. Ongoing research is trying to catalog, both theoretically and empirically, the many dimensions that constitute a supportive organizational climate and contribute to a productive communication climate. James Campbell and Michael Beatty identify the following components: (1) individual autonomy, (2) the degree of structure placed on a position, (3) reward orientation and (4) consideration, warmth, and support.[18] H. S. Dennis would add participative decision making, trust, confidence, credibility, openness and candor, and high performance goals.[19] A final treatment of climate in an organization as it relates with other behavioral variables has yet to be presented.

In organizations, numerous climates are operating. Some deal with the elements of the organization, others with a member's reaction to the elements, and still others with the individual's reaction to his or her workgroup, department, and so on. Yet all of the climates focus primarily on the individual and manager–employee workplace relationships.

McGregor's Theory X and Theory Y

Douglas McGregor, former president of Antioch College and Massachusetts Institute of Technology professor of management, developed a theory of human behavior in organizations that has important implications for communication climate. Based on the writings of Taylor and Mayo, he labeled it Theory X and Theory Y. Theory X and Theory Y present underlying beliefs regarding human nature that affect a manager's decision to adopt one managerial style over another and consequently influence the development of a particular organizational climate.[20]

McGregor believed that hierarchical structure, management control of influence and decision making, close supervision, and performance measurement were based on assumptions about how to motivate human behavior. Specifically, he proposed that *Theory X* managers assume people are inherently opposed to work and must be coerced by any means before they will put forth any effort. The basic assumptions of Theory X are:

1. that the typical person has a natural aversion to work;
2. because of the first assumption, people will work effectively only when ordered, threatened, or forced to do so; and
2. that the typical person is indolent, irresponsible, unambitious, and inclined to value security above everything else.[21]

Theory X, by its traditionally authoritative nature, ignores very important facts about motivation. Direction and control are essentially useless in motivating people whose important needs are social and egotistic. And when people are deprived of certain need satisfaction, they may exhibit behaviors that on the surface seem to be

► UGLY SCENES, UNSPOKEN BARGAINS
By Niki Scott

When Carol told her usually cheerful, undemanding boss about some problems that had developed in her department, she thought she was being helpful. Her boss, on the other hand, was furious.

"I thought I was doing her a favor! I though she'd *want* to know that we were having problems (mostly because of her *laissez faire* attitude), so she could fix them before *her* boss found out," wrote a bewildered Carol from Portsmouth, N.H.

"But she went nuts—paced around her office and ranted and raved and said things like: 'I can't *believe* what I'm hearing!' and 'Is *this* what you call loyalty—this kind of attack?'"

"And she said, 'Before you start criticizing me, you'd better look to your *own* sorry performance! It's about time you got to work on time—not five minutes late all the time.' And 'You'd better watch your step, or you're likely to find yourself out of a job!'"

"I'm still in shock," wrote Carol. "I'm afraid that despite all my good intentions, I've made a permanent enemy of my boss and put my job in jeopardy, too. Where—oh where!—did I go wrong?"

It's clear that Carol has been cursed with that most dangerous species, a boss who's both easily threatened *and* willing to jump to a personal attack when provoked. It's clear that Carol has broken an unspoken bargain, as well.

Unspoken bargains are common in the workplace. This one, between an easygoing boss and her workers, probably went something like: "As your boss, I'll look the other way when you're late to work and lax in other ways about your work. In return, you'll never criticize me, or present me with problems, or make my life more difficult than it already is."

Unspoken agreements are common between co-workers, too. "I've been working with an office 'mother,'" wrote a Raleigh, N.C., reader, "who's always brought cookies from home every Friday, made the coffee for all of us every morning, gotten the mail every day, stayed late when the rest of us couldn't and arranged birthday and retirement parties when we wouldn't.

"She's always cheerful, always helpful, and in return, we never mention the two-hour lunch hours she takes, the hours she spends making personal phone calls to her children and grandchildren, the phone messages she loses and the correspondence she's always misplacing.

"It's been a workable arrangement until last week, when she got angry at one of us about something or other and announced (at the top of her lungs) that she was *sick and tired* of making the coffee every morning, and that if the rest of us wanted birthday and retirement parties in the future, we could damned well organize them ourselves!

"At which point, it suddenly was NOT so OK with us that we were pulling a lot of her share of the load—which we told her in no uncertain terms. Now no one is speaking to anyone or making the coffee. We all bring our own, drink it at our desks and wish we'd never messed with our previous give-and-take arrangement."

If someone in your work or personal life overreacts to a seemingly innocent word or deed from you, it's a good idea to ask yourself if you've broken an unspoken bargain. Because the worst feature of this kind of arrangement is that more often than not, only one person knows about it.

Source: Niki Scott, "Ugly Scenes, Unspoken Bargains," *The Orlando Sentinel*, June 3, 1991, D-5. Copyright © 1991 Universal Press Syndicate. Used with permission.

in harmony with Theory X: indolence, passivity, resistance to change, lack of responsibility, willingness to follow, and incessant demands for economic benefits.

Many human problems in organizations arise because relatively healthy people are asked to participate in work situations that force them to be dependent, subordinate, and submissive, and that do not require them to reach their full potential. Healthy human beings find dependence, subordination, and submission frustrating, and this frustration can lead to regression, aggressiveness, tension, and the restriction of creativity. "People don't function well when they run scared," says Goodyear chairman Charles Pilliod. "You don't get the best out of them. You can needle them, you can push them, but you don't threaten. . . . If people are running scared, they're not going to make the right decisions. They'll make decisions to please the boss rather than recommend what has to be done."[22]

Adherence to Theory X assumptions prohibits clear communication and often leads to internal conflict contributing to major breakdowns. Most of these communication interactions are downward, taking the form of commands. The opportunities for fostering a defensive climate and creating misunderstandings are great. This has led Chevrolet's general manager Robert Lund to conclude, "I don't think there's a place for that kind of toughness. . . . People used to say, 'Do it because I say so, period!' That's an old-fashioned, out-moded approach to getting things done."[23]

McGregor offers an alternative set of assumptions based on the perception that people will naturally expend effort in work and do so because of the personal rewards associated with their efforts. These assumptions, labeled *Theory Y*, are:

1. that work is as natural as play or rest, the given conditions making it onerous or rewarding;
2. that individuals committed to a particular objective will work to achieve it under self-direction and self-control;
3. that organizational objectives offering the individual an opportunity for realization of personal potential can be highly rewarding and motivating;
4. that any human being welcomes responsibility under the right circumstances;
5. that most employees do not make the creative contribution to their organization that they are capable of making; and
6. that organizations waste the potential of most employees.[24]

Theory Y represents a set of assumptions more consistent with current research, assumptions that can lead to higher motivation and greater realization of both individual and organizational goals.

The assumptions of Theory Y are dynamic rather than static. They indicate the possibilities for human growth and development, and they stress the necessity for selective adaptation rather than a single absolute form of control. Most important, these assumptions point out that management can, with some ingenuity, discover how to realize the potential represented by its human resources. Adherence to Theory Y assumptions provides for an easier flow of communication in all directions. The result is more effective, less threatening interactions and communication among people.

Despite the import of McGregor's studies, they have met with criticism centering around their simplistic, polarized either/or approach and the basic assumption that individual and organizational goals can be satisfactorily integrated. Eric Trist and others have suggested that today's young are motivated by different values and value systems than their predecessors in organizations. Consequently, it is possible that the modern postindustrial organization faces a challenge that cannot be answered by theories of integration.[25] McGregor has responded that Theory X and Theory Y are assumptions that may be better understood as ranges of behaviors from X to Y. Managers, as such, should draw on both sets of assumptions, depending on the situation and the specific people involved.

Likert's Participative Organizations

Rensis Likert, professor of sociology and psychology and director of the Institute of Social Research at the University of Michigan, advanced certain conclusions explaining individual behavior in organizational environments. He proposed four possible management systems similar in range to McGregor's Theory X and Theory Y. Each of the four systems was explained in terms of its approach to (1) goal setting, (2) decision making, (3) motivation, (4) interaction among levels, and (5) communication. The key variable identified was the amount of participative decision-making (PDM), a term referring to those decisions made by people who are most affected by them. Based on comparisons between productive and less-productive work groups, Likert identified an exploitative authoritarian system (System I), a benevolent authoritarian system (System II), a consultative system (System III), and a participative system (System IV).[26]

The *exploitative authoritarian system* essentially seeks to "use" people to achieve organizational goals. Similar to McGregor's Theory X assumptions, people are regarded as impersonal resources to be manipulated for the good of the organization and are viewed as not trustworthy and not capable of determining what is in their own best interests. Goals are dictated from above and most decision making of any significance is at the top of the organization. Decisions at lower levels are relatively insignificant and/or closely channeled from above. Communication is primarily formal, being initiated at the top of the organization and flowing downward. Little real communication begins at the lower levels and flows upward.

The *benevolent authoritarian system* is still characterized by hierarchical management control but the feelings and emotions of people are recognized. Goals are dictated from the top, but individuals' personal goals are recognized and accepted as long as they do not interfere with organizational goals. And, although decisions are primarily made at the top, lower levels are allowed to make decisions affecting them within limits clearly prescribed above. Communication is mostly formal and downward, and although lower levels are allowed to voice their opinions and gripes, few changes result. Communication is rarely open, frank, and candid.

In the *consultative system,* management actively seeks input from employees, and people's opinions are considered along with all of the other relevant information. Goals are set at the top after considering input from lower levels. Decisions are made throughout the organization within broad limits imposed from the top. Communication flows more freely in all directions but still with more emphasis on downward communication. There are moderate levels of trust, candor, and openness.

The *participative system,* Likert's ideal, is based on the principle of supportive relationship. According to Likert, a supportive climate would be one in which (1) there is reciprocal confidence and trust between the manager and his or her employees; (2) a sincere effort is put forth by the manager to secure good pay for his or her employees; (3) an effort is made by the manager to understand his or her employees' problems; (4) the manager helps the employee accomplish tasks by providing such things as coaching, help in problem solving, and budgeting; (5) the manager keeps the employee informed about work-related matters; (6) the manager is seen as friendly and approachable; and (7) the manager appears willing to give credit to others instead of taking all the credit personally.[27] Thus, goals are set in participative organizations through true group participation. At various stages all levels are involved in group and individual goal setting. Decisions are made throughout the organization with the important criterion for where decisions are made being access to the relevant information and expertise in the problem area. Communication flows freely in all directions with no subjects being taboo. The atmosphere is one of respect, trust, and support. The participative system, similar to the teamwork style of management, allows feelings of ownership of organizational results and integrates organizational and individual needs to enhance people's dignity and worth.

Vaughn Beals, Jr., CEO and president of Harley-Davidson, understands the strength of participatory management. In the early 1980s, Harley-Davidson was flat on its back, leveled by Honda. Honda was selling better-styled motorcycles for less. Then Beals realized that his biggest and most fundamental problem was management. As he puts it, "We tried all the useful solutions—the culture routine, the robot routine, the low wage routine—and none of them worked. We couldn't avoid the inescapable conclusion. We—the management—were the problem." Beals organized his people into teams and gave the teams responsibility for scheduling, quality, and production line design. He slimmed down the hierarchy, put in a "Just In Time" inventory system, and initiated a trusting atmosphere. Today, Beals says, "The power from those teams is damn near infinite." Thus began one of the great American success stories of the middle 1980s.[28]

Maslow's Hierarchy of Needs

The psychologist Abraham Maslow developed the most widely known and used classification and description of common human needs that may create a more motivating organizational climate. *Maslow's Hierarchy of Needs* theory presents five classes of needs in an ascending order of satisfaction—physiological needs, safety needs, social needs, esteem needs, and self-realization/actualization needs (Exhibit 4-3). The most basic of all the need levels is the lowest one in the hierarchy—physiological or survival needs—with each need class dependent on satisfaction of those more basic than it.[29]

Maslow realized that his theory was a radical departure from the two standard psychological approaches to the study of human nature. The Freudian psychoanalytic school emphasized people's destructive tendencies and paralleled the survival-

▶ **EXHIBIT 4-3**
Maslow's Hierarchy of Needs

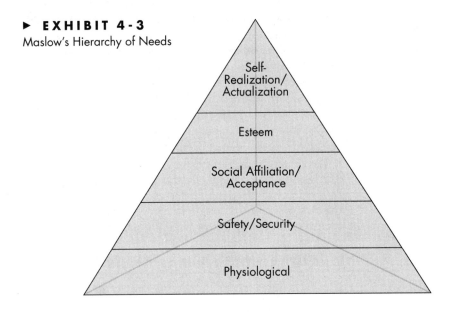

Self-Realization/Actualization

Esteem

Social Affiliation/Acceptance

Safety/Security

Physiological

of-the-fittest views of Charles Darwin. The behaviorism of B. F. Skinner was less pessimistic, suggesting that rewards and positive reinforcement help develop desired responses. Maslow's hierarchy of needs offered an alternative to what he saw as the depressing determinism of both Freud and Skinner. To call attention to the differences between his optimistic view and their denial of human freedom and dignity, he labeled his approach the "third force."[30]

Physiological needs, the lowest level of needs on the hierarchy, represent the basic body needs of food, sleep, sex, and survival. These needs are present in all people and, until they are at least reasonably satisfied, they dominate our behavior. From an organizational perspective, many physiological needs are met by the regularity of a paycheck that provides food and shelter.

Safety and security needs are for freedom from bodily harm and for security. Organizationally, safety and security needs are satisfied when workers believe their jobs are relatively secure and working conditions are free of physical harm.

Social needs exert a significant influence on human behavior only after the safety and security needs have been relatively well satisfied. They include the needs for giving and receiving love and affection; the need to accept, associate with, and be accepted by others; the need to belong or be a part of social groups; and the need to communicate with other people. These needs may be satisfied by the organization through peer and manager–employee relationships and through similarities between the organization's values and the values of the individual members.

Esteem needs are the needs for self-esteem and esteem from others. This class includes the needs for the respect of others, a feeling of achievement, recognition, appreciation, freedom, status, prestige, and a general feeling of worthiness. In organizations, esteem needs may be satisfied through performance evaluations, job titles, status symbols, awards, and the pride people feel in their work contributions.

Self-realization/actualization needs, the highest level of needs in the hierarchy, dominate only after the four lower classes of needs have been at least partially satisfied. This category includes the needs for self-fulfillment by the full use of one's abilities—the needs for creative expression and contribution to worthwhile objectives. Organizationally, they are met by people's feeling that they are exercising their abilities to the fullest and thereby accomplishing all they are capable of accomplishing.

Maslow's theory implies that it is not motivational to communicate about needs that are reasonably well met. Money and fringe benefits are important, but communication designed to motivate at the lower level of these needs frequently does not accurately assess the social, esteem, and self-realization needs of employees. Thus, his theory suggests that a supportive communication climate and individual communication behavior do in some ways reflect an assessment of need satisfaction.

Maslow's theory offers a rational framework within which to examine human behavior in organizations, but research on the validity of the hierarchy is still sparse and inconclusive.[31] Maslow himself recognized the qualitative nature of his theory and the shakiness of its strict application to organizations:

> I of all people should know first how shaky this foundation is as a final foundation. My work on motivation came from the clinic. . . . The carryover of this theory to the industrial situation has some support from industrial studies, but certainly I would like to see a lot more studies. . . . The same thing is true of my studies of self-actualizing people—there is only this one study of mine available. There were many things wrong with the

sampling, so many in fact that it must be considered to be, in the classical sense anyway, a bad or poor or inadequate experiment. I am quite willing to concede this—as a matter of fact, I am eager to concede it—because I'm a little worried about this stuff which I consider to be tentative being swallowed whole by all sorts of enthusiastic people, who really should be a little more tentative in the way that I am.[32]

Does this mean the hierarchy concept is invalid and should be abandoned? Indeed not; there is much intuitive logic behind the idea of a need hierarchy. Rather, Maslow suggests only that his hierarchy of needs is typical of the majority of people and that people do not all follow the order prescribed in the hierarchy.

Herzberg's Hygiene Factors

Frederick Herzberg's *motivation-hygiene theory* has probably created more controversy and stimulated more discussion and research than any other single theory in the human resources movement. It emphasizes the influence of both internal and external factors in shaping organizational climate and explaining human behavior. Herzberg identifies two major sets of factors in an organization's climate that combine to motivate people to work. The first set of factors, having to do with motivational conditions intrinsic to work, include achievement, recognition, the work itself, responsibility, and growth and advancement. He labeled these "motivators." The second set of factors, having to do with the work environment, include company policy and administration, supervision, salary, status, security, and working conditions. Herzberg called these "hygiene factors." His research suggested that these factors influenced satisfaction and/or dissatisfaction-avoidance among workers.[33]

Herzberg's theory proposes that satisfaction and dissatisfaction are not polar opposites: the opposite of job satisfaction and motivation is not dissatisfaction, but simply *no* job satisfaction. And, in turn, the opposite of dissatisfaction is not job satisfaction, but simply the absence of dissatisfaction. The significance of this distinction is that job satisfaction and dissatisfaction seem to be caused by two entirely different sets of factors. The factors influencing job satisfaction and motivation center in the job and seem to have relatively little effect on dissatisfaction. The factors influencing dissatisfaction are peripheral to the job and seem to have relatively little effect on satisfaction and motivation. Thus, the two kinds of factors, motivators and hygiene, can exist independently. Herzberg concludes that many organizations try to motivate workers through hygiene factors but those factors can only relate to whether workers are dissatisfied, not whether they are truly motivated. Motivated workers are those whose motivators are satisfied.

Herzberg's dual-factor theory of motivation has drawn much criticism, largely from the lack of methodological rigor employed in its research basis. Moreover, some conclude that his motivation-hygiene theory is an oversimplification of the relationships between motivation and satisfaction and the sources of job satisfaction and dissatisfaction.[34] Still, there is evidence that overall job satisfaction is strongly related to "the opportunity for independent thought and action on the job."[35] The results may be inconclusive and Herzberg's theory may or may not be complete or totally valid, but the important message seems clear —the organizational climate, the design of jobs, and the nature of the work that people do make a difference in their satisfaction and they influence their motivation and behavior on the job.

Organizational climate is a complex and relatively enduring quality of the internal environment of an organization: it is experienced by its members, influences their behavior, and can be described in terms of the values of a particular set of characteristics or attributes of the organization—delegation of responsibility, standards and expectations, recognition and rewards, and friendly team spirit, good fellowship, and trust. Organizations also have structure, with people acting and interacting according to some defined plan or pattern. This structure is both an important part of the formal communication subsystem and an important influence on climate and interpersonal/intergroup relational skills.

▶ORGANIZATIONAL STRUCTURE

All organizations have a more or less well-defined structure of relationships within which administrators administrate, managers manage, and people work. But what exactly is structure? Organizational design or structure can be considered the "wiring diagram" or "anatomy" of vertical and lateral authority and accountability in relationships.[36] It includes things like official job titles, descriptions, and objectives for employees, along with their conditions of employment; the official differentiation of divisions, departments, and work units; the manual(s) of standard operating procedures; and the corporate charter and other documents establishing the legal basis of the organization. Also included are derivative descriptions such as the organizational chart, official work-flow diagrams, and the like. Finally, structure encompasses the various systems for decision support, management information, work evaluation and compensation, and financial control.

These various aspects of structure share certain defining features. First, they are explicitly stated and recorded, and available for examination by any authorized person. Second, they are prescriptive, telling what the organization should be like, and these prescriptions are legitimately recognized by the organization. Finally, they involve statements that apply to members of the organization, to employees' activities, roles, relationships, and rewards. Thus, structure is a defining characteristic of an organization, "it is what brings about or makes possible that quality of atmosphere, that sustained, routine purposiveness that distinguishes work in an organization from activities in a group, a mob, a society, and so forth."[37]

The purpose of organizational structure is to provide a means for coordinating all of the individual efforts necessary to achieve organizational objectives. Certainly, organizational structures are not ends in themselves; they are one of the means to the end of coordinated individual and organizational activity. In a very simple sense, the purpose of structure in organizations is to help everyone know who is supposed to do what and who reports to whom, so that necessary activities can be meshed together in the best way. This is accomplished through communication. Organizational communication, then, may be additionally defined as "communication which is shaped by, and shapes, task processes and formal structure in the organization."[38]

Tall and Flat Structures

In discussing the structural design of organizations, we can start with *contextual variables*. These are an organization's size and technology. Size predominantly determines

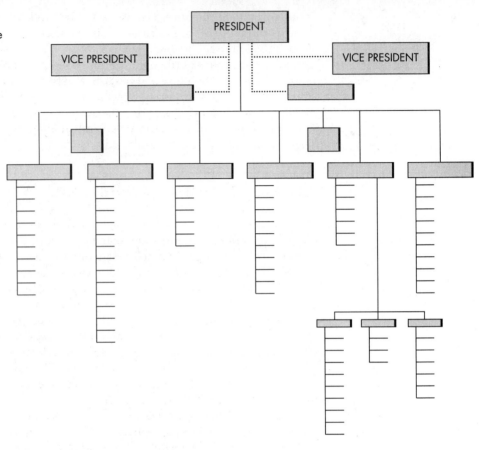

structure and formality. We can think of size in terms of the organization's total number of employees—its scope of operations. As more members are hired, there will be increased horizontal differentiation involving the specialization and grouping together of similar functions. The increased horizontal coordination requirements lead to an emphasis on vertical differentiation to provide coordination. Scalar and functional processes express, respectively, the vertical and the horizontal growth and structure of an organization. *Scalar* refers to the levels of the hierarchy (CEO, vice presidents, department heads, supervisors, line employees) or the "chain of command" in the organization. *Functional* refers to the specific job duties of each person in the organization. The structure of an organization is also influenced by the number of workers an administrator or manager can effectively supervise—*the span of control*. Span of control, in turn, influences the shape of an organization. If most administrators or managers supervise a small number of workers, the overall shape of the organization will be *tall*. If the typical span is great, then the overall shape of the organization will be *flat*. These two structural types are illustrated in Exhibits 4-4 and 4-5, the former typical of a large university and the latter often found in small corporations.

Larger organizations typically assume tall structures; smaller organizations have flat structures. Theodore Caplow outlines the following divisions based on organizational size:

▶ *Small Organizations.* A small organization ranges from three to thirty members and is small enough to permit them to become a primary group within themselves. A family business is an example.

▶ *Medium-Size Organizations.* These organizations are too large for the development of all possible pair relationships but still small enough that any member, including a leader, would interact with any other member. The medium-size organization ranges from about thirty to about a thousand. An average industrial firm might be an example.

▶ *Large Organizations.* A large organization is too large for many members to know each other well but not too large for one or more leaders to be recognized by all other members. These leaders will be recognized by many more people than they are able to recognize. Such an organization ranges from about one thousand to about fifty thousand. Most universities are large organizations.

▶ *Giant Organizations.* The giant organization has too many members which are too widely scattered to permit the direct interaction of any individual with all of the others. The range of the giant organization is from about fifty thousand to infinity. Political parties and business conglomerates are good examples.[39]

Henry Mintzberg has recently developed a more sophisticated typology which expands on size and considers differing arrangements of five components: top management, middle management, the technical core (those who do the basic work of the organization), the technical support staff (engineers, researchers, and analysts responsible for formal technical core planning and control), and administrative support staff (those who provide indirect services including clerical, maintenance, and mailroom employees). Assuming that these five components vary in size and importance depending on the external environment, strategy, and technology, Mintzberg combines them into five different structural configurations:

▶ *Simple Structure.* Small; new; entrepreneurial

▶ *Machine Bureaucracy.* Large, tall, mass-production oriented; emphasis on efficiency and dealing with stable environment; large middle-management group; large technical core and support staffs (e.g., government agencies)

▶ *Professional Bureaucracy.* Large support staff; flat hierarchy; many technically trained professionals (e.g., hospitals and research and development establishments)

▶ **EXHIBIT 4-5**
Flat Organizational Structure

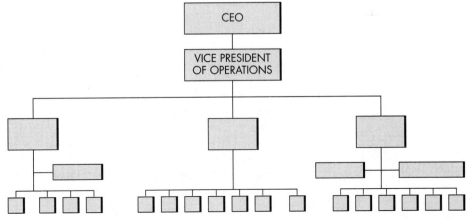

▶ *Divisionalized Bureaucracy.* Extremely large, divided into product or market divisions; varying technologies depending on the divisions; headquarters with staff assistance umbrella for divisions (e.g., conglomerates)

▶ *Adhocracy.* Very complex, adaptable professionalized organizations; extensive division of labor; low formalization; little emphasis on hierarchy (e.g., project engineering firms)[40]

Configurations of the kinds just discussed can be useful in relating size with other structural dimensions and tying them together in a meaningful pattern. Tall, narrow, mechanistic structures are characterized by high complexity, centralization, and formalization. They emphasize routine tasks and programmed behavior and are slow in dealing with unfamiliar situations. In contrast, flat, wide, organic structures are relatively adaptable and flexible. They stress expert-based influence, have loosely defined jobs, and emphasize information exchange rather than top-down directives.[41] Indeed, organizational size has an important impact on an organization's effectiveness and efficiency. The number of levels significantly influences such factors as performance standards and authority delegation.

However, size is only one aspect of the context influencing structure; another aspect is technology—the information, equipment, techniques, and processes required to transform input into output. The focus is on how this transformation is made. Basically, as technology becomes more sophisticated and variable, the organization's structure must be designed to fit.[42] This supports Eric Trist and Kenneth Bamforth's concept of *sociotechnical integration* which assumes that organizational production is optimized through optimizing social and technical systems, and that a constant interchange exists between the work system and the broader environment. They conclude that including people in entire task cycles rather than confining their work to isolated parts provides a sense of self-determination that contributes to a solidarity of purpose and integration of personal and organizational goals.[43]

Other factors that affect organizational structure are (1) supervisory ability, (2) employee ability, (3) complexity of activities supervised, (4) degree to which the activities are interrelated, (5) adequacy of performance standards, (6) amount of authority delegated, and (7) availability of staff assistance. The implications are clear: the higher the personal energy level and the supervisory ability, the greater the number of people the manager can supervise. Likewise, the higher the level of workers' abilities, the more people the manager can supervise. Also, the simpler and more similar the workers' activities are, the wider the span of control. Where employees' jobs are interrelated and the activities of one affect the activities of others, more of the manager's time is required to coordinate activities among the workers. Moreover, the better the performance standards are, the less time the manager has to spend in direct contact with workers. In contrast, if performance standards are poor, or are poorly communicated, more of the manager's time is likely to be needed for direct observation of worker performance. Finally, the more authority delegated, the wider the span can be, because less of the supervisor's time will be needed in decision making and face-to-face communication. The amount of authority delegated, however, should be related to the employee's level of ability, so this factor should operate within limits. Related to the last factor, a manager with a good staff providing both advice and service can supervise more people than one who must do everything related to the job.[44]

What conclusions can be drawn regarding communication? Certainly, the available evidence indicates that structure affects behavior and communication, but the specific effects of particular aspects of structure and of particular combinations of those aspects are not completely clear. It is easy to see that a tall organization, with its multiple levels, increases the number of channels for distortion. Flat organizations reduce the number of levels, but they also reduce the number of face-to-face contacts and can create a communication overload at the manager's office. A natural weakness in the communication process of a structured organization is caused by its serial characteristics. As people send and receive messages through many channels, distortion will occur. Details will be omitted, added, modified, qualified, or adjusted. Consider the following case:

The president of a large company issued the following directive to his vice president:

Tomorrow at approximately 9 A.M. Haley's comet will be visible in this area, an event which occurs only once every 75 years. Have all employees assemble in the company parking lot and I will explain this rare phenomenon to them. In case of rain, we will not be able to see anything, so assemble them in the cafeteria and I will show them films of it.

Vice president to division managers:

By executive order of the company president, tomorrow at 9 A.M., Haley's comet will appear above the company parking lot. If it rains, assemble all personnel in the cafeteria where the phenomenon will take place, something that occurs only once every 75 years.

Division manager to department managers:

By executive order of the company president, tomorrow at 9 A.M., the phenomenal Haley's comet will appear in the cafeteria. In case of rain, in the parking lot, the president will give an order, something which takes place only once every 75 years.

Department managers to office managers:

Tomorrow at 9 A.M., the company president will appear in the cafeteria with Haley's comet, something which occurs every 75 years. If it rains, the president will order the comet into the parking lot.

Office managers to employees:

When it rains tomorrow at 9 A.M., the phenomenal 75-year-old company president, accompanied by his girlfriend Haley, will drive his Comet through the parking lot.

There is little difference between the structured distortion in these apocryphal corporate memos and the message alteration occurring within real-world organizations. I.N.A. vice president Harold Johnson says that "most managers and their subordinates are off about twenty percent of the time in terms of what those subordinates understand the boss wants them to do. And when you multiply that, three or four levels down, you can find somebody working maybe totally opposite to what the organization thinks is important."[45]

Making sense of any message requires employees to interpret it, and interpreting a message usually changes its meaning. Because the information is exchanged repeatedly as it moves through the chain of command, each employee has to make sense of it for himself or herself. With each interpretation the meaning is altered and the amount of absorbed uncertainty grows. If an organization is structured as a

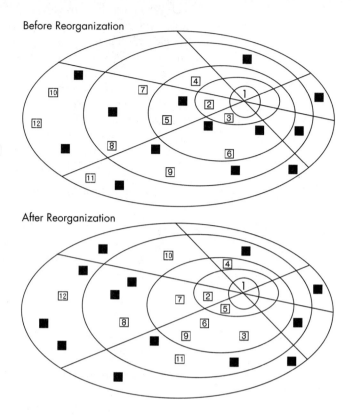

traditional hierarchy, employees will exchange messages many times, and by the time the information arrives at its final destination, it will have been transformed in important ways. Many messages only slightly resemble their original form when they reach their destination and this distortion of messages takes place whether the information is flowing up or down the organizational hierarchy. Indeed, organizational structure has tremendous effect on organizational communication.

Robert N. McMurry observes that conventional organizational charts are frequently misleading because they assume "that everyone on a given level is psychologically equidistant from his immediate supervisor. . . . In actual fact, this is practically never the case. Some supervisors are inevitably 'closer' to their bosses than others. Furthermore, these relationships are often quite unstable; certain individuals are constantly falling in and out of favor with their bosses."[46] He suggests as an organizational structure a circular, three-dimensional "beehive." Exhibit 4-6 depicts such an organizational alignment before and after the reorganization of a management team. The bands constitute supervisory echelons from top to bottom with the number of bands corresponding to the number of levels of management. The pie-shaped segments represent the company's operating divisions or functions. The chief executive is usually considered to be central to the organization's operation, but this is not always true—he or she may favor one division over another and therefore may be placed closer to it. Administrators and supervisors can also be located according to their circumferential bands. The greater their authority and power, the closer they are to the center of the circle.

The beehive organizational chart identifies those who play significant roles in determining what happens in the company, or who simply participate in the making of decisions. It is a "table of power" that shows how things actually work. According to this structure, effective communication starts at the top, with chief executives carefully analyzing the communications of those entering the inner bands. They must be willing to face reality if they expect subordinates to expose them to it. Thus, this structure raises several critical questions: Can the chief executive face reality when it conflicts with personal values or threatens personal job security? Can the chief executive emotionally tolerate an intelligence system that may provide unpleasant information or reveal covertly threatening conditions? McMurry notes that it takes a person of "courage and resolution to accept reality in its less roseate aspects."[47]

Matrix System

NASA's project organization structure introduced the *matrix* concept, a system with multiple chains of command. The distinguishing mark of a matrix is the two-boss manager. It represents an approach whereby divisions or business functions needed to serve respective customer groups work together with/share the technical and professional resources of the organization. Usually the CEO or a designer has the responsibility of directing all the groups toward common objectives. Additionally, selected managers have responsibilities and reporting points in both divisions and resources. In practice, a departmental research and development manager might report to both the corporate research and development manager and the divisional marketing manager. Or, an associate professor teaching in both traditional and nontraditional programs at a university may report to both the dean of the college faculty and the dean of the evening degree program. It is through these two-boss managers that significant integration is achieved.

A matrix is not a loose association of people. Every person has reporting points and is accountable for specific goals or tasks. The system is well suited for a rapidly changing environment because it encourages cross-function communication and innovative thought and action. It permits flexibility and a degree of informality but also requires careful personnel selection and clear goals. Furthermore, attention must be paid to the special requirements of the direct flow of information and personal interaction at all levels. The matrix system, with its informality, works well in small organizations and can be a useful structure for large, diversified organizations, particularly when focusing on short-term projects.

Structural Revolution

Glance at any table of organization. Chances are it consists of straight lines connecting neat little boxes, each exactly like the other. One seldom sees any differentiation of shapes to represent the uniqueness of a company's departments—a spiral, say, to suggest a rapidly growing department, or a mesh to suggest one that has many links with other departments, or a curlicue to symbolize a department that is up-and-down in performance. Like the products of the firm and the bureaucracy it represents, the table of organization is generally standardized. However, Alvin Toffler declares that "company structures will soon 'de-massify.'. . . the day of the cookie-cut company is over. And so are the cookie-cut power structures that ran large corporations."[48]

Indeed, there is a structural revolution underway. Centralized and decentralized structures alike are being challenged. Even the matrix structure which connects groups with one another in an effort to coordinate everything and everyone have, in many instances, developed into dotted lines going this way and that. Tom Peters admits "my co-authors and I downplayed the importance of structure in *In Search of Excellence* and again in *A Passion for Excellence*. We were terribly mistaken." He continues, "Good intentions and brilliant proposals will be deadended, delayed, sabotaged, massaged to death, or revised beyond recognition or usefulness by the over-layered structures at most large and all too many smaller firms."[49] Today's structures, designed for turn-of-the-century mass-production operations under stable conditions, have become antiquated by modern technology and are at odds with current competitive needs.

The growth of companies to gargantuan size and changes in the external environment have tested the structural limits of organizational specialization and overwhelmed channels of communication. As the hierarchical levels expand and the number of supervised employees increases, the number of possible relationships increases geometrically. For example, a manager with four employees has 44 possible interrelationships and the interrelationships increase to 100 with the addition of just one employee.[50] Obviously, the greater the number of levels of management and the number of employees being supervised, the larger the cost and the more difficult effective communication becomes. Consequently, the overall aim is to reduce the layers of management and to achieve "better support with fewer people."[51]

Organizations must become flexible, with rigid, uniform structures being replaced by a diversity of organizational arrangements. These "flex-firms" will not be without structure but will rather embody many different formats within a single frame. In *Powershift*, Alvin Toffler provides a sampling of these new, adaptive organizational systems:

▶ *The Fam-Firm.* Small family-owned firms which were once prevalent are now wind-lassing a resurgence in the form of franchising which links "mom-and-pop" operators to the financial and promotional chart of large firms. In the future these family enterprises will evolve as respected, powerful units within large corporations as well. Among the advantages of flexible fam-firms is their ability to make quick decisions, adapt to new market needs, and willingness to take daring entrepreneurial risks.

▶ *The Pulsating Organization.* This is an organization that expands and contracts in a regular rhythm according to changing economic needs. Examples include companies that gear up for annual model changes, then gear down again; in retail firms that staff up for Christmas and layoff in January; and the U.S. Census Bureau which swells to enormous size every ten years and then shrinks.

▶ *The Two-Faced Organization.* This organization is capable of operating in two modes depending on circumstances. It can shift from hierarchical to nonhierarchical command as needs demand. Examples include the growing number of businesses which exhibit traditional operating structures during routine periods but rely on crisis centers or "shadow management" teams during emergencies.

▶ *The Checkerboard Organization.* Emerging in Austria after World War II, the two main political powers agreed to appoint alternating members from each party to key posts in state-owned companies, banks, insurance companies, schools, and universities. The Japanese bank in California exhibits similar adaptation by alternating Japanese and Americans at each level of the hierarchy, thus guaranteeing an objective flow of information. As firms go global and internationalism expands, this structural approach may become more commonplace.

▶ *The Commissar Organization.* This organization reveals two main information channels rather than a single, formal channel typically characterizing bureaucracy. Here we see "commissars" chosen from above and planted in subordinate units to keep an eye on things and report to the top through separate channels rather than through the normal hierarchy. It is used by organizations to maintain control.

▶ *The Buro-Baronial Organization.* This neo-feudal organizational form relies on "vassalage" which is subjective rather than bureaucratic and impersonal. Departmental baronies are staffed with junior vassals dependent on a "lord" or senior, who is higher up in the tables of organization. Examples include large law firms, major accounting firms, brokerage houses, universities, the military complex, and the Congress of the United States with it 535 elected "barons" ruling over a huge bureaucratic staff.

▶ *The Skunkworks Organization.* Here an organizational team is assigned a specified problem or project and goal, given resources, and allowed to operate outside the normal company rules. Members concentrate their energy and freely exchange information among one another. They develop strong interpersonal ties with one another and a sense of pride, thus becoming emotionally involved with their work outside of the traditional company boundaries. When Steve Jobs directed the Apple/Macintosh "skunkworks" team, a "Jolly Roger" pirate flag flew above the workplace to illustrate their militantly antibureaucratic attitude. And IBM's PC, which has become an industry standard, was similarly developed by a nearly autonomous group working in Boca Raton, Florida, apart from corporate headquarters in Armonk, New York. Other examples can be found at Honda, Hewlett-Packard, Xerox, and other high-tech firms.

▶ *The Self-Start Team.* These are "information clusters" which are typically drawn together by an electronic network. They develop when people intensely interested in a common problem find one another electronically and begin to exchange information across departmental lines, irrespective of either geography or rank. The increasing use of electronic "conferences" illustrates such teams establishing their own objectives and carrying on a free-flowing dialogue. Aetna Life and Casualty company has designed a state-of-the-art teleconference studio for just such electronic meetings.[52]

Instead of neat lines of authority, the flex-firm presents a far more complex, transient, and fuzzy picture. It is heterogeneous, individualistic, antibureaucratic, impatient, opinionated, energetic, creative, innovative, and very competitive. The networks, formal or not, tend to be horizontal rather than vertical—meaning they have either a flat hierarchy or none at all. Above all, they are adaptive—able to reconfigure themselves quickly to meet changing conditions.

Scenarios of flexible organizational structures have contributed to a reconfiguration of the hierarchy itself—the organizational chart is turned upside down with the customer at the top as chairman of the board. Carlzon, Milliken, Imperial, SAS, Nordstrom, and Disney World are among the companies moving this idea forward. There, customer service is number one and frontline people are the corporate heroes. Managers, given this model, turn over many of their traditional tasks as decision makers and referees to self-managing teams. They now readily cross functional barriers making sure that work teams are trained and well equipped, and actively seeking ways to eliminate bottlenecks. This idea promotes a "helping hand" support network with top management wandering across functional barriers and out to the front line.

This ongoing structural revolution reveals an astonishingly high degree of controlled flexibility and informality, with considerable attention to organizational networks, channels, and message flow. Still, the primary focus must be on the people making up the organization. James Swiggert, a management pioneer, knows this well. In 1983, *Inc.* magazine trumpeted his decentralized management style at Kollmorgen Corporation as the new wave of management philosophy. However, several consecutive money-losing years forced a reevaluation and he now astutely observes that "to succeed, it requires something else . . . it requires the right people in the right slots. . . . never compromise with regard to the type of people you have in leadership roles, because if you do, you're going to compromise the company."[53]

▶ NETWORKS AND CHANNELS

On first glance it may appear that all members of an organization are completely free to communicate with each other, but such is not the case. Instead, communication travels in fairly well-defined networks. Harold Leavitt explains that, despite appearances,

> . . . in most face-to-face industrial groups only one communication network seems possible, and that is a fully connected network in which everyone can communicate directly with everyone else. But the argument that this is the only actual network, even in committee, does not hold water. A clear, albeit informal, notion about who can talk to whom exists in most groups. In fact, in most face-to-face meetings, although the *official* network is a fully connected one, the *actual* network may be some other one altogether. Communication networks are much like organizational charts; there is likely to be a formal, officially charted organization, and there is likely also to be an informal, uncharted organization that nevertheless plays a significant role in the functioning of the company.[54]

Farace and MacDonald suggest that the membership of such networks changes, depending on the topic under discussion:

> One readily discernable feature of an organization's communication system, as it is examined over time, is that repetitive patterns of information and communication exchange take place. Some members of the organization interact with one another, but not with other members. They interact more often some times than at other times. Their interaction may cover certain topics; at other times it doesn't. Certain topics never occur in the interactions among some members of the organization. When management sends out messages to subordinates, the messages travel various pathways or networks—some intended and some not.[55]

These networks guide the flow of information throughout the organization. In a large organization comprising thousands of people, many, many networks exist; in smaller organizations there are fewer. Network analysis lets us examine the formal and informal groupings and flow of communication.

Communication networks are the formal and informal patterns of communication that link organizational members. Networks are sets of relatively stable contacts among people through which information is generated and flows. They are the "warp and woof of the fabric of organizational life" and they "define authority, social, political, and other organizational systems, and are the funnels through which flows information used to make decisions. . . . "[56] Supervisors and subordinates, task forces, committees, quality circles, and other types of decision-making bodies are examples of formal communication networks. Informal networks emerge as a result of formal networks and are formed by individuals who have interpersonal relationships, who exchange valuable information across reporting chains, and who disregard formal status and chains of command. Finally, telemediated networks using computers and video systems link geographically separated groups. In our shift to an information society, these technological networks will become increasingly important, changing the way we establish networks and expanding the scope of our network involvement.

Formal Networks and Channels

When messages follow official paths dictated by the organizational hierarchy, they are flowing in accordance with formal network relationships. Messages that flow through such channels are normally routinized. For example, they may be presented on a standardized form completed in triplicate. They frequently take longer to reach their destinations because of the number of stations or "gatekeepers" through which they must pass. They are often given greater consideration and more careful attention than other messages. The use of formal networks as primary message routes ensures the maintenance of the authority structure which is seen as critical to the effective accomplishment of goals. Formal networks also serve to screen and filter messages, thus reducing possible message overload. Formal networks represent the rules and procedures for reaching the upper hierarchy as well as the ways in which the upper levels communicate with subordinates, and peers communicate with peers.

Richard Farace, Peter Monge, and Hamish Russell have identified three general properties of the links found in organizational networks: symmetry, strength, and reciprocity. Links may be symmetrical or asymmetrical. A *symmetrical link* involves people equally exchanging information during an interaction as when peers interact with peers about work problems or social interests. An *asymmetrical link* occurs when one individual gives more information than another, as when managers give directions to workers. The network property of *strength* refers to the frequency and length of interactions among linked individuals. The strength of communication links predicts who is influential among organizational members. Finally, *reciprocity* describes the level of agreement among organizational members about their network links. In other words, do organizational members agree about the types of links they have with each other.[57]

People perform diverse roles in networks, roles determined by their structural relationship vis-a-vis other people in the system. This relationship is defined by the pattern of interaction connecting the individual to the flow of information in the network. *Gatekeepers* control the flow of information through a communication chain by routinely receiving information and determining whether or not to transmit that information to the next link or links. Group members whose interactions are with members of other groups are labeled *bridges*. People whose interactions are mainly

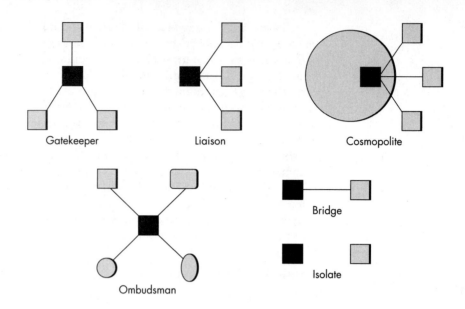

Gatekeeper   Liaison   Cosmopolite

Ombudsman

Bridge

Isolate

with members of two or more groups but who are not members of any one group are considered *liaisons*. *Cosmopolites* are boundary spanners, serving as "windows to the world" by connecting the organization with its relevant external environment. An emerging role in some organizations is that of the *ombudsman* who internally connects disparate groups. Individuals who are relatively unconnected to the organization are *isolates*.[58] All of these roles are depicted in Exhibit 4-7, where the organization member is represented by the solid box and those communicated with are represented by the shaded shapes.

Channels are the means for transmitting messages. Organizations typically have a wide variety of formal channels available for sending oral and written messages. Some of the more common means are face-to-face interactions, formal meetings, talks or speeches, telephone conversations, memoranda, letters, organizational publications, bulletin boards, and electronic/computer-assisted systems.

Face-to-face conversations are by far the most widely used means to connect with others and convey information. Formal meetings, presided over by one or more superiors, are used to define goals and coordinate activities. Though similar to formal meetings, talks and speeches seem to imply larger audiences and more formalized presentations. Telephone conversations involve one of the most commonly used devices for communication today, organizational or otherwise. Picking up the telephone and placing a call is about the quickest way one can communicate with another and, in today's world when time is so important, possibly the cheapest. The memorandum or interoffice memo has long been used in organizations as a quick and effective means for sending messages. There are some advantages to having messages in writing. First, the receiver can look back at a memo if something is forgotten; second, responsibility can be more easily placed if there is a file copy of the message. Consequently, much of what was once communicated only orally is now being sent in writing via the memo, or a memo accompanies or follows the oral message. Although the role of the letter in internal organizational communication has diminished, it is used when a degree of formality is needed beyond what a memo would convey. Organizational publications—newsletters, policy manuals, booklets, and brochures—are used to communicate goals, objectives, procedures, and problems to middle and lower levels of the organization. Bulletin boards are a useful medium for reaching a large audience, but people are often oblivious to them and seldom see anything hanging there. Finally, as we shift to an information society, emphasis is increasingly placed on developing new and improved technical channels that speed information transfer and shorten decision-making response time. It is fair to say the choice and availability of communication channels influences network relationships and the way organizations can and do operate.[59]

Judgments about channel effectiveness are based on the need for immediacy, financial cost, and individual skill levels. Access and availability of channels and the type of response needed influence which channels are effective in particular situations. The following 12 dimensions can be useful in evaluating communication channels:

1. Feedback potential: how quickly can the receiver respond to the message?
2. Complexity capacity: can this channel effectively process complex messages?
3. Breadth potential: how many different messages can be disseminated through this channel?
4. Confidentiality: can the communicators be reasonably sure their messages are received only by those intended?
5. Encoding ease: can the sender easily and quickly use this channel?
6. Decoding ease: can the receiver easily and quickly decode its messages?
7. Time-space constraint: do senders and receivers need to occupy the same time-space?
8. Cost: how much does it cost to use this channel?
9. Interpersonal warmth: does the channel have the potential to communicate interpersonal warmth?
10. Formality: does the channel imbue a sense of formality?
11. "Scanability": does the channel permit the messages to be easily browsed or scanned to find relevant passages?
12. Time of consumption: does the sender or receiver exercise the most control over when the message is consumed?[60]

Finally, as communicators, we all prefer certain modes of communication and feel more comfortable using certain channels, whether oral, written, or electronic. Yet, many find formal networks too time consuming and possibly futile. This leads naturally to the establishment and use of informal communication networks.

Informal Networks and Channels

Informal networks of communication emerge in all organizations. Not all messages flow along the official paths prescribed by the organization's chain of command. When messages deviate from traditional networks we call them informal messages. And when the free flow of information is inhibited within the formal organizational networks, they will almost automatically be supplemented by unofficial informal networks composed of groups or individuals linked together by consistent patterns of communicating with one another. The distinction between formal and informal networks is fragile, as Willard Merrihue points out:

A formal organization starts with a broad purpose or plan, this is subdivided into activities, and the activities are assigned to positions. Structural relationships are established between Position A and Position B, not between Mr. Smith and Miss Jones. Since communication is the vehicle for carrying on relationships between positions, we find in any formal organization a phenomenon which can be designated as positional communication. The entire organization, as it appears on an organization chart, can be referred to as a positional communications network.

Positional communication is upset in practice, however, because positions are staffed with beings with total personalities. The relationship between Position A and Position B does not exist apart from the relationship between Joe and Gertrude and the other folks in the office.[61]

The dilemma outlined is that the formal networks are composed of people and these networks may actually be restrictive, thus prompting the use of informal, personal networks. The rules, procedures, and structures that are designated to produce behaviors oriented toward organizational goals may be cold and impersonal, and actually encourage the use of informal networks.

These informal networks are frequently referred to as the "grapevine." According to Keith Davis, the term arose during the Civil War. Telegraph lines were strung loosely from tree to tree, resembling a grapevine. The messages were frequently garbled, and any rumor was said to be from the grapevine. Oftentimes, the grapevine is considered a loose and ill-defined message system, but research indicates that it is quite accurate. One report estimates its accuracy in the 80 to 90 percent range for noncontroversial company information. Rumors may develop but this is more the result of the types of information transmitted and of the personal associations.[62]

The grapevine represents a network for dispersing messages that would be inappropriate for formal channels, such as personal observations and opinions. Because they do not follow formal channels but rather are diffused through "clusters" of individuals they are usually more personal in their transmission and the messages travel much faster. The grapevine may also satisfy affiliation needs not met through formal channels. Thus, the grapevine carries a virtual smorgasbord of information concerning management's directives, and provides an outlet for expressing emotionally charged messages which, if left unaired, might foster growing hostility and anger among employees. The grapevine can be more important and active than formally established networks, providing valuable feedback to management about employee sentiment. Managers who listen carefully to this informal communication network find it a useful source of information about employee concerns and problems.

Overuse of informal networks may result in growing instability and deterioration of the formal communication networks. When informal channels are overused, poor-quality information can circulate throughout the organization, leading to unwanted anxiety, poor decisions, low morale, perceptions of favoritism, and lower productivity. Phillip Clampitt additionally notes that "the overuse of informal channels by management may send powerful secondary, albeit unintended, messages to employees like, 'We don't have time to communicate with you,' which translates into 'We don't respect you enough to provide you with formal information.'"[63]

Employees understand the prevailing pragmatics of the grapevine and are aware of its limited usefulness. They rank the grapevine last as a preferred source of information, with supervisors being the most preferred. One survey of over 45,000 employ-

Employee Preferences for Source Information

RANK	MAJOR INFORMATION SOURCE (%)	SOURCE	PREFERRED RANK	PREFERRED SOURCE (%)
1	59	Immediate supervisor	1	90
2	42	Grapevine	14	9
3	38	Bulletin boards	8	38
4	37	Small-group meetings	2	70
5	33	Employee handbook	5	46
6	28	Large-group meetings	4	49
7	29	Company-wide employee publication	10	36
8	22	Orientation programs	6	45
9	18	Local employee publication	7	41
10	17	Annual business report to employees	9	37
11	15	Top executives	3	62
12	15	Mass media	13	12
13	14	Upward communications programs	11	29
14	13	Audiovisual	11	29

Source: J. Foehrenbach and S. Goldfarb, "Employee Communication in the '90s: Greater Expectations," *Communication World,* May-June, 1990, p. 7.

ees in 40 organizations found the grapevine to be the second most-frequent source of information but ranked it last in terms of the most preferred (see Exhibit 4-8). In fact, a number of supporting communication assessments have revealed the grapevine to be the only information channel from which employees want to receive less rather than more information.[64]

V. Dallas Merrell, a business consultant, describes a rather special type of informal network in his book *Huddling: The Informal Way to Management Success.*[65] "Huddles" are intimate, task-oriented encounters between two or more people trying to get something done. Huddlers accomplish the most critical, sensitive work of organizations and are the most respected, productive workers. They usually do not have great authority in their positions; rather their power derives from their self-confidence, friendships, connections, access, timing, skills, and knowledge. The ability to make something happen is the essence of the huddler's functional authority.

Huddling can reduce surprise, cut red tape, ameliorate the effects of slow or inefficient leadership, bring order to the conduct of business, keep things in line, and properly channel contributions. It can cut through formal hierarchical channels of communication by allowing diverse corporate members to communicate their ideas to superiors so those superiors can then make final decisions. Lastly, huddlers may compensate for slow or weak leadership by assuming responsibility and unofficially carrying out essential management tasks—carrying messages, ferreting out issues and options, and getting consensus.

Huddling is an organic, normally spontaneous activity growing out of the needs of the people involved and the organization and situations that exist. Huddlers understand each other implicitly—"Got a minute?" or "Which way ya' walking?" are what get a huddle going.

Huddling is not universally accepted, however, and can be dangerous. Rampant huddling will rip an organization apart. Small groups of intimates, operating privately on a "don't quote me" basis, can lead to unethical and illegal behavior. Moreover, sound ideas may be overlooked or placed on hold because of decisions made by informal huddles. A letter to the business editor of *The New York Times* reads, in part: "What makes companies work? Huddling? *No, it does not.* Communicating, which used to be called talking, does. Also, what would pass for the normal business of exchanging ideas. Trust does."[66] Yet, we need to study huddling and refine our perceptions of it because a knowledge of it is helpful to understanding organizational behavior, leadership, and work processes.

Every organization has two basic information networks: formal and informal. These networks may compliment, conflict, or work independently of one another. In truth, then, organizations are networks of networks, each operating with specific purposes. Communication networks, in the final analysis, involve the individual members of an organization who are likely to be members of a wide variety of different networks. How can these very important formal and informal communication patterns be systematically analyzed? Keith Davis suggests some possibilities:

1. *Residential analysis.* In this situation the analyst is a "live in" observer of the existing communication patterns.
2. *Participant analysis.* People are given questionnaires or are interviewed and asked what role they feel they play in the network and certain data about the network.
3. *Duty study.* The analyst sits in a certain spot in the system and observes what passes by like a highway study.
4. *Cross-section study.* All of the communications in a process at any particular time are analyzed.
5. *ECCO analysis.* ECCO is an abbreviation for Episodic Communication Channels in Organizations. This analytic method traces a particular unit of information through such dimensions as time and space while it passes through the system.[67]

Communication networks make organizations work, representing the way communication flows in an organization. The channels reflect the structured flow of downward, horizontal, and upward communication. Taken together, they disclose the patterned dissemination of information throughout the organization.

▶ MESSAGE FLOW

Managing information effectively is a critical task confronting all managers. Management of any kind involves reconciling conflicting forces, and information management is no exception. For instance, to be useful, information must arrive on a timely basis. More often than not, other duties assume greater priority than passing along information, or inefficient channels are used, or the corporation has so many screening devices for messages that they inevitably slow the process. Another overwhelming problem is communication overload or how to deal with the massive quantities of information that inundate most organizations. The relative ease and low cost with which information can be transmitted through new electronic processes will make this problem even more acute in the future. Underload can be equally problematic resulting in stress, poor decisions, and low productivity. Finally, what infor-

Subjects of Most and Least Interest to Employees

RANK	SUBJECT	VERY INTERESTED/ INTERESTED (%)
1	Organization plans for the future	95.3
2	Productivity improvements	90.3
3	Personnel policies and practices	89.9
4	Job-related information	89.2
5	Job advancement opportunities	87.9
6	Effect of external events on my job	87.8
7	How my job fits into the organization	85.4
8	Operations outside of my department or division	85.1
9	How we're doing versus the competition	83.0
10	Personnel changes and promotions	81.4
11	Organizational community involvement	81.3
12	Organizational stand on current issues	79.5
13	How the organization uses its profits	78.4
14	Advertising promotional plans	77.2
15	Financial results	76.4
16	Human interest stories about other employees	70.4
17	Personal news (birthdays, anniversaries, etc.)	57.0

Source: J. Foehrenbach and K. Rosenberg, "How Are We Doing?" *Journal of Communication Management* 12 (1982), p. 7.

mation should be forwarded to employees? Should information be open to all or available only on a "need-to-know" basis? There are dangers at either extreme. A "need-to-know" policy can be stifling and often is a formal excuse to exercise excessive managerial control. Yet, organizations have reasonable and legitimate needs to protect certain information, even from their own employees. Therefore, priority must be given to certain types of information. Certainly, information about decision making, job-related matters, and answers to employee inquiries rank high on the list of priority information to be communicated. One survey found that employees were highly interested in the organization's future plans, productivity improvement, and personnel policies (see Exhibit 4-9).[68] The conflicting forces or tension points of managing communication provide a useful guide as we examine the downward, horizontal, and upward flows of communication.

Downward Communication

Downward communication is the flow of messages from superiors to subordinates, traditionally the predominant form of communication in organizations and, subsequently, the formal channel most frequently studied. Daniel Katz and Robert Kahn have identified five different types of downward communication: job instruction, rationale, information, feedback, and ideology.[69]

Job instruction is concerned with directives that explain specific organizational tasks. Much downward communication is devoted to the giving of instructions. Although it's a routine part of a day's work, especially for lower-level administrators, it is the communication that keeps the wheels of the organization turning. People at all levels of the organization must know what they are to do and how to do it. Numerous studies have pointed out a vast gap in American industry between workers' perceptions of what they are supposed to be doing, and supervisors' perceptions of what they instructed the workers to do.[70] Some of these studies have predicted that these perceptions differ by 50 percent or more. The principal factors affecting the content of job instructions appear to be the complexity of the job and the skill or experience required to perform it. Phillip Lewis recommends the following process for giving clear instructions that can be successfully carried out:

1. Determine what is to be accomplished.
2. Select the right person for the job.
3. Be precise and clear in wording the instructions.
4. Start with what the employee already knows.
5. Start with the simple, then move to the complex.
6. Keep the instructions positive.
7. Give a "reason-why" explanation.
8. Show benefits to the employee.
9. Demonstrate and dramatize.
10. Encourage questions.
11. Establish a target date for completion.
12. Keep tabs on progress.
13. Evaluate the results.
14. Give the employee a sense of success.
15. Have the employee practice his/her new skills.[71]

Job rationale messages explain how tasks are related to overall organizational activities and goals. Rationale communication is determined to a large extent by management philosophy and its assumptions. Organizations currently embracing the theory of management by objectives (MBO), where organizational goals are mutually discussed, are seriously concerned with outlining organizational tasks, providing an explanation of purpose, and indicating areas of progress. For them, job rationale is very important; for the more classically authoritarian organizations, rationale messages are of less concern.

Information messages pertain to the expressing of organizational policy, rules, regulations, benefits, and other data not directly related to job instruction or rationale. Also included would be messages intended to keep members of the organization informed about the organization and its products or services. Each member needs to know not only how to do a specific job, but also enough about the organization and its operations to properly serve clients and customers. Too often this information is not disseminated, especially at the lower levels of the hierarchy where turnover is likely to be high. But it is extremely important that all members be familiar with the products and services as well as the structure and operations. Being well informed is what the "total systems concept" is all about.

Feedback messages provide employees with an assessment of their performance. Sales or job reviews are the instruments most frequently used for this purpose, although supervisory warnings, transfer, and dismissal also indicate job performance. Feedback communication offers information concerning one's success or failure to accomplish certain objectives.

Ideology or indoctrination refers to messages designed to motivate employees by impressing on them the overall mission of the organization and how they relate to the organizational goals. Unlike rationale messages intended to explain and place tasks within the organizational perspective, the emphasis here is on justifying organizational objectives and enlisting subordinate/managerial support. Strengthening loyalty, morale, and motivation is the intent of such downward communication. These messages spell out the attitudes of top administration toward those lower in the organizational hierarchy and the perceptions formed at these lower levels determine the attitudes that are developed toward the top administration. Lower-level personnel may regard top administration in one of two ways. They may regard top administration as competent in performing their duties, compassionate and understanding toward those at lower levels, and sincere in looking out for the best interests of everyone in the organization. Or they may see top administration as competent in performing their task, but insensitive to lower-level people as human beings, regarding them only as assets to be manipulated in support of the enterprise's profitability. These favorable or unfavorable attitudes determine whether lower-level employees will regard themselves as part of the "organization family" and support the goals and objectives of top administration, or as separate and apart from the organization. The role of attitude development may well be the most important role played by downward communication in an organization.

Downward communication makes use of many channels. Some of the more common are informal conversations, direct orders, job descriptions, procedures manuals, orientation programs, training seminars, memoranda, company publications, and public statements. These channels can prove problematic for organizations because they frequently assume an impersonal, objective nature. They are also interpreted as authoritative, with the company appearing overbearing. Therefore, every attempt must be made to carefully select the most appropriate medium for the downward message to be communicated. "Media-rich" channels using face-to-face communication are more personal than otherwise less rich mediums.

Horizontal Communication

Horizontal communication is the lateral movement of messages between people of the same rank or position who possess the same level of organizational authority. These messages usually relate to task coordination, problem solving, information sharing, and conflict resolution. Horizontal communication has received considerably less attention than vertical communication, but we must remember that for the organization to achieve its goals and objectives in a highly competitive climate all parts of the organization are interdependent and must work for the overall benefit of the whole. For individuals to work toward the general good, they must know what is going on throughout the entire organization. This is possible only if there is a good flow of horizontal or lateral communication.

In 1916, Henri Fayol proposed a "bridge" to expedite the flow of messages among equals within a pyramidal structure (see Exhibit 4-10). Fayol's bridge circumscribed traditional channels and permitted equals to communicate directly, i.e., department to department.[72]

Departments meet to discuss how they might work together to accomplish company goals. They assemble to brainstorm ideas and discuss mutual problems. Mem-

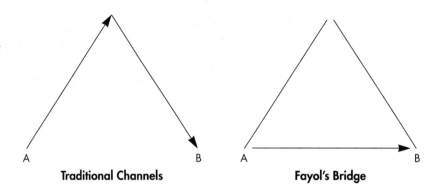

bers of two departments may meet to offer new data or explain current thinking, or to resolve potential conflicts of interest. Such communication causes the organization to operate as a single system.

Interdepartmental meetings and conferences play a vital role in horizontal and lateral communication, keeping each department informed about the plans, problems, and operations of all other departments, and providing excellent opportunities for valuable input from people outside a given department. They also prompt social interaction that enhances good rapport and morale development.

Despite the importance of horizontal communication, a number of factors limit its frequency. For instance, rivalry among departments can result in a tendency toward self-preservation and territorial protection, with subordinates being reluctant to share information. And subordinates may find it difficult to communicate with highly specialized personnel. Specialized people can also inhibit communication among peers. For example, personnel departments might find it difficult to communicate and interact with engineers because of the specialized interests of each. Finally, horizontal communication is not encouraged as long as management perceives that its goals are being met. If management is not encouraging, the lack of motivation can thwart horizontal communication and vertical channels will predominate.

Horizontal communication is needed because it supplements the vertical channels in an organization. Vertical channels would be swamps if all interdepartmental messages had to be sent "through formal channels."

Upward Communication

Upward communication is the flow of messages from subordinates to superiors. Such messages provide job feedback, suggestions, and information about employee satisfaction. In this way, management can learn of on-the-job problems and potential employee difficulties. Employees can offer suggestions that might contribute to organizational efficiency and innovation. Finally, the attitudes of employees pertaining to job satisfaction can be more accurately mirrored. Clearly, upward communication is important, but it may be the most neglected type of communication in many organizations.

Upward flow of information is indispensable for effective planning, decision making, problem solving, morale, and motivation. According to Earl Planty and William Machaver, it provides the following benefits:

1. Management gets an improved picture of the work, accomplishments, problems, plans, attitudes, and feelings of subordinates at all levels.
2. Before becoming deeply involved, management spots individuals, policies, actions, or assignments which are likely to cause trouble.
3. By helping lower echelons of supervision to improve their selection it gets them to do a more systematic and useful job of reporting.
4. By welcoming upward communication, management strengthens the only device for tapping the ideas and help of its subordinates. This gives management a better answer to its problems and eases its own responsibility.
5. By opening the channels upward, management helps the easy flow and acceptance of communications downward. Good listening makes good listeners.[73]

Upward communication can contribute much to the creation of a supportive communication climate within an organizational setting, whether a corporate/industrial complex, university, hospital, or governmental agency. This flow in organizations provides feedback on operations and the effectiveness of policies, feedback to serve as a basis for planning and decision making, and feedback on the human element in the organization. William Spoor, chairman of the Pillsbury Company, has institutionalized freedom of expression for Pillsbury general managers. He holds regular Monday morning meetings to "give them a forum to be heard where they can each say what they want to about their business." As a concrete symbol that people can fearlessly tell him what they think, he has set aside what is known at Pillsbury as the "Chart room," where, Spoor says, "Everyone's entitled, regardless of rank, to say whatever they want. We deal with the major issues in that room. We get very aggressive—and it's marvelous what comes out."[74] Each participant knows there will be no comeback or reprisal for anything said in the privileged room. Whether or not a specific forum is established, one must discover where usable ideas and opinions are most often expressed, by whom, and in what form, and then plug into the flow.

Although the rewards of upward communication are numerous, the traditional reaction on the part of management has been to resist open upward channels. According to Planty and Machaver, "some administrators tend to consider communication to be a one-way street . . . they fail to see the values obtained from encouraging employees to discuss fully the policies and plans of the company. They don't provide a clear channel for funnelling information, opinions, and attitudes up through the organization."[75] Robert McMurry further adds that "there is the inability of many chief executives to comprehend and accept valid information even when it is brought to their attention." He goes on to say, "No wonder top managers are seldom told the whole truth and nothing but by their subordinates."[76]

What are the barriers to upward communication? One basic overall barrier is the fact that communicating upward to a superior is generally a high-risk type of communication. The risk lies in the exposure and revelation by the employee which may yield positive or negative results. Specifically, subordinates desiring to get ahead or holding upward ambitions will filter information, with negative information being highly guarded. Despite the fact that such bad news as failures, mistakes, or divergent opinions is the self-corrective lifeblood of the organizational system, subordinates prefer to withhold this information. Research indicates that the greater the risk in a communication situation, the more apt one is to avoid total open communication. Koehler and Huber outline certain factors that influence the use of upward communication:

1. Positive upward communication is more likely to be utilized by managerial decision-makers than negative upward communication.
2. Upward communication is more likely to be utilized by managerial decision-makers if it is timely.
3. Upward communication is more likely to be accepted if it supports current policy.
4. Upward communication is more likely to be effective if it goes directly to a receiver who can act on it.
5. Upward communication is more effective when it has "intuitive appeal" to the receiver.[77]

A second barrier to upward communication is centered in the organization itself—in the complexity of its very structure. In their review of network studies pertaining to centralization–decentralization, Porter and Roberts describe this particular barrier.[78] Highly centralized, tall structures with traditional pyramids of authority that concentrate information will inhibit or distort upward communication. The organizational distance and many hierarchical levels contribute to such results. Decentralized or flat structures distribute information, thus increasing the likelihood of upward communication and its rewards.

This distance between organizational levels and corporate power with its status, prestige, and position is also physically apparent in the architectural design of office space. Design is frequently a subtle barrier fostering interdepartmental and upward communication problems. It can act as a sort of organizational subconscious restricting otherwise natural communication impulses. Winston Churchill once said, "We shape our buildings, after that they shape us." Office design, to a large degree, determines who has access to whom by creating barriers to some departments and bridges to others. In some fascinating research at MIT, Thomas Allen revealed that people more than ten meters apart have only 8–9 percent probability of communicating at least once a week, versus a 25 percent chance at five meters.[79] This is only one of many studies about the effects of office design on communication.[80] Because every office is unique, special factors have to be considered in each organization to make changes that will promote more effective communication.

A highly controversial and unconventional approach to overcoming this barrier is office landscaping. The open-plan office landscape revolution began more than a decade ago, introduced to the U.S. by Germany and Sweden. Putting workers, supervisors, and upper management in closer working proximity is one of the principal goals of the open-plan. By removing walls, the plan aims to make offices more efficient, more economical, more flexible, and more democratic. Proponents contend that open-planning will increase productivity by grouping people and paper to cut traffic and circulation problems. Executives are less cloistered and more in touch with their workers. At the Chicago headquarters of the McDonald's Corporation, staff efficiency improved 35 percent and the rate of turnover decreased after open-planning was introduced. Montgomery Ward in Chicago, Weyerhauser in Tacoma, Eastman Kodak in Rochester, and the World Trade Center in lower Manhattan are among the companies that have committed themselves totally to major open-plan installations. Moreover, Mercedez-Benz of North America, S. C. Johnson, E. I. Du Pont de Nemours and Co., Pizza Hut, Martin Marietta, and others have initiated open-planning on a limited basis. About three out of ten office workers are now estimated to work in open-plan offices.[81]

Still, according to a survey commissioned by Steelcase Inc., a leading manufacturer of office furniture, fewer than one-third of the office workers queried said they believed that productivity would be improved by changing office design so that they and their supervisors would be less closed off from each other.[82] A Harris survey based on personal interviews with 1,047 full-time workers, 209 executives, and 225 professional office architects reported that workers in conventional offices are "somewhat more satisfied than those in open-plans, who are considerably more positive than those in clerical pool offices."[83]

In her book, *Space Planning: Designing the Office Environment,* Lila Shoskes writes that "the furniture systems that have been developed are less than ideal." Instead of opening up offices, she claims they often create "honey combs, roomettes or mazes, cutting off contact and communication."[84] But the Harris survey concludes that 75 percent of office designers and 57 percent of corporate executives believe that the benefits of the open-plan outweigh its disadvantages.[85] The physical characteristics of an office building are important and can affect communication effectiveness. Perhaps open-planning can overcome some structural barriers within the organization as well as personality distances, but it remains very controversial.

Geography is a final, unavoidable barrier to upward communication. As companies expand domestically and internationally, geographic separation creates real communication difficulties. Obviously, communication becomes more problematic when managers and employees are separated by 1500 miles or more. The weight of these geographical distances has been lightened by the use of overnight mail services, the telephone, fax machines, and other highly specialized technology permitting point-to-point interfacing.

All of these barriers are far from insurmountable and the organizational benefits to managers are significant. The key to fostering upward communication is active listening and maintaining a supportive communication climate. Because upward communication is perceived by subordinates as risky, managers and supervisors must redefine this perception by encouraging such communication and displaying interest and sensitivity. Attention to these factors will generate trust but, in the final analysis, action must be taken on upward messages if employees are to take upward communication seriously. It is inconsistent to ask people to step out and take risks, to speak up, to change things, to blow the whistle on poor quality or service, and then fail to act. Tom Peters notes that managers in today's world don't get paid to be "stewards of resources"; they get "paid for one and only one thing—to make things better . . . to make things different . . . to change things, to act—today."[86]

Effectively managing information involves many perplexities. It is not enough to have a lot of facts. The wise manager seeks a more encompassing perspective by linking fact to fact, like some kind of conceptual scaffolding. Phillip Clampitt presents a simple but interesting perspective on information management when he identifies four categories making up the processing state: (1) processed information, (2) unprocessed information, (3) knowledgeable ignorance, and (4) absolute ignorance.[87] *Processed information* includes those data that have been assimilated, attended to, and duly noted. The letter that has just been carefully read or the conversation that has been completed are common examples of processed information. On the other hand, the reports that go unread, the studies not examined, and the unreturned telephone calls are a few examples of *unprocessed information*. The information is available but, for whatever reason, never consumed. The *knowledgeable ignorance* category represents what we know we don't know—"the known unknowns." It is the missing information that prompts the asking of the right questions. Jacob Bronowski notes that "the hardest part is not to answer, but to conceive the question. The genius of men like Newton and Einstein lies in that: they ask transparent, innocent questions which have catastrophic answers."[88] Finally, *absolute ignorance* represents the traditional way in which "ignorance" is understood, the state of being totally unaware. These categories suggest a unique set of challenges for the manager and encourage the raising of appropriate diagnostic questions given information dissemination difficulties:

Processed Information
▶ Does the information arrive on time?
▶ Does the information arrive at the right place?
▶ Is the information understandable?
▶ Is the information specific enough?

Unprocessed Information
▶ Has the proper information been transmitted?
▶ Has too much information been transmitted? Too little?
▶ Has the information been screened effectively?
▶ Has nonuseful information been discarded?
▶ Do employees have access to needed information?

Knowledgeable Ignorance
▶ Have the proper questions been asked?
▶ Have the "holes" in the information fabric been detected?
▶ Do we know where to find the answers?
▶ Can we prioritize our information needs?

Absolute Ignorance
▶ Is there some mechanism built into the system so that certain information is randomly encountered?
▶ Are new perspectives being sought?
▶ Are new sources of information being tapped?
▶ Should consultants be hired to expose the organization to new trends?[89]

Thus, according to Clampitt, it is not enough to define information management as simply a problem of information flow. In the processed information category, questions of timeliness and ambiguity arise. In the unprocessed information category, the issues of how to manage overload and properly filter information arise. The knowledgeable ignorance category suggests that managers need to be concerned with how to find the gaps in their understanding. And, the absolute ignorance category challenges managers to deal effectively with uncertainty.

Message flow and the processing of information is essential to the modern organization. Downward messages communicate managerial decisions, organizational policy, and operating procedures. Horizontal messages bring different units together and tend to maintain the total organizational system. Upward messages provide nec-

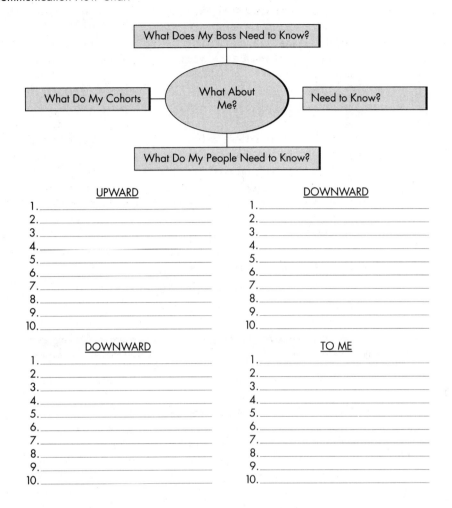

essary feedback. Effectively managed, information processing can bring organizations into integrated functioning units, and this can maximize the effectiveness of the organizational system. The communication flow chart presented in Exhibit 4-11 can aid in identifying the direction of messages. It can provide a means whereby your messages are monitored and recorded. Thus, you can determine the nature of your own "message flow"—creating a personal diagram.

► **SUMMARY**

This chapter began with the premise that organizational climate is one of the major internal components of the communication system. The construct of climate was examined and a number of dimensions

of climate were presented as they relate to managerial style. It was further suggested that employees' attitudes about climate were related to their productivity in the organization. Here, underlying assumptions regarding human nature, work, and motivation were explored.

The structural design of organizations, the communication networks within organizations and the flow of messages were then investigated as equally significant internal variables defining the communication climate (supportive or defensive) that exists within any organization. Organizational structure—tall, flat, or matrix—significantly affects organizational communication, behavior, and effectiveness. Structure was presented as a major tool used by organizations to coordinate individual and group activity, and to achieve organizational goals. It is because of its influential nature that a structural revolution is occurring, but much is yet to be learned of the effects of various types of structures.

All organizations evince certain formal and informal patterns of interaction or networks of communication. These patterns reflect the organization's strategic plan and the role relations existing between and among workers. They also suggest appropriate approaches for information exchange, problem solving, and decision making. These communication networks provide the framework through which communication flows and the multiple communication roles assumed by individuals.

Finally, network members use a variety of oral and written channels to carry messages in vertical, horizontal, and less structured directions. The amount and complexity of messages—the communication load—contribute to the conflicting forces and tensions involved in information management. Yet, the processing of messages and dissemination of information is a critical managerial task affecting the total organization.

In sum, communication is a vital aspect of every organizational function—vital in much the same way that oxygen is vital to life. In the next chapter, we will examine an essential but frequently neglected and taken-for-granted communication skill—listening.

▶ QUESTIONS FOR DISCUSSION AND SKILL DEVELOPMENT

1. What are the basic dimensions forming an organization's climate? Are there any factors that neither Gibb, McGregor, Likert, Maslow, or Herzberg consider which, you feel, play a significant role in establishing a communication climate within an organization? The assessment of the communication climate and measurement of workers' attitudes are often used to determine how best to motivate employees. Are there any other measurements that might be equally appropriate? Explain how organizational identification, job performance, communication satisfaction, and job satisfaction are outcomes that relate to organizational climate. Write a letter telling a real or imaginary boss how to motivate you. How should this information affect your selection of a particular job choice?

2. You have just been promoted to general sales manager with a force of 100 salespeople working for you. What criteria would you set up to encourage participative management?

3. Briefly explain what an organizational structure is and how you think structure affects behavior and communication. Distinguish among tall, flat, and matrix structures. What are the costs and benefits of each structural type? Why does the environment appear to play such a central, causal role in the selection of the most effective organizational form? How does the exercise of authority differ from structural form to structural form? How does structural form affect message flow—downward, horizontal, and upward? How important are organization size and shape in creating job satisfaction? At what level in the organization—top management, supervisor, or worker—do you think communica-tion effectiveness is most important? Least important? Are there any alternatives to the hierarchical organizational structure? What are they?

4. Design a formal organization chart for an organization to which you belong. Include both the chain of command and the job duties of the people in the organization. How many levels does the organization have? What is the average span of control for each manager? What formal network relationships exist? What informal network rela-

tionships? How can these formal and informal communication patterns be systematically analyzed? How would a beehive chart differ from this formal organization chart? How can the informal organization, or unofficial network, bypass the formal organization's system of communication and upset its distribution of authority?

5. What contributes to effective downward, horizontal, and upward communication? What barriers or obstacles prevent horizontal communication? How might they be overcome? Why is it important to have upward communication in any organization? What aspects of upward communication are most important? Why? Is the grapevine or "rumor mill" good, bad, or both good and bad for management? Explain.

6. What critical functions does communication serve within organizations? Which, in your view, is most important for the maintenance and growth of the organization?

▶ NOTES

1. Charles Conrad, *Strategic Organizational Communication,* 2nd ed. (Orlando, FL: Holt, Rinehart & Winston, 1990).
2. Kurt Lewin, *Field Theory in Social Science* (New York: Harper and Brothers, 1951): 241.
3. R. L. Falcione and E. A. Kaplan, "Organizational Climate, Communication, and Culture," in: R. Bostrum, ed., *Communication Yearbook 8* (Beverly Hills, CA: Sage, 1984); L. R. James and A. P. Jones, "Organizational Climate: A Review of Theory and Research," *Psychological Bulletin* 81 (1974): 1096–1112; W. Charles Redding, *Communication Within the Organization: An Interpretive Review of Theory and Research* (New York: Industrial Communication Council, 1972); and R. Taquiri and G. Litwin, *Organizational Climate* (Boston: Harvard University Press, 1968).
4. R. W. Woodman and D. C. King, "Organizational Climate: Science or Folklore?" *Academy of Management Review* 3 (1978): 816–826.
5. R. Guion, "A Note on Organizational Climate," *Organizational Behavior and Human Performance* 9 (1973): 121.
6. H. Schwartz and S. M. Davis, "Matching Corporate Culture and Business Strategy," *Organizational Dynamics* 10 (1981): 30–48.
7. Lytton L. Guimaraes, "Network Analysis: An Approach to the Study of Communication Systems," *Technical Report 12. Project on the Diffusion of Innovations in Rural Societies* (East Lansing, MI: Michigan State University, 1970).
8. Robert Schoenberg, *The Art of Being a Boss* (New York: Harper and Row, 1978): 80–81.
9. Ibid., 209.
10. Ibid., 91.
11. Robert Tannenbaum and Warren H. Schmidt, "How to Choose a Leadership Pattern," *Harvard Business Review* 36 (March-April 1958): 96.
12. Robert R. Blake and Anne Adams McCanse, *Leadership Dilemma–Grid Solutions* (Houston: Gulf Publishing, 1991).
13. L. L. Steinmetz and F. Todd, *First-line Management* (Dallas: Business Publications, 1975): 112.
14. William J. Reddin, *Managerial Effectiveness* (New York: McGraw-Hill, 1970).
15. John M. McGrath and Cal W. Downs, "A Comparative Analysis of Communication Styles and Management Styles" (Paper presented at the Annual Meeting of the Speech Communication Association, Chicago, IL, 1990).
16. Jack Gibb, "Defensive Communication," *Journal of Communication* (1961): 141–148.
17. Redding, *Communication Within the Organization,* 92.
18. James Campbell and Michael Beatty, "Organizational Climate: Its Measurement and Relationship to Work Goal Performance" (Paper presented at the Annual Meeting of the American Psychological Association, Washington, D.C., 1971).
19. H. S. Dennis, "The Construction of a Managerial 'Communication Climate' Inventory for Use in Complex Organizations" (Paper presented at the Annual Meeting of the International Communication Association, Chicago, IL, 1975).
20. Douglas McGregor, *Professional Manager* (New York: McGraw-Hill, 1967).
21. Douglas McGregor, *The Human Side of Enterprise* (New York: McGraw-Hill, 1960): 33–34.

22. Schoenberg, *Art of Being a Boss*, 94.

23. Ibid., 95.

24. McGregor, *Human Side of Enterprise*, 47–48.

25. Eric Trist, "Urban North America: The Challenge of the Next Thirty Years," in: Warren Schmidt, ed., *Organizational Frontiers and Human Values* (Belmont, CA: Wadsworth Publishing, 1970): 77–85.

26. Rensis Likert, *New Patterns of Management* (New York: McGraw-Hill, 1961).

27. Rensis Likert, *The Human Organization* (New York: McGraw-Hill, 1967).

28. James A. Belasco, *Teaching the Elephant to Dance* (New York: Plume, 1991): 244–245.

29. Abraham H. Maslow, *Motivation and Personality*, 2nd ed., (New York: Harper and Row, 1970).

30. Frank Gable, *The Third Force* (New York: Grossman, 1970).

31. C. P. Alderfer, "A New Theory of Human Needs," *Organizational Behavior and Performance* 4 (1969): 142–175; J. V. Clark, "Motivation in Work Groups: A Tentative View," *Human Organization* 19 (1961): 199–208; E. E. Lawler, "A Casual Correlational Test of the Need Hierarchy Concept," *Organizational Behavior and Human Performance* 7 (1973): 265–287; and Daniel Yankelovich, "Stepping Off Maslow's Escalator," *New Rules: Searching for Self-Fulfillment in a World Turned Upside Down* (New York: Random House, 1981): 234–243.

32. Abraham H. Maslow. *Eupsychian Management* (Homewood, IL: Richard D. Irwin, 1965): 85.

33. Frederick Herzberg, *The Motivation to Work* (New York: John Wiley & Sons, 1959); *Work and the Nature of Man* (Cleveland, OH: World Publishing, 1966).

34. Orlando Behling, George Labovitz, and Richard Kozmo, "The Herzberg Controversy," *Academy of Management Journal* 11 (March 1968): 99–108; and R. J. House and L. A. Wigdor, "Herzberg's Dual-Factor Theory of Job Satisfaction and Motivation: A Review of the Evidence and a Criticism," *Personnel Psychology* 20 (1967): 369–389.

35. R. J. Hackman and E. Lawler, "Employee Reactions to Job Characteristics," *Journal of Applied Psychology* 5 (1971): 259–286.

36. R. N. Osborn, James Hunt, and L. R. Jauch, *Organization Theory: An Integrated Approach* (New York: John Wiley & Sons, 1980).

37. Robert D. McPhee, "Formal Structure and Organizational Communication," in: Robert D. McPhee and Phillip K. Tompkins, eds., *Organizational Communication: Traditional Themes and New Directions* (Newbury Park, CA: Sage, 1985): 149–177.

38. Robert D. McPhee, "Organizational Communication: Toward Central Concepts and Phenomena" (Paper presented at the Annual Meeting of the International Communication Association, Dallas, TX, 1983).

39. Theodore Caplow, *Principles of Organization* (New York: Harcourt Brace Jovanovich, 1964): 26–27.

40. Henry Mintzberg, *The Structuring of Organizations* (Englewood Cliffs, NJ: Prentice Hall, 1979).

41. T. Burns and G. M. Stalker, *The Management of Innovation* (London: Tavistock, 1961).

42. S. P. Robbins, *Organization Theory: Structure, Design and Applications*, 3rd ed. (Englewood Cliffs, NJ: Prentice Hall, 1990).

43. Eric Trist and Kenneth Bamforth, "Some Social and Psychological Consequences of the Longwall Method of Coal-Getting," *Human Relations* 4 (1951): 3–38.

44. Aubrey Sanford, Gary Hunt, and Hyler Bracey, *Communication Behavior in Organizations* (Columbus, OH: Charles E. Merrill, 1976).

45. Schoenberg, *Art of Being a Boss*, 121.

46. Robert N. McMurry, "Clear Communication for Chief Executives," *How Successful Executives Handle People* (Boston, MA: President and Fellows of Harvard College): 8.

47. Ibid., 15.

48. Alvin Toffler, *Powershift* (New York: Bantam Books, 1990): 183.

49. Tom Peters, *Thriving on Chaos* (New York: Harper and Row, 1987): 427.

50. V. A. Graicunas, *Relationships in Organizations* (Geneva, Switzerland: International Labor Office, 1933).

51. Richard Schonberger, *World Class Manufacturing: The Lessons of Simplicity Applied* (New York: Free Press, 1986).

52. Toffler, *Powershift*, 191–198. Copyright © 1990 by Alvin Toffler. Used by permission of Bantam Books, a division of Bantam Doubleday Dell Publishing Group, Inc.

53. "New Management Pioneer Jim Swiggert," *Inc.* (February 1987): 34–44.

54. Harold Leavitt, *Managerial Psychology*, 3rd ed. (Chicago: University of Chicago Press, 1972): 195.

55. R. V. Farace and D. MacDonald, "New Directions in the Study of Organizational Communication," *Personnel Psychology* 27 (1974): 7.

56. Rebecca Blair, Karlene Roberts, and Pamela McKechanie, "Vertical and Network Communication in Organizations," in: McPhee and Tompkins, eds., *Organizational Communication,* 55–77.

57. Richard Farace, Peter Monge, and Hamish Russell, *Communicating and Organizing* (Reading, MA: Addison-Wesley, 1977).

58. Edward Rogers and R. Agarwala-Rogers, *Communication in Organizations* (New York: Free Press, 1976).

59. Roger Ailes, *You Are the Message: Secrets of the Master Communicators* (Homewood, IL: Dow Jones–Irwin, 1988).

60. Phillip G. Clampitt, *Communicating for Managerial Effectiveness* (Newbury Park, CA: Sage, 1991): 135.

61. Willard Merrihue, *Managing by Communication* (New York: McGraw-Hill, 1960): 116.

62. Keith Davis, *Human Behavior at Work,* 5th ed. (New York: McGraw-Hill, 1977).

63. Clampitt, *Communicating for Managerial Effectiveness,* 89.

64. J. Foehrenbach and S. Goldfarb, "Employee Communication in the '90s: Greater Expectations," *Communication World* (May-June, 1990).

65. V. Dallas Merrell, *Huddling: The Informal Way to Management Success* (New York: American Management Association, 1979).

66. Jaye Martin, "Huddling," *The New York Times,* March 25, 1979, 16F.

67. Keith Davis, *Human Behavior at Work.*

68. J. Foehrenbach and K. Rosenberg, "How Are We Doing?" *Journal of Communication Management* 12 (1982): 1–10.

69. Daniel Katz and Robert Kahn, *The Social Psychology of Organizations* (New York: John Wiley & Sons, 1966).

70. "Avoiding Failures in Management Communications," in: *Research Report of the Public Opinion Index for Industry* (Princeton, NJ: Opinion Research Corp., January, 1963).

71. Phillip Lewis, *Organizational Communications: The Essence of Effective Management.* (New York: John Wiley & Sons, 1975).

72. Henri Fayol, *General and Industrial Administration* (New York: Pitman, 1947): 34.

73. Earl Planty and William Machaver, "Upward Communication: Project in Executive Development," *Personnel Journal* 28 (1952): 142.

74. Schoenberg, *Art of Being a Boss,* 118.

75. Planty and Machaver, "Upward Communication," 304–319.

76. McMurry, "Clear Communication for Chief Executives," 2.

77. J. W. Koehler and G. Huber, "Effects of Upward Communication on Managerial Decision Making" (Paper presented at the Annual Meeting of the International Communication Association, New Orleans, LA, 1974).

78. L. W. Porter and K. H. Roberts, "Communication in Organizations," in: Marvin D. Dumettel, ed., *Handbook of Industrial and Organizational Psychology* (New York: Rand McNally, 1976).

79. Thomas Allen, "Communication in the Research and Development Laboratory," *Technology Review* (October-November, 1967): 30–35.

80. S. Ornstein, "The Hidden Influence of Office Design," *Academy of Management Executive* 3 (1989): 144–147; W. Schmidt and M. Elizabeth Dorsey, "Office Design: The Spatial Dimension of Organizational Communication and Reflector of Communication Climate," *Perspectives in Business Communication* (Proceedings of the Annual Meeting of the Association of Business Communication-SW, 1986): 25–37.

81. Deborah K. Dietsch, "Workshops of Industry," *Architectural Record* (March 1986): 95–105; Grace M. Andersonk, "Facilities for Talkfests," *Architectural Record* (September 1986): 91–102; and Schmidt and Dorsey, "Office Design," 25–37.

82. Ibid.

83. Carter B. Horsley, "Some Second Thoughts on Open-Plan Offices," *The New York Times,* March 18, 1979: 6.

84. Lila Shoskes, *Space Planning: Designing the Office Environment* (New York: Architectural Books, 1976).

85. Horsley, "Some Second Thoughts."

86. Peters, *Thriving on Chaos,* 566.

87. Clampitt, *Communicating for Managerial Effectiveness,* 79–83.

88. Jacob Bronowski, *The Ascent of Man* (Boston: Little, Brown, 1973): 247.

89. Clampitt, *Communicating for Managerial Effectiveness,* 85.

C ommunication is central to the smooth operation of the modern organization. In this unit, basic communication processes that cut across all organizational contexts are examined. Attention is given to listening, interpersonal communication, and flexible leadership and conflict management.

Basic Communication Processes in the Organization

▶ 5 *Identifies listening as essential to effective organizational activity and suggests how potential barriers to effective listening might be removed.*

▶ 6 *Examines the nature of interpersonal relationships, identifying and describing the influence of self-concept, perception, assertiveness, and gameplaying as dimensions affecting effective communication in the workplace.*

▶ 7 *Identifies approaches to leadership and strategies for productive conflict management.*

C H A P T E R

F I V E

5

Listening

Until recently, listening behavior has been the least studied of the communication skills. Prior to 1950 it was all but neglected in books and journals on communication and our education system seemed to totally ignore this dimension of the communication process. Listening was regarded as an action, but not as a skill subject to development. Listening in the last few decades, largely because of the efforts by people like Dr. Ralph Nichols of the University of Minnesota and others, has become an area of intense interest and a number of training programs in listening have been launched. There seems to be growing agreement that most of us are poor listeners; that with training we could become more effective listeners; that listening training should be provided at some level; that effective listening is an active and dynamic process; and that better listening can be personally rewarding. This chapter identifies the importance of listening, defines listening as more than hearing, examines the different types of listening we engage in regularly, notes the commonly encountered barriers to listening, and finally focuses on keys to more effective listening.

Today, we hear too frequently the complaint that people are not listening. Parents are not listening to their children; children are not listening to their parents; employers are not listening to employees; employees are not listening to employers. From the limitless variety of social, business, educational, and political spheres we hear the plaintive lament that "no one is listening."

Listening is one of the most-often-engaged-in activities, but research suggests that the majority of us are poor listeners. We misunderstand others and are misunderstood in return. We become bored and feign attention while our minds wander. We challenge, interrupt, and dismiss the ideas of others without attending to them. We engage in a battle of talking. Overall, we hear but don't listen.

Clearly, bad listening pervades all phases of our culture. Is there anything we can do about it? Yes, if we come to understand what listening is about; if we become aware of potential barriers to effective listening and look to remove them; and if we give serious attention to improving our listening abilities. Tom Peters keenly observes that "today's effective leader must become a compulsive listener."[1]

▶ IMPORTANCE OF LISTENING

Any communication skill's importance can be determined by considering its frequency, difficulty, and quality. Using this standard, the importance of listening is well documented. Studies show that we spend 80 percent of our waking hours communicating, and researchers agree that 45 percent of that time is spent listening. In the business arena, research reveals that the average American working adult divides communication time roughly along these lines[2]:

Listening	Speaking	Reading	Writing
45 percent	30 percent	16 percent	9 percent

Thus, quantitatively speaking, listening is the most-used form of communication. For such an overlooked skill, listening certainly occupies a large portion of our days.

Modern technology has brought us into closer contact with one another, and the role of listening in interpersonal, face-to-face, group-communicative, and public situations has become more significant in all aspects of our lives. Listening has come to play an increasingly vital role in achieving our desired goals. Andrew Wolvin and Carolyn Coakley report that "listening has been found to be the most critical managerial competency, the communication activity most important to job success, the most important communication skill necessary for entry level positions, the most important communication skill in the organization, the most important communication skill for career competence, the most important communication skill for effective subordinates and supervisors or middle management personnel."[3] There are many who have come to realize that "to listen, per se, is the single best 'tool' for empowering large numbers of others."[4] If talking and giving orders was the administrative model of the smokestack era, listening is the model of the current information age.

Business has come to accept the fact that most people are not efficient listeners and that inefficient and ineffective listening is extraordinarily costly. Tests have shown that immediately after listening to a ten-minute oral presentation, the average listener has heard, understood, properly evaluated, and retained approximately half

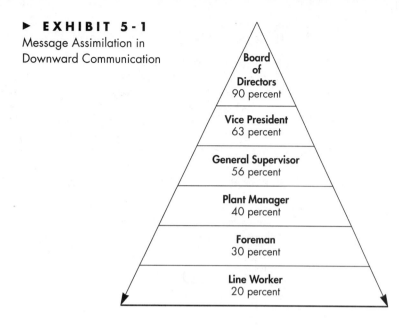

► **EXHIBIT 5-1**
Message Assimilation in
Downward Communication

Board of Directors
90 percent

Vice President
63 percent

General Supervisor
56 percent

Plant Manager
40 percent

Foreman
30 percent

Line Worker
20 percent

of what was said. And within 48 hours, that drops off another 50 percent to a final 25 percent level of effectiveness. In other words, we quite often comprehend and retain only one-quarter of what is said. The Pidgeon Savage Lewis Corporation of Minneapolis, an advertising and communications firm, studied the communicative efficiency of 100 representative industrial management teams. They found that listening can deteriorate to a 20 percent efficiency level in downward communication.[5] Ideas get distorted by as much as 80 percent as they travel through the chain of command. Exhibit 5-1 shows the degree of message assimilation in downward communication.[6]

Communication moving upward through the levels of management indicates similar degrees of listening efficiency or more accurately listening inefficiency. A study of 24 industrial plants verifies this observation. Managers and line workers were asked to rank in importance ten distinct morale factors. The managers ranked as *least* important: (1) full appreciation of work done, (2) feeling "in on things," and (3) sympathetic help on personal problems. The line employees ranked as *most* influential: (1) full appreciation of work done, (2) feeling "in on things," and (3) sympathetic help on personal problems. Incredibly, management guessed exactly wrong, putting the three most important factors in the three least important spots.[7] And this kind of evidence emerges again and again when objective studies are made of how well management seemingly listens to employee groups. For many managers effective listening is the hardest problem.[8] Perhaps the best compliment a supervisor, manager, or executive could receive from a fellow worker would be, "My boss listens to me. We can talk together."

Most forward-looking companies realize that this failure in listening can only hinder their progress. The Sperry Corporation has initiated an ongoing series of programs designed to heighten managers' listening skills. The training concentrates on specific on-the-job applications that show how Sperry employees, in various real-life situations, can do a better job of responding—the endproduct of the listening process.

Richard L. Robertson, staff vice president of public affairs, describes Sperry's new corporate advertising theme—"We understand how important it is to listen"—as more than a slogan. He says, "It expresses a basic managerial philosophy and is fundamental to the way we do business."[9] Moreover, the educational division of Xerox Corporation has developed a short programmed listening course that has been adopted by the Lummas Company, IBM, Mattel, Liberty Mutual Insurance Company, Dow Chemical, Sinclair Oil Company, the City University of New York, Cornell University, Emerson College, and the Community College System of Massachusetts, to name just a few of the businesses, governmental agencies, and institutions of education that provide listening training. These are all efforts to involve employees and counter their increasing sense of alienation from top management.

Specific examples of the importance of careful listening to efficient business operation are numerous. A manager of training for a large New York department store calls attention to one dimension of the problem when he focuses on clerk-customer difficulties. Some years ago, a Long Island plant hired new employees to work over a forge used for heating tool steel. During the initial orientation the men were instructed to hang the hot irons on the wall to the right and as they cooled they were to be moved to the left wall. When an employee needed new grappling irons, he, of course, would take them from the left wall. Well, shortly after the meeting one of the new employees hung a hot grappling iron on the wrong wall and another man walked into the room, reached up and grabbed the hot iron. The burns caused by the hot metal disabled the man permanently. At the accident hearing the man who had placed the iron on the wrong wall said that he had not heard anybody say hot irons were to be hung to the right of the forge.

There is also the large East Coast industrial firm that was suddenly surrounded by striking pickets. Labor negotiations had been underway, but top management had no idea a strike was impending; in fact, it was the first strike in the plant's history. A member of the management team had been alerted to the possibility of a strike by the labor relations representative and informed of preventive actions, but nothing was done and five days of valuable production time were lost. Later, the management member who had been warned said his immediate reaction to the recommendation of the director of labor relations had been "a strike couldn't happen here!" With that thought in mind, he had ceased to listen and evaluate the seriousness of the warning.

An East Coast university some years ago went through a similar scenario. The faculty had been negotiating for months on a new three-year contract. The administration had used a variety of delaying techniques, including the withholding of vital information. The representatives of the administration were warned of an impending strike but dismissed it because the faculty's past conservatism suggested that a strike would not materialize. Because the administration failed to listen to warnings and assess the climate of the faculty, a strike occurred on the first day of classes and delayed the opening of the semester. During day-long negotiations the disputed issues were settled and the contract was signed, but if the administration had been alert to the faculty, the students would not have had to miss class and experience the crossing of picket lines, the possibility of enrolling elsewhere, or the lengthy absence from school and potential delay of graduation.

Such instances could be multiplied almost without end. Clearly, one wonders: How can companies stay in business? How can any firm operate with 20 percent listening efficiency? The answer is that many cannot. Every year in the U.S. 4 percent of our businesses go bankrupt and a new firm has only a 40 percent chance of survival that first year. Every 25 years 90 percent of all our businesses go bankrupt.[10] Certainly, it would be difficult to prove that bad listening or poor communication is the sole cause of nine out of ten business failures. Still, in an attitudinal survey of selected *Fortune 500* companies, 76 percent of trainers and developers (human resource development people) considered listening to be "very important" to the smooth functioning of the organizational system.[11] Further comments from the top executives of a major manufacturing plant in the Chicago area made after they attended a listening seminar confirm these findings and reinforce the crucial role of listening:

> Frankly, I had never thought of listening as an important subject by itself. But now that I am aware of it, I think that perhaps 80% of my work depends on my listening to someone, or on someone else listening to me.

> I've been thinking back about things that have gone wrong over the past couple of years, and suddenly realized that many of the troubles have resulted from someone not hearing something, or getting it in a distorted way.

> It's interesting to me that we have considered so many facets of communication in the company, but have inadvertently overlooked listening. I've about decided that it's the most important link in the company's communications, and it's obviously also the weakest one.[12]

Listening, then, is a subject of substantial importance. It is not, as some people assume, the "natural consequence," the "automatic result," or the "expected conclusion" of a given communication situation. Listening is a specific and important human behavior, one that can be learned and improved on. Listening, in a very real sense, deserves careful and thoughtful consideration by all and particularly by those in the corporate organizational structure.

▶ LISTENING DEFINED

Listening is a complex process. It's more than hearing; we hear with our ears but we listen with our minds. When we truly listen we combine what is coming into our brains from our ears with all of our relevant past experiences, so far as we can recall them. Sounds do not of and by themselves have meaning. Ascribing a meaning is something that we do when our auditory nerves are stimulated by vibrations in the air about us. Without listening there is no speaking; listening and speaking are as closely related as the outside and inside of a cup. The speaker and the listener mutually share the responsibility and are mutually dependent on each other for the results of every attempted act of communication. Communication is really effective only when genuine cooperation is achieved. Marcus Aurelius, the sage Roman emperor of the second century, wrote in Book VI of his *Meditations,* "Accustom thyself to attend eagerly to what is said by another; be in the speaker's mind." And, somewhere in his essays, Thoreau said, "It takes two to speak truth—one to speak and another to hear." Communication is a two-way, reciprocal process and while one party is more obviously active than the other, this should not lead us to conclude that listening is a passive role. The good listener is creatively active.

The problem for many is being able to define what effective listening means. Listening is:

> . . . the accurate perception of what is being communicated. It is the art of separating fact from statement, innuendo, and accusation. A two-way exchange in which both parties involved must always be receptive to the thoughts, ideas, and emotions of the other. To be an effective listener, one must not only open the lines of communication and relax; one must compel others to do the same.[13]

Listening may be an art, but it is also the act of "selectively discriminating among the available aural inputs within any given environment."[14] It involves four separate but interrelated components: what you hear, what you attend to, what you understand, and what you remember. Hearing is only the first part of listening, the physiological part where you sense sound waves (these waves range between approximately 125 and 8,000 cycles per second in frequency and 55 to 85 decibels in loudness). After the sounds are converted into electrochemical impulses and transmitted to the brain, a decision, often unconscious, is made whether to attend to what is heard. Your needs, wants, desires, and interests determine what is attended to. Then, there is the interpretation of what is heard, which contributes to understanding or misunderstanding. You weigh the information and decide how you'll use it. Finally, information is stored in your memory for later recall or, based on what you heard and how you evaluated it, you react.

The model of the listening process (Exhibit 5-2) illustrates the effort required to be an active listener. Mere sounds have no intrinsic meanings. Rather, we supply the meanings when the nerves in our auditory systems are stimulated by vibrations in the atmosphere around us. Thus, listening involves receiving and attending to stimuli, a combination of cognitive and affective processes, and memory or a response that lets the other party know the message was sensed, interpreted, and evaluated. The conch shell is believed to hold a mysterious ability to reflect the sounds of the ocean. By placing the shell to your ear, you can hear the roar of the waves pounding in the surf. It is said that the conch shell's unique power comes from its willingness to listen to its surroundings, completely and undisturbed. By absorbing so perfectly what it hears, the conch is then able to share with the listener the secrets of the sea. Similarly, we can profit from talking less and listening more—listening is the silent success skill that makes all the difference in effective communication.

Receiving/Attending to Stimuli

Listening initially involves the physical process of receiving aural and/or visual stimuli (words, voice cues, nonlinguistic sounds, nonverbal cues), and, at any moment, incredible numbers of stimuli in the immediate environment are vying for your attention. Because you can attend to only a limited number of stimuli at any time, you have to engage constantly in a process of selection. For example, you may pay more attention to various situational stimuli than to others sharing the same communication environment. If all of the stimuli competing for your attention were actually attended to, a neural overload would occur. Attending is not a passive process; it requires effort as well as desire. If you have a limited attention span, a questionable priority system on which to base selection of aural stimuli, or a lack of motiva-

▶ **EXHIBIT 5-2**

The Listening Process

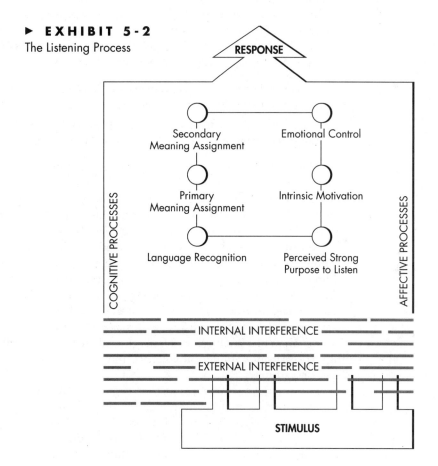

tion to concentrate, your listening ability will be seriously weakened. Listening is hard work.

Cognitive Processes

Active listening involves a combination of cognitive and affective processes. C. William Colburn and Sanford B. Weinberg observe:

> The process of cognitive structuring is comparable to the operation of a computer. When we listen, inputs are received and then sorted via a "program" into usable categories that may be stored for later use or that may be used to produce an immediate "printout" (response). The brain is programmed by our experiences and background, our attitudes and values, our intellect, and our physical capabilities.[15]

How, then, does cognitive structuring affect your ability to listen? In what ways do you identify, categorize, and make appropriate responses?

Messages are perceived, registered on the sense receptors and instantaneously transmitted to the brain through a complex biochemical process, and then decoded. The immediate language code is recognized and identified as familiar or unfamiliar. If unfamiliar, nonverbal cues will become more important.

Even when familiar, the language code may prove problematic. Consider the following two comments, one from a businesswoman and another from a New York City teacher. Both of them point to the fact that stereotypes—in this case language dialects—can make it hard to succeed in the business world:

> I was turned down for a very prestigious national marketing job because I had a Brooklyn accent. I don't want it to happen again.
>
> I don't always expect to live in New York. I expect to move away and I want to move up into school administration. The accent would be a handicap.[16]

The process of assigning meaning to aural stimuli is not fully understood, but researchers suggest that it's done by mental categorization. Categories and subcategories, developed as you acquire and use your language, are stored in your memory. On receiving an aural stimulus, you search the many storage units looking for an appropriate category from which a match can be made and a meaning ascribed.

Your most immediate selection is called a "primary meaning assignment." This is the surface meaning. The secondary meaning assignment involves the processes of interpretation and evaluation. It is, in effect, the meta-meaning of the message. That is, you examine the total message and its situational context, identifying the unique characteristics and how they differ from that category in your memory bank. As a listener, you might interpret a message one way when in a social setting but differently when in a small group or a large audience. Or, you may assign different meanings to apparently similar messages coming from your parents, a close friend, your boss, or a stranger.

The cognitive structuring process organizes the message and assigns a meaning to it. Your interpretation and evaluation of the situation significantly influence any meaning you assign. The cognitive processes involved in listening are maximized or minimized to the extent of your vocabulary, language facility, language usage, knowledge, personal experiences, and flexibility.

Affective Processes

Thus far, listening has been discussed in terms of receiving, attending to, and assigning meaning to a message. Listening is also greatly influenced by certain affective processes. A strong purpose to listen and intrinsic motivation serve to create a listening bond that encourages communicative involvement.

Some messages are "heard" but never really "received," and those that are not received never exist for the listener. There must be a desire to listen. The situation, the speaker, and the message can all contribute to a high interest level for listening. Whether it is a social situation or a classroom or business environment; whether the speaker is known or unknown, well liked or disliked; and whether the message is audible or emotionally intense are some factors that can affect your listening. Listening is a dynamic, active process and you must enter a listening situation prepared to listen.

You are likewise influenced by your personally intrinsic motives. If a message interests you, is perceived as striking current needs and personal concerns, you are more inclined to listen. Messages characterized as vital and relevant, or entertaining, pleasurable, and amusing motivate you to listen. In contrast, messages deemed unimportant and dull receive considerably less attention, if any. From all the possible inputs, those that are chosen depend very much on those intrinsic motives that give direction to your behavior.

Emotional Control

All too often otherwise-effective listening suffers because of a loss of emotional control resulting from a breakdown of cognitive or affective processes. Common causes for this loss of control include: inflammatory or emotionally laden language, prejudices against ideas or groups, biases toward position and/or lines of argument, and personality conflicts. A single emotion-laden word, a disagreement on issues, even the person speaking can short-circuit the listening process. Your listening is most effective when you establish some psychic distance between yourself and the sender, so that comprehending the message can be uppermost in your mind.

Remembering

Finally, listening involves remembering or the storage of aural stimuli in the mind for later retrieval. Human memory involves at least three different memory systems:

▶ *Sensory information storage*—a system which for a very short period of time (.1 to .5 seconds) records an image of the events the receiver has experienced at the sensory level.
▶ *Short-term memory*—a system with the limited capacity to handle approximately six to seven items of information and which involves the interpretation of events.
▶ *Long-term memory*—a system which is virtually unlimited in retention of experiences for more than a few minutes.[17]

Memory is involved in all aspects of listening—in recording sensory images, in interpreting and retaining information for a limited time, and in storing categorized experiences for future use.

We have described the process of listening as sequential, but listening is actually an integrated process with all facets connected and interconnected. Therefore, listening is essentially an intrapersonal communication system that significantly affects the process of interpersonal communication.

▶TYPES OF LISTENING

Let's consider some of the different types of listening. We listen for different purposes and everyday you engage in different types of listening: appreciative, social, comprehensive, critical, and empathic listening.

Appreciative Listening

You listen to the radio or television, purchase tickets to a play or concert, attend the opera. You do this because of sensory/aesthetic enjoyment—it pleases you. Because our individual tastes and what we appreciate vary widely, listening for appreciation is a very individual matter. Further, it can enlarge your experiences, expand your interests, and decrease stress or mental tension. And we are attracted to those people who appreciate listening to the same things we do, so appreciative listening influences our relating to particular others. Overall, appreciative listening is less demanding and requires less responsibility on your part.

Social Listening

Social listening includes conversational listening and courteous listening. It is listening to friends, family members, acquaintances, and guests; it is listening to colleagues and fellow workers. Social listening occurs more because of an interest in the speaker than in a necessary interest in the topic. Attending to social listening communicates your interest in the speaker and your personal concern, and its rewards are personal enjoyment, improvement of personal image as held by others, and improvement of self-concept and self-confidence. Your degree of commitment and responsibility increase with social listening.

Comprehensive Listening

You listen to lectures, briefings, and news broadcasts. This is comprehensive listening—listening to understand a message that is basically informational in nature. Comprehensive listening requires that you set aside any critical judgments of the speaker, message, or the language being used. This type of listening for understanding and remembering requires a variety of related skills and demands an ability to:

1. understand the meanings of words from context;
2. understand the relationship of details to main points;
3. follow the sequence of the message;
4. follow steps in directions;
5. listen for supporting materials;
6. listen to questions with the intent to answer;

7. recognize the speaker's purpose;
8. recognize the repetition of the same idea in different words;
9. repeat what was heard; and
10. take effective notes.[18]

The rewards are many—gaining new insights, learning new concepts, and developing new skills.

Critical Listening

Critical listening attempts to analyze evidence or ideas and to make critical judgments about the validity and quality of the materials presented. It is important as a critical listener that you establish clear criteria for the evaluation of the message. This largely determines whether you choose to accept or reject the message. As a critical listener, you must distinguish between fact and opinion, emotional and logical arguments; detect bias and prejudice; draw inferences; make judgments; and evaluate—not easy tasks. It requires being alert, involved, objective, and responsible. The benefits include increased knowledge, improved human relations, financial rewards, and improved productivity in all spheres of society.

Empathic Listening

Empathic listening is a unique type of listening behavior frequently used in nondirective therapeutic counseling. Psychologists using the techniques of nondirective counseling are trained to listen quietly and objectively. By nodding the head, saying "uh huh," "yes," "continue that thought," and referring to what the speaker has just said, counselors encourage the exploration of personal problems or difficulties. The central function is to provide an empathetic and open ear that allows the client to more accurately assess and resolve his or her own problems. When thoughts are presented to a sympathetic and attentive hearer, positive ends often are realized.

Effective empathic listening is synonymous with what others refer to as nonevaluative listening. Although such procedures are considered to be new, the intent dates back to ancient Egypt and the pharaoh Ptahhopet. More than 4,000 years ago, he advised his staff officers as follows: "An official who must listen to the pleas of clients should listen patiently and without rancor, because a petitioner wants attention to what he says even more than the accomplishing of that for which he came."[19]

You employ a type of empathic listening when listening to personal problems or difficulties of those close to you. Such listening can also be applied to hiring, appraisal, and exit interviews; the handling of workers' grievances; and in labor negotiations and bargaining sessions. This is total listening, encompassing all the cues emitted by the speaker, even those the other would rather conceal and those the listener would rather not hear. Judgment and criticism are withheld.

▶ BARRIERS TO LISTENING

It is interesting to note that the Japanese symbol for the word "listen" incorporates both the character for "ear" and the character for "gate":

耳　　　　　門　　　　　聞
ear　　　　　gate　　　　　listen

There is a variety of external and internal barriers or "gates" to effective listening, and, taken together, they account for some of the most common listening problems and poor listening habits. Being aware of these interfering factors can help you become a more effective, productive, attentive listener. As you read this section, try to identify those problems that affect you most and those weak listening habits you may want to work on eliminating.

External Interference

If a person suffers from a physical impairment that prevents either the hearing of sounds at an adequate volume or the receiving of certain auditory frequencies, then listening will suffer. But most of us have no hearing loss and many of those who do can be diagnosed and treated. However, there is growing evidence that hearing difficulties may be on the increase because of the excessive noise generated by our technological society—airplanes, subways, automobiles, typewriters, printers, loud music.

More important are the scores of distracting stimuli that turn up in every listening situation. Some of the most frequent distractions are uncomfortable room temperatures, air conditioners, restless audiences (gum chewing, chair movement, whispering, paper rattling), annoying speaker mannerisms and appearance, and a myriad of unexpected noises occurring during the speech. These are only some of the external factors that inhibit listening. If such distractions exist and we fail either to correct them or to adjust to them, listening will be less effective.

Also, there is the external problem of speaking rate and listening. The approximate rate at which we speak is 125 to 175 words per minute. And the approximate rate at which we think (if thoughts can be measured this way) is between 400 and 1,000 words per minute. Is it any wonder that we think circles around what a speaker is saying and consequently take mental naps that are interrupted only rarely? It's a situation of false security resulting from reliance on an active listening rate in relation to a slower speaking rate. This differential between speech and thinking can be your greatest problem or your biggest asset, depending on how you handle it. If you realize the potential arising from such a difference and concentrate on what is being said, your thought speed will not get you into trouble.

Psychological/Semantic Interference

Consider those times when someone was speaking and you had no interest in what was being said, or found yourself challenging the speaker, or becoming overly aroused by emotion-laden language. In different degrees and in many different ways, listening is subject to psychological and semantic interference—internal barriers to listening. You can allow this internal interference to consume your attending or you can work to overcome these internal aural filters. The problem is a critical one as illustrated in the following case.

The Case of the Twisted Words

Hank Braun, repairman for a utility, liked the Maple Avenue location to which he had been assigned for 10 years. So when he heard through the grapevine that he was to be transferred in a redistribution of manpower, he was prepared when foreman Dick Herman spoke to him on Wednesday:

"Hank, the company needs to reshuffle some repairmen to take care of a heavy work load in the Bay Street location, and you're one of them. It's only a mile from here, so it shouldn't be a hardship. Effective next Monday, report to Bay Street."

"I heard through the rumor mill that this might be coming," Braun said. "It's only a reshuffling, so it doesn't make any difference who goes. I found someone willing to make the move instead of me."

"Who's that?" asked Herman.

"Saunders." Braun replied.

"I'm not sure. I'll discuss this with the service manager, then get back to you. But, as of now, you transfer on Monday."

Herman took the matter up with Service Manager Joe Sims the following morning. "It won't work," Sims said. "Saunders has special skills we need here. Braun doesn't have them. I think the transfer has to stand."

Herman couldn't locate Braun after the meeting, so he left a note in his work box, asking the man to get in touch with him immediately. But it was the following morning before he saw Braun.

"I spoke to Sims about your request," Herman said as the repairman entered the department. "But he pointed out that Saunders can do work we need here that you can't do, so your transfer still goes."

"We'll see about that," Braun snapped. "This is a fine thing—telling me on a Friday to check into a new spot on Monday. I'm seeing the union rep about this."

"I think you have a grievance there," union rep Jack Delaney told Braun. "I'll get this straightened out with Herman right now."

"Dick," Delaney said to the superior, "one of the men tells me he's being transferred out of here the first of next week, but that you just gave him notice this morning. That's cutting it short, isn't it?"

"You're talking about Braun," Herman said. "Let's get him in here and clear the air."

After the repairman was seated in his office, Herman stated the position:

"Hank, I told you Wednesday that your transfer would be Monday. You mentioned having someone go in your place. I told you I'd check it out, but to consider the move effective. Now you've tried to make it seem as if I said the move wouldn't be made unless you heard from me to the contrary."

Braun admitted this was so—that he wanted to stop his transfer if possible.

"You don't have a grievance, and Delaney knows it," Herman said.

Comment: Employees, not necessarily only the trouble-makers, sometimes twist the words around to suit their needs. The supervisor should be careful of his wording and then remember what he said. He should not make promises he isn't sure he can keep. In this instance, Herman acted correctly.[20]

This case illustrates the problem. There is no easy solution but there is a simple admonition: Get involved. Consider the speaker's full position before you evaluate.

You are not likely to listen unless you're involved. Listening to others is involving yourself. This requires that you come to the situation with a desire to listen as well as a personal understanding of the value that listening holds. Carl Weaver, in his book *Human Listening*, addresses this matter:

> Basic to the listening process is a desire to learn. It is strange that most people do not really want to listen, but to talk. Sometimes someone will ask a question but refuse to listen to the answer, breaking into the first sentence of response with another question or an argument. Sometimes a listener will hear little of what the talker says but will spend his time planning and organizing a response.[21]

There is something to gain—something to learn—from almost every single human encounter. G. K. Chesterton put it well when he said, "In all this world there is no such thing as an uninteresting subject. There are only uninterested people."

When personal biases and attitudes differ from and come into conflict with those of the speaker, listening efficiency declines. Of course differences in position will occur, but the speaker must be given a chance to fully develop his or her ideas. In these situations you must extend to the speaker the benefit he or she would want extended. You must compensate for divergent points of view, "signal" words, anxiety-producing words, or emotion-laden words. Objectivity is the key to facilitating listening. As a listener, you must learn to cope with psychological and semantic interference.

▶ KEYS TO EFFECTIVE LISTENING

Regardless of the type of listening—appreciative, social, comprehensive, critical, or empathic—you can improve your listening skills. But you must personally take the initiative for improvement, recognizing which problems you have, admitting that they are problems, and really wanting to do something about them.

Listening is a complex behavior, highly individual and highly personal. Any improvement will take time. What follow are some suggestions that can contribute to the development of better listening habits.

Come Prepared. We've said again and again that listening is a deliberative activity. It requires that we come to the situation physically and mentally prepared. Too often we come with something less than enthusiasm. A less-than-positive attitude will produce negative results; being alert and active will result in more effective listening.

Eliminate Distractions. Because listening isn't easy, you should eliminate as many distractions as possible. A pleasant environment free of passersby, telephone calls, loud noises, and so on is more conducive to listening. Additionally, you should avoid fidgeting with a pen, playing with a paperclip, doodling, or thinking about the myriad "still-to-do" activities on your daily agenda. Concentrate instead of letting your thoughts wander.

Listen for Main Ideas. Listen for main ideas, principles, or concepts. This may require some work on your part because organization is not always apparent. Don't dwell on the interesting story, anecdote, or humorous saying; concentrate on the content. What is being said? Focus your attention. Use the extra time you gain listening to main ideas to formulate questions you might have.

Evaluate. Listen and evaluate the content of the message instead of judging the speaker's appearance or delivery. Critically listen to messages, evaluating them in terms of your own belief system(s). Unlike a sponge, don't absorb everything—ask questions. Does the speaker have personal interests, biases, prejudices? What are his or her credentials? Why should she or he be believed? Questioning is a valuable tool for increasing understanding.

Be Flexible. Be flexible in your views. Objectivity is an important key to listening. There is no doubt that differences in position will occur, but to be an effective listener you must make peace with diversity. You have to keep your mind open and allow for ideas that are contrary to your personal convictions.

Get Involved. You are not likely to listen unless you are involved. Determine the personal value of the topic for you—find areas of interest. If you can identify personal worth in what the speaker is saying, seeing the potential for personal learning and growth, your desire to listen will be heightened.

React. Listening is an active, not a passive process. By reacting to messages, you demonstrate your concern and your understanding. Reacting can help you communicate your feelings and beliefs more accurately with other people—and permits you to do so more often and more clearly.

Care. Caring requires being sensitive to the communication needs and cues of others. Why are they communicating? What are they saying? It's important that you avoid interrupting and be careful of arbitrarily offering advice or prematurely judging or analyzing. Listening takes time.

Be Aware. Communication breakdowns will inevitably occur. Perhaps the miracle of communication is that we succeed as often as we do. Reflecting on the types of communication behaviors you engaged in when breakdowns and faulty listening occurred can be instructional. You can learn from your mistakes if you view them in light of the communication contexts in which they occurred.

Commit Yourself. Listening is a learned activity. You have to commit yourself to a personal program of improvement because developing good listening habits is like any other strength training—it requires work. To become an effective listener, you must recognize the importance of listening, develop positive listening habits, and practice active listening.

There are many possible approaches to improving your listening skills once the basic problems are identified. Awareness of the problems, and a concentrated effort to correct them, are essential if any progress is to be made. Remember, you can engage in a program of improvement at any age.

▶ SUMMARY

Stuart Chase writes, "Listening is the other half of talking. If people stop listening, it is useless to talk—a point not always appreciated by talkers."[22] Until recently, listening has been very much neglected. Some forward-looking companies and educational institutions have realized the importance of listening, accepted the fact that most people are inefficient listeners, and initiated programs for improvement.

Business is very much aware of the tremendous cost of poor listening. It is costly in terms of time, inefficiency, misunderstanding, and inhibited communication at all levels. In short, less-than-effective listening affects productivity.

Hearing is not listening. Listening is a higher cognitive process which is under our control. Listening is a combination of what we hear, what we understand, and what we remember. It involves the receiving and attending of stimuli, a combination of cognitive and affective processes, emotional control, and memory. Listening is a complex intrapersonal behavior that significantly affects interpersonal communication.

There are external and internal barriers that can interfere with and disrupt otherwise effective listening. The temperature of a room, poor acoustics, the noise of an audience, and such speaker attributes as rate and dialect are situational distractions. Distrust, personal biases, and emotion-laden language are among the internal factors that influence listening effectiveness.

Regardless of its purpose—appreciative, social, comprehensive, critical, or empathic—it is important to view listening as a positive and rewarding activity. Each of us must commit ourselves to a personal program of improvement. Developing good listening habits requires work—to tune out distractions; to concentrate attention; to maintain emotional control; and to create a caring, supportive climate where participants are free to communicate and relationships can develop and grow. In sum, listening is an ongoing learning process requiring constant self-analysis and efforts toward self-improvement.

▶ QUESTIONS FOR DISCUSSION AND SKILL DEVELOPMENT

1. How would you rate yourself as a listener?

   1———2———3———4———5
   poor   excellent

   How do you think the following people would rate you as a listener?

   best friend   1———2———3———4———5
                  poor   excellent
   father/mother 1———2———3———4———5
                  poor   excellent
   brother/sister 1———2———3———4———5
                  poor   excellent
   spouse   1———2———3———4———5
                  poor   excellent
   boss   1———2———3———4———5
                  poor   excellent
   professor   1———2———3———4———5
                  poor   excellent

   Circle the term that best describes you as a listener and explain your answer:

   superior   excellent   above average   average
            below average   poor   terrible

2. Identify five different types of listening. What is the purpose of each? How does responsibility change with each?

3. To improve listening you must recognize which problems you have and really want to do something about them. Which barriers do you personally find most problematic? How do you attempt to overcome them? What barriers do others seem to exhibit toward you? How do you react?

4. What characterizes a poor listener? How might you deal with a poor listener?

5. How can you be a better listener? Outline a five-step program that you believe will make you a more effective listener. What are the relational rewards of effective listening?

▶ NOTES

1. Tom Peters, *Thriving on Chaos* (New York: Harper and Row, 1987): 524.
2. L. Brown, *Communicating Facts and Ideas in Business* (Englewood Cliffs, NJ: Prentice Hall, 1982).
3. Andrew Wolvin and Carolyn Coakley, "A Survey of the Status of Listening Training in Some *Fortune 500* Operations," *Communication Education* 40 (1991).

4. Peters, *Thriving on Chaos,* 526.

5. Ernest G. Bormann, William Howell, Ralph Nichols, and George Shapiro, *Interpersonal Communication in the Modern Organization* (Englewood Cliffs, NJ: Prentice Hall, 1969): 188–189.

6. Ray Killian, *Managing By Design . . . For Executive Effectiveness* (New York: American Management Association, 1968): 255.

7. Bormann, Howell, Nichols, and Shapiro, *Interpersonal Communication,* 190.

8. J. Floyd, *Listening: A Practical Approach* (Glenview, IL: Holt, Rhinehart & Winston, 1985).

9. "Have You Heard About Sperry?" *Management Review* (April 1980): 40.

10. Bormann, Howell, Nichols, and Shapiro, *Interpersonal Communication,* 189.

11. Wallace V. Schmidt, "Trainers: Who They Are, What They Think," *Training* (1979): 18.

12. Ralph G. Nichols and Leonard A. Stevens, "Listening to People," *Harvard Business Review* (September-October 1957): 85.

13. K. Murphy, *Effective Listening: The Key to Career Success* (New York: Bantam Books, 1989): 35.

14. C. William Colburn and Sanford B. Weinberg, *An Orientation to Listening and Audience Analysis* (Palo Alto, CA: Science Research Associates, 1976): 1.

15. Ibid., 4–5.

16. Jane White, "So What's Wrong Wid De Way Your Mudda Taught Ya to Talk?" *Lubbock Avalanche-Journal,* August 30, 1980, D-13.

17. Stewart Tubbs and Sylvia Moss, *Interpersonal Communication* (New York: Random House, 1978): 38.

18. Freda S. Sathre, Ray W. Olson, and Clarissa I. Whitney, *Let's Talk* (Glenview, IL: Scott, Foresman, 1973): 20.

19. Bormann, Howell, Nichols, and Shapiro, *Interpersonal Communication,* 178.

20. "Discipline and Grievances" (Waterford, CT: National Foreman's Institute, 1983): 6–7.

21. Carl H. Weaver, *Human Listening* (Indianapolis, IN: Bobbs-Merrill, 1972): 82.

22. Stuart Chase, "Are You Listening?" *Reader's Digest* (December 1962): 80.

C H A P T E R · S I X

6

Interpersonal Communication and Human Relationships in Organizations

LEARNING OBJECTIVES:

To define interpersonal communication and indicate how it differs from impersonal communication

To define and explain the concept of self-disclosure

To explain how the self-concept is shaped and why it is important to interpersonal communication

To indicate why the self-fulfilling prophecy is important

To explain the process of perception and identify its major influences

To describe and give examples of the three ego states—parent, adult, and child

To identify and provide examples of the three types of transactions—complementary, crossed, and ulterior

To explain why communication games are played in organizations and outline methods for stopping gameplaying

To differentiate aggressive from assertive behavior and outline appropriate assertive approaches

I
nterpersonal communication and the development of human relationships are critical to the modern organization. In fact, the way in which people treat one another at work has a significant bearing on the success or failure of any organization. This chapter provides a framework by which to understand this most fundamental of communication activities.

A factory worker on an assembly line of a major U.S. automobile manufacturer talks with his boss about a way to increase the operating speed of the assembly line. The worker is convinced that this change will improve the efficiency of the company, and the two of them discuss ways to best implement the concept.

The principal of the local high school and the secretary discuss changing the secretary's job title. She is concerned that the word "secretary" is dated and doesn't represent her idea of what the position entails. They agree to change the title to "administrative assistant."

A collections officer for a small-town hospital tells his assistant of his concern that the percentage of collections is too low. They discuss ways to improve the collection of outstanding accounts.

The adult babysitter of a preschool boy and his younger sister tells their mother and father about that day's trip to the neighborhood playground and about how the children played together so well on the jungle gym and the merry-go-round.

The accounting manager of a large real estate development firm is concerned that she cannot spend more time with her seven-month-old child. She presents a proposal for job-sharing the position to her immediate supervisor and the human resource officer of the company.

These people are communicating! The factory worker and his boss are examining a suggestion for making the workplace more efficient; the secretary and the principal are selecting a different job title so she will feel more useful; the hospital collections officer is striving to improve job performance; the babysitter is praising the parents' children while explaining her work that afternoon; and the accounting manager is suggesting a work alternative to her employer so she can spend more time with her new baby. All of these people are busy in one of the most important activities of human beings at work—they are speaking and listening to one another. They are using the oldest method of improving our work and social situations. They are engaging in interpersonal communication.

That all of these people have selected interpersonal communication as the medium by which they can voice their concerns is one indication of its importance.

▶ IMPORTANCE OF INTERPERSONAL COMMUNICATION

We spend most of our time with people on an interpersonal level—individually or in small groups,[1] and we spend most of that time communicating interpersonally. The average business executive, for example, spends 75–80 percent of her time communicating with others—about 45 minutes out of every hour.[2] Intuitively, this makes great sense because people generally want to be with people. Although it is true that everyone needs time alone and that some of our best thinking and work is done while no one else is around, it is equally true that we need other people, and we especially need them in our daily work lives. John Naisbitt argues that this coming together of human beings at work is important now and will be even more important in the future. Naisbitt observes that "people want to go to the office. People want to be with people, and the more technology we pump into the society, the more people will want to be with people."[3] It is clear that more advancement in technology will not mean less communication. At most, technology only alters our organizational duties;

our need for communication continues. Researchers at Cornell University have observed that "computers and other kinds of sophisticated equipment are now performing routine jobs, leaving workers to handle the human challenges of improving the organization and responding to customers."[4]

Specifically, interpersonal communication skills are critical to success in business. Writing and general oral communication skills are important in doing well in the organization, but interpersonal communication skills seem to be the most important. A report in the *Bulletin of the Association for Business Communication* indicated that 70 percent of recent business school graduates rated interpersonal communication skills as mandatory in today's organization; 65 percent rated general oral communication skills and 50 percent rated written communication skills as mandatory.[5] Moreover, most people who lose their jobs in today's marketplace do so because they lack interpersonal skills. Research reveals that of all employees fired, 85 percent are fired because they lack human relations or interpersonal communication skills, not because they lack technical competence.[6]

We have known for a long time that interpersonal communication is important in business and that skills in interpersonal communication are necessary for employees to function well in the modern organization. Dan Curtis, Jerry Winsor, and Ronald Stephens sought to find out what factors and skills were important in business. Their study asked four questions: What factors are most important in helping graduating college students obtain employment? What factors contribute most to success in a business career? What specific college courses are important for entry-level management? What would be the ideal management profile?[7] The following results of that study indicate that interpersonal communication is vital to success in business (the top three responses are presented, with the interpersonal communication skills italicized).

- ▶ Factors most important in helping college students obtain employment after graduation
  1 *oral (speaking) communication*
  2 written communication skills
  3 *enthusiasm*
- ▶ Factors/skills important for successful job performance
  1 *interpersonal/human relations skills*
  2 *oral communication skills*
  3 written communication skills
- ▶ Important courses for entry-level management
  1 written communication
  2 *interpersonal communication*
  3 management
- ▶ Ideal management profile
  1 *ability to work with others*
  2 ability to gather accurate information
  3 *ability to work well in groups*

But what actually is interpersonal communication? What are its attributes? How is it different from other forms of communication?

▶ INTERPERSONAL COMMUNICATION DEFINED

Interpersonal communication has been defined differently by various scholars of speech communication. The term that bears the most significance for us in any definition of interpersonal communication is a "sharing of meaning." Interpersonal communication is characterized by a sensitive sharing between people.

Where the varied definitions differ gives rise to situational and developmental approaches to interpersonal communication. The *situational* school believes that the situation in which communication occurs determines the kind of communication taking place. Followers of this school define each situation, in large part, by the number of people involved in the communication act. They contend that intrapersonal communication happens within a single person, interpersonal communication takes place when two people communicate together, small-group communication results when three to a dozen people get together, public communication occurs when a speaker addresses a large audience, and mass communication happens when a sizable number of people are tuned in electronically. Communication is presented on a continuum ranging from intrapersonal communication to mass communication with the number of participants being the determining factor. This approach, however, doesn't seem completely accurate.

Two people communicating often don't have what we would consider an interpersonal relationship. Two coworkers who dislike each other intensely may have to talk with one another, but this doesn't mean that they are engaged interpersonally. A salesperson may sell a bottle of cologne to a young man after just meeting him, but they don't have what most people would call an interpersonal relationship. A state trooper may pull a car over and give the driver a ticket for speeding, but few would consider this interaction an interpersonal one.

Conversely, a group of three or more people may have what they consider to be an interpersonal relationship among themselves. A teacher may have a close, intertwined relationship with a large number of the students in a particular class with whom he or she communicates every day, and they all may see their connecting as interpersonal. A minister may be so charismatic that dozens, even hundreds, of congregational members are clearly interpersonally involved with the person they listen to every Sunday. Every now and then an outstanding coach, a Vince Lombardi of the Green Bay Packers or a John Wooden of the UCLA Bruins, can interpersonally motivates his players to do almost superhuman feats to win an important game. All of these situations involve more than two people, yet who would deny that an interpersonal sharing of meaning is taking place?

The *developmental* school believes that interpersonal communication is best defined as communication involved in a long-standing relationship between or among the people involved. Followers of the developmental approach believe that interpersonal communication must involve long-lasting reciprocal relationships in which the parties respond selectively and specifically to each other.[8] This approach would consider it interpersonal communication when two close friends converse about one of them getting married, but not when two new coworkers talk about a common job problem.

Just as the situational approach doesn't seem to address adequately the definition of interpersonal communication, there's also something lacking in the developmental approach. The developmental definition requires that the relationship of the communicators be a special one. Yet, you probably have a number of acquaintances, even friends at work with whom you communicate interpersonally but with whom you don't share anything like the special relationships you share with your parents, spouse, or close associates. A realtor may work with a young couple for many months trying to find them their first home, may communicate closely with them every day during that time, and all parties involved may believe that they are communicating interpersonally, but they would not define their relationship as being either special or lengthy.

It seems, then, that neither the situational approach nor the developmental approach adequately defines this very important communication form. The clearest definition of interpersonal communication seems to come from a blending of these two approaches. The following definition draws from the strengths of both schools:

> Interpersonal communication is the sharing of meaning between two or more people who have a personal relationship and who consider each other unique individuals.

This definition focuses attention on a sharing of meaning, and the number of participants and degree of intimacy are less important than the concern and sensitivity expressed by each. Interpersonal communication defines how people relate with each other.

▶ CHARACTERISTICS OF INTERPERSONAL RELATIONSHIPS

Just as not every act of communication is interpersonal, neither is every relationship an interpersonal one. We communicate every day in *impersonal* interactions with others. In fact, these conversations consume a large percentage of our communication time. You engage in impersonal communication when you say hello to the person who works in the office across from yours, even though you don't know her name. You engage in impersonal communication when you purchase a gift from the salesperson at your favorite department store, and if you speak to the person who lives in the apartment below yours when you meet at the mailbox. Consider for a moment the following two interactions:

Interaction I

James: Hi. How's it going?

Janis: Fine. How's life treating you?

James: Oh, can't complain.

Janis: Ready for the Chart meeting?

James: About as much as anyone else, I guess. My report is ready but I'll still be glad when it's over and the execs from corporate leave.

Janis: Yeah. I agree. It looks like it's going to be a nice day. Take care.

James: You, too.

Interaction II

James: Hi. How's Janis?

Janis: Anxious about the Chart meeting. And you?

James: I'm doin' ok. I've managed to get things together for the Chart meeting and I'm ready for the top execs. But, what's the anxiety about? This is just a routine visit.

Janis: I know, but I hate 'em. Reports just frighten me. You know. Standing up in front of everyone.

James: I agree, but you always seem to be in control and present yourself well.

Janis: Thanks. I guess so. Say, would you like to get a cup of coffee?

James: Sure. You going to be able to get away for a vacation?

It's clear which interaction is impersonal and which is interpersonal. In the first dialogue, the two participants reveal virtually nothing about themselves. They express none of their true feelings, particularly toward each other. They report their opinion carefully and tentatively and they offer only information they are confident will be acceptable to the other person. The second dialogue reveals interest and involvement. They express feelings without fear and respect the feelings of the other. The conversation is frank and honest with candid observations being exchanged.

Theorists have identified a number of factors that characterize interpersonal relationships and distinguish them from impersonal exchanges.[9] Among the predominant characteristics are: (1) uniqueness, (2) irreplaceability, (3) interdependence, and (4) self-disclosure. Let's examine each of these important characteristics.

Uniqueness

When we engage in interpersonal communication we act very differently than when we communicate impersonally. Interpersonal relationships are unique in and of themselves, operating by nonstandard rules that are unique to the particular people involved. For example, you might hug your best friend tightly rather than simply saying hello or shaking hands. The language we use to communicate with the people in our interpersonal relationships reflects special verbal and nonverbal cues. We don't label the important people in our lives, but we do use words and gestures to identify our complex relationship. We take the time in these relationships to clarify that these people are multidimensional and we are sensitive to their individual needs.

However, when we engage in impersonal communication we use common and rather standard rules of behavior. We refer to these people in broad, often stereotypical terms and nonverbally distance ourselves from them. When you meet a person for the first time, for example, you might smile, say hello and shake hands. When you enter an elevator, you might stand apart from your fellow riders, looking at the floor numbers and remaining relatively quiet. When you purchase a pair of jeans at the local department store from a clerk you don't know and may never see again, you stand a certain distance from that person and speak in only the most general way. In other words, unlike what we do in interpersonal relationships, we don't see the uniqueness of people in impersonal relationships.

Irreplaceability

It is difficult to replace any interpersonal relationship and most of us go through a type of mourning when important people in our lives must leave us. When a parent or grandparent dies or when your best friend at work moves away or when a lover breaks off a long-term relationship, you rightfully feel that this person cannot be replaced because you have invested your most intense emotions and some of the most important time of your life with this person.

In organizations, some employees begin their work careers being assigned to a mentor, another employee who often works in the same area but who has been at the company a longer period of time and who can help the new employee become acclimated to the norms of the organization. The relationship between the two frequently becomes very special and very interpersonal. But mentors often leave the mentoring relationship to accept a promotion or another position outside the organization. Invariably a sense of loss and irreplaceability ensues.

It's true that these losses may seem less intense over time, but it's also true that the relationship with that particular person can never be fully replaced. We may get new friends, coworkers, or mentors, and, although important in and of themselves, these people are quite different from those in the interpersonal relationships we previously enjoyed.

Impersonal relationships, however, are replaced with little effort and little thought. When you speak to a person in another office over the telephone or when you purchase gasoline from an attendant at a local convenience store or when you see but never speak to a person who sits in your pew at church, you probably don't care if a different person might at some time fill that person's place in your life. This is not being indifferent or apathetic, but simply recognizing that we are not interpersonally attracted to everyone. Interpersonal relationships are special and interpersonal communication is not easy. These personal relationships and the communication that sustains them require care and respect.

Interdependence

We depend on others and they depend on us. This means that we are affected by those people with whom we are interpersonally involved and that they, in turn, are affected by us. We are connected!

In an organization, a worker may genuinely feel wonderful when a close coworker receives a deserved promotion to a better position. In college, you may feel great happiness when your best friend and roommate becomes engaged. At home, you may rejoice with your family when your mother or father lands that long-awaited job. Similarly, we can share significant losses with those with whom we are interdependent. When your best friend at work loses her job, you may well feel terrible; you may even feel angry at the organization. You may legitimately feel upset at a college professor who treats your fraternity brother or sorority sister unfairly. When you are at home, you share the feeling of great sadness when a parent loses an important account or even a job. These are the common experiences people feel when they are engaged in interpersonal relationships with others.

We don't always feel this way, nor should we. If we are not interpersonally connected to a coworker, the feeling is less intense when she doesn't get a promotion. If the relationship is an impersonal one, you don't feel as emotionally spent when another student in one of your classes receives a poor grade on an important examination. You don't have an interdependence with these people—you aren't directly affected by them. Who we communicate with and relate to is not haphazard.

Self-Disclosure

Communicating and relating necessitates being open to one another. The choice to share information about ourselves is one of the most important we can ever make. In fact, disclosure is a type of "peak communication" reserved for those people we know well and trust. It occurs almost exclusively in interpersonal relationships. On the job superiors must communicate with subordinates and subordinates with superiors in a pragmatic, job-related way. It isn't necessary to express personal beliefs, attitudes or emotions. You have some discretion here and can exercise this discretion. As the level of relationship moves toward intimacy the greater the convergence of what is necessary and what is discretionary. For example, family relationships, intimate partner relationships, or close friendships require considerably more disclosure.

Self-disclosure involves voluntarily sharing with another information, opinions, and personal feelings that they would not otherwise know. We need some level of self-disclosure to communicate with another person and have any kind of a relationship. In long-term interpersonal relationships, the level of openness and self-disclosure intensifies. There are two major benefits of appropriately disclosing information to others. First, it helps to establish and maintain lasting personal relationships because a reciprocated bond is created between the parties. Second, you get to know yourself better when you share information and connect with others.

A model allowing us to better understand self-disclosure and permitting you to examine your relationships with others is the Johari Window (see Exhibit 6-1).[10] Created by Joseph Luft and Harrington Ingham, it offers an intrapersonal as well as interpersonal perspective on what may be happening. The "window" is, in effect, a square divided into four quadrants—labeled open, blind, hidden, and unknown—that represent the extent to which you desire or are able to share your knowledge, beliefs, attitudes, and feelings.

The *open quadrant* reflects your general openness to the world and your willingness to be known. It includes the information, feelings, and opinions known by you and openly shared with others.

	KNOWN TO SELF	UNKNOWN TO SELF
KNOWN TO OTHERS	1. Open to self and others	2. Blind to self, seen by others
UNKNOWN TO OTHERS	3. Hidden from others, known by self	4. Unknown to self and others

JOHARI WINDOW

AT THE BEGINNING OF A WORK RELATIONSHIP

1	2
3	4

AFTER RELATIONAL DEVELOPMENT

1	2
3	4

The *blind quadrant* consists of all the things about yourself that other people perceive but are not readily accessible to you. For example, we are generally ignorant of our own unintentional habits and mannerisms. The perceptions of others remain unknown unless feedback is encouraged.

The *hidden quadrant* contains the information and personal feelings that you discreetly disclose to others—ambitions, fears, anxieties. No one is aware of these ideas or feelings unless you choose to disclose them.

The *unknown quadrant* is completely unknown—to others as well as to you. It represents everything about yourself that has never been explored—untapped resources, aptitudes, and potential. It is an area for personal awareness, understanding, and growth—self-discovery.

The quadrants or "panes" are interdependent and when one changes the others change. As depicted in Exhibit 6-1, the size of each quadrant varies according to your communication behavior. As you disclose more (open quadrant), you have fewer secrets (hidden quadrant) and as others respond (blind quadrant) dimensional changes occur.

It is important to appropriately disclose information in the workplace. You may well want to disclose information to your employer or to coworkers so that they can get to know you better. You may also need to convey information at critical times in your life—such as when you need to take time off for an operation that requires hospitalization. You may also need to disclose certain types of information to get promotions or salary raises because unless your employer knows about your achievements, you may not get the rewards you believe you deserve. An important rule of corporate life is to let your employer know your accomplishments.

Of course, self-disclosure involves risk. The risk factor is one of the primary reasons that disclosure doesn't happen very often in impersonal communication. In these relationships, we often feel that we don't know the person well enough to share such personal information; we may even feel that the person will use the information against us in the future and thus it would be too risky to disclose this information. However, communication leading to a growing, maturing, trusting relationship is characterized by self-disclosure and an obvious involvement and commitment. The depth of the involvement and commitment are directly proportional to the disclosure evidenced in the relationship. The development of more than a "Hi/Hello/Good morning" relationship requires that the parties be willing to work at it. Relating necessitates our assuming responsibility for the relationship and being actively involved in its development. Anything less can only be casual, temporary, and impersonal in nature.

Relational communication is a complicated process, with a number of variables affecting us. A survey conducted by Mary Brown Parlee identifies some of these variables[11]:

Quality	Percent Responding Important/ Very Important
Keeps confidences	89
Loyalty	88
Warmth, affection	82
Supportiveness	76
Frankness	75

Additionally, in developing growing relationships there are factors that help the involved parties to move ahead. Two major factors which have a significant bearing on interpersonal communication in the workplace and which assist in a movement toward increased trust, openness, self-realization, and interdependence are our self-concept and perception.

▶ SELF-CONCEPT DEFINED

It is vital to any study of interpersonal communication to understand the concept of the self. In fact, it is "you" who is at the heart of communication. Until you have a relatively solid grasp of who you are and how you got the way you are, interpersonal communication will be difficult at best.

▶ SELF-DISCLOSURE

By John Stewart

Self-disclosure is the act of verbally and nonverbally sharing with another some aspects of what makes you a person, aspects the other individual wouldn't be able to understand or recognize without your help. In other words, self-disclosure is verbally and nonverbally making information about your uniqueness, your choice-making, your addressability, and the unmeasurable or reflective parts of you—for example, your feelings.

It's very important, I think, to remember that self-disclosure is a process that can improve a transaction, that can positively affect what's happening between persons. Disclosure is not meant to meet just one person's needs, but rather to enhance the relationship. Consequently, effective self-disclosure is disclosure that's appropriate, appropriate to the situation and appropriate to the relationship between the persons communicating. A crowded theater or a football game is not the place to discuss a profound religious experience even with your closest friend. Intimate sexual fantasies are usually not appropriate topics for a teacher to discuss with a student or for an employer to discuss with an employee.

One more thing. Sometimes people fear self-disclosure because they feel that their self is their most precious possession and that if they give much of it to others, they are liable to run out, to end up without any self left. This fear is based on the assumption that selves are like money or the hours in a day—there is only so much and when it's gone, it's gone. But the assumption simply isn't accurate. Selves are not governed by the economic law of scarcity. Since each of us is continually growing and changing—becoming—the more we share, the more there is to share. To put it another way, when I give you something of myself, I don't give it "up"; I still "have" it, but as a result of my disclosure, now you "have" it too. As many couples who have enjoyed a long-term relationship have learned, you can never succeed in disclosing everything about yourself. Similarly, the more you know about the other, the more clearly you realize how much more there is to know.

It is true, though, that disclosure is risky. When I share something of personness with you, I take the risk that you might reject it. That kind of rejection could hurt. But I take the risk because I know that if I don't, we cannot meet as persons.

Source: John Stewart, *Bridges Not Walls: A Book About Interpersonal Communication*, 5th ed. (New York: McGraw-Hill, 1990): 213. Copyright © 1990. Reprinted with permission from McGraw-Hill, Inc.

The *self-concept* represents the collection of perceptions you hold of yourself. In other words, as we have grown up, each of us has assembled a set of ideas we use to identify ourselves. These include but are not limited to our beliefs about our appearance, feelings, traits, attitudes, talents, and values. In essence, our self-concept is who we think we are.

No one is born with a self-concept. Indeed, the collection of stories about so-called "wild children" who have been raised by animals and not by humans confirms that the self-concept is learned. When these children were found, they had no concept of self. Their actions and reactions were like those of the animals that had raised them. It was only after these feral children were introduced to people and into families that their self-concepts began to develop.

In typical families, this important formation of self begins quite soon after birth. Michael Lewis and Jeanne Brooks-Gunn have analyzed how infants begin to gain a concept of themselves. In their landmark work, *Social Cognition and the Acquisition of Self,* they conclude that a combination of genetic inheritance, cognitive development, and social environment factors contribute to begin the formation of the self-concept in infants.[12] As early as three months, an infant begins to understand that a cause-and-effect relationship exists between his or her movements and the corresponding movements in a mirror. Quite often, a baby at this age will see herself in a mirror and giggle at the reflected image.

It is usually between the ages of six and nine months that the infant develops a conception of object permanence, the understanding that objects exist even though he or she cannot see them or they are hidden from view. Up to this age, a baby will show no signs of searching for a toy if it is dropped over the edge of a chair. From eight to nine months, a baby will look over the edge to find the dropped toy.[13] Finally, shortly after the first birthday, a child will develop the ability to categorize and one of these sets is self-categorization.

As the person moves through the stages of childhood, adolescence, and adulthood, the process of self understanding and the development of the self-concept continue. In all of these stages of development, the self-concept is further heightened as a result of self-appraisal and reflected appraisal.

Self-appraisal refers to the idea that you develop a self-concept that matches the impressions you get about yourself from what you see. You judge yourself by your reaction to what you think of yourself. These include impressions about what you look like, by how tight or how loose your clothes fit, by what your mirror tells you. If these self-judgments are positive, you tend to develop positive impressions. But, if they are negative and if you can't or don't change, you will probably develop negative impressions about yourself. Similarly, you judge yourself by your reaction to your experiences. In general, the more positive experiences you have, the higher your self-concept; conversely, the more negative experiences you have, the lower your self-concept.[14]

Reflected appraisal refers to the fact that each of us develops a self-concept that matches the way we believe others see us. The noted psychologist Charles Cooley used the image of a mirror to identify this process.[15] This type of appraisal begins in early childhood when we form opinions of ourselves based, in part, on how we believe our parents and other important people feel about us. If children are praised by their parents and told that they are loved, their self-concept will be very different from those children who don't receive this positive stroking. If children are spoken to in tones that express love, affection, and respect, their self-concepts will be very different from those children who are spoken to in tones that express dislike, indifference, and disrespect. Reflect for a moment on Dorothy Law Nolte's famous poem, "Children Learn What They Live"[16]:

> If a child lives with criticism, he learns to condemn.
> If a child lives with hostility, he learns to fight.
> If a child lives with ridicule, he learns to be shy.
> If a child lives with shame, he learns to feel guilty.
> If a child lives with tolerance, he learns to be patient.
> If a child lives with encouragement, he learns confidence.
> If a child lives with praise, he learns to appreciate.
> If a child lives with fairness, he learns justice.
> If a child lives with security, he learns to have faith.
> If a child lives with approval, he learns to like himself.
> If a child lives with acceptance and friendship, he learns to find love in the world.

Nolte focuses on children and their self-concepts, but it would be good for corporate managers to insert the word "employee" for the word "children" to better understand that the way managers treat their employees can directly affect what these workers think of themselves. The significant others in our lives—those important people whose opinions we value—positively or negatively shape our self-concepts.[17]

►IMPORTANCE OF THE SELF-CONCEPT

The implications of the importance of the self-concept are twofold. The first implication is that people with positive self-concepts generally communicate more positively than people with negative ones. The research of Donald E. Hamachek in comparing high–self-concept people and low–self-concept people is especially enlightening.[18] He found that the communication of people with high self-concepts differed significantly from the communication of people with low self-concepts in at least seven important ways. First, the study showed that people with high self-concepts are more likely to think well of others and people with low self-concepts are more likely to disapprove of other people. Think of the people in a typical organization and you'll soon recognize those people who seem to genuinely like the people with whom they work. Conversely, it isn't difficult to notice those workers who constantly criticize their coworkers.

Second, Hamachek found that high–self-concept people expected to be accepted by others and the low–self-concept people actually expected to be rejected by others. This expectation of acceptance or rejection almost seems to achieve a life of its own for people—that is, workers who expect to be accepted usually are, and workers who expect to be rejected usually find that this becomes a reality for them.

Third, research indicated that workers who scored highly on self-concept inventories usually evaluated their own work very highly, and workers with low self-concepts usually believed that their work was just average or even below.

Fourth, it was observed that high–self-concept people aren't afraid of the reactions of other people; in fact, they actually perform very well when they are being watched. The opposite seems true of those people with low self-concepts: they perform poorly when being watched and are concerned that they will be evaluated negatively. High–self-concept employees seem to actually invite their supervisors to watch them at work and see what they accomplish.

Fifth, the research indicated that high–self-concept people work harder for employers who demand high standards of performance, and low–self-concept people work harder for undemanding, less critical employers. In other words, if an employer seems to make significant demands on the employees, it will be the worker with a high self-concept who will most often meet those demands; furthermore, this type of employee doesn't seem to work as hard for those employers who aren't as demanding. The other side of the coin indicates that workers with low self-concept won't work well for demanding employers, but they will work harder for employers who are seen as undemanding and less critical.

Sixth, this study revealed that employees with high self-concepts feel comfortable with people they view as superior but workers with low self-concepts feel intimidated by these people. For example, employees with high self-concepts who see their employers as superior are able to feel comfortable around them. However, workers with low self-concepts are uncomfortable and actually feel threatened when they are around people they view as superior.

▶ A BAG OF POSSIBLES AND OTHER MATTERS OF THE MIND

By Robert Fulghum

Since my apotheosis as Captain Kindergarten, I have been a frequent guest in schools, most often invited by kindergartens and colleges. The environments differ only in scale. In the beginners' classroom and on the university campuses, the same opportunities and facilities exist. Tools for reading and writing and scientific experimentation are there—books and paper, labs and workboxes—and those things necessary for the arts—paint, music, costumes, room to dance—are available. In kindergarten, however, the resources are in separate buildings, with limited availability. But the most radical difference is in the self-image of the students.

Ask kindergartners how many can draw—and all hands shoot up. Yes, of course we can draw—all of us. What can you draw? Anything! How about a dog eating a fire truck in a jungle? Sure! How big do you want it?

How many of you can sing? All hands. Of course we sing! What can you sing? Anything. What if you don't know the words? No problem, we can make them up. Let's sing! Now? Why not!

How many of you can dance? Unanimous again. What kind of music do you like to dance to? Any kind! Let's dance! Now? Sure, why not?

Do you like to act in plays? Yes! Do you play musical instruments? Yes! Do you write poetry? Yes! Can you read and write and count? Yes! Again and again and again, Yes! The children are large, infinite and eager. Everything is possible.

Try those same questions on a college audience. Only a few of the students will raise their hands when asked if they draw or dance or sing or paint or act or play an instrument. Not infrequently, those who do raise their hands will want to quantify their responses—I only play piano, I only draw horses, I only dance to rock and roll, I only sing in the shower.

College students will tell you they do not have talent, are not majoring in art or have not done any of these things since about the third grade. Or worse, that they are embarrassed for others to see them sing or dance or act.

What went wrong between kindergarten and college? What happened to Yes, of course I can!

As I write, I am still feeling exuberant from an encounter with the cast of Richard Wagner's opera "Die Walkure." Last night I watched a stirring performance of this classic drama. This morning I sat onstage with the cast and discussed just how the production happens. I especially wanted to know how they went about learning their parts—what strategies they use to commit all to memory.

The members of the cast are students in kindergarten and first grade. They did indeed perform "Die Walkure"—words, music, dance, costumes, scenery, the works. Next year they will do "Siegfried"—already in production—as part of a run through the entire "Ring" cycle. And no, this is not a special school of the performing arts for gifted children. It's the Spruce Street School in Seattle, Washington.

They are performing Wagner because they are not yet old enough to know they cannot. And they understand the opera because they make up stories and songs just like it out of their own lives.

The skeptical author is thinking maybe the children are just doing a trained seal act—I mean Wagner is heavy stuff—surely they don't really get it. So I ask the young actress playing Brunhilde to tell me how her character fits into the story. "Do you know about Little Red Riding Hood?" she asks. Yes. "Well, it's kind of like that—there's trouble out there in the world for the girl and her grandmother and the wolf and everybody." And then, so I will understand better, she compared the role to that of Lady Macbeth. Yes. She knows about that, too. The school did "Macbeth" last fall.

She also talks about "The Hobbit" and "Star Wars" and a radio play the class is writing that is a spoof on all this—"MacDude." "Do you understand?" she asks with concern. I do. And so does she.

(By the way, the only significant deviation from the script came at the very end of "Die Walkure," where Wotan is supposed to take his sleeping daughter in his arms and kiss her eyelids. No way. Art may have its standards, but no 7-year-old boy is going to kiss a girl on her eyelids or anywhere else. There are limits.)

Seventh, high–self-concept people are able to defend themselves against negative criticism; people with low self-concepts have difficulty doing so. In other words, when employees with a high self-concept are criticized by a coworker or a manager they are able to defend themselves against this type of criticism. When employees with low self-concepts are criticized, they are easily influenced by the critical people and can't defend themselves against the negative comments. This study clearly indicates that people communicate differently and an important key is their self-concept.

The second implication of the importance of the self-concept relates to the self-fulfilling prophecy as it influences our behavior. The self-fulfilling prophecy happens when your expectation of an event makes the event more likely to happen. In other words, a prediction you have made comes true because you made the prediction and because you acted as if it were true. Essentially, there are four basic steps in the self-fulfilling prophecy:

1. You make a prediction or formulate a belief about a person, yourself, or a situation (for example, you tell yourself that you won't be able to finish the report your boss gave you by the deadline).
2. You act toward that situation as if the prediction or belief is true (for example, you don't work as hard on the report as you might in order to meet the deadline).
3. Because you act as if the belief is true, it becomes true (for example, you do miss the deadline).
4. You observe your effect on the situation and what you see strengthens your beliefs (for example, you now believe that you won't be able to finish similar reports by the given deadline in the future).[19]

In this example, your behavior is directly affected by your expectation of the event. Your self-concept, directed by a self-fulfilling prophecy, caused you to behave differently than you normally might have behaved. Certainly, a self-fulfilling prophecy need not be negative, but clearly self-fulfilling prophecies may influence your behavior.

A classic study in the late nineteenth century illustrates the role that self-fulfilling prophecy can play in the organization. After the U.S. Census Bureau purchased a new tabulating machine, the staff of the bureau had to learn skills that the machine's inventor thought were very difficult. He told the staff that each of them could punch approximately 550 cards each day and that to punch more might jeopardize their psychological well-being. Sure enough, after a few weeks each staff member was processing about 550 cards per day, and when the workers tried to punch more than the anticipated number, they indicated they felt very anxious. Soon a new group of clerks was hired to do the same task on the same machines; however, they were told nothing of the new machines, or the anticipated number of cards to be punched, or what might happen if they punched more than 550 cards each day. After only three days, each new clerk was punching over 2,000 cards daily and feeling no ill effects. The self-fulfilling prophecy had worked! The initial group of clerks believed they could only punch 550 cards and behaved accordingly, but the new group, unencumbered by that belief, was able to be much more productive.

Actually, we must identify two different types of self-fulfilling prophecies—the Galatea effect and the Pygmalion effect. The Galatea effect is inwardly directed and is named after the statue carved by a Cypriot king who fell in love with his creation. This type of prophecy is self-imposed and occurs when your own expectations influence your behavior.

The Pygmalion effect results when one person imposes a self-fulfilling prophecy on another person. It is other-directed and gained recognition from a classic study conducted by Robert Rosenthal and his associates at Harvard in the 1960s. Rosenthal wanted to know if students were evaluated by what they actually did in the classroom or by how they had been labeled by teachers and others. In this study, students were given a battery of tests and teachers were told that certain students were likely to improve more than others by the end of the school term. Actually, these students were chosen completely by random and their selection had nothing to do with the battery of tests. The study results proved there was a self-fulfilling prophecy in the classroom. The experimenters found that the teachers evaluated those students labeled as "bright" more favorably and encouraged them to perform better than the others not so identified. The result was that the selected students performed at the level to which they were encouraged—at least in their eyes and the eyes of the teachers.[20]

▶ IMPROVING YOUR SELF-CONCEPT

Now that you have an understanding of how the self-concept is formed and its importance to interpersonal communication, it seems especially important to indicate ways that you might improve your self-concept, if necessary. This is a difficult process for the self-concept isn't easily changed. But, if you commit yourself to the work, it can be done. The following suggestions will provide you with a good start.

Ask Yourself "Who Am I?"

Plato urged his fellow Greeks to "Know Thyself," but today we seem so preoccupied with our busy world that we rarely take the time to ask ourselves the important question, "Who am I?" The first action you must take to change your self-concept is to get into the habit of taking the time to think about yourself; you need to take time to talk to yourself just as you take time to talk with your coworkers, roommate, spouse, parents, and the other significant people in your life. Doesn't it seem paradoxical that you will set time aside for other people, but you won't take time to be with the person who is the most important one in your life—yourself?

The second action needed to better answer the question of who you are is to take a test. The test has two parts and is designed to give you a better insight into yourself.[21] Take a piece of paper and write "I am . . ." 15 or 20 times and then complete each sentence, responding with what comes to mind first—both positive and negative reactions. For example, "I am a good singer," or "I am interested in my work," or "I am nervous when asked to give public presentations." To complete the second part of the test, take another piece of paper and write "I want . . ." as many times as you wish. As you complete each of these sentences, you should write your self-improvement goal and how you intend to achieve the goal. For example, "I want to get to work on time so I'll leave home no later than 7:30 A.M. every day next week," or "I want to be more organized on my job so I'll create a new file system and put my documents into it as soon as I'm finished with them." Understand that your self-concept can change, so your perceptions of yourself and your self-improvement goals can change as well; therefore, you need to update goals at regular and frequent intervals.

Seek Information About Yourself

Each day we encounter other people who can give us information about ourselves, and we can use everyday situations to find out what people in our lives think of us.

You must encourage other people to reveal their comments, candidly and frankly. You can ask a coworker, "Did I handle that situation with the supervisor as I should have this morning?" or you can ask your employer, "Was our customer satisfied with my reaction to her complaints when you spoke to her yesterday?" Information from those you interpersonally communicate with on a regular basis can be insightful and revealing. Remember, you will never find out what other people really think about you unless you elicit such information.

The role of perception is critical when soliciting information and vital to the process of communication. This is because we must perceive and respond to the world around us for interpersonal communication to even occur. It's how we create meaning. Let's examine this influential factor.

▶ PERCEPTION DEFINED

Perception is the mental and cognitive process that enables us to select, organize, and interpret our surroundings. We are constantly perceiving the world around us, actively adding to and subtracting from the stimuli we receive through our five senses. Richard L. Weaver II explains this process of perceiving by comparing it to a large sieve with holes of different shapes and sizes.[22] We each possess a unique sieve unlike any others and each hole in the sieve represents a category with which we've had some experience. The number of holes in the sieve constantly change as we encounter new experiences, just as the size of the holes change according to our changing values. Certain holes are blackened because we choose to ignore some information and certain holes are irregular in size and shape because some information doesn't fit our present categories and must be forced to conform. The uniqueness of each of our sieves means that we all perceive the world differently.

▶ STAGES OF PERCEPTION

The Parable of the Six Blind Men of Indostan

It was six men of indostan
To learning much inclined
Who went to see the Elephant
(Though all of them were blind).
That each by observation
Might satisfy his mind.

The First approached the Elephant,
And happening to fall
Against his broad and sturdy side,
At once began to bawl:
"God bless me! But the Elephant
Is very like a wall."

The Second, feeling of the tusk
Cried, "Ho! What have we here
So very round and smooth and sharp?

To me 'tis very clear
This wonder of an Elephant
Is very like a spear."

The Third approached the animal
And, happening to take
The squirming trunk within his hands,
Thus boldly up he spake:
"I see," quote he, "the Elephant
Is very like a snake."

The Fourth reached out an eager hand,
And felt about the knee:
"What most this wondrous beast is like
Is very plain," quoth he;
"'Tis clear enough the Elephant
Is very like a tree."

The Fifth, who chanced to touch the ear
Said: "E'en the blindest man
Can tell what this resembles most;
Deny the fact who can
This marvel of an Elephant
Is very like a fan."

The Sixth no sooner had begun
About the beast to grope
Than seizing on the swinging tail
That fell within his scope:
"I see," quoth he, "the Elephant
Is very like a rope!"

The problem faced by these six blind men in the poem by John Godfrey Saxe[23] was that they were not *selecting* the same data; they were *organizing* what they did perceive in different ways; and they were *interpreting* their results very differently. Perception involves these three distinct but overlapping steps. These steps occur instantaneously and are almost impossible to discern, but it is important to understand them because each is critical to the perception process.

The Selection Stage

The first step in the perception process is selection. At this stage, your sense organs are stimulated and you draw from the stimuli in your environment. You see the colleague sitting at the next workstation, smell her perfume, hear her conversation with a client, taste the apple you brought for your break, and feel the texture of your chair. Our physical makeup affects how much information we're able to gather. Although the number of stimuli we ordinarily sense is impressive, it's actually small compared with the maximum amount which we are capable of sensing. Our bodies are amazingly sensitive instruments for receiving sensory information. Most people are able to distinguish 7,500,000 different colors. We can hear sounds ranging from 20 to

▶ MIXED SIGNALS LEAD TO LONELY CHILDHOODS

By Maureen Downey

As a child, Mimi Darden longed to be accepted at school. Yet she found herself an outcast and never understood why.

"I thought I was being rejected because I was just a nerd or a bad person," she says.

At age 35, Darden discovered the real reason: She had a learning disability that made it difficult for her to understand non-verbal signals—such as facial expressions, vocal tones and spatial relations.

Just as a dyslexic misreads 17 for 71, Darden misinterprets voice tones and expressions.

"I perceived the other children and even my family members as angry with me," she says. "Even when their tone was friendly and they were trying to explain something to me, I thought they were angry and spent all my time apologizing."

The ability to recognize non-verbal cues is essential to human communication. Studies have shown that only 7 percent of emotional meaning is conveyed with words. The rest is transmitted through facial expression, posture, gesture and tone of voice.

"In relationships where things are not typed on paper and handed back and forth, you need to have non-verbal skills," says Emory University psychologist Marshall P. Duke.

Consider physicians who are halfway out the door before they ask the patient for questions. The non-verbal message—"I'm too busy to respond"—shouts out at most people. But a handful do not hear it.

Duke and Emory colleague Stephen Nowicki call such people "dyssemic"—meaning they cannot translate non-verbal signs. Their research suggests that 10 percent of children demonstrate dyssemia severe enough to interfere with social or academic success.

A dyssemic may not sense how close to stand while talking to someone. Another may fail to detect the rising anger in a coworker's voice. Someone else may fail to pick up on rhythm and use of time, or may be oblivious to clothing styles. Nowicki and Duke, who developed an assessment scale for dyssemia, coauthored *Helping the Child Who Doesn't Fit In* (Peachtree Publishers). The two have tested the non-verbal abilities of more than 1,000 children aged 6 to 10.

The eight-part scale measures a child's ability to understand and send non-verbal messages. The child reviews 40 slides of facial expressions of adults and children and states the emotion expressed. In another segment, a child assesses whether a voice sounds angry, fearful, happy or sad.

"These skills aren't taught to us in any formal way," says Duke. "So we absorb these skills for social success as well as we can." Children who don't absorb them pay a price. The researchers found that the least popular children scored the lowest on the scale.

Nowicki and Duke aren't sure yet whether dyssemia runs in families. It's prevalent in younger siblings of larger families, perhaps because parents are less available. It's also more common in boys.

The researchers cite three possible causes for dyssemia. In a small number of people, it is the result of a brain dysfunction that creates a lifelong non-verbal learning disability, such as in Darden's case. The dyssemia also can be a byproduct of anxiety or depression. For example, a child struggling with academics may be unable to focus on social skills. But the reason most children fumble non-verbal cues is that they simply have never learned them. It is this group that benefits most from instruction.

Sometimes, as they deal with their child's problem, parents discover their own.

"During my son's testing and evaluation, I found myself," says Robert Weiland, 39. "I was looking straight into a mirror." As a child, Weiland was the kid nobody noticed. He skipped most of the last half of his senior year of high school. But while in college, he resolved to change and eventually became CEO of his own high-tech company.

But it has been a daily challenge. "There is no book on social skills, no class," he says. "If you don't learn it, you miss it."

Along with testing, a variety of therapies have evolved to teach non-verbal skills. Nowicki and Duke prescribe exercises that parents can do with children, including flash cards of facial expressions, videotapes and charades.

Rosemary Jackson of the University of Georgia Learning Disabilities Center, who deals with adults with non-verbal learning disabilities, employs similar methods in the support group she conducts. For instance, she turns the sound down on the television and asks clients to decipher the action based on actors' expressions.

But her group members represent extreme cases, unable to hold jobs, drive or live independently. While most adults score 69 percent in the test UGA uses to assess non-verbal ability, group members score in the bottom sixth percentile.

Through the group and a related job-training program, Darden has found as a grown woman what she desperately missed as a child: close friends.

Source: Maureen Downey, "Mixed Signals Lead to Lonely Childhoods," *The Orlando Sentinel,* June 29, 1992, D1–D2. Reprinted with permission from *The Atlanta Journal* and *The Atlanta Constitution.*

20,000 vibration cycles per second. We can distinguish among 5,000 different smells and 10,000 different tastes. Our fingers can feel the separations between objects as small as three to eight millimeters apart.[24]

Yet, even though our senses are indeed remarkable, they are still far from perfect. There are sights we cannot see, sounds we cannot hear, tastes we cannot distinguish, smells we do not sense, and our sense of touch doesn't provide much information if we don't use our sense of sight to determine what we are touching. The result is that some of us are able to perceive data other people are unable to perceive because our senses are different. For example, most communication data come to you from your senses of sight and hearing. Your vision has clear limitations, even if you have 20/20 vision. You can't see all the waves available to you because ultraviolet rays are too short (from 0.00003 to 0.000001 centimeters), as are X-rays, gamma rays, and cosmic rays. On the other end of the light spectrum, infrared rays (with a wave length of 0.00008 to 0.32 centimeters) aren't seen, nor are the longer radar or radio waves. Actually, the visible spectrum for humans is quite narrow in relation to all the wave transmissions occurring all around us. You hear sounds within the range of 20 to 20,000 cycles per second, but your stereo can exceed that range. Your dog can hear frequencies above what you can hear. Thus, even within the realm of our senses, we're only aware of a small part of what is going on around us.

Then, too, each of us selects different data to which we pay attention. In a well-known study of perceptual problems in the workplace, Rensis Likert reported substantial disagreement between subordinates' and supervisors' perceptions and understanding of work problems.[25] The study revealed that 34 percent of the employees surveyed said their supervisors understood their problems well, but 95 percent of the supervisors reported they well understood the problems of their employees. Likert asked this same question of supervisors and their immediate superiors, with 51 percent of the supervisors saying that their immediate superior knew their problems well and 90 percent of the immediate supervisors believing they well understood the problems of their subordinates. Clearly, perceptual difficulties exist in organizations. This perceptual ambiguity can lead to anxiety, dissatisfaction, low morale, lack of interest in the job, and decreased production.

The Organizational Stage

At the second stage, the sensory stimuli you have selected are organized according to certain principles that you have internalized from some time in your past. Three such structures are especially common: figure–ground principle, proximity principle, and resemblance principle.

The organizational principle of *figure–ground* allows you to arrange your stimuli in a more meaningful way. The familiar drawing of the vase–faces/faces–vase is a striking example of figure–ground organization. The drawing can be viewed as a vase or as a set of twins in profile, depending on which you emphasize. Certain data stand out as a figure against a less striking ground. At work you might notice a certain sound even though there are many other sounds you can hear at the same time. When you walk into your office in the morning, you might visually notice that something is different—a slightly turned chair or an object on your desk misplaced. These are examples of figure–ground organization and they illustrate how you make sense of perceptual situations.

Source: Roger N. Shepard, *Mind Sights: Original Visual Illusions, Ambiguities, and Other Anomalies, with a Commentary on the Play of Mind in Perception and Art* (New York: W. H. Freeman, 1990): 69. Copyright © 1990 by Roger N. Shepard. Used with permission of W. H. Freeman and Company.

Roger N. Shepard, writer and illustrator, understands the perceptual process and he observes, "For every situation, our perceptual system automatically applies its previously successful and now thoroughly entrenched methods of process."[26] In his drawings, Shepard displays his knowledge of communication by examining the ideas of perception and reality. The figure–ground principle is well illustrated in Exhibit 6-2 despite Shepard's self-critical analysis: "My attempt to render the six letters of the word 'Figure' as figural patterns against a ground formed by the six letters of the word 'Ground' was not an unqualified success. Nevertheless, the figure–ground ambiguity is quite strong for the first two letters of each of these words, thanks to a fortuitous complementarity of shape between the initial 'F' of Figure and 'G' of Ground and between the 'I' of Figure and 'R' of Ground. Thus, the first letter tends to be seen as 'F' or 'G' but not fully as both at once."[27]

The principle of *proximity* allows you to perceive people or things that are physically grouped together as one or as having something in common. For example, you might see the same three managers having lunch together regularly and conclude that they are best friends who have similar attitudes about the company. The very fact that they are together on a regular basis leads you to believe that they are closer to one another than might actually be the case—they might find meeting over lunch a convenient time to discuss company-related business.

The *resemblance* principle occurs when you group people who are similar in appearance and distinguish them from others who are dissimilar. For example, you might group together executive officers because of their expensive suits and similar ties, and distinguish them from other aspiring managers. Many companies deliberately employ this principle to create a certain image, thus one can identify an "IBM" or "Disney" person based on dress alone. The important point is that you often organize sensory data in a certain way and you do so automatically.

The Interpretation Stage

The final stage of perception is interpretation—where you add meaning to the process. Here, your attitudes, beliefs, values, wants, needs, and past experiences shape how you add meaning to sensory stimuli. This stage is very subjective, being almost entirely dependent on your personal assessment and judgment of the situation. Does the production manager's tone of voice mean that he believes your suggestion is a good one or one that should be discarded? Does the CEO's glance mean that she likes or dislikes you? Was your supervisor's statement that he had an "open door" policy meant to be taken literally or was it just a friendly gesture? These questions may be answered differently by each of us during the interpretation step.

A common way we interpret data during this final step of the perception process is by using cognitive models that psychologists call *schemata;* these allow us to make sense of what we observe in everyday life. A schema is an organized arrangement of knowledge from our experience that we use to interpret our current situation.[28] Sara Trenholm and Arthur Jensen identify three key types of schemata that are especially important to the perceptual process: constructs, prototypes, and scripts.[29]

Constructs are personal observations about people and things that allow us to describe and make judgments about them. George Kelly describes a construct as a "mental yardstick for deciding how two things are similar yet different from a third thing."[30] Constructs are used to answer the questions "What are its characteristics?" and "What do I think about it?" For example, you might describe a fax machine and a computer modem as relatively current and popular forms of business technology compared with a typewriter. A colleague of yours, however, might describe a fax machine and a typewriter as necessities but a computer modem as a luxury. These descriptors—"current," "popular," and "necessity" versus "luxury"—are types of personal constructs.

Prototypes are sets of features commonly associated with members of a category.[31] These schemata are used whenever we attribute certain characteristics to people or things whom we view as similar. For example, each of us has an idiosyncratic image of a good worker. If you view a good worker as a person who arrives early, works hard, and is efficient, then you would be likely to describe new employees as good workers if they displayed these characteristics. Conversely, you would be likely to label new employees as poor workers if they arrive at work later in the day, don't appear to work as hard, and seem inefficient. A common type of prototype is the *stereotype*. This special prototype assigns characteristics to a person solely because of how that person is categorized, and yet stereotypes differ from other prototypes because they go beyond simply categorizing a person to predicting a specific behavior. This suggests that stereotyping comprises four stages: first, a person identifies a class of people, for example, accountants; second, he observes that one or more of the people in this class exhibit a certain trait, such as dullness; third, he generalizes that all people in this group possess this trait of dullness; and fourth, on meeting or hearing about an accountant, he stereotypes the accountant as dull.[32]

A *script* is a kind of schema that serves as a guide to a particular action. These schemata answer the questions, "How shall I go on?" and "What do I do next?" A script allows us to interpret a specific behavior because we can predict a course of action based on our knowledge of the script. For example, a person attending a certain movie often follows this script: purchase ticket for the movie at the ticket booth, enter the theater complex, purchase refreshments, enter the theater featuring your movie, watch the movie, exit the particular theater, and exit the theater complex. Scripts are an important type of schema because they often affect our expectations of others. For example, if you have a script about the ways an employer should act on the job, then you will be more likely to expect your boss to act in a certain way.

These three types of schemata—constructs, prototypes, and scripts—are important to a fuller understanding of perception. Indeed, the social context of our communication directly affects the meaning we assign to our interpersonal messages.

▶ MAJOR INFLUENCES ON THE PERCEPTION PROCESS

We all view the world somewhat differently because we select, organize, and interpret the sensory stimuli in our environment differently. Although many interdependent variables operate during these three steps, there are three major influences that shape our perception of the world—physical, emotional, and cultural influences.

We have already discussed the importance of our physical senses and their limitations, but height, weight, health, age, and even our biological cycles influence our perceptions. Seven-foot-tall professional basketball players notice things about the world most of us never think about—such as the length of beds, height of doorways, and legroom in airline passenger seating. We perceive the world somewhat differently when in good health than when ill—think of the times when you have had the flu and how different your perceptions were at that time than when you felt well. Age, too, affects how we perceive the world. The elderly see the world differently in part because they have more and varied experiences. Finally, even our biological cycles (largely altered by our hormonal makeup) affect our moods and therefore affect our perceptions. Whether you are a morning-person or a night-person will influence your view of the world, especially the world of work when you must adjust your cycle to the hours of the corporation. Therefore, even though a reality may be out there, our physical bodies affect how we select, organize, and interpret that reality.

Just as our physical properties have an impact on our perceptions, so do our emotions affect how we view our world; in short, our feelings at any given moment directly affect our perceptions. Our emotions and their effect on our perceptions are explained, in part, by *attribution theory* which is concerned with whether a specific behavior arises from one's personality (typically recurring behavior patterns) or is prompted by the situation or circumstances.[33] According to attribution theory, what we correctly or incorrectly determine to be the cause of other peoples' behaviors has a direct impact on our perceptions of these people. For example, imagine that you are a manager in your organization and a deadline has been given to an employee to get an important report to your office by 11:00 A.M. It is now noon and you haven't received the report. If you like and respect this employee, you may well believe that something unavoidable has detained the report—perhaps a personal problem at home or a computer breakdown. However, if you aren't fond of this employee, you may attribute the lateness to forgetfulness, lack of consideration, or ineptitude.

Culture, "the relatively specialized life-style of a group of people,"[34] has a bearing on our perceptions. Each culture has its own world view. For example:

▶ In most countries, the thumbs-up sign means "OK" but in Italy this sign is considered a rude gesture.
▶ In Middle Eastern countries, one mustn't accept or pass food with the left hand, since that is the hand commonly used for sanitary functions.
▶ The normal workweek in Saudi Arabia is Saturday through Wednesday.
▶ Tipping is considered an insult in Iceland.
▶ If a business acquaintance in Japan gives you a small wrapped gift, you should thank the giver and open the present later.
▶ When taking flowers to a patient in a hospital, it is considered a major social faux pas to bring chrysanthemums in France or purple flowers in Brazil because each is considered a sign of death in the respective countries.

By Dean C. Barnlund

The assumption that everywhere men and women inhabit the same world and assign essentially the same meanings to events of their lives is perhaps the most pervasive and most intractable barrier to intercultural rapport.

It is not simply that people speak in different tongues but also that they see differently, think differently, feel differently about their experience. "If, by some miracle, Americans and Japanese were to wake up one day and find ourselves talking the same language," observes George Packard, "we would still be faced with the problem of our massive ignorance about each other, we would still have difficulty in knowing what to communicate because we have so much to learn about what motivates the other."

What are some of the probable consequences of encounters between Japanese and Americans? The Japanese are likely to be startled at the ease with which Americans approach and enter into intense conversations with people they scarcely know. Americans' lack of sensitivity to protocol and to status differences, or their deliberate efforts to undermine them, may appear naive or downright insulting. Their constant questions and revealing disclosure may seem intrusive and overbearing, forcing the Japanese to discuss matters they regard as private. Their informality and impulsiveness may deprive social occasions of their congenial predictability. The pace at which Americans move and talk, their verbal and physical flamboyance, may be unnerv-

ing. Their eagerness to contradict, even to argue bluntly, disturbs the harmony that should prevail. Their endless analyzing, insistence on verbal precision, and binding agreements reveal an incredible trust in words over people. They are prone to error because they are always in such a hurry. They are an inscrutable people!

The Americans, in turn, confront Japanese who appear reluctant to meet strangers and slow to get to know them. The Japanese seem preoccupied with the relative status of people and are constantly deferring to those above them. They also are constantly apologizing. They seem to view conversation as some sort of formal ceremony rather than a real meeting of the minds. They are reticent about saying much about themselves, preferring to comment on superficial and irrelevant topics. When questions are put directly to them the answers are so vague that one has little idea of where they stand. They all repeat the same things as if fearful of disagreement. They are as physically opaque as they are verbally—except when drinking—and rarely show feelings of any kind, particularly negative ones. They are composed in the way they sit, the way they stand, the way they talk, as if some accidental and uncalculated act might expose them. There is a reluctance to dig into problems, analyze them step by step, and agree on specific conclusions. And they seem oblivious to deadlines. A highly inscrutable people!

Source: Dean C. Barnlund, *Communicative Styles of Japanese and Americans* (Belmont, CA: Wadsworth, 1989): 189-191. Copyright © 1989 by Wadsworth Publishing Co.

Clearly, members of different cultures have their own ways of looking at the world about them. These differing viewpoints can create major blocks to communication between cultures. The increased interest in global awareness and study of intercultural communication represent efforts to surmount these potential barriers and improve our communication.

► IMPROVING YOUR PERCEPTION

Now that we have defined perception, examined the stages of the process, and looked at its three major influences, it is appropriate to suggest ways by which you can improve the accuracy of your perceptions. Just as changing your self-concept isn't easy, the improvement of the perceptual processes that you have used all of your life is difficult. However, the following suggestions should prove useful.

Question Your Perceptions

Perhaps the greatest obstacle to overcome as you try to improve the accuracy of your perceptions is the tendency to believe that everything you perceive is really the way it is. It is common to hear people say, "I know it happened, I saw it!" or "Believe me, I heard her say it!" We frequently accept unquestioningly the selection, organization, and interpretation of what we see and what we hear. Paul Watzlawick indicated the significance of this barrier when he observed, "The belief that one's own view of reality is the only reality is the most dangerous of all delusions."[35]

Your challenge as a communicator is to actively question your perceptions and avoid the pitfall of believing that your perceptions are always accurate. Just as other people you know are sometimes wrong in their perceptions, so are you. Questioning accuracy begins by asking, "Is what I *believe* I saw, heard, smelled, or felt correct? What else could help me sort this out?" By accepting the possibility of error, you are taking a giant step toward further clarification. In situations where the accuracy of perception is important, take a few seconds to double-check.

Use Perception Checking

Perception checking permits you to objectively check the accuracy of your interpretations of a situation. This clarifying tool is composed of three steps: (1) a description of the behavior you noticed, (2) at least two possible interpretations of the behavior, and (3) a request for feedback from the other person. This is how a perception check might be applied to a typical work situation: The ideas you sent your supervisor outlining ways you could improve your job have not been acknowledged. In fact, your supervisor hasn't even mentioned receiving the interoffice memorandum. Many would immediately assume the supervisor didn't like the ideas, or planned to take credit for the ideas by submitting them himself for administrative review, or the memo was lost in the system. Any or all of these assumptions could be correct. The way to check what really happened is to approach your supervisor and follow the steps previously listed:

> "Jack, two weeks ago I sent you some ideas about how to improve my job, and I haven't heard anything from you about them." (Description of the behavior)
> "This makes me think you didn't care for the ideas, but I realize you've been busy and perhaps just haven't had time to get back to me." (Two interpretations of the behavior)
> "What's up?" (Request for clarification)

As is readily apparent in the example, the judicious use of this skill can significantly reduce the likelihood of misinterpretation. But, as with most interpersonal communication skills, you must practice perception checking for it to be useful.

Don't Confuse Facts with Inferences

As working men or women, you make thousands of inferences each and every day. You assume your car will start as you leave your home in the morning; you assume the doors will be unlocked when you arrive at your office building; you assume the elevator will climb to the selected floor; you assume the ceiling won't fall in on you as you enter your office; you assume your chair won't collapse as you sit down; all of this and your day is just beginning! That's as it should be in order to function because questioning everything in life would literally drive us crazy.

However, you begin to mislead yourself and others when you perceive and then allow your inferences to go beyond what you observed. Being able to distinguish between facts and inferences is critical when important issues are involved. For example, it could make a big difference if you infer that the automobile directly in front of you with its right turn signal on is going to turn into an upcoming intersection instead of the driveway just before the intersection. Then, too, the driver may have just forgotten to turn the signal off and does not intend to turn at all. An error here, could result in a serious accident. William V. Haney has created an effective five-step technique for minimizing this inference–observation confusion[36]:

1. *Detect the inference.* In other words, determine that you are, in fact, making an inference instead of an observation.
2. *Calculate the risk.* In this step, you determine the assessment of the probability that the inference is correct.
3. *Get more data.* Here you turn to certain of your other senses or to other people for verification that what you sensed was correct.
4. *Recalculate the risk.* Now that you have more data, reassess the probability of the risk. When this step is completed, you should be able to better determine if your inference was a reasonable one.
5. *Label your inferences.* Finally, qualify your statements and index your observations. A major problem contributing to the confusion of facts with inferences is a failure to appropriately use our language to distinguish between observations and inferences. Instead of using tentative language, frequently we use definite language. Thus, instead of saying, "I *believe* Sarah left the office earlier today," or "I'm *not certain but it seems* Sarah left the office earlier," we will say "Sarah left the office earlier today." We don't let others know that our statements are based on inferences, not observations.

The application of Haney's technique is not easy; even with constant care and attention, it's possible to blend and blur observations and inferences. Our natural inclinations and the nature of our language make this a continual challenge. However, the payoff is healthier communication and a clearer understanding of our alternatives, given a particular situation.

Effective interpersonal communication and relating require us to adapt to changes as they occur. By engaging in self-concept improvement and continually honing our perceptual skills, we are responsibly responding to the interpersonal demands of the workplace. Additionally, it is important that we periodically pause to assess the effectiveness of interpersonal communication and review relational development within the organization.

▶ DYADIC ANALYSIS, COMMUNICATION GAMES, AND ASSERTIVENESS

The study of dyadic relationships, or face-to-face exchanges between individuals, can be a useful and relatively simple method of analyzing problems of communication and assessing communication effectiveness within organizational settings. Eric Berne presents the model of "transactional analysis" which can be applied to the study of dyadic relationships within organizations.[37] He defines the transaction as a basic scientific unit and provides a common vocabulary for explaining transactions. A transaction is the smallest unit of social interaction and transactional analysis is a method of examining any single transaction as "I do something to you and you do something back." Transactional analysis can serve as a structure for critiquing dyads and can help in answering the question, "What's going on here?"

Dyadic Analysis

Dyadic analysis begins with the contention that each person is composed of three ego states that are separate and distinct sources of behavior—parent, adult, and child. This evolves out of the findings by Wilder Penfield's research that everything that has been in our conscious awareness is recorded in detail and stored in the brain, capable of being played back in the present.[38] These ego states of being are not roles but psychological realities produced by the playback of recorded data in that past involving real people, real times, real places, real decisions, and real emotions. Berne observes that "Parent, Adult, and Child are not concepts like Superego, Ego, and Id . . . but phenomenological realities."[39]

Muriel James and Dorothy Jongeward, in their book *Born to Win*, define the three ego states as follows:

> *Parent ego state:* Contains the attitudes and behavior incorporated from external sources, primarily parents. Outwardly, it often is expressed toward others in prejudicial, critical, and nurturing behavior. Inwardly, it is expressed as old Parental messages which continue to influence the inner Child.

> *Adult ego state:* Oriented to current reality and the objective gathering of information. It is organized, adaptable, intelligent, and functions by testing reality, estimating probabilities, and computing dispassionately.

> *Child ego state:* Contains all the impulses that come naturally to an infant. It also contains the recordings of his early experiences, how he responded to them, and the "position" he took about himself and others. It is expressed as "old" (archaic) behavior from childhood.[40]

Each of these three ego states is needed to complete the personality profile of any individual and each state has its legitimate place in a full and productive life. The parent has the dual function of enabling people to act effectively as "actual" parents and to make the automatic responses necessary to cope with routine matters. The adult is necessary for the processing of outside, real-world, factual data; the computing of probabilities essential for action, and the regulation of the parent and the child states—i.e., survival. In the child resides intuition, creativity, spontaneous drive, and enjoyment. Each type of ego state has its own vital value for the human organism and consequently the effectiveness of any transaction is contingent on one's sorting out and selecting the most appropriate ego state. This is true whether transactions are personal or evolve out of an organizational setting.

We come now to the central technique of using Berne's categories to analyze a transaction and understand what's going on in a dyadic interaction. Anything that happens between people will involve a transaction between their ego states. The pur-

1 That new secretary we hired certainly has a know-it-all attitude.

2 Yes, we'll probably have to find a replacement before everyone is alienated.

1 The meeting was very productive.

2 I agree; it's good that so many positive suggestions were made.

1 This report must be completed by noon tomorrow.

2 You're always hurrying me. Couldn't I please have a little more time to work on it?

pose of the analysis is to discover which part of each person is acting in each situation. All transactions can be classified as being complementary, crossed, or ulterior.

A *complementary* transaction occurs when a message sent from a particular ego state is appropriately responded to by the other person. Complementary transactions are characterized by open, parallel lines of communication—parent–parent, adult–adult, child–child, parent–child, or child–parent. Some typical complementary transactions are shown in Exhibit 6-3.

A *crossed* transaction occurs when the person who initiates the transaction receives an unexpected or inappropriate response. The lines of transaction are crossed, and the participants are often left feeling discounted or put down. At this point, people tend to withdraw, turn away from each other, or move the conversation in another direction. Crossed transactions in business can lower both morale and productivity. William R. Tracey, director of training at the U.S. Army School of Intelligence, observes that "whether conscious or unconscious, failure to show sensitivity to the feelings of subordinates, even lapses in common courtesy or consideration, do a great deal of damage in organizations. At the very least, they cause communication gaps, wasted time, unnecessary work, loss of productivity, poor morale and a host of other organizational ills."[41] Some typical crossed transactions are shown in Exhibit 6-4.

Ulterior transactions are more complex, involving the activity of more than two ego states simultaneously. When an ulterior message is sent, it is disguised under a socially acceptable transaction but with a psychological factor introduced. Thus, it is necessary to examine the meta-communication that is occurring. These transactions frequently lead to misunderstandings and strained relations because open interpersonal disclosure is constrained and all of the participants may not be fully aware of the messages being exchanged. Exhibit 6-5 illustrates an ulterior transaction.

The three types of transactions discussed and diagrammed can serve as a means of analyzing interpersonal communication within organizational settings. An understanding of transactions and dyadic analysis is equally important to managers and coworkers or employees. It can assist you in better assessing the interpersonal communication of others. You can reasonably measure their reaction to you and others, and that might influence your behavior. You are more aware of what's happening in a given situation, and can answer the why question.

Communication Games

People play psychological games with one another in many situations, including the organizational setting. Eric Berne defines a psychological game as a "recurring set of transactions, often repetitive, superficially rational, with a concealed motivation; or more colloquially, as a series of transactions with a gimmick."[42] All games arise out of ulterior transactions and have a beginning, a given set of rules, and a con-

▶ **EXHIBIT 6-4**
Crossed Transactions

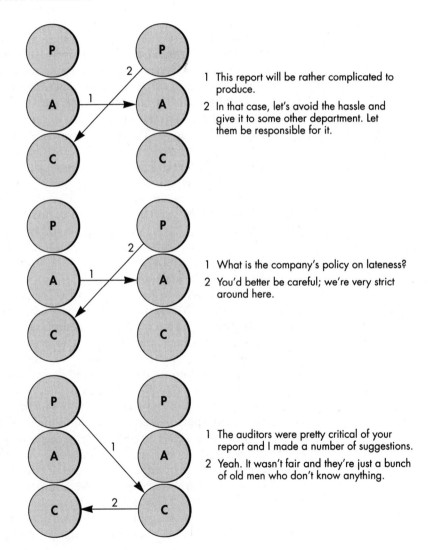

1 This report will be rather complicated to produce.
2 In that case, let's avoid the hassle and give it to some other department. Let them be responsible for it.

1 What is the company's policy on lateness?
2 You'd better be careful; we're very strict around here.

1 The auditors were pretty critical of your report and I made a number of suggestions.
2 Yeah. It wasn't fair and they're just a bunch of old men who don't know anything.

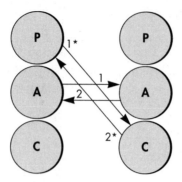

SURFACE MESSAGE

1 Traffic must be heavy today because you're late again this morning.

2 No, I had car trouble but am getting it repaired over the weekend.

ULTERIOR MESSAGE

1* Please don't be late again or I'll have to write a reprimand or possibly dismiss you.

2* I promise not to be late again if I can help it; don't punish me.

cluding payoff. The term "game" in this context does not refer to playful behavior but rather refers to sequences of behavior which are governed by rules and which frequently inhibit accurate and open interpersonal communication between people.

It is important that we distinguish between communication games and other types of communication behavior—rituals, pastimes, and intimacy. Rituals are simple, noncommittal transactions that do not permit "real" involvement and therefore keep people "safely" apart. There are greeting, dating, cocktail party, and business rituals. These socially programmed and approved behaviors can be seen in all facets of our lives. Our earlier discussion of impersonal communication characterizes the rituals we engage in frequently.

Pastimes are also nonthreatening and noncommittal in nature and represent a means of making new acquaintances and confirming our own social roles. Talk of cars, sports, cooking, travel, social acquaintances, and business are ways of passing time and can be observed at parties, luncheons, and at work. As useful as pastimes may be in certain situations, they too are impersonal and rarely materialize into prolonged, intimate relationships.

Genuine intimacy involves "getting close" to people, sharing thoughts and feelings, showing warmth and concern. Intimacy involves a much deeper human relationship than rituals and pastimes permit and is free of the ulterior dynamics characterized by games. There exists an open climate where people can exchange hopes, fears, dreams, and ambitions; and where potentially interfering barriers to communication are recognized, intercepted, and eliminated. Although intimate relationships are usually thought of as being associated with marriage and family, it is not necessary to reserve intimacy solely to the home environment. Relationships of intimacy, sincere interpersonal communication meeting the criteria stated earlier, can be equally beneficial in the business or organizational arena. It is through such game-free relationships that we "can reach out to the vast areas of knowledge about our universe and about each other, explore the depths of philosophy and religion, perceive what is new, unrefracted by the old, and perhaps find answers, one at a time, to the great perplexity, 'What's the good of it all?'"[43]

Unfortunately, gaming behavior abounds because people lack trust and faith, and consequently choose life positions dissimilar with the risk-taking involved in intimacy. In short, people are frightened to assume the commitment necessary for real interpersonal communication and fail to assume a life position that can lead to positive and productive interpersonal relationships. Psychological games are played for either of two purposes, both of which are damaging to the person and to the organization: to discount the player or to discount others. Those who play games to discount themselves are usually in their child ego state and are trying to get forgiveness, sympathy, or putdowns. They are insecure. Those who play games to discount others are usually in their parent ego state and are trying to provide blame, save face, find fault with, or get even with others—gain power. Games of this sort result from a lack of trust within the organization.[44]

Communication games are played out by people with a low self-concept whose life positions are generally less than positive or self-rewarding. Such psychological gaming behavior threatens the smooth functioning of the entire organizational system, so every effort should be made to stop a gaming situation. How can gaming behavior be prevented or corrected? It is not easy, but there are three primary ways to halt such behavior, depending on the nature of the game, the players, and the intensity. They are: refuse to play, refuse to provide the payoff, and stop discounting. Games cannot be played unless there are players and payoffs. There must be at least two people engaging in this behavior and seeking some end. Refusing to discount others and attempting to stop one's own discounting can prevent gaming behavior. This approach replaces an otherwise less-than-positive self-concept with a more positive outlook and those playing the game come to realize they are responsible for their own actions. The prevention of games opens communication and leads to more desirable, productive, and positive interpersonal relationships—personally, socially, on-the-job, and professionally.

Assertiveness

Anyone entering the organization soon learns that the cosmo-corporate game of success encourages, even demands, such qualities as competitive drive; cooperative spirit; strategic, logical, and analytical skills; and a compulsion to assume leadership and achieve authority and power. In short, the players, male or female, must be assertive.

The increased attention given to assertiveness and assertiveness training has also given rise to much confusion. Some suppose that men "naturally" possess assertiveness and that women lack the self-confidence necessary for managerial effectiveness and need to develop a more assertive style of communication. Others consider assertiveness to be a handicapping quality when possessed by women, directing attention to an "assertive–aggressive" duality:

> Assertiveness is a valuable personal trait for women to develop (like motherhood and apple pie, it can be lauded), but it's not much of a threat in the business game. Assertion, after all, means to insist on recognition of oneself, or to maintain your right to legitimate feelings, needs, and ideas by making positive statements. As now taught to women, assertiveness means to express yourself to get what you want but don't make anybody mad in the process. . . . assertive is nice, aggressive is naughty.[45]

Assertiveness is not an innate ability of men or women, nor is it synonymous with aggressive behavior. Assertiveness is a positive, responsible, bold, enterprising set of behaviors; aggressiveness tends toward quarrelsome, hostile practices. A more assertive

► HOW TO TUNE SOMEONE IN TO YOUR WAY OF THINKING WITHOUT GIVING ORDERS

By J. Mitchell Perry

How many times has your boss told you what to do at work and your first reaction has been to resist? As a manager, how many times have you been frustrated with coworkers who were unwilling to sign up for your ideas on how they could work more efficiently?

How often have you told your adolescent child not to do a certain thing and he or she ends up doing it anyway?

Most of us who are managers, influence peddlers, or parents are constantly giving directives, orders and generally telling people what to do. Our advice may be sound, but often we are met with reluctance.

This isn't because of what we are saying, but because we have come up with the answers, not them. People will change, adjust and commit when, in their terms, it makes sense for them to do so. Our job when influencing them is to expedite the process.

A powerful way to make this happen is to ask a series of questions that will lead someone to the same answer you would have proposed. Let's say that I am your manager at a Fast-Food Fried Chicken Restaurant. The conclusion I want you to reach is that it's a good idea for you to wear a chicken suit to drum up business.

But if I told you this from the outset, you would probably find a host of reasons why you shouldn't—for example, that you would look like an idiot. Deep down inside you may think my idea is a good one, but you resist it because it wasn't your idea.

Instead, as your manager, let me ask you some questions: Question: What's a good way to get families to bring us their business? Answer: We could offer a discount. Q: That's good. What would be a way we could really stick

out? A: We could come up with a funny promotion. Q: What kind of promotion would your kids think is funny? A: Well, I could always dress up in a chicken suit.

Initially, this process may appear more time consuming, but I guarantee that it's quicker than if I had told you what to do from the outset and then had to overcome your opposition.

You might be wondering what kind of questions you need to ask. There are two types: open-ended and closed-ended. Open-ended questions lead to greater discovery. They are the questions that begin with Who, What, Where, When, Which and How. These kinds of questions accelerate the process. On the other hand, asking closed-ended questions—ones that prompt "yes" and "no" answers—takes more skill on your part. Generally they're more difficult and it takes longer to arrive at conclusions.

"Why" questions put people on the spot and immediately make them defensive. You may, for example, ask your child, "Why do you like Madonna?" Instead, you could say, "What made you choose that Madonna CD?" "What made you . . ." is a much less aggressive way of finding out. Encouraging people to make their own discoveries is quite a challenge.

We have been conditioned to give answers and tell people what to do rather than ask questions and let people come to their own conclusions.

The task may be difficult, but if you want people to change, commit or adjust their behavior, they will do it only when they have thought of it and think it's a good idea.

Why waste time fighting people's resistance when you could spend that time signing people up for your programs.

Source: J. Mitchell Perry, "How to Tune Someone in to Your Way of Thinking Without Giving Orders," *The Orlando Sentinel*, November 26, 1992, C1. Reprinted by permission: Tribune Media Services.

---

posture can give both men and women increased confidence and the skills necessary to build a strong personal power base. This combined with an understanding of organizational realities can lead to managerial success.

Interacting and coping in a nondefensive, nonmanipulative way allow problems and conflicts to be worked out with mutual compromise. It makes interpersonal communication more effective and helps halt communication gameplaying. Manuel Smith, a clinical professor of psychology at UCLA and a pioneer in the field of systematic assertive therapy, has identified several assertive strategies applicable to organizational settings—the broken record, fogging, and negative assertion.[46]

The *broken record* is a technique whereby you calmly and persistently repeat your arguments or demands over and over. You remain calm and ignore manipulative side traps while sticking to your desired point. By being assertive in a persistent way you take positive action to achieve your goals. Consider the following dialogue:

You: John, I need that report you put together covering our most recent sales figures. I must have it by three o'clock this afternoon so I can include it in my presentation.

John: I'm sorry, Mariam, I won't be able to give it to you by then because I have to check over the figures again and I'm really tied up today.

You: I realize, John, that you're very busy, but I have to have the report by three o'clock.

John: I told you I don't have time to do it.

You: I understand that you told me you're busy, John, but I must have the report by three o'clock.

John: Well, this other work I'm doing is more important and it's for my supervisor. I don't see how I can do the report for you today.

You: Certainly, John, your other work is important; however, I still need the report by three o'clock.

You remain calm and stick to your desired objective. Ultimately, you'll probably get the report.

Fogging is a technique whereby you refuse to be defensive when criticized, refuse to be apologetic, and refrain from counterattacking with criticism of your own. You handle criticism assertively simply by offering no resistance. The dialogue may go something like this:

John: Your attitude has been terrible lately.

You: Yes, I see how you might say that.

Here, you have disarmed your adversary by appearing to agree without actually doing so. You have not denied the emotionally provoking assertion, nor have you confirmed it, while at the same time not becoming emotional and defensive in your behavior.

Negative assertion is a positive technique that allows you to look more comfortably at negatives in your own behavior or personality without feeling defensive. It effectively counters our natural reaction to reject personal criticism. Suppose the following dialogue occurs between you and your supervisor:

John: You didn't do too well in your two o'clock meeting.

You: You're right, I wasn't very skillful in the way I handled the situation, was I? How do you think I should have handled it?

Here, a defensive argument was averted and you'll get some valuable suggestions for the future. Additionally, you've won respect for accepting criticism gracefully and your supervisor will probably be pleased and flattered at your request for advice.

Assertiveness involves the use of interpersonal techniques required of both men and women in the organizational setting. It represents a positive, responsible posture and set of behaviors. We all are governed by a "Bill of Assertive Rights"[47]:

I. You have the right to judge your own behavior, thoughts, and emotions, and to take the responsibility for their initiation and consequences upon yourself.

II. You have the right to offer no reasons or excuses for justifying your behavior.

III. You have the right to judge if you are responsible for finding solutions to other peoples' problems.

IV. You have the right to change your mind.

V. You have the right to make mistakes—and be responsible for them.

VI. You have the right to say, "I don't know."

VII. You have the right to be independent of the goodwill of others before coping with them.

VIII. You have the right to be illogical in making decisions.

IX. You have the right to say, "I don't understand."

X. You have the right to say, "I don't care."

▶ SUMMARY

Interpersonal communication is the sharing of meaning between two or more people who have a personal relationship and who consider each other as unique individuals. This is the most familiar and most common way that people communicate. It is especially important in business because the average executive spends up to 80 percent of the day communicating with others, and the majority of that communication is interpersonal in nature. This reliance on interpersonal communication will continue, regardless of future technological advances.

Interpersonal communication can best be understood by contrasting it to impersonal communication where people are treated as objects and not as unique human beings. We hold in high esteem our interpersonal relationships because they are unique, irreplaceable, interdependent, and contain more self-disclosure.

Our self-concept, the set of perceptions we each have of ourself, is an important factor when considering interpersonal communication. No one is born with a self-concept but it develops through self-appraisal and reflected appraisal. Self-appraisal is the judgment of ourselves on the basis of how we see ourselves, including our physical being, our self-image, and our talents. Reflected appraisal is how we believe significant others see us, such as parents, siblings, prominent teachers, best friends, and employers. Our self-concept is important because it directly affects how we communicate. Research indicates that people with positive self-concepts communicate very differently than people with more negative self-concepts. Moreover, the self-concept is meaningfully related to the phenomenon of the self-fulfilling prophecy, where our expectations of events result in their actually happening. The Galatea (self-directed) and Pygmalion (other-directed) effects are both types of self-fulfilling prophecies.

We can improve our self-concept by taking time to get to know ourselves better and by actively seeking information about ourselves from others. In this way, we come to a greater understanding of who we really are and can be more effective interpersonal communicators.

Perception, the mental and cognitive process that enables us to select, organize, and interpret our surroundings, is a second major factor influencing interpersonal communication. We all see the world somewhat differently as a result of individual physical influences (our senses, age, health, and biological cycles), emotional influences (emotions and feelings), and cultural influences (the varied lifestyles of groups of people). This enables us to communicate with others and accounts for many of our communication misunderstandings. We can improve our communication with others by questioning the accuracy of our perceptions, by using perception-checking to clarify our perceptions, and by distinguishing between facts and inferences. These are not easy tasks to perform but the results will be interpersonally rewarding.

Dyadic or face-to-face exchanges pervade all organizational activity, serving a multiplicity of functions, operating at numerous levels within the organizational hierarchy, and significantly affecting the lives of the organization's employees. Therefore, the analysis of dyadic relationships can be a useful method for measuring personal communication effectiveness and understanding interpersonal communication problems within the organization. The transactional analysis model is a tool for examining complementary, crossed, and ulterior interactions, and for identifying communication gameplaying within the organization.

Communication games, unlike such other types of communication behavior as rituals, pastimes, and intimacy, are dysfunctional in nature, involving concealed motivations and a host of ulterior dynamics. Games are played for many reasons: to gain power, to discount oneself, to seek revenge, to exploit, or to gain prestige. However, not participating, withholding the payoff, and refusing to discount others' gameplaying behavior will yield to more accurate and open communication.

The organizational setting, however, requires that both men and women assertively express their ideas.

Assertiveness, unlike aggressiveness, involves responsibly engaging in positive, nondefensive behaviors. A more assertive posture can give men and women increased confidence and the skills necessary to accomplish their objectives.

You are with other people your entire lifetime, at home and at work. It is people and your interactions with them that make your life happy or sad, meaningful or meaningless, full or empty. Thus, interpersonal communication and the resulting interpersonal relationships exert a powerful and significant influence on organizational systems.

▶ QUESTIONS FOR DISCUSSION AND SKILL DEVELOPMENT

1. In what specific ways has interpersonal communication been important to you in your personal life? In your school life? In your work life?
2. You have been participating in interpersonal communication all of your life. What is your personal definition of "interpersonal communication"? How does your definition differ from others?
3. Make a list of people with whom you regularly communicate interpersonally and a list of those people with whom you regularly communicate impersonally. How do the lists differ? Beside the qualities listed in the text, what other qualities differentiate these groups of people?
4. Write a paragraph responding to the question, "Who am I?" Take some time to reflect and carefully organize your thoughts.
5. What are five important self-fulfilling prophecies you now have? Are these representative of the Galatea effect or the Pygmalion effect? Explain.
6. Create a perception-check for a recent event in which your perception of the event was incorrect. Use exact perception-checking language.
7. What are two instances in which you made an inference instead of an observation? Write a short paragraph about the result of making the inference instead of the observation? In what ways could the outcomes have been affected if you hadn't made the inferences?
8. Recognize and provide examples from your own experience of the three types of transactions—complementary, crossed, and ulterior.
9. Explain the concept of "communication games" and "gameplaying." Identify games commonly played in organizations, citing the transactions, roles, and payoffs for each. Suggest specific ways for stopping these games.
10. Distinguish between aggressive behavior and assertiveness. Give examples of assertive approaches to selected situations. What are your "assertive rights"?

▶ NOTES

1. Roy M. Berko, Andrew D. Wolvin, and Ray Curtis, *This Business of Communication,* 5th ed. (Madison, WI: Brown and Benchmark, 1993).
2. A. Pertofi, "The Graphic Revolution in Computers," in: E. Cornish, ed., *Careers Tomorrow: The Outlook for Work in a Changing World* (Bethesda, MD: World Future Society, 1988): 62–66.
3. John Naisbitt, *Megatrends: Ten New Directions Transforming Our Lives* (New York: Warner Books, 1982): 45.
4. T. Bailey, "Changes in the Nature and Structure of Work: Implications for Skill Requirements and Skill Formation," *Columbia University Conservation of Human Resources Technical Paper No. 9* (November 1989).

5. Anita S. Bednar and Robert J. Olney, "Communication Needs of Recent Graduates," *Bulletin of the Association for Business Communication* (December 1987): 22–23.

6. Kathryn Martin, "Video Teaches Personal Skills to Students," *Colorado Springs Gazette Telegraph,* September 8, 1987, B1.

7. Dan B. Curtis, Jerry L. Winsor, and Ronald D. Stephens, "National Preferences in Business and Communication Education," *Communication Education* (January 1989): 6–14.

8. Arthur P. Bochner, "The Functions of Human Communication in Interpersonal Bonding," in: Carroll C. Arnold and John Waite Bowers, eds., *Handbook of Rhetorical and Communication Theory* (Boston: Allyn and Bacon, 1984): 550.

9. Ronald B. Adler and Neil Towne, *Looking Out, Looking In,* 7th ed. (New York: Harcourt Brace Jovanovich, 1993).

10. Joseph Luft, *Of Human Interaction* (Palo Alto, CA: National Press Books, 1969): 6.

11. Mary Brown Parlee, "The Friendship Bond," *Psychology Today* (1979): 43–54.

12. Michael Lewis and Jeanne Brooks-Gunn, *Social Cognition and the Acquisition of Self* (New York: Basic Books, 1979): 222–240.

13. Miriam Stoppard, *Know Your Child* (New York: Ballantine Books, 1991).

14. Rudolph Verderber, *Communicate* (Belmont, CA: Wadsworth, 1993): 36–37.

15. Charles H. Cooley, *Human Nature and the Social Order* (New York: Scribner's, 1912).

16. Dorothy Law Nolte, "Children Learn What They Live," in: Adler and Towne, *Looking Out, Looking In,* 44.

17. Adler and Towne, *Looking Out, Looking In,* 43–44.

18. Donald E. Hamachek, *Encounters with the Self,* 2nd ed. (New York: Holt, Rinehart & Winston, 1982): 3–5.

19. Joseph A. DeVito, *Messages: Building Interpersonal Communication Skills* (New York: Harper and Row, 1990): 70.

20. Robert Rosenthal and L. Jacobson, *Pygmalion in the Classroom* (New York: Holt, Rinehart & Winston, 1968): 5–6.

21. DeVito, *Messages,* 37–38.

22. Richard L. Weaver II, *Understanding Interpersonal Communication,* 5th ed. (Glenview, IL: Scott, Foresman/Little, Brown Higher Education, 1990): 57–59.

23. John Godfrey Saxe, "The Parable of the Six Blind Men of Indostan," *Poems* (Boston, 1852).

24. Frank A. Geldard, *The Human Senses* (New York: John Wiley & Sons, 1953).

25. Rensis Likert, *New Patterns of Management* (New York: McGraw-Hill, 1961): 52.

26. Roger N. Shepard, *Mind Sights: Original Visual Illusions, Ambiguities, and Other Anomalies, with a Commentary on the Play of Mind in Perception and Art* (New York: W.H. Freeman, 1990): 69.

27. Ibid.

28. Kay Deaux and Lawrence Wrightman, *Social Psychology,* 4th ed. (Belmont, CA: Wadsworth, 1988).

29. Sara Trenholm and Arthur Jensen, *Interpersonal Communication,* 2nd ed. (Belmont, CA: Wadsworth, 1992): 58–60.

30. George Kelly, *The Psychology of Personal Constructs* (New York: Norton Press, 1955).

31. N. Cantor, "A Cognitive Social Approach to Personality," in: N. Cantor and J. F. Kihlstrom, eds., *Personality, Cognition, and Social Interaction* (Hillsdale, NJ: Erlbaum Press, 1981).

32. P. F. Secord, C. W. Backman, and D. R. Slavitt, *Understanding Social Life: An Introduction to Social Psychology* (New York: McGraw-Hill, 1976).

33. Joseph P. Forgas, *Emotion and Social Judgments* (New York: Pergamon Press, 1991).

34. DeVito, *Messages,* 238.

35. Paul Watzlawick, *The Situation Is Hopeless, But Not Serious: The Pursuit of Unhappiness* (New York: W. W. Norton, 1983).

36. William V. Haney, *Communication and Organizational Behavior* (Homewood, IL: Richard D. Irwin, 1967): 195.

37. Eric Berne, *Games People Play* (New York: Grove Press, 1964).

38. W. Penfield, "Memory Mechanisms," *A.M.A. Archives of Neurology and Psychiatry* 67 (1952): 178–198.

39. Eric Berne, *Transactional Analysis in Psychotherapy* (New York: Grove Press, 1961): 24.

40. Muriel James and Dorothy Jongeward, *Born to Win* (Reading, MA: Addison-Wesley, 1971): 20.

41. William R. Tracey, "Put-down Techniques: Are You Guilty of Them?" *Personnel Journal* 58 (May 1979): 311.

42. Berne, *Games People Play,* 48.

43. Thomas A. Harris, *I'm OK–You're OK* (New York: Harper and Row, 1967): 153.

44. Berne, *Games People Play,* 78–168.

45. Betty Harragan, *Games Mother Never Taught You* (New York: Warner Books, 1977): 308.

46. Manuel Smith, *When I Say No, I Feel Guilty* (New York: Bantam Books, 1975): 72–120.

47. Ibid., i.

CHAPTER SEVEN

7

Flexible Leadership and Conflict Management

LEARNING OBJECTIVES:

To define leadership and discuss the ways it emerges

To compare and contrast approaches to leadership—trait approach, style approach, situational approach, and transformational approach

To determine leadership style in terms of task behaviors, relationship behaviors, and group maturity

To distinguish the various forms and contexts of conflict

To understand the place of conflict in groups and in the organizational arena

To identify communication strategies for managing conflicts

Organizations are a tapestry of explicit and implicit power structures. In the explicit structure, leadership is conferred and represented by title and authority. In the implicit structure, leadership is a delicately sculpted image built by cultivating respect of peers, and projecting a sense of reliability, goal orientation, and vision. Inevitably, this latter leadership construct entails effectively managing conflicts as they arise. The skills for both leadership and conflict management are basics for success in tomorrow's workplace. Those who have these skills can help employers create the conditions for achieving goals and for succeeding in the marketplace. This chapter (1) examines various approaches to leadership, (2) explores dimensions of flexible leadership, and (3) focuses on productive conflict resolution.

Leadership has fascinated scholars for centuries, but despite all this attention it remains an enigma. James MacGregor Burns, historian and professor of government, observes that "leadership is one of the most observed and least understood phenomena on earth."[1] Leadership has been defined in different ways. Paul Hersey defines it as "any attempt to influence the behavior of another individual or group."[2] Bernard Bass would add that actual change in behavior is needed for successful leadership.[3] These definitions attempt to consider the character traits of leaders as well as the environmental factors and symbolic forces or vision that make a leader effective or ineffective. We will define leadership as *the process of influencing the activities of a person or a group to achieve a goal in a given situation.*

It must be noted that, despite their often being mistakenly equated, there is a difference between leadership and management. Warren Bennis observes: "Leading does not mean managing; the difference between the two is crucial. There are many institutions that are very well managed and very poorly led. They may excel in the ability to handle all the routine inputs every day, yet they may never ask whether the routine should be preserved at all."[4] The fundamental difference between management and leadership is that the former is concerned with activities designed to produce "consistency and order," whereas the latter is concerned with "constructive or adaptive change."[5] Managers are safe, conservative, predictable, and conforming; leaders are movers and shakers—imaginative, innovative, real risk takers. Warren Bennis and Burt Nanus say that "managers are people who do things right and leaders are people who do the right thing."[6] Ultimately, leadership is a vital part of management; it is the motor that makes the car run. Management without leadership is doomed to go nowhere, it's doomed to failure.

▶ APPROACHES TO LEADERSHIP

Theoretical explanations of leadership have been presented through various models. Some researchers have tried to discover the character traits of leaders; others have focused on leadership behavior or styles to determine how leaders act in particular situations. More recently, attention has been given to examining environmental factors and those situations which give rise to leadership. Finally, much of the emerging literature about the "New Leadership" has centered on charisma and how leaders create a symbolic focus or vision for a group.[7]

Character Trait Approach

The *character trait approach* theory of leadership emphasizes the personal qualities of leaders and implies that leaders are born rather than made. Gordon Allport, one of the most influential of the trait theorists, observes that "traits are the building blocks of personality, the guideposts for action, the source of uniqueness of the individual."[8] Three broad types of traits have emerged: (1) physical factors such as height, weight, physique, appearance, and age; (2) ability characteristics such as intelligence, knowledge, scholarship, and communication skills; and (3) personality features such as alertness, emotional control, personal integrity, sensitivity, self-confidence, self-assurance, assertiveness, and initiative. Recent leadership studies have evinced a resurgence of the trait approach, with the emphasis being placed on the learned and acquired personal traits of acknowledged leaders. Having interviewed such leaders from various walks of life, Warren Bennis identified the following common characteristics[9]:

> ▶ *Passion*—the leader loves what he or she does
> ▶ *Integrity*—this trait is composed of self-knowledge, candor, and maturity
> ▶ *Trust*—this is a quality which the leader earns from others
> ▶ *Curiosity and daring*—the leader actively seeks knowledge and is willing to take risks

Similarly, Philip Crosby has identified certain common qualities of leaders: ethical, available, sensible, willing to learn, determined, energetic, reliable, humble, intense, and pleasant.[10] Although some traits appear to differentiate between effective and ineffective leaders, there still exist many contradictory and qualifying research findings.[11] Certainly, these are important qualities, but they do not provide a comprehensive explanation of how leaders interact with followers and meet the needs of specific circumstances.

Leadership Style Approach

From the late 1940s, the study of leadership in organizations moved increasingly toward the understanding of *leadership style* or behavior to describe what leaders do. Leadership style researchers study the behavior exhibited by effective leaders, and then train others to model such behavior. A range of leadership styles have been developed and chief among these has been the autocratic-to-democratic continuum proposed by Ralph White and Ronald Lippitt. They identify three primary styles: autocratic, democratic, and laissez-faire. The *autocratic leader* makes decisions with little influence from others, viewing followers as simply necessary elements for goal achievement. *Democratic leaders* are sensitive to the interpersonal and relational needs of followers and involve them in decision making and problem solving. Finally, the *laissez-faire leader* is a nonleader who takes a "hands off" approach, providing little or no direction and showing little direct concern for individuals or goals.[12]

The optimal leader behavior is that which achieves high scores on both consideration and initiating dimensions. Consideration relates to the extent to which leaders promote camaraderie, mutual trust, liking, and respect in the relationship between themselves and their followers. Initiating denotes the degree to which leaders organize work tightly, structure the work context, provide clear-cut definitions of role responsibility, and generally play a very active part in getting the work at hand fully scheduled. Leaders' behaviors have been related to such outcomes as job satisfaction, group productivity, and performance.[13] This approach offers guidelines for leadership by suggesting the necessary functions that a leader should perform.

However, the assertion that both consideration and initiating dimensions of style promote work-group effectiveness, job satisfaction, morale, and the like has been found empirically wanting by some studies.[14] The failure to take situational factors into account may in part explain the inconsistent findings. The trait and style approaches focus primarily on the individual characteristics of leaders and followers. Trait characteristics and style dimensions do not operate singly; they exist in combination with a situation to influence followers.

► ARE YOU AN UNCONSCIOUS LEADER?

By Nina Harris

Corporate boards are crying for them. Nations' citizens propel them to powerful positions. Toastmasters breeds them. But defining them is a challenge.

Despite the multitude of research accumulated over the years, the concept of leadership remains elusive. Just what makes a good leader? Is it intelligence? Prestige? Dependability? Charisma?

One way of defining leadership is functionally, which is a bit different from the standard definition of leadership.

A leader is usually thought to be someone who most helps a particular group achieve its objectives. But think about your last committee meeting. Weren't those terrific ideas that George contributed? And Marge was a whiz at soothing ruffled feathers when Jay and Linda tangled over marketing strategies. Bill waltzed in twenty minutes late as usual, and Nancy kept yawning and staring into space.

From the functional point of view, each of these people was a leader, in his or her own way—even Bill, Jay, Linda and Nancy. These four were dysfunctional leaders. Their late arrival, quarreling and daydreaming led the group away from its goal.

Task Skills

But George exhibited a positive functional leadership skill. His input helped push the group toward completion of the project. Although George didn't think of himself as a leader, he did act as a leader, however briefly, because his ideas took the group one step further toward its goal. You act as a leader occasionally, too, if you do any of the following during a meeting:

- ► *Initiate.* Are you the one who proposes a plan that will help your group with its project? If so, you're leading the group toward its ultimate goal.
- ► *Clarify.* Are you able to unearth the real problem the group faces? Sometimes the basic problem is buried by other trivial matters. If you're the one who pinpoints and defines the actual problem, you're clearing the way for action.
- ► *Gather data.* Do you provide information concerning the group's task? Ask for or offer opinions? When you do so, you're helping to accumulate the data the group needs to perform its job. (Note, though, that most groups never get beyond the opinion-giving stage. That's one of the reasons groups aren't as effective as individuals for getting jobs done.)

- ► *Summarize.* Are you the one who pulls together related ideas or draws a conclusion for the group to consider? If you do either of these, you're directing your group toward its objective.

Group Maintenance

The difficulty involved with using the above skills is that they frequently create conflict within the group. That's where another set of functional leadership skills comes into play. Remember Marge? She handled group maintenance—that is, she helped keep the group working smoothly. You're reinforcing your group's efficient operation whenever you:

- ► *Encourage.* Are you friendly, warm and responsive to others in the group? If you are, you're encouraging your fellow group members to contribute their ideas without fear of rejection or ridicule. By keeping communication channels open, you're insuring everyone will participate.
- ► *Harmonize.* Do you dispel the friction that develops when personalities clash? When you do, you guide the group back to the business at hand and away from self-destructive disagreements.
- ► *Set standards.* Ever find yourself establishing rules and guidelines for the group to follow? Then you are the one who supplies the group with an operational framework that will help it efficiently achieve its goal. You periodically check the group's behavior against these standards, too, to keep everything organized.

Conscious Effort

You instinctively carry out many of the above functions in your everyday life. Think of all the times this past week that you've offered suggestions, listened empathetically, offered support or eliminated some confusion. The problem is, you usually don't do so consciously. In any group situation, you must be able to stand back and ask yourself a few key questions: What is happening in the group right now? What functional leadership roles are being played? What functional leadership skills could I employ that would make me an effective leader and thus help the group? When you are able to do this, you'll enhance the efforts of the groups you belong to and contribute to your own personal growth.

So study the above skills and figure out which ones you have and which ones you need to develop. As our society grows larger and more technologically complex, the need for rewarding human systems—systems in which men and

Situation Approach

The *situation approach,* often referred to as a contingency approach, assumes that leadership behavior is contingent on variations in the situation.[15] One of the earliest, and most frequently cited situational models is Fred Fiedler's Contingency Model of Leadership.[16] His rating of least-preferred coworker (LPC) became the primary element of the model. Fiedler claims that our ratings of others with whom we do not like to work provide us with valuable information about our leadership behavior. Those with low LPC scores are more concerned with tasks and are negatively evaluated by others; leaders with high LPC scores demonstrate greater concern for relationships and are more favorably evaluated. The effectiveness of a leader in a given situation is influenced by three factors: (1) the leader's position power, (2) task structure, and (3) the interpersonal relationship between leader and members.

A leader gains power by virtue of his or her position within a group or organization. From this perspective, power can be understood as the influence an individual has over another as a result of dependency on the powerful person. John French and Bertram Raven describe five power bases available to leaders: legitimate, reward, coercive, referent, and expert power.[17] *Legitimate power* resides in the position, title, or role a person occupies. People holding legitimate power have the right to prescribe our behavior within specified parameters: judges, teachers, parents, our supervisors at work. *Reward power* rests on the ability to control and distribute something of value to others. Although rewards are often tangible, like money and health benefits, they might also be intangible, like warmth and supportiveness. Regardless of type, rewards must be desirable to serve as sufficient motivators. *Coercive power* is based on the ability to administer punishment or to give negative reinforcement. In its most extreme form, coercive power translates into brute physical force. *Referent power* is role-model power resulting when others identify with the leader. It is assigned by others, arising when one person admires another. Finally, *expert power* rests on what the leader knows. In our culture, experts are influential because they supply needed information and skills. Expert power is based on the person not the position, in contrast to legitimate power. To this list, some add *connection power,* resulting from the people the leader knows and their networking within the organization. Its strength is derived from the "connections" or links with other powerful people throughout the organization.[18] Warren Bennis and Burt Nanus summarize the relationship between power and leadership this way: "Power is . . . the capacity to translate intention into reality and sustain it. Leadership is the wise use of this power. . . . Vision is the commodity of leaders, and power is their currency."[19]

Task structure is another important situational variable. Some tasks are highly structured, having very specific procedures and agreed-on outcomes; others are highly unstructured and may be accomplished in a number of ways. Task structure influences the degree of direct control and the need for participation.

Finally, a situational leader builds a relationship with his or her followers through interaction. A positive relationship is characterized by loyalty, affection, trust, and respect. Positive relationships result in situations that are highly motivating and that produce member commitment.

Fiedler plotted each of the three situational variables for leaders on a continuum from favorable to unfavorable. The most favorable conditions for leaders exist when the relationship between the leader and followers is good, the task is highly structured, and the leader's position power is strong. The least favorable conditions exist when the relationship between the leader and followers is poor, the task is highly unstructured, and the leader's position power is weak. The effectiveness of a leader in a given situation, according to Fiedler, is influenced by LPC scores. Much of the criticism of Fiedler's theory has focused on the LPC measures because situations must be adapted to fit leaders instead of leaders modifying behavior to fit situations.[20]

The situational approach depends so heavily on specific situational factors that no general principles can be discovered. Moreover, there are exceptions to the rule that unique circumstances alone determine leadership effectiveness in different situations. Charles Pearce, who functioned well as president of Bell and Howell Corporation, was just as effective as the U.S. senator from Illinois. Robert McNamara, who successfully led the Ford Motor Company, was just as effective as the U.S. Secretary of Defense and head of the World Bank. As with the trait theory, the situational approach fails to specify critical behavioral factors. Both theories focus on individuals as leaders and how they affect group behavior rather than on leadership behavior as a total process of achieving goals.

Transformational Approach

In the past decade, the transformational approach has emerged as a new perspective for understanding and explaining leadership. The transformational approach was first outlined by James MacGregor Burns who compared traditional or "transactional" leadership with a more "complex" and "potent" type of leadership called "transforming."[21] Transactional leadership rewards subordinates for compliance with the leader's expectations but fails to inject those extra increments of effort that make the difference between mundane and extraordinary performance. By contrast, transformational leaders motivate subordinates to commit themselves to performance that exceeds expectations. *Transformational leadership* comprises:

▶ *Charisma*—Max Weber was one of the first organizational scholars to discuss this leadership by virtue of personality. The charismatic leader provides vision and sense of mission, instills pride, gains respect, and trust.

▶ *Inspiration*—The leader communicates high expectations, uses symbols to focus efforts, and expresses important purposes in simple ways.

▶ *Vision*—The leader articulates an idealized goal or vision and is future directed. The leader is part visionary, part standard-bearer, part cheerleader, and part taskmaster.

▶ *Individualized Consideration*—Individualized consideration entails the leader giving personal attention to followers and their needs, trusting and respecting them, and helping them to learn by encouraging responsibility.

▶ *Intellectual Stimulation*—The leader provides a flow of new ideas which challenge followers and which stimulate a rethinking of old ways of doing things.[22]

Transformational leaders formulate end values which serve to inject their environment with meaning and provide a lens through which the world is interpreted. They work to convert others to this acquired worldview by conveying their enthusiasm to their followers. They engage in activities that represent considerable personal risk, often use unconventional methods to move towards achieving their vision, and are sensitive to the organization's environment and the threats and opportunities that it offers.

Increasingly, leadership is extolled which exhibits vision, empowers others, inspires, challenges the status quo, and adopts a proactive stance.[23] This represents a bold and exciting perspective for understanding and explaining leadership. However, different labels have been given to this kind of leadership—transformational, charismatic, visionary, and magic.[24] Together, these overlapping approaches have been dubbed the "New Leadership" and they emphasize similar themes and motifs:

- ▶ Leadership and management are not synonymous.
- ▶ Vision is an important, if not essential, component of the leadership of organizations and often of divisions within organizations.
- ▶ Vision must be properly communicated to be an effective motivator.
- ▶ Leadership can be a route to the empowerment of others.
- ▶ Leaders must be trusted and seen as having personal integrity.
- ▶ The leader does not usually work alone.
- ▶ Charisma is an important component of effective leadership, but it is only one facet.[25]

Despite these very real contributions of the New Leadership, there is a relative absence of any situational analysis and perhaps too much attention to leader behavior. Certainly more studies are needed to establish the long-term effectiveness of New Leadership practices. Past experience of leadership and organizational research suggests that it is unlikely that we really have discovered a "one best way."[26]

▶ FLEXIBLE LEADERSHIP

Whether you've seen the movie version with Marlon Brando, the televised revisionist version with Mel Gibson, or read the Nordoff and Hall trilogy, most of you are familiar with the great sea saga, *Mutiny on the Bounty*. What you may not know is that the Nordoff and Hall trilogy is an accurate account of a historical event. There was a mutiny on HMS *Bounty* on April 28, 1789; Captain Bligh and Fletcher Christian actually lived. What makes them appropriate to our purposes is that we can balance the fictional account with the historical record; also, a ship at sea is akin to a closed-structure organization and here the two protagonists exhibit exactly opposite styles of leadership in a particular situation.

William Bligh was captain of the ship, his rank at the time actually that of lieutenant. He had worked his way up through the ranks, not being gentry-born, so his nautical skills were unquestioned and served along with his position as a basis of power. This voyage to Tahiti, which had only been made twice before, had as its mission to bring back breadfruit cuttings to be cultivated in England as a cheap source of food. To achieve this goal, Bligh was allowed to handpick most of his crew, including Fletcher Christian who had been his pupil on several previous voyages.

Bligh became a tyrannical boss—skillful but without praise for the skills of others, strong-willed but without tolerance for the will of others, temperamental, self-righteous, and above setting an example. Not long into the voyage, over dinner with the officers, the differing attitudes toward the crew and the two leadership styles of Bligh and Christian are sharply contrasted:

> The talk had turned to the members of the *Bounty*'s company.
>
> "Damn them!" said Bligh. . . . "A lazy, incompetent lot of scoundrels! . . . That fellow I had flogged yesterday; what was his name, Mr. Fryer?"
>
> "Burkitt," replied the master, a little red in the face.
>
> "Yes, Burkitt, the insolent hound! And they're all as bad. I'm damned if they know a sheet from a tack!"
>
> "I venture to differ with you, sir," said the master. "I should call Smith, Quintal, and McCoy first-class seamen and even Burkitt, though he was in the wrong. . . . "
>
> "The insolent hound!" repeated Bligh violently, interrupting the master. "At the slightest report of misconduct, I'll have him seized up again. Next time it will be four dozen, instead of two!"
>
> Christian caught my eye as the captain spoke. "If I may express an opinion, Mr. Bligh," he said quietly, "Burkitt's nature is one to tame with kindness rather than with blows."
>
> Bligh's short, harsh laugh rang out grimly. "La-di-da, Mr. Christian! On my word, you should apply for a place as master in a young ladies' seminary! Kindness, indeed! . . . A fine captain you'll make if you don't heave overboard such notions. Kindness! . . . Fear is what they do understand! Without that, mutiny and piracy would be rife on the high seas!"
>
> . . . Christian shook his head. "I cannot agree," he said courteously. "Our seamen do not differ from other Englishmen. Some must be ruled by fear, it is true, but there are others, and finer men, who will follow a kind, just, and fearless officer to the death."[27]

Fletcher Christian is portrayed as a democratic leader who derived his power both from position and personal loyalty. He was sensitive, decisive, and ambitious. In terms of today's standards, he was the model executive most would want to emulate, until he violated the norms and ignored the organizational goal.

The mutiny occurred while en route back to England with the breadfruit cuttings on board. Up to this point, regardless of your feelings toward Bligh, he was a successful leader—he was accomplishing the organizational goal. The mutiny, however, proves that Bligh was not an *effective* leader. He failed to use a leadership style appropriate to the developing situation and this impinged on his success as a leader.

On the other hand, Christian was an effective leader, but he also failed. He accepted the personal power and leadership offered by members of the crew and chose to mutiny over other options, thus failing to successfully accomplish the organizational goal(s). Christian was murdered not long after in a sequence of events started by one of his own crew members. His democratic style proved inappropriate to the new situation and he was no longer effective.

Bligh consistently used a tyrannical style up to and throughout the mutiny; Christian always used a democratic style of leadership. Both failed as leaders because they were rigid in their styles. That's the lesson demonstrated by this classic case: leadership must be flexible.

The notion of *flexible leadership* is an accommodating approach that builds on previous research and remains open to the still-developing transformational/charismatic thinking with all its vision, inspiration, and empowerment. It recognizes that certain successful and effective leadership qualities can be advantageous in specific situations, but personal traits alone do not predispose people to success as leaders. Leadership is a delicate balance of successfulness and effectiveness. A leader must choose a style not only appropriate to achieving the goal or task but also one that is appropriate to the situation. Such behavior calls for a whole new way of thinking and operating, which James Hunt calls "Janusian" after the two-faced Roman god Janus.[28] Those who are successful are labeled "master managers."[29]

Choosing an appropriate style is helped by the Situational Leadership Model developed by Paul Hersey and Kenneth Blanchard.[30] Hersey and Blanchard divide leader behavior into task and relationship dimensions. The appropriate degree of task and relationship behavior exhibited by a leader is dependent on the readiness level of the followers.

Task behavior is the amount of direction a leader provides to accomplish a specific task. It can be low or high depending on what each group member is to do, and when, where, and how it's to be done.

Relationship behavior is the extent to which a leader engages in two-way communication, facilitative behavior, and supportive behavior, and provides positive psychological strokes. The leader provides "reasons why," actively listens to the comments of others, and is sensitive to the stroking needs of his or her followers. This, too, can range from low to high.

This commingling of task and relationship behaviors produces four basic leadership styles:

1. *High task/low relationship:* This is the "telling" style of leadership; a lot of direction and only a small amount of consideration. Bligh's tyranny exemplifies the worst aspect of this style; managers who simply command by telling typify it. *Example, supervisor to subordinate:* "I want you to do ____ and I want it done by the end of the day."

2. *High task/high relationship:* This is the "selling" style of leadership; the leader still provides considerable direction, but also provides "reasons why" so that the follower "buys" into the decisions implicit in the directions. *Example, sales manager to sales representative:* "The BRY account has dropped in sales lately. Why? . . . Okay, but you should have noted that in your call reports. Nonetheless, here's what you can do . . . because. . . . Try this approach on your next call and be sure to detail what happens in your next call report."

3. *Low task/high relationship:* This is the "participating" style of leadership; the leader and followers share in the decision-making process. Mr. Christian's democratic style properly belongs here, particularly because of the shared decision to mutiny. *Example, department head to secretary:* "We may computerize and this might affect your areas of responsibility. Let's meet to discuss its feasibility."

4. *Low task/low relationship:* This is the "delegating" style of leadership; the leader allows followers considerable freedom in making decisions and handling responsibility. *Example, senior legal adviser to legal assistant:* "Draw up the new contract with the BRY Corporation. I trust your judgment and believe you can do a fine job."

These are the four basic leadership styles that emerge from the Situational Leadership Model. Certainly, individual nuances exist within each style. However, to operationalize these styles, a leader must select a style of leadership that fits the situation and the goal(s) to be achieved. How do you choose which of the four basic styles to use? How do you select a style of leadership that fits the situation? How do you determine a style appropriate to the goal(s) or task(s) to be achieved? There are no simple answers to these questions, but the third factor in the Situational Leadership Model can serve as a guide—follower readiness.

Follower readiness consists of two major components: job readiness and psychological readiness. Job readiness refers to demonstrated task-related abilities, skills, and knowledge. Psychological readiness relates to feelings of confidence, willingness, and motivation. The follower's level of readiness involves the ability and willingness to assume responsibility and set attainable goals. Simply stated, knowledge isn't everything; earnest enthusiasm counts, too.

According to Hersey and Blanchard, four combinations of job and psychological readiness indicate follower readiness (R):

▶ R1: Low job readiness and low psychological readiness (follower lacks skills and willingness); neither task-relevant experience nor ability to set goals confidently.

▶ R2: Low job readiness and high psychological readiness (follower lacks skills, but is willing); some task-relevant experience but no ability to set goals despite some confidence.

▶ R3: High job readiness and low psychological readiness (follower is skilled, but lacks willingness); significant task-relevant experience and ability to set goals but still insecure.

▶ R4: High job readiness and high psychological readiness (follower is skilled and willing); solid task-relevant experience and thoroughly able/confident to set goals.

These four levels refer to the follower(s); task and relationship behaviors refer to the leader. Readiness levels can fluctuate as a follower moves from task to task or from one situation to another. Certainly, as followers gain experience their readiness levels change. However, the readiness level of followers dictates effective leader behavior. The mechanism for tying the follower's readiness to the leader's task/relationship behavior is a bell-shaped curve (Exhibit 7-1). The steps in choosing an appropriate style of leadership for a specific situation are (1) determine the task and desired relationship, (2) determine the follower's level of readiness, and (3) draw a vertical line from the determined level of readiness to the bell-shaped curve. The quadrant in which the vertical line meets the curve indicates the style of leadership with the highest probability of being both effective and successful for that situation. Consider the following example.

Quality Electronics has just hired a brilliant electrical engineer who previously worked for the firm's leading competitor. The new engineer has a solid reputation for working on very sophisticated research and development (R&D) projects. The R&D supervisor is excited about immediately starting some projects that fit this new person's unique expertise. However, the R&D procedures followed in the company where the engineer previously worked were completely different. What style(s) of leadership should the R&D supervisor initially use with this new engineer?

▶ **EXHIBIT 7-1**
Situational Leadership®

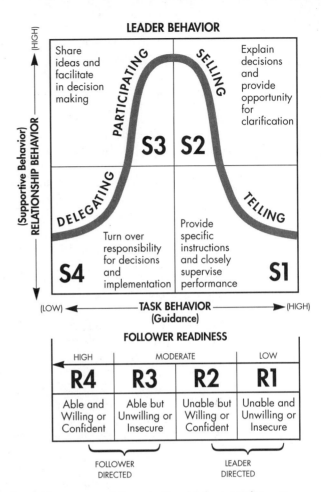

Source: Paul Hersey and Ken Blanchard, *Management of Organizational Behavior Utilizing Human Resources, 6/E,* © 1993, p. 186. Reproduced by permission of Prentice Hall, Inc., Englewood Cliffs, New Jersey.

First, determine the task. In this instance, there are really two tasks. The supervisor wants the engineer to begin working on new projects; but to do this, the engineer has to become familiar with entirely new procedures.

Second, determine the engineer's level of readiness for each task. The new engineer is unfamiliar with company procedures as well as with the others who make up the work team, so the supervisor would assess the engineer's level of readiness to be R1. Drawing a vertical line up from R1 on the bell curve, the supervisor will find an S1 or "telling" style of leadership to be most appropriate. However, the engineer's level of readiness for doing R&D projects is very high (R4) and for this task the supervisor selects an S4 or "delegating" style of leadership. Using two different styles of leadership may appear paradoxical, but it represents the essence of flexible leadership. Consider the following dialogue:

Supervisor: Since you're new here, take a few days to see what we have in the way of equipment, how we organize research teams, and how we operate. Then, go to it.

Chapter 7   Flexible Leadership and Conflict Management   **7-12**

Engineer: Sounds great.

Supervisor: Yeah, I think you'll like it here. Listen, our procedures are different from what you're used to, especially regarding requisitioning materials. So, until you get the hang of it, I'll want to review your requisition forms before you place any orders.

Engineer: Fine. I appreciate your help.

Note that the supervisor did not conclude this dialogue by saying "Okay?" One word alone usually does not alter a leadership style, but in this example it would have been sufficient to suggest an S2 or "selling" style of leadership regarding procedures. Using "Okay?" would be asking the engineer to buy into the decisions implicit in the supervisor's directions about procedures. Also note, that by saying "until you get the hang of it" the supervisor is using a supportive style and provides reassurance that this is only a temporary inconvenience.

The new engineer spends the next week organizing the R&D teams. The engineer will lead one team; leaders will be appointed from the existing staff for the other two teams. One team leader will be Roberta, a good worker who has led teams before and has been in the industry for six years, four with the present firm. The other team leader is Jake. He has approximately the same experience as Roberta but he's weak on microcomputer technology. What styles of leadership should initially be used when dealing with Roberta and Jake?

Based on their task-relevant experience, neither of them is fully ready, so an S3 or "participating" style of leadership is selected for each of the team leaders. This works well with Roberta, but problems develop with Jake because of his weakness in microcomputing. Realizing the inappropriate choice, a change is made to an S2 or "selling" style of leadership, because Jake has to buy into the importance of strengthening his knowledge. This may require outside course work or in-house, on-the-job training. Once Jake has resolved this deficiency, the S3 leadership style can be resumed. The future behavior and growth in maturity of Roberta and Jake will probably necessitate further changes in leadership style. Choosing an appropriate style of leadership for a specific situation is a continuous and fluid process. Effective leadership is not rigid; it's flexible.

It should be obvious that flexible leadership in an organizational environment is accomplished through communication. Nowhere is communication competency more important than when people are trying to lead and establish vision and direction for organizations. So, it is a leader's responsibility to communicate clearly what is expected of followers and what rewards can be anticipated when tasks are successfully completed. Robert House and his associates have developed a Path–Goal Theory, derived from expectancy theory, which claims that followers are motivated to be productive when they believe that successful task completion will provide a path to a valuable goal.[31] Consequently, to motivate followers they identify four communication styles that relate well to our previous discussion of task, relationship, and follower maturity. These four communication styles are[32]:

1. *Directive leadership*—task-related communication behavior that includes planning and organizing, coordination of activities, policy setting, and other forms of specific guidance. Use when the task is unstructured and the followers are inexperienced and insecure. (S1/R1)

2. *Supportive leadership*—interpersonal communication, sensitive to the social needs and well-being of followers, and the development of a positive climate for interaction. Use when the task is structured but stressful, tedious, or difficult and the followers are knowledgeable and experienced but lack confidence or commitment. (S2/R2)
3. *Participative leadership*—communication designed to solicit opinions and ideas from followers and involve them in decision making and problem solving. Use when the task is unstructured and the followers are skilled and experienced but uncertain and apprehensive. (S3/R3)
4. *Achievement-oriented leadership*—communication focusing on goal attainment and accomplishment, emphasizing followers to achieve the articulated vision. Use to create a positive performance expectation when the task is unstructured and the followers possess necessary skills and express confidence in their ability to excel. (S4/R4)

By providing specific expectations for individual task assignments and reinforcing the group goal, the group leader can increase the followers' motivation and satisfaction levels.

Leadership is the process of influencing the activities of a person or group to achieve a goal in a given situation. *There is no one right way to lead.* No single style of leadership can sufficiently guarantee a leader being both successful and effective. As with the human body, such rigidity invariably leads to broken bones and other complications. Leadership requires that one be flexible and supple, yet not be a contortionist. Flexible leadership is fluid movement, a movement you can develop through an understanding of the relationships among communication style, task behavior, relationship behavior, follower readiness, needs, abilities, values, and personality, given a specific situation.

▶COMMUNICATION AND CONFLICT MANAGEMENT

One of the more challenging problems that organizational members face is handling conflicts with subordinates, supervisors, peers, and clients. For employees involved in task coordination and decision making, conflict management is an everyday occurrence. Communication plays an intrinsic role in conflict and conflict management. It is pivotal in conceptualizing the controversy, and in choosing ways to handle disputes. It shapes the formation of issues, the emotional climate of conflicts, and the cyclical development of interaction. Linda Putnam observes that "since communication permeates every aspect of conflict, it is more than a variable, it constitutes the essence of conflict."[33]

There are several definitions for the term "conflict." Lewis Coser introduced the conflict perspective into American sociology with his definition of conflict as "a struggle over values and claims to scarce status, power, and resources in which the aims of the opponents are to neutralize, injure, or eliminate their rivals."[34] K. W. Thomas provides a process definition of conflict—a process that originates when one person perceives that another party has frustrated, or is about to frustrate, some goal or concern of his or hers.[35] Morton Deutsch maintains that "conflict exists whenever incompatible activities occur . . . an action which is incompatible with another action prevents, obstructs, interferes with, injures, or in some way makes it less likely or less effective."[36] He distinguishes five types of conflict: intrapersonal (within self), interpersonal (between individuals), intragroup (within a group), intergroup (between groups), and international (between nations).[37] Finally, Joyce Hocker and William Wilmot provide a communication perspective when they observe that "conflict is an expressed struggle between at least two interdependent parties who perceive incompatible goals, resources, and interference from the other party in achieving their goals."[38] They further note that the term "conflict resolution" is often used to describe the process of dealing with conflicts, when "conflict management" might be a better term because the most productive direction to take may be to escalate differences so that they can be productively dealt with. Ultimately, of course, conflict ought to be reduced.

Causes and Contexts of Conflict

A good portion of the early literature on conflict theory attempted to identify, isolate, and examine the causes of conflict. Frequently, such investigations concluded that conflicts are caused by a wide variety of complex psychological, social, and situational factors that are closely interrelated and interactive. Consequently, a simple enumeration of causes yields little to our understanding, is often confusing, and is probably of little value. What is important is that a conflict is not a conflict until at least one person perceives it as such, and a social conflict requires at least two people who perceive it as such. People in conflict perceive their goals as incompatible with those of the other party. Moreover, power disparity promotes struggles over power and increases the underlying bases of conflict.[39] Researchers suggest that conflict can occur in any organizational setting where there are two or more competing responses to a single event.[40] Conflict can be intrapersonal or interpersonal; it can involve individuals, groups, or be organizationwide.

Conflicts occur in a variety of contexts. Context refers to the shared perceptions among participants in a situation concerning behavioral norms and attitudinal expectancies. Various schemes have been suggested for describing these contexts. Social psychologist Morton Deutsch observes that "conflict can occur in a cooperative or competitive context and the processes of conflict resolution which are likely to be displayed will be strongly influenced by the context within which conflict occurs."[41] John Keltner adds to cooperative and competitive contexts that of warfare, thus creating a continuum with cooperation at one end, competition somewhere in between, and warfare at the other end.[42] A closer examination of these three major points along this continuum may further our understanding of the causes of conflict and clarify the distinctions between the forms and processes of conflict.

Conflicts occurring within cooperative contexts reveal open, free-flowing, and honest communication. Feelings are revealed and discussed in a warm, supportive climate. Disagreements are resolved through lively and open discussion with the personal needs and concerns of the involved parties being considered and respected. Solutions sought are acceptable and beneficial to everyone and further solidify close and supportive relationships.

Conflicts in contexts characterized by competition exhibit a contest-like striving for mutually exclusive goals. Participants contend against each other to win something. Even "friendly" competition is expected to produce winners and losers. Certainly, there are varying levels of conflict intensity, with some competition being mild, some bitter and destructive. However, the outcome is predictable—there is a winner and a loser.

Warfare is the most dangerous and destructive context of conflict. Warfare promotes perceptions of intense personal danger, including threats to personal survival. Participants are defined or define themselves as enemies with few or no rules governing the behavior of the combatants culminating in the destruction of one or more of the participants. Communication under these conditions is difficult and may cease or be poisoned by mutual mistrust. Warfare is uncontrolled and uncontrollable conflict. Although we often don't think of warfare in the business arena, consider the Japanese motto, "Business is war."[43]

Conflict may be productive or dysfunctional. Our premise is that the parties involved are responsible for the direction of their relationship. If you are in an unproductive or destructive conflict with another, you have the responsibility to put restraints on your own choices that feed the destructive spiral, and create a more positive and supportive system of interaction. Conflict is a pervasive aspect of organizational life and serves vital needs in promoting change and in adapting to dynamic organizational environments.

Role of Conflict in Organizations

Conflict is certainly a critical issue in organizational life. The American Management Association reports that chief executive officers (CEOs) spend approximately 18 percent of their time dealing with conflict, and middle managers give 26 percent of their time to managing it. Practicing managers further report that conflict management continues to become increasingly important to organizational effectiveness.[44] Consequently, one might think that understanding and handling conflict would be a major priority in organizational life, but few people try to understand it and many avoid or resist it. Why? People often view conflict as an almost totally negative activity with no redeeming qualities. Words frequently associated with conflict are "anger," "hostility," "anxiety," and "disagreement," rather than "exciting," "strengthening," "helpful," "growth-producing," or "enriching." Thomas Crum observes, however, that "there is truly a magical quality about conflict which can call out the best in us, that which is not summoned under ordinary circumstances."[45] These perceptual differences exist because some have perpetuated myths that are very detrimental to the successful management of conflict. Robert Doolittle identifies five myths or misunderstandings regarding the nature of conflict[46]:

1. *People are naturally in harmony because of their humanity and conflicts are therefore dysfunctional.*

    This stems from an overly romanticized view of the nature of human beings and their social structures. Conflicts are both natural and functional. In fact, no social structure can continue to exist unless it acknowledges, manages, and profits from the conflicts that inevitably and regularly occur within it.

2. *Conflicts occur because people do not understand each other.*

    If conflicts are caused primarily by lack of understanding, then they can be resolved rather easily by communication that informs and clarifies. Although some conflicts result from mere misunderstandings, the most serious ones occur among individuals and groups who understand each other very well but who strongly disagree. Disagreements among people who understand each others' interests and intentions require intensive communication directed toward conciliation and mediation as well as clarification. Further, even simple disagreements often require careful and sensitive handling aimed at soothing ruffled feelings, reassuring damaged egos, and rebuilding strained relationships.

3. *Conflicts can always be satisfactorily resolved.*

Certainly, we would like to believe that all conflicts are resolvable through some means, but experience and common sense suggest a far-different reality. Some are so deeply ingrained, so fundamental, and perhaps so necessary that they consistently defy resolution. The best that can be hoped for is that these struggles may eventually be mediated and defused so that those with opposing goals, values, and philosophies can respect each other and learn to coexist while retaining their differing points of view.

4. *Conflicts represent a breakdown in the social fabric.*

A society that attempts to suppress conflict cannot survive. Far from representing the deterioration of the social fabric, the presence of conflict is evidence of the resiliency and fundamental strength of a social system. Conflicts suggest both the need for and the possible directions of necessary change. Conflict is inevitable and potentially functional, especially where it is approached intelligently, honestly, and confidently.

5. *Conflicts stem from a breakdown in communication.*

Communication is a process that is, ideally, mutually inclusive, beneficial, and obligating. We have to be prepared to listen as well as speak. Far from representing breakdowns in communication, conflicts may be the very stimuli that prompt us to communicate with others and to sustain communicative relationships. Although it is true that conflicts often result in the termination of communication among individuals, groups, and even nations, they need not do so. Indeed, greater efforts and warmer and stronger relationships suggest that it is not conflict that produces breakdowns in communication but the unwillingness or inability to manage and use conflict for constructive purposes.

The misunderstandings discussed here prevent many from making constructive use of conflict and from discovering effective means for managing and resolving it when it does occur. Conflict is a pervasive activity which is often mistakenly viewed as abnormal or destructive. A more constructive perspective defines conflict as a normal event that occurs in any relationship. From this positive perspective, conflict may be viewed as an activator or energy source for transforming the ordinary into the extraordinary. Consequently, when placed in the synergistic context of group problem-solving, the equation becomes[47]:

$$\frac{\text{Ordinary People + Ordinary Resources + Ordinary Circumstances}}{\textbf{Conflict}} \longrightarrow$$

Extraordinary States of Being + Extraordinary Results

Louis Pondy provides a particularly useful understanding of how conflict episodes occur. He identifies five basic stages that mutually interact with one another and influence the outcome of any conflict situation: latent conflict, perceived conflict, felt conflict, manifest conflict, and conflict aftermath.[48] *Latent conflict* refers to the underlying conditions that can trigger a conflict. These conditions may frequently exist in one form or another, although they may or may not produce conflict. *Perceived conflict* occurs when the involved parties become aware of their differences and consequently begin to experience significant frustration. *Felt conflict* is the stage where the participants become ego-involved and begin to assess their individual motives, the motives of others, and the importance of the problem; it represents the merger of their perceptions and emotional reactions. *Manifest conflict* is that stage where "actual" conflict behaviors are exhibited—open aggression, overpowering competition, making of threats, silence, and agreeing to solutions are some of the possibilities. It is that stage where participants readily recognize "conflict" and use their communication skills and peacemaking abilities to manage it productively. Finally, *conflict aftermath,* resulting from the complex interactions of the previous stages, is that point where outcomes are evaluated as being productive or counterproductive. These five stages are helpful in visualizing conflict as a process and can be useful when selecting appropriate communication styles and constructive methods for conflict management.

Styles of Conflict Management

Styles of conflict management are our patterned responses or consistent and repetitive predispositions toward conflict situations. Conflict styles frequently are described as five fundamental orientations based on the balance between satisfying individual needs/goals and satisfying the needs/goals of others in the conflict. The five stylistic choices generally identified are: avoidance, competition, compromise, accommodation, and collaboration.[49]

Avoidance is a style characterized by denying the conflict, equivocating, and being noncommittal. Although avoiders may have a genuine concern for goals and relationships, they refrain from either psychologically or physically participating in conflict situations. It is useful when the issue is trivial or when others can manage the conflict without your involvement, but avoidance frequently suggests that you don't care and it may let conflict simmer and heat up unnecessarily instead of opening an avenue for resolution. It usually preserves the conflict and sets the stage for a later, more violent explosion.

A *competitive* style is characterized by assertive or aggressive behavior and overt disagreement. Competitive people often conceptualize conflict as win–lose and prefer to view themselves as winners. Competition can be useful in situations where the involved parties recognize competitive behavior as a sign of strength and treat it as a natural response, such as in games and sports or a court battle. In other circumstances it may be used to demonstrate personal interest and commitment regarding the conflicting issues. A competitive style of managing conflict can often damage relationships, locking participants into attack/counterattack sequences and depriving them of collaborative, cooperative solutions to their problems. Alfie Kohn believes that any competition is dysfunctional; there is no such thing as "healthy" competition.[50]

Compromisers prefer to balance people concerns with task issues and often approach conflict with a give-and-take attitude that contributes to negotiation. Compromise is a useful style for restoring harmony when the conflicting participants are willing to make some concessions to achieve a mutually satisfying solution. However,

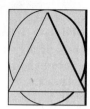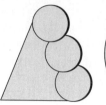

Source: Thomas Crum, *The Magic of Conflict* (New York: Touchstone Books, 1987). Copyright © 1987 by Thomas Crum. Reprinted by permission of Simon & Schuster, Inc.

when the parties are pressured or coerced into compromising, the problem(s) will likely surface again. In such a case, compromise may provide only a temporary respite rather than a productive and positive resolution.

The *accommodative* style is characterized by the sacrifice of personal goals in order to resolve conflict and maintain relationships. People who want to be liked, have high affiliative needs, or genuinely are concerned for the needs of others often prefer an accommodative approach to conflict. This abandonment style may be useful when disputed areas seem unimportant or trivial, but becomes problematic if consistently employed when issues/goals/tasks are regarded as personally significant. Then, the accommodator begins to feel victimized and exploited.

The *collaborative* style is clearly the ideal because it recognizes conflict as potentially productive and encourages people to examine issues thoughtfully and to work toward accomplishing common goals or objectives. Collaboration assumes an exploratory, problem-solving orientation and works well when one wants to find an integrative solution that will satisfy all parties. It is an active affirmation of the importance of relationship and content goals, and thus builds a team or partner approach to conflict management. However, collaboration is a difficult, emotionally intense, time-consuming style and people can only behave collaboratively when others are also willing to assume a collaborative orientation. One avoider or competitor can frustrate the intentions of the entire group.

Thomas Crum integrates the various styles discussed and presents an interesting perspective on conflict management from a geometric standpoint.[51] Using three basic shapes—a triangle, a circle, and a square—he illustrates the complexity of conflicts and our choices about how we can respond to them (see Exhibit 7-2).

The triangle represents those responses that have a particular focused movement, such as direct resistance or competition, as well as avoidance and disengagement. The square indicates a lessened ability to move dynamically and symbolizes holding a position or conscious resistance, as well as passive disengagement or avoidance. Finally, the circle represents a flowing, rolling, or blending response as is often found in compromise, collaboration, and acceptance or accommodation. The geometry of the circle results in the greatest ease of movement and ability to create alignment without the possibility of being "pierced." Crum concludes that we have the potential for all shapes within us and should not lock ourselves into any one form of response for fear of becoming rigid. Rather, we should remain flexible to respond in many different ways and explore the variety of appropriate possibilities.

Any of the conflict styles or geometric shapes discussed can be appropriate and useful, or appropriate and nonproductive, depending on the circumstances. Nonproductive or destructive conflicts leave the participants dissatisfied with the outcome, feeling that they have lost. Productive conflicts leave participants satisfied and feeling that they have gained something: the problem is solved, the relationship is enhanced, and a new vision for working cooperatively in the future is developed.

Measuring Organizational Conflict

The role of conflict style research in organizations has progressed from an emphasis on resolving disputes to one on managing recurring controversies. Researchers are now concerned with the value of conflict in promoting organizational change and in managing divergent goals. This focus has resulted in the development of a vast array of conflict style instruments designed for measuring conflict in organizations and used in research and training. Besides the original Blake and Mouton inventory described previously, other conflict style instruments include the Hall Conflict Management Survey, the Thomas-Kilmann Conflict Management-of-Difference Survey, the Rahim Organizational Conflict Inventory-II, the Putnam-Wilson Organizational Communication Conflict Instrument, and the Ross-DeWine Conflict Management Message Style. A brief examination of each of these instruments can help reframe our concepts of conflict, communication, and organizations, and to create a systemic view.

The Conflict Management Survey (CMS) was developed and tested by Jay Hall of Teleometrics, International. Hall describes five conflict styles:

▶ *Win–Lose*—Conflict is managed by emphasizing personal goals to the exclusion of relationships. The protection of personal goals is the measure of success of the conflict.

▶ *Yield–Lose*—Conflict is managed through the sacrifice of personal goals to the relationship. Relationships carry more importance than personal goals and must be maintained even at high cost to personal ambitions.

▶ *Lose–Leave*—Conflict is managed by a hopeless attitude which is characterized by the individual leaving the conflict either physically or psychologically or both. Neither personal nor relationship goals are given much importance.

▶ *Compromise*—Conflict is managed in a manipulative style which attempts to make trades between personal and relationship goals. This compromise position seeks to moderate the effects of losing by limiting gains.

▶ *Synergistic*—Conflict is managed by attacking major importance to both relationship and personal goals. A problem-solving approach is utilized to seek solutions that favorably impact both the relationship and personal goals.[52]

The CMS proposes that conflict is best understood through preferences for conflict and communication behaviors during conflict, and provides individuals opportunities to choose from a set of essential communication strategies and tactics as they relate to the particular context. Hall states, "Too often conflict is thought of and treated as if it possessed inherent qualities all its own. A more accurate view is that the way we, as individuals, think about and choose to handle conflict is more important in determining its outcome than the nature of the conflict itself."[53]

The Thomas-Kilmann Conflict Management-of-Differences (or MODE) Survey uses the dimensions of assertiveness and cooperativeness to assess conflict. Assertiveness refers to an attempt to satisfy one's own concerns; cooperativeness is an attempt to satisfy the concerns of the other. Five modes of managing differences to satisfy one's own and others' concerns are identified:

▶ *Collaborating*—assertive and cooperative, mutual problem solving to satisfy both parties' needs
▶ *Compromising*—intermediate in both assertiveness and cooperation, exchanges concessions
▶ *Competing*—assertive and uncooperative, tries to win own position
▶ *Accommodating*—unassertive and cooperative, satisfies the other's goals
▶ *Avoiding*—unassertive and uncooperative, postpones or avoids unpleasant issues[54]

According to Thomas and Kilmann, modes of conflict behavior are strongly influenced by both personality and situational factors and each person is capable of using all five modes. Modes are viewed as flexible conflict-handling methods.

The Rahim Organizational Conflict Inventory-II (ROCI-II) measures five conflict management styles identified as *integrating* or collaboration, *obliging* or accommodating, *dominating* or competing, *avoiding* or withdrawal, and *compromising*. The ROCI-II is also associated with a comprehensive model for diagnosing organizational conflict that relates conflict styles to other important variables.[55] Rahim argues that a complete understanding of conflict management within an organization requires a distinction between the amounts of conflict at various levels and the styles of interpersonal conflict used by organizational participants. By indexing the amount of conflict operating at various levels, organizations can estimate the degree of conflict relative to optimum productivity. By analyzing the conflict-handling styles of organization members, information can be obtained about the appropriateness or effectiveness of each style for particular situations. The advantage, then, in investigating both the amount of conflict and the style of conflict management within a particular organizational context is that "effectiveness can be maximized if a moderate amount of conflict is maintained and organizational members use different styles of conflict depending on situations."[56]

Putnam and Wilson developed the Organizational Communication Conflict Instrument (OCCI) to assess conflict strategies in specific situations. They see conflict behaviors as strategies or "lines of action for pursuing and coordinating goals within a specific situation."[57] They identify three categories of conflict strategies: nonconfrontation strategies, solution-oriented strategies, and control strategies. *Nonconfrontation strategies* manage conflict indirectly, either by physically avoiding disagreements or by downplaying controversy and sidestepping volatile issues. *Solution-oriented strategies* manage conflict both by searching for creative, integrative solutions and by making compromises. *Control strategies* manage conflict by arguing persistently for their positions and using nonverbal messages to emphasize demands. The strength of the OCCI is its move from a stylistic to a strategic conception of conflict management. The OCCI also assesses verbal and nonverbal tactics, and is sensitive to situational influences on conflict behaviors.

Finally, the Ross-DeWine Conflict Management Message Style (CMMS) instrument is unique in that it relies on messages as the primary mode for assessing interchanges in conflict and asserts that conflict management style can and should be addressed with message-oriented behaviors. It is a self-report instrument that identifies three message types: self-oriented, issue-oriented, and other-oriented messages. A message with focus on *self* reflects emphasis on the speaker's personal interests. A message that focuses on *issue* maintains that the problem can be solved without jeopardizing the relationship and emphasizes that both parties must deal with the problem. A message that focuses on *other* emphasizes overlooking the problem and keeping the other party happy. Although only recently developed, the CMMS offers advantages for communication specialists over existing conflict style instruments because of its focus on verbal messages. The CMMS is a tool for assessing the verbal components of conflict behavior.[58]

Steps of Conflict Management

Effective conflict intervention and conflict management requires methodically examining the nature of the conflict, assessing the pattern of relationships between the parties, and determining which approach or communication style will prove most constructive. Deborah Borisoff and David Victor present a concise and useful model for conflict management which consists of five steps: assessment, acknowledgment, attitude, action, and analysis.[59]

▶ *Assessment*—Assessment is an important initial step in managing differences and requires that we carefully consider the following five aspects of the communication environment:

1. the individual traits of the participants and the nature of the relationship
2. the nature and cause of the conflict
3. the clarification of each party's personal agenda, goals, and objectives
4. an examination of the prevailing communication climate
5. a preliminary determination of an appropriate conflict-handling style

▶ *Acknowledgment*—Acknowledging the other party's involvement and constructively dealing with the perceptual differences is essential to effective conflict management. It is incumbent on the participants to appreciate the diversity which may exist and nonjudgmentally recognize the cultural, ideological, value, gender, experiential, and communicative differences.

▶ *Attitude*—For conflict to be productively managed, it is important that the participants assume a positive attitude that generates trust and cooperation. Demonstrating conciliation, compassion, concern, and a willingness to assume responsibility for one's actions is crucial for satisfactorily resolving differences.

▶ *Action*—Ultimately, direct, deliberate, positive action must be taken toward managing conflict. Integrating the information gathered from the previous stages should be useful in selecting and applying productive communication techniques that will actively move the participants toward a mutually satisfying solution. Certainly one's actions should be conducive to, rather than inhibitive of, interpersonal exchange.

▶ *Analysis*—The final step in this conflict management model is analysis. Decisions should be reviewed and evaluated with an eye to future impact upon the participants—their goals and relationship. Thus it is important to consider if:

1. the concerns of all parties have been met as adequately as possible;
2. the decisions can be implemented swiftly and/or effectively;
3. the short- or long-term effects of the solution are viable; and
4. the relationship between the conflicting parties has been modified productively.

▶ HOCKER-WILMOT CONFLICT ASSESSMENT GUIDE

This guide is composed of a series of questions designed to focus on the components of conflict. It can be used to bring specific aspects of a conflict into focus and serve as a check on gaps in information about conflict. The guide is best used in toto so that the interplay of conflict elements can be clearly highlighted. For important, recurring, long-term conflicts, you might want to use each question for your assessment. Another way of using the guide is to pick several questions from each section which appear to apply to your conflict. Even seemingly small interpersonal conflicts benefit from a careful, objective assessment. You might do this in writing, in guided discussion with others, or simply use the questions for your own reflection.

I. Nature of the Conflict

A. What are the "triggering events" that brought this conflict into mutual awareness?
B. What is the historical context of this conflict in terms of (1) the ongoing relationship between the parties and (2) other, external events within which this conflict is embedded?
C. Do the parties have assumptions about conflict that are discernable by their choices of conflict metaphors, patterns of behavior, or clear expressions of their attitudes about conflict?
D. Conflict elements:
   1. How is the struggle being expressed by each party?
   2. What are the perceived incompatible goals?
   3. What are the perceived scarce resources?
   4. In what ways are the parties interdependent? How are they interfering with one another? How are they cooperating to keep the conflict in motion?
E. Has the conflict vacillated between productive and destructive phases? If so, which elements might be transformed by creative solutions to the conflict?

II. Goals

A. How do the parties clarify their goals? Do they phrase them in individualistic or system terms.
B. What does each party think the other's goals are? Are they similar or dissimilar to the perceptions of self-goals?
C. How have the goals been altered from the beginning of the conflict to the present? In what ways are the prospective, transactive, and retrospective goals similar or dissimilar?
D. What are the content goals?
E. What are the relational goals?

F. What is each party's translation of content goals into relationship goals?
G. From an external perspective, where would this conflict system be placed in terms of cohesion and adaptability?
H. Would any of the other system descriptions aptly summarize the system dynamics?

III. Power

A. What attitudes about their own and the other's power does each party have? Do they talk openly about power, or is it not discussed?
B. What do the parties see as their own and the other's dependencies on one another? As an external observer, can you classify some dependencies that they do not list?
C. What power currencies do the parties see themselves and the other possessing?
D. From an external perspective, what power currencies of which the participants are not aware seem to be operating?
E. In what ways do the parties disagree on the balance of power between them? Do they underestimate their own or the other's influence?
F. What impact does each party's assessment of power have on subsequent choices in the conflict?
G. What evidence of destructive "power balancing" occurs?
H. In what ways do observers of the conflict agree and disagree with the parties' assessments of their power?
I. What are some unused sources of power that are present?

IV. Tactics and Styles

A. What individual styles did each party use?
B. How did the individual styles change during the course of the conflict?
C. How did the parties perceive the other's style?
D. In what way did a party's style reinforce the choices the other party made as the conflict progressed?
E. Were the style choices primarily symmetrical or complementary?
F. From an external perspective, what were the advantages and disadvantages of each style within this particular conflict?
G. Can the overall system be characterized as having a predominant style? What do the participants say about the relationship as a whole?

H. Do the participants appear to strategize about their conflict choices or remain spontaneous?
I. How does each party view the other's strategizing?
J. What are the tactical options used by both parties?
K. Do the tactical options classify primarily into avoidance, competition, or collaborative tactics?
L. How are the participants' tactics mutually impacting on the other's choices? How are the tactics interlocking to push the conflict through phases of escalation, maintenance, and reduction?

V. Assessment

A. What rules of repetitive patterns characterize this conflict?
B. What triangles and microevents best characterize the conflict?
C. How destructive is the tone of this conflict?

VI. Self-Regulation

A. What options for change do the parties perceive?
B. What philosophy of conflict characterizes the system?
C. What techniques for self-regulation or system-regulation have been used thus far? Which might be used productively by the system?
D. How might anger be managed more productively?

VII. Attempted Solutions

A. What options have been explored for managing the conflict?
B. Have attempted solutions become part of the problem?
C. Have third parties been brought into the conflict? If so, what roles did they play and what was the impact of their involvement?

D. Is this conflict a repetitive one, with attempted solutions providing temporary change, but with the overall pattern remaining unchanged? If so, what is that overall pattern?
E. Can you identify categories of attempted solutions that have not been tried?

The Conflict Assessment Guide can be used in a variety of contexts. Students who are writing an analysis of a conflict can use the questions as a check on the components of conflict. Using extensive interviews with the conflict parties or constructing a questionnaire based on the guide enables one to discover the dynamics of a conflict. The guide can also be used for analyzing larger social or international conflicts, but without interviewing or assessing the conflict parties, one is restricted to highly selective information.

A consultant to organizations can also use the guide by modifying it for direct use. Similarly, an intervener in private conflicts such as those of a family can solicit information about the components of a conflict in an informal, conversational way by referring to the guide as an outline of relevant topics. In either case, care should be taken to modify the guide for the particular task, for the conflict parties, and for your intervention goals.

If one is a participant in a conflict, the guide can be used as a form of self-intervention. If both parties respond to the guide, you can use it to highlight what you and the other party perceive about your conflict. It is recommended that a questionnaire be constructed for both persons to answer, and once the data is collected, the parties can discuss the similarities and differences in their perceptions of the conflict.

Applying this model to group problem solving and organizational settings can result in both a heightened awareness of the dimensions of conflict and a greater ability to use appropriate conflict-handling behavior.

In addition to the model presented, alternative methods for conflict management and assessment are available, and may be useful to the immediate participants or to third parties. Paul Wehr has developed a Conflict Mapping Guide that provides "both the intervener and the conflict parties a clearer understanding of the origins, nature, dynamics, and possibilities for resolution of conflict."[60] Also, the Hocker-Wilmot Conflict Assessment Guide (included here) can be of benefit when collecting information about your own and another party's view of the conflict.[61] These are both highly comprehensive assessment guides that use open-ended, participant-based methods for understanding conflict processes. Careful assessment can significantly assist one in visualizing the creative and productive options available for conflict management.

Parties to conflicts have three basic options for altering the conflict. A natural but usually unsuccessful response is trying to change the other party. Because all parties to a conflict consider their stance and options to be reasonable, such efforts result in all parties fruitlessly attempting to change one another. Trying to alter the conflict conditions can prove more successful. If you can increase scarce resources, change perceptions of incompatible goals, or make some other alteration in the conflict elements, you will be able to change a conflict. Finally, you can change your own behavior. This is usually the most difficult but also the most successful way to alter a conflict. This requires a true change in your orientation to the other as well as interpretation of issues and reaction to the conflict processes. Self-change can profoundly affect and alter the conflictual elements in the relationship. It represents an effort to regulate conflict "from the inside out." If successful, conflict regulation offers the following distinct advantages:

► alters the escalatory conflict spiral and halts destructive behavior
► allows self-discovery; when you use restraint, you have the time to understand sources of power you can use, and you can understand your own needs and goals for this particular conflict
► allows for more creative conflict management options than either party could generate singly; each individual is induced into innovation
► prevents you from taking actions that you will later have to justify or feel remorse for using
► releases energy for productive uses that was being diverted into frustration[62]

Conflict management and regulation is an activity that depends on people sensitive to the concerns of others and open to diverse ways of approaching this difficult process. Learning about the process is one way to regulate conflict.

► SUMMARY

At its most elementary level, leadership means that a person can influence others to act in a certain way. Every person may need at times to influence his or her workgroup and to provide a vision of what the organization as a whole or the specific task at hand requires. Leadership skills are necessary, therefore, at every level of the organization from the chief executive to the line worker.

Leadership and its influence on decision making and problem solving have probably been the most studied individual organizational and group role. Researchers have generated a variety of models or approaches toward leadership—trait, style, situational, and transformational. The contributions of each of these approaches are evinced in a flexible leadership orientation that balances task, relational, and individual maturity dimensions. Certainly, the study of leadership will intensify as companies search for ways to develop successful leaders in a highly competitive business environment. Strong leadership will be required to move us through such issues as deregulation, the savings and loan crisis, corporate takeovers, a rising national debt, and slower economic growth. Our futures will depend on people who are visionary, possess integrity, instill trust, and have curiosity and daring.

Conflict is a natural part of group and organizational activity. Conflicts, both major and minor, are a fact of worklife. They can sap productivity and short-circuit strategic plans. Although many fear its destructive potential, conflict can be productively managed by carefully assessing the situation and selecting an appropriate conflict-handling style. Conflict isn't negative, it just is, and when effectively managed can produce creative outcomes. Thomas Crum observes that "seeing conflict as an opportunity to create art from our very being is a challenge for the artist in all of us."[63]

An organization's ability to achieve its strategic objectives depends on the problem-solving, leadership, and conflict-managing skills of its workforce. Unresolved problems create dysfunctional relationships in the workplace, which ultimately become impediments to flexibility and leadership, and to dealing with strategic change in an open-ended and creative way. Creative solutions derived from effective leadership and the constructive management of conflict help the organization move toward its strategic goals.

▶ QUESTIONS FOR DISCUSSION AND SKILL DEVELOPMENT

1. There was a time when the acknowledged superiority of American business was exemplified by the superiority of American management. As Steve Lohr writes in *The New York Times,* leaders with vision were "the real key to American management." Today, many critics say we have lost our superiority and refer to this as a "crisis in leadership." Do you agree? Disagree?

2. What personality characteristics or traits do you believe leaders should possess? Which leadership style do you find to be most effective? Why? How does the situation influence leadership? Can leaders be truly flexible? Explain.

3. On a scale of 1 (above average) to 5 (needs improvement), rate the kind of leader you think other people believe you to be. People think my leadership is:

   _____ intellectual   _____ creative
   _____ caring   _____ sincere
   _____ knowledgeable   _____ goal-centered
   _____ democratic   _____ value-centered
   _____ productive   _____ realistic
   _____ visionary

4. What are some of the more prevalent misunderstandings about conflict? List and explain types of disagreements that can become the sources of conflict. What kinds of goals are the most frequent causes of conflict? Why?

5. Aren't the terms "conflict" and "cooperation" mutually exclusive? What communication skills are most useful in managing conflicts? What conflict management style or predisposition do you use? Avoidance? Competition? Compromise? Accommodation? Collaboration?

6. Using the Hocker-Wilmot Conflict Assessment Guide, analyze a conflict in which you were involved. Can you see more clearly the stages through which the conflict evolved? Would you now handle the conflict differently? Explain.

▶ NOTES

1. James MacGregor Burns, *Leadership* (New York: Harper and Row, 1978): 2.

2. Paul Hersey, *The Situational Leader* (Escondido, CA: Center for Leadership Studies, 1984): 14.

3. Bernard Bass, *Leadership, Psychology, and Organizational Behavior* (New York: Harper and Row, 1960): 90.

4. Warren Bennis, *The Unconscious Conspiracy: Why Leaders Can't Lead* (New York: AMACOM, 1976): 154.

5. J. P. Kotter, *A Force for Change: How Leadership Differs from Management* (New York: The Free Press, 1990): 4–5.

6. Warren Bennis and Burt Nanus, *Leaders: The Strategies for Taking Charge* (New York: Harper and Row, 1985): 21.

7. Alan Bryman, *Charisma and Leadership in Organizations* (Newbury Park, CA: Sage, 1992).

8. Gordon Allport, "Traits Revisited," *American Psychologist* (January 1966): 1–10.

9. Warren Bennis, *On Becoming a Leader* (Reading, MA: Addison-Wesley, 1989).

10. Philip Crosby, *Leading: The Art of Becoming an Executive* (New York: McGraw-Hill, 1989).

11. Bernard M. Bass, *Bass and Stogdill's Handbook of Leadership: Theory, Research and Managerial Applications,* 3rd ed. (New York: The Free Press, 1990); S. A. Kirkpatrick and E. A. Locke, "Leadership: Do Traits Matter?" *The Executive* 5 (1991): 48–60; R. D. Mann, "A Review of the Relationship Between Personality and Performance in Small

Groups," *Psychological Bulletin* 56 (1959): 241–270; and R. M. Stogdill, "Personal Factors Associated with Leadership: A Survey of the Literature," *Journal of Psychology* 25 (1948): 35–71.

12. Ralph White and Ronald Lippitt, *Autocracy and Democracy: An Experimental Inquiry* (New York: Harper and Row, 1960).

13. E. A. Fleishman, E. F. Harris, and H. E. Burtt, *Leadership and Supervision in Industry* (Columbus, OH: Ohio State University, 1955); and R. M. Stogdill and A. E. Coons, *Leader Behavior: Its Description and Measurement* (Columbus, OH: Ohio State University, 1957).

14. B. M. Fisher and J. E. Edwards, "Consideration and Initiating Structure and Their Relationships With Leader Effectiveness: A Meta-Analysis," *Best Papers Proceedings* (Anaheim, CA: Academy of Management, 1988); A. K. Korman, "Consideration, Initiating Structure, and Organizational Criteria—A Review," *Personnel Psychology* 19 (1966): 349–361; L. L. Larson, J. G. Hunt, and R. N. Osborn, "The Great Hi–Hi Leader Behavior Myth: A Lesson From Occam's Razor," *Academy of Management Journal* 19 (1976): 628–641; and P. C. Nystrom, "Managers and the Hi–Hi Leader Myth," *Academy of Management Journal* 21 (1978): 325–331.

15. T. Burns and G. M. Stalker, *The Management of Innovation* (Chicago, IL: Quadrangle Books, 1961); P. R. Lawrence and J. W. Lorsch, *Organization and Environment* (Cambridge, MA: Harvard University Press, 1967); and J. Woodward, *Industrial Organization: Theory and Practice* (London: Oxford University Press, 1965).

16. F. E. Fiedler, *A Theory of Leadership Effectiveness* (New York: McGraw-Hill, 1967); F. E. Fiedler, "Personality, Motivational Systems, and the Behavior of High and Low LPC Persons," *Human Relations* 25 (1972): 391–412; and L. Berkowitz, *Advances in Experimental Social Psychology* (New York: Academic Press, 1978).

17. John French and Bertram Raven, "The Bases of Social Power," in: D. Cartwright and A. Zander, eds., *Group Dynamics* (New York: Harper and Row, 1968): 259–268.

18. Pamela Shockley-Zalabak, *Fundamentals of Organizational Communication*, 2nd ed. (New York: Longman Publishing, 1991): 279.

19. Bennis and Nanus, *Leaders*, 17–18.

20. A. S. Ashaur, "The Contingency Model of Leadership Effectiveness: An Evaluation," *Organizational Behavior and Human Performance* 9 (1973): 339–355; S. Kerr and A. Harlan, "Predicting the Effects of Leadership Training and Experience from the Contingency Model: Some Remaining Problems," *Journal of Applied Psychology* 57 (1973): 114–117; and J. G. Hunt and L. L. Larson, *Leadership: The Cutting Edge* (Carbondale, IL: Southern Illinois University Press, 1977).

21. Burns, *Leadership*.

22. Bryman, *Charisma and Leadership*, 99.

23. Benjamin Tregoe, John Zimmerman, Ronald Smith, and Peter Tobia, *Vision in Action* (New York: Simon & Schuster, 1989).

24. Bernard M. Bass, "From Transactional to Transformation Leadership: Learning to Share the Vision," *Organizational Dynamics* 18 (1990): 19–31; J. A. Conger, *The Charismatic Leader: Behind the Mystique of Exceptional Leadership* (San Francisco: Jossey-Bass, 1989); D. A. Nadler and M. L. Tushman, "Beyond the Charismatic Leader: Leadership and Organizational Change," *California Management Review* 32 (1990): 77–97; M. Sashkin, "True Vision in Leadership," *Training and Development Journal* 40 (1986): 58–61; and G. A. Yukl, "Managerial Leadership: A Review of Theory and Research," *Journal of Management* 15 (1989): 251–289.

25. Bryman, *Charisma and Leadership*, 174–176.

26. A. Bryman, *Leadership and Organizations* (London: Routledge and Paul Kegan, 1986); D. V. Day and R. G. Lord, "Executive Leadership and Organizational Performance: Suggestions for a New Theory and Methodology," *Journal of Management* 14 (1988): 453–464; A. B. Thomas, "Does Leadership Make a Difference to Organizational Performance?" *Administrative Science Quarterly* 33 (1988): 388–400; and N. M. Tichy and M. A. Devanna, *The Transformational Leader* (New York: John Wiley & Sons, 1990).

27. Charles Nordoff and James Norman Hall, *Mutiny on the Bounty* (New York: Pocket Books, 1975): 43–44.

28. James Hunt, *Leadership, A New Synthesis* (Newbury Park, CA: Sage, 1991): 164.

29. R. E. Quinn, S. R. Faerman, M. P. Thompson, and M. R. McGrath, *Becoming a Master Manager* (New York: John Wiley & Sons, 1990).

30. Paul Hersey and Kenneth Blanchard, *Management of Organizational Behavior: Utilizing Human Resources,* 6th ed. (Englewood Cliffs, NJ: Prentice Hall, 1993).

31. Robert J. House, "A Path–Goal Theory of Leader Effectiveness," *Administrative Science Quarterly* 16 (1971): 321–328.

32. Michael Z. Hackman and Craig E. Johnson, *Leadership* (Prospect Heights, IL: Waveland Press, 1991): 51–53; and Robert J. House and T. R. Mitchell, "Path–Goal Theory of Leadership," *Journal of Contemporary Business* 3 (1974): 81–97.

33. Linda L. Putnam, "Communication and Interpersonal Conflict in Organizations," *Management Communication Quarterly* 1 (February 1988): 295.

34. Lewis Coser, *Functions of Social Conflict* (New York: The Free Press, 1956): 8.

35. K. W. Thomas, "Conflict and Conflict Management," in: M. Dunnette, ed., *The Handbook of Industrial and Organizational Psychology* (Chicago, IL: Rand McNally, 1976): 889–935.

36. Morton Deutsch, "Conflicts: Productive and Destructive," in: F. E. Jandt, ed., *Conflict Resolution Through Communication* (New York: Harper and Row, 1973): 156.

37. Morton Deutsch, "Toward an Understanding of Conflict," *International Journal of Group Tensions* 1 (1971): 42–54.

38. Joyce L. Hocker and William W. Wilmot, *Interpersonal Conflict,* 3rd ed. (Dubuque, IA: Wm. C. Brown, 1991): 12.

39. Ibid.

40. W. Wayland Cummings, Larry Long, and Michael Lewis, *Managing Communication in Organizations* (Dubuque, IA: Gorsuch Scarisbuck, 1983).

41. Deutsch, "Conflicts," 157.

42. John W. Keltner, *Interpersonal Speech Communication* (Belmont, CA: Wadsworth, 1970).

43. Clyde V. Prestowitz, Jr., *Trading Places: How We Are Giving Our Future to Japan and How to Reclaim It* (New York: Basic Books, 1989); Karl van Wolferen, *The Enigma of Japanese Power* (New York: Alfred A. Knopf, 1989); Michael L. Dertouzos, Richard K. Lester, and Robert M. Solow, *Made in America: Regaining the Productive Edge, Report of the MIT Commission on Industrial Productivity* (Cambridge, MA: MIT Press, 1989); and Paul Kennedy, *The Rise and Fall of the Great Powers* (New York: Random House, 1987).

44. K. Thomas and W. Schmidt, "A Survey of Managerial Interests with Respect to Conflict," *Academy of Management Journal* 19 (1976): 315–318.

45. Thomas Crum, *The Magic of Conflict* (New York: Touchstone Books, 1987): 30.

46. Robert J. Doolittle, *Orientations to Communication and Conflict* (Palo Alto, CA: Science Research Associates, 1976): 7–10.

47. Crum, *Magic of Conflict*, 25. Copyright © 1987 by Thomas Crum. Reprinted by permission of Simon & Schuster, Inc.

48. Louis Pondy, "Organizational Conflict: Concepts and Models," *Administrative Science Quarterly* 12 (1967): 296–320.

49. R. R. Blake and J. S. Mouton, *The Managerial Grid* (Houston, TX: Gulf Publishing, 1964); C. T. Brown, P. Yelsmer, and P. W. Keller, "Communication—Conflict Predispositions: Development of a Theory and an Instrument," *Human Relations* 34 (1981): 103–117; L. D. Brown, *Managing Conflict at Organizational Interfaces* (Reading, MA: Addison-Wesley, 1983); D. J. Canary and W. R. Cupach, "Relational and Episodic Characteristics Associated with Conflict Tactics," *Journal of Social and Personal Relationships* 5 (1988): 305–322; R. W. Fogg, "Dealing with Conflict: A Repertoire of Creative Peaceful Approaches," *Journal of Conflict Resolution* 29 (1985): 330–358; J. S. Hime, *Conflict and Conflict Management* (Athens, GA: University of Georgia Press, 1980); L. L. Putnam and J. P. Folger, "Communication, Conflict, and Dispute Resolution: The Study of Interaction and the Development of Conflict Theory," *Communication Research* 15 (1988): 349–359; and J. Wieman and J. Daly, *Communicating Strategically: Strategies in Interpersonal Communication* (Hillsdale, NJ: Lawrence Erlbaum Associates, 1990).

50. Alfie Kohn, *No Contest: The Case Against Competition* (Boston: Houghton Mifflin, 1976).

51. Crum, *Magic of Conflict,* 136–138, 206–213.

52. Pamela Shockley-Zalabak, "Assessing the Hall Conflict Management Survey," *Management Communication Quarterly* 1 (February 1988): 305.

53. Jay Hall, *Conflict Management Survey: A Survey of One's Characteristic Reaction to and Handling of Conflicts Between Himself and Others* (Conroe, TX: Teleometrics, 1986): 14.

54. Deanna F. Womack, "Assessing the Thomas-Kil-

mann Conflict MODE Survey," *Management Communication Quarterly* 1 (February 1988): 322. Copyright © 1988 by Sage Publications, Inc. Reprinted by permission of Sage Publications, Inc.

55. Deborah Weider-Hatfield, "Assessing the Rahim Organizational Conflict Inventory-II (ROCI-II)," *Management Communication Quarterly* 1 (February 1988): 350–366.

56. M. A. Rahim, *Managing Conflict in Organizations* (New York: Praeger, 1986).

57. Steven R. Wilson and Michael S. Waltman, "Assessing the Putnam-Wilson Organizational Communication Conflict Instrument (OCCI)," *Management Communication Quarterly* 1 (February 1988): 368.

58. Roseanna G. Ross and Sue DeWine, "Assessing the Ross-DeWine Conflict Management Message Style," *Management Communication Quarterly* 1 (February 1988): 389–413.

59. Deborah Borisoff and David Victor, *Conflict Management, A Communication Skills Approach* (Englewood Cliffs, NJ: Prentice Hall, 1989): 2–17.

60. Paul Wehr, *Conflict Resolution* (Boulder, CO: Westview Press, 1979): 19.

61. Hocker and Wilmot, *Interpersonal Conflict*, 173–176.

62. Ibid., 179–183.

63. Crum, *Magic of Conflict*, 21.

C ommunication is an integral part of the world of business. How well you present yourself and your ideas and how well you work with other people are the two basic essentials of any career. Here fundamental communication formats operating within the organizational arena are identified and developed. Specifically, attention is given to interviewing, group communication, and public communication.

UNIT THREE

Contexts for Business and Professional Communication

▶ 8   *Explores the importance of interviewing in the workplace, defining strategies and techniques pertaining to the selection, appraisal, discipline, counseling, and exit interviews.*

▶ 9   *Describes the selection interviewing process, focusing on the cover letter, résumé, interview, and follow-up and evaluation activities.*

▶ 10   *Focuses on types and functions of groups in organizations, identifying and describing key variables affecting group communication and problem solving.*

▶ 11   *Examines the nature of public communication in the organization, noting the essential stages in the preparation and delivery of public messages, including the preparation and use of visual aids.*

▶ 12   *Further examines public communication, specifically identifying and describing the nature of informative and persuasive presentations and the speaking demands of selected special occasions.*

CHAPTER EIGHT

8

Interviewing Strategies, Techniques, and Applications

LEARNING OBJECTIVES:

To define the basic processes of an interview

To develop strategies and approaches to elicit the maximum amount of information

To focus listening on the important factors of the interview

To view the interview as a management tool—describe the similarities and differences among the various basic types of interview situations

To be sensitive and responsive to the basic ethics of interviewing

Mary Smith is graduating soon and about to enter the work world. The selection interview is her doorway to that world. Mike Johnson is completing his fifth year with an engineering firm and expecting a promotion. The appraisal interview is his doorway to advancement. Kathy Collins is managing a department with serious personnel problems. The discipline interview is her doorway to correcting employee abuses. Bill Bradly is supervising a group of employees experiencing personality conflicts that are disrupting team objectives. The counseling interview is his doorway to restoring productivity. Acme Computer Systems is losing a third of its first-year employees to resignation. The exit interview is Acme's doorway to discovering internal problems and finding solutions. The comparison of interviews to doorways is purposeful. Doorways are not where the action is but rather places through which you must pass to find the action. Doorways are symbolic of opportunity, change, advancement, and further challenge. This chapter explores interviews as doorways to organizational solutions, focusing on selection, appraisal, discipline, counseling, and exit interviews.

I nterviewing demands intellect, patience, empathy, and concern. Skillful interviewing requires training, practice, and perseverance. Felix Lopez compares the skilled interviewer to a master musician:

> Interviewing is very much like piano playing—a fair degree of skill can be acquired without the necessity of formal instruction. But there is a world of difference in craftsmanship, in technique, and in finesse between the amateur who plays "by ear" and the accomplished concert pianist. The self-instructed player mechanically reproduces on the keyboard certain melodies that have been committed to memory; the artist, by skillfully blending mastery of musical theory, countless hours of practice, is pleasing to the audience, and expressive to the pianist's inner feeling.[1]

Various degrees of proficiency exist in the interviewing process, as do different qualitative levels of interviewing skill. And even the novice or moderately competent interviewer/interviewee can experience some success. However, the problem is missing information, either because of ill planning and implementation or because the participants lack the understanding and critical insight to get more than the facts. There is a vast difference between skilled and unskilled interviewers, and our purpose in this chapter is to provide you with a basic frame of reference for analyzing a situation, determining what your alternatives are, and then choosing how you wish to proceed.

An organization is structured around a network of people talking to people in an attempt to solve common problems. When this occurs, we have an interview. An *interview* is a communication process by which an interviewer purposefully interacts with an interviewee, asking and answering subject-specific questions, in an attempt to solve problems for the mutual benefit of both participants and the organization.

Let's explore this definition. Interviews represent a communication process, denoting a dynamic, ever-changing interaction, with many variables operating with and acting on one another. They do not occur in isolation from other influences and, despite the way we sometimes think of them, there is no such thing as "the" interview. There are a lot of different situations in which people interact in what can be called an interview. The types of interviews most common to the business arena are selection, appraisal, discipline, counseling, and exit interviews. Each of these is influenced by the intent, setting, and participants, among other variables.

The interviewer may be one person, several people, a team, or a panel. The interviewer role identifies the person or persons with the responsibility and power to plan, schedule, and execute the interview. Within the organization, interviewers are people with designated power to ask questions, to obtain information, and to communicate that information to others. The interviewer initially establishes the interactional relationship between the involved parties, but it must be stressed that the interviewer and interviewee roles are supplementary and that you can only view the interviewer role in terms of its relationship to the interviewee role.

Interviewees make up the second part of the relational equation and typically have less power than the interviewer, although each role is shaped by very personal interpretations. Interviewees possess information that the interviewer needs to get if the purposeful objectives are to be achieved and problem solving is to occur. The interviewee and interviewer are integral participants in the interviewing process and interdependently influence one another as well as the final outcome.

People interview for task-related purposes; they have something they want to accomplish—select a person for a job, appraise and apprise an employee, correct disruptive behavior, or determine the undermining causes of organizational unrest. Each party in the interview has a purpose and some content to communicate, either planned in advance or developed during the interview. The degree to which each party's purposes are achieved is a measure of how productive and successful the interview is. This purposeful and subject-specific nature of the interview differentiates it from social conversation.

For the interviewer and interviewee to interact effectively, both must have communication skills and an interviewing strategy. By "strategy" we do not mean to imply the use of manipulative or deceptive behavior. Rather, we mean that each participant has a positive, constructive plan for interacting and uses that plan as the basis for skillful communication. The communication skills most important are planning, question asking, and question answering. Asking and answering questions are crucial to the interviewing process.

Finally, the object of any interview is to provide information of mutual benefit while furthering the goals of the organization. For example, in the case of the selection interview the applicant-interviewee seeks to communicate information about self that will demonstrate the applicant's usefulness to the organization. The interviewer works to determine compatibility before the organization invests in the applicant's training by discovering positive information as well as characteristics which might devalue the applicant. Underlying this process is a definite ethical dimension. If the end result is to benefit all concerned, then each has the responsibility to participate fully, honestly, and openly. When both participants assume responsibility for the outcome of the interaction, potential barriers to communication are removed and success is enhanced.

▶ IMPORTANCE OF THE INTERVIEW

How important is the skill of interviewing to the modern organization? Interviewing can easily be considered one of an organization's most important communication activities, crucial to information gathering and information sharing. Interviews are the doorways to organizational solutions. Decisions to employ, promote, alter behavior, retain, or terminate a person are based on what may or may not occur during specific interviews. Much of what organizations do is essentially dependent on talking to other people.

Interviewing is fundamental to acquiring information. Collecting complete and accurate information is a critical and ongoing organizational process. Information-gathering interviews are designed to get facts, opinions, attitudes, reasons for actions, or trends of belief. They are an exchange of information, opinions, or experiences from one person to another with the skillful interviewer looking for a revelation or an insight, a thought, or a viewpoint that is interesting, not commonly heard, and not already known. Equally important is the basic need to share information. Information-giving interviews are used to orient new members of organizations or to train, instruct, or coach. Ultimately, interviews are efforts to solve problems or bring about change.

Interview types are many and varied, and often supplement questionnaires, application forms, and written responses. So, when should you use an interview? The answer is multifaceted and dependent on a variety of factors, but Charles Stewart and William Cash, Jr. observe that generally, we should use an interview at the following times:

1. when we need to motivate a person to respond freely, openly, and accurately
2. when we want to probe into answers or clarify questions
3. when we want to adopt questions and responses to each interviewee or interviewer
4. when we might need to explain or justify questions or answers
5. when we want lengthy answers to questions
6. when we want to maintain control over questions, answers, interviewees, interviewers, and situations
7. when we want to match interviewees with specific requirements such as age, sex, race, educational level, income range, political beliefs, and so on
8. when we want to observe interviewer's or interviewee's appearance, dress, manner, or nonverbal communication or to assess communication skills
9. when we need to examine in detail emotions, beliefs, feelings, and attitudes that may be undetectable in writing
10. when we need to verify that the interviewer or interviewee is who he or she claims to be[2]

The interview is a useful tool, but like any tool it is best used by skillfully trained and trustworthy people.

Skillful interviewing, grounded on established and tested techniques, is the basis for information collection and problem solving. The skilled interviewer understands the need to determine control and is keenly sensitive to planning options, questioning strategies, and the alternative role of listener/respondent. This does not imply that the interviewer can or should anticipate everything that is going to happen in an interview, try to be Machiavellian, or play the role of amateur psychologist. It does stress, however, the proactive role of the interviewer. It's the interviewer who sets the course, taking the initiative in scheduling the interview, identifying the topics to be discussed, establishing the purpose of the interview, and preparing questions.

Regardless of interview type, interviewers select a communicative style characterizing the extent to which they try to control the nature and content of the interviewee's answers. Using a *directive style,* the interviewer establishes the purpose of the interview, defines and analyzes the situation, gives opinions and information, makes suggestions, and assertively controls the pacing. The *nondirective style* involves probing and the use of questions to indirectly influence the interview process rather than the actual content itself. Here the interviewee may assume greater control of purpose, subject matter, and pacing. Thus, at one extreme, some interviewers adopt such a rigid control of the interaction that interviewees hardly have a chance to talk, and at the other end of the continuum interviewers make little or no effort to control the content of the interview, acting more as facilitators or advisors. The choice between the two is one of the most important decisions that any interviewer makes because it influences every other behavior in the interaction.

Which style is better—directive or nondirective? The answer is neither one. They are simply two basic options at either end of a graduated continuum, and both are available to the interviewer. Each approach can be appropriately applied and has its own advantages and disadvantages (see Exhibit 8-1). Typically, selection and discipline interviews, surveys, and opinion polls are more directive; appraisal, counsel-

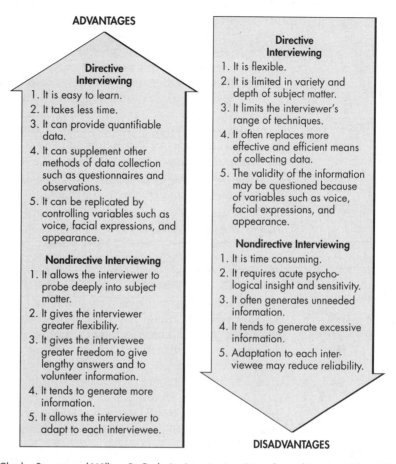

ADVANTAGES

Directive Interviewing
1. It is easy to learn.
2. It takes less time.
3. It can provide quantifiable data.
4. It can supplement other methods of data collection such as questionnaires and observations.
5. It can be replicated by controlling variables such as voice, facial expressions, and appearance.

Nondirective Interviewing
1. It allows the interviewer to probe deeply into subject matter.
2. It gives the interviewer greater flexibility.
3. It gives the interviewee greater freedom to give lengthy answers and to volunteer information.
4. It tends to generate more information.
5. It allows the interviewer to adapt to each interviewee.

Directive Interviewing
1. It is flexible.
2. It is limited in variety and depth of subject matter.
3. It limits the interviewer's range of techniques.
4. It often replaces more effective and efficient means of collecting data.
5. The validity of the information may be questioned because of variables such as voice, facial expressions, and appearance.

Nondirective Interviewing
1. It is time consuming.
2. It requires acute psychological insight and sensitivity.
3. It often generates unneeded information.
4. It tends to generate excessive information.
5. Adaptation to each interviewee may reduce reliability.

DISADVANTAGES

Source: Charles Stewart and William B. Cash, Jr., *Interviewing: Principles and Practices,* 6th ed. (Dubuque, IA: Wm. C. Brown, 1991), p. 7.

ing, and exit interviews are more nondirective. And rarely is an interview completely one or the other. But these different orientations affect the structure of the interview, the amount of participation, and the role that the interviewer plays. Ultimately, the choice of which style to use must rest with the interviewer's personality, objectives, relationship with the interviewee, amount of time and energy expendable, and, most importantly, the interviewee's expectations.

►STRATEGIES AND TECHNIQUES OF INTERVIEWING

Successful interviewing requires careful planning for, like any other communication event, an interview can be no better than the preparation that precedes it. How does one prepare for an interview? First, determine the purpose of the interview and your approach. Why is this event happening? What is your role in it? How are you going to achieve your objective(s)? Second, identify what information is sought and develop a strategy or set of questions and responses designed to elicit that information. Do you have the necessary information? What kinds of questions must be asked to bring forth the needed responses? How might you probe for additional information? Third, assess the interview situation and select a conducive environment. Where should the interview take place? What time of day/week/month? Who should be present? And fourth, consider your role as a listener and respondent. How much talking should you do? What would be a proper balance? What information will the interviewee request? Planning means visualizing possible interview situations, deciding which is the most desirable, and then determining how to move toward that situation and away from paths leading to less-desirable outcomes. The important point is that you go into the interview with a predetermined plan, although you might alter it during the course of the interview itself. In fact, some interviewers construct alternative plans to be used in contingency situations. Better to have too many than not enough plans, for without a plan you succeed only by luck.

Purpose and Approach

Interviews are purposive, focusing on certain kinds of information. They differ from other conversations because the participants have a specific reason for being there. Although it may seem obvious that determining your purpose and goals benefits interviews, deciding on the purpose and goals is often the part of the planning process to which the least attention is paid. As a result, both parties may be frustrated and encounter problems in the interview itself when they discover certain purposes for the interview that may not have been apparent when it was planned.

The overriding purpose of any interview is the acquisition of information. We interview because, as the interviewer, we may obtain information that is otherwise unavailable; as the interviewee, we have an opportunity to send a message in a way that might otherwise be impossible; and the typical face-to-face setting allows ways of assessing the other person or the information being communicated that would not otherwise be attainable.

The interview purpose and goals, however, need to be more specifically identified. Typically, one's purpose is stated in terms of the reasons for the interview—selection, appraisal, discipline, counseling, or exit. But there may be many specific purposes and goals associated with each of these interview types that need to be carefully defined. What you want in terms of content and your relationship with the other person must be considered. Some common goals for interviewers include (1) establishing rapport and credibility with the interviewee, (2) establishing a climate in which information will be disclosed freely, and (3) determining what is appropriate information. Your purpose and goals need to be both generally and specifically identified.

The key to determining your purpose and using goals effectively lies in precisely phrasing the purpose/goal statements. This requires not just the ability to write clear sentences but also to make them reflect the desired substance of the interview. The results of your interviews will ultimately be tested by how well you have achieved your purpose and objectives. Here are some guidelines to follow:

1. Develop a brief statement that tells why you are conducting the interview.
2. Make a list of the information components you need.
3. Specifically identify how you will use the information once you obtain it.

4. Prepare a list of goals or objectives, taking all of these factors into account.
5. Determine what data you need from interviewees to achieve each goal or objective.
6. Draft questions whose answers will provide you with the necessary information to satisfy your purpose and goals.

Lack of a clear purpose and specific goals can turn your interview into a jumbling nonconversation that confuses both parties. However, not only must you have a clear purpose and goals but you must also select a suitable approach to communicate them. You must decide how to structure your interview. Communication researchers have identified certain basic interview approaches or structural frameworks—funnel, inverted funnel, quintamensional design, tunnel, chain-link, and freeform.[3] The exact structure that you choose to build will depend on the particular situation and the type of interview. The best interviews often combine more than one approach.

Funnel Sequence. The funnel sequence employs a questioning approach that moves from the general to the specific. It begins with a broad, open-ended question at the top of the funnel, with each subsequent question becoming more closed and restrictive to the available responses. This sequence of questioning permits the interviewer to discover the interviewee's frame of reference, encourages the interviewee to communicate opinions, and avoids possible conditioning or biasing of responses. An example of the funnel sequence is seen in the following exchange:

Mary: If you could have an ideal job, what would it be like?

John: I enjoy working with people, so would want a people-oriented position that's personally challenging and permits room for growth and development. It would also allow me to contribute to problem solving and reward individual and collaborative accomplishments.

Mary: Well, that's fine. Why are you interested in this job?

John: I'm interested in this job because I want to learn and become an ad executive. This is a medium-sized agency where I think I'll be exposed to a wider range of responsibilities than I would at a larger agency. Considering the accounts you have, I think I'd learn a great deal here and eventually be able to take on more challenging assignments.

Mary: Given our varied accounts, what educational/work experience helps qualify you for this position?

John: My college degree in advertising and marketing gave me the training to handle the problems and decisions you'd expect of me. An internship during my senior year was particularly helpful in exposing me to the real-world responsibilities of such a position. Also, I have excellent office skills for the huge amount of routine paperwork I know goes with this kind of position.

Mary: Why should I hire you over other candidates?

The funnel sequence is effective in a variety of interview settings. Because open questions are easier to answer, pose less of a threat to interviewees, and get them talking, it is a particularly good way to begin an interview and sensitizes the questioner to the need for follow-up probes.

Inverted-Funnel Sequence. The inverted-funnel sequence follows an inductive thinking process, beginning with a specific question and proceeding to more open-ended, general questions. The purpose of an inverted funnel approach is to reach an opinion, based on a foundation of gradual expansion from a specific incident or fact. It forces the interviewee to think through specific attitudes or facts before articulating a general reaction or a conclusion. An example of the inverted-funnel sequence is seen in the following exchange:

Beth: I want to verify that this appraisal covers the period from April 1 to March 31.

Britt: Yes, that's correct. My last appraisal was a year ago.

Beth: Have you completed the refresher course you were taking to qualify for your real estate broker's license?

Britt: Yes. It kept me up at nights studying, but I've finished it and am scheduled to take the real estate broker's exam next week. I'm confident that I'll do well.

Beth: I'm sure you will. What additional courses do you have to take before receiving your bachelor's degree?

Britt: I'm enrolled to take three evening courses this fall which will complete my degree requirements in business. However, the commencement ceremonies won't take place until May. At least I'll be finished. The company's tuition reimbursement policy has sure been helpful.

Beth: Congratulations. We like to encourage the development of our employees. What self-development activities do you plan to engage in during the upcoming year?

Britt: I would like to attend several seminars and perhaps a couple of workshops. They could be valuable in helping me perform my current job and broaden my area of expertise.

Beth: Speaking of performance, how would you evaluate your overall performance over the last 12 months?

Britt: I've been personally pleased. The immediate, short-term goals we agreed on last year have been accomplished and I'm making steady progress on the longer range goals. As I gain experience, I begin to see my career taking shape.

Beth: What do you think of your career progress to date? How can I help you?

The inverted sequence is useful when you need to motivate interviewees to respond. Respondents may be shy or reluctant to share opinions and attitudes or feel they do not know the answers to your questions. Beginning with a narrow topic and broadening to a wider subject can prompt general reactions and plans.

Quintamensional Design Sequence. The quintamensional design sequence was developed by George Gallup in 1947 to probe the intensity of attitudes or opinions.[4] This approach is built, as the name suggests, on five questions that proceed from an interviewer's awareness of an issue to attitudes uninfluenced by the interviewer, specific attitudes, reasons for those attitudes, and intensity of attitude. For example:

1. *Awareness:* what do you think about our employee retraining program?
2. *Uninfluenced attitudes:* which type of retraining is likely to be most effective?
3. *Specific attitude:* do you approve of the money spent on the retraining program?
4. *Reason why:* for what reason?

5. *Intensity of attitude:* on a scale of one to five, from not concerned to very strongly concerned, how strongly do you feel about this issue?

The quintamensional design is similar to the funnel sequence, differing in that it has limited objectives. The last question in the sequence is the determinant since the objective is to produce quantifiable data.

Tunnel Sequence. The tunnel sequence uses a series of similar questions, either all open or all closed, to quantitatively solicit immediate reactions or attitudes toward people, places, incidents, or issues. The questions always involve a "forced choice," which means that the respondent is given a finite number of possible responses and must select the one that is most satisfactory. Consequently, the tunnel sequence allows little probing for in-depth information and often consists of a series of bipolar, either/or, agree/disagree, approve/disapprove questions. An example of the tunnel sequence is seen in the following exchange:

Howard: Were rotary bars recently being attached incorrectly at your assembly station?

Grif: Yes, but I was away from the station at the time—on break.

Howard: Do you realize that someone is supposed to be at the assembly station at all times?

Grif: Well, I suppose so. But, I didn't know Don was going to be away.

Howard: But weren't both you and Don away from the station taking a break together?

Grif: We were, but Don wasn't scheduled for a break at that time and—

Howard: Still, did you disregard the quality control supervisor's request to return to your station?

Grif: I did because—

Howard: Do you understand why I have to write you up for this infraction? Do you agree with this disciplinary report? Will you please sign it.

In addition to getting an interpretation of an incident or quick index of someone's attitude toward a particular subject, the tunnel sequence can be useful in psychological profiling. A long series of forced-choice questions containing several reworded questions on the same issue, to check consistency of response, can reveal personality types.

Chain-Link Sequence. The chain-link sequence provides a framework that encourages reflective probing and results in more depth across a broader range of responses. This approach begins with an open-ended question followed by several probes that lead to a closed question calling for a specific response. The sequence ends with a mirror or summary question that ensures accurate understanding by the interviewer and allows the interviewee an opportunity to clarify, confirm, or modify the information. Following the mirror question, a new chain-link sequence is begun with an open question. An example of the chain-link sequence is seen in the following exchange:

Stacey: Pat, why have you decided to leave Faraday Manufacturing?

Pat: Well, my new position at Bannister pays better and is a more challenging position. It offers greater responsibility and more room for personal development—growth.

Stacey: I see. Go on. What about your position here at Faraday?

Pat: Well, it seems to be a dead end. You know, nowhere to go. I mean, I like it and all, but I have a career to think about.

Stacey: Why do you feel that way? What do you mean by "dead end"?

Pat: Well, it's the same routine over and over—never anything new. I'm rarely included in decision making and there doesn't seem to be anywhere to go.

Stacey: Does your supervisor know about this? Did you ever communicate these concerns to your supervisor?

Pat: Yes, sort of. I went to him and asked to be given different kinds of assignments and to be included in more of the decision making. He seemed to care about me and I thought I could talk to him. He smiled and said he would look into it but nothing happened. I went back again several times, but it was always the same old story—big smile and no change. So, I gave up—but I'm not angry at him.

Stacey: Okay, Pat, let me see if I got this straight. What you're saying is, you feel under utilized and left out of the loop, and your supervisor hasn't been able to address these concerns? Have I got it right?

The chain-link sequence invariably takes more time and places fewer constraints on the direction of the interview. It is less rigidly structured and produces more dialogue in the interview situation.

Freeform Sequence. The freeform sequence is loosely structured and open-ended, but it is not without direction. A freeform approach is largely controlled by the interviewee and invites open-ended responses. The objective of the interviewer is to test the interviewee's intellect or to understand the interviewee's reasoning, or to judge the intensity of the interviewee's opinions. An example of the freeform sequence is seen in the following exchange:

Charlene: We're currently having personnel problems here at Baystate Rubber, Dave, and we would appreciate your helping us locate the source of these problems. What did you think of Baystate when you first came here?

Dave: I had heard a lot about Baystate and Baystate quality when I first came here three years ago. But, I don't know what that means now. This is just a job to me.

Charlene: Why is that, Dave? What has changed?

Dave: My superior only wants me at my machine at 7:15 A.M., he rarely says anything to me unless I goof up. I just sit here all day long and operate this machine. I don't think the president of the company even knows my name.

Charlene: Uh-huh. Tell me more.

Dave: I got a kid at home who is five years old. I call in sick every once in a while to take my kid fishing at the beach. He plays in the sand, I fish. I love it. No company can make me give that up.

Charlene: Why do you feel this way? Explain further. . . . .

The freeform sequence is a valuable approach when you have unlimited time to do a profile or counsel an employee. Follow-up questions are essential and the alert freeform interviewer must avoid digression while working to maintain the interviewee's interest and cultivating her or his confidence.

An interview is a journey of discovery. A clear purpose and approach ensure that you know where you are going, and together they serve as a guide to ensure that you successfully reach your destination. An unstructured interview is not a guide at all, resulting in your taking multiple detours down one sideroad or another. Those side-trips may be more interesting than the highway, but you can easily find yourself lost and confused—unable to reach your original destination. Once you're sure that you know where you are going and have mapped out an approach to get there, you can plan the interview questions.

Questions and Questioning Techniques

Questions are the interviewer's primary tool in gathering information, with the ability to use them effectively the key to successful interviewing. There is a great difference between merely asking questions and making questions work for you effectively. Anyone can ask questions. The skillful interviewer understands the rationale for selecting certain types of questions over others, the precise functions that specific types of questions serve, and is able to phrase questions that produce useful results. Different kinds of information require different types of questions and questioning techniques.

Several factors must be taken into account when preparing questions. Interviewers need to consider how broad they are in scope, how leading they are in directing the interviewee toward or away from one or more answers, and how personal they are in their potential for creating a supportive or defensive communication climate.[5] We will weigh each of these considerations in discussing the types of questions and their functions.

The following list identifies general, basic, and recurring types of questions that you can expect to ask and be asked. It should only be used as a guide for conducting your interviews.

Open Questions. Open questions ask for broad or general information and allow the interviewee considerable freedom to respond in an appropriate way. They are often used to obtain information about feelings, goals, and perspectives. Answers to open questions can reveal uncertainty, intensity of feelings, frames of reference, prejudices, or stereotypes. The following are some examples of open questions:

- ▶ Tell me about yourself.
- ▶ What do you know about our company?
- ▶ How do you feel about working in a culturally diverse environment?
- ▶ Where do you see yourself in ten years?

Open questions generally elicit longer responses than other types of questions because they communicate interest and appear to be nonthreatening. This can result in your receiving a lot of information you either do not want or do not need. However, not all people respond to open questions in a comfortable way. If a participant has some conflict or emotional involvement with a particular subject area or is generally suspicious of you or the purpose of your question, the response will be more defensive and less extensive. Consider the following exchange:

Larry: How are things going in your department?
Barry: Why do you ask? What have you heard?

This exchange would require you to be more specific in probing for information.

Closed Questions. Closed questions are very specific and restrictive in nature. When you use closed questions, you intentionally limit the range of available responses. They are particularly useful when you want a large amount of specific information in a relatively short period of time. Answers to closed questions are brief and succinct, and can be easily coded, tabulated, and analyzed. The following are some examples of closed questions:

► Are you applying for other jobs?
► Do you mind working weekends?
► Do you approve or disapprove of mandatory drug tests?
► Would you rather work alone or in groups?
► Do you want this job?

There is no doubt that closed questions are more efficient than open questions but they don't reveal why an interviewee has a particular attitude, and so they require additional probing by the interviewer.

Probing Questions. Probing questions may be open or closed and grow out of a felt need for more follow-up information, a feeling that the answer received from the initial question is superficial, vague, or inaccurate and not the full or correct response needed. Probes are of two types: directive and nondirective. Directive probes focus answers on specific items of information. Nondirective probes keep the interviewee talking without biasing his or her responses or interrupting the line of thought. Basic directive probes include elaboration, clarification, repetition, and confrontation; nondirective varieties include mirror statements, neutral phrases, and silence.

Elaboration is an assertive probe that asks the interviewee to extend, amplify, or provide additional details. Some examples are: Could you go into that more? What happened then? How did you feel about that?

Clarification is used to obtain a further explanation when you don't understand words or phrases used in an answer or how certain events are related. For example, you might ask, "What do you mean when you use the term 'progressive'?"

Repetition is used when an interviewee doesn't hear or understand, or tries to evade, a question. You simply repeat the query exactly or ask a reasonable facsimile.

Confrontation probes call attention to an apparent inconsistency, a misrepresentation, or a contradiction among items of information in the answers. Interviewers point out these errors not to trap the interviewee but rather to provide an opportunity to clarify the situation or misunderstandings. Many interviewers find it difficult to use this type of probe because of a desire to avoid the stress of conflict and a potentially unpleasant situation. However, confrontation need not be emotionally wrecking and may be a useful and constructive questioning technique.

Mirror statements, also called reflective or summary statements, repeat to the interviewee an answer or information he or she has given to indicate your degree of listening and accurately understanding what has been said. They should clearly be perceived as probes and invite further clarification or elaboration as needed. For example, you might say: "In other words, you're saying. . . , " or "Okay, let me see if I understand. . . , " or "You think, then, that you can. . . ."

Neutral phrases show that you are listening, indicate your interest, and encourage the other person to continue talking. Typical examples include "Hmmm," "Oh," "I see," "Go on," "And then?" "Wow!" "Uh-huh," and other nonverbal assents. These phrases are generally a natural part of the conversation and are frequently uttered when the interviewee is talking.

Silence can be an extremely powerful probe in an interview, permitting interviewees time for reflection and thinking while prompting them to continue talking. Research indicates that there is a positive correlation between the amount of silence used by the interviewer and the respondent's general level of spontaneity.[6] Most interviewers do not use silence effectively because they become too anxious to participate in the interview, feeling that nothing is happening unless someone is talking. Skilled interviewers, on the other hand, have learned to use silence deliberately and productively. The use of silent probes distinguishes the novice from the skillful interviewer.

In sum, probes are questions that are either open or closed and may be assertive and direct or neutral and indirect—even silent. Effective probes are suited to the situation and let you delve deeper into areas while maintaining control of the interview.

Hypothetical Questions. Hypothetical questions present interviewees with a set of circumstances requiring them to make selective choices. They are designed to see how a person might respond in a given low- to high-pressure situation. Hypothetical questions are particularly useful because the answers are less abstract and they reveal the closest thing to actual job behavior that can be observed in an interview. To assess someone's style for handling conflict, you might describe a confrontational situation, or to discover their supervisory orientation, you might ask them how they would respond to a group of new, inexperienced employees. The use of such questions can both enrich the information you obtain and enhance the interview experience.

Leading Questions. Leading questions suggest explicitly or implicitly the expected or desired answer and make it difficult for the interviewee to present his or her own ideas. Robert Kahn and Charles Cannell note that the leading question "makes it easier or more tempting for the respondent to give one answer than another."[7] The leading question telegraphs its expected answer: "You like close detail work, don't you?" "Wouldn't you agree that an MBA is necessary for this position?" "Travel is necessary in this job; you don't mind being on the road, do you?" Interviewers will use such questions to check for assertiveness, to prod reluctant interviewees, to see how respondents cope with stress, or to provoke unguarded replies. When used judiciously and with care, leading questions can be effective tools; they become a serious problem only when the interviewer fails to realize that he or she is, in fact, leading the interviewee to potentially distort responses.

Loaded Questions. Loaded questions provide strong direction toward a particular answer but differ from leading questions in that they use emotionally charged language and higher degrees of entrapment. They are sometimes used by interviewers to check for defensiveness. When you ask, "How do you feel about these stupid policies?" or "When was the last time you got drunk?" you are exercising an extraordinary kind of control. Loaded questions should only be used by skillful interviewers with extreme caution because they can easily create a dysfunctional communication climate that will negatively affect both parties in the interviewing situation.

The question is the tool with which interviewers, like archaeologists on a search for hidden treasures, remove layers of material in order to arrive at the information they seek. Different types of questions perform different functions, and when carefully employed they significantly influence the validity and reliability of any interview. Validity refers to the extent to which you are observing, receiving, or measuring what you think you are observing, or measuring. Are you getting the information you need? Want? Reliability is the extent to which you would get the same results if you or another interviewer were to conduct a similar interview with the same individual. Validity and reliability can be important criteria when judging the effectiveness of any particular interview. In sum, question asking is an art, requiring skill, practice, and attention to how people respond.

Selecting and Creating the Environment

All interviews arise out of an *exigency*—a combination of people, places, and events marked by a degree of urgency requiring resolution. The nature of interviewing situations changes with differing combinations of people, places, and events affecting the behaviors of the participants. Therefore, it is important to define the situation and select an environment that is conducive for interviewing.

Interviews do not occur in a vacuum but rather are influenced by and in turn influence the external environment. When analyzing the interview situation, you must recognize what has preceded and will follow the interview and consider these variables: physical setting, social setting, time dimensions, and psychological climate.

Architecture, furnishings, room dimensions, temperature, lighting, noise, privacy, physical placement of participants, and territoriality all affect the interview situation. A well-lighted, moderate-sized room, pleasantly decorated, comfortably climate-controlled, and properly ventilated, creates a supportive environment that encourages communication among participants. Surroundings free of noise and distractions enhance concentration and help maintain lines of thinking. The spatial and territorial dimensions dictate control and influence the formality or informality of the situation. The physical setting creates the desired atmosphere or mood needed to encourage dialogue and move the interaction beyond surface exchanges. Fortunately, the interviewer has considerable freedom to plan and arrange the interview and adjust the physical characteristics of the meeting place.

Social or cultural customs and the nature of the occasion influence the communication climate and the personal relationship established between the participants. To avoid interpersonal problems, both parties should be sensitive to the other's sociocultural background, as it is easy to offend unconsciously. Differences in cultural norms can be problematic and you must make an effort to appreciate and be open, understanding, and accepting of diversity. It is also important to remember that each person comes to an interview with unique perceptions of the situation. The interviewer may consider the interview routine, but the interviewee may see it as a major life event. It is in the social setting where the necessary credibility and trustworthiness is established to prompt a candid, truthful exchange of information and ideas.

The length of the interview and the time when it occurs may also influence its outcome. People feel more alert and motivated at different times of the day/week/month/year. Some prefer to deal with important matters early in the morning and, if possible, early in the week; others prefer midmorning or early afternoon and later in the week. Interviews are often inappropriately scheduled for Mondays when motivation is low or Fridays when interviewers are looking forward to the weekend and anticipating relaxing. Holidays such as Christmas, Chanukah, Thanksgiving, and Yom Kippur are also particularly poor occasions for reprimands or dismissals. Time dimensions should be carefully considered because they affect concentration, mood, and the ability to communicate.

The most common way of thinking about psychological climate in an interview is in terms of comfort or stress. Comfort represents the degree to which the participants feel at ease. Stress is the degree of anxiety they experience. Shyness, communication apprehension, nervousness, and ego threats are potential problems that plague interviews and reduce their effectiveness; tact, patience, sensitivity, and language skill can help alleviate these tensions. Whatever can be done to build a congenial relationship will positively affect the psychological climate and be a powerful motivator in the interview. It is here that rapport building becomes important. Perhaps the overriding way to construct a comfortable climate is for the participants to express genuine consideration for one another's needs.

Yet, research indicates that some people experience high levels of communicative anxiety that seriously impede effective performance during interviews; these people require both anxiety management training and interviewing skills training.[8] Toward this end, a variety of anxiety-reduction techniques are available.[9]

One proven method of anxiety reduction is systematic desensitization. *Systematic desensitization* refers to a treatment package that systematically includes (1) training in muscle relaxation; (2) construction of hierarchies of anxiety-eliciting stimuli; and (3) the graduated pairing, through imagery, of anxiety-eliciting stimuli with the relaxed state. It may be presented on a one-to-one basis, through group methods, or even via tape recordings.[10]

Another technique used to modify social-communicative anxiety is cognitive-behavior therapy. *Cognitive-behavior therapy* is based on the formulation of "anxiety as a two-dimensional construct, incorporating both physiological and cognitive responses."[11] Several cognitive-behavioral anxiety-reduction techniques have been developed, all based on the principle that cognitive factors such as irrational beliefs or expectations directly mediate change in other physiological and motoric response channels. One such method is Rational-Emotive Therapy (RET). The goal in this technique is to identify the irrational schemes of the apprehensive communicator and instruct the person to replace the irrational beliefs with some rational, nonthreatening self-statements. An alternative to RET is Cognitive Restructuring (CR). The major steps in CR for treating communication anxiety are (1) explaining to the person that communication anxiety is a learned reaction and can be overcome if he or she is more aware of the negative self-statements, (2) identifying negative self-statements that are listed and discussed in terms of their effect on communication behavior, (3) learning coping statements to substitute for the negative self-statements, and (4) practicing an active rehearsal of the coping statements through role playing.[12] Both RET and CR are based on the notion that "it is not the incidence of irrational beliefs that distinguishes normal and abnormal populations; rather, that people differ in the coping responses they make to their irrational thoughts."[13]

Interviewer as Listener and Respondent

Interviewing is a two-way process requiring a balance in turn-taking, meaning interviewers must also be listeners and respondents. Part of the coordinated action in an interview comes from the orderly interchange in which both participants know when they can speak and when they should listen. The desired or specific balance varies with every interview type and situation. Participants with highly developed social and communication skills will enjoy a more balanced exchange than will those who are introverted and less articulate.

In addition to interpersonal skills and communication competency, the type of interview influences the balance. The discipline interview may require an 80/20 balance with the interviewer doing most of the speaking; selection and exit interviews often reveal a 70/30 balance with the interviewee dominating the speaking. Appraisal interviews are frequently a 50/50 balance. Counseling interviews permit the interviewee the greatest freedom to speak, assuring a nondirective approach. No interview can be successful without meaningful feedback.

The importance of listening is self-evident. We previously discussed types of listening as well as potential barriers and keys to effective listening, presenting it as an active or aggressive rather than passive activity. The skilled interviewer listens to comprehend, analyze, interpret information, display interest, and provide reassurance. This requires placing oneself in the situation of the other party and listening with a "third ear" to what is not said. John Stewart and Gary D'Angelo observe that genuine understanding "involves grasping fully what the other person is trying to say—from her or his point of view—and how he or she feels about it. It comes about when you are able to interpret accurately and empathically the cues the other person makes available."[14] Listening well is your most important responsibility—a skill that cannot be taken for granted or given too much attention.

The interview process is an integral part of organizational life, affecting organizational outcomes, job satisfaction, and the productivity of employees.[15] It is a managerial tool used to gather information and to motivate. Consequently, it is useful to explore the different kinds of interview situations. In the next sections we will focus more directly on the various types of interviews—those designed for selection, appraisal, discipline, counseling, and exit.

▶ SELECTION INTERVIEW

The selection interview is used for screening, hiring, and placing applicants, employees, and members of the organization. It is the most common form of interview in organizational life, with over 99 percent of today's organizations relying on the selection interview as part of their hiring procedures.[16] Indeed, a majority of companies no longer use other methods of identifying potential personnel, but rely solely on the selection interview for making hiring decisions.[17] The interview is crucial to the hiring process and such interviewing is costly. According to the Employment Management Association, companies spend an average of $672.00 per person to hire hourly workers and $7,488.00 per person to hire professional or managerial employees.[18] John Drake explains why when he states that because "the success of any manager depends on the depth of talent with which he surrounds himself, it becomes absolutely critical for him to learn to effectively evaluate manpower."[19]

Although numerous tools and procedures are used to recruit and select new employees, the interview is consistently the most frequently used selection device, Given its apparent importance as a recruitment and selection tool, it is not surprising to discover that a plethora of empirical research has been conducted to explore the dynamics of the interviewing process. Essentially, the selection interview benefits the interviewer, the interviewee, and the company. It provides an opportunity to obtain information about the candidate that might not be obtained otherwise. Most people will say more about themselves than they will write down, so probing often yields more depth to the answers. The "why" is often more important than the "what." Moreover, the interviewer can assess communication abilities, appearance, personality factors, thinking patterns, and level of motivation. In conversation, the interviewee can more fully present his or her credentials and can reveal the real extent of interest in the job and the company. Finally, the interview personalizes the company. As the representative of the company, you provide the image that the interviewee has of the company. Through you the interviewee gets a sense of the working atmosphere and of the people in the organization. The interview supplements and expands any written materials.

The interview is at the heart of the selection process but it does not begin when the candidate walks through the door. Rather it is preceded by serious preparation and is attended by the appropriate use of questioning techniques and the application of analytical skills. The key points include: preparing ahead; establishing rapport and a climate for communication; stating the purpose of the interview, gathering information; describing the job and organization; matching the candidate to the job; answering the candidate's questions; closing effectively; evaluating the candidate; and evaluating yourself. In the next chapter we examine in detail the selection interviewing process and its accompanying communication demands.

▶ APPRAISAL INTERVIEW

Organizations are becoming increasingly aware of the critical importance of performance appraisals for the effective management of human resources. Studies indicate that 89 percent of companies with more than 500 employees and 74 percent of smaller companies use performance appraisal systems.[20] Also, all state government organizations and 76 percent of city government organizations surveyed used such systems.[21] Performance appraisals are key components in maximizing organizational efficiency and effectiveness. When appropriately designed and conducted, they can serve as a strategy for: (1) improving employee job performance by revealing training needs; (2) facilitating objective decision making regarding employee retention, promotion, and/or transfer; (3) increasing employee motivation and personal growth by providing feedback about job performance; (4) reducing the potential threat of legal complications by providing documentation; and (5) enhancing attainment of organizational goals and objectives by providing a means to foster and monitor goal-directed behavior.[22] Robert Johnson observes that inherent in the employer–employee relationship is the need for performance appraisal and he summarizes the effective use of appraisal interviews as follows:

> The employee has a legitimate need to know how his performance compares with his supervisor's expectations. It is not merely a matter of idle curiosity, but a true need, an essential link of communication between employer and employee. . . . In the absence of specific feedback on performance, some serious problems may develop. The employee may be forming undesirable work habits, but he may assume quite erroneously that the

supervisor's silence means approval. . . . The employer—specifically, the supervisor—needs to carry out the essential process of communication between employer and employee. If the employee is doing less than satisfactory work and his performance is correctable, the supervisor needs to convey this in the appraisal interview and arrange for improvement. If the employee's work is satisfactory, the supervisor has a stake in that person's future and will use the appraisal interview to promote continued satisfactory performance.[23]

But in spite of the importance accorded performance appraisals, the attitudes of many supervisors toward conducting such interviews range from reluctance to pure disdain. This disdain can be explained in several ways. Supervisors are not comfortable openly discussing performance analysis with their subordinates. Many feel that the process serves no constructive purpose; others realize that they lack the necessary communicative skills. According to surveys of more than 400 companies by Drake, Beam, Morin, and Opinion Research Corporation, the major failure of these evaluations is an inability of managers to communicate with their subordinates about their strengths and weaknesses. Stephen Morriss, executive vice president of Drake, Beam, Morin, observes that "it's just something that people really dislike because they have to sit down one-on-one with another individual and tell him what he is doing right or wrong."[24] Roy Serpa adds that if superiors (1) do not define objectives, (2) establish vague personal goals, (3) reward arbitrarily, (4) promote on the basis of personal relationships, and (5) do not develop their subordinates, then the prevailing belief will be that performance appraisals are useless and unnecessary. He says that raises and promotions are often granted for longevity or partiality on the part of the supervisor rather than individual performance and, in some cases, high achievers receive no better recognition or reward than mediocre performers.[25] Still, research shows that employees at every level like to know where they stand.[26] Even if the appraisal proves to be negative, subordinates prefer to be evaluated and counseled on how to improve. No performance appraisal at all leaves them angry, frustrated, and dissatisfied.[27]

Properly conducted appraisal interviews reduce the emphasis on evaluation that creates conflict and substitute a concern for common interests. Beverly Kaye and Shelly Krantz have identified several ways in which appraisal interviews contribute to improved performance, job satisfaction, and employee growth. First, appraisals help to build productive superior–subordinate relationships by exploring topics of mutual concern. Second, constructive appraisals provide an opportunity to discuss issues affecting both the participants and the larger organization. Third, properly conducted appraisals encourage self-motivation by helping both participants define their goals and objectives. Fourth, appraisals may improve the working relationships among members of the organization by helping to establish clearer boundaries of accountability. Fifth, appraisals may improve the working climate in the organization by making the personnel process less mysterious. Finally, appraisals create an environment that promotes personal and professional development by encouraging employees to think about their own growth.[28]

Typically, employees are evaluated after a probationary period and then periodically on an annual or semiannual basis. The success of appraisal interviews rests entirely on the attitudes of the participants. When approached constructively by both parties, the interview can be a significant doorway to better morale and productivity. The following six-step process for performance appraisals can help ensure that these evaluations are both fair and productive.[29]

1. *Schedule the performance appraisal in advance and be prepared.* The employee should prepare a report on his or her performance, submit it to the supervisor a week ahead of the interview, and be prepared to discuss it. The interviewer can then compare ratings. This increases the employee's involvement in the process. The appraisal interview is at its worst when it comes as a surprise to the employee.

2. *Create the proper atmosphere for two-way communication.* To create a co-equal atmosphere, the appraiser should (a) state the purpose of the interview, (b) use the employee's first name or nickname if appropriate, (c) position the furniture so that both parties have an unimpeded view of each other, and (d) provide a comfortable physical interview setting in which both parties can relax. Oftentimes the employee will feel more at ease if the interview is conducted in a conference room rather than in the supervisor's office.

3. *Begin with a statement of purpose.* The employee will probably be anxious, so a clear statement of the purpose of the interview, its format, its uses, its expected outcome, as well as thoughtful responses to the employee's questions will help put him or her at ease. If the employee knows what the interviewer is trying to accomplish, he or she will avoid false expectations and be properly prepared.

4. *Encourage the employee to participate.* The skillful manager will indicate from the outset an interest in the employee's opinions and concerns. An effective method for conducting appraisals is to follow a nondirective approach. A nondirective approach encourages the employee to identify strengths and weaknesses and to investigate means for working out solutions to strengthen the weak areas. In this approach the interviewer refrains from telling the employee what the problem is, or what the solution is. Instead, the interviewer provides a sounding board for the employee to investigate problems and solutions. When the employee provides insightful responses, the interviewer reinforces those responses through verbal and/or nonverbal agreement. Allowing the employee an opportunity to provide a verbal self-appraisal can be a good starting point.

5. *Discuss total performance, setting future performance goals and formulating a development plan.* Do not dwell primarily on negative aspects of performance, and do not allow the employee to do so. Discuss strengths and identify specific opportunities for growth and improvement, outlining methods for achieving agreed-on goals. Above all, base your appraisal on the performance, not the person. It is useful if you can separate salary issues from performance evaluation.

6. *Summarize the interview and provide documentation.* Summarize the discussion and clarify any disagreements. Initial established goals for the coming year. Appraisals offer one of the best means of documenting why organizational decisions have been made, and serve as a form of management protection.

The work plan sets the standards by which the employee is measured during the appraisal process. But, more than a simple measure of performance, the work plan also takes into account the employee's development. Marion S. Kellogg observes that "ultimately what an employee and his manager agree to do represents a psychological contract between them. If the work package requires the employee to add to his knowledge, develop his skills, fill an experience gap or undertake a desired modification, the groundwork for the employee's development is established. And the man-

▶ MY PERFORMANCE APPRAISAL—ONE DISAPPOINTING EXPERIENCE

I would like to share with you what was for me a very disappointing experience—my performance evaluation. It was the worst evaluation experience I ever had.

In my organization, we use a performance management system based on an objective we have selected for the year. My supervisor and I met and agreed on my objective. She thought it was appropriate and above what had been done previously by the person who held the position. I worked toward the objective during the year, meeting my deadlines along the way. Before I was to meet with her for my final evaluation, she was transferred to another to another department. Her former boss was now my immediate supervisor.

The deadline for evaluations came and went without a word from him. I asked if he would like me to set up an appointment with his secretary for us to get together regarding my MBO. He said, "No, but I'll be getting with you soon." More time passed, no word.

Then one day as I'm going into my office from having conducted a new employee orientation program, he yells to me from down the hall—"You got a minute?" I said, "Sure" and put my things down, picked up a notepad and followed him to his office. He had yet to say what this meeting was about. As we walked into his office, he says to me, "I hate doing this but it has to be done. I just hate doing evaluations."

Finally, I knew why were meeting. He stands over his desk sifting through piles of papers saying, "Now where did I put that file, I know it was here the other day." Right about now, I'm feeling pretty uncomfortable. This is the one time of the year to formally meet with my supervisor to get feedback on my performance. This is important to me and I had every indication from him that it was a major pain. After a few more grumblings about having to do evaluations, he found my paperwork.

The three ways to be rated are "at expectation," "above expectation," and "below expectation." He rated my objective "at expectation" even though my previous supervisor had said it was above and had told me that I had met it. Bottom line—no merit pay.

I asked him for an example of an objective which would be above expectation so I could work toward that in the future. He slumped down in his chair and talked in circles without saying anything of substance while *not* looking at me.

This was a very disappointing and unproductive interaction. Here was an opportunity for a meaningful exchange, a chance for me to get positive feedback on my performance, and an opportunity for him to share with me the areas in which I needed improvement. None of this happened. He had me sign the form and said, "That's all."

I was hurt and then angry. I found the whole process to be a waste of time and energy. His communication with me seemed to be an example of how *not* to do an employee evaluation. His attitude about having to do it, his body language, the fact that words were exchanged but no real communication happened all equaled a very negative experience. I really felt cheated. I agree with W. Edwards Deming when he says that "performance appraisal is the number one American management problem."

Source: Student journal entry, Hamilton Holt School of Rollins College, Winter Park, FL, Fall 1991.

ager's guidance will contribute not only to organization results but to employee growth as well."[30]

There are no shortcuts to successful performance appraisals and there are a number of options as to the form that actual evaluations can take. Laws do not require performance appraisal by organizations, but Equal Employment Opportunity (EEO) guidelines state that those that are conducted must be standardized in form and administration, measure actual work performance, and be applied to all classes of employees.

The job performance review provides a unique opportunity for two-way communication. The employee can make the session a profitable one by developing a constructive attitude of cooperation with the interviewer. Before being interviewed, complete a self-evaluation, identifying your strengths and weaknesses, your points of high and low performance over the time period in question. Be able to identify the areas in which you have shown improvement and be able to offer solutions for your problem areas. The appraisal interview provides you with the opportunity to create a positive image and participate in goal setting.

The appraisal interview is part of a broader, organizationally sanctioned but individually focused performance review process that usually incorporates assessment and evaluation of performance; problem solving requiring analytical, facilitating, and counseling behaviors; and career planning. A successful performance review process is characterized by (1) candor, trust, and openness in the discussion between supervisor and subordinate about performance and career planning; (2) clarification for the employee of his or her performance measurement, career alternatives, and career planning; and (3) employee feedback regarding supervision and organizational goals and objectives. The purpose is not to prove a point but to seek solutions beneficial to both parties and to the organization.

▶ DISCIPLINE INTERVIEW

The discipline interview occurs when the employer perceives an ongoing problem of which the employee is aware and which is in clear violation of organization policy, rules, or regulations. Major behavioral offenses are easily dealt with and almost always met with termination and often criminal charges. However, it is handling the less severe or less obvious behavioral breaches that managers find difficult and unpleasant.[31] As a supervisor, it may be your most distasteful task, but it should be approached as a constructive interaction to personally benefit the employee and the organization. Today, many companies are proactively including a discipline process as an integral part of their personnel policies and procedures in an effort to avoid potential litigation.[32]

No matter how effective a discipline policy seems to be on paper, if it is not implemented fairly and efficiently, it is worthless. Joseph Seltzer notes that "if employees feel that a supervisor is unfair or weak, there is a tendency to lose respect for the rules—and for the supervisor."[33] Consequently, maintaining control is an important factor for the interviewer to consider in conducting the discipline interview. The employee should be told of the specific offense and given an opportunity to explain why the offense occurred and also to clarify any misperceptions. The interviewer should not allow the employee to debate the issue but merely to present any necessary additional information. The interviewer should then state what disciplinary action is to be taken and specify the terms of the discipline. The interviewer must be firm and not submit to any compromise, pleading, or bargaining from the employee. Otherwise, the discipline will lose its impact.

Although specific techniques differ with interviewers and guidelines may vary among companies, the following characteristics seem to be common to discipline interviewing and the proper implementation of disciplinary actions: (1) discipline should be immediate; (2) it should have prior warning; (3) it should be consistent; (4) it should be impersonal; and (5) the punishment should be appropriate.[34] The interviewer should maintain cordial and sincere seriousness throughout the interaction. Discipline is a serious business designed to correct behavior, not punish it, and should contribute to developing a more productive employee.[35]

The discipline interview may assume a direct approach, but it is still a two-way interaction. The interviewee is in trouble and really not in any position to bargain or negotiate, but the interviewer should make every effort to determine the accuracy of the charges. If the employee is being unjustly disciplined, then procedures for appeal within the organization should be pursued. The Affirmative Action officer or union steward would be appropriate sources for further information. If the charges are warranted, then the best approach is to be cooperative, demonstrate a willingness to correct the error(s), and accept the discipline without argument. Typically, the record of a discipline interview is initialed by both parties and becomes a part of the employee's file. A constructive attitude will do much to soften a discipline report.

The discipline interview and a clearly stated disciplinary policy are beneficial to all. They ease the manager's difficult job of disciplining by informing the employee of what is expected. If used wisely and implemented well, they can have a positive impact on the health of the entire organization.

▶ COUNSELING INTERVIEW

Counseling is a communication activity that is both deeply humane and essential to sound organizational management. The counseling interview typifies the "helping" or "coaching" relationship. Its main objective is to change the counselee's behavior or the attitudes that motivate the behavior, and contribute to a greater understanding of her or his talents, roles, or performance in the organization.[36] Unlike psychotherapy, counseling in business does not seek to remedy personality problems; nor does it require a professionally trained practitioner to be effective. The counseling situation occurs when someone realizes that a work-specific performance problem exists that he or she cannot handle alone.

Counseling is a management skill, a process that occurs repeatedly at many levels of responsibility. Counseling in the organizational arena presumes that there is a hierarchy; that there is a supervisor and a person being supervised or coached. It is not communication between equals. A characteristic of organization is the existence of power centers that control the efforts of the organization and direct them toward its goals. These power centers must also continuously review the organization's performance and repattern its structure, where necessary, to increase its efficiency. Ultimately, counseling or coaching is a problem-solving skill.[37]

The spectrum of possible situations that may involve the counseling interview is wide and the reasons why someone may be counseled vary greatly. Likewise, describing interviewer and interviewee roles in counseling interviews is complicated. Current literature describes two very different approaches to conducting such interviews. At one extreme, some theorists emphasize the use of very directive counseling strategies in which the counselor assumes complete control of the interview. At the other extreme, theorists following the lead of Carl Rogers rely on nondirective methods in which the counselor lets the interviewee take control of the interview. Most use interviewing strategies that fall somewhere along a line drawn between directive and nondirective.[38] Common to any counseling is the potential power to help other human beings help themselves solve problems that are goal oriented and organization centered.

Remedial Counseling

Counseling is often remedial. The supervisor notices a deficiency in a subordinate's performance and wishes to help or ensure that performance is brought up to par. A heart-to-heart talk may ensue, or perhaps a dressing down. Chances are high that such actions alone will have little effect; these approaches are far less effective than is *true* counseling. To focus our discussion, let's examine an individual-specific, although hypothetical, case:

> Pat Jones is a junior executive with the Holt Corporation. She has been employed in the marketing department for three years, is single, is working on an MBA part-time, and is career oriented. However, on several occasions, Pat has shown some difficulty meeting due dates or deadlines, with the result that others' work was delayed and unnecessary burdens were placed on coworkers and superiors. Pat's work is of high quality when completed, and there always appears to be a reasonable explanation for each late submission. As Pat's immediate supervisor, you wish to remedy the problem of late work submission, and at the same time maintain Pat's quality of work and company loyalty. Pat has just submitted a fine analysis two days late, and you are under some pressure from other departments to move the project along expeditiously.

Let's look at some factors that might influence your counseling Pat. You have a right to be angry. After all, Pat is a competent employee who is aware of the problems previous late submissions of work have caused. Pat is a business-educated person, an adult who knows that others depend on both the quality and timeliness of assignments. You are getting flak from your colleagues and boss because Pat has delayed your submitting the final program proposal.

"I've had it!" you feel. "I'm going to rake Pat over the coals, for sure! I won't be embarrassed again. Either Pat shapes up, or I'll arrange a transfer, maybe one to the unemployment office." Not an unreasonable reaction. If given time, you might even rationalize that you are in touch with your feelings and would be reacting in a healthy, open, and honest way. Your motives are clear and reasonable, and certainly no one could fault you for expressing such genuine feelings.

The fault in this scenario is that it ignores totally the organizational context in which it occurred. As Pat's supervisor, you showed no clear sense of *why* you were calling Pat in or why you were letting off steam—at least no clear sense beyond the venting of your own feelings and possibly finding some emotional relief for yourself. The danger is in losing an excellent employee, which would not be in your best interest and could be costly to the organization. So, this option seems to lack an organizational orientation and a clear purpose centering on the task and the employee, not the supervisor. More could be said about this option, but let's consider others. Alternatively, you choose to dictate the following memorandum to Pat:

> TO: Pat Jones, Marketing
> FROM: Algonquin Phalanthrope, Director
>
> As you know, Pat, the Marketing Division of Holt Corporation is one of the most important in the entire firm. Our work is what the company is all about—selling Wolfram Waggles to women, worldwide.
>
> And, Pat, your role is an important one within the Marketing Division. Your contributions over the three years you've been with us have been an important part of our success. However, there has been a problem with the timeliness of your work, and the Celebes Islands Market Share Analysis you just completed is a prime example. Your two-day lateness delayed our total Asiatic Report by three days and the senior executive deputy assistant to the chairman has criticized this delay.

Now, Pat, our firm's policy is clear on this and you know it well. We can't allow delays of this sort and the pattern of tardiness you've created cannot help either our division or your career. I'm certain you'll be sure to avoid such unfortunate delays in the future.

Cordially,

Algonquin Phalanthrope
cc: personnel file

Phalanthrope is appropriately pleased with his handling of Pat's lateness. He has avoided embarrassing her in a personal confrontation; she can reread the memo and so be very clear on what needs to be corrected; it will be a lasting reminder, a continuing incentive to get work in on time. There are added benefits for Phalanthrope as well: (1) his busy schedule was not interrupted by a possibly long and acrimonious confrontation; (2) he is "covered" officially and in writing should a superior question him on how and when he handled Pat's late reports; and (3) the tone of the memorandum is objective and professional, reflecting well on his managerial style.

However, the memorandum seems to have done more to relieve Phalanthrope of responsibility than to change Pat's behavior. Pat may well read the memorandum at a bad time, feel chagrined or put down, or just angry, and tear it up. She may focus on the "cc: personnel file" and conclude that this is part of a plan leading to dismissal. Or she may feel deep resentment because the lateness of the Celebes Islands analysis was beyond her control—after all, the computer was down most of Thursday and the typist was out for three days that week. This approach, then, lacks proper grounding in facts, is impersonal, and is subject to reasonable alternative interpretations.

Still another possible approach to Pat's lateness might be to call her in and ask for the reasons for the late report—prompt a personal encounter:

Phalanthrope: Pat, the Celebes Islands Analysis was very good, but you delivered it to me two days late. What happened? Can you explain it to me?

Pat: Sorry, Mr. Phalanthrope, I thought it was due on the 17th, so I thought it was only a day late. But, with my regular secretary out and the computer down, it was a miracle I completed it as early as I did.

Phalanthrope: The Celebes Islands Analysis held up the whole Asiatic Report, and I was chewed out for that being late. I've got to get all of my projects in on schedule. When program proposals are due, they are due!

Pat: Yeah. I know how important your big report is, but I can't work without data or without a good statistical typist. I did my best.

Phalanthrope: This can't continue and this isn't the first time you've held up the works. But, Pat, after what was said to me, this had better be the last time you delay *my* work. I don't care how good your reports are, if they're not in my hands when I need them. . . .

The very fact that the director initiated a face-to-face encounter, permitting personal dialogue, is a powerful plus. The personal interaction allows the participants opportunities to modify their views and to change their approach based on the received and understood messages exchanged. But, there are some shortcomings in the way the interview actually occurred.

Phalanthrope began the interview by stating his problem and opening the door for Pat to respond. However, after Pat offered reasons for the late report, the director simply restated and expanded on *his* problem. It is almost axiomatic to communication that you shouldn't ask a question and invite a response unless you intend to acknowledge and actively involve the other party. In this particular interview there's little evidence of shared thinking. Rather, it appears to be an exchange of monologues. This is particularly evident in Phalanthrope's reference to his being "chewed out." It's difficult to decide whether the lateness of Pat's report would have been a problem if he hadn't found himself in trouble. Is the director's agenda Pat's lateness or avoidance of criticism for himself? Again, Pat offers reasons which are ignored. Apparently, Pat feels that there are justifiable reasons for the delay and mentions them. At least on one level, she acknowledges the director's difficulties even though Phalanthrope ignores her protestations. Her comments seem not to be acknowledged or taken into account in any way. This interview lacks reciprocity and statements seem to contain several levels of message-meaning.

Counseling is not an activity apart from, but is an integral part of, a manager's habit of successful communication. It is a superior's effort to modify or improve another's behavior, and communication is a major means of identification with others. For either of these objectives to be reached, there are two conditions that must be met. First, the counselee must want to change and must seek help to do so. Second, the counselor must want to help and, after agreeing to do so, must demonstrate excellent listening and probing skills and empathy in order for the counselee to resolve the issues that prompted the need for help. Specifically, to produce change, the counselor must (1) understand fully what is or is not now being done; (2) have a clear sense of what ought to be the case; (3) compare "is" with "ought," and conclude that there is a significant, demonstrable difference; and (4) compare the deficit in performance with resources, the original behavior, and personal qualities, and develop plausible ways of bringing "is" into greater congruence with "ought." That is, to bring the present situation closer to what should be the case.[39] Let's examine each of these specific change-producing elements to better understand what each entails and why they are necessary conditions for effective, thoughtful counseling.

The counselor or coach must thoroughly understand what *is* currently being done or not done—the facts of the situation. This demands accurate observation and description of an employee's behavior. If done properly, later difficulties will be avoided because factual disputes will not arise. Furthermore, the problem may seem quite different after a full investigation. Pat Jones may not be a chronically tardy worker; perhaps the reports Phalanthrope has received were late because of a confusion about deadlines or other circumstances. Knowing when you have a sufficiently complete and accurate view of the problem is a matter of experience and judgment. However, even when you are persuaded that you know enough, be certain to remain open to new and even contradictory information that may expose multiple causes for the problem, influence your preferred remedy, or change your entire orientation toward the person you are counseling. Simply put, obtain as full and accurate a picture of the original situation as is practical; remain open to new information; and remain flexible in your handling of new data.

The counselor must have a clear sense of what *ought* to be. This requires that understandable and fair standards exist to cover the situation(s) that might lead to counseling. Obviously, standards should not be ambiguous or secret, nor should they be invented arbitrarily for each situation. Moreover, the counselor must avoid reacting on the purely personal level of "I don't like what's going on."

In the Pat Jones example, several rules or work standards are involved. One refers to work being produced on a timely basis. Is an hour, day, or week's delay unacceptable? Does it apply to all work or should a qualitative distinction be made among tasks? Are excuses or reasons ever acceptable? Does the misfeasance or nonfeasance of others ever justify one's submitting work after a due date? What are the employee's obligations in such cases? What obligations do managers and first-line supervisors have in translating and applying general work rules to particular circumstances? How free are such supervisors to depart from or modify company work rules for special cases? To the extent that these questions go unanswered, problems will surely arise.

The counselor must compare "is" with "ought" and conclude that there is a significant difference between "reality" and the "ideal." This process, sometimes called *logical subtraction,* may reveal deficiencies in information or ambiguities in standards. It is fairly uncomplicated but should not be done hastily or automatically. It is important to ground your conclusion(s) in the facts and in the explicitly stated standards.

In almost every case, you will find that reality somehow falls short of the written standard. Your task as supervisor-counselor is to use good, professional judgment about how much of a difference really "makes a difference." For counseling to be effective, any is/ought discrepancy must be demonstrable to the employee being coached and it should be one worth remedying. Remember, acceptance of your counseling is based on the shared perception of a solvable problem rooted in factual agreement and mutually accepted rules.

The counselor should assess a deficit in performance with a view toward developing plausible ways of bringing the "is" into greater agreement with the "ought." Review the problem, check your assets, and fashion ways of using these resources to solve the problem. "Functional fixedness" is a term used to describe individuals who tend to see things in only one way. An important trait of an effective counselor is an open, inquiring mind. Imagination, flexibility, and openness lead to creativity and are critically important when exploring solutions to problems. In the case of Pat's late reports, you might:

1. Team Pat with a peer, anticipating that a coworker's good influence might change Pat's behavior.
2. Monitor Pat's work yourself throughout the report-producing process and not merely after the fact.
3. Change Pat's work assignments, at least temporarily, to less time-dependent tasks.

When generating these plausible solutions, the counselor should take the following questions into consideration:

▶ Based on your experience, which of these approaches will most likely succeed? This should prompt further questions about the efficacy of similar approaches in the past, your understanding of the employee being counseled, and research findings reported in the professional literature.
▶ What would each alternative cost? Costs are not always obvious, not always financial, and seldom easily predicted. What additional work might be involved with each solution? How will other employees' work and feelings be affected?
▶ Which alternative seems likely to have the broadest positive effect beyond the immediate problem? Affect the greatest number of people? Have the most long-lasting effect?

▶ Which alternative can be evaluated most readily? A solution that cannot be assessed, both along the way and on completion, probably should be avoided. To the extent that we fail to evaluate effectiveness, we fail to *know* if we've succeeded.

Failure to consider these criteria leaves the counselor to sheer guesswork and the pious hope that the approach chosen actually works.

Having decided on your approach, you discuss it with those affected and remain open to suggestions, modifications, and improvements. This may involve only the employee, or other employees and supervisors. Sensitivity to others' feelings and to the need for confidentiality is important. To the extent that you can control them, all conditions surrounding the interview should promote the experience. Select an area free of noise distractions and interruption, one that offers a supportive communication climate. Make every effort to create an environment that will not jeopardize the outcome of the session. Counseling is intensely personal and, as such, delicate.

Let's return to Pat's late production problems. Assume that you decided to change her work assignments and monitor her work more closely. You intend to avoid crowding her because this might reduce her self-confidence and you hope to "help Pat change Pat." Because the best counselor is nonmanipulative, you explain the plan and discuss it with her. She agrees with it and the two of you decide on a sequence of four assignments over the next six weeks, each having a closer due date. Your monitoring schedule is tentatively set for daily visits during the first project, tapering to a single check midway through the last project. This will measure the approach's success.

As a counselor, you should be alert to the fears, needs, and preferences of the employee being counseled. This means that a conscious effort is made to take the other person into account and give serious consideration to their opinions. It's important to solicit the employee's ideas and suggestions about possible solutions. And, after the fact, who is better to ask whether the process could have been improved on than the counselee? Certainly, the employee may have a more narrow view than yours, but neither should you deny yourself the in-sights this deeply involved person may provide. Moreover, this feedback can assist you in future counseling efforts.

What if all of your efforts seemingly fail? What if the employee's job performance does not improve and even deteriorates? At some point, you conclude that you did not succeed in your counseling. Here it is important to retain an objective and professional view. Perhaps you really erred or personal factors intruded and the problem could be attacked more successfully if another manager-counselor took charge. Or, it may be the employee's deeply rooted personality problem that manifests itself in substandard job performance. If you and the employee cannot sort out the job-related aspect(s) and resolve it, recognize your limits and *do not tamper with problems beyond your competence.* If you conclude that the difficulty is not one appropriate for you or the company to address, be sure your reasons are sound and then consult with other members of management to decide among other remedies, such as a professional referral, or transfer, or dismissal. Here, careful recordkeeping is important, and respect for the person's rights and sensitivity to Affirmative Action and EEO standards are essential.

Counseling as Coaching

A problem need not always mean a deficit, a rule violation, or a fault. Another sort of problem is that of an employee whose talents can and should be developed. It is still a problem, albeit a positive one. Instead of trying to bring another person's performance from substandard up to par, you want to develop his or her strengths, or prepare your subordinate for advancement. The deficit in such cases is the difference between what is satisfactory and what might be exceptional. Reconciling these two involves coaching.[40]

For example, you might encourage an employee to complete a college program to qualify for higher steps on the career ladder, or to enroll in selected training seminars and workshops. You might offer an employee the opportunity to expand the scope of assignments so that you can later make a case for a salary increase or promotion. You might coach an employee on how to raise performance levels from "good" to "outstanding."

Coaching is part of a larger sphere of activities often called human relations development (HRD). The same strategies and communication skills outlined earlier in Pat's case apply and are employed in doing it well, but the developmental side of counseling can be more demanding of the coach.

Developmental activity is easier to postpone. After all, there's no real problem, right? You're busy and it would be time consuming; couldn't it be postponed? You can sometimes run the risk of creating a competitor for yourself and put your job in jeopardy, and who would rush into doing that? Also, you got where you are now without anyone else "developing" you, so why work with your subordinates? Certainly, these are self-centered, narrow-minded, and singularly focused reasons. Coaching requires someone who is self-confident, committed, and professionally oriented toward achieving the larger organizational mission. The rewards can be personally gratifying.

Developmental coaching may be perceived as similar to, yet different from, mentorship. They are similar in that both entail the exercise of beneficial influence by a superior over a subordinate. However, coaching differs from mentoring in several ways: (1) coaching is readily done for many subordinates; mentoring is usually limited to a few selected people; (2) coaching is subordinate-centered; mentors often demand and receive a certain loyalty or allegiance; and (3) coaching only involves occasional intervention; mentoring usually exerts a sustained influence on one's career over a period of time.[41]

Coaching has elements of objective diagnosis, of authority and leadership, and it is a very personal, feeling-filled attempt to achieve the objectives of the organization by helping another human being change and improve their job performance. It's a process that can prove valuable if you consistently make it a part of your personal style.

Counseling is an important managerial/supervisory role not limited to formal meetings; it should permeate virtually every interaction, every communication you have with members of your staff. Counseling is an effort to help others improve their job-related performance, enhance their career opportunities, and find greater satisfaction in doing their jobs.

▶ EXIT INTERVIEW

Organizations lose many valuable employees each year to turnover. Studies indicate that large companies may lose up to 50 percent of their college graduates during the first four or five years of postcollege employment.[42] The organizational costs incurred by turnover are fringe benefits, severance pay, overtime costs, underuse of facilities, administrative expenses, training cost, and productivity losses. Some estimate that a rank-and-file employee who quits can cost a company at least $3,000, and the cost is significantly greater for managers and professional employees.[43] This is not to suggest that all attrition is harmful—moderate attrition can actually be positive.[44] The key to effective management is selective control of attrition. To be productive, an organization needs to identify high-performance employees whose departure would be a real loss, and marginal employees who the company could afford to lose. It is important to know who is leaving, why, and whether that loss will be a plus or a minus. At this juncture the exit interview can be a helpful instrument.

The exit interview can help to control attrition and identify areas where changes need to be instituted. It has several specific functions: (1) to discover why the employee is leaving, (2) to discover any problems within the organization that may be causing employees to leave, (3) to discover causes external to the organization that are responsible for employee turnover, (4) to discover possible means for improving the organization, and (5) to enhance the goodwill image of the organization by showing concern for the future career of the person leaving.[45] So, the exit interview includes information gathering, information giving, and counseling.

The exit interview requires specific skills in probing the employee's responses to discover any underlying meanings or problems that he or she may prefer not to talk about. Most people leaving one job for another keep their real reasons to themselves. One survey compared the results of exit interviews among people who had terminated in a factory environment with the results of a questionnaire subsequently mailed to them. It found only moderate correlations between the reasons for leaving as recorded during the exit interview and as reported on the questionnaire.[46] Interviewees most frequently cite higher earnings as the reason for leaving rather than conflict with management, dissatisfaction with advancement, or dissatisfaction with the content of the job. There can be a big difference between the reasons for leaving a company that an employee will give at the time of departure and a year later. James Black claims that less than one out of four times can an interviewer get a complete and factual statement from an employee regarding reasons for leaving.[47]

Explanations for such discrepancies vary. Perhaps the employee has had a chance to reevaluate and develop a clearer perspective on leaving. Or, the employee may be initially hesitant to present valid information at the time of the exit interview, fearing a poor reference which might affect future employment. Finally, she or he may simply want to avoid a face-to-face confrontation.[48] The challenge that the exit interview presents is one of getting necessary information, or as much as possible, and conveying your appreciation to the departing employee.

Persuading an employee to tell the truth about why he or she is leaving is a difficult and complex task. But, if you are perceptive, you can detect signs that may provide information, which taken with data furnished by other exit interviews, forms a story-telling pattern. From this, an organization can learn much about operational situations and make necessary changes that can improve circumstances and keep valuable employees. The following are key factors in effective exit interviewing[49]:

▶ *Prepare carefully*—The key to successful exit interviewing is thorough preparation. The interviewer should review the employee's file for clues as to why the employee is leaving.

▶ *Put the employee at ease*—The attitude of the interviewer as well as the location of the interview creates the climate for discussion. If the employee detects a lack of interest or senses that this is simply a routine matter, the responses will be in kind and the answers will not be very informative. Moreover, there is no point in the interviewer challenging or arguing with the employee. The interviewer must not appear threatening or hard, nor express sarcasm or prejudice. A trusting, supportive climate is essential and the employee needs to be assured of confidentiality if the exit interview is to produce results. Consequently, the interview should be conducted in a quiet and private location.

▶ *Seek information*—Do not ask questions that can be answered with a simple "yes" or "no." Rather, employ an open-ended questioning technique that encourages the employee to offer opinions and suggestions regarding policies/procedures. The worker is familiar with the department and understands the attitudes of employees working in it, so his or her experience can be profitable.

▶ *Use tact*—The employee is under no obligation to give information, so if she avoids answering a specific question or he is reluctant to discuss a subject, drop it. Also, do not attempt to convince the employee to stay. The decision has been made, and your task is to determine why that choice was made.

▶ *Be honest*—Do not try to trick or mislead the employee. For example, the sharing of confidences should be avoided.

▶ *Conclude the interview*—When it is obvious that the interview is over and all willingly provided information has been supplied, work toward a mutually satisfying close. Wish the employee well and say goodbye. Remember, the retention of goodwill is one purpose of the exit interview.

▶ *Complete the exit interview report*—As quickly as possible following the interview, write down the reasons given for leaving, information given on how operations could be improved, and personal impressions gained from the interview. This ensures an accurate record of the proceedings that might prove useful at a later date.

These guidelines can result in a more effective exit interview. However, even when carefully observed, employees may prefer to give safe rather than real reasons for their leaving. The traditional exit interview format using dialogue cannot always bridge this barrier.

Martin Hilb of Schering-Plough International offers an interesting alternative exit interview procedure. It includes built-in mechanisms that make it more accurate than the typical interview. The standardized exit interview presented by Hilb is characterized by: (1) the standardized interview situation, (2) "image cards" as an aid in managing the interview, and (3) the "profile" method for evaluating the results and measuring the success of personnel predictors.[50]

This procedure uses standardized techniques and guidelines such as those previously discussed, but by using a "special incident technique" the interviewer can ask direct questions that result in more specific responses. For example: "If you think back, what did you like most during the five years you stayed with us?" Then, "What was it you disliked during your time with us?" This makes the comparing of results easier and improves validity, reliability, and efficiency.

Following the standard questions, the departing employee is handed a number of image cards, each with an internal characteristic or value factor the organization considers important. These cards might include such characteristics or factors as good external image of the organization, job security, good relationship with manager or with colleagues, fair salary, and good career possibilities. The exiting employee is asked to group the cards according to those characteristics (1) realized, (2) partially realized, and (3) not yet realized. The interviewer then candidly discusses the employee's categorization of the characteristics or factors and encourages the departing employee to make suggestions about how situations might be improved.

Annually, a profile of the arrangement of image factors can be made of the final outcomes of all exit interviews conducted in that year. The results will reveal the organization's strengths and weaknesses, thus assisting managers in formulating departmental objectives and making necessary changes. This profile method can depict organizational progress from year to year and serve as an evaluative measure.

The standardized interview procedure is time consuming and requires considerable sophistication on the parts of the interviewer and the interviewee. However, it can produce a good deal of feedback information that can be factor-analyzed, cross-tabulated, and correlated. The image cards stimulate interest in the exit interview process, permit greater objectivity by the interviewer, and motivate departing employees to reveal real rather than safe reasons for leaving. Finally, the interviewer is better able to evaluate and assess policies and procedures, and make recommendations for change. It does, of course, represent only one alternative procedure that may overcome the difficulties otherwise encountered when using traditional exit interview techniques.

▶ ETHICS AND INTERVIEWING

To the extent that organizations develop in an attempt to satisfy human needs, all people within the organization share mutual responsibility for protecting each other's rights. Failure to accept responsibility invariably results in labor–management disputes, poor employee morale, interdepartmental conflicts, and other counterproductive activity. Within the context of the interview, the need for ethical behavior is of utmost importance. Two areas of responsibility are: (1) the need to be an informed member of the organization, and (2) the need to be sensitive and responsive to the human rights of other members.

Need to Be Informed

Regardless of the type of interview, the interviewer must be informed—must know organization policy, structure, and goals. The power designated to the interviewer carries with it a heavy responsibility to be as informed as one is powerful. The same applies to the interviewee. One's answers are only as good as one's information. The point to be made is that all parties must be honest and accurate in the information they convey.

A second important area of information concerns the civil rights of employees as protected under EEO legislation. Every employer with supervisory responsibility has an ethical responsibility to know and understand these laws, and abide by them. Likewise, the organization has the responsibility to inform its employees of these laws. Most organizations conduct such communication through Affirmative Action programs.

Need to Be Sensitive

Sensitivity is essentially a concern for others and the ability to communicate that concern. The sensitive person tries to identify with others; to share in another person's needs, wants, values, and problems. Sexist, racist, and ethnic remarks and attempts at humor can never be excused or tolerated. Power never gives one the right to harass another person. At the outset, we observed that the objective of interviewing is to reach goals that are beneficial to all concerned. With this attitude toward interviewing as your foundation for ethical communication, few, if any, ethical problems should arise.

▶ SUMMARY

This chapter compared interviewing to doorways leading into areas of opportunity, change and advancement in the world of work. The interview was defined as an interaction between people asking and answering questions in an attempt to solve problems for their mutual benefit. We considered the importance of interviewing and explored basic strategies and techniques common to the interviewing process. Here, we discussed (1) purpose and approaches to interviewing, (2) questions and questioning techniques, (3) selecting the environment, and (4) the reciprocal role of interviewer as listener and respondent. The intent was to examine the nature of interviewing and to provide a basis for conducting and participating in selected types of interviews.

We then focused on five specific types of interviewing situations: (1) the selection interview, (2) the appraisal interview, (3) the discipline interview, (4) the counseling interview, and (5) the exit interview. Each was discussed from the perspective of the interviewer and the interviewee. These applications revealed interviewing to be a critically important managerial tool, influencing the entire organization.

Finally, we considered the ethics of interviewing in the organization. The ethics of interviewing are both subtle and complex, but the need to be informed and the need to be sensitive are fundamental requisites to any situation.

Successful interviewing requires training, practice, and continuous self-study. There is no magic formula or single "how-to-do-it" recipe to follow. Thorough preparation, developed communication skills, adaptive flexibility, and a willingness to face the risks involved in intimate person-to-person interaction will contribute to everyone's effectiveness and yield personal rewards.

▶ QUESTIONS FOR DISCUSSION AND SKILL DEVELOPMENT

1. Describe two recent interview situations in which you were involved, one a positive experience and the other negative. What participant behaviors, message components, and climate caused the situation to be positive or negative? How did questioning techniques affect the relationship? "Openness" is often used when describing an interviewing climate. What do you mean by "open"?

2. What is the purpose of a selection interview? Describe a selection interview situation in which you were involved. How did it benefit you? How did it benefit the company?

3. What is the purpose of an appraisal interview? What kind of communication climate should be established? What are the assumptions on which a good appraisal system should be based?

4. Often managers treat the appraisal interview tangentially. A few general comments are made and the employee is rated on an appraisal chart. Why do you believe this practice occurs? What should be the optimum amount of participation by the interviewee?

5. What kind of performance appraisal process is used by your organization, or an organization with which you are familiar? What performance standards or objectives does the organization use? How often does it measure each person's performance? How is the appraisal interview structured?

How does it deal with personnel who are not performing satisfactorily?

6. What is the purpose of the discipline interview? What do you think is the most critical stage in the discipline interview? Why? If you were a manager who had to discipline a problem employee, what approach would you take? What general guidelines would you set?

7. What is the purpose of a counseling interview? How does the counseling interview differ from other types of interviews? To what extent should the counseling interviewer be directive/nondirective?

8. The term "helping" is at the heart of the counseling interview. What does it mean in relation to remedial counseling? Coaching? Identify two situations you experienced in the last several weeks in which you engaged in counseling behaviors. What were the general circumstances? What techniques did you use? What outcomes did you achieve?

9. What is the purpose of the exit interview? Why is an exit interview important? What questions should be asked? Why do you think many interviewers do not probe as well as they ought to?

Given the following exchange, what direct/indirect probing techniques would you use?

Interviewer: Sarah, we regret your leaving us because you've been such a fine employee. It's important to us to know why someone chooses to leave. The information you can share will help us improve in the future. Let me assure you that whatever we discuss will be held in the strictest confidence. Could you tell me why you're leaving?

Sarah: Well, I just got this opportunity to work at Republic Engineering.

Discuss the extent to which you would be willing to reveal/not reveal negative information. Why?

10. What are the ethical responsibilities of the interviewer and the interviewee? How are they similar to or different from the legal responsibilities? What ethical and legal considerations should guide you during selection interviews? Appraisal interviews? Discipline interviews? Counseling interviews? Exit interviews? Is ethics a serious problem in interviewing? Why? Why not?

► NOTES

1. Felix M. Lopez, *Personnel Interviewing* (New York: McGraw-Hill, 1975): 1.
2. Charles Stewart and William B. Cash, Jr., *Interviewing: Principles and Practices,* 6th ed. (Dubuque, IA: Wm. C. Brown, 1991): 7
3. Shirley Biage, *Interviews That Work* (Belmont, CA: Wadsworth, 1986); Cal Downs, G. Paul Smeyak, and Ernest Martin, *Professional Interviewing* (New York: Harper and Row, 1980); and Marvin Gottlieb, *Interview* (New York: Longman Publishing, 1986).
4. George Gallup, "The Quintamensional Plan of Question Design," *Public Opinion Quarterly* 11 (Fall 1947): 385.
5. Robert L. Kahn and Charles F. Cannell, *The Dynamics of Interviewing* (New York: John Wiley & Sons, 1957).
6. Gordon Raymond, *Interviewing* (Homewood, IL: Dorsey Press, 1969).
7. Kahn and Cannell, *Dynamics of Interviewing*, 127.
8. John Daly and James McCrosky, *Avoiding Communication* (Beverly Hills, CA: Sage, 1984); V. Freimuth, "The Effects of Communication Apprehension on Communication Effectiveness," *Human Communication Research* 2 (1976): 289–295; James McCrosky and Virginia Richmond, "The Impact of Communication Apprehension on Individuals in Organizations," *Communication Quarterly* 3 (1979): 55–61; James McCrosky, "Oral Communication Apprehension: A Summary of Recent Theory and Research," *Human Communication Research* 7 (1977): 77–96; D. C. Murray, "Talk, Silence, and Anxiety," *Psychological Bulletin* 75 (1971): 244–260; P. Pilkonis, "The Behavioral Consequences of Shyness," *Journal of Personality* 45 (1977): 596–611; and M. S. Scott, J. McCrosky, and M. E. Sheahan, "Measuring Communication Apprehension in the Organization Setting," *Journal of Communication* 28 (1978): 104–111.

9. J. R. Barbee and E. C. Keil, "Experimental Techniques of Job Interview Training for the Disadvantaged: Videotaped Feedback, Behavioral Modification, and Microcounseling," *Journal of Applied Psychology* 58 (1973): 60–69; W. J. Fremouw and R. E. Zitter, "A Comparison of Skills Training and Cognitive Restructuring-Relaxation for the Treatment of Speech Anxiety," *Behavior Therapy* 9 (1978): 249–259; J. G. Hollandsworth, R. C. Glazeski, and M. E. Dressel, "Use of Social-Skills Training in the Treatment of Extreme Anxiety and Deficient Verbal Skills in the Job-Interview Setting," *Journal of Applied Behavior Analysis* 11 (1978): 259–269; James McCrosky, "The Implementation of a Large-Scale Program of Systematic Desensitization for Communication Apprehension," *Speech Teacher* 21 (1972): 255–264; L. W. Morris, E. W. Harris, and D. J. Rovins, "Interactive Effects of Generalized and Situational Expectancies on the Arousal of Cognitive and Emotional Components of Social Anxiety," *Journal of Research in Personality* 15 (1981): 302–311; and Will Powers, "The Rhetorical Interrogative: Anxiety or Control?" *Human Communication Research* 4 (1977): 44–77.

10. S. R. Glaser, "Oral Communication Apprehension and Avoidance: The Current Status of Treatment Research," *Communication Education* 30 (1981): 321–341.

11. W. J. Fremouw, "Cognitive-Behavior Therapies for Modification of Communication Apprehension," in: John Daly and James McCroskey, eds., *Avoiding Communication* (Beverly Hills, CA: Sage, 1984): 209.

12. W. J. Fremouw and M. D. Scott, "An Alternative Method of the Treatment of Communication Apprehension," *Communication Education* 28 (1973): 129–133.

13. Fremouw, "Cognitive-Behavior Therapies," 211.

14. John Stewart and Gary D'Angelo, *Together: Communicating Interpersonally* (Reading, MA: Addison-Wesley, 1975): 191.

15. C. D. Tengler and F. M. Jablin, "Effects of Question Type, Orientation, and Sequencing in the Employment Screening Interview," *Communication Monographs* 50 (1983): 245–263.

16. C. E. Wilson, "The New Generation of Selection Interviews: Structured, Behavior-Based, Valid" (Paper presented at the Annual Meeting of the Speech Communication Association, Chicago, IL, 1990).

17. H. Lancaster, "Failing System: Job Tests Are Dropped by Many Companies Due to Antibias Drive," *The Wall Street Journal*, September 14, 1975, A1.

18. T. F. Boyle and C. Hymowitz, "White-Collar Blues," *The Wall Street Journal*, October 4, 1990, A1.

19. John D. Drake, *Interviewing for Managers*, rev. ed. (New York: AMACOM, 1982): 4.

20. A. H. Locher and K. S. Teel, "Performance Appraisal—A Survey of Current Practices," *Personnel Journal* 56 (1977): 245–247.

21. K. H. Lacho, "A Study of Employee Appraisal Systems of Major Cities in the United States," *Public Personnel Management* 8 (1979): 111–125.

22. W. H. Holley and H. S. Field, "The Law and Performance Evaluation in Education: A Review of Court Cases and Implications for Use," *Journal of Law and Education* 6 (1977): 427–448; G. P. Latham and K. N. Wexley, *Increasing Productivity Through Performance Appraisal* (Reading, MA: Addison-Wesley, 1981); and H. P. Smith and P. J. Brower, *Performance Appraisal and Human Development* (Reading, MA: Addison-Wesley, 1977).

23. Robert G. Johnson, *The Appraisal Interview Guide* (New York: AMACOM, 1979): 3–5.

24. "Performance Reviews: Waste of Time?" *Duns Business Monthly* (October 1984): 57.

25. Roy Serpa, "Why Many Organizations—Despite Good Intentions—Often Fail to Give Employees Fair and Useful Performance Reviews," *Management Review* (July 1984): 43–44.

26. Harold Mayfield, "In Defense of Performance Appraisal," *Harvard Business Review* 37 (1960): 82–93; and Cal W. Downs and David Spohn, "A Case Study of an Appraisal System" (Paper presented at the Annual Meeting of the Academy of Management, Kansas City, MO, 1976).

27. Wallace V. Schmidt, "Communication and Job Satisfaction: The Federal Employee," *Proceedings of the Association for Business Communication-SW* (1989): 77–83.

28. Beverly Kaye and Shelly Krantz, "Performance Appraisal: A Win/Win Approach," *Training and Development Journal* (March 1983): 32–35.

29. H. Kent Baker, "Two Goals in Every Performance Appraisal," *Personnel Journal* (September 1984): 75–81.

30. Marion S. Kellogg, *What to Do About Performance Appraisal*, rev. ed. (New York: AMACOM, 1975): 169–170.

31. Rodney P. Beary, "Office Discipline: Getting the Lead Out," *Modern Office Technology* (May 1986): 96–99.

32. Roger B. Madsen and Barbara Knudsen-Fields, "Productive Progressive Discipline Procedures," *Management Solutions* (May 1987): 18–25.

33. Joseph Seltzer, "Discipline with a Clear Sense of Purpose," *Management Solutions* (February 1987): 32–38.

34. Wade Humphreys and Neil J. Humphreys, "The Proper Use of Discipline," *Management Solutions* (May 1988): 6–10; and Peter A. Veglahn, "The Five Steps in Practicing Effective Discipline," *Management Solutions* (November 1987): 24–30.

35. Richard D. Arvey and Allan P. Jones, "The Use of Discipline in Organizational Settings: A Framework for Future Research," *Research in Organizational Behavior* 7 (1985): 367–408.

36. V. R. Buzzotta, R. E. Lefton, and M. Sherberg, "Coaching and Counseling: How You Can Improve the Way It's Done," *Training and Development Journal* 31 (1977): 50–60; J. J. Leach, "Career Development: Some Questions and Tentative Answers," *Personnel Administration* 25 (1980): 31–34; and John Quay, "The Art and Science of Effective Interviewing," *Journal of Management Consulting* 2 (1985): 14–17.

37. T. N. Blodgett, "The Problem in Defining the Problem," *Training and Development Journal* 31 (1977): 18–20; P. M. Muchinsky, "Organizational Communication: Relationships to Organizational Climate and Job Satisfaction," *Academy of Management Journal* 20 (1977): 592–607; and The Woodland Group, "Management Development Roles: Coach, Sponsor and Mentor," *Personnel Journal* 59 (1980): 918–921.

38. Robert Doyle, "The Counselor's Role, Communication Skills, or the Roles Counselors Play: A Conceptual Model," *Counselor Education and Supervision* 22 (1982): 123–131; Robert Elliott, "Helpful and Nonhelpful Events in Brief Counseling Interviews: An Empirical Taxonomy," *Journal of Counseling Psychology* 32 (1985): 307–322; and J. Fitz-Enz, "Taking a Positive Approach to Employee Counseling," *Business* 30 (1980): 43–47.

39. Alfred Benjamin, *The Helping Interview*, 3rd ed. (Boston: Houghton Mifflin, 1981); Robert Carkhuff, Richard Pierce, and John Cannon, *The Art of Helping* (Amherst, MA: Human Resource Development Press, 1989); and Arthur Combs, *Helping Relationships: Basic Concepts for the Helping Professions* (Boston: Allyn and Bacon, 1985).

40. Z. B. Leibowitz and N. K. Schlossberg, "Training Managers for Their Role in a Career Development System," *Training and Development Journal* 35 (1981): 72–79; M. Lorey, "Coaching: A New Look at an Old Responsibility," *Supervisory Management* 22 (1977): 26–31; and A. B. Randolph, "Managerial Career Coaching," *Training and Development Journal* 35 (1981): 54–55.

41. Robert Bolton, *People Skills* (Englewood Cliffs, NJ: Prentice Hall, 1979); Peter Cairo, "Counseling in Industry: A Selected Review of the Literature," *Personnel Psychology* 36 (1983): 1–18; James Nicholson and Gordon Golsam, *The Creative Counselor* (New York: McGraw-Hill, 1983); and B. L. Rosenbaum, "How Good People-Handlers Motivate Others," *Nation's Business* 66 (1978): 78–80.

42. M. D. Dunnette, R. D. Avery, and P. A. Banes, "Why Do They Leave?" *Personnel* 50 (1973): 25–39.

43. A. N. Nash and S. J. Carroll, *The Management of Compensation* (Belmont, CA: Wadsworth, 1975).

44. J. R. Hinrichs, "Employees Going and Coming: The Exit Interview," *Personnel* 48 (1971): 31–35.

45. S. B. Wehrenberg, "The Exit Interview: Why Bother?" *Supervisory Management* 25 (1980): 20–25; and H. Wilke, "Making Use of the Exit Interview," *International Management* 26 (1971): 32–34.

46. J. Lefkowitz and M. L. Katz, "Validity of Exit Interviews," *Personnel Psychology* 22 (1969): 445–456.

47. James Black, *How to Get Results from Interviewing* (New York: McGraw-Hill, 1970): 154–168.

48. W. L. McNaughton, "Attitudes of Ex-Employees at Intervals After Quitting," *Personnel Journal* 35 (1956): 61–63.

49. Wallace Schmidt, "The Exit Interview as Monitor for Change: A Review of Literature," *Proceedings of the Association for Business Communication-SW* (1984): 23–33.

50. Martin Hilb, "The Standardized Exit Interview," *Personnel Journal* 57 (1978): 327–329.

9

The Selection Interview

LEARNING OBJECTIVES:

To engage in a career search

To write a cover letter that effectively presents you as a job applicant

To develop and prepare a personal résumé, using a format that appropriately presents your educational background and experience

To prepare adequately for a selection interview

To apply techniques of effective interviewing to the selection process

To recognize and follow nondiscriminatory practices

To follow up and evaluate the selection process

From a systems perspective, the actual selection interview is only one of several important written and verbal communication variables in the selection process. Hiring and selection decisions are based not only on oral communication factors during the actual interview, but also on such written communication factors as the cover letter and the résumé. The actual interview must be viewed only as part of the selection interview process. This chapter provides a framework for conducting the selection interview and examining it from the dual perspectives of the interviewer and interviewee.

Whether you are about to graduate, are a recent graduate, a fast-tracker, a workforce reentrant, or a career changer, if you are considering new horizons, you must know yourself and give serious thought to your needs, interests, skills, and goals. You might begin this self-inventory by asking a few basic questions: What is special or unique about me? About my background? Training? Experience? What kind of work do I enjoy doing? What do I want from a job? What do I need from a job? Do I prefer to work alone or as part of a team? Would I rather work with machines or people? Am I attracted to a large corporate environment or would I be happier with a small company? What do I want for myself in the future? What does "success" mean to me? There are also many books available to help with this self-analysis, such as Richard Bolles' *What Color Is Your Parachute?*, John Crystal and Richard Bolles' *Where Do I Go from Here with My Life?*, Tom Jackson's *28 Days to a Better Job*, Lester Schwartz and Irv Brechner's *The Career Finder*, Barry Gale and Linda Gale's *Discover What You're Best At*, and Emily Cho's *Looking, Working, Living Terrific 24 Hours a Day*. A thorough personal inventory will save you from job-selection errors such as accepting a job incompatible with your needs, aspirations, and temperament. Remember, employers are interested in candidates who know what they want and what they have to offer. They are not in the business of career planning and quickly lose patience with undirected job seekers.

You should also gather all possible information about a potential organization prior to the interview. You do research on the potential employer not only to demonstrate your knowledge and seriousness, but also to determine if the company is right for you. Your research can include:

size	location(s)	product(s) or service(s)
corporate culture	competitors	history
training	compensation	advancement paths
job content	organizational goals	management style
leadership	industry ranking	corporate affiliations

To gather this information speak with people working in the career field or employed by the organization that interests you. Study organizational literature and annual reports. Read articles about the organization published in newspapers, magazines, or professional and trade journals. Consult organizational directories appropriate to your field of interest, such as *Thomas' Register of American Manufacturers, Standard and Poor's Register, Moody's Industrial Manual, Macmillan Job Guide to American Corporations, 25,000 Leading American Corporations, United States Government Manual, Who's Who in Educational Administration*, or the *Literary Market Place*. All of these resources are readily available in the reference sections of most libraries. This information will permit you to relate your skills and abilities directly to the needs of a potential employer.

▶ THE COVER LETTER

The cover letter precedes and initially represents you; you are judged by it. It should not be slighted or hastily written. This letter is the personalizing factor in the presentation of an otherwise essentially impersonal document—your résumé. When the envelope is opened, your cover letter is the first thing seen and can make an indelible first impression (see Exhibit 9-1). Moreover, cover letters are carefully read, not

March 6, 19—

Dear Sir:

I am applying for the position you recently listed in *The Orlando Sentinel*. The enclosed résumé should provide you with all the necessary information.

I look forward to hearing from you.

Sincerely,

October 5, 19—

My Dear Sir or Madam:

With reference to your listing, I am enclosing a brief résumé.

I write in the strictest confidence and trust you will appreciate my situation. If you need additional information, please don't hesitate to contact me.

Cordially,

September 30, 19—

Dear Sir:

I am the best mortgage loan field representative in Florida. I have a knowledge of loan organization procedures. I have sold lake resort property. I am a real hard-charging, hustling go-getter, not afraid of hard work. I am honest, dependable, reliable, ambitious, and trustworthy. I am ready, willing, and able to come and be the top representative for Consumer Savings & Loan. I always try harder than the other man. I never stop trying until I have succeeded. I have my roller skates on now and am ready to start rolling for Consumer Savings & Loan. How about a chance?

Yours Very Truly,

scanned like most résumés. Some European companies may even request that the cover letter be handwritten. They often submit the cover letter to a graphologist who analyzes the writer's personality from the handwriting. A good cover letter may take time and be difficult to write, but it sets the stage for the reader to accept your résumé as something special.

A cover letter should be brief, rarely more than one page (see Exhibit 9-2). You should always try to follow accepted business letter protocol, with the date, employer's name, and address first. Keep your sentences short—an average of 14 words per sentence is about right. Short words are best because they speak more clearly than those polysyllabic behemoths that say more about your self-image problems than about your abilities. Likewise, your paragraphs should be direct and concise.

The first paragraph of the letter of application is, without a doubt, the most difficult for most applicants to compose. It is, however, the most important paragraph to write and one which should follow proper guidelines. Specifically, there are three elements that should be included in the first paragraph: (1) what motivated you to write the letter to this specific source, (2) exactly what position you are applying for, and (3) how clear it is that you have something to offer to the company.

Paragraphs two and three can deliver a one–two punch. Paragraph two should serve as a general summary of your education, experience, or other areas of signifi-

▶ **EXHIBIT 9-2**
Well-Written Cover Letter

120 Ridgeline Road
Orlando, FL 32803
July 30, 19—

Westinghouse Electric Corporation
Employment Department/OS
4400 Alafaya Trail
Tampa, FL 32826–2399

Dear Carol Moorhead:

I am interested in the position of Training and Development Specialist which was advertised in *The Orlando Sentinel*. I feel that I could very successfully perform the duties of this position and contribute significantly to the training function at Westinghouse.

I hold a Bachelor of Arts degree in English from Auburn University and have four years of experience in the training and development field. My background has been of a generalist nature, providing me with experience in all areas. I have administered benefits programs and have also conducted training and development seminars. My written and oral communication skills are exceptionally strong. I have edited newsletters, written policy and procedure manuals, and developed written training materials. In addition to one-on-one communication, I am very experienced in giving group presentations.

Other strengths include effective problem-solving skills and the ability to interact successfully with people at all organizational levels. I am career-oriented and motivated to perform with a high degree of energy and commitment.

Enclosed is a résumé that describes my background in detail. If you need additional information to act on my application, I can be reached at (555) 369-4861.

Thank you very much for your consideration. I look forward to hearing from you.

Sincerely,

Susan R. Smith

► JOB MARKETABILITY EVALUATION FORM

By William N. Yeomans[1]

Scholastic Standing	Score
Phi Beta Kappa; top 10 percent of class	6
Top 25 percent of class	4
Top 50 percent of class	2
Lower 50 percent of class	0

Academic Rating of Your College	Score
Very high; Ivy League-caliber	6
Good, well-respected academically	4
Not known for academic excellence	1
Barely accredited or not accredited	0

Work Experience	Score
Full-time work in your major field	6
Summer or part-time work in your major	4
Work in unrelated field	2
No work experience	0

College Expenses Earned Yourself	Score
75–100 percent	6
50–75 percent	4
25–50 percent	1
Under 25 percent	0

Campus Activities	Score
Major elected offices; many activities	4
Major elected offices; some activities	2
No elected offices but some activities	1
No elected offices and no activities	0

Appearance	Score
All-American handsome or beautiful	4
Good-looking	3
Nice, but forgettable	1
Weird-looking	0

Personality	Score
Popularity plus, well-liked; meet people easily	4
Pretty well-liked; meet people easily most of the time	3
Some friends; not too great at meeting people	1
Zero personality	0

Height (if weight is proportionate)	Score
5'10" to 6'4" for men	3
5' to 6' for women	3
4'1" or under; 6' or over, or overweight, for women	0
Under 5'10", over 6'4", or overweight, for men	0

Bearing (voice, posture, eye contact)	Score
Commanding, immediately impressive	3
Mostly impressive	2
Not too impressive	1
A laugh	0

TOTAL SCORE _____

Results

35–42 *Outstanding!* You should be able to pick and choose a suitable position. However, people rarely score this high, so evaluate yourself again to be sure.

20–34 *Excellent prospect.* You should have several job possibilities without much trouble.

8–19 *Average candidate.* Job opportunities will depend on the economy and labor market. Need to try to develop areas to increase your hirability.

0–7 *Not so good.* You will probably have difficulty in getting a desirable job. Need to think of ways to improve your score, or you may have evaluated yourself too severely.

---

cance that should be shared with the prospective employer. Paragraph three is an amplification of paragraph two in that it provides more detailed illustration of your background and experience. For an experienced person, there are three points this paragraph should definitely stress. First, state any experience that you have had in working with human resources (either supervising people or working with others as an organizational leader). Secondly, you should state any experience that you have had working with material resources (budgeting, financial management). Finally, you should include a sufficiently detailed description of your responsibilities in those positions. The goal of these two paragraphs is to selectively tailor your strengths to the needs and interests of the potential employer.

► THE HIDDEN HURDLE

By Roger Rickles

The personnel executive was as good as hired. During a pro forma final-stage interview, the board chairman observed that the job might involve a relocation later. "That sounds fine," said the candidate, "but of course I'd have to check with Mommy."

"*Mommy*"? His wife.

"Let's skip this guy," the board chairman said after the interview to Frank B. Beaudine, the executive recruiter. "If he calls his wife 'Mommy,' he might think I'm 'Daddy.'" The chairman wanted a team of hard-hitting executives, and the Mommy talk suggested to him an executive hopelessly dependent on his wife, Mr. Beaudine says.

And that was goodbye to a $55,000-a-year job—not the only one ever lost over a single word. Corporations like to say that competence overwhelmingly decides who gets managerial jobs. But executive recruiters say subjective chemistry—deciding whether the candidate is "our kind of person"—often is far more important than the executives doing the hiring realize.

The Big Factor

"Chemistry is the paramount factor in hiring," says Wilhemus B. Bryan III, executive vice president of William H. Clark Associates, New York recruiters. Mr. Beaudine, who is president of Eastman & Beaudine, Chicago, adds, "More than half of the time, the technically best-qualified person isn't hired."

Decisive factors can range from significant questions of managerial style to finesse in eating an artichoke, recruiters say. In many cases, especially at the senior level, all the final candidates have such comparable, proven track records that "chemistry becomes one of the major things to separate them," says T. G. Bartholdi, a recruiter based in Wellesley Hills, Mass.

Chemistry counts more than ever these days, recruiters and executives say. Given today's operating styles and large staff bureaucracies, management involves more consultation and staff coordination than in years gone by, they note. This means the chemistry between the executive and his associates counts more heavily in getting the job done smoothly—and companies know it, personnel officials say. "There's much more participation and less management by edict than in the past, so chemistry is substantively more important," says Frank Toner, vice president of human resources at Boise Cascade Corp., Boise, Idaho.

Seeking Risk Takers

Forced to evaluate this chemistry on the basis of a few interviews, employers latch on to all kinds of criteria that one might never expect, recruiters say. Burton L. Rozner, executive vice president of Oliver & Rozner Associates, New York, recalls an entrepreneur who wanted an executive who personally was borrowed to the hilt. This entrepreneur, who operated a company with annual sales of $350 million, figured that heavy borrowers were just the risk-taking, self-confident, aggressive executives he had in mind.

One California engineering executive lost a job because he spoke with enthusiasm about coaching his son's Little League baseball team. In most cases, Little League might seem safe enough. But in this case, it "made the company president feel the executive's work wasn't really his top priority," says Robert Kremple, partner in Kremple & Meade, Los Angeles recruiters.

Physical appearance can cost jobs too. Recruiters say trim executives often think chubby ones "lack self-discipline." John Wareham, president of Wareham Associates, New York, recalls an executive who was rejected as "too short" even though he was five feet, eight inches tall. "I feel you should look up to people in the finance industry," said the hiring executive—himself six feet three inches tall.

Mr. Rozner cites a five-foot, five-inch candidate for a $60,000-a-year Midwestern manufacturing vice presidency who encountered clear sailing until a rainstorm ruined his chances. The short executive lent his tall prospective employer one of his raincoats. The employer later explained that until he put on the coat, he never fully realized how short the applicant was—or how uncomfortable he was with short people. The boss was so uncomfortable he couldn't hire the man, even though the two would have worked 700 miles apart.

Sifting Candidates

Of course, chemistry probably won't get an obvious bungler a good job, and where one candidate is clearly superior, it may play no role at all. But in the common situation where three or four candidates all could handle the job, executives often lean to people who share their personal values, manner of dressing and even personal habits, recruiters say.

For instance, Mr. Rozner cites a $55,000-a-year-pharmaceutical executive who landed a $90,000-a-year division presidency partly because he liked Victorian houses. The fact that both the company chairman and the executive loved the old houses, hated television and rarely allowed their children to watch TV suggested to the chairman a great similarity of values that would allow the two to work comfortably together, Mr. Rozner explains.

Recruiters say many executives sneer at candidates who wear short-sleeved shirts, short socks or light-colored suits. J. Gerald Simmons, president of Handy Associates, New York, recalls a personnel vice president of a major financial institution who asked a candidate: "How far would I have to look up your sleeve before I found a shirt?" Many executives think pipe smokers tend to be slow-moving, pensive souls who belong in a library instead of an executive suite, recruiters add.

Artichokes were the Waterloo of one company president seeking the $300,000-a-year presidency of another consumer-goods company. Though the executive was generally well polished, he revealed at dinner with the chairman a pitiable incompetence at handling the unfamiliar first course. At one point, he even tried carving the leaves with a knife and fork.

"The chairman said he just didn't want a guy who didn't know how to eat properly," says Robert A. Staub, president of Staub, Warmbold & Associates, New York recruiters. "I just couldn't believe it. I never did tell the guy the real reason he didn't get the job."

Recruiters say prejudice against Jews and ethnic groups still prevails in many companies, especially in smaller communities. "Sometimes, people never get beyond the names," one recruiter observes. Many recruiters privately concede that they usually go along with the client's prejudices without much protest.

Prejudice against divorced executives has declined, and junior-level management ranks have gained more diversity in recent years. But in most companies, senior management still is drawn from a remarkably narrow range of society, personnel officers note. In a survey of senior executives of the largest 750 companies, only eight of the 1,708 respondents were women and only three were black. Some 95% were married, but only 11% had been married more than once. Nearly 70% were Republicans, and 92% identified with "conservative or moderate" views on social issues, said the study, conducted by the University of California at Los Angeles and Korn/Ferry International, recruiters based in Los Angeles.

A Weakness

But chemistry in hiring involves relevant questions of operating styles as well as irrelevant prejudices. Mr. Bryan of Clark Associates recalls a company that hired the second best qualified of two women as public-relations director. The better-qualified candidate believed that retaining outside public-relations agencies was the most efficient way to handle special situations. The company's management prized self-sufficiency and thought retaining outsiders was a sign of weakness.

Sometimes executives seek operating styles that might seem disastrous elsewhere. Mr. Rozner cites a chemical-company chairman who specified an executive "who can talk back to me" and hired a man who told him exactly what he was doing wrong. The chairman recognized that the job called for a hard-hitting negotiator who wouldn't be intimidated.

But recruiters say executives often don't recognize the chemistry that influences their hiring decisions, especially when they're avoiding a strong executive who might prove threatening. "They often want an aggressive, dynamic person who is slightly less aggressive and dynamic than they are," says Mr. Wareham, the New York recruiter.

Of course, potential employees reject companies too. Eugene C. Judd, president of Judd-Falk Inc., New York recruiters, cites a candidate for the presidency of a company who bowed out largely because the office layout bothered him. The offices of the top four executives were so physically isolated and differently decorated from those of the other senior executives that they appeared planned to create a barrier. This executive, who thrived on frequent interaction with peers and subordinates, felt he would never fit into the "highly structured, hierarchical operating style that he correctly perceived," Mr. Judd recalls.

Keys to Success

Employers and recruiters use all sorts of methods to find executives who will fit. "The key thing is figuring out what it takes to succeed in that environment," says Roger M. Kenny, senior vice president of Spencer Stuart & Associates, recruiters.

Carl Menk, president of Boyden Associates, another large recruiter, believes there are three basic types of company: growth, turnaround and maintenance. "Very few people can fit into even two of these well," he adds. Among other things, Boyden therefore looks carefully at the type of company where the prospective new executive worked before, Mr. Menk says.

Many companies arrange for the prospective new hire and his wife to meet socially with other executives. A significant minority of companies also use psychological testing.

Given the increased attention to chemistry, the job that called for three interviews in the company five years ago often calls for five or six today, recruiters say. NCR Corp., Dayton, also has prospects meet with more prospective peers than in the past. "That's where the applicant will spend the majority of his time; jobs require more interaction than in the past," says William H. von Reichbauer, director of corporate recruitment.

Many companies, like Bendix Corp., seek the opinions of potential subordinates too. "The more people you have involved, the better your collective judgment will be," says

(continued on page 9-9)

Paragraph four serves as a summary statement to your cover letter. It contains some essential information that an employer will want for an oral interview prior to employing you. In this paragraph indicate that a résumé is enclosed; include a sentence about your willingness to provide the prospective employer with any other materials that might be needed; say that you are available for an interview; and provide your telephone number.

Conclude your letter with a brief statement of appreciation for the reader's time and consideration.

The following checklist can be helpful as you write your cover letter and can serve as a guide for review after you have completed it.

▶ Select high-quality paper and a good typewriter/word processor. The typewriter should have a good ribbon or the printer should have an adequate toner cartridge.
▶ Include at least the street, city, state, and ZIP code in the return address.
▶ Include the date.
▶ Make an effort to include the addressee's name and title, the company name, street, city, state, and ZIP code.
▶ Tell why you are writing.
▶ State the specific position for which you are applying.
▶ Provide insights into your experience and qualifications.
▶ Include your education as a positive supplement to experience.
▶ Tell how you meet the specific criteria listed in the job advertisement.
▶ Reflect your ability to work with human, financial, and material resources.
▶ State your date of availability.
▶ Mention any enclosures, such as a résumé.
▶ Review the letter for correct spelling, typographical errors, and standard English grammar.
▶ Proofread aloud.

▶ THE RÉSUMÉ

Résumés help to sell the most important product you have—yourself. A résumé provides you with an opportunity to organize the relevant facts about yourself in a concise written presentation and to communicate your value as a potential employee. It helps a prospective employer to know: who you are, what you know, what you can do, what you have done, what is your present status, what kind of job you would like, what your goals and objectives are, and what your special assets or attributes are. As a biographical summary of one's professional and educational background, the résumé is one of the most important documents that a person creates.

Résumés are likely to play an increasingly important role in the recruitment process during the next decade. A marked decrease in on-campus recruiting during the past several years has forced applicants and employers to rely increasingly on résumés for preliminary screening. Moreover, over 75 percent of those newly jobless are managers, professionals, or administrative or technical staff, and this influx of white-collar workers affects the selection process.[2] Under these circumstances, the traditional one-page résumé is likely to be a very inadequate hiring tool. It simply doesn't allow an applicant to present himself or herself well nor does it provide employers with enough information for adequate evaluations and comparisons of applicants. Authorities note that student applicants more often err on the side of making résumés too short rather than too long.[3] Burdette Bostwick, one of the nation's foremost career consultants, says that "there is no standard résumé length. . . . a six-page résumé can be concise; a three-page résumé, verbose."[4]

There are no panaceas or absolutes for writing the résumé. Experts acknowledge three essential formats for presenting your credentials to a potential employer: chronologically, functionally, and in combination (chrono-functionally).[5] Your particular circumstances will determine the right format for you.

Chronological Résumé

The chronological résumé is the most common and readily accepted form of presentation. It starts with your educational background; lists your employment history, working backward from most-recent to most-distant and noting job titles as well as responsibilities; and finally includes other relevant information. A chronological résumé usually incorporates contact information, a job/career objective, education, a description of work experience, and optional categories determined by the unique aspects of your background (see Exhibit 9-3).

Functional Résumé

The functional résumé focuses on the professional skills you have developed over the years, rather than when, where, or how you acquired them. It deemphasizes dates, job titles, and specific employers, focusing attention instead on the skill rather than the context or time of its acquisition (see Exhibit 9-4). This less-orthodox format is suited to a number of different personal circumstances, specifically those of:

▶ experienced professionals with a storehouse of expertise
▶ entry-level types with considerable volunteer service but no direct work-related experience
▶ career-changers who want to emphasize acquired skills rather than limited experience
▶ people with lengthy experience at a single company who wish to change jobs and revitalize their careers
▶ military personnel entering the civilian workforce
▶ people returning to the workplace after a long absence
▶ people close to retirement with considerable skills acquired over time[6]

The functional résumé is more free-form and thus presents a major challenge for the writer. Because it focuses so strongly on skills and the ability to contribute in a particular direction, you must have an employment objective clearly in mind. When this is directly communicated, such a résumé can be very effective. Without this focus, however, or if you are engaged in an open-ended career search, this format loses its direction and tends to drift without purpose.

▶ **EXHIBIT 9-3**
Chronological Résumé

SUSAN R. SMITH

120 RIDGELINE ROAD • ORLANDO, FLORIDA 32803   (555) 369-4861

OBJECTIVE   A challenging, responsible position in the field of training and development

EDUCATION   **Auburn University**   Auburn, Alabama 32831
Bachelor of Arts degree granted *summa cum laude*, 1990
Major: English   Minor: Communication

EXPERIENCE   1992–PRESENT
Howard Systems International   Orlando, Florida
Personnel Coordinator
- Perform personnel functions including: benefits administration, wage and salary administration, workers' compensation, Affirmative Action activities, recruitment and selection.
- Coordinate training and development functions including: needs assessment, design and implementation of organizational training programs, development of policy and procedure manuals.
- Edit company newsletter.

1990–1992
Arkwin Technical Corporation   Huntsville, Alabama
Personnel Assistant
- Performed various personnel functions including: records maintenance, data entry, monthly reports.
- Developed and conducted employee training programs in management and supervisory skills, oral and written communication, and clerical skills.
- Edited company newsletter.

SKILLS   Computer experience, word processing, typing, 10-key

LANGUAGES   Conversational knowledge of Spanish and able to sign for the deaf

HONORS   Included in *Who's Who in American Colleges and Universities*, 1990; Phi Beta Kappa; named to Dean's List all four years of college.

PROFESSIONAL ORGANIZATIONS   Society for Human Resource Management (SHRM)
American Society for Training and Development (ASTD)
Business and Professional Women's Club (BPW)

COMMUNITY ACTIVITIES   United Way (Loaned Executive in 1992 campaign)
Recipient of Employer of the Year award from Goodwill Industries for efforts in recruiting and hiring handicapped employees

HOBBIES   Tennis, jogging, and reading

REFERENCES   Available on request

SUSAN R. SMITH

120 RIDGELINE ROAD • ORLANDO, FLORIDA 32803   (555) 369-4861

OBJECTIVE
A challenging, responsible position in the field of training and development, where my dedication and attention to detail will create opportunities for growth

SUMMARY
Considerable experience in the human resource marketplace. Responsible for administration, management, training and development, and publication activities at various levels.

ADMINISTRATION
Administered a variety of benefits programs as well as conducted wage and salary administration, payroll (ADP system), and workers' compensation. Involved in policy development.

MANAGEMENT
Maintained both manual and computerized records, data entry, and monthly reports. Managed Affirmative Action programs and conducted recruitment and selection activities. Hired supervisors, sales personnel, and staff members. Turnover was maintained below average for the industry.

TRAINING AND DEVELOPMENT
Conducted needs assessments, and designed and implemented departmental and organizational training programs. Developed and conducted employee training programs in management and supervisory skills, oral and written communication, listening, and clerical skills. Conducted employee orientation program. Used a variety of training techniques and multimedia applications.

PUBLICATIONS
Edited company newsletters, and developed and wrote policy and procedure manuals.

PERSONAL SKILLS
Possess basic computer skills, word processing, typing, and 10-key. Can speak Spanish at a conversational level.

PERSONAL ATTRIBUTES
Accurate, analytical, creative, conscientious, punctual, energetic, and ambitious

EDUCATION
B.A., 1990, Auburn University

REFERENCES
Available on request

Combination Résumé

The combination (or chrono-functional) résumé is uniquely designed for the upwardly mobile professional with a track record. If you have a performance record and are pursuing a career track, then this can be an effective résumé format (see Exhibit 9-5). In addition to contact information and objective, it incorporates the following:

► a career summary that includes a power-packed description of skills, achievements, and personal traits. It spotlights a past with solid contributions and projects a clear focus on future career growth.

▶ a chronological history with names of companies, dates, titles, duties, and responsibilities. This section also includes further evidence of achievements or special contributions.

▶ a description of your educational preparation as well as other optional categories as determined by you and the individualized aspects of your background.[7]

SUSAN R. SMITH

120 RIDGELINE ROAD • ORLANDO, FLORIDA 32803   (555) 369-4861

OBJECTIVE	Human resource management
SUMMARY	Considerable experience in human resource development with increasing responsibilities in administration, management, training and development, and publication. Concentration in high-technology corporations.
ADMINISTRATION	Administered various benefits programs and conducted wage and salary administration, payroll (ADP) system, and workers' compensation. Involved in policy development at all levels. Colleagues considered me to be conscientious, energetic, and cooperative.
MANAGEMENT	Maintained both manual and computerized records, data entry, and monthly reports. Managed Affirmative Action programs and conducted recruitment and selection activities. Hired supervisors, sales personnel, and staff members. Turnover was maintained below average for the industry. Colleagues found me to be detail oriented, analytical, and dependable.
TRAINING AND DEVELOPMENT	Conducted needs assessments, and designed and implemented departmental and organizational training programs. Developed and conducted employee training programs in management and supervisory skills, oral and written communication, listening, and clerical skills. Conducted employee orientation programs. Used a variety of training techniques, exercises, and multimedia applications. Participants found me to be creative, versatile, and enthusiastic.
PUBLICATIONS	Edited company newsletters, and developed and wrote policy and procedure manuals. The publications were thoroughly researched, and clearly and concisely written. The newsletters came out on a monthly basis.
PERSONAL SKILLS	Computer experience, word processing, typing, 10-key; conversational Spanish and able to sign for the deaf.

EXPERIENCE	HOWARD SYSTEMS INTERNATIONAL	Orlando, FL
	Personnel Coordinator	1992–Present
	Responsible for administering selected personnel functions and coordinating all training and development functions. Edit company newsletter and am involved in the publication of policy and procedure manuals.	

A résumé is a brief profile of oneself that is made available to a potential employer prior to an interview to present a review of one's background and potential. The following checklist identifies some items that might be included in a résumé:

▶ At the top put your name, address, and telephone number with area code.

▶ A job objective may be applicable and should be carefully prepared so as not to be too constricting. The best résumés have objectives written in broad, nonspecific terms. They are often little more than a categorization.

Smith • Page 2

ADDITIONAL RESPONSIBILITIES:
- Schedule and conduct selection and recruitment activities
- Involved in personnel policy development

ARKWIN TECHNICAL CORPORATION   Huntsville, AL
Personnel Assistant   1990–1992
Responsible for maintaining records; designed and implemented selected training and development programs. Edited company newsletter which was distributed on a monthly basis.

EDUCATION   AUBURN UNIVERSITY   Auburn, AL 32831
Bachelor of Arts degree granted *summa cum laude,* 1990
Major: English   Minor: Composition

Course of Study: composition, creative writing, photography, public speaking, group dynamics, consumer behavior, public relations, organizational communication, and communication theory

Honors: Included in *Who's Who in American Colleges and Universities,* Phi Beta Kappa, and Dean's List

Activities: Gamma Gamma Nu sorority, Intercollegiate Debate, and Radio Club

THOMAS JEFFERSON HIGH SCHOOL   Dallas, TX 75701
Diploma granted with High Honors, 1986

BIOGRAPHY

PROFESSIONAL   Society for Human Resource Management (SHRM)
ORGANIZATIONS   American Society for Training and Development (ASTD)
                Business and Professional Women's Club (BPW)

COMMUNITY   United Way (Loaned Executive in 1992 campaign)
ACTIVITIES   Recipient of Employer of the Year award from Goodwill Industries for efforts in recruiting and hiring handicapped employees

HOBBIES   Tennis, jogging, and reading

REFERENCES   Available on request

- ▶ Include your educational record—secondary school, postsecondary school work, dates of graduation, certification/degree, professional schools, civil service schools, and military schools. List all college degrees and your major and minor areas of study. If you graduated with honors or had a high grade-point average (GPA), note this as well. You may even include selected course work.
- ▶ Outline your employment record and work history. Maintain a list of previous employment; however, you may select your most recent years of employment. Try to illustrate how your work is compatible with the position being sought. Include the name/address and endorsements. Use action verbs to describe yourself and give punch to your résumé. Begin with your latest position and work back chronologically, noting the beginning and ending dates of each position. There is no real point to stating your reasons for leaving a job on a résumé.
- ▶ Military service should be included if applicable. Summarize your experience, noting highest rank, positions or classifications, and discharge record.
- ▶ List accreditation and licenses. If you are close to a particular accreditation or license, list it with information about the status.
- ▶ Professional affiliations and memberships to show your career dedication.
- ▶ Include all published works and patents. Such achievements reflect original thought and commitment to your career.
- ▶ If you are fluent in a foreign language(s), include that. For many positions, the mastery of a second language is a major asset, particularly in this age of the global village and increased cultural diversity.
- ▶ Technological and computer skills are an asset and should be listed, even if at a basic level of word processing. Being computer literate is a strong plus.
- ▶ Note any unusual asset or skill that is not apparent unless specifically identified.
- ▶ Note honors and awards you've received to focus attention on your success orientation.
- ▶ Community service can be important as corporations come to accept the idea that community activities are good public relations. A seat on the city/village council, work with the Boy Scouts/Girl Scouts, charitable cause involvement or fundraising work are all activities that show a willingness to involve oneself and can often demonstrate organizational abilities. Omit references to any religious, political, or otherwise potentially controversial affiliations.
- ▶ Hobbies and activities can be worthwhile noting if they fit into certain broad categories. These would include team sports (baseball, basketball), individual determination activities (tennis, golf, jogging, swimming, skiing, bicycling), and "brain activities" (bridge, chess, backgammon, reading). They reveal how you use your leisure time. In an age when burnout has become a recognized phenomenon, they suggest stress-reducing outlets. Omit listing any high-risk or dangerous activities, such as hang-gliding, skydiving, or auto racing.
- ▶ Note that references are available on request. You should have a list of references to be made available, but do not include them in your résumé unless the job listing requests that you do so.
- ▶ *Never include written testimonials, references to salary, charts and graphs, mention of age, race, religion, gender, national origin, photographs, descriptions of health/physical condition, marital status, weaknesses, or demands.*

"Give me a moment of your busy day! Listen to me, I got something to say!" That's what your résumé must scream—in a suitably professional manner, of course. You may be the subject of the résumé, but the employer is its object. A résumé is a directed communication to a particular audience that has specific needs, so take care with its visual appearance, using top-quality paper and a lot of white space to make it easier to read. Your résumé is a personal written communication that represents you and clearly demonstrates your ability to produce valuable results in an area of concern to potential employers in a way that motivates them to meet you. Ultimately, the purpose of the résumé is to get you an interview.

▶ THE INTERVIEW

The purposes of selection interviews differ in both type and degree. Generally, they are both information-giving and information-seeking. In this sense, they are informational conversations in which the interviewer seeks information from you, the job applicant; but they are also times at which you, the applicant, seek information from the interviewer. Skillful interviewers need to be cognizant of the organization's needs. They must know what kinds of knowledge, skills, abilities, and other characteristics (KSAOs) are necessary to perform the job. Moreover, no two interviews are the same. Individual personalities and philosophies inevitably influence the conduct of an interview. Most large organizations and many smaller ones invest heavily in well-trained personnel interviewers who have one major responsibility—to select the best employees from those in the applicant pool. Still, John Lafevre observes that "interviewers are merely professional gamblers who have been provided a thirty-minute tip sheet analysis to help them decide on which candidate to place the bet."[8]

Interviewer's Perspective

When the interviewer approaches an applicant, the interviewer has two basic challenges: (1) ask the questions that will provide the most accurate information about the applicant, and (2) present an image of the organization that will make the applicant want to accept the position if an offer is made. The following four-part structure can be used as a guide to accomplishing these objectives:

▶ *Introduction*—The interviewer will want to establish rapport and create a positive, supportive atmosphere. Discussing subjects of mutual interest can help put the candidate at ease.

▶ *Background*—The interviewer, using questions and answers, will examine the candidate's basic qualifications for the job (KSAOs) and try to determine if the candidate meets or exceeds the requirements.

▶ *Discussion*—It is here that the interviewer will start helping the candidate match career goals with organizational opportunities and invite the candidate to ask questions. This is a very important part of the interview because it permits the interviewer to personalize the company and give more detailed explanations about the local offices, the unique aspects of the jobs available, advancement and self-development, and corporate philosophy. Not every candidate will be interested in the same things about a job or company. Consequently, these questions may vary considerably.

▶ *Close*—At this point, the interviewer will provide information needed to ensure a clear understanding of the actual employment procedures. The candidate may

► ATTACK OF THE KILLER JOB-HUNTERS

By Linda Shrieves

When it comes to job-hunters, most can be lumped into three categories: the good, the bad, and—yes, you knew they were out there—the horrendous.

Just about anybody can guess the qualities of the good and the bad candidates. They are, after all, predictable: Their résumés are either stellar or snooze-inducing; their interviews outstanding or off-putting.

But then there are the *truly* bad ones. People whose résumés are so bad, so weird or just so outlandish that they immediately get pinned up on the office bulletin board. People whose cover letters appear to have beamed in from outer space. People whose job interviews become office legend. These people could lead seminars on how NOT to land a job.

Take the job prospect who brought her dog along with her when she filled out the application. "She actually sat the dog down on the seat beside her while she filled out the application," said Michelle Linnert, an interviewer for Sun Bank. When Linnert suggested that the woman come back for an interview—some time when she wouldn't have the dog with her—the woman became indignant.

In fact, banks seem to attract more unusual candidates than other businesses. Vicki Neidert, a personnel interviewer for C&S Bank, guesses that's because the average citizen figures he knows how a bank operates—and therefore assumes he can operate a bank.

In seven years of interviewing job candidates, Neidert has accumulated what may be more than her fair share of horrific interviews. She regularly finds herself dealing with people who seem to be missing the essential job-hunting gene.

Perhaps the worst involved an applicant who had a pacemaker. "She came in, sat down and said, 'My name is so-and-so and my pacemaker's name is George. See, you can see it in my skin,' and she actually moved it back and forth," Neidert said.

Not one to hold a pacemaker against a person, Neidert continued to listen. The candidate continued to rattle on.

"She said she could work anywhere, do anything, as long as she didn't work near a microwave. She rattled on and just wouldn't quit. I hardly got to say a word. Then she said, 'I know that I've only done baby-sitting, but I know I can be a teller. . . . Want to see me count some money?'"

Or there was the woman who insisted that Neidert had turned her name in to the FBI because she was on the most-wanted list.

It all started when the woman filled out an application at C&S. Within a few days, she appeared at a branch office, complaining that people were following her and that Neidert was responsible. "She said she knew I was the one who had turned her in because I was the only one who had access to all this personal information about her," Neidert said. "She said she was going to turn me in to the FBI for turning her in to the FBI."

Needless to say, she didn't get called back for the interview.

In many cases, job candidates with bad résumés never make it to the interview stage. Bland résumés may be boring, and the résumé with typos in it may have been oversights, but the really horrible résumé requires some effort.

As the owner of an Orlando ad agency, Doug Minear expects adventuresome résumés, but what he gets frequently are awful attempts at creativity.

"Once or twice a year, I get someone who puts their face on a wanted poster and uses that as a résumé," Minear said. "We also get a number of résumés every year from people who have made a newsletter about themselves. It will have headlines and photographs of themselves and even an ad for themselves—the whole works."

Brevity may be important if you want the job, but if you want to leave an impression that an interviewer will never forget, send a James Michener-esque résumé.

Ask Joseph Wise. Wise, who supervises the employment office for the Orange County School System, has run across lots of terrific résumés, but one sticks out in his memory.

It was 42 pages long.

"There were many letters of recommendation, transcripts, newspaper clips from the projects this teacher had done, all kinds of stuff," Wise said. "This person may have been a great teacher, but you had to wonder what had happened to his ability to edit something, anything, out of this. Why couldn't he decide what was important and what wasn't?"

Neidert had a similar prospect who had gone so far as to have the résumé published—and bound. The attached cover letter instructed the personnel department to "please find my enclosed qualifications."

"It was a book! It was 30 pages long. Of course I didn't sit there and read the whole thing," Neidert said. "And then she never showed up for the interview."

And, when it comes to really flubbing a job interview, nothing works like being inappropriately dressed.

Doug Minear, for instance, assumed that job candidates would all dress as if they were going to church. How wrong he has been.

"These people with fancy résumés will show up for an interview wearing blue jeans and chewing gum!" Minear said. "I'm always amazed. I've discovered that it's a real adventure trying to bring someone on board.

"Once, we advertised in the paper for a secretarial position and you wouldn't believe the line of people outside the office the next morning. It looked like the line for *The Rocky Horror Picture Show*," Minear said. "There were women wearing halter tops, short, short skirts, boots, you name it. We hired, literally, the only woman who came in wearing a business suit. And she was terrible! I can only imagine what the others would have been like."

However, there is hope for those who choose to dress down for an interview.

When Jim McLaughlin, president of Peterson Outdoor Advertising, was looking for someone to work on the management staff, he had a most shocking interview.

"The job candidate came in for the interview wearing work boots, blue jeans, a flannel shirt, long hair with ponytail and full facial hair," McLaughlin said.

McLaughlin wasn't impressed. "I thought it was going to be a short interview," he recalled.

But the candidate persuaded McLaughlin to look past his appearance and consider his ideas and his intelligence.

"Now he's the company's sales manager," said McLaughlin, "and I can honestly say he has turned out to be one of the best employees I ever hired."

Source: Linda Shrieves, "Attack of the Killer Job Hunters," *The Orlando Sentinel*, November 27, 1989, C1–C2.

receive an explanation of when to expect to hear from the company, stated arrangements for any testing, or an invitation to a subsequent interview.

Interviewing requires careful preparation and attention. If the interview is not structured, essential information may not be covered. The interviewer must probe analytically and thoroughly, being aware of personal interpretations of what the interviewee says and tempering personal biases or prejudices when making decisions. Research suggests, however, that although interview reliability may be high in given situations, the validities obtained are usually low.[9]

The interviewer is also responsible for protecting the civil rights of the applicant. Since the passage of the Civil Rights Act of 1964, employment interviewing has been regulated by federal law. Any question that has the potential to discriminate among groups of people may not be asked. The U.S. Supreme Court has said that "the touchstone is business necessity." In other words, the interviewer may only ask questions that are pertinent to the bona fide occupational qualifications. This means that an employer may not ask questions concerning an applicant's gender, race, religion, marital status, handicap, or age unless such information is a legitimate requirement for employment. For example, the interviewer may not ask a female applicant about her plans for marriage and/or having a family. Such information has no bearing on how well she will perform a job. Moreover, men are seldom, if ever, questioned about such topics.

The inexperienced interviewer may occasionally ask such questions because he or she lacks the skills to seek necessary information in a nondiscriminatory way, but this is no excuse. In such a case, the interviewee should not provide the inappropriately requested information. Rather, the interviewee might respond to the legally appropriate question which should have been asked. Here are some discriminatory questions and possible responses:

Q: What are your marriage plans?

A: If what you're concerned about is my ability to travel or my commitment to my employer, I assure you that I am quite aware of the job responsibilities and personal commitments involved.

Q: Who will take care of your children while you are at work?

A: If what you're concerned about is my being to work on time, there are no outside commitments which should interfere with my employment.

Q: How old are you?

A: I believe that you will find my skills, competence, and experience qualify me for the position listed.

Q: Do you have a handicap?

A: Any disabilities I may have would not interfere with my ability to perform all aspects of this position.

Q: What is your religion? What church do you attend?

A: If you are concerned about my availability to work on weekends, I can assure you that I could fit into your work schedule.

An applicant would want to consider carefully whether to work for an employer who persists in asking such questions.

Although there are many complexities in the law, it is fairly clear that an employer can be found guilty of discrimination in at least two ways:

1. *Adverse (or disparate) treatment.* Essentially this means that the employer can be shown to have intentionally refused to hire, promote, or retain someone because of their race, sex, religion, color, or national origin.

2. *Adverse (or disparate) impact.* In this situation, the employer may have no "evil motive" which influenced them but an adverse impact may occur. For example, an employer may require that all truck drivers have a high school diploma. This may have an adverse impact on minorities. Or, an employer may require that all plant employees be at least five feet eight inches tall and weigh 160 pounds. This will have an adverse impact on women. If an employer's selection practices have adverse impact, the burden of proof is on him to show that these practices are job related. Is a high school diploma necessary for one to be a good truck driver? Is a height and weight requirement necessary to be a successful plant employee?

Legal difficulties can be avoided if the interviewer asks only pertinent, job-relevant questions. Furthermore, the interviewer should ask all applicants the same basic questions to ensure that each has the same opportunity to provide equivalent information. This will also make it easier to evaluate and compare candidates at a later date.

EEO legislation along with job market trends and the need to hire the best possible candidates have prompted recruitment managers to explore new approaches to selection interviewing. Two alternatives to the traditional interview are: (1) the behavioral or creative interview and (2) the structured interview. Each is situation oriented, placing greater emphasis on performance and behavior rather than on personal attitudes.[10]

Behavioral interviewing is based on the principle that the best predictor of future behavior is past behavior. Two corollaries to this principle take change into account:

Corollary 1: The more recent the past behavior, the greater its predictive power.

Corollary 2: The more long-lasting the behavior, the greater its predictive power.[11]

► QUESTIONS INTERVIEWERS ASK

1. What do you see yourself doing in 5, 10, 15 years?
2. Why did you decide to go to your college or university?
3. If you could change anything about your education, what would it be?
4. Do you work well under pressure? (give some examples)
5. Would you rather be a leader or a follower?
6. What motivates you to give the most effort?
7. Are your grades a good indicator of your academic achievement? (explain)
8. Do you have plans for continued study? (explain)
9. Who is the person you admire most? Why?
10. How do you evaluate success?
11. Why should I hire you over other candidates?
12. Do you work better alone or with supervision? (explain)
13. How have your past job experiences prepared you, directly or indirectly, for this position?
14. Describe an unpleasant work situation in the past and how did you handle it?
15. What methods do you use to make decisions?
16. If you could structure the perfect job for yourself, what would you do, and why?
17. Give some standard examples of situations in which you have been criticized. How did you react and why?
18. What kinds of challenges do you feel bring out your potential?
19. In what areas do you feel you would like to develop further? How do you plan to do that?
20. Tell me about two serious interpersonal-relationship problems you've had on the job and how did you deal with each? Were you satisfied with the outcome? Would you do anything differently now?
21. In groups, do you often emerge as a dominant figure? What do you feel causes this?
22. Why are you interested in working for our company?
23. What have you learned from your mistakes?
24. What qualities should an effective manager have?
25. How do you spend your free time?

At all times, then, the interviewer must be intellectually alert to reasonable extrapolation from the job analysis findings of KSAOs to the individual's background and vice versa. The interviewer asks the applicant about real-life work situations and from the applicant's answers assesses judgment and analyzes skills according to company criteria. For example, the following types of questions elicit behavior description information:

► Tell me about your best accomplishment in your last job. Start with where you got the idea; describe how you planned to carry it out, how you executed your plan, and how you dealt with the major obstacles(s) you had to overcome.

► Tell me about the last time you faced the situation of an employee who wasn't performing. What was the situation, how did you deal with it, what did you say, what did the employee say, and so forth?

► Tell me about the most emotional confrontation you had with your boss in that job. How did you respond to the situation? What was the outcome? How satisfied were you with the results?

► Tell me about the least-effective performer you have ever supervised. What steps did you take to increase motivation? What type of counseling? How did the employee respond to your efforts?

► Tell me about the hardest you worked in that part-time job. Was the time and attention worthwhile?

The responses to these kinds of questions, when followed up with further behavior description questions, allows the interviewer to "watch" the applicant perform in the workplace. Such an approach is time consuming, but behavioral interviewing accu-

► WHY APPLICANTS ARE REJECTED

Results of a survey conducted by Northwestern University of 153 companies. Shown in rank order are the factors that most often lead to rejection of applicants.

1. Poor personal appearance
2. Overbearing-overaggressive-conceited "superiority complex"—"know-it-all"
3. Inability to express oneself clearly—poor voice, diction, grammar
4. Lack of planning for career—no purpose and goals
5. Lack of interest and enthusiasm—passive, indifferent
6. Lack of confidence and poise—nervousness, ill-at-ease
7. Failure to participate in activities
8. Overemphasis on money—interest only in best dollar offer
9. Poor scholastic record—just got by
10. Unwilling to start at the bottom—expects too much too soon
11. Makes excuses—evasiveness—hedges on unfavorable factors in record
12. Lack of tact
13. Lack of maturity
14. Lack of courtesy—ill mannered
15. Condemnation of past employers
16. Lack of social understanding
17. Marked dislike for school work
18. Lack of vitality
19. Fails to look interviewer in the eye
20. Limp, fishy handshake
21. Indecision
22. Loafs during vacations—lakeside pleasure
23. Unhappy married life
24. Friction with parents
25. Sloppy application blank
26. Merely shopping around
27. Wants job only for short time
28. Little sense of humor
29. Lack of knowledge in field of specialization
30. Parents make decisions for him
31. No interest in company or in industry
32. Emphasis on whom he knows
33. Unwillingness to go where we send her
34. Cynical
35. Low moral standards
36. Lazy
37. Intolerant—strong prejudices
38. Narrow interests
39. Spends much time in movies
40. Poor handling of personal finances
41. No interest in community activities
42. Inability to take criticism
43. Lack of appreciation of the value of experience
44. Radical ideas
45. Late to interview without good reason
46. Never heard of company
47. Failure to express appreciation for interviewer's time
48. Asks no questions about the job
49. High-pressure type
50. Indefinite response to questions

racy exceeds traditional interviewing accuracy by three to seven times. Scott Paper initiated behavior interviewing to find applicants whose judgment and sense of teamwork would fit their corporate culture. Hershey Food began similar training in behavior interviewing so that managers "can judge between a 'fast horse and a champion' who'll fit Hershey's culture."[12]

Structured interviewing also has received increased attention from interviewers. The structured interview has several characteristics: (1) it contains a structured series of job related questions; (2) each question is evaluated by a predetermined rating scale; and (3) specific steps are taken to ensure that questions are consistently asked of all applicants for a position. The questions asked are: Who was responsible? What skills were needed? Where was this applicable? When did you do this kind of work? Why did you make that decision? How did you solve that problem?[13]

Using this approach, the interviewer evaluates applicants on job-related data and therefore decreases the potential occurrence of "halo" and "pitch fork" rating errors. The halo error occurs when a person who is outstanding on one dimension is consequently overrated on other dimensions. The pitch fork error occurs when too much emphasis is placed on some singular negative information over the many positive attributes or dimensions of an applicant. Here, applicants are evaluated on job-specific dimensions and the situational behaviors they describe. When consistently administered among applicants, the structural interview may help employers have stronger cases against legal suits alleging disparate impact and invasion of privacy in hiring practices.[14]

Interviewee's Perspective

Because selection interviews function as a specialized form of interpersonal communication, we must also examine the interviewee's perspective. A selection interview is a two-way proposition. Rather than feeling subservient, remember that you, the interviewee, were invited in for a talk. The company is interested in you.

You have two major objectives in the selection interview: (1) to provide accurate information, developing a positive self-image and articulating your abilities; and (2) to discover if the position is desirable, appropriate, and consistent with your career objectives or goals. A positive self-image is absolutely necessary if you are to perform well in the interview. Keep in mind that no one is perfect; the interviewer knows this and will discount the applicant who admits to no faults. Employers seek human beings, and productive employees are most often those who have positive and constructive attitudes concerning their strengths and weaknesses. In the interview, you need to capitalize on your strengths. With preparation and a knowledge of what to expect, you can keep things in perspective and prevent the interview from becoming "The Great Confrontation." Anticipating interview questions and participating in mock interviews can significantly strengthen your interview performance and help you relax and enjoy the experience. Practice makes perfect so practice answering potential questions, including difficult ones.

It is also important to communicate a professional image in the interview. From the time you arrive for the interview—between five and ten minutes early—you must sell yourself as a capable person. This, of course, includes a perfectly groomed, classic, professional look. Avoid high-fashion clothing or overly casual clothing. Different jobs require different degrees of formality, so dress to suit the company and the position. Dark or neutral colors are always a safe choice. Don't relax yourself with a beverage before the interview—liquor smells, coffee invariably spills, iced drinks make

▶ YOU WANT A JOB—AND CHINESE FOOD?

By Katherine Morrall

When it comes to recruitment, personnel directors may think they have heard it all.

But Robert Half Inc., a New York-based financial, accounting and data processing recruiting firm, has some new tales to add to the files.

Robert Half, chairman, commissioned an independent research firm to ask some of the nation's 1,000 top executives about the most unusual requests or demands they've received from job candidates as conditions of employment.

Weird But True

The responses gave new meaning to the definition of perks. Half reports that the answers ranged from the strange and eccentric to the bizarre and amusing. According to executives surveyed, some job candidates have:

▶ Not taken a job unless both Italian and Chinese restaurants were within walking distance.

▶ Wanted to be paid extra for any time spent thinking about work at night or during the weekends.

▶ Insisted that any company hiring him ship his prize-winning horses by air from Australia.

▶ Asked for paid membership at the city zoo for the entire family.

▶ Demanded specific days off with pay in addition to their birthdays, the first day of the World Series, Bastille Day and, in every leap year, February 29.

▶ Asked the company to contribute to his ex-wife's alimony payments, but didn't insist on it.

▶ Refused to take any job with travel to New York, Los Angeles or Houston.

▶ Asked that the firm's medical plan cover visits to a faith healer.

▶ Wanted the new employer to pay shipping charges to move a 24-foot sailboat from Boston to Chicago.

▶ Insisted the employer pay his wife's law school tuition.

▶ Refused to accept a position unless the mailroom saved all foreign stamps on incoming mail so he could add to his child's stamp collection.

▶ Asked the new employer for compensation for half the income lost while unemployed for four months.

▶ Declined to take a job unless the corporation paid kennel boarding fees for his two dogs while he was traveling.

In addition, a top executive preferred a large office, with no windows, because she found interesting views too distracting. On the other hand, a middle-management executive wanted her office equipped with a refrigerator, projection television set, video cassette recorder and microwave oven.

Half says job candidates probably make the requests out of fear of change. From his experience as a recruiter, he adds that it's also typical for job candidates to make excuses for why they can't make an interview.

Possible Explanations

"I can't tell you how many times people have told me they can't make an appointment because they are painting a house," he says.

Out of all the responses on the survey, Half says he has only been asked for a zoo membership, which he didn't consider unreasonable.

The outcome of the other demands, however, are a bit more nebulous. Half says the requests for shipping the sailboat from Boston to Chicago and flying the horses from Australia were made by high-priced executives.

"You can almost understand it in that context," he contends. "The executives were probably trying to see how many perks they could get. What I want to know is whether the horses flew first class."

Source: Katherine Morrall, "You Want a Job—And Chinese Food?" *BBB Bulletin* (October 1987):1.

your hands feel cold and clammy. Don't smoke or chew gum during the interview. And, although the meeting may be relaxed and friendly, take care not to slip over into a slouching, at-home informality. If you feel nervous, it's because you're concerned about your performance. Your body is adjusting by providing essential energy so channel that energy into listening and responding to the best of your ability.

You have only a short time in which to impress, so make the most of it. Lean slightly forward from the middle of your chair with your arms free from your sides. Speak up clearly and with answers that are right to the point. Be prepared with paper and pencil to take notes and you'll appear genuinely interested and efficient.

As important as the image you project is the image you get of the prospective organization. This is your opportunity to learn about the organization so you can make an intelligent decision about accepting or rejecting an offer. Take on the role of the interviewer. Have questions ready to ask, but avoid asking questions that could have been researched in advance. Ask thoughtful questions that reflect your knowledge of the organization. In addition to soliciting necessary details, such questioning communicates a professional image. Interviewers expect questions and frequently invite them.

▶ **EXHIBIT 9-6**
Thank-You Letter

120 Ridgeline Road
Orlando, FL 32803
August 21, 19—

Westinghouse Electric Corporation
Employment Department/OS
4400 Alafaya Trail
Tampa, FL 32826–2399

Dear Carol Moorhead:

Thank you for meeting with me today to discuss the Training and Development Specialist position with Westinghouse Electric Corporation. I was very interested to hear about the company and its products.

With my administrative and managerial background, I feel that I could very competently perform the duties you described. As I mentioned in our conversation, I have four years of experience in training and development, and can handle all types of situations. I possess excellent communication skills and am accustomed to producing accurate detail work. My adaptability and flexibility would be useful traits during the current transition period being experienced by the company. Having an opportunity to apply my skills to the sales field is also very appealing at this point in my career.

Thank you for the time you spent with me during the interview. I would like to put my training and experience to use in a company of the caliber of Westinghouse. Please feel free to call me at (555) 369-4861 concerning the status of my credentials. I look forward to hearing from you soon.

Sincerely,

Susan R. Smith

CANDIDATE REVIEW

Candidate _____ Date _____

INTERVIEW SUMMARY (technical knowledge, maturity, ability to communicate, initiative, experience related to position, management style, etc.)

CANDIDATE STRENGTHS (key abilities and characteristics)

1. _____
2. _____
3. _____
4. _____
5. _____

CANDIDATE WEAKNESSES (concerns about the candidate)

1. _____
2. _____
3. _____
4. _____
5. _____

SUMMARY (all things considered)

NO GO		MARGINAL			SATISFACTORY		DESIRABLE		OUTSTANDING	
0	1	2	3	4	5	6	7	8	9	10

INTERVIEWER'S SIGNATURE   DATE

►FOLLOW-UP AND EVALUATION

When the interviewer rises to indicate that the time is up, shake his or her hand warmly, smile as though you had just been given the job, and express your thanks. The interview, however, does *not* end when you leave the employer's office. Send a thank-you letter to the interviewer(s) within 24 hours (see Exhibit 9-6). This is an important detail that many interviewees overlook. A recent survey revealed that 80 percent of the employers questioned strongly believed that applicants should send a letter shortly after the interview expressing appreciation for being considered for the job.[15]

Each thank-you letter is highly individualized and tailored to the company, the industry, and the person(s) with whom you interviewed. A typed letter is preferred, but if that is not possible within 24 hours, a handwritten letter is acceptable. Use the standard business letter format. In this letter you should:

▶ Thank the interviewer and demonstrate your enthusiasm and continued interest in the position.
▶ Refer to specific points discussed during the interview. Highlight facts about your background that are pertinent to the position you are seeking. Be specific.
▶ If you have already been told "no," reiterate your continuing interest in the employer's operation—perhaps in another capacity or at another time.
▶ State, in closing, that you will be in touch with the interviewer.

The thank-you letter is your chance to add something you might have neglected. It will also bring you to mind again. But, most of all, the interviewer will be impressed with your thoughtfulness.

After the candidate leaves, the interviewer must carefully record the information and impressions received (see Exhibit 9-7). This becomes important when you later compare and contrast candidates. Relying solely on memory to select the best candidate is particularly risky and can only lead to difficulties. Additionally, this evaluative process provides you an opportunity to assess your skills and determine the effectiveness of the interview. This can be helpful when conducting future interviews.

When selecting a candidate, there are only two issues: *capability* —what the candidate can do—and *personality* —what the candidate is like. A well-written cover letter, carefully prepared résumé, and effective interviewing skills can give both the interviewee and the interviewer the winning edge.

▶ SUMMARY

This chapter has presented the selection interview as an integral part of any career search and as necessary when trying to hire the right person for the right job. The cover letter, résumé, interview, and follow-up/evaluation activities are critical components to this process. Ultimately, each contributes toward achieving an effective outcome beneficial to both parties.

The cover letter introduces you to the organization and permits you to tailor a description of your qualifications to the organizational needs. It should be carefully written, following standard business-letter guidelines. Cover letters are brief, generally not more than one page. Keep your sentences short and your paragraphs concise and to the point. A good cover letter sets the stage for the employer to accept your résumé as something special.

The résumé must speak loudly and clearly of your value as a potential employee. And the value must be spoken in a few brief seconds because, in the business

world, that's all the attention a résumé will get. Creating an effective résumé requires that you carefully select an appropriate format—chronological, functional, or a combination of the two. Each format has certain benefits based on you and your particular circumstances. Regardless of format, however, the résumé must reflect your educational background and work experience. In addition, you will want to direct attention to those areas that distinguish you from other candidates. What makes you unique? The résumé is a valuable vehicle for demonstrating your knowledge, skills, abilities, and other personal characteristics. It takes you the first few paces toward a job—it gets your foot in the door.

The selection interview is where decisions regarding hiring will be made. The interviewer must structure the interview, develop questions within legal guidelines that elicit the needed information, and conduct the interview. The interviewee must seek information about the organization, and present both a positive personal and professional image. Each party must carefully plan and prepare for the selection interview if it is to be successful.

However, the interview "isn't over until it's over." Simply put, after the interview each must pursue follow-up and evaluation activities. The interviewee should send a thank-you letter within 24 hours. The interviewer should write an evaluation of the candidate and assess the interview itself.

Companies are always looking for employees. Even a company with no growth rate can still be expected (according to national averages) to experience a 14 percent turnover in staff over the course of a year. The selection-interviewing process discussed remains the most viable means of filling these vacancies. Consequently, selection interviewing is a vital part of organizational life and equally important in career development and growth. The higher up the professional ladder you climb, the more important this process becomes.

► QUESTIONS FOR DISCUSSION AND SKILL DEVELOPMENT

1. Prepare a résumé and an accompanying cover letter to be used in applying for a real job listed in the classified section of your local newspaper. Do they positively reflect you? Do they adequately present your assets, experience, and education? How might other versions/formats present you?

2. Why is it always a good idea to update the job description for any position you are trying to fill? What other preparatory steps should you, as an interviewer, take? Why is it a good idea to review the Equal Employment Opportunity guidelines prior to conducting an interview?

3. What is the difference between an open-ended question and a direct question? What is your preference between open and closed questions? Hypothetical questions? Have you ever been asked a discriminatory question? How did you respond? Why? What was your perception of the interviewer? The organization?

4. What should be the distribution of talking time between the applicant and the interviewer? What kind of information should the interviewer be prepared to give the applicant?

5. All of us make judgments about others that are not objective, or are sometimes unjustified. Such judgments interfere with good communication.

They appear as stereotypes, when we prejudge someone on the basis of his or her appearance, background, or position. List those situations and influences, both favorable and unfavorable, to which you must be alert as possible sources of communication barriers. What kinds of people do you sometimes avoid? What kinds of people do you enjoy being with or talking to? (Watch out for the "halo effect" with these people.) What kinds of behavior or outward appearance do you find distracting or annoying in others? What are your most apparent hang-ups (attitudes, prejudices) of a negative nature? What are your most apparent hang-ups of a positive nature? What people do you have difficulty listening to, and why? In what situations do you find it hard to listen to others?

6. When is the best time to complete your evaluation of an applicant? Why? What criteria should you use in evaluating the applicant? Why is documentation of hiring decisions so important?

7. Why is it important to let a candidate know when he or she might expect a decision?

8. After reading this chapter, how might you change your approach to selection interviewing as the interviewer? As the interviewee?

► NOTES

1. This evaluation form was designed by William N. Yeomans to help prospective employees evaluate their job marketability, thus establishing some realistic expectations concerning employability. Certainly some of the categories and descriptive labels

are highly subjective and perhaps exclusionary, but appearance, personality, height/weight, and bearing do influence prospective employers. You will notice that the more objective and quantifiable measures of scholastic standing, academic rating, work experience, and college expenses earned yourself carry more weight in determining the final score. Remember, ultimately you make the difference.

2. T. F. Boyle and C. Hymowitz, "White-Collar Blues," *The Wall Street Journal*, October 4, 1990, A1.

3. William C. Himstreet and Wayne M. Baty, *Business Communication: Principles and Methods* (New York: Kent, 1981).

4. Burdette E. Bostwick, *Résumé Writing: A Comprehensive Guide to How To Do It*, 2nd ed. (New York: John Wiley & Sons, 1980): 155.

5. Martin J. Yate, *Résumés That Knock 'Em Dead* (Boston: Bob Adams, 1990); and Gary T. Hunt and William Eadie, *Interviewing* (New York: CBS College Publishing, 1987).

6. Yate, *Résumés That Knock 'Em Dead*, 10–11.

7. Ibid., 12.

8. Jack Gratus, *Successful Interviewing: How to Find and Keep the Best People* (New York: Penguin Books, 1988): 36.

9. Eugene Mayfield, "The Selection Interview—A Re-Evaluation of Published Research," *Personnel Psychology* 17 (1964): 171–180; and Orman R. Wright, Jr., "Summary of Research on the Selection Interview Since 1964," *Personnel Psychology* 22 (1969): 394–401.

10. S. D. Maurer and C. Fay, "Effect of Situational Interviews, Conventional Structured Interviews, and Training on Interview Rating or Agreement: An Experimental Analysis," *Personnel Psychology* 41 (1988): 329–344; W. L. Tuller, "Relational Control in the Employment Interview," *Journal of Applied Psychology* 74 (1989): 971–977; and P. M. Wright, P. A. Lichtenfels, and E. D. Pursell, "The Structured Interview: Additional Studies and a Meta-Analysis," *Journal of Occupational Psychology* 62 (1989): 191–199.

11. Tom Janz, Lowell Hellervik, and David Gilmore, *Behavior Description Interviewing* (Boston: Allyn and Bacon, 1986): 33.

12. "Creative Interviewing Takes Firmer Hold as the Job Pinch Worsens," *The Wall Street Journal*, May 8, 1990, A1.

13. C. E. Wilson, "The New Generation of Selection Interviews: Structural, Behavior-Based, Valid" (Paper presented at the Annual Meeting of the Speech Communication Association, Chicago, IL, 1990).

14. J. Hollwitz, "Legal and Ethical Implications of Structural Interviewing" (Paper presented at the Annual Meeting of the Speech Communication Association, Chicago, IL, 1990).

15. Barron Wells and Nelda Spinks, "Interviewing: What Small Companies Say," *The Bulletin* 55 (1992): 18–22.

C H A P T E R   T E N

10

Group Problem Solving and Meeting Dynamics

LEARNING OBJECTIVES:

To identify and describe the types and functions of small groups found in organizations

To show the relationship between group and systems functions

To define small-group activity, focus on the nature of small groups; the laws of their development; and their interrelations with individuals, other groups, and larger institutions

To recognize what constitutes a small group and be able to increase effectiveness in groups by understanding what produces group facilitation and group effectiveness

To discuss group identity, structure, norms, roles, networks, methods, and cohesion

To recognize the needs and demands of conference dynamics and apply appropriate techniques when conducting meetings

People in organizations must inevitably spend at least some of their time as members of various groups—social, information-sharing, learning, and problem-solving groups. The coffee break, cocktail party, departmental meeting, training seminar, in-house management program, and task group are all typical discussion situations. Each discussion type represented here is going on in hundreds of organizations right now and these are only a few of the types of situations and groups from which discussions emerge. Of all types of sustained direct oral communication, none is more common or important to our way of life generally and that of an organization specifically than small-group discussion and conferences. This chapter examines the different types and functions of groups in organizations, reveals groups to be effective in solving problems, and presents practical conference techniques useful when conducting meetings.

Meetings account for much of the time spent in organizations. Rollie Tillman, Jr., found that 94 percent of organizations with more than 10,000 employees and 64 percent of those with less than 250 employees had formal committees that met regularly.[1] Other studies indicate that over 90 percent of the *Fortune 500* companies used problem-solving and decision-making groups in their daily operations, and that executives typically spend an average of ten hours per week in formal committee meetings.[2] Then there are the many informal meetings conducted daily, weekly, and monthly. It is likely that in your lifetime, regardless of your occupation, you will spend more than 9,000 hours—roughly one year—in meetings.[3] Norman Maier describes the situation well when he notes that "executives hold conferences at all levels in an organization; scientists work in teams; educators serve on committees; parents serve on action groups; teachers educate by the use of participation methods; psychologists and psychiatrists practice group therapy; and teenagers hold meetings."[4] So, despite the criticism often leveled against small groups in organizations, they do represent one of the most prevalent forms of communication within the organizational structure. Additionally, in the last decade telecommunications has become a fact of organizational life with conference calls and videoconferencing becoming common. This unequaled technological development has led E. K. Clemons and F. W. McFarlan to observe that if organizations "don't capitalize on the promise of telecommunications, laggard companies may find themselves in trouble."[5]

▶ SMALL GROUPS DEFINED

A camel, some say, is a horse that was built by a committee—the implication being that group solutions are far less effective than those made by individuals. Max S. Marshall suggests in *The Hydra of the Campus* that a "committee is a body of men [or women] who can do nothing individually, but who can collectively decide that nothing can be done. A committee is a group of the unwanted chosen from the unwilling by the unfit to do the unnecessary." And many would agree with Lewis Carroll's description of small-group activity, when he wrote in *Alice's Adventures in Wonderland:* "I don't think they play at all fairly. . . . and they all quarrel so dreadfully one can't hear oneself speak—and they don't seem to have rules in particular; at least, if there are, nobody attends to them—and you've no idea how confusing it is all the things being alive. . . ." Despite the fact that group associations can prove difficult, you can avoid creating "camels" and reap enormous rewards and benefits. Now, more than ever before, it is important that groups perform their functions well if the larger system is to work.

Ernest Bormann defines group discussion as "one or more meetings of a small group of people who thereby communicate, face-to-face, in order to fulfill a common purpose and achieve a group goal."[6] Stewart Tubbs and Sylvia Moss present an even more complete definition when they observe that a small group is a "collection of people who influence one another, derive some satisfaction from maintaining membership in the group, interact for some purpose, assume specialized roles, are dependent on one another and communicate face-to-face . . . *small group communication* may be regarded as *the process by which (three or more) members of a group exchange verbal and nonverbal messages in an attempt to influence one another.*"[7] The key terms common to these traditional definitions of small groups as well as the current literature in group dynamics are a "process" involving a "face-to-face interaction" of a "collection of people" for a particular "purpose" and/or "objective."[8] Small groups develop characteristics that differ from the sum of the characteristics and personalities of its members. Referred to as *synergy,* the recurrent finding that the whole is more than the sum of its parts has revealed that groups often come up with solutions that are superior to the thinking of any one member.[9]

A group is not just any collection or aggregate of people. Consider five people standing on a street corner waiting to cross or seven people working in the same setting—are these small groups? Certainly each situation has few enough people to qualify, but there is no communicative bond or interdependent purpose so these are not small groups. "Groupness" emerges from the relationships among the people involved, thus a small group is a collection of people who relate to one another in ways that make them interdependent to some significant degree. If an automobile accident should occur and the five pedestrians waiting on the street corner in our earlier example should join together to help the injured, then a group has been formed. Or, if our seven employees combine their talents to work on a particular project, again a group has emerged. Groups possess specific and definite sets of characteristics. John Brilhart identifies five characteristics common to small groups:

1. A sufficiently small number of people so that each will be aware of and have some reaction to each other (from 3 to rarely more than 20).
2. A mutually interdependent purpose in which the success of each person is contingent upon the success of the others in achieving this goal.
3. Each person has a sense of belonging or membership, identifying himself/herself with the other members of the group.
4. Oral interaction (not all interaction will be oral, but a significant characteristic of a discussion is reciprocal influence exercised by talking).
5. Behavior-based norms and procedures accepted by all members.[10]

Marvin E. Shaw points to six characteristics and raises six questions that serve to define group activity:

1. *Perception*—do members make an impression on other members?
2. *Motivation*—is membership in the group rewarding?
3. *Goals*—do group members work together for a purpose?
4. *Organization*—does each member have a specialized role—moderator, notetaker, and so on?
5. *Interdependency*—is each member somewhat dependent on the others?
6. *Interaction*—is the group small enough to allow face-to-face communication between members?[11]

Groups may, then, be viewed as systems or interdependent subsystems. They are "a set of units bound by a definable context within which the component units interact with each other."[12] Groups are open and dynamic, having a multiplicity of purposes, functions, and objectives. B. Aubrey Fisher developed an Interact System Model to describe the sequence of phases that groups experience. This concept depicts group activity as a continually evolving process moving through four phases of decision emergence—orientation, conflict, emergence, and reinforcement.[13]

The first phase is *orientation* and is characterized by large amounts of clarification and agreement. It reduces uncertainty and allows disagreements to be aired without disturbing the peace. The clash of opinions, formation of coalitions and solidification of roles occurs during the second phase, *conflict.* The move to phase three, *emergence,* is more prolonged but eventually the group attains a unanimity of opinion. This is the longest-lasting phase. Finally, phase four, *reinforcement,* serves to build solidarity and real agreement among members. These phases describe groups moving through a developmental process. Bruce Tuckman and Mary Ann Jensen further confirmed Fisher's view when they synthesized previous research and concluded that groups go through a developmental cycle of forming, storming, norming, performing, and adjourning.[14]

Although many theorists accept this classical view of group development which assumes that all groups follow the same sequence of phases, a growing number of researchers are examining a multiple-sequence model. A *multiple-sequence model* suggests that groups do not pass through a uniform, graded sequence of stages en route to a decision or problem solution, but rather that different groups can experience different developmental sequences. It assumes that the stages are not distinct and groups do not necessarily progress in the same fixed sequences. From this perspective, ideas may be introduced, anchored, shelved, and readvanced in a group's halting progress toward a final solution. Consequently, various orderings of phases are possible depending on the group.[15] Whatever the process, groups do experience some cycle of evolving and dissolving.

Small groups involve a mutually motivated aggregate of individuals, cognizant of accepted norms and procedures, orally interacting, purposefully, interdependently, and systematically. Communication in groups is complex with all of the dimensions operating simultaneously and basic dimensions continuously changing during the interaction.

▶ GROUP NORMS, ROLES, AND NETWORKS

The outcomes of small-group problem solving are very much dependent on the group norms that evolve, the group roles performed by members, and the group networks employed. A group is more than a collection of individuals working toward some common purpose; it consists of people who relate to one another in many ways. Each person in a discussion group holds a definite position in relation to the others in the group and together they all work to achieve a group purpose.

Group Norms

Norms are rules or patterns of behavior that develop over time. Edgar Schein defines norms as "a set of assumptions or expectations held by the members of a group or organization concerning what kind of behavior is right or wrong, good or bad, appropriate or inappropriate, allowed or not allowed."[16] Group norms constitute the conventional methods a group uses to deal with both task and interpersonal concerns. According to Muzofer Sherif, every social group, small or large, with some degree of in-group and out-group delineation, has an "organization defining the roles (statuses and functions) of individual members . . . and requires certain conformities in action and aspiration from the individuals who belong. All this is determined or regulated by a set of standards or norms of the group."[17] Groups develop norms about a variety of activities and events, such as meeting times, attendance, leadership, and rules of order governing participation. The norms may be formal or informal, explicit or implicit. The former often take the shape of written bylaws to a constitution or a statement of standard operating procedures; the latter are transferred from established group members to newcomers by word of mouth. Thus, the new member will be wise to identify group norms and wait until they become evident before charging into meetings with ideas, suggestions, and particularly with recommendations for change.

Norms do not emerge on their own, but are the products of the group. Consequently, groups maintain and perpetuate norms through indoctrination and enforcement. Indoctrination consists of socializing new members in the ways of the group and against those group members who violate group norms—fail to conform. John Wenburg and William Wilmot have identified five sequential steps taken by groups to handle deviants:

1. Delay action (do nothing and hope that the member will automatically "get back in line");
2. Talk among themselves and use light humor with the deviant;
3. Ridicule the deviant (recognizing his/her behavior as different and shameful);
4. Apply "serious" persuasion (severe criticism or even threats); and
5. Ignore, isolate, and finally reject the deviant.[18]

Whether formal and explicit or informal and subtle, all groups include procedures for indoctrinating new members to group norms and for enforcing adherence to them. The more closely a group conforms to its norms, attitudes, and values, the more cohesive it is. Cohesiveness is a process in which group members are attracted to each other, motivated to remain together, and share a common perspective of the group's activities.

A natural consequence of group norms, then, is conformity of member behavior. Conformity can contribute to the development of group cohesiveness, but it does not exist without certain liabilities. The desire for conformity can lead to group pressure being exerted on members who hold dissenting opinions. Stewart Tubbs and Sylvia Moss, in summarizing studies of conformity research on individuals distinguish between private acceptance of a judgment or opinion and public compliance; i.e., between whether people change their thinking as a result of hearing opinions different from their own or whether they say they agree with the group when in fact they disagree. Public compliance usually results from a desire to avoid social pressures and the unpleasantness of conflict. Individual characteristics of compliance reveal dependence, need for social approval, and a lack of self-confidence. The influence of conformity is increased when members have a high degree of salience toward the group—a perception of the importance of the group and the personal desire of members to belong to a particular group.

Conformity can also affect group behavior in a number of ways. One effect of conformity is a tendency for members to increase their individual willingness to assume risks as a result of group activity. This inclination away from conservatism and toward risk taking when in groups is referred to as the *risky-shift phenomenon*. Several explanations have been proposed ranging from the suggestion that Western culture values risk taking over conservative behavior to the possibilities that members arguing in favor of risk taking are more persuasive or that the diffusion of responsibility among the group members promotes risky actions. Although research findings seem to agree that the risky-shift phenomenon is real, some exceptions have been noted in the group behaviors of managers and executives tackling business-related problems. In these instances, a measure of individual decision making proves to be more risk oriented than the endproduct(s) of small groups involved in the same task(s). When queried, such managers and executives express a willingness to personally accept the responsibilities of risky decisions and their accompanying praise, rewards, or punishments. However, when acting as a part of a group, there is reticence to impose undue risk on or jeopardize the other group members. Consequently, groups in organizational settings may not necessarily experience the risky-shift phenomenon to the same extent as groups in other settings.

A second effect of conformity on groups is the Pollyanna-Nietzsche effect. The *Pollyanna-Nietzsche effect* refers to the overwhelming belief by group members that their solution is indeed the "best" and will work flawlessly. Certainly, the energy and commitment required of group members along with agreements made through consensus contribute to explaining this effect. However, effective group problem solving does not always produce finely tuned solutions, and perhaps there are even better alternatives that have not been advanced or considered. Groups must carefully evaluate the implementation of any solution and constantly be vigilant to other alternatives. Problem solving is often an ongoing activity.

Finally, Irving Janis has been studying for a number of years a phenomenon he calls "groupthink." *Groupthink* is "a mode of thinking that people engage in when they are deeply involved in a cohesive in-group, when the members' strivings for unanimity override their motivation to realistically appraise alternative causes of action."[19] It occurs only when cohesiveness is high and represents a "deterioration of mental efficiency, reality testing, and moral judgment that results from group pressure."[20] Janis is convinced that a group's cohesiveness can make their desire for conformity exceed their task interest to reach a high-quality decision. Discussion members are troubled by conflict, doubts, and worry, and consequently seek complete concurrence without regard for the decision(s) at hand. Examples of groupthink include the failure to prepare for the Japanese attack on Pearl Harbor, the Bay of Pigs invasion, and the disastrous helicopter attempt to rescue the Iranian hostages.

Although Janis sees groups that are highly attractive to group members as especially prone to making bad policy decisions, he doesn't believe that all cohesive groups end up succumbing to groupthink. Groups can take the following positive steps to avoid groupthink[21]:

▶ The leader should be impartial and avoid endorsing any position until after complete, active discussion by all participants who act as "skeptical generalists."
▶ The leader should instruct everyone to critically evaluate ideas and encourage the expression of objections and doubts.
▶ One or two group members may be appointed as devil's advocates; playing the role of critical evaluators, they guarantee "hard-look" assessments of cherished ideas and proposed plans.
▶ The group may, from time to time, be subdivided to work separately on the same question and to air their differences.
▶ Outside experts may occasionally be invited to attend meetings and provide interpretive insights.

Implementation of these suggestions prevents easy consensus and can help close-knit groups avoid making terrible decisions—becoming victims of groupthink.

Group Roles

Every member of a discussion group will perform a variety of functions; the profile of all these functions and the relative frequency of each in relation to the behaviors of other members describes one's group role. Group roles are most often classified into one of three broad categories: (1) task roles, (2) group-building and -maintenance roles, and (3) individual self-serving roles. In 1948, Kenneth Benne and Paul Sheats explained these communication roles in their classic article, "Functional Roles of Group Members."[22]

Task behaviors are purpose oriented and refer to goal-related activities serving the accomplishment of the group's objectives:

1. The *initiator-contributor* suggests or proposes to the group new ideas or an alternative way of regarding the group problem or goal.
2. The *information seeker* asks for authoritative information and facts pertinent to the problem being discussed and seeks clarification of suggestions.
3. The *opinion giver* asks for a clarification of the values pertinent to what the group is undertaking or of the values involved in a suggestion made or in alternative suggestions.
4. The *information giver* offers facts or generalizations that are authoritative or relates his or her own pertinent experiences to the group problem.
5. The *opinion seeker* states his or her beliefs or opinions as they relate to a suggestion made or to alternative suggestions.
6. The *elaborator* spells out suggestions in terms of examples, offers a rationale for suggestions previously made, and tries to deduce how an idea or suggestion would work if adopted by the group.
7. The *coordinator* clarifies the relationships among various ideas and suggestions, tries to pull ideas and suggestions together, and generally works to coordinate the activities of various members or subgroups.
8. The *orienter* defines the position of the group with respect to its goals by summarizing what has occurred, pointing to all departures from agreed-on directions or goals, and raising questions about the direction the group discussion is taking.
9. The *evaluator-critic* examines the group's accomplishments and critically subjects them to some standard or set of standards functioning in the context of the group task.
10. The *energizer* prods the group to action and stimulates or arouses the group to greater or higher-quality problem solving.
11. The *procedural technician* expedites group movement by doing things for the group, such as performing routine tasks.
12. The *recorder* writes down suggestions, maintains a record of group decisions, and generally serves as the "group memory."

Group-building and -maintenance behaviors maintain cooperative interpersonal relationships, cohesiveness, and a group-centered orientation. They contribute to the social well-being of the group:

1. The *encourager* praises, agrees with, and accepts the contributions of others.
2. The *harmonizer* mediates the differences among other members, attempts to reconcile disagreements, and works to relieve tension in conflict situations.

► DeBONO'S SIX HATS

(A thinking strategy developed by Dr. Edward DeBono of the International Center for Creative Thinking)

By Sheila Wright

To become a better thinker, try to separate positive from negative thoughts and recognize that maybe you are limited in your expression of certain thoughts based on your previous categorization.

Example: In a meeting environment do you suppress certain creative ideas because you have the reputation of being strictly a left-brained practical thinker?

Dr. DeBono has assigned 6 imaginary hats, each a different color, to the different types of thoughts we are capable of entertaining.

Here's how it works: You are conducting a meeting and would like to have everyone's total participation. By assigning the entire group a particular color hat, you can then solicit a specific type of thought on one project.

Once you are familiar with each color hat and what each represents, you can orchestrate your meeting with confidence. For example, you might say, "Regarding the cookware project, let's all put on a green hat and think of as many creative food combinations as possible." Or, "Now let's switch to a white hat."

If you use the hats from time to time while conducting meetings, your attendees will become familiar with each color hat and will know immediately what response you are soliciting without your reminder.

White hat: objective thinking. *White—neutral, objective.*

While wearing the white hat, you concentrate on the facts. You can also point out any gaps in information presented. White-hat thinking does not involve arguments, views or opinions.

Red hat: feelings. *Red—fire, anger, emotions.*

While you wear the red hat, you can express hunches and intuitive feelings. You may not be able to explain your feelings as they may be based on experiences you can't put your finger on.

In many discussions, particularly in business, we're not supposed to include our feelings, but we put them in anyway disguised as logic. The red hat lets us express our feelings openly.

Black hat: caution. *Black—gloomy, negative, the color of a judge's robe.*

While wearing the black hat, you can think about logical negatives—why something is illegal, why it won't work, why it won't be profitable, why it doesn't fit the fact or experience. It is sometimes important to consider the negative outcomes of a particular project.

Wearing the black hat allows attendees to contribute along those lines without being viewed personally as negative.

Yellow hat: logical, positive thoughts. *Yellow—sunny, positive.*

While you wear the yellow hat you must be logical. Here's an example. Your department is moving to another building. Yellow-hat thinking involves looking at logical considerations—plenty of electrical outlets for all the computers? Controlled thermostat? Proper distance between the shared printer and each workstation? Just saying that it would be nice to have a change is red-hat thinking.

Green hat: creativity. *Green—grass, fertile growth, energy.*

While wearing the green hat, you are free to generate new ideas, alternatives and possibilities. Right-brained creative folks thrive here.

Let's say you are conducting a marketing strategies meeting. You ask everyone to put on the green hat and contribute only wild, crazy, and off-the-wall ideas for new products. Could this be how the hula hoop was born?

In normal discussion it's very difficult to slip in creative ideas. Wearing the green hat is a way of making off-the-wall ideas acceptable.

Blue hat: objective overview. *Blue—cool, the color of a clear sky, which is above all else.*

The blue hat allows you as a meeting facilitator or an attendee to select one of the other five hats to wear. It's like controlling the direction of the conversation. A blue-hat statement would be, "We haven't gotten anywhere by being logical. Putting on my blue hat, I suggest we have some red-hat thinking to clear the air."

Wearing the blue hat lets you lay out your goals, evaluate how far you've gotten, summarize the results and reach a conclusion.

A tip for using the hats: Make sure that every idea that is brought up is analyzed under each hat. Once you've narrowed your options down to three or four, go back and do one more yellow- and black-hat check on each. At the end of this process you will have a well-thought-out plan of what you want to do.

Source: Sheila Wright, "DeBono's Six Hats," *Network Orange* (November/December 1991): 6.

3. The *compromiser* operates from within a conflict in which his or her idea or position is involved and displays a willingness to come halfway to move the group toward a mutually satisfying solution.
4. The *gatekeeper and expediter* maintains the flow of communication by keeping communication channels open and encouraging or facilitating the participation of others.
5. The *standard setter* expresses standards for the group to achieve in its functioning or applies standards in evaluating the quality of group processes.
6. The *group observer and commentator* keeps records of various aspects of the group process and, along with proposed interpretations, feeds such data back into the group's evaluation of its own procedures.
7. The *follower* goes along with the movement of the group, more or less passively accepting the ideas of others.

Individual self-serving behaviors satisfy only personal needs and consequently inhibit task progress as well as group building and maintenance. These are dysfunctional activities that thwart group activity:

1. The *aggressor* expresses disapproval of the values, acts, or feelings of others and attacks the group or the problem it is tackling.
2. The *blocker* is pessimistic and stubbornly resistant.
3. The *recognition seeker* works in various ways to call attention to himself or herself by boasting, reporting on personal achievements, or acting in unusual ways. Often these people arrive 10 or 15 minutes late and make a grand entrance.
4. The *self-confessor* uses the opportunity that the group setting provides to express personal, non–group-oriented feelings, insights, or ideologies.
5. The *clown* displays his or her lack of involvement in the group's process by disrupting the group and refusing to take ideas seriously.
6. The *dominator* tries to assert authority or superiority by manipulating the group or certain of its members.
7. The *help seeker* tries to call forth "sympathy" responses from other members or from the whole group.
8. The *special-interest pleader* speaks for the "small businessperson," "the grassroots community," or some other specific interest, usually cloaking his or her own biases and prejudices in the stereotypes that best fit individual needs.
9. The *philosopher* focuses attention on his or her knowledge and persists in discussing abstract, theoretical issues.
10. The *storyteller* insists on relating personal experiences and uses the group situation to reminisce.

A number of additional obstructive roles have been identified and labeled. James McBurney and Kenneth Hance describe such role-players in discussion groups as "Mr. Pontifical," "Mr. Doom," "Mr. Smug," "Mr. Milquetoast," "Mr. Wordy," "Mr. Lunatic Fringe," and "Mr. Suspicious."[23] Also writing in the 1950s, William Sattler and Ed Miller add to the list such undesirable participants as "Mr. Orator," "Mr. Fearful," "Mr. Isolate," "Mr. Contrary," and "Mr. Emotional Antagonist."[24] You can probably further expand this list from your group experiences.

The recommendation should be clear: observe, identify, and analyze the task and maintenance roles, and expand your participatory flexibility. Practice a wide range of roles and choose those activities that are constructive rather than obstructive to the group process.

Group Networks

Group interaction may also be viewed from a network perspective. Networks are formal or informal communication patterns linking three or more members together. Network analysis is one of the best ways to examine the flow of messages within and throughout the organization and to assess the discussion effectiveness of small groups. Frequently used networks are the wheel, chain, Y, circle, and all-channel networks (see Exhibit 10-1).[25]

Looking at these visual representations, we immediately see the degree to which they are *centralized* or *decentralized*—the two principal characteristics of their design. Centrality refers to the degree to which all messages must flow through a single position or linkage in the network. In the wheel all messages must flow through the person occupying the middle position; he or she usually becomes the leader as a result of the high degree of centrality. The Delphi technique in which group members never meet face to face would be an example of the centralized network, as would the Y or chain. In contrast, the circle has low centrality because each person sends and receives in either direction with no one person occupying the center, and in the all-channel network all communication lines are open. Most face-to-face problem-solving groups would represent one of these networks.

Research findings show that differences in the degree of interconnectedness or centrality in each of these networks result in different effects on the group process and product. Highly centralized networks inherently possess a greater propensity for leadership and organization, resulting in faster task performance with the fewest

▶ **EXHIBIT 10-1**
Group Networks

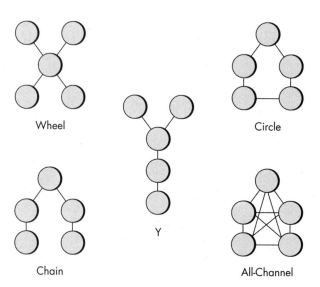

Wheel   Y   Circle

Chain   All-Channel

number of errors. Low-centrality communication networks, although seemingly more disorganized and unstable, reveal increases in group morale and prove most efficient when the group must solve complex rather than simple problems. Because organizations more frequently treat complex problems that require high group morale, it seems that decentralized, more fully connected networks would have certain advantages. Their open, sharing, and democratic procedures permit extensive message exchange and give them certain benefits that contemporary organizations are seeking. They enhance the exchange and management of information, contributing to a more cooperative environment and a more creative outcome.[26]

▶ FUNCTIONS OF GROUPS IN ORGANIZATIONS

Within any organization one usually finds a number of groups that exist to maintain and further the objectives of the larger organization. Organizations are composed of both formal groups and informal groups. Formally organized groups are those whose members have been assigned to permanent or temporary task groups to achieve some specific organizational goal(s). All organizations also have informal work groups that naturally emerge to satisfy individual needs not met by the formal networks. The former are primarily task oriented; the latter satisfy socioemotional needs. Gerald Goldhaber categorizes some small-group activities found in many different, complex organizations according into two categories:

Formal Small-Group Activities

- ▶ Quality circles
- ▶ Brainstorming sessions
- ▶ Decision-making meetings
- ▶ Orientation session(s)
- ▶ Training programs
- ▶ Regular department meetings
- ▶ Directors or executive meetings
- ▶ Special purpose meetings (crisis, budget, safety)
- ▶ Interdepartmental meetings
- ▶ Roundtable discussions

- ▶ Advisory councils
- ▶ Committee meetings (regular and ad hoc)
- ▶ Counseling groups
- ▶ Transactional analysis groups
- ▶ Conferences
- ▶ Problem-solving sessions
- ▶ Information-sharing meetings
- ▶ Sales meetings
- ▶ Labor and management negotiations

Informal Small-Group Activities

- ▶ Informal meetings
- ▶ Rap sessions
- ▶ Luncheons
- ▶ Coffee breaks
- ▶ Grapevine
- ▶ Retreats and informal conferences

- ▶ Bowling and golf teams (or similar social groups)
- ▶ Gripe sessions
- ▶ Social events (picnics, meals, family nights)[27]

You will notice a preponderance of formal group activities and these do by necessity occupy more of one's time, but it would be a mistake to diminish the importance of informal group activities. Research indicates that an organization with strong informal groups will be more effective than an organization with weak ones. Moreover, needs not met by formal and informal groups will create frustration and disrupt organizational objectives,[28] so, rather than existing apart from the larger construct, these two types of groups are an integrated part of the total organizational system.

Researchers in group dynamics are in general agreement that every group serves one of two primary functions: it is either task oriented or essentially socioemotional/personal. This division is neither exhaustive nor mutually exclusive, but it does reflect the group process and serves as a helpful way of viewing the basic functions of groups in organizations.

Task Purposes

Task purposes are goal centered, objective, and impersonal in nature. In organizations, group tasks are usually assigned by the larger organization. However, the origin of tasks may also be internal to the group, being created by the group's leadership or by the members of the group itself. Task functions in small groups include decision making and problem solving, informing, appraising, creating interest, and stimulating creativity.

Decision Making and Problem Solving. One of the most important and pervasive purposes of small-group activity is that of decision making and problem solving. All groups, regardless of specific purpose, must make a multitude of decisions involving the process of the group, the subject matter of the discussion, and the people in the group—decisions made by group members alone and in concert with one another. The solving of a problem requires that many specific decisions be made relative to the nature of the problem, the criteria for a solution, possible solutions, the selection of a best solution, and its implementation. Problem solving requires that participants agree on a cause of action and make a number of decisions.

Informing. This purpose for discussion is also very prevalent. Almost all military staff meetings, many business and professional groups, and many student and faculty committees perceive themselves as essentially information or advisory groups. Such groups keep important people informed or consulted, and may also serve an orientation or learning purpose. Further, they can provide a public information service when an external audience is involved. These groups are distinguished from other task-oriented groups because of the peculiar forces operating on the members. They gather data, examine the nature of the problem, and may even generate and debate the merits of possible solutions, but they do not have the power to make any definitive decisions, although they are usually affected by any final decision. In effect, these groups recommend solutions to problems and people at higher levels make the final decisions.

Appraising. Some groups are organized primarily for the purpose of examining a situation, such as fact-finding boards, committees of inquiry, investigating committees, and juries. Congressional investigating committees, a fact-finding commission charged to investigate a labor–management dispute or accident, management consultants called in to conduct a corporate survey, and grand juries are all representative of this group function. Appraisal may either take place before the fact, in which case it is proactive and a prelude to policy formation, or after the fact, in which case it is reactive and intended to set a value judgment on something that has happened.

Appraisal groups recommend action(s) to be taken or decisions to be made as a result of their investigations and, like information groups, are not or are seldom directly responsible for the final decision. Moreover, group members often are not directly affected by the final decision(s).

Creating Interest. Public discussion is often used to stimulate interest in important and timely questions or to activate others. In the first instance, experts present relevant information about a significant problem and discuss representative solutions. Although they may not agree on a final solution, the listeners become more aware of the problem and investigate it further. In the second instance, the group's task is primarily to recruit people and mobilize resources necessary for completing a particular project. Here, attention is given to persuading people to assume the necessary responsibilities and motivating them to act.

Stimulating Creativity. A final task function is to stimulate creativity and new ideas, with hope to deriving new solutions to specified problems. Advertising agencies, marketing departments, and sales divisions as well as legislative staffs, fundraising associations, and curriculum-development committees are typical examples of this group function.

Socioemotional/Personal Purposes

Socioemotional or *personal purposes* have their origins primarily within the individual and relating most directly to the satisfaction of self-centered needs or drives. People may also enter groups to seek personal satisfaction, to resolve personal need discrepancies, and to achieve a sense of psychological equilibrium. These groups are social, cathartic, consultative, educational, and therapeutic in nature.

Social. People in organizations engage in group discussion for what are primarily social purposes. Discussions over coffee, casual talk in the hall, and talk of sports in an elevator are examples of such discussions. Individual goals may range from passing the time to deliberately trying to strengthen interpersonal relationships, promote status, or secure goodwill. The substance of most social discussions is of little moment, but such social discussion is often the prelude to considerations of more significant subjects.

Cathartic. This discussion function provides personal support through interpersonal dialogue. The intent is to allow people an opportunity to relieve their tensions, fears, gripes, apprehensions, and aspirations in a group. Bull sessions or counseling interviews are examples of such discussions. One should not dismiss cathartic discussion lightly because an invitation to "get things off your chest" is one which most people need and often seek.

Consultative. Employee counseling has come to occupy a very important function in today's organization. The current state of competition for attracting qualified personnel has resulted in an increased concern on the part of business to make every effort to reduce turnover and retain productive employees. It is in this capacity that counseling plays a major role. Employee counseling is a management function intended to satisfy personal needs and encourage individual growth and development through honest and rational discourse. Unlike cathartic discussions, employee counseling seeks to accomplish more than a reduction of frustration; it aims to increase individual potential and in so doing increase organizational productivity. Although counseling is most often a dyadic process, it can involve a number of people from a department or a number of line employees.

Educational. Certainly an important function performed by groups and one of the principal reasons for participating in groups is the opportunity to learn. Group members join together and participate in discussion intended to expand their thinking and develop new skills. Probably the class you are now taking uses discussion as a primary instrument for learning. Orientation sessions and training workshops in many businesses may also be considered learning groups. Other examples include professional seminars or conferences and public symposia.

Therapeutic. The aim of the therapeutic discussion is to help alter people's attitudes, feelings, or behavior about some aspect of their lives. These discussions may be distinguished from cathartic and consultative group functions in that a highly skilled professional facilitator is needed to remedy the specific personal difficulties. Thus, this group function comes under the heading of psychotherapy or psychiatric treatment.

Common Work Groups

We have identified certain task and socioemotional functions performed by groups. Earlier we said that organizations comprise many different formal and informal groups. Some of the specific work groups functioning in organizations include work teams, quality circles, study circles, management committees, focus groups, task force groups, and steering committees.

Work Teams. Organizational life, by necessity, involves us with work teams composed of a supervisor or director and our peers. Such teams vary in size and formality. Some work closely together, others meet infrequently to exchange information. Work teams may be long-standing with permanently defined responsibilities and few changes in membership, or project specific, formed around the technical specialties of other members of the organization. The latter are of short duration and must quickly clarify goals, roles, and responsibilities in order to establish effective working relationships.[29] Carl Larson and Frank LaFasto identify three features common to the members of effective work teams: (1) the possession of needed skills or abilities, (2) a desire to contribute, and (3) the capability of collaborating with others.[30]

Quality Circles. Probably no issue in contemporary American management is more prominent than that of worker participation as it relates to productivity. The success of the Japanese use of quality circles has led American managers to study the procedures in depth and implement such processes in American industry. Developed by W. Edwards Deming, quality circles are small groups of workers who voluntarily meet on a regular basis to discuss questions of quality, productivity, and output.

Groups from the same general area select their own facilitator and meet on company time in a company location. The success of these groups requires considerable commitment throughout the organization so that managers and executives will be open to the recommended solutions from the groups and able to implement those solutions that can be effective in meeting problems. It is important that the workers not perceive quality circles as a management ploy to cut the workforce by increasing productivity.[31] General Electric, General Motors, Kaiser Aluminum, Westinghouse, and Motorola are only a few of the corporations that have documented increased productivity and worker satisfaction as a result of using quality circles.[32]

Study Circles. Developed in Scandinavia, some corporations use study circles in which personal as well as employers' needs and interests are discussed. Study circle participants decide what they will discuss, where to meet, the materials, the resources, the learning plans, and the problem-solving methods. In study circles there is a lack of structured discussion and no authority figure. The results, according to those who have observed study groups in operation, are well worth the investment of time, resources, and effort.[33]

Management Committees. Management committees use the talents of employees while building a strong spirit of cooperation and shared goals. The 8 to 15 members handle organizationwide concerns on a regular basis. For example, a computer/management committee may interact with automation vendors, prepare companywide procedure manuals, and conduct computer training. The newsletter committee would be responsible for writing, designing, and printing the in-house newsletter. Other committees, such as a company committee and social planning committee, could also be formed. These are not business-planning committees nor do they play any part in managing the daily work-flow. Rather, they have limited responsibilities and draw from across the organization. Committee assignments are rotated and no employee can serve on more than one committee. They represent a team effort that can "bring out the best in employees" and lead to the "development of a self-disciplined, self-motivated staff."[34]

Focus Groups. Focus groups bring people together at a central location to probe intensively for qualitative data related to specific problem areas or to react to proposed courses of action. Group members discuss problems openly and provide useful information. The interaction in focus groups is multiplicative, with each member becoming a richer source of information than he or she would be alone. To be successful, the facilitator must serve as a catalyst generating different viewpoints and uncovering reasons behind opinions rather than just discovering the opinions themselves.[35] Focus groups are frequently used by marketing and advertising professionals to gather information.

Task Force Groups. Task force groups bring diverse organizational members from the various operational divisions together for the purpose of strategic planning. They are study groups given specific responsibilities by management to make recommendations regarding organizational change. To be effective, group members must agree that change is needed and must work cooperatively toward the organizationwide objectives and projected vision.[36]

Steering Committees. Steering committees are similar to task force groups in their composition, but their charge is to implement organizational plans and processes for change. They direct, oversee, and evaluate the progress of plans, goals, programs, and mission. To be successful, steering committees must have the authority and power to strategically promote and manage change. Forward-looking companies proactively use task force groups and steering committees for organizational development (OD) or planned change.[37]

Regardless of the nature of the group or its purpose, it is only through the interaction of its members that groups can become effective. To encourage interaction, a number of discussion techniques have been devised and can be used in conjunction with the various types of groups.

▶ TYPES OF GROUPS IN ORGANIZATIONS

The types of groups used in organizations and selected for conducting discussions vary with the group's purpose, the question being discussed, and the people involved (see Exhibit 10-2). Traditional discussion formats used in the organizational setting include the panel, roundtable, colloquy, symposium, brainstorming, case discussion, role-playing, and encounter self-development training.[38]

Panel

The panel is usually a public discussion in which a small group of experts or well-informed people examine some problem or issue in a free, direct exchange of ideas. The distinctive feature of the panel is the communication pattern. Participants engage in an open conversational interchange that can be lively and extemporaneous. Informality is the keynote and the members of the group can freely interrupt one another. This freedom can be both a virtue and a liability to the panel format. The panel is designed to solve problems, arrive at a consensus, and illuminate

▶ EXHIBIT 10-2
Types, Patterns, and Purposes of Groups

TYPE	PATTERN	PURPOSE
Panel	Open, direct, public or private exchange of ideas	Problem solving
Roundtable	Closed, investigative exploration of ideas	Understanding
Colloquy	Open, public exchange involving lay members and experts	Information sharing
Symposium	Controlled, public exchange of opinions of experts	Information gathering
Brainstorming	Noncritical, nonjudgmental generation of ideas	Creativity
Case discussion	Collaborative exploration of real/hypothetical situations	Teaching/learning
Role-playing	Participants enact varying roles in a "safe" environment	Attitude development
Encounter self-development training	Intense awareness encounters with others	Self-improvement

ideas. Panelists are usually chosen because they can supply needed information for well-informed discussion or because they represent views held by members of a larger group. The panel is also suitable for problem solving in less-public discussion situations.

Example: Economists, bankers, and government representatives meet to discuss the problem of a sluggish economy and, specifically, interest rates, mortgages, and the availability of money. There is an audience composed of the national press corps and interested people; additionally, the discussion is being carried on C-Span so the audience is significantly increased. Participants follow an agenda but engage in a free exchange of ideas. Although they disagree on a particular solution, they do reach an agreement on certain guidelines that might facilitate a solution. The discussion has been characterized by an active exchange or interchange.

Roundtable

The roundtable is usually a closed-group, enlightenment discussion in which participants with a common problem enter into a free exchange of ideas for the purpose of learning from each other. Said to have originated with King Arthur and the Knights of the Round Table (although whether this is fact or legend is uncertain), this type of discussion encourages a climate of equality and is used extensively in small decision-making groups and small learning groups. The purpose is to increase understanding about ways of approaching and investigating a problem that influences all of the involved members.

Example: The district supervisors of Southland Corporation meet to discuss a problem common to all Seven-Eleven stores in the area—the high rate of employee turnover. It is noted that the problem is not new and each describes current attempts to resolve it. Finally, solutions are advanced with the supervisors agreeing that increased attention should be given to applicant screening, working conditions, and job enrichment. Additionally, a study should be conducted relative to this problem. The discussion has been freewheeling and open, allowing all participants to voice their ideas.

Colloquy

The colloquy is an arrangement similar to the panel, intimately involving an audience and a platform of experts. Originally involving the reporting of information by experts and then questioning by an audience, an alternative format has evolved using a lay panel and a selected panel of experts. Although knowledgeable professionals formerly gave direction to the discussion, in the new format the lay panel prepares and directs the discussion with experts adding necessary information on request or as needed. This format was originally created to work out problems, but it has become essentially an information-sharing process.

Example: The area CETA planner, knowledgeable about minority training programs, meets with lay members of a Public Industrial Council representing a large midwestern city. The meeting is open to the public and addresses the allocation of training funds. The Council and members of business and industry developed the agenda, and the CETA planner serves as a resource person answering questions relative to career availability and governmental guidelines.

Symposium

The symposium also resembles the panel in that it is a public discussion, but participants present a prepared talk on one area or phase of the discussion question. Usually, group members are chosen because they are acknowledged authorities in their fields, representing particular positions on a problem or possessing special competence, expertise, or information relative to the issue. Following the prepared presentations, the gathered experts may question one another or questions might be asked by another group of interrogators. The symposium is less spontaneous and more formal than other formats, but the questions and answers add a measure of spontaneity. The symposium is very much an information-gathering process rather than a problem-solving endeavor. It usually precedes problem solving.

Example: Experts from the Department of Agriculture, Soil Conservation Service and Agricultural Stabilization Agency, and the Army Corps of Engineers meet in west Texas to discuss the water shortage with county commissioners. The respective authorities in their fields give prepared presentations outlining the gravity of the problem and they advance potential remedies, given their specialized areas. During the ensuing discussion, there is general agreement that action must be taken soon to ensure an adequate water supply for the future. The county commissioners later meet to develop specific recommendations for their local jurisdiction based on the information gathered from the involved experts.

Brainstorming

Brainstorming is a type of small-group effort to encourage the free exchange of ideas and solutions leading to creativity and innovation. It is a creative problem-solving approach developed in the late 1930s by Alex F. Osborn, a New York advertising executive. The brainstorming procedure follows a definite structure intended to produce many ideas or alternatives by reducing some of the inhibitory influences normally associated with small groups. The basic premise is that a large list of potential alternatives increases the probability of achieving an effective solution.

Brainstorming, as a device for stimulating the production of ideas, involves two stages and is based on the observance of a few fundamental rules. During the first stage, the facilitator appoints a recorder to write down all ideas, then briefly explains the problem, which should be limited, specific, and restricted in scope. Members then suggest possible solutions. It is at this point that certain rules must be rigorously enforced to avoid some of the weaknesses of conventional problem-solving groups. The following rules permit creative idea generation without fear of censure.

1. No criticism! There is no such thing as a bad idea. Criticism contributes to a negative atmosphere that results in self screening and inhibits the generation of ideas.
2. The more ideas the better. Be patient and push participants. Often the best ideas only emerge after the participants have been going for a time and are even slightly weary. Initially members are skimming the familiar and superficial ideas off the surface of their minds and only after these are listed do their brains really get busy and begin to think creatively.
3. The wilder, the better. Encourage free-wheeling and welcome the unconventional. Don't permit questions or discussion regarding ideas because this focuses the group's attention on a particular idea and prevents the exploration of other

> ▶ **BRAINSTORMING REALLY CAN WORK**
>
> At my previous employment, I had the opportunity to attend brainstorming sessions. My first one was a three-day event, held in a remote location with approximately one-fourth of the company attending. We were seated in a large conference room at a horseshoe-shaped table. In the middle of the room, one of the vice presidents conducted the session.
>
> Using a flip-chart and markers, he would write the heading of the topic to discuss. We were to spurt off any idea that came to mind. Each piece of paper would then be hung on the outer walls. At first, people were quite afraid of saying anything for fear of humiliation. The president and owner of the company was present, which had a way of intimidating you. However, around midday of the first day, people had forgotten who was there and were spilling off anything that came to mind. Many unique answers were given. Of course, no answer was considered bad, but you could always tell when the group didn't like it—there was dead silence. On the other hand, when an approving answer was given, you could hear the group members chatter, "Oh, that's pretty good."
>
> By the end of the third day, we were all pretty burned-out with ideas and creativity. My only thoughts were how much longer would we go on with this. However, after it was over, seeing how this type of session is performed was an enlightening experience; a very unique style of group meeting for problem solving. The advantage with using this format was that it allowed for some interesting ideas to be generated. I guess brainstorming really can work.
>
> ───────────────────────────────
>
> Source: Student journal entry, Hamilton Holt School of Rollins College, Winter Park, FL, Fall 1991.

alternatives. Uninhibited thinking leads to unique solutions. Remember, it is easier to tame a wild idea than to energize a dull one.

4. Hitchhike on each other's ideas. Build on the thoughts of others to produce even better ideas. Everyone is to present new concepts or variations on a theme, even if the original idea was presented by someone else.

5. Employ "plus-ing." Continually add to an idea to make it better. Ask, "What could be altered or added?" Your idea + my idea = WOW!

The second stage of brainstorming examines the list of ideas and the merits of each one's possible implementation. Other ideas may be added to the list during this stage and prior to any critical examination of the relative feasibility of solutions. It is advisable that a different group of people perform this essentially evaluative function because they would be in a better position to analyze ideas objectively and without personal biases or prejudices. Creative decision making and problem solving is necessary for the growth, development, and prosperity of any institution or organization.

Example: Akio Morita and his partners wanted a new name for their developing enterprise that could be recognized anywhere in the world and one that could be pronounced the same in any language. The brainstorming path they took led from "sonus," meaning "sound," to "sunny" and "sonny-bay." "Sonny" (pronounced "sohnnee" in Japanese) means "to lose money" and so was discarded. But take away one letter and you have "Sony," the name carried by the world's number-one brand in a host of products since the introduction of the first transistor radio in 1957.[39]

Case Discussion

The case discussion, popularized by the Harvard School of Business, consists of presenting a discussion group with a description of a situation requiring members to research, analyze, suggest potential solutions, and present final resolutions. Applicable to a wide variety of problems, this format serves principally as a learning device.

Example: A professor in the MBA program at New York University lectures on varying managerial styles. A specific situation involving a superior–subordinate interaction is then outlined. Students are asked to research the problem collaboratively and propose recommendations. Their analysis will be compared with actual solutions to similar situations and used to assess their understanding of basic concepts.

Role-Playing

Role-playing presents a problem situation, assigns appropriate roles, and asks the participants to act out in impromptu fashion the implications of the situation. Members in role-playing assume roles different from and possibly even contradictory to those normally played out in routine daily activity. Because role-playing can be more informal, flexible, and permissive, group members are more relaxed, openly communicating feelings, attitudes, and beliefs that might otherwise be masked. Today it is frequently used as a learning device in education and a training procedure in business and industry. Role-playing helps participants to better understand themselves, to see problems more clearly, and to develop empathy—that is, to gain insight into the ways other people view the world. It can be effective if the situations are clearly presented, a safe environment is created, and the participants fully understand the objective(s).

Example: Sarah Miles, a mid-level manager for Delta Corporation, is participating in a power-negotiation seminar recommended by her supervisor. During the course of the seminar, she is asked to assume the role of a union representative in a contract negotiation situation. While playing this role, Sarah gains an understanding of the pressures experienced by a union representative and an increased awareness of her own behavior. This nonthreatening environment permitted an open disclosure of opinions, attitudes, and beliefs.

Encounter Self-Development Training

Finally, the encounter self-development training group functions in various settings. It may focus on specific training in human relations skills, or on the exploration of past experiences and the dynamics of personal development, or on creative expression. Although the focus may vary, there are certain similar external characteristics. The group, in almost every instance, is small, relatively unstructured, and chooses its own goals and personal directions. The leader's responsibility is primarily to facilitate the expression of both feelings and thoughts on the part of the group members. The dynamics of this type of group are such that it moves from confusion and discontinuity to a climate of trust and support. Group members eventually drop some of their defenses and facades, and relate more directly on a feeling basis with other members of the group. This is an intensive, personally revealing group experience that can contribute to a better understanding of oneself and one's relationships with others. Currently, a number of intensive training programs are being conducted by industries, universities, and churches and synagogues. A word of caution: encounter groups can be dangerous if the facilitators are not trained professionals.

Example: Raymond Thomas, an aspiring manager, is concerned about his lack of assertiveness when dealing with others. He decides to participate in an assertiveness-training program sponsored by the local community college to correct this perceived weakness. The seminar is conducted by a trained psychologist who places Ray and a small group of participants in a number of hypothetical situations requiring them to act assertively. These experiences are then transferred to Ray's work situation.

▶ GROUP TECHNIQUES AND METHODS

"Technique" is defined as the systematic procedure by which a complex or scientific task is accomplished. Synonyms include "skill," "style," "routine," "plan," and "mode." Here we will explore selected interactional modes that can improve group discussion when skillfully applied. These specialized techniques include PERT, buzz groups/Phillips 66 technique, nominal group technique, Delphi procedure, and teleconferencing techniques.

PERT

Problem-solving discussions are a means of working toward a program-end that can be evaluated in terms of how closely it meets desired goals. The worth and merit of the discussion process are measured against the desirability of the program. A quasimathematical procedure called PERT offers a framework for problem solving, program planning, and implementation.[40] This procedure diminishes interpersonal conflict and encourages cooperation and the accomplishment of program goals. PERT (program evaluation and review technique) was introduced by the U.S. Navy in 1958 as a response to some of the problems arising in coordinating activities involved in the Polaris Missile program. It has subsequently been adopted by numerous other government agencies as well as private business concerns because it is well suited to large-scale program planning and management control.

The PERT procedure consists of a group working together to plot a network of the activities that necessarily precede a specific desired outcome or goal. The completed network defines and coordinates what must be done to accomplish the desired goal and reveals weaknesses in the implementation of the plan. PERT enables a planning group to identify potential bottlenecks, to appropriately allocate personnel, to estimate times for operations, to determine starting points for procedures, and to test the total logic of a plan or procedure. Based on the concept of probabilities, the logical structure of a proposed program can be tested in advance, and faulty or unfeasible steps revised or eliminated.[41] The PERT procedure, then, is based on a computer logic providing a step-by-step approach for program development involving the listing, ordering, diagramming, and statistical analysis of necessary events.

Buzz Groups/Phillips 66 Technique

A constant problem when working with large public groups is generating necessary participation. Buzz groups or the Phillips 66 technique are devices frequently used with success in resolving this difficulty. If a group of 20, 40, or more people, for example, is discussing a complex question, a small number of people usually dominate the group activity. But if the audience is divided into small buzz groups that discuss an aspect of the problem for a limited period of time and then report their findings to the whole assembly, involvement is increased. This procedure invites participation and allows all an opportunity to express their ideas.

The Phillips 66 method, originally developed by J. Donald Phillips, requires that the audience be divided into groups of six members and that each group discuss a specific topic for six minutes. This technique differs from buzz groups in that members both discuss a topic or problem and develop pertinent questions. The individual groups raise questions relevant to the discussion topic and the chairperson presents them to the primary discussion group, which then addresses these questions in the presence of the audience. Although buzz groups and the Phillips 66 technique can encourage involvement, they better serve to point up problems than to solve them.[42]

Nominal Group Technique

The nominal group technique, developed by Andre L. Delbecq and Andrew H. Vande Ven in 1968, has been used by organizations in health, social service, education, industry, and government. It is both a problem-solving and idea-generating technique emphasizing the private generation and ranking of solutions according to a rather rigid procedure. The group leader initially presents a statement of the problem to the assembled group and, using this statement as a basis, the group members follow the steps outlined below:

1. Members, individually, write down ideas, options, alternatives, and solutions without any open discussion.
2. Without discussion, members present their ideas to the group in a round-robin fashion and these ideas are recorded on large sheets of paper or a chalkboard for everyone to see.
3. Members may ask another person for clarification of an idea or proposal, but there should be no evaluative discussion or debate for the purpose of arriving at a sense of agreement or disagreement. At this point proposals may be combined or integrated to avoid overlap and reduce the number of possibilities.
4. Members individually rank the various proposed solutions and the results are tallied to determine the relative support for each solution.
5. Members individually vote on the higher-priority ideas until a convergence occurs.

The leadership role is critical to the success of the nominal group technique, for the leader must ensure that the behaviors vital to each step are observed—discouragement of talking, discussion of ideas, and critical observations. This technique permits a high degree of social and emotional involvement among members who might otherwise experience considerable communication anxiety. The nominal group technique has been referred to as "a group in name only."[43]

Delphi Procedure

The Delphi procedure, developed by Norman Dalkey and his associates at the Rand Corporation, was originally devised to help make long-range forecasts under conditions of uncertainty. The procedure as adapted to group problem solving provides an interesting approach because the group members do not have to meet face-to-face. The success of the Delphi process depends on the coordinator(s) and the selection of qualified participants in the problem area. Five basic steps are involved:

1. A question or problem statement is determined and sent to each of the selected participants who write down possible solutions, ideas, and suggestions that are forwarded to the group coordinator(s).
2. Individual ideas are collated and sent to each participant who must then combine and integrate the ideas in a way that seems to make sense and return the results to the group coordinator(s).
3. The proposals are further synthesized and integrated by the group coordinator(s) and then developed into a questionnaire that is sent to all participants.
4. The participants rank-order or rate the proposed solutions and return the questionnaire to the group coordinator(s).
5. Another questionnaire based on the averaged rankings or ratings is sent to all participants for reranking or rating and this procedure continues until convergence occurs and a solution emerges.

The role of the group coordinator(s) is obvious. Those who collect and distribute the information have a high degree of control over the process and its outcome. Still, the Delphi technique has its advantages: (1) it can involve a large number of participants in diverse geographical locations; (2) it prevents social conformity effects in the evaluation of proposals; (3) it circumvents the politics of cliques and subgroups; and (4) it incorporates mathematical group techniques to reach a group judgment, thus reducing the chances for errors in group decision making.[44]

Teleconferencing Techniques

It is estimated that 20 million meetings are held everyday in the U. S. and 80 percent of all meetings last less than 30 minutes.[45] This proliferation of meetings has prompted an increasing interest by business in teleconferencing techniques. Teleconferencing encompasses any form of electronically assisted communication, including: (1) audioconferences where groups of three or more people participate simultaneously by voice alone over a telephone line; (2) videoconferences that use cable, satellite, or microwaves to transmit freeze-frame or full-motion color images of the participants; and (3) computer conferences that connect computer terminals so that participants to all locations can transmit information for immediate access or later retrieval.[46]

Teleconferencing obviously reduces travel costs and improves productivity through reduced travel time, but it also promotes faster decision making which results in shorter and better-organized meetings than those that are held face-to-face.[47] However, is teleconferencing appropriate for problem solving? Are good-quality group decisions made via the teleconference? Research comparing decision quality under conditions of face-to-face and technologically mediated conferences indicates no substantial differences in the quality of decisions. In addition, communication styles were found not to be significantly altered by the presence of teleconferencing. The initial conclusions, then, are that supervisors and subordinates can be involved in decision making via telecommunications rather than being physically present in the same location with no changes occurring in decision quality, communication style, or participant satisfaction.[48] As one teleconferencing participant put it, "If I say something that makes the vice-president mad, at least I've got a 3,000-mile head start."[49]

Many of the guidelines for face-to-face meetings apply to teleconferencing, but there are some that are unique to electronic meetings[50]:

▶ Speakers should be close enough to the microphones to be easily heard.

▶ Participants should be careful to control noise of papers, tapping on tables, nervous coughing, clearing of the throat, and other distracting habits that the microphones will pick up. For the same reason, don't engage in side conversations with others because these will trigger the voice-activated microphones and disrupt the audio transmission.

▶ High-quality graphics must be prepared that fit the television format when using videoconferencing.

▶ Handouts should be sent early enough to be available for an audioconference.

▶ Dress for the camera's eye during videoconferencing and avoid strong patterns that may cause a wavy movement or light colors that bleed into a light-colored background. Neutral tones are preferable.

▶ Participants should be introduced at the start of the meeting and continue to identify themselves as they proceed through the teleconference.

▶ Departures and entrances should be announced.

▶ Participants, especially in videoconferencing, will have to wait until the cameras are turned to them before they participate.

▶ Keep a friendly expression, especially for a freeze-frame setup, because your picture will be transmitted only intermittently and you wouldn't want to be caught with a frown or in the midst of some nervous gesture. Also, try to look both at the camera and at others in your location to avoid glassy-eyed stares.

▶ Limit the agenda because people tire more easily during teleconferencing than they do in face-to-face meetings. The conference should be limited to no more than an hour; if longer, a break should take place.

▶ DECISION MAKING AND PROBLEM SOLVING

We previously defined small groups, identified the functions performed by groups and the reasons why individuals form groups, and explored various group types. We further examined selected techniques that may enhance group performance. And, throughout our discussion, problem solving was singled out as the most prevalent reason for group activity. It deserves even closer attention. Here we address some basic questions pertaining to effective decision making and problem solving: Just what is a problem? How can a problem best be resolved? What are some of the possible outcomes of group problem solving?

Problems and Questions for Discussion

A problem exists when there is a difference between what is currently happening and what the group or organization wants to happen; a difference between actual and desired conditions. Any charge, goal, or mission, whether externally imposed on the group or internally derived, can be viewed as a problem to be solved.

Problem-solving discussions usually begin with a question that expresses the problem. The question should be carefully formulated and frequently reexamined. The following criteria can be useful in formulating the problem-solving question:

- ▶ The problem should be stated as a question. Problem-solving involves answer seeking, so when presented in the form of a question discussion rather than debate can take place.
- ▶ The question should focus on the real problem. All too often discussion questions focus attention on some symptom of a problem; but good problem solving demands questions that focus attention on the causes of the problem. For example, if John, a usually productive employee, is constantly showing up late for work, a group of immediate supervisors might consider discussing the question of "should we fire John?" A better question, getting at the possible causes of the problem, would be "what can be done to motivate John to be prompt and responsible?" The former question limits discussion to a single solution resulting from the group's reacting to symptoms. The latter question permits the group to examine causes and alternative solutions.
- ▶ The scope of the question should be limited. It should specify whose behavior is subject to change. The question should focus attention on the problem and specify the group(s) whose behavior is to be directly affected by the solution. For example, the marketing department may work with production if the question is mutually contiguous, if both groups are directly affected by the solution. This has given rise to teambuilding and many of the common types of work groups previously described.
- ▶ The question should be stated impartially, not suggesting potential solutions. If the question is presented so that agreement or disagreement is asked for, the problem-solving process is short-circuited. Such questions as "should the federal government require private industry to be more responsible to consumer interests?" or "should the federal government require that the closed-shop concept be abolished?" assume the dimensions of a national debate resolution and encourage conflict and polarization. The discussants enter the situation with a view toward accepting or rejecting a particular solution rather than creating a solution to the problem. Better questions for the purposes of problem solving would be "what can private industry do to be more responsive to consumer interest groups?" or "how can the problem of union membership versus no union membership be resolved?" These are open questions. Unfortunately, many questions that purport to stimulate problem solving are phrased so that they include solutions.
- ▶ The question should encompass both the problem and a solution. The question should call for more than a listing but require a complete analysis and a solution to the problem. A problem-solving group should deal with the entirety of the problem.

Determining the question for discussion is a most critical process because of its influence on the nature of the goal(s) and consequently the quality of the solution(s). If the question is ambiguous, lacking definition, discussants will likewise be uncertain of their goal(s) and this uncertainty will be reflected in the end solution(s).

Standard Discussion Procedure

It is to be expected that people who get together as a group for the first time flounder for a while, trying to figure out how best to get the job done. Even established groups assigned new tasks may spend the first couple of meetings interpreting their task and deciding how to proceed. This was noted earlier when we identified the various stages groups inevitably go through. So, after the question for discussion has been appropriately phrased, the next step in small-group problem solving is determining a satisfactory and desirable problem-solving procedure. Procedures have been developed and perfected through use in literally thousands of groups in community, governmental, business, industrial, and educational settings. These procedures include agendas that can be intentionally and rationally used to systematically consider ideas as well as to encourage the maximum involvement of all group members.

The reflective thinking procedure, based on John Dewey's analysis of how people think and how they solve problems, is the most popular pattern for problem-solving discussion and one which is the basis for most alternative problem-solving procedures. In *How We Think*, published in 1910, Dewey coined the term "reflective thinking" which he defined as "active, persistent and careful consideration of any belief or supposed form of knowledge in the light of the grounds that support it, and further conclusions to which it tends."[51] Continuing to equate problem solving with reflective thinking, Dewey identifies five distinct steps: (1) a felt difficulty, (2) its location and definition, (3) suggestion of possible solutions, (4) rational development of the suggestions, and (5) further observation and experimentation leading to acceptance or rejection of a solution. The influence of Dewey's work is evidenced in the development by scholars in the field of the *standard discussion procedure* which helps groups work through problems using the reflective thinking approach. Comprising the following steps, it outlines the course of productive group discussion:

1. *Problem*—statement of the question for discussion, clarification and definition of terms, possible delimiting of the question's scope.
2. *Analysis of the problem*—examination of the history and status quo relating to the problem. What is the background of the problem? Where are we today? Who's involved? Why? To what extent?
3. *Criteria*—establishment of general guidelines for any possible solution. To what ideals, values, principles, requirements must any solution we choose adhere or square?
4. *Possible solutions and evaluation*—solicit and list proposals, and evaluate each. What are the advantages of each proposed solution? What are the limitations or disadvantages of each proposal?
5. *Choosing the best solution*—through group consensus or majority vote, select a solution consistent with the criteria listed and decisions previously reached.
6. *Implementation*—operationalize the selected solution and evaluate its effectiveness.

The standard discussion procedure is particularly useful for ensuring that all people are operating from a common set of definitions and assumptions, have agreed on the nature and extent of the problem, and have established evaluative criteria to use in assessing solutions.

Rational Management Procedure

The *rational management procedure*, developed by C. H. Kepner and B. B. Tregoe, is one of several adaptations of the standard discussion procedure based on the Dewey model that is specifically designed for technical problems in business and industry.[52] Kepner and Tregoe define a problem as a deviation from a standard and identify the nature and extent of the problem by an elaborate set of step-by-step comparisons. The first comparison made is the "should" to the "actual"—that is, the ideal situation to actual conditions. Next, they compare the "musts" with the "wants" to determine those criteria that are required of an effective solution. The boundaries of the problem are located and a final solution arrived at by repeatedly measuring potential solutions against required criteria as well as against desirable criteria. This alternative procedure is particularly useful in arriving at an objective solution because the criteria are weighted by member ratings, thus giving any proposal a quantitative dimension. Often one solution emerges as clearly superior but, if not, the group can select from among equally rated solutions.

If problem solving is to be a rational process, rational procedures must be employed. The standard discussion and rational management procedures can serve as guides or process models to be followed to improve decision making and problem solving. Certainly, the more specific the wording of the question, and the more specific the goal or objective, the easier it is to select a suitable problem-solving mode.

Possible Outcomes of Group Problem Solving

Consensus is one of the most desirable outcomes of interaction in small groups. Consensus refers to a coming together of the minds of those in the group after a period of time, or it denotes general agreement or at least a "willingness to give it a try" among all members of a group concerning a given decision. If consensus can be genuinely achieved, it is valuable because member satisfaction and commitment to action are likely to be stronger than when sharp differences remain. This is important because often the people who help make a decision are those who are also expected to carry it out.

Consensus is not always possible to achieve. The majority vote, where the solution with the greatest support is adopted, represents a frequently used alternative method of decision making. Rupert Cortwright and George Hinds observe that "the ideal outcome of discussion, theoretically, may be consensus, the common high ground of unanimous agreement. This, however, is never to be sought at the price of the slightest coercion of even one member. When discussion does not lead to unanimity within the time limits which are practical, the democratic process calls for decision or action by majority rule. Discussion ought not to become an instrument of endless delay foisted on a majority by a willful minority."[53] Consensus is preferred, but the majority vote is often necessary. It gives members an opportunity to voice their disagreement and allows the group to proceed.

Certainly, the least-desirable methods of arriving at a decision are those involving manipulation. Selected members within a group may form a coalition of interest in order to overpower other members. Although coalitions may be quite successful, they can have disastrous effects on group morale. Also, groups may be railroaded when one or a few influential group members force their will on the entire group. This, of course, is most likely to produce resentment and resistance.

Lastly, there may be no real outcome. Sometimes a group becomes hopelessly and bitterly split; the members see no way to resolve differences and produce a decision that comes close to representing a reasonable majority point of view. The group may have to abandon the project or resort to using outside third parties in mediation and/or arbitration.

► THE STANDARD AGENDA CAN YIELD RESULTS

By Sherry L. Knight

As the litigation legal assistant supervisor, I have many diversified duties. I am responsible for the operation of several different litigation procedures, as well as supervising the three paralegals in my department. One of my duties includes making sure that our docket and case list procedures are working and that the procedures are being followed by everyone in the litigation department. The individuals, two litigation paralegals and the librarian, who are responsible for the day-to-day activity of the case list and docket, came to me complaining of problems with these procedures. They indicated that there was a great potential for information to fall through the cracks because of the poor communication between these individuals and others in the litigation department. It is very important that all cases being worked in litigation are included on the case list, for one reason so that when pleadings or other documents with deadlines come in, the docketing person will know who is assigned to the case and who should receive reminders about the deadline.

We four worked as a group and discussed the various problems with the two systems and how those problems could be resolved. We came to a consensus and developed new forms to be implemented into the system. These forms would help the secretaries, and would make the two procedures operate more efficiently, more accurately and with less time than is presently being consumed.

We prepared our agenda to discuss the new procedures to be implemented; and developed and prepared the forms to be explained and distributed at the next meeting. I set the meeting well in advance, at a time recommended by the personnel director, and I provided doughnuts and coffee.

All but one secretary, who was on vacation, attended the meeting and all of the litigation paralegals were there. We began with my explaining the purpose for the meeting and giving some information about the new changes. I then turned the meeting over to the individuals who work with the two systems to explain the particular problems they are experiencing with communication breakdown among the departments. Initially, the secretaries did not visually appear to be very interested in our problems or proposed solutions but as they became more actively involved in the discussion, their interest increased. I personally tried to emphasize to the group that this had to be a team effort. I tried to help them identify with the problem and realize that they are an integral part of these particular organizational processes.

The secretaries asked questions and received clarification on the new procedures. They also voiced their opinions and made their own suggestions as to how these two departments could operate more efficiently and these suggestions and opinions were addressed and discussed at our meeting. After the meeting, we all felt that the communication in the meeting was excellent. There was a very positive climate and we all worked together and agreed to implement the new procedures. We also agreed to all work towards making these new procedures as well as the existing procedure run more smoothly.

It was very interesting to watch my group and the participants at the meeting work through the group problem-solving process. Whether intentional or unintentional, our group followed the Standard Discussion agenda based on Dewey's reflective thinking procedure. It worked!

Sherry L. Knight is a legal assistant supervisor for an Orlando, Florida, law firm.

Mediation is a method of resolving disputes and conflicts. It requires the participation of a mediator who tries to promote agreement. The mediator has no authority to impose a settlement on the parties, nor can the parties be forced to enter into mediation or to reach an agreement. Mediation will be successful if the mediator can help the disputants to compromise and reach agreement on their own. Compromise is at the heart of a successfully mediated dispute and the end result of a mediation session is that there are neither winners nor losers but rather, it is hoped, generally satisfied individuals.[54]

Arbitration is used when participants mutually agree that a neutral third person is needed to solve their conflict. Arbitration has some distinct features that make it useful as a form of third-party intervention. First, both parties enter into arbitration voluntarily, with neither party forcing the other into the process, and neither party feeling coerced into a settlement situation. Second, it keeps one party from using passive–aggressive or impasse tactics on the other—sooner or later the issue will be resolved for the arbitrator will ultimately make a binding judgment. Third, in many cases the arbitrator has special training in the content area of the dispute, such as contract arbitration. When the arbitrator has such special expertise, he or she can offer creative solutions. Fourth, arbitration is readily available for use in situations in which the participants experience a communication breakdown and are no longer able to solve their own problems. Finally, arbitration is a process that can be used for a wide variety of content areas, ranging from contract disputes to conflicts in domestic relations.[55]

The output in discussion is less inclusive, more refined, and more focused than the input. Martin Andersen has developed an elaborate model of group discussion that assumes a systems perspective and identifies six output characteristics[56]:

1. The purpose of every discussion is twofold: (a) to ensure group goal achievement and (b) to provide some member satisfaction.
2. Under conditions of maximum productivity, the component of content should be characterized by a cognitive–affective balance.
3. The output characteristics of the thought pattern are that the decisions and understandings reached should be based on the highest level of logic and evidence and optimum suasion—sound reasoning, well-supported facts and opinions, a proper inquiry–advocacy relationship, and sufficient motivating relevancy to ensure that decisions made will be supported.
4. Two qualities should characterize the group under conditions of maximum productivity—analytical maturity and socioemotional balance.
5. When a discussion group is functioning at its peak, there should be optimum opportunity for leadership development.
6. Finally, at its best the communication component should be characterized by clarity and acceptability.

This model focuses on fundamental constructs and can serve as an operational guide for practice and prediction in effective discussion.

▶ CONFERENCE TECHNIQUES AND MEETING DYNAMICS

The term "conference" is used most frequently to designate two types of activities. One type of conference is typical of a committee meeting; the group is usually small and the discussion is a closed group with members tackling a mutual problem. A second meaning of the word designates a large, more-public meeting that may also be referred to as a convention or seminar. Conferences are types of formal discussions. Almost all conferences use discussion methods and evidence the group processes previously described. Our concern will primarily be with outlining ways in which conferences and meetings can be made more effective.

Survey after survey have indicated two prevalent attitudes or preconceptions on the part of managers about conferences. First, there are too many meetings. Second, too much time is wasted during the course of these sessions. These negative attitudes prevail despite the fact that conferences and meetings are essential to effective communication and information management within an organization. Why, then, are meetings so often considered boring, unproductive, and almost always too long? Some reasons offered are:

- ▶ No specific, clear-cut objective for the meeting, its leaders, or its participants
- ▶ No meeting agenda
- ▶ Too many or the wrong choice of participants
- ▶ No consideration for allies or antagonists
- ▶ Failure to prepare properly
- ▶ Inability to present ideas concisely
- ▶ Lack of sound leadership and control
- ▶ Improper use of visual aids
- ▶ Too many digressions and interruptions
- ▶ Time wasted on "why" rather than "how"
- ▶ Mixed final decisions[57]

However, meetings don't have to be long and unproductive. Careful planning and the following of basic guidelines represent another, more dynamic way.

Initially, one's planning must address the question of group problem solving versus individual decision making. Is a conference or meeting the best and most desirable way to achieve your objective? It should be quite obvious that under certain conditions groups may not prove particularly useful. The following are important aspects to consider in deciding whether to use a group to solve a particular problem or to act singly. Depending on the particular circumstances, some aspects will be more important than others and so may require group activity. A "yes" response to several of the following questions indicates that an individual would probably have difficulty solving the problem alone and a group should be used:

1. Are many steps required to solve the problem?
2. Are there many parts to the problem?
3. Will the solution be difficult to verify?
4. Are the individuals involved likely to perceive the problem as an impersonal one?
5. Will the problem be of moderate difficulty for the individuals who constitute the group?
6. Is a great deal of information required to solve the problem? Would a single individual be unlikely to possess it?
7. Does the problem demand a division of labor?
8. Are many solutions desired?
9. Are many hours required for the problem's solution?
10. Will individuals have to assume a great deal of responsibility for the solution?
11. Are the proposed solutions likely to be diverse?
12. Are the attitudes concerning the problem likely to be diverse?
13. Does the problem immediately affect a number of people; will the solution immediately affect a number of people?
14. Is it unlikely that group members will engage in non–task-oriented behavior?
15. Does the problem lend itself to group methods? Are potential group members familiar with group activity?

If group problem solving is selected, careful planning must precede the conference or meeting.

When should meetings be called? When shouldn't they be called? Despite the time they take away from other work and the poor way in which they are often handled, business meetings are almost always unavoidable. There is no way to conduct business without occasionally participating in or leading meetings. Meetings may center on coordinating activities among departments or among the members of a department. The discussion might focus on how well everyone in a department or in a company is doing in meeting organizational goals. Different companies have different needs for charting their progress and coordinating efforts, so these meetings may occur quarterly, monthly, weekly, or daily. Business people also have meetings whenever changes arise, such as market changes, internal company changes, or external changes in suppliers. The best way to find out how to handle these changes is to have all people affected by the changes meet to discuss them. Such meetings may include clients and suppliers who could benefit from the information shared.

Before you call or attend any meetings, make sure you know the objective of that meeting. To find your objective, ask yourself:

▶ Why am I holding the meeting?
▶ Why am I going to participate in the meeting?
▶ What do I want to achieve at the meeting?
▶ What do I want to achieve after the meeting is over?

A meeting without a specific objective is almost certain to achieve nothing specific. And that's a waste of time.

Once you have determined the value of having a meeting, look again at any alternatives. Perhaps you can achieve your objective by phone calls to some of the potential participants. Maybe you can ask for a written response to a memo you will send or use E-mail and then handle the problem yourself. Ask yourself the following questions to determine if you should hold a meeting:

▶ Is a meeting the *only* means of fulfilling my objective?
▶ If not, what are the alternatives?
▶ How effective are the alternatives?
▶ Is a meeting the *best* means of fulfilling my objective?
▶ Will a meeting use my time and my colleagues' time to best advantage?

Once the value of the best alternative is assessed, you can decide which of the two, the meeting or the alternative, is better. You can then act accordingly.

When meetings prove necessary, what's the proper way to call a meeting? How should agenda be prepared? Use a memo or agenda as both a blueprint and a plan of action for every meeting. A written memo or agenda is the best means of giving and securing information and, if properly put together, will focus everyone on the objective and the means to achieve it. During the meeting it can also be used as a guide and reference, and after the meeting it can serve as a reminder of what was to be accomplished and a means of checking on follow-up actions. Time spent preparing a memo or agenda will be saved during the meeting.

A good memo or agenda should state the objective of the meeting, the issues to be discussed, the time the meeting will begin and end, the place, the participants involved, and what is expected of them in the way of preparation before the meeting. Certainly, asking yourself the right questions will help you find, formulate, and focus your ideas as well as assist the participants in their preparation for the meeting. Questions can stimulate thinking and motivate others into coming up with new and imaginative ideas. Above all, however, keep the memo or agenda to no more than one page with any supporting materials, charts, or graphs stapled or paperclipped to it. Careful preparation is the best way to keep any meeting on target and on time.

Milo O. Frank notes that "unfocused exploratory meetings are like trying to find your way out of a labyrinth in the dark."[58] Members planning a conference would be wise to use the following checklist as a guide. The conference or meeting can then serve as an effective channel of communication and information management.

1. What is the purpose of the meeting?
2. What outcomes are to emerge from the meeting? When should these goals be reached?
3. What type of format will best achieve the meeting's purpose?
4. Who will participate? Have you left out someone who should be invited? Have you included someone who need not be involved?
5. Who will serve as leader, chairperson, moderator, or facilitator?
6. What is the best place to hold the meeting? What is a good time? How long should the meeting last?
7. How and when will the participants be briefed on the meeting and given directions for preparing to take part?
8. Who will prepare the agenda? Will it be circulated in advance?
9. What physical details need to be taken care of? Seating arrangements? Sound system? Ventilation and heating? Audiovisual aids and equipment? Other?
10. How will the proceedings and results be recorded?
11. How will the conference or meeting be evaluated?
12. What will be done to follow up?

Certainly, planning and attention to detail contribute to constructive meetings. However, they do not guarantee meeting success. What, then, is the difference between stimulating discussions and a productive meeting? Results! The following guidelines for effective group participation can be helpful in accomplishing results.

1. *Come to the meeting with questions.* If the meeting has been well planned, you will know the topic(s) of discussion in advance. Do some preliminary thinking, read, ask questions, and make notes of the points you want to raise during the discussion.
2. *Speak your mind freely.* Everyone's ideas are important. Your opinions and remarks are the substance of effective group activity; they can provide directions or energize others.
3. *Listen thoughtfully to others.* The hardest part of discussion is to concentrate on what is being said and *not* on what you plan to say as soon as you get a chance. Let yourself be stimulated by the thinking of others. Be an involved, critically active listener.
4. *Address your remarks to everyone.* Don't just talk to the discussion leader or chair, or any single individual. Address the whole group, even when replying to a specific remark by another participant. This helps curb arguments or two-way conversations. It further serves to energize the involvement of the entire group.
5. *Don't monopolize the discussion.* The goal is group productivity, so make frequent but brief remarks—a minute or two is long enough to speak at any one time. If

you like to talk, you'll have to watch yourself very closely because time seemingly goes by twice as fast when you are talking.

6. *Assume diverse, positive role activities.* Involve yourself in a variety of communication roles—task and social maintenance roles. Don't allow self-centered or ego-enhancing behaviors to intrude and disrupt group activities. This may require that you refrain from describing at length interesting but unrelated personal experiences. Before you tell a story or joke, satisfy yourself that it will contribute to participation.

7. *Help the discussion leader.* Always be alert for the need to summarize or clarify the points under discussion. Help keep the discussion on track by being certain that everyone understands what's going on.

8. *Appreciate diversity.* Be sensitive to the individual personal characteristics, attitudes, and values of others. Our increased contact with other cultures makes it imperative for you to make a concerted effort to get along with and to try to understand people whose beliefs and backgrounds may be vastly different from your own. Remember, if you try to understand diversity, appreciation follows.

9. *Be friendly when you disagree.* Conflict can be productive and friendly disagreement is a good way to stimulate sound thinking when agreement has been too hasty. Study ways to be tactful and then *be* tactful. Remember, there are at least three sides to most questions—yours, mine, and the right one.

10. *Be friendly when others disagree with you.* Be flexible and open to constructive criticism. The test of intelligence is how quickly you see what is right, not how often you are right to begin with. Critical thinking needs to be encouraged.

11. *Don't let silence embarrass you.* Silence often occurs and provides time to collect your thoughts. Patience is necessary if productive results are desired.

12. *Build group pride.* Be supportive of others and celebrate in the decisions made and progress achieved. Praise collaborative efforts and team membership.

13. *Welcome criticism of your discussion technique.* Discussion groups can often enhance their performance by using part of their time for self-analysis. Assessing group effectiveness can contribute to future productivity.

14. *Reach decisions.* Act, try to reach agreement or a common understanding on the problems and topics of discussion. When meetings are successful, understanding, agreement, compromise, and concession will take place. Be willing to take responsibility for group outcomes.

15. *Follow through after the meeting.* Be clear on your own responsibility for future action(s).

Even if participants follow the above guidelines, meetings can run astray if not properly managed. How can participation at meetings be managed effectively? The four elements that will make a meeting successful are: time constraints, preparation, proper presentation, and control. Set time limits in advance and stick to them. This may include limiting the length of time that a speaker has the floor—ten minutes, five minutes, two minutes—whatever length of time seems appropriate to the length of the meeting and the number of attendees. Additionally, consider limiting to two the number of times a speaker may speak on any given question or issue. (This does not mean twice in the meeting, but on a specific point of discussion.) Finally, once a question or issue has been discussed, ask for a motion and vote— take action.

▶ THE KENNEDY SPACE CENTER THUMB TWIDDLER

Bill Brett runs a major operation at the Kennedy Space Center and has developed a high-tech device to focus, tighten, and shorten meetings. It is a thin, flat plywood square with two holes in it—"the Kennedy Space Center Thumb Twiddler." When meetings wander off track, and lose sight of their objectives, a participant places his or her right thumb in one hole and left thumb in the other hole from the opposite side, intertwines the fingers, and rotates the Twiddler. Those watching get the point and soon the meeting is back on track.

If you're curious to try it out, it takes only a minute or two to manufacture this ingenious high-tech object out of a piece of cardboard or even a narrow strip of plywood. It will save many minutes when you demonstrate its use the next time one of your meetings begins to wander. It works. It may not get you into space, but it will keep your meetings on track.

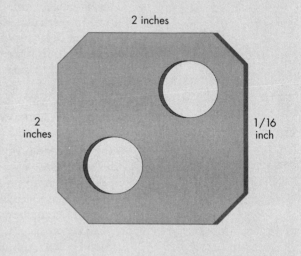

2 inches

2 inches

1/16 inch

Source: Milo O. Frank, *How to Run a Successful Meeting in Half the Time* (New York: Pocket Books, 1989): 156–157. Copyright © 1989 by Milo O. Frank. Reprinted by permission of Simon & Schuster, Inc.

If the leader points the way, participants will follow. This means being prepared for the meeting and providing the needed direction. It is the leader's responsibility to maintain a focus and keep the meeting on track.

Each participant is expected to present his or her viewpoint in a clear, concise, and interesting manner within the prescribed length of time. A most-important consideration, here, is to discuss only one question or issue at a time. If a question or issue requires extended discussion, consider creating a subcommittee of interested participants. This can maintain the momentum of the meeting and prevent it from becoming interminable.

The leader or director controls the meeting and each person's participation. Priorities should be set and a firm but polite attitude should prevail. This may mean interrupting when you want to take the floor and gain control. Judiciously interrupting is a meeting tool to achieve a purpose—to cut off a digression and save time. The leader or director should also end a meeting when the objective has been accomplished. Know when to say, "Thank you for attending this meeting."

It is vital to determine the value of any meeting. At every meeting's end, restate the objective and summarize the results. Also restate any assignment that have been made and the follow-up actions required. To evaluate further, ask each participant to submit in writing brief answers to the following questions:

▶ Did we achieve the meeting' objective as stated in the agenda? If not, why not?
▶ What three positive things can we do to improve the next meeting?
▶ What are the two most important things the leader can do to improve the meeting?
▶ What are the two most important things the participants can do to improve the meeting?
▶ Could we have done without this meeting? If so, how?

The answers to these questions can provide an assessment of meeting effectiveness and promote the increased involvement and responsibility of all participants. The net result will be better and briefer meetings.

Meetings are a fact of organizational life. Whether it's a gathering of ten people or a conference with hundreds in attendance, no meeting has to be boring, time-wasting, or unproductive.

▶ SUMMARY

Group activity is a way of life, with each of us simultaneously a member of many kinds of groups. And people in organizations spend a good part of their time as members of various small groups—social, informational, educational, and problem-solving or task groups.

Numerous factors influence the outcome of small-group efforts. Small-group communication can be viewed as a subsystem operating within an organization to achieve organizational goals. There are inputs, outputs, and feedback.

A small group is a collection of individuals in face-to-face relation that makes them interdependent to some degree. A group is not just any collection or aggregate of people, but rather a collection of individuals who develop a certain dynamic over a period of time. Group dynamics encompasses group types, functions, norms, roles, and networks.

The groups we operate in may be formal or informal in nature. They develop norms that outline and direct member behavior. Normative group development melds individual members into a cohesive unit that often proves productive, but may produce a risky or groupthink outcome. A variety of role behaviors are played out within any group. Members may assume task, group maintenance, or self-serving behaviors. Although role flexibility is desirable, most people interpret the role of group member rather narrowly, performing only a few of the behaviors described. These are, it is hoped, constructive rather than destructive behaviors. Finally, group networks also influence the endproduct of group activity. Highly centralized networks (wheel, chain, Y) make the fewest errors and take less time; decentralized networks (circle, all-channel) better handle complex tasks, generate more messages, and produce a higher sense of morale or member commitment.

Functionally, groups are essentially task oriented while at the same time addressing socioemotional pur-

poses. In addition to being goal centered, group activity satisfies personal needs. Among the different types of groups are panel, roundtable, colloquy, symposium, brainstorming, case discussion, role-playing, and encounter self-development training sessions. A variety of techniques can be employed to promote the effective functioning of groups, including PERT, the buzz Group/Phillips 66 technique, the nominal group technique, the Delphi procedure, and teleconferencing techniques.

Problem solving is the most prevalent of group activities. A problem exists when there is a difference between what is currently happening and what the group wants to happen. Although a number of solution procedures may be used, John Dewey's reflective thinking process generally serves as a basic foundation for most problem solving. The problem is defined, clarified, analyzed, placed in relation to a standard set of criteria with solutions being advanced and discussed, and finally a best solution is adopted and implemented. The optimum outcome of the problem-solving process will be group consensus—general agreement among all members of a group concerning a given decision—but in its absence, other alternatives for arriving at a decision range from majority rule to withdrawal and disbanding in response to unreasonable conflicts.

Group activity is most closely associated with conferences and meetings—facts of everyday business life. Many of us perceive them as a useless waste of time, but they can be dynamic and stimulating interchanges that yield productive results.

Throughout this chapter, emphasis has been given to the significance of small-group activity—a position supported by Dorwin Cartwright and Alvin Zander who wrote in 1968:

A democratic society derives its strength from the effective functioning of the multitude of groups which it contains. Its most valuable resources are the groups of people found in its homes, communities, churches, business concerns, union halls, and various branches of government. Now, more than ever before, it is recognized that these units must perform their functions well if the larger system is to work.[59]

▶ QUESTIONS FOR DISCUSSION AND SKILL DEVELOPMENT

1. Why are groups necessary and valuable in society? How do groups function in the organizational setting? What kinds of groups do you belong to?
2. Your boss is trying to decide if it would be worthwhile to set up an interdepartmental small group to discuss employee grievances. What would be the advantages and disadvantages to using such a group? Also, make suggestions that would help in planning a meeting of the group.
3. What types of groups have you participated in? Panel? Roundtable? Colloquy? Symposium? Brainstorming? Case Discussion? Role-playing? En-counter self-development training? Was the outcome satisfying and rewarding? Why or why not?
4. Think of the last group meeting you attended. What norms or rules can you identify? Did most members observe them? How did the group handle deviates? What role(s) did you play? Did anyone display self-serving behaviors? How were most decisions made? How was conflict resolved? Were most members satisfied with the outcome(s)?
5. What do you consider to be the major problems inhibiting productive conferences or meetings? How can conferences and meetings be made more productive?

▶ NOTES

1. Rollie Tillman, Jr., "Problems in Review: Committees on Trial," *Harvard Business Review* 21 (May-June 1960): 6–12.
2. M. Kriesberg, "Executives Evaluate Administrative Conferences," *Advanced Management* 15 (1950): 15–17; and E. Lawler and S. Mohrman, "Quality Circles After the Fad," *Harvard Business Review* (January-February 1985): 65–71.
3. Michael Doyle and David Straus, *How to Make Meetings Work* (New York: Wyden Books, 1976).
4. Norman Maier, *Problem-Solving Discussions and Conferences* (New York: McGraw-Hill, 1963): v.
5. E. K. Clemons and F. W. McFarlan, "Telecom: Hook Up or Lose Out," *Harvard Business Review* 64 (1986): 91.
6. Ernest Bormann, *Discussion and Group Methods.* (New York: Harper and Row, 1969): 3–4.
7. Stewart L. Tubbs and Sylvia Moss, *Human Communication*, 2nd ed. (New York: Random House, 1987): 251–252.
8. H. Lloyd Goodall, Jr., *Small Group Communication in Organizations* (Dubuque, IA: Wm. C. Brown, 1985); R. Y. Hirokawa, "Discussion Procedures and Decision-Making Performance," *Human Commu-nication Research* 12 (1985): 203–224; and R. W. Napier and M. K. Gershenfeld, *Groups: Theory and Experience* (Boston: Houghton Mifflin, 1989).
9. R. Y. Hirokawa, "Group Communication and Decision-Making Performance," *Human Communication Research* 14 (1988): 487–515; Patrick Laughlin and Richard McGlynn, "Collective Induction: Mutual Group and Individual Influence by Exchange of Hypotheses and Evidence," *Journal of Experimental Social Psychology* 22 (1986): 567–589; and D. G. Leathers, "Quality of Group Communication as a Determinant of Group Product," *Speech Monographs* 39 (1972): 166–173.
10. John K. Brilhart, *Effective Group Discussion*, 2nd ed. (Dubuque, IA: Wm. C. Brown, 1974): 17.
11. Marvin Shaw, *Group Dynamics: The Psychology of Small Group Behavior*, 3rd ed. (New York: McGraw-Hill, 1981): 11.
12. B. Aubrey Fisher and Leonard C. Hawes, "An Interact System Model: Generating a Grounded Theory of Small Groups," *Quarterly Journal of Speech* 57 (1971): 445.
13. B. Aubrey Fisher, "Decision Emergence: Phases in Group Decision Making," *Speech Monographs* 37

(1970): 53–66; and B. Aubrey Fisher, "The Process of Decision Modification in Small Discussion Groups," *Journal of Communication* 20 (1970): 51–64.

14. Bruce W. Tuckman and Mary Ann Jensen, "Stages of Small-Group Development Revisited," *Group and Organization Studies* 2 (1977): 419–427.

15. Kenneth Cessna, "Phases in Group Development: The Negative Evidence," *Small Group Behavior* 15 (1984): 3–32; Marshall Scott Poole, "Decision Development in Small Groups I: A Comparison of Two Models," *Communication Monographs* 48 (1981): 1–20; Marshall Scott Poole, "Decision Development in Small Groups II: A Study of Multiple Sequences in Decision Making," *Communication Monographs* 50 (1983): 206–226; and Marshall Scott Poole, "Decision Development in Small Groups III: A Multiple Sequence Model of Group Decision Development," *Communication Monographs* 50 (1983): 321–341.

16. Edgar Schein, *Process Consultation* (Reading, MA: Addison-Wesley, 1969): 41.

17. Muzofer Sherif, *An Outline of Social Psychology* (New York: Harper and Brothers, 1948): 59.

18. John Wenburg and William Wilmot, *The Personal Communication Process* (New York: John Wiley & Sons, 1973): 256.

19. Irving Janis, *Victims of Groupthink* (Boston: Houghton Mifflin, 1972): 9.

20. Donald Harvey and Donald Brown, *An Experimental Approach to Organization Development* (Englewood Cliffs, NJ: Prentice Hall, 1988): 256.

21. Irving Janis, *Groupthink*, 2nd ed. (New York: Houghton Mifflin, 1982). Copyright © 1982 by Houghton Mifflin Company. Used with permission.

22. Kenneth Benne and Paul Sheats, "Functional Roles of Group Members," *Journal of Social Issues* 4 (1948): 41–49.

23. James H. McBurney and Kenneth G. Hance, *Discussion in Human Affairs* (New York: Harper and Row, 1950).

24. William M. Sattler and Ed N. Miller, *Discussion and Conference* (New York: Prentice Hall, 1954).

25. Everett M. Rogers and Redkha Agarwala-Rogers, *Communication in Organizations* (New York: The Free Press, 1976); and Raymond Ross, *Small Groups in Organizational Settings* (Englewood Cliffs, NJ: Prentice Hall, 1989).

26. Norman Gilroy and Jim Swan, *Building Networks: Cooperation as a Strategy for Success in a Changing World* (Dubuque, IA: Kendall/Hunt, 1983).

27. Gerald M. Goldhaber, *Organizational Communication*, 4th ed. (Dubuque, IA: Wm. C. Brown, 1986): 281.

28. C. Hendrick, *Group Processes and Intergroup Relations* (Newbury Park, CA: Sage, 1987).

29. John Cragan and David Wright, *Communication in Small Group Discussions* (St. Paul, MN: West Publishing, 1986).

30. Carl Larson and Frank LaFasto, *Teamwork: What Must Go Right/What Can Go Wrong* (Newbury Park, CA: Sage, 1989).

31. Berkeley Rice, "Square Holes for Quality Circles," *Psychology Today* (February 1984): 17–18.

32. Arnald Kanarick, "The Far Side of Quality Circle," *Management Review* 70 (1981): 16–17; and Hobart Rowan, "The Japanese Advantage," *Washington Post,* October 7, 1981, G2.

33. Roy Berko, Andrew Wolvin, and Ray Curtis, *This Business of Communicating* (Dubuque, IA: Wm. C. Brown, 1986).

34. Bob Rush, "Making Use of Management Committees," *American Agent and Broker* (March 1991): 24–28.

35. Jane Farley Templeton, *Focus Groups* (Chicago, IL: Probus Publishing, 1987).

36. Pamela Shockley-Zalabak, *Fundamentals of Organizational Communication*, 2nd ed. (New York: Longman Publishing, 1991).

37. Stephen Stumpf and Thomas Mullen, *Taking Charge* (Englewood Cliffs, NJ: Prentice Hall, 1992).

38. John K. Brilhart and Gloria Galanes, *Effective Group Discussion*, 6th ed. (Dubuque, IA: Wm. C. Brown, 1989); Bobby R. Patton, Kim Griffen, and Eleanor Patton, *Decision-Making Group Interaction*, 3rd ed. (New York: Harper and Row, 1989); and Beatrice Schultz, *Communicating in the Small Group: Theory and Practice* (New York: Harper and Row, 1989).

39. Akio Morita, *Made in Japan: Akio Morita and Sony* (New York: E. P. Dutton, 1986).

40. Gerald M. Phillips, "PERT As a Logical Adjunct to the Discussion Process," *Journal of Communication* 15 (June 1965): 89–99.

41. Harry F. Evarts, *Introduction to PERT* (Boston: Allyn and Bacon, 1964); and K. R. MacCremmon and C. A. Ryavec, *An Analytical Study of PERT*

Assumptions (Santa Monica, CA: Rand Corporation, 1962).

42. Ronald L. Applbaum, Edward M. Bodaken, Kenneth K. Sereno, and Karl W. E. Anatol, *The Process of Group Communication*, 2nd ed. (Chicago: Science Research Associates, 1979).

43. Andre L. Delbecq, Andrew H. Vande Ven, and David H. Gustafson, *Group Techniques for Program Planning* (Glenview, IL: Scott Foresman, 1975); and Andrew H. Vande Ven and Andre L. Delbecq, "The Effectiveness of Nominal, Delphi, and Interacting Group Decision Making Processes," *Academy of Management Journal* 17 (1974): 605–621.

44. Gerald Wilson, H. Lloyd Goodal, and Christopher Waagen, *Organizational Communication* (New York: Harper and Row, 1986); and J. T. Wood, G. M. Phillips, and D. J. Pedersen, *Group Discussion: A Practical Guide to Participation and Leadership,* 2nd ed. (New York: Harper and Row, 1986).

45. Kathleen Wagoner and Mary Ruprecht, *Office Automation: A Management Approach* (New York: John Wiley & Sons, 1984).

46. J. Fulk and C. Steinfield, *Organizations and Communication Technology* (Newbury Park, CA: Sage, 1990).

47. Eleanor Tedesco and Robert Mitchell, *Administrative Office Management—The Electronic Office* (New York: John Wiley & Sons, 1984).

48. L. E. Albertson, *The Effectiveness of Communication Across Media* (Melbourne, Australia: Australia Research Laboratories, 1991); A. Chapanis, R. N. Parrish, R. B. Oshman, and G. D. Weeks, "Studies in Interactive Communication II: The Effects of Four Communication Modes on the Linguistic Performance of Teams During Cooperative Problem Solving," *Human Factors* 19 (1977): 101–126; R. S. Hiltz, K. Johnson, and M. Turoff, "Experiments in Group Decision Making," *Human Communication Research* 13 (1986): 225–252; M. Moss, *Telecommunications and Productivity* (Reading, MA: Addison-Wesley, 1981); and Larry R. Smeltzer, "Supervisory-Subordinate Communication When Mediated by Audio-Graphics Teleconferencing," *Journal of Business Communication* 29 (1992): 161–178.

49. Marya Holcombe and Judith Stein, *Presentations for Decision Makers* (New York: Van Nostrand, 1990): 181.

50. Bonnie Roe White, "Teleconferencing: Its Potential in the Modern Office," *Century 21 Reporting* (Fall 1984): 5.

51. John Dewey, *How We Think* (Boston: D. C. Heath, 1910): 68–78.

52. C. H. Kepner and B. B. Tregoe, *The Rational Manager: A Systematic Approach to Problem Solving and Decision Making* (New York: McGraw-Hill, 1965).

53. Rupert Cortwright and George Hinds, *Creative Discussion* (New York: Macmillan, 1959): 14.

54. John W. Keltner, *Mediation: Toward a Civilized System of Dispute Resolution* (Annandale, VA: Speech Communication Association, 1987); and J. A. Wall, "Mediation: An Analysis, Review, and Proposed Research," *Journal of Conflict Resolution* 25 (1981): 157–180.

55. R. T. Clark, *Coping with Mediation, Fact Finding, and Forms of Arbitration* (Chicago, IL: International Personnel Management Association, 1974); M. A. Rahim, *Managing Conflict in Organizations* (New York: Praeger, 1986); and B. H. Sheppard, "Third Party Conflict Intervention: A Procedural Model," *Research in Organizational Behavior* 6 (1984): 141–190.

56. Martin P. Andersen, "A Model of Group Discussion," *Southern Speech Journal* 30 (1965): 279–293.

57. Milo Frank, *How to Run a Successful Meeting in Half the Time* (New York: Pocket Books, 1989): 18.

58. Frank, *How to Run a Successful Meeting*, 39.

59. Dorwin Cartwright and Alvin Zander, *Group Dynamics* (New York: Harper and Row, 1968): ix.

CHAPTER ELEVEN

11

Public Communication—Message Preparation and Delivery

LEARNING OBJECTIVES:

To indicate the importance of public communication to the organization

To describe different types of presentations

To explain communication anxiety and ways to control your fear when making public presentations

To select a proper topic for a presentation

To analyze the audience you will address

To gather interesting examples, statistics, quotations, and stories for your presentations

To organize your presentation for the greatest impact

To explain the functions and types of visual aids

To deliver your presentation with power

One afternoon a Roman emperor was entertaining himself at the Coliseum by feeding Christians to the lions. Several Christians were sacrificed and the crowd screamed for more. The next martyr entered the arena and said something to the lion. The beast cowered away. Then a second lion approached, with the same result; and then a third. The amazed throng began to shift its sympathies to the Christian. The emperor announced that the Christian's life would be spared, and that the would-be martyr should appear before him.

"I am sparing your life," said the emperor, "but before I release you, I demand to know what it was you said to those beasts."

"I merely said to each lion: After dinner, of course, you'll be expected to say a few words."

Again and again throughout our lifetimes each of us is called upon to "say a few words." A knowledge of public communication is critical to your success in today's organization because it is very likely that you will be called upon to deliver a number of presentations at work. How well you succeed in these presentations will determine, in part, how far and how quickly you advance in your particular organization. Preparing public presentations and delivering them to audiences are skills you need to master.

Tom Parker, in his book *In One Day*, writes about the many and varied activities in which Americans engage every day. One of the most important of the activities he chronicles, especially for Americans in the workplace, is speaking in public. He writes that "in one day Americans make 100,000 presentations. If they were all waiting their turn at the same lectern, the speakers would form a line 28 miles long. It would take the last speaker nine hours just to walk to that lectern."[1]

▶ PUBLIC COMMUNICATION IN THE ORGANIZATION

Whatever your occupation, you will find yourself presenting information about your work to others. After he studied public communication in a number of organizations, Ernest Bormann concluded that "you will be giving presentations to offer yourself, a sales proposal, a program, an important budget or organizational change to others who have the power to accept or reject the substance of your message."[2] Speaking in public has become increasingly common and especially important in organizations. In her essay on training twenty-first–century managers, Elizabeth M. Fowler observes that they must be skilled in public communication and, citing a report on the qualifications needed by top managers in the year 2000, she observes, "it was found that our corporate leaders will have to be accomplished public speakers who have learned the art of addressing small and large groups as well as the news media."[3] Management understands that a lack of public speaking skills affects the company in many ways—including the bottom line. Roger E. Flax, president and CEO of Motivational Systems, a management and sales training firm that trains over 50,000 people a year in communication skills, observes that "companies are finally saying it's costing us billions of dollars a year because employees don't know how to stand up and give speeches."[4]

In the past, corporate administrators, board directors, and public relations practitioners did most of the speaking for the corporation, and it is still true today that highly placed personnel do a lot of speaking in representing their organizations. Western Electric Company has over 100 speakers who make some 2,000 presentations each year. Standard Oil has between 50 and 100 representatives delivering some 500 speeches annually. Dow Chemical employees face 1,000 audiences each year, and 300 Georgia Pacific speakers make approximately 1,500 presentations every year. In the 1990s, however, it seems that nearly every employer of every corporation has a responsibility to present information to others. One study found that 50 percent of a group of blue-collar workers reported giving at least one public presentation within the past year, and 31 percent said they gave more than three speeches.[5] It is now common practice for corporations to encourage all of their employees to participate in the delivery of presentations. For example, over 90 percent of the 2,200 presentations given by General Motors' employees each year are delivered by middle managers, and 2,000 mid-level personnel of Phillips Petroleum Company deliver almost 10,000 presentations annually.[6]

It has become axiomatic that if you work, you will speak. When you first begin your career, many of these presentations will be in-house in front of coworkers. However, as you grow within your organization, you will also be expected to give speeches to listeners outside your workplace. Consider these examples: the vice president of marketing for a cable television company presents a new marketing strategy to the division heads of the company; the company president addresses the local Rotary group about the economic future of the area; the accounting manager for a large development firm explains zero-based budgeting to a group of department managers; and the corporate trainer for a bank speaks to a group of new tellers about their duties. These employees are representative of all kinds of workers in all sorts of businesses in all parts of the country, and they understand that being skilled in public communication enables them to perform better at work and to move up the corporate ladder.

▶ DIFFERENCES BETWEEN PUBLIC AND WRITTEN COMMUNICATION

That public communication is now common in America's organizations doesn't mean that written communication is unimportant. There are times when writing a memorandum, a written report, or a letter is absolutely necessary to communicate your message. However, you need to be aware that at times there are clear benefits to the use of oral public communication. Efficiency, effectiveness, and influence are some of the critical factors you must consider.

Efficiency. Oral communication often saves time because written forms of communication can be lost or buried under other materials on a desk or a conference table. No doubt there have been times when you have misplaced important files or reports. The result can be minimal if the written communication is quickly found, but it can be disastrous if it is found too late or never found at all. Furthermore, responding to a written communication can be put off for any number of reasons, and important feedback can be postponed. With oral communication, however, feedback is much more immediate because people hear the presentation and respond to it at once. Even if the audience members wait to respond for hours or days after the presentation, the speaker knows that the audience has received the message, and that may not be true with written communication.

Effectiveness. Oral communication is often more effective than written communication because of its face-to-face nature. When you give a speech or make a report, you are able to see how your audience reacts to your ideas immediately because of the nonverbal and verbal communication that takes place. You can clarify your message on the fly if you see confused looks on listeners' faces, or you can begin to wrap it up if the audience looks bored or restless. Similarly, you can increase your enthusiasm while presenting your message when you see that the audience is excited about what you are saying. And oral communication gives you the chance to answer the questions of the audience and clear up issues immediately—both during and after the presentation.

Influence. Oral communication can be much more persuasive than written communication. The charisma, appearance, and knowledge of the speaker cast an influence over the members of an audience that a written memorandum simply cannot achieve. Think back to the last time you heard a really persuasive speaker and try to remember how you felt. You probably were moved to put into action what the speaker was requesting. This is a common response when the spoken word persuades us. Another reason that oral communication is more influential is that it is difficult to turn someone down or to say no face to face—the immediacy of the situation often calls out for interaction and rebuttal.

There is also more variety possible in spoken than in written language. Some of the differences between oral and written presentational styles are the following:

- ▶ Sentence length should be shorter in oral style.
- ▶ Oral style permits a greater variety in sentence structure; imperative and explanatory sentences are better suited to oral style, emphasizing the personal elements and relationships of face-to-face communication.
- ▶ Sentences are structurally less involved in oral style.
- ▶ Personal pronouns are more numerous in oral style.
- ▶ Fragmentary sentences may be used in oral style.
- ▶ Contractions are used more often in oral style.
- ▶ Repetition is necessary in oral style because speech is a linear temporal act.

A speech or report is not an essay, and it is imperative that your language and phrasing communicate your concern and involvement. The most effective oral presentations are those that communicate, linguistically and nonlinguistically, a sense of commitment.

▶PUBLIC COMMUNICATION DEFINED

What comes to mind when you hear the term "public communication"? Many people imagine a public speaker standing behind a lectern and reading a prepared speech to an audience of hundreds or thousands of strangers. Others conjure up thoughts of a manager using visual aids and handouts as she talks to a group of a dozen coworkers in a company boardroom. You also might think public communication refers to a company president addressing the board of directors or stockholders about the company's strategic plans. Actually, all of these speakers are engaging in public communication, which we define as face-to-face communication in which a speaker has control of the speaking situation and the primary responsibility of presenting a message to one or more people.

Let's examine our definition of public communication in more detail so you can comprehend its parameters.

First, public communication is face-to-face with one or more people, i.e., it involves a speaker talking directly to an audience of other people. There may be a secondary external audience that doesn't actually see the speaker (such as people listening to a speech over a radio), but there must be a primary audience located proximally and listening to the speaker.

Second, the speaker has control of the speaking situation in public communication. By this, we mean that it is the speaker, no one else, who controls what is happening during the occasion. In other communication situations, such as an interpersonal encounter or a selection interview or a small-group discussion, the control of the situation is shared with other people.

Third, in public communication the speaker's primary responsibility is to present a message. Here, it is the speaker who assumes the role of being responsible for getting the message across to the listeners. In other forms of communication, certain responsibilities may be more important than the delivery of a message. For example, in interpersonal communication the development of the relationships between and among people is often more important than the messages they exchange. In other settings, this responsibility of getting a message across is shared with the other participants in the situation.

Finally, the number of listeners may be only a few or even just one other person. It isn't the size of the audience that determines whether public communication has happened; the audience can be any size. You are engaging in public communication when you attempt to persuade your boss that you deserve a salary raise or when you inform your manager about the recent disagreement between two people in your department.

▶ FORMS OF PUBLIC COMMUNICATION

There are a number of different forms or types of public communication that commonly occur in organizations. You have probably used or seen and heard a number of the following examples of public communication:

- ▶ research and technical reports
- ▶ briefing announcements
- ▶ orientation sessions
- ▶ question-and-answer sessions
- ▶ informational reports
- ▶ training and development programs
- ▶ conference presentations
- ▶ introductions of speakers
- ▶ convention programs
- ▶ sales presentations
- ▶ after-dinner speeches
- ▶ special project proposals
- ▶ progress reports
- ▶ award ceremonies
- ▶ press conferences

Throughout the chapters on public communication, we will be using the general term "presentations" to refer to these many and varied forms of public communication. These presentations fall into two groups—formal speeches and reports. Although all speeches and reports meet the criteria of our definition of public communication, they differ in some important ways. Frank E. X. Dance explains that the differences between speeches and reports are "not of the genre but of the situation or setting."[7] Dance recognizes that speeches and reports are inherently similar in nature and in certain respects overlapping, but let's examine a few of the more explicit distinctions between them.

First, formal speeches generally are designed for larger and more heterogeneous audiences than are reports. These public speeches are often delivered to a larger number of people and these people may not have a lot in common. The audience members may be attending the speech voluntarily or they may have been assigned to attend the speech. On the other hand, reports are usually delivered to smaller and more homogeneous groups of people. These presentations can be delivered to a few people seated around a board table or to only one person in an office. The listener in these smaller audiences is most likely to be there because her or his job requires attendance.

Second, the places where formal speeches and reports are delivered can also vary. Speeches are sometimes delivered in business settings, but they can also be deliv-

▶ SPEECH WRITERS IN THE THICK OF IT

By Jeannette Spalding

President Steve Ewing of Michigan Consolidated Gas Company (MichCon) often drops by and makes himself at home in the office of Ed Stanulis, seemingly a nobody. Then the two men hash over some weighty issues of the Detroit-based gas utility. At other times, Stanulis talks turkey with Al Glancy III, chairman and CEO.

Where does a non-management professional like Stanulis get off being such a casual acquaintance with the president?

Why does he get in to see the chairman and CEO?

He's the speech writer.

"There's clout, prestige, and power in being a speech writer," Stanulis says. "The speech writer becomes a confidant and an adviser."

The clout, power and prestige of speech writing should make business communicators stand up and take notice. Business communicators sit in ideal positions to gain speech writing skills and to become speech writers. When the clout is added to a potential $100,000-a-year plus income, no business communicator can afford to overlook the possibilities.

But while prestigious, speech writing can be thorny.

Speech writers circulate among the company's movers and shakers and get in the thick of company decisions.

"We are at the forefront of what's happening," Stanulis says. "Often, I know what will happen way ahead of some of the vice presidents."

Speech writers publicize the company's policies by preparing speeches for top management. Speech writers intimately observe policy in the making and policy carried out. In this process, speech writers can't help but learn the top-level management skill of policy formation. It's a skill that can boost business communicators into the executive suite.

"Speech writing is a valuable arrow to have in your quiver if you want to be vice president of communication," says Steve Hallmark, an independent speech writing consultant based in Chicago and a former American Bar Association speech writer.

Stanulis' speeches go through an elaborate approval system to avoid inaccuracies. Top executives and appropriate technical people put their eagle eyes to these speeches. This approval process seems laborious at times because everyone feels a need to make changes, whether or not those changes are really warranted.

Negotiating copy changes and working with top management join responsibilities that speech writers and other business communicators share. These common skills give

business communicators some savvy to give speech writing a try.

Floyd Walker suggests ways corporate writers can get speech writing experience. These writers should put themselves in positions of writing for the spoken word—newscasts or video scripts, says the administrator of Community Relations and Media Services for Allied Signal Aerospace Co., based in Kansas City, MO. Such writing gives the writer experience about what works and what doesn't work for the spoken word. Also, writers should seek out opportunities to write speeches.

Aspiring speech writers should watch people speak, listen to speech content, read speeches, know the speakers, and know the company, Walker says. By observation, the writer learns some dos and don'ts of speech writing and how specific people talk. The writer's knowledge and tenure with the company give the powers-that-be confidence to let the novice speech writer have a go at it.

As the corporate writer adds a growing number of speeches to a portfolio, who knows where opportunity will lead?

Stanulis, for example, eased into speech writing from a technical writing and technical training background. He worked for the Federal Reserve Bank addressing audiences about the bank and its monetary policy. Later, he wrote speeches on the same topic for other speakers, a chore that turned into a full-time speech writing job. He hired on as company speech writer at MichCon. Speech writers like Stanulis learn speech writing on the job. In fact, many middle to upper-level managers get conscripted into speech writing service without particularly asking. Not only do these managers come from business communication, but they also come from law, operations, human resources and strategic planning.

Hallmark knows one such draftee. The chairman needed a speech about strategic planning, so the strategic planner wrote the speech. The chairman loved it. The next time the chairman needed a speech, the strategic planner received the assignment, even though the speech had no connection to strategic planning. Thus, a speech writer was born.

"The Chicago Speech Writers Forum has 70 writers and not a single one of us set out to be a speech writer," Hallmark says. Stanulis says the same things about the 45-member Detroit Speech Writers Forum.

It's no accident that upper managers are well-versed in the intricacies of corporate policy making. They work and negotiate on the same level with the CEO, which is what the speech writer must do.

"Speech writers are seasoned observers and participants in the corporate environment," Hallmark says. "They have made major management decisions. They have made policy. They have been there."

Speech writers also have a temperament and willingness to set aside their ego to allow the speaker's ego to shine forth—not a universal trait in everyone, Hallmark says.

His speech writing experience over the years has led him to a point where he now writes 50 speeches a year and draws top dollar for each one. A speech writer's income in the U.S. ranges from the median $56,000 a year to the top end income of $115,000 a year, according to an informal survey by Ragan Communications published in its November 17, 1989 *Speech Writer's Newsletter.*

The speech writing demand these days is as good as the money. Hallmark says that Peggy Noonan's popular book, *What I Saw at the Revolution,* spurred an interest in speech giving among entrepreneurs, a field ripe for the harvest by independent speech writers. Also, the Chicago speech writer says that CEOs talk more to audiences in-house to motivate them on issues such as customer service, an opportunity for speech writers who prefer the inside corporate scene.

And speech writers really get inside the inside corporate scene. How much more on the inside can a professional get than someone like speech writer Stanulis? He has frequent visits to his office by one of the company's top officers, and he is one of the first to know what will happen in his company. Being this much "in the know" is something business communicators thrive on.

Source: Jeannette Spalding, "Speech Writers in the Thick of It," *Communication World* (October 1990):23–25. Reprinted with permission from the International Association of Business Communications.

ered in convention halls, stadiums, and auditoriums that accommodate larger audiences. Reports, however, are more frequently presented in business settings such as boardrooms, conference and meeting rooms, and other general business environments. These smaller places are appropriate for reports because the audiences usually comprise a small number of listeners.

Third, the topic and manner of its choosing is different in most formal speeches and reports. In speeches, the topic is quite often left up to the speaker—at least, the speaker is given a general topic area and is allowed to provide the focus. Listeners will generally accept a slight variation from the announced topic. In reports, however, the topic is usually assigned to the presenter by a corporate superior, often a manager or department head, and the purpose is quite specific.

Public communication, then, is commonly associated with the term "presentations" and is marked by its face-to-face nature, the control the speaker exerts over the situation, and its purpose of extending a message to one or more people. Presentations comprise formal speeches and reports that are similar in nature, but which differ in certain specific ways including the types of audiences, the places where the presentations are delivered, and the choice and orientation of the topics presented.

▶ SPEAKER APPREHENSION

One of the major concerns of employees who make presentations is the fear of speaking before other people. This fear is known by many names—stage fright, nervousness, anxiety, or speaker apprehension—and it is very common among people who make presentations.

For years, a number of surveys have indicated that Americans fear speaking in public more than anything else and, in *The Book of Lists,* David Wallechinsky, Irving Wallace, and Amy Wallace cite one survey in which 3,000 Americans listed fear of

► **EXHIBIT 11-1**

Physical Signs of Anxiety and Fright

Voice	quivering or tense
	speech too fast
	speech too slow
	monotonous; lack of emphasis
Verbal fluency	nonfluencies; stammering; halting speech
	vocalized pauses
	hunts for words; speech blocks
Mouth and throat	swallowing
	clearing throat
	breathing heavily
Facial expression	lack of eye contact; extraneous eye movements
	tense face muscles; grimaces; twitches
	deadpan facial expression
Arms and hands	rigid or tense
	fidgeting; extraneous movements
	motionless; lack of appropriate gestures
Gross body movement	sways; paces; shuffles feet

speaking before a group ahead of such other fear-provokers as heights, snakes, sickness, financial distress, and death.[8] About 20 percent of Americans suffer so significantly from communication apprehension that their presentations are adversely affected.[9] James McCroskey and Lawrence Wheeless further note that "communication apprehension is probably the most common handicap suffered by people in contemporary American society."[10] Exhibit 11-1 presents some of the behaviors characteristic of excessively frightened people.[11]

Everyone has some apprehension about making a presentation before other people. You can never eliminate your fear of speaking before others, nor should you. Some anxiety is good because you need the adrenaline produced by your body in stressful situations to push you to your peak performance. Just as athletes get "psyched up" before an important game or meet, you also need to be somewhat tense before you make your presentations.

Now, it's important for you to begin the process of understanding your own personal anxiety so you can learn to control it and not allow it to control you. Everyone has a different degree of anxiety and, if it's within certain limits, it's considered normal. Here's an opportunity to measure your speaker apprehension:

How Apprehensive Are You in Making Presentations?[12]

This instrument consists of six statements about your feelings on giving a presentation. Indicate the degree to which each statement applies to you by marking whether you (1) strongly agree, (2) agree, (3) are undecided, (4) disagree, or (5) strongly disagree with each statement. There are no right or wrong answers. Don't be concerned that some of the statements are similar to others. Work quickly and just record your first impression.

_____1. I have no fear of making a presentation.

_____2. Certain parts of my body feel very tense and rigid while making a presentation.

_____3. I feel relaxed while making a presentation.

_____4. My thoughts become confused and jumbled when I am making a presentation.

_____5. I face the prospect of making a presentation with confidence.

_____6. While making a presentation, I get so nervous that I forget facts I really know.

Scoring: To obtain your presentation apprehension score, use the following formula—To a base of 18 add your scores for items 1, 3, and 5; then subtract your scores for items 2, 4, and 6. A score above 18 shows some degree of apprehension, and places you in the company of the vast majority of people.

Now that you have a better idea about your own personal degree of speaker apprehension, we offer you the following suggestions for controlling your fear of speaking before others.

Understand What Causes Your Fear. To control your anxiety, you need to understand what causes your fear. Raymond Beatty identifies five contributing factors that influence presentational anxiety.[13] An understanding of these factors will give you a better idea of your own fear and how to best control it. First is perceived novelty. Most of us show some anxiety when we face new situations. When your boss first asks you to make a presentation to the rest of the managers, you will probably be influenced by the newness of speaking in this particular situation. To minimize this factor, it is important that you gain as much experience as possible in making oral presentations. Volunteer to make presentations at work, join your local Toastmasters organization, or speak in your civic and church groups. Do anything you can to gain the experience necessary to become a veteran at speaking, because then the novelty of making presentations won't be a factor in making you apprehensive.

Second is a potential sense of subordinate status. You can also become apprehensive when you believe that certain people in your audience are better speakers than you or that they know more about your subject than you do. This feeling of inadequacy can damage your self-esteem and prove personally demoralizing, so it's important that you bolster your self-confidence when you enter speaking situations and realize that speaking isn't a contest against others. Keep focused on your message and not on what you believe others may be thinking about you. You must know as much as you can about your subject and be well prepared. This should help to quell otherwise subordinate feelings.

Third is a feeling of conspicuousness. Your nervousness increases if you believe everyone is looking at you. Have you ever noticed how much easier it is to speak when you are at your seat instead of standing behind a lectern in the middle of the room? Again, this is a common feeling among all people who make presentations. Many of us don't like to be in the limelight and become more anxious if we believe we look conspicuous. To reduce this factor, think of the audience as a small group of colleagues who only want the best for you—this is probably true anyway. And again, concentrate on the message you are presenting and not on yourself as the presenter.

Fourth is the factor of dissimilarity. People feel more nervous when they think they have little in common with their listeners. This factor doesn't have as much impact when you present reports because you usually know the members of these audiences. However, dissimilarity is common when you give speeches because you may not know very many, if any, of the listeners. In these situations, you need to find similarities between you and the listeners and stress them in the preparation and delivery of your speeches.

▶ TAKING THE TERROR OUT OF TALK

By Michael T. Motley

Surveys show that what Americans fear most—more than snakes, heights, disease, financial problems, or even death—is speaking before a group. This is surprising, in a way, since even a dreadful speech isn't as serious as illness, poverty, or the grave. Yet about 85% of us feel uncomfortably anxious speaking in public. Even professionals, evangelists, and entertainers suffer extreme stage fright, or, to use its more formal label, "speech anxiety."

While it's comforting to realize that such anxiety is almost universal, a magic formula to dispel it would be even more comforting. There is no such formula, but recent research that helps us understand speech anxiety better also suggests ways to control it.

The most familiar aspects of speech anxiety are its physical symptoms. Most people report some combination of sweaty palms, dry mouth, increased heart rate, shaky hands, weak knees, shortness of breath and butterflies in the stomach. Laboratory measurements add increased blood pressure and muscle tension to the list of symptoms. With all of this going on, it's no wonder the experience is unpleasant—for some, so unpleasant that they avoid public speaking completely, whatever the cost. I have treated attorneys, ministers, and public-relations executives who were ready to quit their professions to avoid public speaking. Other clients were losing chances for advancement by passing off speaking assignments to colleagues.

Physical symptoms are just one component of speech anxiety. More important is how people interpret the symptoms. A few speakers, the confident ones, see their physical reaction as a positive sign that they are emotionally ready for the speech. Most of us, however, interpret the feelings as fear. To justify this fear, we need something to be afraid of, so we begin to imagine what will happen if our speech is less than perfect. These imagined consequences are usually exaggerated and irrational. People say, for example, "The audience will ridicule me if I make a mistake. I'll be embarrassed to death," when in fact audiences usually ignore errors and awkwardness as long as they get something out of the speech. These irrational fears and physiological symptoms often feed on each other—the fears increase the symptoms, which in turn increase the fears—until extreme physiological arousal combines with thoughts of catastrophe. Heart rates can approach 200 beats per minute in speakers convinced that they will make fools of themselves.

Excessive anxiety is especially common among people who view speeches as performances, in which they must satisfy an audience of critics who will carefully evaluate gestures, language and everything else they do. Though they can't describe precisely what these critics expect, people with a performance orientation assume that formal, artificial behavior is somehow better than the way they usually talk. Research has shown that expecting to be evaluated or being uncertain about the proper way to behave arouses anxiety in almost any situation. A much more useful orientation, and a more accurate one, is to view speeches as communication rather than performance. The speakers' role is to share ideas with an audience more interested in hearing what they have to say than in analyzing or criticizing how they say it—a situation not very different, at least in this regard, from everyday conversation.

A number of techniques are being used successfully to control anxiety. One popular approach, systematic desensitization, is aimed specifically at lessening physiological arousal. The technique involves training in muscular relaxation, coupled with visual imagery. People are taught to relax as they imagine giving a speech, the assumption being that psychological anxiety doesn't go with physical relaxation. Typically, people start by imagining an event fairly remote from the planned speech, such as being in the audience for someone else's speech. Once they achieve relaxation with that image, they repeat the process while imagining events closer to giving the speech, until they finally visualize their own speech, still feeling relaxed.

Another popular approach, rational emotive therapy (RET), works on irrational thoughts that contribute to anxiety. RET and its variations try, in particular, to get speakers to realize that many of their fears are ill-founded. After people explain precisely what they fear, the therapist points out flaws in the reasoning and helps them adopt a more realistic attitude.

In my public speaking courses, for example, students will often say that what they are afraid of is getting a bad grade on the impending speech. If this were the real problem, my offer to leave the room and allow the speech to remain ungraded would eliminate the anxiety. It doesn't, of course, since their fear of audience evaluation remains.

Other speakers will mention some more generalized fear, such as "I just never seem to speak well," or make self-fulfilling prophecies, such as "I'm going to bore them to death." The therapist helps them replace such statements with more positive and reasonable ones, such as "Since this information is interesting to me I can make it interesting to others."

Another approach I find effective shifts the speaker's orientation away from performance and toward communication. "Communicative pragmatics orienting" works to persuade people that effective public speaking is more like ordinary communication than like a public performance. Once people genuinely view making a speech as communication, they can think of it in terms of their normal, everyday conversation rather than in terms of past anxiety-ridden performances. I have found that with this approach, speech anxiety almost always subsides and the speeches improve.

There is an exercise I use to demonstrate the point: as the speaker approaches the podium, I dismiss the audience temporarily and begin a "one-way conversation" with the speaker. I tell him or her to forget about giving a speech and simply talk spontaneously to me, using the speech-outline notes as a guide. In this situation, most people feel rather silly orating, so they start to speak conversationally, using natural language, inflections and gestures. I ask the speaker to maintain this conversational style while the audience gradually returns, a few people at a time.

The speakers usually do this successfully as the audience returns. When they don't, the transition from talk to speech is invariably identified later by the audience as the point when effectiveness began to decrease and by the speaker as the point when anxiety began to increase.

All the speech-anxiety therapies I've mentioned involve more than I have described here, of course, and require qualified therapists. For most of us, giving a speech is an important and novel event. It's natural and appropriate to feel some anxiety. A speaker's aim should be to keep this natural nervousness from cycling out of control; not to get rid of the butterflies but to make them fly in formation.

Source: Michael T. Motley, "Taking the Terror Out of Talk," *Psychology Today* (January 1988):46–49. Reprinted with permission from *Psychology Today* magazine, copyright © 1988 (Sussex Publishers, Inc.).

Finally, one's prior experience may be a contributing factor to speaker apprehension. You will exhibit apprehensive behaviors more often if you've felt such nervousness before. Unfortunately it is true that communication apprehension feeds on the past. More importantly, even if your listeners didn't perceive you to be nervous but you felt nervous, it is your perception of anxiety that will influence you the next time you speak. To minimize this factor, gain positive experience by participating in successful speaking situations. If your memories are positive, you will feel much less apprehension when you make your presentations.

Correct Your Misconceptions About Making Presentations. Misconceptions, myths, or misplaced beliefs about speaking in public contribute to our feelings of anxiety. These ideas have arisen over the years and become near-truths to many people. But, realizing that they are *not* true, you can further control your speaker apprehension.

Myth One: Good Speakers Are Born, Not Made. This myth assumes that certain people are born with an innate ability to speak well and others aren't, i.e., you either have it or you don't. People who accept this myth believe that actively working to improve your presentational ability is a waste of time if you aren't one of the gifted. Actually, all good speakers are made through hard work and practice. Isocrates, the progenitor of Greek eloquence, observed that effective speakers required some natural talent, much training, and considerable courage. By volunteering for more speaking opportunities and working hard on your speeches and reports, you can develop the skills necessary to deliver a solid presentation.

Myth Two: Presentational Speaking Is Unnatural. People who accept this myth believe that public communication is totally different from the everyday, conversational communication in which we all engage. They see people who make speeches or reports as stiff speakers standing behind a lectern droning on to uninterested listeners, or they see glib, silver-tongued orators persuading others with slick visuals, fancy words, and smooth delivery. In both situations, presentational speaking is seen as different from everyday speaking. Presenting speeches and reports, howver, is really very similar to the conversational speaking you do all the time. Think about the similarities: both forms have the essential components of speaker, listener, message, and channel; they both involve and depend upon feedback between speaker and listener; they both use verbal and nonverbal symbols; and they both depend upon clarity of expression and sound logic. In fact, you aren't a novice at presentational speaking because you have already had considerable experience speaking to other people. James Fallows, President Jimmy Carter's chief speech writer, further notes that traditional public speaking has been replaced by a less ritualized, less formal type of speaking when he observes that "fifteen years ago, the public responded to the graceful artifice of noble speech. . . . Now it's more important to people to hear rough approximation of how the person actually speaks than to have something glamorous. It's reassuring to feel that you are seeing a slice of the real person."[14]

Myth Three: Presentational Speaking Just Means Sounding Good. To the believers of this myth, the delivery of the message is everything, and content counts for nothing. This is the dangerous assumption that the public speaker should be concerned primarily with technique. Here a speaker is effective if she has a dynamic delivery, meaningful gestures, direct eye contact with the audience, and an attractive appearance. The purpose of speaking becomes the management and maneuvering of people rather than a responsible act. It is this kind of thinking that has led to the phrase "mere rhetoric." This myth is symbolized by the stereotypical used-car salesman and the slick politician who try to con us into buying or believing something. Actually, content—your message—is the reason for speaking, and the delivery of that message is the way it gets to the audience. Speakers should be well informed, speak with the best knowledge possible, respect the responses of others even when contrary, and make clear personal commitments. By hard work in your practice sessions and by concentrating on your message and not on yourself, you can both sound good and say something meaningful.

Visualize Yourself Being Successful. When you are apprehensive about your upcoming presentation, you are visualizing a negative outcome. If you have an especially powerful imagination, your mind can create frightening scenarios in which you see yourself forgetting your message, failing to answer a difficult question, stumbling over your words, and even blushing when the audience laughs at what you have just said.

Instead, use visualization to your benefit. Professional athletes and actors have used positive visualization for years to preview their success, and effective presenters use visualization as well. When you practice your speech or report, try to see the audience applauding your effort, picture your boss congratulating you on your successful presentation. As you prepare, try to replace negative thoughts with positive ones by turning them around. For example, instead of thinking, "I'm going to forget what to say," think to yourself, "I've practiced so much I know what to say"; and instead of thinking, "Someone will ask me a question I won't know how to answer," think, "I know this subject, and I'm prepared."

Lately, presenters have adopted scripts to use before they make their speeches or reports to prompt their visualizing a successful performance. We have provided you with the following script to use before you make presentations.[15] The best way to use a visualization script is to read it several times before your presentation or tape record it and listen to it again and again. Business executives and other presenters believe these scripts allow them to change their negative thoughts to positive ones. Try this exercise:

> Close your eyes. Allow your body to get comfortable in your chair. Take a deep breath and hold it . . . now slowly release it through your nose. Now take another deep breath and make certain you are breathing from the diaphragm . . . hold it . . . now slowly release it and note how you feel while doing this . . . feel the relaxation flow throughout your body. Now take one more really deep breath . . . hold it . . . and now release it slowly . . . as you begin your normal breathing pattern. Shift around in your chair so you are comfortable.

> Now you see yourself at the beginning of the day when you are going to give your presentation. See yourself getting up in the morning, full of energy and confidence, and looking forward to the day's opportunities. You are putting on just the right clothes for your presentation that day. As you are going to work, you note how clear and confident you feel and how others around you comment positively on your appearance and demeanor. You feel completely prepared for the task at hand. Your preparation has been exceptionally thorough, and you have really researched the topic you will be presenting today.

> Now you see yourself in the room where you will make your presentation, and you are talking very comfortably and confidently with others in the room. The people to whom you will be presenting your message appear to be quite friendly and are very cordial in their greetings and subsequent conversation. You feel absolutely sure of your material and of your ability to present the information in a convincing and positive manner. Now you see yourself approaching the area where you will make your presentation. You are feeling very good about yourself, and you see yourself moving forward eagerly.

> You now see yourself delivering your presentation. It is really very good and you have all the finesse of a polished speaker. You are aware that your audience is giving you head nods, smiles, and other positive responses that clearly give you the message that you are truly on target. You are now through the introduction and the body of the presentation and are heading into a brilliant summation of your position on the topic. You now see yourself fielding audience questions with the same confidence and energy that you exhibited in the presentation itself. You see yourself receiving the congratulations of people around you. You see yourself as relaxed, pleased with your presentation, and ready for the next task you need to accomplish that day. You feel filled with purpose, energy, and a sense of general well-being. You silently congratulate yourself on a job well done!

> Now . . . you have returned to this time and place. Take a deep breath and hold it . . . and let it go. Do this once more and feel yourself comfortably back where you began. Take as much time as you need before you leave the room.

Practice Thoroughly. This final suggestion is one that we can't emphasize enough. A legitimate reason for speakers to feel nervousness and low confidence is inadequate preparation. Prepare and practice thoroughly—preparation without practice is sure to doom even the best presenter. Speech practice must be undertaken systematically. Practice time will vary from presentation to presentation. For example, there will be times when your employer will ask you to present the next day, and your time to get ready and practice will be very short. For more elaborate presentations, especially speeches, you'll have a longer time frame in which to practice. Even if you're asked to speak in one or two days, the following three-step schedule will allow you to properly practice most of your presentations:

Step One: Read Your Speaking Outline Aloud. After you have researched your topic and transferred your information to notecards or another similar aid, you need to begin your practice sessions by going through the presentation aloud several times. You'll want to explain your examples and state fully all quotations and statistics. Try to complete the presentation even if you stumble or make a mistake.

Step Two: Polish and Refine the Presentation. This is the time to check on physical movement, eye contact, gestures, and distracting aspects of your delivery such as vocalized pauses ("uh . . . ah . . . um"). You should also smooth out your delivery and speak as much as possible without using your notes. This second step is also an excellent opportunity to ask other people—coworkers, your boss, friends, and family—to listen to you and make suggestions. If these people aren't available, you can use a full-length mirror to get a visual idea about how you will look to your listeners.

Use a tape recorder during rehearsal to make you conscious of slang expressions and annoying repetitions that creep into your speech, Videotaping provides even more specific feedback—your gestures and movements can be very revealing. You may initially be somewhat uncertain about videotaping, but once you've adjusted to seeing yourself as others see you, you'll find videotaping a terrific bonus. Seeing what patterns you fall into when you are nervous will make it easier to correct them—you can't change something you don't know you do.

Step Three: Have a Dress Rehearsal. This is the last opportunity to practice before you speak, and this session should take place under conditions closely approximating your real speaking situation. Go through the entire presentation, making the final changes you need for the presentation, to be as solid as possible. When this session is over, you should feel confident and be looking forward to your presentation.

Remember, presentational success comes from earning the right to the time. You earn that right by knowing the topic. You earn that right by research and careful reflection. And, you earn that right by careful preparation and speaking—practice, practice, practice. A reporter asked the world-famous pianist Arthur Rubinstein, near the end of his life, "Are you the greatest musician who ever lived, as some people have said?" The wise old maestro responded, "Music is an art, not a science and no one ever becomes the greatest at an art—they could always be greater!" We can say the same about the art of public speaking. No amount of practice will make you perfect, but it will make you consistently good, and sometimes great.

▶ STEPS IN PREPARATION AND DELIVERY

Perhaps before analyzing the specifics of preparing the presentation—selecting a topic, defining the purpose, analyzing your audience, researching the topic, organizing the body, planning your introduction and conclusion, delivering the presentation, and evaluating your presentation—it is important to ask: What is an effective speech? This is a difficult question to answer. You can learn all the proper techniques and still not give an effective speech; and even if it is effective, there may no concrete evidence of the results; and even if the results are immediately apparent, there may be considerable disagreement about whether they are desirable. This doesn't mean that there are no standards for distinguishing an effective speech from an ineffective one. It means that the results depend not so much on how well you apply the techniques as on the use to which you put them. The answer to our question ultimately rests with the qualities that characterize an effective speaker:

1. The effective speaker has developed the capacity for observation, has sharpened senses, and has learned to use them accurately and fully. He or she is sensitive.
2. The effective speaker has built up a broad background of knowledge in the area(s) in which she or he wishes to communicate. The speaker is knowledgeable.
3. The effective speaker not only understands the subject matter but also his or her own capabilities and limitations. Closely connected here is an ability for self-criticism.
4. The effective speaker has developed the capacity for thinking purposefully and logically.
5. The effective speaker will have a generally accurate image of the audience.
6. The effective speaker will use every opportunity for practice.
7. The effective speaker will keep in mind his or her ethical responsibilities. Two thousand years ago the great Roman teacher, Quintilian, defined the orator as a "good man skilled in speaking."

On November 19, 1863, two men spoke at the dedication of a national cemetery in a small Pennsylvania town. The first speaker was Edward Everett. He was considered a genius and heralded as a brilliant speaker. He stepped to the platform and for more than an hour his powerful, carefully organized remarks and eloquent oratory held the attention of his audience. The second speaker was a man so awkward in appearance that one of his critics called him "the big baboon." This man had been too busy to do much preparation, only jotting down a few notes on the brief train ride from Washington that day. When he strolled to the podium, he had no smile for the audience, no humorous stories, no heartwarming illustrations. His speech contained only 266 words and lasted less than five minutes. "Fourscore and seven years ago, . . . " he began, and the rest is history. The second speaker was Abraham Lincoln and his message was the famous Gettysburg Address. His speech effectively touched the hearts of the people; it spoke to their needs, their dreams, their fears, their sufferings. So, an effective speech fits the speaker, the audience, its purpose, and the occasion. To borrow from the Gettysburg Address, it is "altogether fitting and proper."

What are the steps in preparing and delivering a speech? How do you determine your topic, your purpose? How do you organize the material? What are the functions of the introduction and the conclusion? What can be used as supporting material? What about style and delivery? How can you be effective? Business presentations being delivered in today's corporate world are all different. A briefing by the company president may be succinct and limited to one issue but a speech to the company's stockholders may be lengthy and cover many diverse topics. A sales presentation may have two listeners and be interrupted constantly by questions, and a slide presentation in a 50-person department may have all questions delayed until the end. Although these presentations differ in a variety of ways, the preparation for them is very similar. Effective speakers generally follow the same steps in planning and developing any presentation. All of your presentations will make some use of each of the following stages of preparation. As we discuss these stages, it is well to keep in mind the advice of Dionysius: "Let thy speech be better than silence, or be silent."

Step One: Select and Narrow Your Topic

The first step in preparing your presentation is to select and narrow your topic. Rarely will you find a situation in which topic selection is a function solely of your choice. Oral reports require that you address a specific subject and, even when speaking to outside audiences, general parameters are usually suggested. Your subject matter is fairly rigidly dictated when you are asked to present an orientation session to new employees about company benefits or to inform the members of the department about the current new software package; choice is equally limited when you're asked to respond to citizen concerns about a new runway proposed by the local airport authority or address the local Chamber of Commerce about your company's role in the community during the next decade. But there will be times when you'll have the opportunity to choose your own subject for an upcoming presentation or be allowed to specify the exact nature of the general topic suggested to you. At these times, you need to make wise decisions about topic selection.

Certainly, your personal knowledge, experiences, attitudes, and beliefs will be reflected in your approach to any topic. Although speeches may vary in purpose, each is essentially a personal statement from you as a speaker to others who choose or are asked to listen. Regardless of attempts at objectivity, you cannot totally divorce yourself from the personal history that has shaped your perceptions, so your frame of reference helps determine the focus you adopt on any particular topic. The following criteria can also be used when you make your topic selection.

The topic should interest you because you'll give more of your time to preparing a presentation if the topic interests you. If you're enthusiastic about the topic, or if you could become excited about it, you'll probably research, organize, and practice your presentation with more vigor. It is also true that you'll have more fun with your topic if you find it interesting, and having fun is a part of presenting well.

The topic should be important to your listeners. Topics of import to you may not seem so to your audience, and topics perceived to be unimportant aren't listened to enthusiastically. A legitimate question for any listener to ask is: why is this topic important to me? The effective presenter always addresses the timeliness and significance of the topic early in the presentation, before the listener asks.

Narrow the topic so it is appropriate for the speaking situation. This requires you to analyze the topic in relation to the time allotted. There may be elements of your presentation that could better be handled in forms other than the oral presentation. For example, certain parts might be better communicated by a written memo to specific listeners. This analysis can also reveal those parts of the subject with which you feel uncomfortable and which you may choose to ignore.

The length of time you'll be given to speak depends on a number of variables, over most of which you'll have little control. The length can be from a very few minutes to well over an hour for many reports and speeches. You do, however, have control over your rate of speaking. The average speaker says approximately 125 words per minute. The typical journalistic paragraph of simple sentences also runs about 125 words. Thus, a very general rule is that an average speaker speaks about one short paragraph per minute. Of course, if the material is highly technical or statistical, or if you speak slowly, the time can stretch to almost two minutes per paragraph.

Another way to determine the number of ideas you can present is to section the presentation. If you have ten minutes to inform your staff about a new corporate smoking policy, then you'll usually devote one to two minutes to introduce the policy and about one minute to conclude the presentation. That leaves seven to eight minutes to discuss the core information. If you decide to cover three or four main issues, you'll only be able to devote a couple of minutes to each and that may not be enough time to fully develop any of them. Therefore, you may decide to narrow your topic to two or three main issues, thus giving you more time for each. The important point here is that your topic needs to be well chosen and narrowed to fit the speaking situation. Note: Let the rambler beware! No one likes someone who exceeds the time limit.

Step Two: Define Your Purpose

An effective speaker must assume a purpose and a structure. Your task as a public speaker is to determine why you are going to speak to a particular audience. You should determine what your stated purpose is, what your audience thinks your purpose is, and what your real purpose is. It's important to have the purpose clearly defined in your mind because your purpose will influence what you say, how you say it, and what responses you want.

Traditionally, presentations are divided into three major categories: informative, persuasive, and entertaining. The informative presentation is designed to educate your audience by expanding their knowledge or teaching them specific facts. Here you explain, instruct, define, clarify, or demonstrate new information. Your goal is to help your listeners understand your topic, not to change their attitudes or behavior. Your purpose is to produce clear ideas in the minds of your listeners. This necessitates identifying what knowledge your hearers already have about the subject, and using what they already know in constructing the new meanings you want them to grasp. Instructing the staff about the basic principles of zero-based budgeting, demonstrating the operation of the video camera to the interns, and training the new sales representative are typical examples of the presentation to inform.

The persuasive presentation is intended to influence audience members to change their opinions, attitudes, or actions. In persuasive presentations you wish to influence, convince, motivate, sell, or stimulate your listeners to alter their beliefs or to act. You go beyond giving information to actually espousing a position. The difference between informing and persuading is the difference between "explaining" and "exhorting."[16] The persuasive effort attempts to solidify, to modify, or to change the audience's attitudes and behaviors; the speaker chooses to stimulate, convince, or actuate the audience. Persuading the vice president of marketing to try a new marketing strategy, convincing the CEO that new markets need to be opened, and selling a computer system to a new client are examples of persuasive presentations.

The entertaining presentation provides pleasure and enjoyment with little serious intent to disseminate information or prompt change. This speech, built around a kind of theme often involving the recounting of a series of personal experiences or humorous anecdotes, is no small task because peoples' notions of what is humorous and what they find to be entertaining vary widely. After-dinner speakers and those participating in "roast and toasts" often speak to entertain, with varied success.

However, because the purpose of communication is so complex and multileveled today, these traditional labels can be confining and misleading. A less-traditional approach to presentational content is more accurately reflective of the modern business and professional arena. The purpose of a presentation is determined not by its content, but by the motivation of the person sending the message. Why are you giving this presentation? What rewards do you hope to achieve as a result of it? What punishments do you wish to avoid by engaging in this speech making? What do you want the audience to do, to feel, or to believe as a result of hearing your presentation? For example:

▶ The professor lectures. Why does he? Perhaps he wants his students to have information he thinks is valuable. Maybe he wants his students to achieve good grades as evidence to his peers that he's a good teacher. Perhaps he wants his students to see the world from a particular perspective. He may be motivated by any number of factors.

▶ The corporation treasurer reports. Why? She wants the stockholders to know the state of affairs. Why? Perhaps she wants them to continue holding stock or to buy additional stock certificates. Maybe she wants them to support the current board of directors—or to withdraw their support from the board.

Thus, the determining question is: Why are you giving a speech or report? The answer to the *why* influences what information you will include and exclude from a presentation. Your motivation also influences how you present the material.

Moreover, the purpose of any presentation is also dependent upon the members of the audience. Some may see the presentation as providing only information; others may be persuaded by it. Given the nature of the communication process, the audience plays a significant role in the perception of purpose. Audience members do not determine the purpose for you, but they do determine the purpose they perceive. Communication is a receiver-based phenomenon; the receivers' perception of your purpose will influence their subsequent behavior. Naive receivers may perceive a presentation as purely informational. A cynical audience may perceive your planned informational approach as information control, attempted manipulation, or attempted opinion modification. A contented, self-satisfied audience may perceive a witty and humorous presentation as purely entertaining in purpose, when, in fact, you might have been trying to inform, to attack, or to prompt action. Consequently, the three traditional presentational modes—to inform, to persuade, and to entertain—can more properly be viewed as devices used for achieving objectives. In a sense, all presentations seek to control a listener's attention and they all request his or her understanding. But, depending on a speaker's goals, a particular presentation may be primarily informative, more persuasive, or little more than entertaining.

When you determine your purpose, you must narrow your choices and decide specifically what you want to accomplish, what you wish your listeners to understand, or the attitudes and behavior you want the audience to change. The following suggestions can prove useful when framing your specific purpose statement. First, express your purpose statement as an infinitive phrase, not as a fragment. You might use a few words or fragments of a sentence to tell others what your subject will be, but when you begin working on your presentation you need to state it in the form of an infinitive phrase. This will clarify your purpose and your goal for you.

NOT: My purpose is work clothes.

BUT: My purpose is to have you understand how to dress appropriately for your job.

NOT: My purpose is union dues.

BUT: My purpose is to persuade you that union dues should be increased by ten percent this year.

Second, express your purpose as a statement, not a question. Questions may make good titles for presentations, but they are usually too vague to serve as a working purpose statement. Moreover, questions don't show the direction the presentation is headed.

NOT: Is buying IBM stock a good idea?

BUT: To persuade you to buy IBM stock today.

NOT: Should you start your own childcare business?

BUT: To persuade you that you can establish a childcare business on your own.

Third, identify exactly what you wish to accomplish in the presentation. This requires your limiting the purpose statement and phrasing it with your listeners in mind. Less-accomplished speakers believe they, rather than the audience, are at the center of the speaking situation. When this happens, you lose sight of whether your desired goal is accomplished. But, limiting your purpose statement and relating it to listener concerns, you improve your chances of reaching and accomplishing your goal.

NOT: To sell you this product.

BUT: To convince you to purchase the Panasonic KX-P1524 computer printer.

NOT: To explain the telephone answering system.

BUT: To have you understand the operating advantages of our newly installed telephone answering system.

Determining your topic and narrowing, focusing, and adapting it to your purpose and audience are probably your most difficult tasks. Completing these steps successfully is essential to developing an effective presentation. Rarely will a presentation have the power and give the satisfaction you desire if you do these initial steps hastily or haphazardly.

Step Three: Analyze Your Audience

Audience analysis is essential because all oral presentations are transactions between a speaker and listeners. Your central concern as speaker is, therefore, twofold: your interest and their interest. Ralph Waldo Emerson said it well when he observed that the key to successful communication is to "translate a truth into language perfectly intelligible to the person to whom you speak."[17] Every topic must, then, be approached with equal concern for personal and audience needs and values. Both speaker and listener must be "alive" to the topic if the communication exchange is to be meaningful and reciprocal. Jo Sprague and Douglas Stuart describe the relationship between speaker and listeners this way: "When you ask an audience to listen to your ideas, you

▶ PUTTING MORE OOMPH IN YOUR ORATORY

By Dick Janssen

Robert Burns once wrote of the yearning to see ourselves as others see us. Today, thanks to the camcorder, the poet could see himself, hear himself—and then be critiqued. How would he like that? I think I know.

I found out, as many managers do, by taking a crash course in communicating. Much of the time, I felt like a butterfly under a magnifying glass. By the time I was released, though, I had confronted some dismaying habits and had a headful of pointers on how to handle any audience.

A number of image gurus run such programs for corporate clients. Among the largest firms are New York's Communispond (212-687-8040), Atlanta's Speakeasy (404-261-4029), and Chicago's Executive Technique (312-266-0001). Decker Communications, based in San Francisco (415-546-6100), taught my one-day senior executive course, which costs $2,500. Pricey—but the limit is six students; a two-day session for 15 costs less.

Our instructor, Bert Decker, displays all the empathy of a drill sergeant: "I've trained over 32,000 people, and there isn't anyone who comes here who really wants to be here," says Decker, a former documentary filmmaker. Yet, the motivation to tough it out is strong: managers spend 94% of their time communicating, "giving off cues about ourselves dozens of times a day."

I soon found out what sort of cues. After taking my turn standing up and telling the class about my job and family, I am whisked off to watch a video replay. There I am, in living color, looking at the floor and occasionally heavenward. Staring longingly at the (off-limits) shelter of the lectern. Clutching my prop, a ballpoint pen, and using it to make feeble gestures. Rocking backward, with my voice a guarded monotone. And, sin of sins, I often stall with a meaningless "uh."

The tape ends. I am shaken and don't believe that I will be redeemed as a speaker in just one day. But my coach finds glimmers of hope. After the first minute, I had let a smile break through, and I had even said something mildly amusing. (Personal and audience-tailored anecdotes are in; jokes are out.) And, while I didn't use my hands expansively enough, I never put them in my pockets. It is time for one of Decker's upbeat generalizations: "We are all better than we think we are."

My peers, meanwhile, display flaws of their own. An advertising exec fails to leave room in her speech for the commas or periods that would let listeners keep up with her rapid-fire thoughts. A manufacturing honcho's delivery is so wooden that he might have been reading aloud from a physics text.

Soon, Decker tosses us some surprise ad-lib topics. Mine is "feet," and what counts here is not accuracy but free association and enthusiasm. ("They're vital to the shoe industry," I offer.) Later, in pursuit of persuasion, we have to outline and deliver a speech on a real-life situation, such as urging a skeptical sales force to push low-end merchandise.

In between, we absorb Decker's minilectures on principles. A speech, he proclaims, should convey an overall impression rather than just facts and figures: "You have to reach people emotionally, not mechanically, if you want to cause change." Our words are only a small part of the message we convey and are easily undercut by visual cues such as poor posture or darting eyes.

To avoid such a problem, he reminds us of things our mothers probably taught us, plus some finishing touches. Like not slouching. We learn to stand with our knees flexed, tilting slightly forward, a nuance of body language meant to serve us as well at a cocktail party as on the speaker's platform. Instead of averting our eyes from one amorphous glob of an audience, we learn to seek eye contact with an individual—for three to six seconds, max, that is. We find we do gain encouragement from this fleeting but intimate human contact. Then we move on to nurture rapport with another listener.

More videotapes show we are improving. And we are made privy to some of the subtler secrets of well-coached CEOs and pols. Never say: "That's a good question." (It reflects poorly on other questions.) Look away fast from a hostile questioner, so you don't get locked into a counterproductive debate. When you avoid making a direct reply, use the question as a bridge to a point you wish to make. To make the most of a crash course, follow up on your own later. All it takes is a videocamera or just a mirror and a simple cassette tape recorder. When will I start finding the time for this? Well, uh . . .

Source: Dick Janssen, "Putting More Oomph in Your Oratory," *Business Week* (June 4, 1990): 165. Reprinted by special permission. Copyright © 1990 by McGraw-Hill, Inc.

are asking them to come part way into your experience. It is your obligation to go part way into theirs."[18]

There are a number of audience-related dimensions to be considered. The purpose of analyzing an audience is to help the speaker better understand the target listeners and, consequently, to design and deliver a message that will be understood and given fair consideration. The most crucial problems of choice facing the speaker arise from his or her estimation of the nature of the audience and the accommodations to be made. The speaker addresses a group and the purposes, positions, attitudes, and expectations of that group. So the speaker's knowledge of the audience reflects certain assumptions about those assembled and about the ways in which they will think about the substance of the discourse. Effective speakers often use an audience analysis that identifies the demographic features of the audience and estimates which of these factors are important to the situation. The following are some of the demographic factors you may choose to consider:

▶ *Age.* What is the average age of the audience? What is the range of ages? Does the audience include different age groups? Is age an important factor to members of this group?

▶ *Size.* How many people will be listening to you? Is this group a part of a larger group?

▶ *Gender.* What is the distribution of men and women? Is the audience predominantly one sex? Do these men and women view this topic differently? Would certain statements be seen as offensive to parts of the audience?

▶ *Education.* What is the average educational level? What percentage of the audience has some college education? Have the listeners attended primarily one school or one type of school?

▶ *Religion.* What religions are represented in the audience? Is there a dominant religion? What is the strength of their beliefs? Is religion an important factor in this situation?

▶ *Culture.* What is the audience's racial and ethnic background? Is one race or culture dominant in the audience? In what ways might culture be affected by this topic? Will the audience see you as an outsider to their race or ethnicity? Would certain issues be seen as insensitive?

▶ *Occupation and Income.* What are the major occupations of the listeners? Is one occupation more dominant than others? What is the general status of the occupations of the audience? What is their income level? What is the range of incomes in the audience? Does occupation and/or income have a bearing on this topic?

▶ *Knowledge and Experience.* How much does the audience know about this topic? What don't they know? Are certain of the members likely to be experts on the subject? What biases or prejudices might they have about this topic? What does the audience know about me as the speaker? Will they be hostile, indifferent, or friendly toward me?

Much of the information needed to answer these questions will be unknown to you, so it's vital that you seek a number of different sources for help. First, you may be able to observe the group directly. Second, you might use your contact person. Whether giving a speech or a report, you'll usually be approached by another person who may know more about your audience than you do. Ask this person as many specific questions as necessary to make you feel comfortable. Third, you may be able to speak with a few members of the group before your presentation. This will permit some immediate information which might prompt adaptations to your presentation.

Finally, even if you know nothing of your audience, don't despair—use your own intuition and experience. At these times, draw upon your own knowledge of communication, human behavior, and groups.

In a sense, the groups with which any person seeks affiliation become his or her reference groups; the individual "refers" to the positions, values, and attitudes of some group in choosing his or her own personal positions, values, and attitudes. In short, you need to be audience-centered in your approach to making presentations. Public communication, including oral reports, occurs primarily not as the product of the autonomous needs of individuals, but as the product of efforts to organize, sustain, and shape the lives of groups or social institutions.

Other than demographic information, there are three additional components involved in an audience analysis: (1) the listeners' interest level, (2) their relationship to the speaker, and (3) their measure of identification with the speaker.

The interest level may range from concerned, to moderately interested, to apathetic, to hostile. What determines the interest "set" of an individual? What is it that makes one attend to specific portions of his or her surroundings and ignore others? Research in this area suggests that two factors are especially important: self-interest and familiarity. Anything that affects us vitally is interesting to us. Matters associated with the satisfaction of our deep physiological needs or with fundamental psychological concerns command attention. The power of the familiar as a factor probably results from its giving specific meaning to the situation that confronts us. There is, of course, a point where this factor ceases to function as a means of gaining and holding interest. When situations have become completely familiar and offer no further challenge, we choose to be disinterested in them. Thus, the message must adapt to that level of interest present in the audience. For example, consider Eliot Asinof's vivid description of Dick Gregory's 1968 M.I.T. address:

> The scene is the Massachusetts Institute of Technology—the spacious Kresge Auditorium packed with students waiting for the guest lecturer. He is not a leading world scientist or engineer, nor is his subject matter of any technological concern. He is Dick Gregory, the ubiquitous Negro comedian, author, actor, Presidential candidate (without a party) and crusader for human rights who—to emphasize his commitment—has virtually given up comfortable nightclub engagements to tour college campuses.
>
> Since Gregory has been tied up in traffic driving down from Portsmouth, New Hampshire, where he lectured earlier in the day, the audience grows good-humorously restless, tossing paper airplanes with a technical artistry befitting M.I.T. In time, there is a rhythmic clapping and foot stamping in the classic undergraduate appeal for action.
>
> "What brings you here?" I ask a few students seated around me. "Well, I hear he's very funny," replies a very serious-looking boy with horn-rimmed glasses. There are more young men wearing glasses than not. A small percentage are long-haired, and it is difficult to find one with a necktie and a jacket. It is almost impossible to find a Negro.
>
> Finally, an hour late, Gregory strides on stage to an extremely warm greeting. He is wearing blue coveralls—with uncut hair and a six-week-old beard—and he is far leaner than I remember him, especially around the face, after his recent 40-day fast. He stands there for a long moment in the anticipatory silence, looking them over. Finally, he walks to the front of the huge stage and takes an even closer look. "Why, you're normal. You're just a bunch of cats like anywhere else. . . . Man, it's M.I.T. and I expected robots!"
>
> They roar with laughter and he is off and running.[19]

Here, Gregory immediately secures and holds the interest of his audience by gaining their attention, addressing their expectations, and adapting to the situation.

The relationship between you, the speaker, and the immediate audience may be that of (a) superior to subordinate, the reverse of that, or as an equal; (b) politically or socially obligated; or (c) obligation free. Relationships within a structure influence how a message will be received. The speaker must candidly assess whether he or she is a member of the group which that audience represents, is in the decision-making circle, on the fringes or, possibly in a competing group. Then, the speaker must determine how he or she would like to be thought of by that audience, and the construction of the message, whether directly or subtly, ought to provide answers to the relationship desired by the speaker.

Finally, an audience analysis should measure the degree of identification existing between the speaker and the audience. Identification is vital to achieving effectiveness. Kenneth Burke succinctly describes the proximity between identification, persuasion, and communication: "As for the relation between 'identification' and 'persuasion' we might well keep in mind that a speaker persuades an audience by the use of stylistic identifications. . . . So, there is no chance of your keeping apart the meanings of persuasion, identification, and communication."[20] In short, regardless of form, public communication is a matter of understanding another's reasoning; comprehending another's beliefs, attitudes and values; and sympathizing with another's verbal and nonverbal codes. Identification is a process of becoming more alike. As Burke puts it, "You persuade a man only insofar as you can talk his language by speech, gestures, tonality, order, image, attitude, idea, *identifying* your ways with his."[21] In practical terms, then, you are attempting to discover commonalities.

Step Four: Research Your Topic

It is not enough to believe something is the case. When delivering a speech or report, you must be fortified with information. For certain presentations, the information you'll need is obvious. If you're informing the members of your firm's board of directors about last month's banking activity, your information will include the receipts and disbursements from that month. If you're demonstrating a new piece of equipment recently purchased by your office, your information will be the operating instructions for the machinery. Most of your presentations, however, will require you to research your topic, and the information available for most topics can seem overwhelming. This year, more than 50,000 books will be published in the U.S.[22] Add to this the millions of pages of information printed in newspapers, magazines, and other periodicals; volumes of public and private agencies' reports, hearings, and pamphlets; and hours of news and opinions broadcast via television and radio.[23] It is clear that a wealth of information exists for your presentations. Not all the information you acquire will appear in the text of your speech or report, but you'll need it all to select the material you'll include. Furthermore, you'll need extra information to respond successfully to questions and challenges arising as a result of your presentation.

When gathering information, you're responsible for determining the accuracy of the material, the plausibility of stated or implied conclusions, and the expertise of the author. You are not a mindless collector of other people's verbiage, but must function as a thoughtful, inquisitive, critical investigator. Not everything in print is true, reasonable, or acceptable, and it's your task to make discriminating and knowledgeable choices. You must seek, and gather, and think. You can help yourself immensely in this critical process by making a habit of cross-checking all significant information. Newspapers have been mistaken, books have contained erroneous material, and people have lied. Don't be caught in this web of potential falsehood. Double- and cross-check.

Look for the information you need in personal experiences, interviews, general references, and specific references. Personal experiences and knowledge acquired through the years offer good starting points for your research, but don't generalize too broadly from your personal experiences. Your personal information needs support from other information to give it a broader perspective.

As a rule of thumb, most presentations should use independent primary references. Independent references are not connected with each other. For example, three books written by the same author are not independent, nor are a series of pamphlets published by the same organization. Some of your references may be interrelated or interdependent, but at least three should be independent. Consult the complete texts of pertinent material, avoiding abridgements.

General references such as dictionaries and encyclopedias, and specific references such as books, newspapers, television and radio broadcasts, records, magazines, and scholarly journals are excellent information sources. Also, much of the research for your business presentations will be provided by the company for which you work. Among the types of materials you are seeking are quotations or expert testimony, statistics, examples, comparisons, analogies, and interesting descriptive stories.

Quotations. Quotations are the word-for-word or the paraphrased use of an expert's statement on your topic. They are used to support an assertion you've made in your presentation. You need to indicate the source of the quotation in your speech or report to enhance the credibility of the evidence, and you need to be sure that the source is unbiased. Additionally, you need to be sure that the quotation applies directly to your assertion, is appropriate to the situation and to the audience, and is neither too long nor too short. When using expert testimony:

1. Be sure that testimony comes from a reasonable authority in the subject area of the presentation. Verify the competency of the source.
2. Be sure that the testimony is reflective of current opinions; date the testimony.
3. Be sure the testimony is used in the proper and intended context.
4. Keep quotations brief.
5. Identify for the audience both the credibility of the source of estimony and the place that the quotation was located.

Statistics. Statistics are data collected in the form of numbers and are especially useful in business presentations because so much of business is concerned with numbers. Statistics, essentially, are used to give your ideas numerical precision. They're especially powerful in bringing your topic alive and dramatizing it. Your statistics need to be current, understandable, representative of what they claim to measure, and from a credible source. When using statistics, you should answer the following questions:

1. Are the statistics dependable?
2. Are the statistics current?

3. Are the statistics valid?
4. Can the statistics be simplified to round numbers?
5. Are statistics so copious that the audience will be overwhelmed and lose interest?

Examples. Examples are single instances that develop a general statement, and they can be very persuasive. In fact, research has shown that vivid examples have more impact on the beliefs and actions of the audience than any other kind of supporting material.[24] Examples can be about real or hypothetical circumstances and can be brief, such as a single specific instance, or extended, such as illustrations, narratives, or anecdotes.

Comparisons. Comparisons relate the known to the unknown by fusing already familiar material with unfamiliar material. Accepted ideas are integrated with new concepts, permitting greater identification with the audience, so ideas take on greater clarity and more acceptable dimensions when related to those already understood.

Analogies. Analogies present parallel situations for purposes of illustration and clarification. However, the parallel is indirect or implied and the instances are only figuratively similar. For example, our earlier comparison of communication to the lifeblood of a human organism was an analogy. Analogies are useful as a means of illustration and can make a presentation memorable.

Stories. Stories are very detailed examples and can be used to expand an idea you've made in the presentation. This form of research is especially powerful because it can build suspense and keep the attention of the audience focused on the speaker. For this reason, stories are especially valuable in the introduction and the conclusion. They must be relevant to the point you're making, neither too long nor too short, and appropriate to the situation and the audience.

Research of the materials discussed isn't done randomly. You need to have a plan. The following research strategy will optimize your efforts: First, fit your research to the time allotted. If you have considerable time to peruse materials, you can go to a variety of sources and use a number of different sources for the speech or report. But when time is at a premium, you will be limited to using a few sources and less materials. Second, approach the topic so that you progress from the general to the specific. You need to start from the largest data base possible—research summaries or state-of-the-art books and articles that synthesize current thought on the subject—then move to more specific sources of information. Third, develop important questions to be answered from your initial analysis. If you're preparing a speech to persuade the audience to join the teacher's union, the following questions will probably surface from your initial research efforts: What are the benefits of unionization? What are the disadvantages of joining a union? How many school districts are currently unionized? Why hasn't this district joined the union in the past? How much does it cost to join the union? Once these questions are answered, your information gathering can address other more specific questions. Throughout the process, remember your responsibility to interpret the information you collect.

Research is at the heart of the speech preparation process and should be undertaken with care and diligence. Effective research will provide proof for your arguments, vividness for your speaking, and credibility for you in the eyes of the audience.

Step Five: Organize Your Presentation

Plato observed centuries ago, in the *Phaedrus,* that "Every discourse ought to be a living creature, having a body of its own and a head and feet; there should be a middle, beginning, and end adapted to one another and to the whole."[25] Every presentation must be well organized if it is to be effective. All of us seem to realize intuitively that organized essays, articles, and oral presentations are more understandable than those that are not organized. Moreover, a number of research studies verify that a presentation is more effective when it is well structured. One study tested the comprehension of two audiences hearing the same message; as you might expect, the group hearing the organized presentation scored higher on the post-comprehension test.[26] Other studies have also indicated that effectively organized messages help listeners learn and retain material during informative presentations.[27] Finally, a clear and specific method of organization increases the speaker's confidence and the ability to fluently deliver the message.[28]

There is no set formula for the meaningful arrangement of one's presentation, but you may profitably think of organization in terms of the following simple diagram:

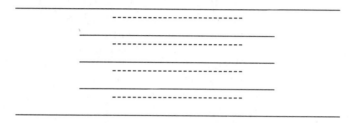

The longer first line represents the central idea. If the presentation has unity, it should have a single main theme, thesis, controlling purpose, or thrust (the first long line). Then this central idea should be based systematically on appropriate main headings, here represented by the three shorter, solid lines. The main headings are further developed by the use of supporting materials or information gathered during research. Lastly, the presentation provides a summary of ideas, stimulates action, and challenges the audience, as represented by the final long line. The short, broken lines in the diagram represent transitions from one part to another. If you think of your speech or oral report as a series of linked ideas, some more important than others, you should begin to understand the principle of subordination that underlies the theory of speech organization. The specific purpose or thesis states the goal of the presentation; the main points divide the specific purpose into its key parts; and the rest of the body of the presentation develops, explains, or proves the main points. The following guidelines should be useful as you organize the body of your presentation.

The central idea should describe your thesis and be phrased as a full, declarative sentence. The thesis statement, or central idea, encapsulates what the presentation is about and expands and clarifies the specific purpose statement. In an informative presentation, the central idea is a statement of what you want the audience to learn; in a persuasive presentation, it is a statement of what you want the audience to believe or how you want them to act. It should be limited to one clear idea and be phrased in a single, declarative, full sentence. Phrasing it as a question or a sentence fragment doesn't provide the precision necessary for this important aspect of the presentation.

The body of your presentation should contain no more than five main points. As you begin to phrase prospective main points, you may find your list growing to five, seven, or even ten. If you remember, however, that every main point must be developed in some detail and that your goal is to help the audience retain the subject matter of each main point, you will see the impracticality of more than five main points. You should be able to organize your presentation around a few main points that develop the thesis. Moreover, these main points need to be mutually exclusive, i.e., the ideas in your main points must be inherently different. Thus, having more than five main ideas usually is a sign that your purpose needs to be limited, or that like ideas need to be grouped under a single heading.

Main points should correspond exactly to your thesis statement, being phrased as complete sentences using a parallel style. As a rule, main points are complete sentences that best develop the specific purpose. Your analysis of the topic will allow you to use the thesis statement as the standard against which to measure the main points. Vague, meaningless main points will have the same effect on the development of your presentation as a vague purpose. Using parallel wording when phrasing your main points will further help you and the audience to recall the main points. Consider the following thesis statement and main points:

Thesis: Changing our company's hiring policy to assure more diversity will increase the quality of our workforce.

   I. Our present hiring practice doesn't consider diversity when seeking prospective candidates.

   II. The company is very homogeneous, with many employees having similar skills and experiential backgrounds.

   III. We can hire a more diverse workforce this year, given the current turnover in positions.

Certainly the main points presented are important because they suggest a possible violation of EEO guidelines and a failure to have an operative Affirmative Action program. However, they do not address the issue of "diversity and a quality workforce." Without this relationship, the thesis statement is wanting. More appropriate main points supporting the thesis and conforming to a parallel style would be:

Thesis: Changing our company's hiring policy to assure more diversity will increase the quality of our workforce.

   I. A diverse workforce will encourage a multiplicity of perspectives, given company issues.

   II. A diverse workforce will enlarge our current skill-base.

   III. A diverse workforce will enhance our customer service and relationship with the community.

Here, the main points directly support the thesis and the parallel wording improves audience retention. Your main points anchor the structure of the presentation and should be carefully selected, phrased, and arranged.

Logically arrange your main points in an order appropriate to your subject and stated purpose or thesis. Effective speakers have found that their ideas blend together better, will be more easily phrased, and will be more easily understood if they follow one of several common presentational patterns: chronological, spatial, cause-and-effect, problem–solution, pro–con, or topical. The particular pattern that is best for your presentation depends on your purpose and the effect you want to achieve. What is important is that the material be organized.

Chronological Pattern. This pattern follows a time sequence where information is arranged from a beginning point to an ending point. Presentations using the chronological pattern present events in the order in which they occur. If the focus of the presentation is "how" or "when," this type of pattern can be effective. For example, a report on how to prepare a financial statement according to the accounting cycle might be arranged this way:

    I. The first step in preparing a financial statement is to journalize the entries.
    II. The second step is to post the entries.
    III. The third step is to prepare a trial balance.
    IV. The fourth step is to prepare the adjustments.
    V. The fifth step in preparing the statement is to prepare the adjusted trial balance.

Or, you might present the history of your corporation using a chronological order:

    I. The Abbott Corporation began in the 1970s as a small, family-owned business.
    II. It grew steadily in the 1980s into a medium-sized company.
    III. It emerged in the 1990s as a large, international corporation.

Spatial Pattern. This pattern organizes ideas according to physical properties, location, or geographical relationships. Space and direction become your ordering principles—from left to right, east to west, top to bottom, or inside to outside. This pattern is often appropriate with problems focusing on area. A presentation that explains a new marketing strategy using flyers for a pizza company might use the following spatial pattern:

    I. The first area where the flyers will be distributed is in ZIP codes 32570–32579.
    II. The second area is in ZIP codes 32580–32589.
    III. The third area is in ZIP codes 32590–32599.

Cause-and-Effect Pattern. This pattern is used to show events that are causally related. Causal analysis determines whether one factor caused another factor to occur—an effect. The key word is "caused." A cause-and-effect arrangement tries to show that an incident or series of incidents contributed to or triggered a related event or series of events. Determining such relationships is particularly difficult because of the complex nature of human affairs. A chronological relationship does not necessarily equal a causal relationship. One event following another may as easily be chance as cause. Although two factors often appear together with regularity, this is no evidence that one causes the other. For example, when it rains the sidewalks are wet, but wet sidewalks do not necessarily mean it rained. Moreover, confusion can also arise from a misunderstanding of *necessary* and *sufficient* conditions. The presence of oxygen is a necessary condition for fire to burn, but fire does not occur whenever there is oxygen; the presence of oxygen alone is not sufficient to cause fire. The cause-and-effect pattern can be very effective, but you must be careful not to confuse relationship and correlation with causation. In an informative report to the company about recent layoffs, the CEO might arrange the issues as follows:

I. The layoffs were caused by recessionary pressures and a large reduction in orders from our major buyers.

II. The layoffs have resulted in a 10 percent reduction in the company workforce.

Problem–Solution Pattern. The problem–solution pattern is often used in persuasive presentations and is divided into two main points. The first describes the existence and seriousness of a problem; the second develops an acceptable and workable solution to that problem. Such an arrangement should (a) define relevant terms, (b) analyze the problem historically and in terms of the status quo, and (c) offer a desirable solution that the audience is willing to adopt. In explaining the new company drug-testing policy, the director of human resources might organize the main points of the presentation like this:

I. The number of company employees who use drugs that impair their work has increased to an intolerable level.

II. Drug testing will better guarantee that company employees remain drug-free.

Pro–Con Pattern. This pattern discusses the positive side of a situation and then the negative side of the situation, or presents your arguments and your opponents' arguments. The pro–con approach can be useful when the audience is well informed on the issue(s) and familiar with opposing arguments, or when a speaker for the opposition precedes or follows you. It may also be used when, as a result of your research, a preferred solution does not naturally emerge and you wish to leave the selection of a preferable alternative up to the audience. The vice president of safety for a railroad line who is concerned about the number of older freight engines that may be unsafe could organize a presentation to colleagues as follows:

I. The older freight engines that pose safety hazards should be retired.

II. The older freight engines that pose safety hazards should be overhauled and retained.

Topical Pattern. This is the most common pattern and consists of selecting a limited number of equally important issues related to the stated purpose. The topical arrangement deals with types, forms, qualities, or aspects of the selected subject and collectively presents a particular perspective. It can be useful to present familiar ideas first and then progress to the unfamiliar, or to present the easiest material first and then move on to the more-difficult material. The topical pattern is well suited to both informative and persuasive communications. A presentation intended to persuade an audience that company benefits need to be increased might argue from the following topical pattern:

I. The company's medical benefits have a very high deductible payment.

II. The company has no dental policy benefit.

III. The company has no tuition payment policy for higher education.

Taken collectively, your main points outline the structure of your presentation. Whether your audience understands, believes, or appreciates what you have to say will depend on your development of these main points. They cannot stand alone; you have to support them with examples, illustrations, statistics, comparisons, analogies, testimony, and the use of visual aids.

Use transitions between major parts of your presentation. Transitions are words or phrases that form a bridge from one section of your presentation to the next. These connectives are similar to ligaments and tendons in the human body. Without connectives, a presentation is disjointed and uncoordinated. When building transitions between thoughts consider the following words and their use.

These expressions indicate that what follows is supplementary to what precedes. They link matters of like kind and grammatical form:

also	*and*	*moreover*	*furthermore*
likewise	*again*	*in addition*	

These expressions indicate that what follows is the result of what precedes:

therefore	*and so*	*so*
consequently	*subsequently*	*as a result*

These words indicate a change in direction. They suggest conflict and sometimes imply concession:

but	*however*	*yet*	*on the other hand*
still	*nevertheless*	*notwithstanding*	*nonetheless*

These words indicate concession:

although	*even though*	*though*

These words indicate a reason for a subsequent sentence:

because	*for*

These words show cause or relationship in time:

then	*since*	*as*

These words restrict or enlarge:

so that	*in order that*	*for this reason*	*of course*
in other words	*in fact*	*for example*	

Transitions are usually necessary between the introduction and the first main point, between main points, and between the last main point and the conclusion. They summarize one idea and preview the next.

An ordered presentation has an introduction, a body, and a conclusion. The introduction gains our attention; the body develops major ideas that support the stated purpose; and the conclusion provides a summary and a forceful, positive close. This organizational pattern is much like the saying you've probably heard, "Tell them what you're going to tell them. Tell them. Tell them what you told them." Having discussed the body of the presentation, you're ready to prepare the introduction and conclusion.

Step Six: Plan Your Introduction and Conclusion

On the evening of October 9, 1986, a conductor stepped to the podium at Her Majesty's Theatre in London, tapped his baton, raised his arms, and signaled the orchestra to play. Moments later the audience heard the dramatic opening chords of "The Phantom of the Opera." Several hours later the theatre rang with applause while the curtain descended and the orchestra played Andrew Lloyd Weber's dramatic finale. Like most musical stage plays, *Phantom of the Opera* begins with an overture—an orchestral introduction that captures the audience's attention and gives them a preview of the music they are going to hear—and closes with a musical climax. Similarly, you must set the stage, introduce the theme, focus the audience's attention, tap their interests, and then provide a powerful close. Just as musicals need an effective beginning and ending, your presentations need a solid introduction and conclusion. Without them, the body of your speech or report will be incomplete, and you won't effectively achieve your purpose.

Introduction. This portion should (a) capture the attention of your audience, (b) provide a clearly stated and fully qualified statement of purpose, (c) establish your credibility, and (d) forecast the focus of your presentation. The introduction should cause your audience to feel that they have a reason for listening to your speech or report. These first two minutes of your presentation are the most crucial for it is now that the audience will decide either to sit up and listen or drift off into their own thoughts.

The introduction is the time to figuratively grab the audience and make them want to listen to you. Remember that some members of your audience may be ambivalent, believing they already know what you have to say or feeling that they can't afford the time to listen to you. If you don't capture their attention at the outset, you'll probably lose them for the entire speech or report. By motivating them to listen during the first minute or so, you can be reasonably certain that they are psychologically prepared to listen to the heart of the presentation. How you go about gaining audience attention and focusing that attention on your specific purpose can vary. Commonly used techniques include: the rhetorical question; the startling statement; the quotation; the anecdote, narrative, or illustration; and humor.

The *rhetorical question* plants an idea for consideration and immediately involves the thinking processes of the audience. Next you pause and then proceed to answer this question, or series of questions, in the body of the presentation. Rhetorical questions do not seek an outward verbal or behavioral response from the audience, but rather are meant to stimulate thought and pique curiosity. Questions should be pertinent to the topic and meaningful to the audience.

The *startling statement* is a headline technique that serves the same function in a presentation as large print does in a newspaper. You present certain bold statements or startling statistics intended to arouse attention and interests. Shocking, unusual, or dramatic statements should be evaluated for their potential effectiveness, their reflection of good taste, and their indication of good sense. Avoid opening statements that are trite, boring, or distracting.

A *quotation* can provide a challenging thought and prepare the audience for the presentation to follow. It can enhance your personal credibility by association, so take care to choose a quotation from a source the audience will respect and trust.

The *anecdote, narrative,* or *illustration* can provide detail and personalize your subject for the audience. These devices may focus on a personal experience or they may recall an example or event read or remembered. They may be true or hypothetical, literary or historical. Because we all like to hear stories, they can vividly set a tone to your remarks and draw the audience into your presentation.

Humor must be selectively and carefully used. There is always the risk that using humor in the introduction may detract from the seriousness of your subject. And there is probably no worse way to begin a presentation than by telling a joke that flops; the pitfall is being corny or trite. When tastefully chosen and told well, a funny story that is relevant to the topic and the occasion is extremely effective.

These and other techniques may be used to gain the attention of your audience. In selecting an attention-getting strategy, keep in mind the need for appropriateness. Your approach should be in harmony with the nature and tone of the presentation, with your talents and personality, and with the tastes and expectations of the audience. Rarely is your only choice the dull and unimaginative opening clichés, "Today I am going to talk about. . . " or "I am pleased to be here to talk about. . . ."

In these first several moments you reveal your purpose and state your central thesis. This may seem elementary, but many speakers are unclear in the beginning, leaving the audience no defined path to follow the subsequent development of ideas. So, the rambler should beware, heeding the expectations and demands of the audience.

It is also in the introduction that your audience will decide if they want to listen to you, if they like you, and if they find you credible. Therefore, at this point you must establish why you, in particular, are in a position to address this topic. What knowledge, skills, and experiences do you bring to the situation? How honest and trustworthy are your opinions, attitudes, and beliefs? You must, however, use subtlety and diplomacy in establishing your credibility—the line between seeming to brag and merely stating your qualifications is narrow. Indicate your interest, express concern, display sensitivity, and gently tell your audience who you are. Abbreviate this if you are already familiar to your audience.

Finally, you want to forecast your main points for the audience. This preview will help your listeners follow your subsequent progression of ideas. A presentation is an immediate event and your audience is *listening* to you, not reading your speech or report; so if they lose your train of thought at some point, they can't go back and reread the material. Previewing the main points lets your listeners better understand your approach to the topic and your point of view.

Having noted what you should do in an introduction, let's briefly examine some introductory don'ts. *Don't apologize or discredit yourself.* Some speakers begin their presentations by saying: "I'm really nervous today, . . ." or "I'm not very good at public speaking, but. . . ," or "I don't know much about . . . so bear with me as I speak. . . ." They believe that a brief apology will endear them to the audience, but the opposite is true. Listeners generally reject speakers who begin with an apology or who discredit themselves. *Don't make the introduction too long.* The introduction should represent only 10 to 15 percent of the total presentation. Longer introductions will probably prompt listeners to ask, "When are you going to get to the point?" *Don't use a false start.* Some speakers begin with a false start by saying, "Before I begin, I'd like to say. . . ." Such unnecessary beginnings only detract from a more effective introduction.

The introduction is not going to make your speech or report an instant success, but an effective introduction will get an audience to look at you and listen to you. That's about as much as you can ask of an audience during the first few minutes of a presentation.

Conclusion. The conclusion of the speech or report is especially important. A presentation must have feet—it must have a conclusion. Speakers often mistakenly believe their presentation is over when they complete the body of the speech or report. As a result, they fail to close effectively, choosing instead to mumble, "That's all I have" or "Thank you," or simply walking from the lectern to their seat. The conclusion should succinctly bring your remarks to a close and leave a forceful, positive image with the listeners.

One of the most common ways of concluding a presentation is to summarize the main ideas you have chosen to communicate. In summarizing, you may reiterate the main points in a straightforward, almost literal manner, or you might restate them in a more concise fashion. Your summary may also include a quotation, illustrative anecdote, or narrative to make for a more memorable closing. Poems, lyrics, or striking memorable slogans can also be effective if carefully chosen and well integrated. The important issue is that the audience should hear one last time what you want them to remember.

The challenge is a call for action. You may challenge the audience to act, to believe, to meet a need, to demonstrate concern, or even to live a different kind of life. The challenge may be specific or general; it may be a direct plea for some type of action or a rhetorical question raised for the audience to answer in their lives. The anticipated result is an acceptance of the challenge issued—action.

The conclusion is also an excellent opportunity for you to leave a positive, strong, and lasting impression. End your presentation just as you started it—with strength and confidence. A too-short conclusion will deny you the chance to fulfill the important functions of the conclusion and will leave a weak impression with the audience. The way you conclude should leave your listeners in a particular frame of mind.

There is much you can do to make the conclusion effective, but there are also a number of pitfalls you should avoid. *Don't use concluding phrases in other parts of the presentation.* Phrases such as "in conclusion" or "to summarize" announce your intentions to close. You can confuse listeners when you use these phrases before your wrap-up and force them to reorient themselves to your ongoing presentation. *Don't end with an apology.* Concluding statements such as, "Well, I guess I've rambled on long enough," or "I hope I haven't bored you today," will only decrease your credibility and undo what you have accomplished in the presentation. *Don't introduce a new issue.* The conclusion is not the place to introduce new ideas into your speech or report. You may present new evidence and extensions of arguments made earlier, but completely new and different ideas should be avoided. Carolyn Planck, president of Communication for Professionals, observes: "Few things are as annoying as the speaker who behaves like a car with a faulty idle . . . when the key is turned off, the engine continues to sputter, cough, and go on and on and on. When the speaker has summarized and created the proper mood, he/she should give a final, concluding statement and STOP."[29]

Conclusions, like introductions, cannot do much for a poor presentation, but they can heighten the effect of a good presentation. They tie the presentation together into a compact, concise package by summarizing the main points and providing direction, action, or visualization.

Step Seven: Select Your Visual Aids

We live in a society that places a premium on the visual. Toddlers are viewing computer screens in their preschools, adolescents are playing video games in arcades, adults are watching large-screen televisions in their living rooms, and renting videos has become commonplace. We see huge billboards with moving parts and blinking lights on our highways, and read books, magazines, and newspapers with visual images that inform us about news events and persuade us to buy new products. Our information age exists within the confines of an electronic age that is integrally related to visual imagery. Consequently, visual support is a critical component of most management presentations.

The last half of the 1980s witnessed major changes in audience expectations for quality visual support. Before desktop publishing, overheads were often difficult to read and time-consuming to create. Charts were handmade and text visuals were usually typed or carefully hand-printed. Thirty-five–millimeter slides were used occasionally at great expense, as were videotapes. Audiences understood these constraints and accepted the results. But now anyone with a personal computer can quickly create graphics or produce handouts, and inexpensive portable camcorders permit easy videotaping. Moreover, programmed and interactive computer presentations are playing an increasingly frequent role in conference-room activity. Visual aids have become an expected part of most informative and persuasive speaking and, if used well, can powerfully increase the effectiveness of a presentation.

The purpose of any visual is to help the audience understand and believe you in the shortest possible time. Visuals should add value to the presentation, and to do this, they must be easy to see or read and easy to understand. Furthermore and, most importantly, their content must support your words. If an aid does not present the idea more clearly than it can be presented without the aid, or if it does not add a dimension of credibility or interest, then it becomes a distraction that will inhibit the interaction between speaker and audience. Speakers often want to use visual aids just because everyone else uses them. But when considering using visuals, you should ask yourself: "Do I *need* to use visual aids in this presentation?" If the answer is yes and you choose them carefully, they can enhance your presentation in a number of ways.

Visuals Create Interest. Visual aids can be helpful in gaining and maintaining the attention of your listeners. Words alone may seize attention and develop interest, but visuals can enhance your words significantly. An engineer speaking on the future of energy can increase interest by displaying a piece of oil shale or showing a model of a high-tech wind generator. A speaker on the environment could show samples of water or particles removed from the air. A corporate executive emphasizing the need for a crisis management plan might show a videoclip of the destruction left in the wake of Hurricane Andrew. The more abstract the ideas, the more a concrete demonstration, object, picture, or recording can hold acceptable levels of attention. Visuals can grab the audience's attention and create an interest in the presentation.

Visuals Aid Understanding. Listeners understand better if they both hear your words and see visual aids that reinforce your message. Some topics, especially those involving physical objects or processes, simply cannot be well explained with the oral message alone. William Seiler reports that even simple drawings enhance recall, and charts and photographs help listeners process and retain data.[30] Because we can only remember a limited number of thoughts and impressions, we remember only those things important to us, deeming the rest trivia and disregarding it. We tend to remember: (a) what we pay close attention to, (b) what we clearly understand, and (c) what we vividly experience. Visual aids help listeners remember more of your speech and remember it for a longer period of time.[31] If receivers can watch a demonstration, see pictures, hear a tape recording, view a film, feel an object, or

► THE ROLE OF VISUAL AIDS IN PRESENTATIONS

By John J. Makay

In an attempt to discover whether visual support materials give presenters a persuasive edge, Douglas R. Vogal, Gary W. Dickson, and John A. Lehman, researchers at the Management Information Systems Research Center at the University of Minnesota and the 3M Corporation conducted the following study:

They gathered nine groups of thirty-five undergraduate business students each. The groups were shown a ten-minute speech to influence the audience to sign up for a series of time-management seminars. (The seminars involved two three-hour sessions at a cost of $15.) To make sure the quality of the speaker was consistent, each group watched the same presentation on videotape. The difference in the presentations was the use of visual support. While one group watched the presentation with no visual support, the other eight groups watched videotapes enhanced by some form of high quality visuals. (One of the researchers manually displayed the visual material for these presentations.) The variables in visual support treatments included color vs. black-and-white, plain text vs. text enhanced with "clip art" and graphs, and 35-mm slides vs. overhead transparencies.

At the conclusion of each videotape researchers surveyed the subjects to learn their degree of interest in the time-management seminars (a questionnaire had been administered before the videotapes to determine initial attitudes) and to assess their comprehension of the videotape. Ten days later, a final questionnaire was administered to test how much of the videotaped information the students retained.

According to the researchers, compared to their pre-speech attitudes, the groups who had seen a speech supported by visuals were willing to spend 43% more time and 26% more money on the seminars than those who had seen the presentation without visual support. In addition, the various components of persuasion were improved by the presence of visual support. Action (the commitment to sign up for the course) improved by 43%; positive comprehension by 7.5%; and agreement with the presenter's position by 5.5%. When the speeches were delivered with visual support, the audiences perceived the presenter as more concise, clearer, making better use of supporting data, more professional, more persuasive, and more interesting.

Specific characteristics of the visuals also influenced the persuasive force of the presentation. Color overhead transparencies had the greatest positive impact on action. In addition, comprehension and retention improved with color vs. black-and-white visual support. The researchers also found that 35-mm slides increased the audience's perception of speaker professionalism.

These findings were in response to an "average" or "typical" speaker. To determine the impact of visual support on the persuasive ability of a superior speaker, the researchers videotaped a second speaker with better skills. Both speakers read identical remarks. The researchers found that "typical" speakers who integrated visuals into their speeches were as effective as "better" speakers who use no visuals. They also found that the better presenters were most persuasive when they used high quality—machine produced rather than hand-drawn—visual support. Audiences were less willing to commit their time or money to the seminar when the "better" speakers used inferior visual material.

Source: John J. Makay, *Public Speaking: Theory into Practice* (Fort Worth, TX: Harcourt Brace Jovanovich, 1992): 173. Copyright © 1992 Holt, Rinehart & Winston, Inc., reprinted by permission of the publisher.

even do an activity along with the speaker, they will comprehend more and retain the message longer.

Visuals Boost Personal Impact. Visual aids also enhance your credibility and increase your personal impact. They add dynamism and sizzle to your presentation, and that transfers to you personally. There is a carryover effect to you as a speaker from visuals that are vibrant, exciting, and even artistic. So the effective use of visual materials often promotes a favorable audience response. They appreciate the noticeable time and attention given to careful preparation, and the obvious concern for increased understanding. Listeners perceive you to be earnest, confident, and speaking with knowledge.

Speakers sometimes avoid using visual aids in presentations because they require more time, energy, and risk to develop and use. But they can be a crucial component of the public-speaking process, and they are consistent with our increasingly visual culture and with the norms or expectations of audiences in the business and professional setting.

Once you have decided that your presentation will be enhanced by visual support, you have two decisions to make: (1) the form of the visual, and (2) the substance of the visual. Visual aids may assume various forms, shapes, and sizes with the specific choice being determined by the nature of the presentation, the audience, and the occasion. Each form serves a particular purpose and has specific design guidelines that apply equally to any medium. Here we will examine those visuals common to informative and persuasive presentations—personal demonstration; physical objects; models; text visuals; conceptual visuals; tables, charts, or graphs; pictures or diagrams; maps; audio/videotapes; and on-screen computer displays.

Personal Demonstration. When speakers personally exhibit a particular behavior, like swinging a tennis racquet, performing first aid techniques, or operating a machine, they become the visual support as well as the primary information source. The advantages are increased animation, adaptability, and realism. You can move around to appropriate positions and postures, change your behavior to meet unexpected situations, and actually show how a particular activity should be performed. Certain delivery problems to consider are the difficulty in using notes during the demonstration and the physical effort required. However, more critical is the danger of failing, or performing awkwardly and with embarrassment, distracting the audience and damaging your credibility. These problems can be solved by careful preparation and practice.

Physical Objects. Audiences appreciate seeing appropriate physical objects that have the advantages of realism and exactness. The obvious value of using physical objects, when the subject of your presentation, is the real-life experience gained by the listeners. The sales representative for a carpet manufacturer can be much more effective if samples are shown to potential buyers, or a personnel supervisor can more effectively explain how to complete a medical form if employees can see a form at the same time. Objects are sometimes too big or too small to be practical for a particular speaking environment. If it is too large to take into the room (such as an airplane) or too small to be easily seen (such as a computer chip), use a reproduction such as a model airplane or an enlarged replica of the computer chip. Physical objects are particularly useful when your purpose is to develop audience skills in such activities as operating equipment or creating an arts-and-crafts project.

Models. Models can be replicas of the real thing or theoretical representations of a process and its relational components. Physicians often use plastic models of body parts that can be further disassembled to show the inner workings when describing particular procedures for patients. Genetic engineers have created theoretical molecular models, and communication scholars have designed various models of the communication process. Models are useful for instructional purposes and can help listeners organize and relate information. Moreover, theoretical models can serve to stimulate further research.

Text Visuals. Text visuals contain only words or phrases and serve to preview or summarize information. They can keep important information in front of the audience and help them follow the presentation. It's especially important that text visuals convey a readily understandable message and be simple in content and in design. You should use action or message phrases rather than topic words or complete sentences, and keep lists parallel and in the order you intend to follow. It can also be helpful to highlight the most important message on the visual. Your goal is to have an easy-to-read, esthetically pleasing visual.

Conceptual Visuals. Conceptual visuals use clip art or images to make a point by analogy or to show the relationship of ideas. Boxes, arrows, pyramids, or pictures are often used to convey a message. They clarify a point by putting it in a nonbusiness context that has meaning to the audience. It is critical that the analogies or pictured relationships show what you mean to show and are meaningful to your audience. Although relatively new, conceptual visuals permit a latitude of creativity that can capture and maintain the interest of your audience.

Tables, Charts, or Graphs. Tables, charts, or graphic representations of data show statistical or conceptual relationships among variables. They are the visuals most often used in business presentations. Computer software programs offer you a broad range of variations and combinations of chart forms, so it is important to understand the purpose of each form and how each can be used most effectively.

- *Tables* can give exact numbers for multiple variables and work well as backup visuals to provide details (e.g., a table showing the quantitative growth of selected product lines over a ten-year period of time).
- *Bar and column charts* are most useful for illustrating the relationship between two or more sets of figures, comparing several variables at one time, or one variable at discrete points in time (e.g., a bar graph comparing sales of different product lines or a column graph comparing the sales of one product line over time).
- *Gantt charts* focus attention on the parts of a process over time (e.g., a Gantt chart displaying the development and implementation of a management training program noting the time frame for each component in the process).
- *Pie charts* show the relationship of one or more parts to each other and to the whole by dividing a circle (or pie) into the representative portions (e.g., a pie chart can indicate the percentage of listeners in specific age groups who listen to a particular radio station).
- *Scatter charts* show the correlation or lack of correlation between two variables (e.g., a scatter chart can compare faculty salary to academic rank to assess the degree of equity or degree of compression).
- *Line graphs* indicate the changes over time of one or more variables (e.g., a line graph can indicate the turnover rate in a company over time or compare/contrast the turnover rate with similar companies over time).

Pictures or Diagrams. Photographs, paintings, and drawings improve a presentation by giving listeners a visual sense of what you are talking about. Topics involving particular places, people, or themes may rely more heavily on pictorial content. If you wanted to show your listeners the effects of smoking, contrasting pictures of lungs from a smoker and a nonsmoker would concretely and effectively make your point. Indeed, a picture can be worth a thousand words. Diagrams or drawings of actual objects can show three-dimensional views and concentrate on important features. It is important that pictures, drawings, and diagrams be simple, relevant, and large enough to be seen by the audience.

Maps. Maps show dimensions, distances, terrain, contrasts, and geographical relationships. They are often indispensable when speaking on the weather, international politics, travel, transportation, military activities, historical topics, and various business and government issues. To be effective, maps must be current, contain relevant detail, and be easy to read or see from a distance.

Audio/Videotapes. The electronic age makes audiovisual materials especially appealing and informative. Audio/videotape systems permit the audience to experience your topic. The strategic impact of carefully planned audiovisual materials can be significant, but the use of electronic media brings with it some possible problems: poor quality of sound or inadequate amplification, tape breakage or malfunction of equipment, and loss of electric power. Because such speakers as training officers, teachers, and sales representatives need to use these aids regularly, they develop ways to systematize their use and have experience in coping with these problems. For the rest of us, the use of electronic media requires practice.

On-Screen Computer Displays. Over the past few years, computers have become an increasingly useful tool for producing visuals before presentations and for developing visuals during presentations. Computer-generated graphics used before your presentation can increase the sophistication and clarity of your visuals if you follow a few simple guidelines. First, you can supplement your computer-generated graphics by providing the audience with computer-generated handouts to take with them when they leave the meeting. And, second, remember that the information presented by the graphics is most important. Edward R. Tufte offers this warning:

> Computers and their affiliated apparatus can do powerful things graphically. . . . But at least a few computer graphics only evoke the response, "Isn't it remarkable that the computer can be programmed to draw like that?" instead of "My, what interesting data. . . ." These graphics are really all non–data-ink or redundant data-ink, and it is often chart-junk. Graphical decoration . . . comes cheaper than the hard work required to produce intriguing numbers and secure evidence."[32]

Computers can also be programmed for use during a speech to produce a series of visuals from memory, resulting in a presentation similar to one using slides but with an increased sense of forward movement. Programs such as "Freelance Plus," "Harvard Graphics," or "Show Partner" can add color, motion, and sizzle to your presentation. But maybe the most attractive use for computers in the presentation arena is the ability to play "what if?" games with a small number of participants. A graphic display can illustrate powerfully the effect a small change in one variable can have on other variables. To use the computer this way, the presenter must decide which graphic form best displays the data, and what and how much data manipulation to use. Done effectively, these presentations can be both exciting and persuasive.

Currently, the use of computers in presentations requires considerable skill, training, and sophistication and a substantial investment in both software and hardware.

Their use will undoubtedly increase as managers become more comfortable with computers and as cost-effective, user-friendly programs are developed.

The effective use of visual aids requires careful planning and preparation of materials, always with an eye to the purpose and main ideas of the presentation and the audience for which it's intended. And, no matter how well prepared, visual aids that are ineptly presented are at best useless, and at worst a distraction.

Prepare Well in Advance. Last-minute attempts to find appropriate pictures, draw charts, or arrange for demonstration equipment are not only hectic; the audience usually senses the lack of careful preparation and is left with a negative impression of the speaker and the message. Making professional-looking visuals takes time and may require the help of artists, photographers, statisticians, drafters, audiovisual technicians, and computer programmers. Some presenters try to save money, cut corners, or rush production, and it doesn't work. Today's business and professional audiences *expect* high-quality, carefully crafted, and creative visuals that present information in a fresh and interesting form.

Consider the Medium and the Occasion. Make the visual aid and all its components suitable to the unique characteristics of the medium and relevant to the topic and occasion. Overheads, slides, and flip-charts require your attending to size of type, visual dimensions, and consistency as well as to artistic and mechanical concerns. Audiovisual materials demand that you consider production techniques, sound systems, and visual angles. And you must prepare your visuals for the audience—for what they know, what they don't know, and what they expect to know. The communications director explaining a new television advertising campaign will include a video because the audience will expect to see a sample advertisement. The corporate executive proposing a policy change will include a handout because the audience will want to see the policy itself. When you approach the use of visual materials from a receiver-centered perspective, the aids become a means of ensuring that receivers will understand and appreciate the intended message. Screen visual materials carefully, asking: Are these devices really necessary? What do I hope to achieve that cannot be gained without them? Have I selected appropriate visual forms to clarify ideas? Do they provide fresh and interesting information? Will I insult my audience's intelligence by using these aids? Too often, speakers toss in extra materials as an afterthought simply because the aid is available, looks good, and "might as well be shown."

Patricia Rowell, director of business and special projects at Seminole Community College, recommends using storyboards and visual imaging when developing a presentation with visual support.[33] These provide a mechanism for checking the flow of information and assessing the use of multiple channels or mediums to support your message. You write the key ideas of your presentation as headings at the top of each boxed storyboard. Next, note the selected visual form for support and sketch the visual. Finally, add a transition. The series of storyboards outlines your presentation and indicates where visuals might be inserted. Visual imaging is a method of diagramming that permits a broader view of the presentation and the multiple channels or mediums you might use. Each channel or medium is assigned a geometrical shape or image—for example, a square might represent lecturing, a circle an overhead or flip-chart, a triangle might indicate slides or videotape, a rectangle a discussion, and an octagon could stand for handouts. When the flow of a presentation is diagramed using these shapes, you can better determine the appropriateness of each channel or medium, predict time requirements, and weigh potential impact:

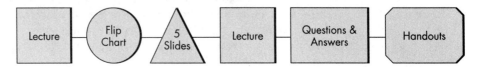

Once you've diagrammed your presentation, you may want to reassess the use of certain channels to better break up the presentation and add interest as well as to invite more audience involvement. Or, you might gain additional speaking confidence by seeing that your presentation, as illustrated above, reflects an effective balance of channels and use of visual support. Certainly the visual dimension of your presentation can be a key factor in achieving your communication goals.

Keep Aids Clear, Simple, and Visible. Each visual should illustrate one idea with a clear point of focus. Guard against creating overly elaborate visuals with unnecessary information or extraneous lines and vibrating patterns that will only confuse and distract the audience. A series of simple charts, graphs, or pictures may be more useful than one large complicated one. Or a complex aid can gradually be built up with overlays as you guide the audience through the parts of the picture step by step. Remember: you want to focus attention on the message, not on the visual, and you do this by keeping it simple and ensuring that most of the ink on the page relates to the message. Visual aids must also be large enough to be easily seen, and using bold lines and dark or contrasting colors can help. It's very frustrating to try to see a visual that's too small. Avoid having to ad lib an embarrassed, "I know you can't see this clearly, but. . ." by making the message easy to read and eliminating unnecessary design details and text. Visuals should aid, not burden, your presentation.

Be Wary of Handouts. A common tactic of business and professional speaking today is to hand out duplicated materials so that everyone can read along while the speaker elaborates on the information. Although this procedure is productive in certain workshops, trainings, and conference settings, it can present a problem. George Grice and John Skinner describe this difficulty when they observe: "If you distribute handouts before your remarks, the audience is already ahead of you. Passing out information during a presentation can be distracting, especially if you stop talking as you do so. Disseminating material after the presentation eliminates distractions but does not allow the listener to refer to the printed information as you are explaining it."[34] Given the paradox, if a handout must be distributed, it usually should be made available at the end of the presentation. Increasingly, however, busy executives are demanding handouts in advance, allowing them an opportunity to review the ideas and make notes. When this is necessary, consider writing an executive summary that uses headings and summary pages to focus attention and highlight major ideas. Be careful not to provide so much information that people stop listening to you in order to read.

Introduce Visuals Effectively. The use of visual materials usually either leads to improved audience understanding and interest or distracts the audience from the speaker's message. A visual aid is only effective when you introduce it at the proper psychological point in the presentation. Visuals should be in view only when they help the audience understand the speaker's idea—introduced, used, then removed. Too many presenters speak to the audience with their visuals in full view when they aren't being used, thus deflecting attention away from themselves.

Speak to the audience and not to the visual aid. The audience should always be the speaker's primary concern. Few sights are more ludicrous than an adult standing before an audience but engaged in a serious discussion with a blackboard, a chart, or a slide. If you must turn your back to the group to write, don't speak while you write—the silence won't bother your audience because they'll be busy watching what you're writing. When you are well prepared, only an occasional glance at a visual to tell that everything is in order or to see where to point will be necessary. Because eye contact has such potency for maintaining audience attention, you cannot abandon this crucial tool.

Certain delivery techniques with particular media can enhance their effectiveness. Standing close to a flip-chart, blackboard, or projection screen can prove helpful when pointing out information. But when you position yourself and use visual support, remember not to block anyone's view. Using a remote control for slides or videotape presentations gives you greater flexibility and movement. Using overheads, slides, films, and VCRs professionally means being certain that your equipment is in good working order and that you know how to use it correctly.

Practice Beforehand. This step in preparation and use is frequently overlooked. Speakers practice the verbal message orally and occasionally *think,* "At this point I'll pick up the object and show how it's used, or bring up a chart or graph." But thinking is not *doing,* and many speakers have been surprised by unexpected problems at crucial moments in their presentations. Perhaps the color slides are not in order; or a device won't work properly; or an important detail has been omitted from a diagram; or the aids are too bulky to hold, clumsy to manipulate, or difficult to set up. Practicing will not guarantee that unexpected problems never arise, but it can significantly reduce their likelihood and improve your speaking confidence. We especially encourage your rehearsing in the presence of a listener.

Step Eight: Deliver Your Presentation

A well-reasoned, well-supported, well-arranged collection of thoughts is only the skeleton of a presentation. The speech or report does not become a presentation until you deliver it. Delivery is the use of voice and body to convey the message; it is what we see and hear; it is the physical medium through which the ideas are perceived. That 40 percent of managers surveyed in a study admitted to falling asleep during a meeting or presentation suggests that presenters need to respond more effectively to the demand for exciting presentations.[35] Here we will discuss the common types of delivery and provide guidelines for the effective use of vocal and physical elements of delivery. Throughout our discussion, we will emphasize the concept of *enlarged conversation* as the method you should strive to emulate in your presentations. Conversation depends on verbs, nouns, and adverbs for impact—it is direct and straightforward.

Three common presentational formats are manuscript speaking, impromptu speaking, and extemporaneous speaking. Manuscript speaking, although difficult, permits the greatest control over the presentation. Impromptu speaking requires that the speaker construct the outline of the speech while speaking. Extemporaneous speaking requires a well-developed outline and the ability to conversationally present your ideas.

Manuscript Speaking. A manuscript speech or report is used when tight control of language, ideas, or time is necessary. Business and professional speakers frequently use the manuscript. Harold Haskett, Jr., professor of communication for the General Motors Institute, offers this rationale for manuscript delivery:

> If the apparent problems of preparation and delivery of a speech from manuscript are excessively involved, why do executives in large corporations make widespread use of it? The answer is in the *control*. Management feels that it must have control over the content put in speeches given by executives in company-related situations. This control is exercised through approval or disapproval of the prepared speech manuscript by an executive's superiors prior to its use. He commits himself to reading the approved manuscript word-for-word. The other control factor is time. In a tight time situation in a meeting a manuscript tends to assure that the time restrictions will be followed. Since these two factors are easy to measure and manipulate, manuscripts are used extensively. Also to a busy executive the temptation to delegate the writing of the speech manuscript is extremely hard to resist.[36]

Manuscripts are often required if the speaking occasion is especially important. It is excellent for such situations as upper-level corporate gatherings, meetings concerning technical and detailed material, or formal addresses to an external public.

Manuscript speaking requires skill at capturing the listener's interest and emotions, and maintaining a sense of involvement demands even greater skill. Especially useful is mastery of visualization and conversationality. A speaker must be listener-oriented during delivery, acknowledging the audience. Visualization creates, through voice, gesture, and movement, the images expressed in the presentation. And, by using a conversational style, the speaker recognizes the presence of the audience and personalizes an otherwise formal situation.

Manuscript speaking is not merely reading words; the audience needs to experience the ideas. Common problems associated with manuscript speaking include limited eye contact, word choice and sentence structure better suited to written works, difficulties associated with reading, and inflexibility. Good ideas alone do not make a presentation effective; the life of the ideas must be communicated. The following guidelines can be useful when preparing a manuscript:

1. Have the manuscript typed in capital letters with triple spaces between lines.
2. Don't attach the pages to each other. Loose pages enable you to move from page to page by merely slipping each completed page to the side and beginning the next page. You have faster, easier access to each page without the distraction of turning pages.
3. Practice delivering the speech or report orally. On the manuscript, underline or highlight the words and phrases you want to emphasize.
4. Become sufficiently familiar with the manuscript to deliver at least several lines from the presentation directly to the audience, without referring to the text. But, *don't memorize the speech or report.*
5. Don't practice so much that you become bored with the material.

When properly used, the manuscript speech or report represents a condition of maximum control and should foster an increased sense of confidence. When you use a manuscript, you can plan tangential elements more accurately, and use more vivid and precise language.

Impromptu Speaking. In 1789, the delegates to the United States Constitutional Convention, trying to create a workable government for the new country, were torn into angry factions by deep disagreements. They became so disheartened that many delegates wanted to patch together an easy compromise and go home. But their chairman, George Washington, rose and delivered one of the briefest speeches in the history of statesmanship. "If we offer to the people something of which we ourselves do not approve," he said, "how can we afterwards defend our work? Let us raise a standard to which the wise and honest may gladly repair. The event is in the hands of God." There was silence when he finished; then the members resumed their work with increased determination. They produced the U.S. Constitution, one of the greatest documents in history. Washington's direct, timely, and concise impromptu remarks, spoken with the confidence of a leader, had inspired them to action.

Impromptu speaking is informal and without prior preparation, planning, or intent. It requires you to think quickly, often planning while speaking. You may have a moment or two to prepare a few key ideas before speaking, but that's the maximum possible preparation time. Because you are usually formulating ideas and patterns of presentation while speaking, you need to help the audience follow the development of your thought patterns. The following guidelines can be useful when placed in an impromptu speaking situation:

1. Quickly select a theme around which to build your presentation. Try to link your topic to a subject you already know well.
2. Plan your first and last sentences. Concisely stated opening and closing summary statements allow you to avoid the aimless rambling so common with impromptu speaking. If possible, you might write these out along with a brief outline before speaking.
3. Select a simple organizational pattern. It's best to use a basic, logical arrangement of thoughts because you won't have the time to develop complex ideas associated with more complicated organizational patterns. Because of the free-flowing manner of this presentation, include summaries throughout to permit your listeners to fill in information they have missed, to clarify relationships among points, and to reinforce points you've already made.
4. Keep ideas direct, concise, and simple. Limit yourself to one, two, or three main points supported with personal knowledge or experience. Introduce these major points at a slow rate of speech and with pauses to permit the audience to digest each idea.
5. Maintain your composure and speak with confidence. Audience members understand the difficulty associated with impromptu speaking and don't expect a polished presentation.

Impromptu speaking is not easy because it excludes the opportunity for research, audience analysis, strategic planning, and practice. However, a recent survey of alumni at five universities ranked impromptu speaking as the most important mode of delivery in business situations.[37]

Impromptu speaking is a common occurrence in daily organizational life. There are situations when no realistic amount of preparation would lead you to believe that you would have to speak. Often impromptu speaking is a response to some question or a reaction to a statement during a business meeting. As a result, you have minimal control over critical communication variables.

Extemporaneous Speaking. An extemporaneous speech or report is planned, practiced, and well-outlined. Cal Downs and his associates observe that "by *extemporaneous* we mean a speech carefully prepared, thoroughly outlined, rehearsed but not memorized, and delivered from notes rather than manuscript."[38] Because the speaker is not committed to a manuscript, extemporaneous speaking can be modified during presentation permitting greater accommodation to audience needs, attitudes, and responses. The speaker is constantly creating, analyzing, adjusting, and searching as he or she "realizes" ideas in the presence of an audience. It is a challenging and demanding style of delivery. The following guidelines can be useful when speaking extemporaneously:

1. Carefully plan and prepare the presentation. Select and narrow your topic, define your purpose, analyze your audience, gather information, and organize the presentation. Your audience *expects* a well-developed and well-thought-out presentation.
2. Convert your full-sentence outline to speaking notes. A full-sentence outline is useful when preparing the presentation, but after that make notes on the key ideas and components of the outline for use during delivery. Quotations, statistics, and other technical data should be included, but keep your notes brief, legible, and not distracting to the audience. Some speakers use index cards; others prefer to type their notes in large print on letter-size paper so they can see the entire outline at a glance.
3. Rehearse your presentation. Practice thoroughly, but avoid memorization. Using your outlined notes, take each point and talk about it. Notice here the verb "talk." A speaker *talks*. A speaker does not read. The outline guides ideas so that the speaker can establish and sustain contact with the audience, can share ideas with them. This is the hallmark of an enlarged conversational style.

The extemporaneous style of delivery is used for formal and semiformal planned occasions. Well suited for the oral report, it tends to be the preferred style of delivery and is most frequently recommended.

Regardless of the type of speaking format you choose, any presentation requires your attending to the vocal and physical elements of delivery. The best of ideas poorly delivered will have little chance with an audience. The following guidelines should enable you to acquire a powerful and compelling delivery.

Guidelines for Delivery: Vocal Elements

Develop a Skilled and Controlled Voice. Most of us have potentially effective speaking voices. We need only listen to our voices and concentrate on how we are using them. A good speaking voice should be balanced between extremes of volume, pitch, and rate, and have a pleasing sound quality. Nothing is more disconcerting to an audience than a speaker who cannot be heard. And your listeners won't fully understand your message if you don't project enough to be heard clearly. Volume should be varied to add emphasis or dramatic impact to your presentations. Good speakers also vary the pitch of their voices and rate of speaking to convey emotion and conviction. The most important recommendation for voice quality is to think in terms of friendliness and confidence, and to relax the tension out of your voice. A good speaking voice has the following characteristics:

1. The tone is *pleasant,* conveying a sense of friendliness.
2. It is *natural,* reflecting the true personality and sincerity of the speaker.
3. It has *vitality,* giving the impression of force and strength, even when it isn't especially loud.
4. It has *various shades of meaning,* never sounding monotonous and emotionless.
5. It is *easily heard,* due to both proper volume and clear articulation.[39]

Speak with Enthusiasm. Effective speakers are enthusiastic and communicate that to the audience. A speaker who looks and sounds enthusiastic will be listened to and the ideas will be remembered.[40] Speaking this way comes from a sincere desire to communicate your ideas to your listeners.

Use Proper Enunciation and Pronunciation. Enunciation and pronunciation refer to the proper articulation of words. Just as standard grammar is important to your presentation of ideas, proper articulation is critical to a successful delivery. The way the majority of educated people talk is the standard against which you should measure your own speaking. Also, your speech patterns should relate to those used in your own circle of associates. You are part of a community that has a particular way of talking, and your speech should sound enough like the other members of that group to avoid distracting your listeners from your message. However, at the same time, your speech should be sufficiently "national" in sound to fit in when you travel beyond your immediate circle of associates.

No matter what dialect you speak, listeners will have difficulty understanding you if you fail to observe proper rules of enunciation. For our purposes, this means to articulate words and phrases distinctly and clearly with your lips, teeth, tongue, and palate. Common errors caused by lazy lips and jaws, or clumsy use of the tongue include:

1. *Omitting sounds.* We all hear (and probably say) such words as "goin'," "comin'," and "s'prise."
2. *Slurring.* When whole syllables and sounds are omitted, the word is slurred, such as "prob'ly" for "probably" and "d'jeat?" for "did you eat?" A more subtle form of slurring is called "assimilation," where a speech sound is modified by its neighboring sounds for ease of saying it—e.g., making the phonetic transition from *n* to *c* in "include" is not easy, so many speakers will slur the word to "ingclude."
3. *Muffling.* This common weakness results from lazy lip, tongue, and jaw action and produces such words as "weat" for "wheat" and "liddle" for "little."

Articulation problems arise from lazy speech patterns, but pronunciation problems are usually born of ignorance. In poor pronunciation, you don't *know* how to say a word correctly. Pay special attention to these common errors, and avoid them:

1. *Adding sounds.* People sometimes insert extra syllables into a word, such as "athalete" for "athlete," "realator" for "realtor," and "fillum" for "film." Some-

times people are misled by the spelling of a word to include silent letters: mort_gage, salmon. People also add extraneous sounds to words, such as "idear" for "idea," "warsh" for "wash," and "acrosst" for "across."

2. *Transposing.* We have all heard people say "revelant" when they meant "relevant," "hunderd" for "hundred," and "prespiration" for "perspiration."

3. *Improper stressing.* This fault of accenting the wrong syllable is so common that the dictionaries have a difficult time keeping up with changing usage. Consult a current dictionary of the English language or a source on American pronunciation to get preferred pronunciations. Also, such words as "rebel" or "digest" can be nouns or verbs, depending on where the stress is placed.

Errors in enunciation and mistakes in pronunciation not only confuse people about your meaning, but leave the impression that you are poorly educated and seriously undermine your personal credibility.

Pause Effectively. Effective use of pauses can be a powerful delivery tool, allowing the audience time to digest your message. Pauses can also add color and feeling to your presentation. Don't underestimate the power of silence: it can underscore important ideas, provide direction, arouse interest, create suspense, and signal appropriate places for applause or laughter.

Eliminate Unnecessary Vocalizations. Such sounds as "ah," "uh," "um," or "er" are distracting to an audience, and give the impression that the speaker is unprepared, nervous, or uncertain of the facts being presented. Unnecessary words or phrases should also be avoided. Don't overuse "okay," "see," "like," and "you know." These are often mistakenly used by inexperienced speakers as transitions, but truly effective transitions summarize and forecast.

Much but not all of your message is carried by voice; physical elements also speak quite loudly. Eye contact, facial expression, gestures, and body countenance should further your speaking goal and reinforce the verbal message. They should:

1. convey information and attitudes you want to convey
2. conceal information and attitudes you don't want to convey
3. limit the number of unintended messages you send—the number of sender-associated random factors to which you attribute no conscious meaning, but to which the receiver does ascribe meaning
4. limit, modify, or eliminate factors to which you and the receiver ascribe potentially different meanings
5. minimize factors that send interfering messages—factors with no direct relationship to the issue being considered and that might distract the receiver should be eliminated[41]

Physical messages are an integral part of the totality of public communication. Remember: in the business and professional arena "every body communicates." The following suggestions can be useful when considering the physical elements of delivery.

Guidelines for Delivery: Physical Elements

Maintain Eye Contact with Your Audience. You must talk to your audience, allowing the focus of your attention to move from one segment of the group to another. This requires that you as a speaker look at the faces before you—not at the ceiling, the back of the room, or the tops of their heads, but *at them.* And learn to do this not as if you were programmed, but as a person with ease and grace, and with the purpose of inclusion. Effective speakers maintain eye contact approximately 85 percent of the time, looking down only to read technical material or to refer briefly to their notes. Speakers who look directly at members of the audience are generally perceived as honest, knowledgeable, and involved with their listeners. Remember that public communication is a mutual exchange, not a soliloquy or personal monologue, and eye contact confirms this exchange.

Be Poised and Confident Behind the Lectern. The lectern should be used to place your notes and perhaps rest your arms or hands. The lectern is an aid, not a crutch, so avoid slouching, leaning on it, or draping your body over it. Effective speakers stand on both feet, observe good posture, and generate confidence. Good posture gives the impression of authority.

Use Facial Expressions to Convey Your Mood. The face is a mirror to the soul, and your facial expressions can communicate sincerity, pleasure, happiness, sadness, certainty, anger, resentment, fear, and concern. Oftentimes inexperienced speakers remain stoically expressionless, or reveal their nervousness and anxiety. Don't be afraid to smile—it breaks down barriers and does not, as many presenters seem to think, suggest that you're not serious about what you're saying. When you smile at someone, he or she feels included and generally smiles back. You want to maintain an accessible, open presence.

Gesture Naturally and Comfortably. A speaker who maintains a white-knuckle grip on the lectern or who stays glued to the overhead projector is terrified, and everyone soon knows it. To project self-confidence and authority use your hands as you speak. Gestures should be as natural and spontaneous as they are during a conversation. Your arms and hands may seem to resist, but don't be afraid to use gestures. They can help your audience follow your outlined ideas and can emphasize your major points. Tailor the gestures to reinforce your message. Avoid pointing, which might seem accusatory and threatening, or making repetitive gestures that become distracting. Rather, gesture with both arms and hands purposefully and with confidence.

Move with Purpose. Your presentation will be enhanced if you make use of bodily movement. If the movement is done at strategic times, such as after the introduction, between main points, or before the conclusion, it can draw appropriate attention to you and add a dynamic dimension to your delivery. Taking a few steps away from the lectern—to the left or right, forward or diagonally—can signal interest or intensity of concern. Movement will make you appear less rigid or statue-like, and more relaxed, confident, and convincing. However, avoid moving about the room randomly or pacing like a caged tiger. To guard against moving too much, stop each time you make a point. The stillness of a complete pause in your movement, like silence, emphasizes the importance of what you are saying. Effective movement is well-timed and meaningful.

Reduce Distracting Mannerisms. Swaying to and fro, clicking a pen, tapping a pencil on the lectern, putting your hands in and out of your pockets, twirling your hair, or jingling change can become distracting to even the most interested audience. These

▶ SPEAKER TRAITS

A group of Rollins College students conducted interviews with professional people to determine the businessperson's perception of effective and ineffective speaker traits. The results of the interviews are presented here:

Traits of an Effective Speaker

▶ Enthusiastic
▶ In control of the situation
▶ Knowledgeable and credible
▶ Keeps strong eye contact
▶ Audience-centered
▶ Honest
▶ Organized/prepared
▶ Has a strong voice
▶ Direct and open manner
▶ Concise

Traits of an Ineffective Speaker

▶ Nervous
▶ Lacks preparation and organization
▶ Has an "I don't care" attitude
▶ Used distracting mannerisms
▶ Reads or memorizes materials
▶ Bluffs or avoids questions
▶ Rambles or wastes time
▶ Lacks facts and figures
▶ Is sloppy with visuals, grammar, or appearance
▶ Apologetic

and other idiosyncratic mannerisms may be difficult to eliminate but every effort should be made to reduce them. Videotaping your presentations can greatly assist you in achieving this goal.

Step up to and away from the Lectern with Confidence. The audience begins making judgments about you from the moment you rise from your seat to speak, so it's important that you approach the lectern with confidence. Moreover, you should pause a few seconds before speaking to focus the attention of the audience and gain control of the situation. This also permits you a moment to quell any personal anxieties. At the close of your presentation, don't rush back to your seat; instead, pause and maintain eye contact with your audience for a brief moment. Remember: *you* are in control of the speaking situation.

The physical elements of delivery, like the vocal elements, should emphasize meaning and should direct the audience's attention to meaning. Delivery must be adapted to all the demanding elements in the public situation: the occasion, the audience, the material, and the speaker. Effective delivery focuses attention and helps listeners concentrate on what is being communicated; it does not attract attention to itself.

Step Nine: Evaluate Your Performance

Now the analysis begins. Evaluation permits you to review, mull over, and critically consider all aspects of the presentation, letting you identify personal strengths and weaknesses. The question, then, is: how do I rate as a speaker? By examining the following checklist you can determine how good a speaker you really are.

▶ I effectively capture the listeners' interest and attention through the appropriate use of questions, quotations, examples, or illustrations.
▶ I clearly state and explain the purpose of the presentation, and my purpose statement is a complete statement.

- I make the audience aware of why they need the data.
- I establish a sense of credibility as a speaker, indicating my qualifications as an expert in the area.
- I suggest the order in which ideas will be developed.
- The plan of organization is clear, coherent, and easy to follow.
- The main ideas are clearly distinguishable.
- The main ideas are well developed and supported by good examples, current statistics, timely testimony, and interesting analogies, comparisons, or stories.
- I have adequate supporting data to substantiate what is said.
- The main points of the speech reflect logical reasoning and lead naturally to the conclusion.
- All the content is meaningful in terms of the topic (the problem and its solution).
- I recognize the importance of transitions and summaries within the message.
- I take time to create the best visual materials to enhance my spoken message.
- I present ideas in a clear, grammatically correct, understandable, and vivid way.
- I carefully choose my words.
- I am aware of emotionally loaded words.
- I avoid trite, wordy expressions.
- My language is appropriate for this particular audience and occasion.
- I provide a good summary and synthesis of main ideas.
- I restate the importance of the topic and the value of the findings.
- The conclusion is forceful, challenging, and thought provoking.
- The conclusion leaves the audience in the desired frame of mind with a positive final impression.
- I use a natural, pleasant, conversational style of delivery.
- I work to establish eye contact with all audience members.
- I can be heard easily by everyone; my diction is clear; my rate and pitch of speaking are appropriate and meaningfully varied.
- My voice shows variety in volume and rate.
- I am poised, self-confident, and convincing.
- My facial expression is friendly and sincere.
- I am open and confident in my gestures, posture, and body action.
- Gestures and movement are natural, well-timed, and meaningful.
- I display enthusiasm.
- I practice my presentation sufficiently before giving it.
- The presentation is stimulating, informative, thought provoking, or persuasive.
- The presentation achieves its rhetorical goal(s).
- I have a strong desire to be an effective speaker.

By carefully attending to the outlined stages of preparation, your evaluations will be more positive than that of the young minister invited by the pastor of his home church to give his first sermon. After weeks of preparation, the great day arrived and he delivered the sermon. As the members of the congregation filed past after the service, they told him how nice he looked, how fine his message was, and how they wished him well in his career. When his spunky, no-nonsense grandmother approached, he asked: "Well, how did I do, Granny?" "Sonny," the old woman said, "I only saw three things wrong. First, you read it. Second, you didn't read it well. And third, it wasn't worth reading, anyhow!"

We have been talking about one-speaker-presentations throughout our discussion, largely because we feel team presentations have distinct disadvantages and are very difficult to do well. One critical problem is that the members of the audience may be confused and unable to determine who's in charge. Furthermore, any lapse in the intricate coordination necessary to shift from one presenter to another may result in pathetic silences or comical babble. Finally, the presentations may overlap and be unnecessarily repetitive. When several people are scheduled to present, each should present the material he or she knows best, each should be involved in developing the total program, and all should rehearse together to ensure smooth transitions. If you are part of a group presentation, consider your piece as a presentation in itself, with a beginning, a body, and an end.

▶ SUMMARY

Public presentations play an important role in the modern organization—a primary medium whereby information is processed. Your effectiveness as a public speaker can significantly influence how rapidly you advance within the business and professional environment, so the skills involved in manuscript, impromptu, and extemporaneous speaking are critical. Of particular importance to business and industry are informal internal reports, semiformal and formal reports or speeches, and external public relations speeches.

Public communication is defined as the face-to-face communication in which a speaker has control of the speaking situation and the primary responsibility of presenting a message to one or more people. Although the purposes for public communication have traditionally been to inform, to persuade, or to entertain, the ultimate objective is to influence and impress. As a public speaker, you will to varying degrees offer information, solidify or modify beliefs, move audiences to action, and entertain in every presentation.

The fear of making presentations is common because of the perceived novelty of the speaking situation; the subordinate status, conspicuousness, and dissimilarity felt by many speakers; and a prior history of nervousness. A certain amount of anxiety is considered normal and even desirable, but excessive speaker apprehension can significantly impair your effectiveness. You can control your nervousness by correcting your misperceptions about speaking, by visualizing success, and by practicing thoroughly.

The process of making presentations comprises a number of steps, an understanding of which is necessary if you hope to be effective. Step one: select and narrow your topic, determining what about the topic is both interesting to you and important to your listeners. Step two: define your purpose in terms of the desired audience reaction and behavioral goals. Step three: analyze your audience demographically—by size, age, gender, education, religion, culture, occupation, and knowledge—to focus on their needs and interests. Step four: research your topic, carefully gathering information to support your purpose and provide proof for your arguments. Step five: arrange your information and ideas according to standard chronological, spatial, cause-and-effect, problem–solution, pro–con, or topical patterns. Step six: plan your introduction and conclusion to grab and focus your listeners' attention and to provide a positive closing impact. Step seven: select your visual aids and practice using them. They should create interest, increase understanding, and boost the impact of your speeches and reports. Visual support includes the use of personal demonstration; physical objects; models; text visuals; conceptual visuals; tables, charts, or graphs; pictures or diagrams; maps; and audio/videotapes. Effective visuals are suitable to the medium and the occasion, clear, simple, and large enough to be seen. Step eight: deliver your presentation in an enlarged conversational style with an understanding of both the vocal and physical elements of delivery and an awareness of their powerful influence. Step nine: evaluate your performance with a critical eye toward improvement. Each of these steps is important, but effectiveness and presentational success ultimately depend on practice, practice, practice.

Now you're ready. You're on. You're great!

► QUESTIONS FOR DISCUSSION AND SKILL DEVELOPMENT

1. In what ways does presentational speaking make a difference in your corporate life? Is being an effective speaker important to you? To others at your place of work?
2. How would you describe your own speaker apprehension? Specifically, what makes you nervous about making a presentation? Do you agree that it is normal to be somewhat nervous at the start of a presentation? Why? Why not?
3. How does written communication differ from oral communication? Why is this important to understand? Which do you prefer?
4. How do reports and speeches differ? What purposes do they most frequently serve?
5. Why must a speaker be audience-centered? How can you get information about your audience? What are the most important demographic factors of audiences? Why?
6. What are some useful research materials for presentations? Which materials will be most useful in the types of presentations you will deliver at work? Why?
7. Why is it important that presentations be organized clearly? What are the most common organizational patterns? Which patterns do you prefer? Why?
8. Why is the introduction so critical? The conclusion? What are the primary objectives of an introduction? A conclusion? What are common introductory and concluding techniques? Are some more effective than others? Why?

9. In what ways can visual aids support your presentational purposes? Select a chart, graph, or diagram from a newsmagazine and describe how you would adapt it for use in an informative presentation. In a persuasive presentation.
10. Describe the best type of visual aid to use for the following presentations: (a) to inform an audience about the national debt, (b) to inform an audience about the status of drug testing in U.S. corporations, (c) to persuade an audience that computer-generated graphics and presentationsl programs can significantly enhance a business report. Are visuals more helpful when informing or when persuading an audience? Why?
11. How would you define an effective delivery? What vocal and physical elements are most influential? What is meant by *enlarged conversation*? Which speaking style do you prefer—manuscript speaking, impromptu speaking, extemporaneous speaking? Why do we emphasize practice, practice, practice?
12. Watch a business presentation and critically analyze it. Focus on the speaker's purpose, organization, supporting material, introduction, conclusion, and delivery. How did this presentation compare with other business presentations you have heard? Now, record yourself delivering a short presentation and evaluate the recording. Determine your personal strengths and weaknesses. What presentational skills do you want to improve?

► NOTES

1. Tom Parker, *In One Day* (Boston: Houghton Mifflin, 1984): 31.
2. E. G. Bormann, W. S. Howell, R. G. Nichols, and G. L. Shapiro, *Interpersonal Communication in the Modern Organization,* 2nd ed. (Englewood Cliffs, NJ: Prentice Hall, 1982): 196.
2. Elizabeth M. Fowler, "Training 21st-Century Executives," *New York Times,* June 20, 1989, D13.
4. Carol Kleiman, "Information Skills Back in Demand," *The Orlando Sentinel,* September 30, 1990, E-21.
5. W. I. Gordon and J. R. Miller, *Speak Up for Business* (Dubuque, IA: Kendall-Hunt, 1977).
6. Ronald B. Adler, *Communicating at Work: Principles and Practices for Business and the Professions,* 4th ed. (New York: McGraw-Hill, 1992).
7. Frank E. X. Dance, "What Do You Mean by Presentational Speaking," *Management Communication Quarterly* (November, 1987): 260–271.
8. David Wallechinsky, Irving Wallace, and Amy Wallace, *The Book of Lists* (New York: Morrow, 1977): 469–470.

9. Virginia P. Richmond and James C. McCroskey, *Communication: Apprehension, Avoidance, and Effectiveness,* 2nd ed. (Scottsdale, AZ: Gorsuch Scarisbrick, 1989).

10. James C. McCroskey and Lawrence Wheeless, *Introduction to Human Communication* (Boston: Allyn and Bacon, 1976).

11. Raymond S. Ross, *Speech Communication* (Englewood Cliffs, NJ: Prentice Hall, 1977): 100.

12. James C. McCroskey, *An Introduction to Rhetorical Communication,* 6th ed. (Englewood Cliffs, NJ: Prentice Hall, 1993): 37.

13. Joseph A. DeVito, *Essentials of Human Communication* (New York: HarperCollins, 1993).

14. Judith Martin, "Plain Speech for Carter," *Newsday,* July 13, 1977, 3A.

15. This script reflects visualization scripting principles. See Joseph Ayers and Ted Hoff, "Visualization: A Means for Reducing Speech Anxiety," *Communication Education* 34 (October 1985): 318–323.

16. James C. Humes, *Roles Speakers Play* (New York: Harper and Row, 1976).

17. Robert T. Oliver, *History of Public Speaking in America* (Boston: Allyn and Bacon, 1965): 122.

18. Jo Sprague and Douglas Stuart, *The Speaker's Handbook,* 3rd ed. (New York: Harcourt Brace Jovanovich, 1992): 32.

19. Eliot Asinof, "Dick Gregory Is Not So Funny Now," *New York Times Magazine* (March 17, 1968): 37–45. Copyright © 1968 by The New York Times Company. Reprinted by permission.

20. Kenneth Burke, *A Grammar of Motives* (Englewood Cliffs, NJ: Prentice Hall, 1946): 56.

21. Kenneth Burke, *A Rhetoric of Motives* (Englewood Cliffs, NJ: Prentice Hall, 1950): 23.

22. *The New York Public Library Desk Reference* (New York: Stonesong-Simon, 1989): xi.

23. G. L. Grice and J. F. Skinner, *Mastering Public Speaking* (Englewood Cliffs, NJ: Prentice Hall, 1993).

24. Thomas Koballa, Jr., "Persuading Teachers to Reexamine the Innovative Elementary Science Programs of Yesterday: The Effect of Anecdotal versus Data-Summary Communications," *Journal of Research in Science Teaching* 23 (1986): 437–449.

25. I. Edmon, ed., *The Works of Plato* (New York: Simon & Shuster, 1928): 309.

26. Ernest C. Thompson, "An Experimental Investigation of the Relative Effectiveness of Organized Structure in Oral Communication," *Southern States Speech Journal* 26 (1960): 59–69.

27. Christopher Spicer and Ronald Bassett, "The Effect of Organization on Learning from an Informative Message," *Southern Speech Communication Journal* 41 (Spring 1976): 290–299.

28. John Greene, "Speech Preparation Processes and Verbal Fluency," *Human Communication Journal* 11 (1984): 61–84.

29. Carolyn R. Planck, president of Communication for Professionals, Winter Park, FL.

30. William J. Seiler, "The Effects of Visual Materials on Attitudes, Credibility, and Retention," *Speech Communication Monographs* 38 (November 1971): 331–334.

31. Grice and Skinner, *Mastering Public Speaking.*

32. Edward R. Tufte, *The Visual Display of Quantitative Information* (Cheshire, CT: Graphics Press, 1983).

33. Patricia Rowell, "Using Storyboards and Visual Imaging to Develop High-Impact Presentations" (Presentation to the Central Florida Chapter of the American Society for Training and Development, Orlando, FL, May 26, 1992).

34. Grice and Skinner, *Mastering Public Speaking,* 279.

35. Marya W. Holcombe and Judith K. Stein, *Presentations for Decision Makers* (New York: Van Nostrand Reinhold, 1990).

36. Harold O. Haskitt, Jr., "When Speaking from Manuscript: Say It and Mean It," *Personnel Journal* (February 1972): 109.

37. John Johnson and Nancy Szczupakiewicz, "The Public Speaking Course: Is It Preparing Students with Work-Related Skills?" *Communication Education* 3 (1987): 131–137.

38. Cal Downs, Wil Linkugel, and David M. Berg, *The Organizational Communicator* (New York: Harper and Row, 1977): 223.

39. *Communication and Leadership Program* (Santa Ana, CA: Toastmasters International, 1977): 27.

40. Read G. Williams and John E. Ware, Jr., "Validity of Student Ratings of Instruction Under Different Incentive Conditions: A Further Study of the Dr. Fox Effect," *Journal of Educational Psychology* 68 (February 1976): 50.

41. Wallace V. Schmidt and Jo-Ann Graham, *The Public Forum, A Transactional Approach to Public Communication* (Sherman Oaks, CA: Alfred Publishing, 1979): 97.

CHAPTER TWELVE

12

Informative, Persuasive, and Special Occasion Presentations

LEARNING OBJECTIVES:

To explain the nature of informative presentations

To describe the role of informative speaking

To identify the different types of informative presentations

To explain the nature of persuasion

To identify the different types of persuasive presentations

To explain Monroe's motivated sequence

To understand the speaking demands of selected special occasions

To evaluate the ethics of public communication and select a personally appropriate perspective

eggy Noonan, speechwriter for former president Ronald Reagan, observes in *What I Saw at the Revolution* that a speaker's listeners "are distracted by worries and responsibilities and the demands of daily life, and you have to know that and respect it—and plan the narrative, sharpen the details, and add color and momentum."[1] Noonan recognizes the importance of purpose and place in making effective presentations, as did Ralph Waldo Emerson over a century ago when he wrote that "any piece of knowledge I acquire today has a value at this moment exactly proportioned to my skill to deal with it. Tomorrow, when I know more, I recall that piece of knowledge and use it better."[2] In this chapter, you will come to a fuller understanding of the two most common purposes in public communication—to inform and to persuade. We will also examine selected presentations for special occasions.

The term "public" in "public communication" suggests that the messages we are going to be dealing with go beyond the sphere of individual privacy and are matters of concern to groups of people. Public communication differs from other communication contexts in the following ways:

▶ It is a powerful instrument for social change.
▶ It focuses on the speaker but engages the audience as an active agent in determining the direction of change.
▶ It is a dynamic, purposeful act—usually informative or persuasive in nature.

The scope of public communication is potentially overwhelming. In business, industry, government, the military, and education, a variety of presentations to diverse internal and external audiences occur. From a briefing which describes the status of an organization's operations to an address proposing a new appropriation to a legislative body, public communication is a significant part of organizational activity. Whether face-to-face or via radio, television, or the print media, the scope and range of public communication is enormous.

▶NATURE OF INFORMATIVE AND PERSUASIVE PURPOSES

In 1968, Marshall McLuhan and Quentin Fiore referred to a large number of different and varied societies linked together by communication as "the Global Village."[3] They properly included the word "village" in the discussion because they emphasized not only the technology of communication but also the degree to which this communication allowed people to become involved in the affairs of others. In the quarter-century since McLuhan and Fiore coined this now-famous phrase, technological advances have greatly expanded our ability to gather and disseminate information. It is not enough to get information somewhere by 10:30 tomorrow; the recipient wants it faxed now, if not five minutes ago. Ideas must be put together quickly for swift decisions. This has ramifications for presentation technique and strategy as well. People everywhere, and managers in particular, are less inclined to be patient listeners—presentations must be crisp, short, and well organized. The demand for a disciplined approach to putting thoughts together is obvious and a minimalist approach is clear.

Although we live in a highly sophisticated communication environment, public communication still has impact. A live speaker before a live audience remains a vital force in today's organization. Informative and persuasive presentations are important vehicles for the dissemination of information and major weapons in the communication arsenal of any organization. But, is there a difference between the purposes of informing and persuading? The answer isn't easy because the distinction between the two is blurry, at best.

All communication is dependent on information of some kind, and when you inform, you also exert a persuasive influence. Richard M. Weaver notes that persuasion "is cognate with language; it is impossible and even ridiculous that the utterances of men could be neutral. All of us are preachers in private or public capacities. We have no sooner uttered words than we have given impulse to other people to look at the world, or some small part of it, in our way."[4] To put it differently, you're always persuading your audience in one way or another, whether your purpose is primarily informational or persuasive, and you're always attempting to induce your listeners to accept your way of looking at things when you address a group with a free choice of accepting or rejecting your message.[5] For example, when promoting a no-smoking policy, you must initially inform the corporate officers about the dangers of smoking and about similar policies in other smoke-free organizations. Or, when explaining a new computer system to coworkers, you are also persuading them to accept you as a credible source and to use the new, more efficient system.

Ultimately, all speaking is both informative and persuasive. All information is persuasive and all persuasion is informative. However, a certain presentation may be more informational or more persuasive, depending on the intent of the speaker. Thus, all we can really say about presentations is that their purpose may be mainly informational or mainly persuasive.

▶ ROLE OF INFORMATIVE SPEAKING

We live in a society that is vitally interested in information. Because people in the U.S. place such a high premium on education, we're almost engulfed with data and information. This becomes especially clear when you understand that our nation has more newspapers, magazines, book publishers, radio stations, television channels, computer networks, and public libraries than the nations of Great Britain, France, Germany, and the Commonwealth of Independent States combined.[6] Collectively, we have more means of information than any other people on earth. Individually, we consume these with what could only be described as a voracious appetite. Richard Saul Wurman reports that the average American adult reads over 100 newspapers, 36 magazines, and 3,000 forms and notices every year[7]; that representative adult also listens to over 700 hours of radio, watches nearly 2500 hours of television, and talks on the telephone for almost 61 hours every year.[8]

Of course the information we process is just a very small part of the available material. The sources of data are, literally, all around us, but most of us just don't have the time to absorb as much of it as we might like. Louis Martin, associate editor for the Association of Research Libraries, provides just one example when he observes that "if the average reader tried to catch up with one year's output of learned publications just in the sciences, it would take about 50 years of reading at 24 hours a day for seven days a week."[9]

One of the important reasons for us to keep current with information is because it usually has a very short lifespan. The data you present to your coworkers or your managers will be outdated in just a short period of time. Indeed, the knowledge we gain today can be obsolete tomorrow. Connie Koenenn has concluded that "at least 80% of what you were taught in school will be proved wrong. Knowledge is doubling at the rate of 100% every 20 months."[10] You must keep current with the information that is important to you, to your particular job, and to your organization.

The world of business understands that the presentation of information is meaningful for the people who work in today's corporations. After studying a number of organizations, Michael F. Warlum was able to conclude that "a factor vital to the health of any corporation is the constant exchange of information. Although written forms of business communication remain important, the oral exchange of infor-

▶ SPEAKERS AND THE BOTTOM LINE

By Rex Kelly

To many people in the business world, any corporate activity is a success or failure based on just one thing. How does a specific activity affect the bottom line? A company that does not have a strong communication program with its employees, its customers, and the general public is a company courting disaster.

Every act of communication from a company affects the environment in which the company operates. They affect the company's ability to reach its goals, the bottom line. They affect the bottom line because the only way a company can achieve its goals is to get people to feel, think, and act in ways that contribute to those goals. And the public forum, making speeches, is one of the very best ways to influence people.

The speech gives people both what they want and what they need. It gives them a human concept to associate with a company or product. It changes the company from some abstract "thing" out there, to a real, believable, likeable person right here. Credible speakers give us one of the best ways to personify the company—to personify it in a way that builds a positive public environment.

Through speakers, the public will hear what we say because they can see how we look and talk to us about their concerns. The company becomes a person, and that person can win people to his side and thereby to the company's side.

A speech is one of the most effective forms of communication, and the character of the speaker determines whether real communication happens or not.

Why do politicians go out on the campaign trail? Surely they would experience less wear and tear if they just mailed everybody 8-by-10 glossies and a copy of their platform.

Why do preachers preach? And why are television evangelists so remarkably successful? I know for a fact that the Christian message is readily available in printed form. What is it about the way they present their message?

And finally, with records, television, and movies, why will perfectly intelligent people pay $25 to $200 to go see an entertainer "in person?"

All of these questions have the same answer. *There is an elemental power in having a living, breathing human being—right here, right now—interacting with other human beings.*

And when that living, breathing human being is a skilled communicator, he or she possesses real power. The power to change the way people feel, to change the way they think, and even to change the way they act.

For a company to achieve its goals, whether they are financial or social, this power is exactly what they need.

Most companies have similar goals. They provide a product or service. They seek to make money. They may advocate social changes. If they want these things to happen, they have to get people to think, feel, and act in a way that will allow the company to accomplish its goals. I maintain there is no better way to make this happen than through communication.

Getting the public to support a company's goals, creating a favorable political climate, or even meeting sales goals are helped enormously by speakers presenting the message—live.

We must insist as strongly as we are able that any speaker we send out will consistently communicate high personal credibility. The speaker must be able to create a strong positive perception of the company he represents.

On the other hand, an assistant supervisor can do a lot of good by being a credible and likeable spokesman for his company.

The point is that the speaker must understand the process of communication and be eager to make the effort that makes communication happen.

If our goal is to have our speaking activities help the bottom line, to create an environment supportive of your companies' goals, then we must use every legitimate means at our disposal. I am suggesting that one of the strongest weapons we have in the fight for the public mind are the individuals who go out and meet our critics and customers in person.

A company's credibility rests on the credibility of each of its employees. It has been demonstrated time and again that a business's reputation can be critically damaged by the dishonest, arrogant, or ignorant action of just one employee.

So, what are the characteristics we should insist on? An effective speaker must be committed, honest, and well informed.

A speaker who is committed cares about the task at hand. He believes in the power of the spoken word, and in the value of getting out in the community. He is willing to focus his intellectual and emotional resources to produce the best result he can. He will demand his best effort from himself in every situation. Doing his best at whatever task is set is a matter of both personal and professional pride.

A speaker's honesty is intimately connected with this personal commitment. Neither one can be faked. If a speaker doesn't really believe what he is saying, the audience will sense it. With the type of audiences we face, it is foolish, even dangerous, to think we can fool very many people even some of the time. Honesty is not only the best policy, it is the only policy.

A speaker must tell the whole truth, not just part of it, even when it involves admitting a mistake. Lee Iacocca probably saved many thousands of dollars by simply stating, "Did we screw up? You bet we did!" We have to resist in every way possible being placed in the position of defending obvious mistakes.

It is next to impossible for a speaker to credibly present the truth unless he is truly well informed. The best of intentions do no good if a speaker doesn't know his subject backwards and forwards.

In short, an effective speaker must be willing to put in the time to be both an interested and interesting representative of the company. This is always what an audience hopes for, and it is what will awaken their natural willingness to respond to and agree with the speaker.

A typical audience hopes to meet an interesting person or hear a good speech. But from years of experience attending civic club lunches, they aren't too surprised if it doesn't happen. This low level of expectations creates a terrific advantage for a speaker who is well prepared and is excited about what he is doing.

This preparation and sense of excitement immediately raises the speaker above the prevailing mediocrity and gives an immediate boost to their credibility, no matter what their title.

When an audience that is expecting to hear a standard company line, for example, is faced with someone who understands their point of view and gives it fair treatment, they open up. They pay attention. They will respond to a speaker who is concerned about responding to their feelings and values.

If we want the best possible response from our audiences, we have to give it our best shot. We cannot, in all fairness, ask more of the audience than we have been willing to give of ourselves. If we haven't given our best, if we don't mean what we say; we are engaged in deception, not communication. And the audience will know it. And the harm will be done.

Source: Rex E. Kelly, Director, Corporate Communications, Mississippi Power Co., "Speakers and the Bottom Line: The Character of the Speaker," *Vital Speeches of the Day 54*, no. 2 (November 1, 1987).

mation occupies an increasingly important role in the functioning of today's companies."[11] Indeed, the need to clearly communicate information is critical and the need for people who can retrieve and explain information is going to greatly increase in the future.

If you are like most others, you probably believe you know who gives the speeches in our society—the lawyers, ministers, politicians, and highly placed corporate executives. Although public speaking is important to people in these professions, you might be surprised to know who *really* gives the speeches in contemporary society. Communication professor Kathleen Edgerton Kendall tried to discover if "real people ever give speeches" by examining the presentational experiences of a group of 202 randomly selected people. She found that these people—much like you—did speak to audiences and some of them spoke quite often. Her findings revealed that:

- ▶ 55% of the subjects had spoken to a group of ten or more people at least once in the past two years.
- ▶ 70% of the people who had spoken to a group had delivered four or more speeches during the two years.
- ▶ The speaking was often related to their work.
- ▶ Most of the speaking was informational—the subjects described their purpose as to teach or instruct.
- ▶ Younger people spoke more often than older people.
- ▶ Women spoke more often than men.
- ▶ People with high incomes spoke more often than people who earn less money.

▶ Educated people spoke more often than people with less education—the implications of this fact for the college-educated may be that they should expect to give speeches—and would probably benefit from training.[12]

Real people *do* give speeches and all available evidence suggests that they will be speaking increasingly more often. Many of these speaking activities will share information about the organization with other members. They will disseminate information from one department to all other departments, from management to employees, from employee representatives to management, and from senior members to new members.

▶TYPES OF INFORMATIVE PRESENTATIONS

Presentations that are primarily informative are the most common means of knowledge exchange in organizations. Such speaking activities usually address one of the following topics:

▶ Recent developments in a particular field
▶ Cause and/or effects of a phenomenon
▶ Feasibility of a project
▶ Organizational or departmental responsibility
▶ Description of a process or a mechanism
▶ Instructions
▶ Investigation of the faults and/or merits of a proposal
▶ Collection and/or summary of information for a supervisor
▶ Proposal presented to a superior
▶ Status or progress on a project

These presentations may assume a variety of forms, including informative briefings, oral reports, lectures, question-and-answer sessions, and explanations. In your work-life, you will probably deliver many such informative presentations, so how can you best approach these speaking assignments?

Informative Briefings

A common way for information to be communicated at work is through the informative briefing. This type of presentation is delivered to people who have a common interest, and it concentrates on new ideas, concerns, concepts, or data. The informative briefing is usually short and often followed by an active exchange and discussion of important issues in the briefing. When presenting a briefing, be sure to:

1. Analyze your audience carefully so you understand how much they know. Because these people have a common interest, they may have considerable knowledge about your topic. You will want to spend less time on understood information and develop those areas where information gaps may exist. A careful analysis will reveal the critical issues that must be discussed.
2. Explain all new concerns and concepts fully. Be careful of jargon and technical terms that may confuse your listeners. Remember: your task is to explain completely and concisely.

The briefing should offer knowledge to someone who is less informed and who has a personal interest in the subject area. The topic should be adequately limited and researched, the audience identified and analyzed in regard to the selecting and phrasing of ideas, and the findings or the facts generally drawn from surveys and interviews systematically organized and presented. An effective briefing helps listeners retain the information. Briefings might include a police commander informing officers about a certain high-crime area of the city, or an owner-manager of a new restaurant telling servers about a common customer complaint.

Oral Reports

The oral report is a presentation in which you gather, analyze, and interpret data for another person or group. Such a report often takes the form of a request or assignment from a superior. Two common types of oral reports are the factual report that assembles, arranges, and interprets raw information; and the advisory report that makes a set of recommendations relative to the information that has been prepared.[13] In the oral report, you assume the role of a reporter—finding, organizing, and making sense out of information. Because these reports can be either formal or informal, they may take place in the executive boardroom of a major corporation, in the conference room of a small business, or in the office of the company secretary.

Presenting oral reports isn't easy and you need to approach your assignment carefully. In one study, John T. Mallow discovered that American corporate executives believed over 80 percent of the people in their organization were incapable of presenting a clear oral report; furthermore, he reports that these executives claimed they had far greater difficulty training people to do this than to write a clear letter.[14] The following guidelines should prove helpful when you present your reports:

1. Meticulous research is imperative. Because these reports are often required by a superior in your organization, your preparation will reflect directly on you. Moreover, these reports can have important implications for the organization because corporate action may depend on your report.
2. When your report contains a recommendation, begin with a statement of the proposal, unless there is a compelling reason not to do so (e.g., if your audience is hostile to you or your recommendation). After presenting the proposal, tell your listeners how you arrived at it. This will allow your audience to more fully understand your point of view.
3. Use visual aids effectively. Oral reports often require a great amount of data, and visual aids are an excellent way of presenting this information. The guidelines on using visual aids presented later in this chapter should prove useful to you.

The oral report requires that you be focused and that you deliberately direct the attention of your listeners to the areas of critical concern. Few meetings will produce eloquent oratory, but the ability to stand up and speak cogently and to the point is a must at any meeting. The man or woman who rambles on, unable to communicate ideas, is worse than a nuisance; he or she is a dead loss.

Lectures

Lectures are formal presentations of material intended to aid the listeners in learning. They are a common informative mode, well entrenched in academia. In high school or college, you have undoubtedly been exposed to this type of informational speaking. Lectures are also used in other organizational settings—the speaker at a professional seminar, the invited lecturer at the corporate luncheon meeting, and the public lecturer at the city museum typify this informational format used to promote learning.

When using a lecture approach, consider the following suggestions:

1. It is important to analyze your audience carefully. You don't want to bore them with information they already know, nor do you want to overwhelm them with new material.
2. The organization of your lecture is vitally important. Your introduction needs to capture the attention of the audience; the body of the lecture needs to focus on a few main points supported by compelling ideas and evidence; and your conclusion needs to summarize your main points.

Effective lectures will use a variety of materials and techniques to involve the audience in the learning process. As an ancient Chinese proverb states: "Tell me, I forget; show me, I remember; involve me, I understand."

Question-and-Answer Sessions

You have probably already participated in question-and-answer sessions in the role of questioner, respondent, or audience member. Such sessions usually follow a formal procedure and are primarily designed to provide the audience with an opportunity to ask the speaker questions for greater clarification or to challenge a point of view. Your goal is to encourage positive discussion while remaining in control of the presentation. Based on his experience as a White House speechwriter, William Safire reported on the preparation required for a president to face a question-and-answer session in the form of a press conference:

> The fact is that a presidential press conference requires at least two days of hard homework. [The president's] staff will prepare about 75 questions, covering the approximately 25 that will be asked in a half hour and all those that go unasked. These, along with suggested answers, go into his "black book" for review, occasional challenge and memorization. All presidents of the last two decades have done that homework.[15]

Safire suggests the general direction to be followed by anyone who wishes to be well prepared before facing a barrage of questions. More specifically, when participating in a question-and-answer session, you want to:

1. Read your audience accurately and identify with their thinking and speaking patterns. People are most comfortable with others who think and speak the way they do, so you can enhance your credibility and personal identification with the audience by mirroring their language patterns, moods, and body language. This requires learning to listen to the pace of questions or comments and adjusting your own pace to match that of the questioner. It also involves listening for images or speech patterns that might reveal the questioner's thinking patterns. You will find it helpful to remember that some people are aural thinkers and use such images as "it sounds good," or "can you amplify that idea?" Others, the visual thinkers, say "I see what you mean," or "give me the big picture." The kinetic

thinkers are fond of expressions like "it feels right," or "I wouldn't touch it." It takes practice to be able to hear these patterns and use them in your own speech, but it can be a valuable, subtle way to break down a listener's resistance and put you both on the same side.

2. Adopt an active listening attitude. Often we are too busy thinking ahead to what we want to say in response that we don't really hear more than the first few words of the question being asked. Instead, it is important to remain open-minded and let the questioner finish without interrupting. It is often helpful to summarize mentally what is being said so you can then formulate the questioner's comments in your own words. Also, looking attentive and moving or leaning toward the speaker indicate that you are genuinely interested in the comment or question.

3. Handle difficult questions and effectively overcome objections. When responding, it is helpful to restate the question. This ensures that everyone present heard it and allows you to confirm that you understood the question correctly. Don't feel rushed. If you pause to think before you respond, it's a compliment to the questioner, not a sign of indecision. But what do you do when you don't know the answer to a question or if the questioner is openly hostile to your point of view? If you don't know the answer, by all means say so. Nothing can cause you to lose credibility faster than someone catching you making up an answer or giving erroneous information. And you may never be able to regain the trust you lost in that short thoughtless moment. An appropriate response in such a situation would be, "I don't have the answer to that question, but I'll find out for you if you would like me to." Your listeners will appreciate your honesty and you will probably gain additional respect from the audience. When the questioner is antagonistic or upset, you have a different type of challenge. Don't become defensive or lose your temper. Rather, listen fully and then rephrase the question in neutral, more objective terms to defuse hostility or emotionally charged language. Try to create a spirit of mutual understanding of the problem, which may enable you to move toward agreement on goals or solutions that you can both accept. Resist closing the exchange by asking, "Does that answer your question?" unless you are ready for a prolonged and lengthy discussion which may exclude other members of the audience.

4. Concisely answer each question. Brief and intelligent responses will impress your listeners more than long, drawn-out answers. You may feel an urge to answer the easy questions at great length to be protected from the hard ones. Remember that the intent of a Q&A session is to respond to as many questions as possible within the designated time limits. Unnecessarily long answers defeat this purpose and may suggest to the audience that you are stalling or trying to avoid difficult inquiries. An occasional very short answer should be encouraged: "Yes, I fully agree," or "No, we would not take that course if we had any other choice."

5. Calmly deal with interruptions and distractions. Invariably you will at one time or another encounter unexpected interruptions or distractions. Common distractions include late arrivals, conversations that interfere with the presentation, or arguments occurring between audience members. In these situations you can, respectively, pause until the late arrivals are seated and calmly remind the audience members of the purpose of the meeting. The goal is to deal with the situation without losing your professionalism or your control of the meeting. At other times, however, more unexpected interruptions may occur—a jackham-

mer suddenly starting up just outside the meeting room window or a power failure in the middle of your slide presentation. Don't try to compete with the distraction or pretend it didn't happen—that makes you look insecure and perhaps a little foolish. Call a break and quickly try to correct the situation or improvise. The slight delay is much more desirable than continuing to fight a losing battle. You will probably find your audience to be very understanding and perhaps even more willing to support your ideas.

In managing an effective question-and-answer session, the key is to be confident, maintain a sense of humor, keep cool, and never let anyone take away your control of the group. Toward the end of the presentation, it is useful to get closure on the issue by summarizing what you believe to be the group consensus and by tying the consensus to the purpose of your presentation. These sessions are effective because of their interactive nature and audience involvement.

Explanations

These types of informative presentations increase the audience's understanding of a given subject. Explanations have two general purposes: they clarify the nature of a concept, process, object, or proposal; or they offer a supporting rationale for a contestable claim.[16] For instance, the vice president of finance for a major pharmaceutical company explains why last quarter's profits were lower than expected—and thereby clarifies. This same executive officer explains why the company has decided to forego testing of orphan drugs—and so presents the rationale in support of a policy decision. Explanations are complex, informative presentations intended to clarify and gain audience understanding in times of confusion, misunderstanding, and perhaps anger. The following guidelines are critical to effective explanations:

1. Clarity is an immediate concern when you present explanations. The audience expects you to clarify the issue(s) and to rationally gain their support through convincing arguments. Consequently, you must carefully organize your explanation, using language that is understandable to your listeners.
2. Evidence and reasoning must be solid. The complex and often controversial nature of explanations, coupled with the intense interest of audience members, require substantial support and use of evidence. Relying solely on emotional appeals will prove unsatisfactory to an audience seeking to be convinced and looking for compelling, logical reasons that make sense to them.

We include the following outline of an effective explanatory presentation, titled "The Changing Consumer: Predicting the Marketplace of the Future," for you to read and analyze. This presentation was delivered by Wendy Liebmann, president of WSL Marketing, to the "Drug Store of the Future" symposium at Tarpon Springs, Florida, in January 1992. The full text of Liebmann's presentation is included in a sidebox (see page 12-13).

Outline for "The Changing Consumer: Predicting the Marketplace of the Future" Presentation

General Purpose: To inform
Specific Purpose: To inform the audience about ways the American marketplace must specialize in order to meet the diversification of U.S. consumers.

Central Idea: The American marketplace will specialize in the future because U.S. consumers are diversifying.

Main Points:
 I.   The twentieth-century marketplace emphasized a mass consumer.
      A. The twentieth century began as an age of immigration.
      B. The twentieth century marketplace emphasized mass marketing.
 II. The twenty-first–century marketplace will emphasize a diversified consumer.
      A. The twenty-first century will begin with a new age of immigration.
      B. The twenty-first century will contain an aging population.
      C. The twenty-first century will be an age of diminished expectations.
 III. Specialty marketing will become critical to the new marketplace.
      A. Marketing will be tailored to specific consumers.
      B. Value will be a key to all successful retailing.

Wendy Liebmann's informative presentation was carefully crafted and delivered. As you analyze this contemporary speech consider the following questions: Does the speaker achieve her purpose? How was the speech adapted to her audience and to the occasion? What was the organizational pattern of Liebmann's speech? How did the speaker capture and hold the the attention of the audience? Did she speak to the correct comprehension level of the audience? Was the use of the repetitive phrase "picture it" a useful linguistic technique? Was the presentation current and up-to-date?

▶ STRATEGIES FOR EFFECTIVE INFORMATIVE SPEAKING

We previously provided general guidelines for effective presentations. Here we specifically identify certain strategies that should prove valuable when you are called on to deliver an informative presentation.

Capture and Hold the Audience's Attention. A compelling beginning, an action-oriented ending, and an effective blending of words and visual support are the components of a powerful informative presentation. Use the introduction to tell the audience how the subject affects them. It must include what the presentation is about and why it is important, establish rapport with the audience, and show how you will develop your argument. Then, be vivid with your language. Many a listener has become bored with a presentation because the language wasn't stimulating. Paint pictures with your words—provide color, shape, size, and movement, and use a graphic and vibrant vocabulary to motivate your audience to listen. Words have the ability to evoke all of the human senses. Consider, for example, the vivid description of milk production used by Karl Eller, president of Combined Communications Corporation, to illustrate the free enterprise system:

> I'm going to leave you with a little reminder. That reminder is a glass of milk. . . . But look at that milk and think about what it took to bring that glass of milk to your table. Some farmer bred and raised the cow. Some farmer owned and tended the land it grazed on. . . . Some farmer milked the cow or cows and sold the milk to someone who processed it, pasteurized it and packaged it. . . . And all along the line the product was

▶ THE CHANGING CONSUMER: PREDICTING THE MARKETPLACE OF THE FUTURE

By Wendy Liebmann

PICTURE IT. Twentieth century America. It began as an age of immigration. People flocking to these shores from Poland and Russia, from Ireland and England, from Italy and Germany. Sometimes by choice. Often by necessity. Often through no free will of their own. Arriving in the millions, they landed in New York, Galveston, New Orleans, and made the way throughout the country.

They came looking for the American Dream. A chance to work for a living, to earn enough to feed their families, to practice their own religion, hold their own political views—with no fear of persecution. They came to be Americans.

And they were. They assimilated as fast as they could learn the language. The immigrant children cast off their foreign ways. They wanted to dress like Americans, look like Americans, eat like Americans, speak like Americans, live like Americans. And so was born the dominant face of 20th century America. And so was born an opportunity—to sell the American Dream to the American consumer. One idea to one group of people.

It began with a man named Henry Ford, and a revolutionary concept: mass-producing an affordable product—an automobile—for a universal consumer. As the century evolved mass marketing became the way of business. Returning from a war that crystallized the American ethos, young, aggressive men and women, eager to succeed, demanded their "chicken in every pot, car in every garage" . . . and a television in every living room.

As a result, brands like Coca-Cola, Levi, Ivory, Revlon, Ford, Gillette and McDonalds came to define America and Americans—both in this country and throughout the world.

With mass market brands came mass media to spread the word, and mass market retailers to sell the product. In the '50s and '60s it was Sears, Roebuck & Co., Montgomery Ward, J.C. Penney, E.J. Korvette, K-Mart, Kroger, A&P, Publix, Winn-Dixie and Safeway. In the '70s, '80s and '90s it was Eckerd, Wal-Mart, Walgreens, Drug Emporium, Food Lion, Sam's, The GAP, Price Club.

Brand name products in the hundreds and thousands came to be purchased in just about any mass retail store—from the drug store to the discount store, from the deep discount drug store to the warehouse club.

The over-extended distribution of branded merchandise contributed to the blurring of retail channels, and by the 1980s the "massification" of American business was complete.

Unfortunately, however, it was complete just in time to confront the "demassification" of the American consumer.

Like the Old South of a century ago, the homogeneous America of the 20th century is now gone with the wind. The mass market is dead. The consumer of the 21st century is not one, but many. A kaleidoscope of demographic and psychographic segments each with distinct, and often mutually exclusive, needs and desires. While 20th century America was a melting pot, 21st century America will be a mosaic.

Picture it. Twenty-first century America. It will begin as an age of immigration. People will flock to these shores from Haiti and Cuba, from Mexico and China, from Hong Kong and Uzbekistan. Sometimes by choice. Often by necessity. Often through no free will of their own.

Arriving in the millions, they will land in Los Angeles, Seattle, Miami, and stay just where they land, in a ghetto-like community reminiscent of their homeland.

Like their 20th century counterparts, they will come looking for the American Dream. A chance to work for a living, to earn enough to feed their families, to practice their own religion, and hold their own political views—with no fear of persecution. They will come to be Americans. But different Americans, diverse Americans, maintaining a strong sense of their own heritage and the character of the land from which they came.

They will not assimilate as fast as they can learn the language. In fact, English will never be their primary language. They will be proud of their national tongue.

They will not cast off their foreign ways. They will not dress like Americans, eat like Americans, speak like Americans, live like Americans, as those in the 20th century. Instead they will retain the essence of their own distinctive culture.

And so will be born a new face for 21st century America. And so will be born an opportunity—a necessity—to sell a new American Dream to many diverse American consumers. The specialization of American business will arrive to meet the diversification of American consumers.

America in the 21st century will be characterized by its differences, not its similarities. America in the 21st century will be a mosaic of different ethnic groups and cultures that no longer view assimilation as their American Dream.

By the year 2000, nearly one-third of the U.S. population will be non-white or Hispanic. By the year 2056, the "average" American will be African, Asian, Hispanic, or Arabic. In California, parts of Florida and Texas, Spanish—not English—will be the predominant language.

But America in the 21st century will be characterized not only by its ethnic diversity, but also by the aging of its population.

Picture it. Twenty-first century America. An aging nation. No longer a nation of youth.

By the year 2000, nearly 30 percent of the population will be over 50. No longer young, aggressive men and women eager to succeed, demanding their "chicken in every pot, car in every garage," and a television in every living room.

Instead, they will be older men and women who are determined to, who must—through necessity—stay fit and healthy to live their longer lives.

Wellness will be of great concern. As much because of the fear of the high cost of health care, and how to afford it, as for its psychological rewards.

These will be cautious men and women who understand the value of money, and the need to save it. Men and women who know that price alone is not the issue, but that value for their money is paramount.

Men and women who will not pay more for anything than they believe it is worth. To whom worth and value have a new meaning. No longer confined to the old "price + quality" equation, but expanded to include service, convenience, selection and the overall purchase experience.

Intelligent, experienced—oftentimes cynical—men and women who will demand quality information on which to base their choice of stores and products.

Men and women who will choose a store based on its brand image—its ability to deliver a unique promise, a promise confirmed by the products and service it offers. Men and women who will not accept the promise of health care from a store that sells liquor and tobacco; will not accept the promise of every day low prices from a store that offers weekly sales.

Loyal men and women who know when to value a brand and a store—and when to reject it—when it does not address their specific needs.

And so will be born a mature face of 21st century America. And so will be born an opportunity—to sell a realistic, real, caring American Dream to older and more experienced American consumers.

But America in the 21st century will be characterized not only by its ethnic diversity and the aging of its population, but also by a diminishing level of aspirations. What began in 20th century America as an age of immigration, of hope, of new beginnings and boundless aspirations, of streets paved with gold, will be no more.

Picture it. Twenty-first century America. An age of diminishing expectations. A realization that doing better than your parents is no longer guaranteed. That having a job for your entire working life, owning your own home, sending your children to college and retiring to a warm climate at age 65 are no longer assured—even if you are willing to work hard all your life.

And so will be born a concerned face of 21st century America. And so will be born an opportunity—to sell the American Dream to a consumer who does not believe he or she can afford it.

So, how will we market to, and satisfy this consumer of the 21st century, this ethnically diverse, aging consumer with significantly diminished expectations? Certainly for the one-size-fits-all mass marketer of the 20th century, it is an all but impossible task. *The mass market is dead.*

And so must be born a new face for retailing in 21st century America. The mass market is dead, long live specialty marketing.

Picture it. Twenty-first century America. The retailer will be part of, and reflect the community. The store's environment, the products it sells, the employees and the message it evokes will be tailored to the specific nature and needs of the community it serves.

If an Hispanic community, the employees will be Hispanic. The merchandise will be tailored to the color preferences and taste preferences of Hispanic consumers. The signing and advertising will be in Spanish. The promotions will support traditional Spanish holidays and festivals. And manufacturers sales representatives will come from or be part of that community.

If an older community, the employees will be older. The merchandise and service levels will be tailored to the needs and preferences of older consumers. The store will be designed to make for a comfortable, relaxed shopping trip. A coffee shop (a meeting place), motorized shopping carts, a personal shopper, numbered parking spaces, store-to-car delivery, home delivery 24 hours of the day.

In all, a store's image and credibility will come from its roots within the community—its commitment to that community. Not merely from its success as a well-known "national brand" retailer.

Even today, there exist examples of successful retailers who have begun to practice this 21st century philosophy. Von's Tianguis (tee-an-geese) in California and England's The Body Shop are two examples of specialized, community-oriented retailers.

Tianguis with its tortilleria, instead of a bakery. Stores loaded with chili peppers, cilantro, beans, salsa, Mexican cheeses, over 600 items of product tailored to its predominantly Mexican customers.

And The Body Shop, an environmentally and socially-conscious bath and body store, where store personnel are required to spend several hours per week working for a local charity or social program.

(continued on page 12-15)

CHANGING CONSUMER *(continued from page 12-14)*

In 21st century America value will be the key to all successful retailing. Picture it. A retailer who emphasizes value of purchase and shopping experience above all else. Whether that retailer sells apparel, health and beauty aids, prescription drugs, electronics, toys, sporting goods, stationery or food. Not necessarily the lowest prices in town—but the best value in town.

The customers will know—before entering the store—that they will find exactly what they want and pay no more for it than it is worth—every day of the week. In fact, when they leave the store they will believe they got more than they paid for. Sale-driven retailing of the 20th century will be no more.

Twentieth century examples of value-based retailers: Wal-Mart, Toys 'R' Us, warehouse clubs, deep-discounters. The first signs of 21st century value-based retailers.

Picture it. A 21st century retailer where service is given regardless of the price of the merchandise. Customers will know—before entering the store—that if they need help, they need only ask. Someone will show them where the appropriate merchandise is, answer their questions, offer suggestions and give recommendations—but only if the customer wants it.

Customers will know that if they don't have time to go to the store they have only to call their personal shopper who will take their order, charge it to a credit card and deliver it—free of charge—within 48 hours.

If they want to return or exchange an item today, tomorrow—or six months from now, they need only return to the store to get their money back. No receipt necessary. No questions asked. If too busy, they have only to call the store to arrange a door-to-store pick-up to return the merchandise—free of charge.

Sound familiar? Perhaps a 21st century Wal-Mart store?

Picture it. An apparel store designed to attract value-conscious, style-conscious consumers. A narrow mix of quality fashion basics in multiple colors and fabrications. No sales. Just everyday great values.

A quick and easy store to shop. A mistake-proof selection. Mix anything with everything for faultless fashion. A constantly changing mix of merchandise to pique the shopper's interest. Need help, just ask and it's there. A different size, a different color, a different fabric. Not in that store.

Not in another store. "We'll special order it from our factory." And it will be delivered to your door, within days, free of charge.

Sound familiar? Perhaps a 21st century GAP Store? Picture it. A 21st century retailer where the store is a brand unto itself. A "good health store." Every imaginable product for fitness, beauty and health: vitamins, food supplements, medications, beauty products, weekly health and beauty lectures, a health food bar. Next door a fitness club. "Good health" advisors. Beauty advisors. No cigarettes. No liquor, no soda and no chips!

Sound familiar? Perhaps an Eckerd Store of the 21st century?

The 21st century consumer will not be satisfied with me-too stores and copy-cat products, with empty promises of service and selection, with poor quality and snake-oil mentality, "Come and get it, come and get it. Today only. . . ."

Consumers will shun me-too stores and me-too products and instead expect, demand, credible, innovative products with realistic benefits, tailored to their specific needs.

In the 21st century consumers will reject new products that are merely knock-offs of existing items. Another brand of two-in-one shampoo and conditioner will not be tolerated. Product innovations that make life easier, more comfortable, are more economical and efficient, that consciously reflect the needs of specific customers will succeed. Quality will be paramount.

Innovation, quality, service and value will be the price of entry to the 21st century. Distinctive, credible messages from a retailer and a manufacturer to its community. Not department stores selling service and selection when they offer none. Not drug stores selling promises of health care and cigarettes at the same time. Not manufacturers promising an innovative new product—the 10th of its kind on the market. Instead, marketers who will be accountable for their message, who will provide affordable quality, who will listen to and respect their customers.

Picture it. Twenty-first century America. An age where the specialization of American business will arrive to meet the diversification of American consumers. An opportunity—a necessity—to sell a new American Dream, an affordable American Dream, a credible American Dream to the mosaic that will be America.

Source: Wendy Liebmann, "The Changing Consumer: Predicting the Marketplace of the Future," *Vital Speeches of the Day* 58, no. 13 (April 15, 1992): 409-412.

either made better or its distribution was simplified and narrowed and a lot of people had jobs. Wealth was created. Someone was paid to haul the milk to the restaurant and paid to carry it inside and put it in the refrigerator. The waitress was paid wages. . . .

You ordered milk. You got milk. But you got more than milk. You got a miracle in a glass. The miracle of created wealth.[17]

Finally, hold audience attention until the very close. As a speaker, your most pressing task is to create and sustain the interest of your audience. Cultivate the audience's sensitivity, awareness, and understanding, and identify with your listeners. The use of examples, stories, and quotations can help you accomplish this important task. Franklin D. Roosevelt once said, "I've always thought that the greatest symbol of common sense is building a bridge." And this is what effective informative speaking is all about. It's the combination of personal attributes, knowledge, and carefully planned techniques that enables you to build a bridge across the gap that stands between you and your audience.

Use Basic Organizational Principles to Build a Logical Structure for Your Presentation. Begin with the overall picture, letting your listeners understand where you're going and what you're doing. Jo Sprague and Douglas Stuart compare this to putting a jigsaw puzzle together: "Have you ever tried to put together a jigsaw puzzle without looking at the picture on the box? What you have is a jumble of unrelated pieces. Once you see the big picture you have some idea of how things are supposed to fit together."[18] You can then make a natural transition into the body of the presentation by providing a preview statement that outlines the main points to be developed. Continue, then, to structure your arguments, carefully guiding your listeners along.

Use Different Channels of Communication. Use multiple channels of communication to increase comprehension and add impact to your presentation. You might use a television monitor to show a short videotape, an overhead projector to clarify a set of statistics, and an audiotape to let the audience hear the new radio advertisement. Remember that people recall best what they see and hear. Richard Saul Wurman further explains the importance of different channels when he observes: "There are only three means of description available to us—words, pictures, and numbers. The palette is limited. Generally, the best instructions rely on all three, but in any instance one should predominate, while the other two serve and extend. The key to giving good instructions is to choose the appropriate means."[19] As with every other factor in a presentation, the needs of the audience come first in choosing appropriate channels of communication. Industries and organizations vary in the formality they expect: in some, a stand-up performance is the norm; in others, anything more formal than rolled-up sleeves around a table is considered overdone; and still others prefer an electronic component with the use of slides and an overhead projector or computer modeling. Ultimately, the determining questions should be: What are you trying to achieve? What do your data demand? Do you have the time, money, and equipment available? Remember: the potential for disaster increases exponentially with the number of electronic gadgets involved in your presentation.

Avoid Being Too Technical. One of the easiest ways to lose an audience is to be too technical in your language. What seems simple to you may be very difficult for someone else. Perhaps you remember how confused you were when you first tried to read the technical manual to program your VCR. Or, when you tried to remedy a computer error by listening to instructions from a computer expert. These situations illustrate the confusion and exasperation that can occur when one fails to analyze the audience and use effective language. When technical language is necessary, take time to carefully define each term.

Avoid Information Overload. Your task as an informative speaker is to assemble data, glean what is important to your purpose, and present it to your listeners. To overwhelm them with too many data is to overlook the important step of being selective in what you present. This information overload causes your listeners anxiety, confusion, irritability, and anger, finally prompting them to just tune you out. A good rule to follow in informative speaking is "less is more."

Two of the most urgent tasks you face in making informative presentations are to make people understand you and to make them care enough to act on your ideas and requests. That's what effective informative speaking is all about—it's your ability to share information and get people to act. Effectiveness does not come from the magic of an inborn gift but rather from a mastery of basic presentational skills.

▶ ROLE OF PERSUASIVE SPEAKING

Armed with the most recent government studies proving that secondhand smoke is related to cancer in nonsmokers, the director of human relations convinces the corporate president to adopt a companywide no-smoking policy.

Three partners in the city's most prestigious law firm persuade the managing partner to hire a female attorney, the first in the firm's long history.

Aware that a local company has used advanced computer technology to deny workers retirement benefits, a group of laid-off workers encourages an attorney to file a class action suit against the company.

All of these people are engaged in persuasive speaking which we define as the delivery of messages to an audience by a speaker who intends to influence their choices by changing, reinforcing, or shaping their attitudes. This definition refers to the three endproducts of persuasion: changed, reinforced, and shaped responses. *Changing* responses are those whereby the speaker intends to alter an existing attitude, "smokers are persuaded to become nonsmokers, automobile drivers are persuaded to walk or to use public transportation, Christians are persuaded to become Moslems, and so on."[20] These are the most difficult of all persuasive interactions. *Reinforcing* responses are used to modify an existing attitude or behavior by strengthening it. Wallace Fotheringham calls this response "continuance" or a process of keeping the audience doing what it is already doing.[21] In a sense, these responses reward the audience for sustaining presently held beliefs, attitudes, or values. Finally, *shaping* responses are used to mold the ideas, attitudes, and opinions of listeners who have little or no prior knowledge or understanding of the topic. The situation that prompts a communicator to try persuasion is an audience's confusion about what to believe or how to act. Persuasion is ultimately intended to modify overt behavior. Depending on the audience, the persuasive speaker may seek to reduce hostility, to reinforce and intensify favorable attitudes, or to convince receivers.

As you prepare your persuasive presentation, you will choose from these possible perspectives. Once selected, the perspective will influence the form of the presentation and your relationship with the audience. Perspective, closely allied to intention, is a central choice that you must make after careful consideration. Donald K. Smith clarifies the concept and emphasizes its importance when he observes:

> The speaker's *position* is the central content and stance of his action. In this sense, the idea of position includes, but is broader than, the conception that a speech is organized around a central statement or thesis. The speaker takes a position by defining not only the central idea he wishes to communicate, but also by revealing his point of view (or stance) toward his subject matter, his audience, the occasion, and himself. Thus the speaker's position has both a cognitive dimension and an emotive dimension; it reveals not only what the speaker believes, but also the point of view and attitudes through which he expresses his belief.[22]

Your position or perspective is more inclusive than the stated purpose. Besides being a central statement of belief, a chosen position says something about how you see the world. Your position is the product of most of your experiences, your encounters with other people and their ideas, your perspective on previous occasions, your friends, and those whom you admire or with whom you have previously acted. In selecting and stating your perspective, you reveal yourself to your audience. Your attitudes and perceptions are disclosed and made available for public scrutiny. The audience becomes aware of your particular stance and your intentions.

Although some may think of persuasion in the corporation as the province of the marketing or public relations departments, a fuller understanding of persuasion will convince you that it is meaningful to everyone who works. It's certainly a common activity for all of us. A large part of each of our days is devoted to persuasive activities—either we are being persuaded or we are persuading others. In our personal lives, we try to convince our family members and friends of everything from which television program to watch, to which restaurant to visit, to what to name the baby. We're also busy persuading other people in our business lives, convincing our bosses, coworkers, and customers about a variety of issues and concerns. Indisputably, persuasion plays an important role in both our personal and our occupational lives. Eugene Weinstein correctly observes that "no set of skills is as essential to participating in society as the skills enabling people to get others to think, feel, or do what they want them to do."[23]

▶ TYPES OF PERSUASIVE PRESENTATIONS

Using persuasion, a speaker seeks to influence the listener's beliefs, attitudes, values, and behavior. Persuasive objectives have not been achieved if listeners merely understand ideas or facts. They must instead respond to the persuader's message with agreement, with conviction, and usually with a particular behavior or action, before persuasive communication can be termed successful. Persuasive presentations generally fall into three categories: proposals, sales presentations, and motivational talks.

Proposals

The persuasive proposal is a common type of presentation in any organization. Proposals are usually intended to persuade the listeners to adopt a new plan, concept, or procedure or to provide additional resources of some kind such as funding, staff, or equipment. They are important presentations because the action desired is often largely dependent on the persuasiveness of the proposal.

To convince an audience that a particular proposal should be accepted or rejected starts with the recognition that there must be a specific issue at stake. The issue, stated in the form of a proposition, may be of three types. First is the proposition of fact. Here, the audience does not accept a factual statement as true and demands verification. "We have a new marketing strategy" is a factual statement not likely to be disbelieved. On the other hand, a speaker who argues, "We are not guilty of any of the false advertising allegations alleged by the Better Business Bureau" may be stating a fact very much in doubt. Second is the proposition of policy which concerns future action or behavior and contends that something should or should not be done. A speaker arguing that Equal Employment Opportunity guidelines should be broadened or that environmental regulations should be strengthened is advancing propositions of policy. Third are propositions of value which focus on desirability, contending that something is good or bad. A speech proclaiming the virtues of our free enterprise system would be an example. These presentations with their corresponding propositions are often delivered to an audience of many listeners. However, they can also be presented to just one person, as when you ask your superior for a raise, promotion, or more staff for your department.

Sales Presentations

These presentations are often the lifeblood of the organization and include informal, one-to-one situations as well as more formal speeches to groups. The diversity of the products that are the subjects of these presentations is significant and underscores the importance of this type of persuasive format. Their specific intent is to get action. When you call for an audience to do something, three criteria should be kept in mind. First, the action should be clear. The desired action must be specified unambiguously. Second, the action should be easy. The individual or group should be able to take the desired action without going to a lot of trouble. Third, the action should be made necessary. This speech should not be timid; it should establish a clear connection between arguments developed in the talk and the need to act.

Ethos or source credibility is critical to effective sales presentations. The sales message includes all of the speaker and context characteristics that the audience perceives and gives meaning to, and this includes our personal source credibility, image, or reputation. Some ethos is antecedent; it exists in the receivers' minds before the speech begins. But for most speakers, ethos is derived from the actual speech behavior; it must be earned. The better you understand the criteria by which receivers ascribe ethos to a speaker, and the better you adapt to those unique criteria in each communication situation, the more persuasive you will be.

Motivational Speeches

These inspiring speeches have become popular in corporate America and are used to persuade company employees to do more, work harder, manage more efficiently, and feel better about themselves, their jobs, and the company. Popular speakers in the decade of the 1990s include motivator Zig Ziglar, corporate gurus Tom Peters John Naisbitt, and Charles Givens, and sports personalities Dick Vitale, Fran Tarken-

▶ POWERSPEAK: THE TWELVE MOST PERSUASIVE WORDS IN THE ENGLISH LANGUAGE

By Dorothy Leeds

In her best-selling book, Powerspeak, *Dorothy Leeds lists 12 words that are especially useful when persuading other people. We include these 12 examples of "power speaking" and the reasons why they are important in persuasion.*

1. **Discovery.** When we hear the word "discovery" we often think back to our childhood and get a feeling of excitement and adventure. If you tell the audience that you want to share a "discovery" with them, you make your enthusiasm contagious.
2. **Easy.** To be honest, most of us would prefer that life be easy rather than difficult. People generally like to believe that they can accomplish a lot without much effort. Your audience will often favor quick and uncomplicated answers over long and complex responses.
3. **Guarantee.** This is one of those "magic bullet" words which catches our attention because we're all reluctant to try something new if there is a risk involved. Take away that fear by guaranteeing what you believe is a sure thing, and you can sell your audience on your point.
4. **Health.** Self-preservation is a great motivator. We all want to be healthy, and sustaining our health is important to us. Promises of good health have been a part of persuasive messages for centuries and have led people to buy everything from gold bracelets to magic elixirs. You can persuade your audience to believe in your legitimate pursuits by making their health an issue of importance.
5. **Love.** Clearly, this is a word that can alter attitudes and provoke action. Love is one of the few things that we cannot do without. All of us seek love from other people and feel better when we are able to give it to those who are very close to us. The word "love" invokes the thought of romantic fantasies in many people.
6. **Money.** It seems people have always been interested in money. Many people are interested in making more money in their jobs and winning money through lot-

teries and gambling, saving money through shrewd investments, and spending money on the necessities and luxuries of life. The word "money" is an attention-getter.

7. **New.** We are always interested in the new and the different and the novel in life. People would usually rather have something new than something used. Possessing new things and knowing new ideas has a special and unique appeal for all of us.
8. **Proven.** The word "proven" is one of the no-risk words of our vocabulary because it assures listeners that something has already been tested and given the go-ahead. We generally prefer the proven over the unproven.
9. **Results.** Ours is a results-oriented society, and many of us are waiting, in fact, for results. Whether you are speaking about an advertising campaign, an innovative idea, or a marketing approach, results are the bottom line in business.
10. **Safety.** The idea of safety is very comforting to people. We put dead bolts, burglar bars, and security systems on our homes and alarms, ignition cut-off systems, and steering wheel locks on our automobiles. Safety has become a major industry in America. Appealing to the concept of safety in the language of your presentation can act as a reassurance to your listeners.
11. **Save.** Everyone is a bargain hunter in some way. Whether you seek a saving in money, resources, or time, the concept of saving has an intrinsic appeal to people. It will be a benefit to you as a presenter if you can persuade your listeners that your ideas provide a savings of some kind for them.
12. **You.** The most important word is the final one on the list of twelve. The best persuasive speakers personalize their messages by using the word "you" often. You can best energize your audience by addressing them directly.

Source: Dorothy Leeds, *Powerspeak: The Complete Guide to Persuasive Public Speaking and Presenting* (New York: Berkley Books [originally published by Prentice Hall, 1988]): 99–100.

ton, and Tommy LaSorda. The common theme of motivational speakers is that the audience members can do better than they are presently doing. Zig Ziglar will tell you how to be a better sales representative and feel better about yourself and your job; Charles Givens will persuade listeners to strive for financial security; and Dick

Vitale will urge a high school audience to live drug-free. All of these "feel-good" speakers are interested in improving your self-confidence, worklife, and personal worth.

Sometimes an audience needs a pep talk. In such a case, the aim is to stimulate listeners by stirring their feelings. Some feelings are generally positive and desirable in terms of the receiver: love, happiness, joy, sympathy, trust, pride, desire. The appeal of the message is that, if followed, the receivers will feel good. Persuasive speakers have also learned that appealing to negative emotions can occasionally be very effective. Negative emotions include: fear, anxiety, anger, sorrow, disappointment, guilt. Using such appeals, you can prompt listeners to assume personal responsibility for their lives and act in more positive directions. There will never be a science of motivation, but over time you can learn to recognize the salient features of various audiences and to develop messages that enhance your persuasive goals.

▶ STRATEGIES FOR EFFECTIVE PERSUASIVE SPEAKING

Just as with informative presentations, persuasive messages should be prepared and delivered with an awareness of what happens during the communication process. Successful persuasive presentations exhibit a fine mixture of carefully selected, varied, compatible, complementary strategies that address the question: How do people come to change their thoughts and behaviors? A strategy is a method or plan used to achieve a goal, and the following strategies should be useful as you prepare to speak persuasively.

Assume a Receiver-Centered Perspective. We've noted before that everyone who initiates communication with others seeks a response from them. A receiver-centered perspective of communication assumes that how listeners respond to a speech determines the degree and quality of the communication that has occurred. But many people think of persuasion as something that one person *does to* another. The problem with this view is that even the best-constructed, fluently delivered persuasive message may not achieve the intended response. Rather than viewing persuasion as something that one person does to another, you should think of it as a process in which one person attempts to elicit a specific response, and one or more people respond in various ways. Persuasion occurs when the receivers say it has, when their verbal or nonverbal behaviors reveal that you have achieved your purpose. The outcomes of persuasive communication accrue not only from the speaker's message and context, but also from the complex variables in the receiver. This explains why the "best-laid plans" of many speakers do not achieve the expected results.

Identify Your Role and Your Risk. Donald K. Smith identifies six speaker roles and their corresponding modalities that should be considered when preparing persuasive presentations.[24] Associated with each role is a certain degree of risk. You may serve as an *agent* of the audience, in which case your position reflects and reinforces the thinking of the audience. As an agent of the audience, you are assuming very little risk because the audience is friendly, or predisposed toward your point of view. You may serve as a *catalyst, mediator,* or *defendant* in which cases you seek strategies of management. In these roles you are, respectively, attempting to move an audience in a particular direction, to bring a sharply divided audience together, or to gain support for your personal conduct or beliefs, and the risk involved is considerably increased. As a *critic*, you directly confront the audience and consequently assume a highly risky and openly aggressive posture. From such a perspective, you may consider your audience hostile. Finally, when assuming the role of *leader*, you hope to transcend existing difficulties and move the audience to a new interpretation of the problem. Considerable risk is also associated with this speaker role because audience members may reject your analysis or be reluctant to venture into new ground. Persuasion requires you to assume a position, select appropriate types of proof and structural forms, and to determine a relationship with your audience.

Adjust the Content to the Audience's Attitude. The audience for a persuasive presentation can be classified as either favorable, neutral, or hostile, and it is important that you understand these different types of listeners. The *favorable* or *friendly audience* is predisposed toward you and your point of view, and is seeking personal involvement. You can instill that feeling of involvement with emotional appeals and by being very specific about what you want them to do. They already agree with the facts and want to be inspired to act. The *neutral* or *apathetic audience* is undecided, uninformed, or perhaps just uninterested, and you need to gain their attention, showing them how they are directly affected by your subject. It's fine to use vivid examples and illustrations, but remember that they also need factual information to raise their awareness and understanding. Factual support can make them more informed listeners and concerned advocates. Finally, the *hostile audience* disagrees with your point of view and may be openly confrontational. Your objective should be to present your argument(s) logically and with sufficient factual support, while appearing to be an open-minded, knowledgeable, and fair person. Expecting to change the thinking of such an audience in a single presentation is probably unrealistic. Persuasion takes time and what you are seeking is a reasoned, sustained, conciliatory discussion of the issues. Understanding your listeners' attitudes and comprehending the relationship between claims and support ought to broaden your options when preparing persuasive presentations.

Use Alternative Organizational Patterns. We have previously discussed a number of suitable organizational patterns, but, when your purpose is to persuade, other patterns may be effective. These alternatives include primacy–recency strategies, a two-sided or counterargument approach, and Monroe's motivated sequence.

Primacy–recency strategies ask which is more effective, the argument that is presented first (primacy) or the argument that is presented last (recency). There's no absolute answer to this question because it depends on the interaction of myriad variables. However, in some instances, presenting arguments favored by the audience first and more controversial arguments second opens receivers to be more receptive.[25] Perhaps, when presented with controversial material first, listeners are so busy trying to resolve the controversy or construct their responses that they fail to tune in to the subsequent material. Whichever strategy you choose, don't put your most important argument in the middle. Research has clearly shown that an audience will remember longer what it hears first and last.

At times your audience will know a lot about the topic and be keenly aware of arguments against your position, or perhaps those counterarguments soon will be made public. In this case it is wise to use a *two-sided approach* and get the counterarguments out in the open. Research suggests that intelligent and well-informed audiences will be more easily convinced if they hear both sides in a controversy. They are also more likely to stay convinced longer if they hear both points of view while making up their minds.[26] These results square with common sense. A speaker confident and candid enough to bring out opposing arguments exerts a strong, personally credible appeal, and the counterarguments an audience hears later from others will lose some of their power to dissuade because they have already been taken into account. However, when presenting counterarguments, avoid phrases such as "we concede" and "I admit"; use "we recognize," or "I realize," or "we are aware." Of course, as with all strategies, you'll want to consider other variables operating in the situation, including the needs and expectations of the receivers. For example, a major corporation was hiring an industrial psychologist. Several psychologists were interviewed by the top management team. Each candidate presented information about the major psychological concerns of the company as evenhandedly as possible by saying, "On the one hand it has been said . . . and on the other hand it has been said. . . ." Finally the committee sent a memo to the chief personnel officer saying, "Please send us a one-handed psychologist." Clearly, in this situation the receivers wanted a one-sided presentation. In other situations, however, a two-sided presentation can be a particularly powerful approach.

The *motivated sequence* was developed by Alan Monroe and introduced in the 1935 edition of his now classic text, *Principles and Types of Speech*.[27] Based on John Dewey's "psycho-logic" approach to the resolution of problems, the motivated sequence functionally forecasts the thinking processes or mental stages of listeners.[28] In the preface to the first edition, Monroe explains the rationale for the five steps in the motivated sequence:

> The names of the conventional divisions (introduction, body, conclusion) have been discarded in favor of a "motivated sequence" of five steps, each of which is named to correspond with the function of that step in securing a particular reaction from the audience. These steps are named attention, need, satisfaction, visualization, and action. Thus, the student is made to realize by the very names of the divisions themselves that he [sic] must first gain attention, then create a feeling of need, satisfy that need, make his audience visualize that satisfaction, and finally impel his listeners to act. It is obvious, or course, that not all five of these steps are needed in every speech . . . . the functional characteristic of the motivated sequence has stood the test of time.[29]

Let's consider, for a moment, each of these steps:

Step 1: *Attention.* Capture the attention of the group, adapt to the audience, and build credibility. You want to motivate and compel the audience to listen to your presentation by introducing the problem in an interesting way.

Step 2: *Need.* Describe the problem and support it with the necessary evidence and reasoning to prove its significance. Present the audience with a problem and give them a strong need for solving it. Why is it necessary to consider a change?

Step 3: *Satisfaction.* Provide a desirable solution for the previously outlined difficulties. Support is provided here to prove that the solution satisfies the need—that it is workable and remedies the problem. You may want to remember the words of Claude Bernard when he said: "[A fact is] nothing. It is valu-

Example of the Motivated Sequence Pattern

Topic for Persuasive Presentation:
"BE A PART OF OUR BLOOD DRIVE — DONATE BLOOD TODAY!"

ATTENTION

If you or a member of your family were in an emergency situation and needed blood, there might not be enough available!

NEED

Currently there is not enough blood available to satisfy the existing needs. Disasters and other emergency situations have exhausted our blood supply.

SATISFACTION

By joining with your coworkers in giving blood during our blood drive, you can help guarantee that there will be sufficient supply during any upcoming emergencies. This means that area hospitals will be able to supply blood as needed in a prompt and timely manner.

VISUALIZATION

If the blood drive is unsuccessful, there won't be enough blood available for people like you and your family. If it is successful, lives can be saved — perhaps yours or a family member's.

ACTION

Go out to the Red Cross Bloodmobile today and donate. Be a friend in deed.

able only for the idea attached to it, or for the proof which it furnishes." What is the answer to the problem?

Step 4: *Visualization.* Paint a picture of—or visualize—the outcomes of the proposed solution. Make your solution attractive and arouse a strong desire in your audience for its adoption. How will change or lack of action directly affect members of the audience?

Step 5: *Action.* Specify action to be taken and make that behavior convenient. Call for a clear response from your audience, inviting them to act on your presentation.

The motivated sequence is a proven method of organizing persuasive presentations, and you should seriously consider using it. Take a careful look at Exhibit 12-1 which presents a shortened example of this organizational pattern used to encourage blood donors.

Be Realistic About the Outcome. Remember that it is difficult, perhaps impossible, to predict audience responses because they're generated by both rational and nonrational factors. We are reasoning animals and capable of solving puzzles by thinking logically, analytically, abstractly, and rationally. But persuasive speakers should recognize that, although their messages may truly be "reasoned discourse," the receivers will often respond, in part, on nonrational grounds. They may be affected by their own emotions and beliefs in ways that render the logical development of the presentation irrelevant. If their emotions dominate, the logical dimension may not be a factor in how they perceive your message. This is why persuasive speaking is to a large extent an artistic process rather than a science.

The following student outline for a speech using a problem–solution format is a good example of a persuasive presentation on a business subject. The full text of the speech is also presented here in a sidebox (see page 12-27). After you read the outline and the speech, use the questions for analysis in the paragraph following the outline. The speech was delivered to a college-level introductory public speaking class.

Outline for "The Problem With Pennies" Speech

General Purpose: To persuade

Specific Purpose: To persuade the audience that pennies should be discontinued as a U.S. coin.

Central Idea: Pennies should be discontinued as a U.S. coin because they cause problems for individuals, business, and the nation.

Main Points:

I. Using pennies should be discontinued because they cause significant problems.
    A. They cause problems for individuals.
    B. They cause problems for business.
    C. They cause problems for the nation as a whole.
II. The discontinuance of pennies can be brought about by four easy steps.
    A. The federal government should legalize and standardize the rounding off of all purchases to the nearest nickel.
    B. The sales tax should also be rounded off to the nearest nickel.
    C. The U.S. Mint should stop making new pennies.
    D. People should cash in the pennies already in circulation.

In analyzing the above presentation, the following questions should guide you: What is the relationship of the speaker to the audience? Is she addressing a proposition of fact, policy, or value? How well is the problem defined? Is the significance of the problem demonstrated? How? In what ways is the topic related to her audience? Is her use of evidence clear and compelling? Why? Is her use of language effective? How? Does the introduction gain our attention, and is the close action-oriented and positive? What could the speaker do to improve on this presentation? Were you persuaded? Why? Why not?

▶ SPEAKING ON SPECIAL OCCASIONS

Most of the speaking you will do in the course of your organizational life will be informative or persuasive, but there will be times when you are called on to deliver a speech for a special occasion. The purpose of such a presentation is neither to inform nor to persuade—it is to fit the needs of the special occasion. Stephen Lucas describes how these occasions stand out from other speaking situations: "Special occasions are the punctuation marks of day-to-day life, the high points that stand out above ordinary routine. Christenings, weddings, funerals, graduations, award ceremonies, inaugurals, retirement dinners—all these are occasions, and they are very special to the people who take part in them. Nearly always they are occasions for speechmaking."[30]

Here we discuss the most common types of special occasion presentations you may make and provide suggestions for each.

Speeches of Introduction

The speech of introduction usually presents a formal speaker at a business function, luncheon, or dinner. Generally, this speech has two objectives: (1) to inform the audience about the speaker and (2) to warmly greet and make the speaker feel relaxed and welcome. Keep this speech short but well organized because the attending audience wants to hear the presentation by the invited speaker, not the introduction. Do not trace the speaker's life history from birth to the present. If you don't know the speaker well, get information from a contact person, the person in charge of the gathering, or the speaker personally. This information should include degrees and titles, publications and creative projects, and pertinent occupational and life experiences. It is imperative that the information about the speaker be completely accurate. This includes the correct pronunciation of her or his name. One of the more famous faux pas occurred when the speaker introduced the then-president of the United States this way: "Ladies and gentlemen, the President of the United States—Hoobert Heaver." If you have any doubts about the accuracy of information be certain to check it well before the occasion. Many a speech of introduction has failed for its inaccuracy. In short, you want your introduction to be brief, accurate, and adapted to the occasion.

Speeches of Acceptance

The acceptance speech is intended to thank the presenting person or group, and to accept an award, honor, or tribute. The recipient is usually fully aware of the presentation, but there are situations when the presentation is a surprise. In these instances, follow the suggestions regarding impromptu speaking: quickly select a theme ("Thank you for this important award"), and choose a simple organizational pattern ("Let me thank two groups of people—those who selected me for this honor, and those who made it possible for me to receive this honor"). You should accept the honor with a sense of pride, without being boastful and without embarrassment or a sense of undeservedness—remember that the selection committee took some time to choose you for the award. Finally, when closing an acceptance speech, note what the honor will mean to you in the future. You might say, "This award is the highest honor our company bestows on an employee and I will always look on it with fond memories of this evening. Thank you." In short, accept the award with gratitude and follow the guidelines of brevity, humility, and graciousness.

Televised Presentations

In this era of nearly omnipresent mass media, it is likely that at some time you will be asked to speak on television. The invitation may come from the staff of a televi-

► THE PROBLEM WITH PENNIES

By Susan Ingraham

"A nickel for your thoughts." "A nickel saved is a nickel earned." "Nickels from heaven."

Okay, maybe these phrases don't have quite the same ring as the original saying: "A penny for your thoughts," "A penny saved is a penny earned," and "Pennies from heaven." But it's a fact of our nation's economic life that the penny is becoming obsolete. Inflation over the past few decades has been the death of penny candy, penny arcades, and penny bubble gum. The fact is that pennies don't buy much of anything any more. The age of the penny is over. It's time to let this dinosaur of our economy go extinct.

Sure, most of you say, pennies can be annoying. But why do we have to get rid of them? Why must we change something that's worked for so long? And what would we do without pennies? I had the same questions when I started work on this speech. But as a result of my research, I'm convinced that the continued use of pennies is a costly problem and that we can get along just fine without them. Today, I hope to convince you of the same thing.

The place to begin is by noting that pennies cause problems for individuals, for businesses, and for the nation as a whole. Many Americans consider pennies to be an almost useless annoyance. According to my class survey, about two-thirds of you find pennies bothersome. They take up space and add weight to your pockets, wallets, and purses. They get in the way when you're trying to find other coins. They slow down checkout lines when you have to search for exact change. And most of the time when you really need coins—for copy machines, pay phones, vending machines, and video games—you can't use pennies anyway.

In fact, many people don't use pennies. A survey by the U.S. Mint showed that only half of the 12,000 people questioned use pennies on a daily basis. Most of the other half collect pennies around the house, waiting until they have enough to cash in at the bank. It can be a long wait. In a *Los Angeles Times* article, writer Noel Gunther explained that during his last two years in college, he and his roommate saved all their pennies so they could throw a "Pennies from Heaven" party for graduation. They filled six jars with what looked like a fortune. The day before graduation, they emptied the jars and counted out $21.56—barely enough to buy beverages.

Pennies are a nuisance for the business community as well as for individuals. The National Association of Convenience Stores estimates that an average of two seconds is spent handling pennies during each of its members' 10 billion annual cash transactions. That comes out to a total of 5.5 million hours spent handling pennies—at an average cost of $22 million. According to *Fortune* magazine, some banks charge up to 30 cents for every dollar's worth of pennies they process. This makes it very costly for many businesses to accept pennies.

Keeping pennies in circulation also costs the nation as a whole. Every year the Treasury Department takes about 7 billion pennies out of circulation because they are bent or worn out. According to the Treasury Department, several billion more pennies go into mayonnaise jars, coffee cans, piggy banks, and dresser drawers. Or they are simply thrown away. In the survey mentioned earlier in my speech, the U.S. Mint reported that 6 percent of American adults simply jettison their pennies with the trash!

To keep an adequate supply of pennies in circulation, the U.S. Mint creates approximately 12 billion new pennies each year. The cost of manufacturing these new pennies is .66 of a cent apiece, which adds up to almost $80 million a year. As Treasury officials told *U.S. News & World Report,* when you add on storage and handling expenses, it costs our society considerably more than a penny to transact a penny's worth of business.

You can now see the magnitude of the problem with pennies. Fortunately, it is a problem that can be easily solved. The solution I recommend is similar to a plan supported by the Coin Coalition, a group working to eliminate pennies from our economy.

The plan has four steps. First, the federal government should legalize and standardize the rounding off of all purchases to the nearest nickel. This rounding off should take place after all items in a given transaction are totalled but before the sales tax is added. Because the number of purchases rounded up would roughly equal the number rounded down, this would not cause any increase to consumers.

Second, the sales tax should also be rounded off to the nearest nickel. Both the customer and the state would stand an equal chance of gaining or losing a maximum of two cents on each purchase. In essence, this is no different from what you do when you file your income taxes—except that in computing your income taxes, you round everything off to the nearest dollar.

Because the first two steps of this plan will eliminate the need for pennies, the third step is for the U. S. Mint to stop making new pennies. As we have shown, this will save the taxpayers some $80 million a year in minting costs alone.

The fourth step of this plan is for people to cash in the pennies already in circulation, thereby removing pennies entirely from the money supply.

I admit that it may be hard to imagine a world without pennies, but there is plenty of evidence that this plan will work. James Benfield, Executive Director of the Coin Coalition, notes that when the U.S. stopped minting half-cent coins in 1857, a similar procedure of rounding off purchases and phasing out the coins worked extremely well. None of us miss the half-cent, and in a few years none of us will miss the penny.

Whether we realize it or not, many of us already round off some of our purchases to the nearest nickel. Think for a moment of the "Take a Penny, Leave a Penny" containers next to the cash registers at local convenience stores. Every time you take a few pennies from the box to pay for your purchase or leave a few pennies from your change, you are actually rounding off the amount you pay to the nearest nickel.

In conclusion, pennies create problems for individuals, for businesses, and for the nation as a whole. The time and money currently wasted in using and minting pennies could be put to more productive ends. By rounding off purchases and sales taxes to the nearest nickel, by ending production of new pennies, and by letting old pennies drop out of use, the problems created by pennies could be eliminated without upsetting the economy. And just as we have gotten used to life with penny candy, penny arcades, and penny bubble gum, so I think, given time, we will also get used to the phrase, "a nickel saved is a nickel earned."

Source: Susan Ingraham, "The Problem with Pennies," in: Stephen E. Lucas, *The Art of Public Speaking*, 4th ed. (New York: McGraw-Hill, 1992): 393–396.

sion station because you are a recognized expert in a particular field, or because you are the designated spokesperson for a group or organization. Gaining on-camera television skills may well be the greatest emerging challenge now facing corporate communicators.[31]

Business communicators increasingly find themselves today in the televised interview. When participating in such an interview, try to make *your* main point at least once during your television time although the interviewer may lead you down other paths. Also, realize that events happen suddenly on television and, therefore, you need to make your points quickly. A half-hour on radio or an hour with a newspaper reporter becomes approximately four minutes on television.[32] Be firm and assertive, but don't appear angry when personally challenged because a large television audience may be watching. A calm, controlled demeanor projects most positively.

You may be asked to deliver a speech in front of television cameras. These presentations may be presented live before a large audience and broadcast to different locations via multiple monitors, or recorded on videocassette for playback at a later time. When delivering televised presentations, you will want to follow a few suggestions: *Don't be intimidated by the television setting.* It's natural to find a television studio distracting and intimidating with the bright lights, hurried movements of technicians and personnel, and large pieces of equipment. Consequently, your visiting a studio, taking a studio tour, reading available materials about working with the media, and speaking with people who are familiar with television can help. *Dress appropriately for the medium.* Wear clothes that look good against the background within the studio or location where you will be taping. The "cool" colors—blue, gray, and pastels—are preferred. Patterns and busy weaves, as well as prints, should be avoided because they blur on camera. Wear minimal jewelry because its glare distracts the viewing audience. It is always a good idea to ask media professionals in charge of the session specific questions about your appearance. Remember: television magnifies your appearance, so take care to dress appropriately for the cameras. *Be aware of eye contact.* Knowing where to look during a televised presentation is critical if you hope to be effective.

The general rules are to maintain eye contact with your interviewer during an interview and with the audience, camera or teleprompter when giving a speech. The camera will usually find you during your presentation so maintaining eye contact with the audience is a good plan. If you are speaking with a teleprompter located above or on the camera, you will be looking at the camera; but if you are speaking with teleprompters located to the left or right of the lectern, you can alternate your eye contact between them, and the cameraperson will follow your gaze.

Television is a very important medium and you will undoubtedly find yourself speaking there sometime in the future, so you need to become knowledgeable about the television situation, prepare yourself as thoroughly as possible, and do your best.

Speeches of Tribute

Speeches of tribute are designed to commemorate, praise, celebrate, or eulogize. They draw on examples, testimony, statistics, and illustrations to create respect and to inspire. Farewell addresses, dedications, and eulogies are common examples of speeches of tribute.

Farewell addresses happen when people leave or retire from an organization or are promoted to a new position that takes them away from colleagues and workmates. These speeches are either given in gratitude to others by the person who is leaving, or by colleagues and associates who wish to extend best wishes to the person who is leaving.

Dedications are presented when schools, parks, monuments, or buildings are constructed. They are testimonials to the occasion, celebrating the completion of a project and addressing the purpose it will serve for the community. The intent is to take pride in the accomplishment and promote continued interest, support, and involvement.

Eulogies are presentations given to honor the dead. These speeches express appropriate personal and collective grief, deepen appreciation and respect for the deceased, and/or give the audience strength for the present and inspiration for the future. Peggy Noonan observes: "They are the most moving kind of speech because they attempt to pluck meaning from the fog, and on short order, when the emotions are still ragged and raw and susceptible to leaps. It is a challenge to look at a life and organize our thoughts about it and try to explain to ourselves what it meant, and the most moving part is the element of implicit celebration. Most people aren't appreciated enough, and the bravest things we do in our lives are usually known only to ourselves. . . . A eulogy gives a chance to celebrate. . . .[33]

Although these speeches of tribute differ significantly in content, certain guidelines will prove useful if you are asked to make such a presentation. *Call attention to the most important attributes or accomplishments of the person.* Choose a few and emphasize them, instead of listing all of their achievements with "good deeds" seemingly blending together. *Emphasize the effect the person had on other people.* A person's effect on other people is usually of more long-standing importance than that person's singular accomplishments. Therefore, stress how this person's life affected the lives of others, including in your remarks people in your audience who were touched in some way by the person to whom you are paying tribute. *Connect your theme with the occasion in your conclusion.* The overall message of your tribute should be connected

▶ TRIBUTE TO THE *CHALLENGER* ASTRONAUTS
Delivered by Ronald Reagan, January 28, 1986

Ladies and Gentlemen, I'd planned to speak to you tonight on the State of the Union but the events of earlier today have led me to change those plans. Today is a day for mourning and remembering.

Nancy and I are pained to the core by the tragedy of the shuttle *Challenger*. We know we share this pain with all of the people of our country. This is truly a national loss.

Nineteen years ago, almost to the day, we lost three astronauts in a terrible accident on the ground. But we've never lost an astronaut in flight; we've never had a tragedy like this. And perhaps we've forgotten the courage it took for the crew of the shuttle; but they, the *Challenger* seven, were aware of the dangers, but overcome them and did their jobs brilliantly. We mourn seven heroes: Michael Smith, Dick Scobee, Judith Resnik, Ronald McNair, Ellison Onizuka, Gregory Jarvis, and Christa McAuliffe. We mourn their loss as a nation together.

(For) the families of the seven, we cannot bear, as you do, the full impact of this tragedy, but we feel the loss, and we're thinking about you so very much. Your loved ones were daring and brave, and they had that special grace, that special spirit that says, "Give me a challenge and I'll meet it with joy." They had a hunger to explore the universe and discover its truths. They wished to serve, and they did. They served all of us.

We've grown used to wonders in this century. It's hard to dazzle us, but for 25 years the U.S. space program has been doing just that. We've grown used to the idea of space, and perhaps we forget that we've only just begun. We're still pioneers. They, the members of the *Challenger* crew, were pioneers.

And I want to say something to the schoolchildren of America who were watching the live coverage of the shut-tle's takeoff. I know it is hard to understand, but sometimes painful things like this happen. It's all part of the process of exploration and discovery. It's all part of taking a chance and expanding man's horizons. The future doesn't belong to the fainthearted; it belongs to the brave. The *Challenger* crew was pulling us into the future, and we'll continue to follow them.

I've always had great faith in and respect for our space program, and what happened today does nothing to diminish it. We don't hide our space program. We don't keep secrets and cover things up. We do it all up front and in public. That's the way freedom is, and we wouldn't change it for a minute. We'll continue our quest in space. There will be more shuttle flights and more shuttle crews and, yes, more volunteers, more civilians, more teachers in space. Nothing ends here; our hopes and our journeys continue.

I want to add that I wish I could talk to every man and woman who works for NASA or who worked on this mission and tell them: "Your dedication and professionalism have moved and impressed us for decades. And we know of your anguish. We share it."

There's a coincidence today. On this day 390 years ago, the great explorer Sir Francis Drake died aboard ship off the coast of Panama. In his lifetime the great frontiers were the oceans, and an historian later said, "He lived by the sea, died on it, and was buried in it." Well, today we can say of the *Challenger* crew: Their dedication was, like Drake's, complete. The crew of the space shuttle *Challenger* honored us by the manner in which they lived their lives. We will never forget them, nor the last time we saw them, this morning, as they prepared for their journey and waved good-bye and "slipped the surly bonds of earth" to "touch the face of God." Thank you.

---

to the people and the occasion. If you are delivering a farewell, tell the person who is departing that you will strive to carry on what he or she has begun; at a dedication, stress that the object being dedicated should remind the listeners of the accomplishments of the person or group being honored; in a eulogy, emphasize that the person who died would wish the audience to continue what he or she started, or promote the principles by which he or she lived.

The "Tribute to the *Challenger* Astronauts" speech, written by Peggy Noonan and delivered to the nation by then-president Ronald Reagan in 1986, is a fine example of a eulogy. It eloquently fulfills the purposes of the eulogy, expressing appropriate grief at the disaster, deepening the listeners' appreciation of and respect for the fallen astronauts, and giving the audience both strength for the present and inspiration for the future. We've include it here for your analysis (see above).

Today, the explosion of the space shuttle *Challenger* remains a sudden emotional event in the lives of many Americans, and Reagan's speech is remembered as a moving tribute to the heroic crew. Use the following critical questions to guide your analysis of this address: In what ways did Reagan fulfill the purposes of a eulogy? How did the choice of language make the speech memorable? Was the final quotation a good choice for the conclusion of the speech? Why? Was the length of the speech appropriate? To how many different audiences was the speech directed? Who were they?

▶ETHICS AND PUBLIC COMMUNICATION

The moral measure of public communication, informative and persuasive strategies, rests with the goal of the user, the result of the use, and the value system of the evaluator. These factors determine the acceptability or correctness of public communication in a particular situation. There are no universal absolutes. There is no universal ethic. We won't try to tell you what is moral or immoral, but we urge you to establish within your own ethical bank a set of principles on which you can draw when you must make a decision about the ethics of your potential choices.

Karl Wallace, in "An Ethical Basis of Communication," provides his perceptions of the basic guidelines for determining what might be considered ethical. These guidelines are founded on two basic philosophical constructs:

1. . . . ethical standards of communication should place emphasis on the means used to secure the end, rather than on achieving the end itself.
2. . . . communication inevitably must stand for and must reflect the same ethical values as the political society of which it is a part.[34]

Wallace considers these constructs not only compatible with, but the very essence of, a democratic society having "respect for the individual, a profound faith in equality, the belief in freedom . . . [and] the conviction that every person is capable of understanding the nature of democracy; its goals, its values, its procedures and processes."[35] Having established this frame of reference, Wallace presents four fundamental ethical principles of communication:

First, a communicator in a free society must recognize that during the moments of his utterance he is the sole source of argument and information.

Second, the communicator who respects the democratic way of life must select and present fact and opinion fairly. . . . He must therefore be accurate in reporting fact and opinion. . . .

Third, the communicator who believes in the ultimate values of democracy will invariably reveal the sources of his information and opinion.

Fourth, a communicator in a democratic society will acknowledge and respect diversity of argument and opinion.[36]

The attitudes and values expressed by Wallace are good and noble ones. Given a society equally good and noble, they are probably most applicable, appropriate, and apperceptive.

Saul Alinsky also takes a society view of the ethical question, but from a somewhat different perspective. His societal position is situationally oriented. In *Reveille for Radicals,* he writes: "We must accept open-ended systems of ethics and values, not only to meet constantly changing conditions but also to keep changing ourselves, in order to survive in the fluid society that lies ahead of us. Such systems must be workable in the world as it is and not unrealistically aimed toward the world as we would like it to be."[37]

Thomas Nilsen, in *Ethics of Speech Communication*, focuses on the individual and his or her freedom to make informed choices. He observes: "When we communicate to influence the attitudes, beliefs, and actions of others, the ethical touchstone is the degree of free, informed, and critical choice on matters of significance in their lives that is fostered by our speaking."[38] He defines "good" as that "which makes possible and contributes to the individual's making informed, independent, and critical choices that are meaningful in his life."[39]

The positions taken by Wallace, Alinsky, and Nilsen reflect three possible ways of approaching the subject of ethics in public communication. Wallace's assumption that we live in a democratic society and that our communication must adhere to the tenets manifested in democratic documents and pronouncements is one approach. It very much resembles a traditional, Aristotelian ethic. Alinsky's position that there are no absolutes and that the communicator must adapt to the ethics, values, and needs of the times is another way of considering ethics. Essentially, his system claims that if the ends are just, the means are just. Nilsen's concern for individual choices is still another approach. These approaches are not necessarily contradictory and in some respects are complementary. Any ethical view should include a realistic assessment of the current state of the society, express a concern for a continuous striving to achieve the democratic ideal, and maintain a respect for the role of individual choices.

We will not posit here a definitive ethical code. However, you might want to consider certain categories when you're making ethical determinations. The categories might be labeled, "The Ethical Dozen":

1. Does the strategy demonstrate *respect for yourself?*
2. Does the use of the strategy have the potential for bringing *benefit or harm?*
3. Does the strategy *violate or conform to religious beliefs?*
4. Does the strategy address *real issues or counterfeit issues?*
5. Does the strategy *violate or conform to the law?*
6. Does the strategy knowingly *present the truth or a lie?*
7. Will the use of the strategy *produce harmony or discord?*
8. Is the strategy *designed to reveal or conceal?*
9. Is the language *designed to clarify or obscure?*
10. Is the *information relevant or irrelevant?*
11. Is the strategy *respectful of individual rights?*
12. After using the strategy, *will you be able to respect yourself?*[40]

We make no statement as to what the answers to these questions ought to be. We can't evaluate the potential answers. We do ask that what you do, you do knowingly.

▶ SUMMARY

Informative and persuasive presentations are both common and important to the world of business. Although they differ in many ways, these presentations are similar because all speaking has elements of both information and persuasion.

Informational presentations serve a variety of purposes, and require careful attention to form and technique. The informational briefing is made to people who have a common interest, and it concentrates on new ideas, concerns, concepts, and data. The oral report is intended to gather, analyze, and interpret data for another person. The lecture is a more formal presentation in which you help your listeners to learn a new concept. Question-and-answer sessions generally follow more formal presentations and are designed to allow the audience to query the speaker. Explanations are provided to increase the audience's understanding of a given subject. Effective strategies for giving informational presentations include: capturing the audience's attention, following the principles of clear organization, using different channels of communication, trying not to be too technical, and avoiding information overload.

Persuasion is a deliberate effort to influence audience choices by changing, reinforcing, or shaping listeners' attitudes. Proposals, sales presentations, and motivational speeches are the most common types of persuasive presentations. Proposals are intended to persuade the audience to adopt a new plan, concept, or procedure. Sales presentations may be formal or informal and seek specific action. Motivational speeches are pep talks urging employees to feel good about themselves, and to be more productive and efficient. Important guidelines for effective persuasive presen-

tations include: (1) assuming a receiver-centered perspective; (2) developing an appropriate relationship with the audience; (3) adjusting the content to match the audience's attitude toward the topic; (4) considering alternative organizational patterns such as primacy–recency, two-sided counterarguments, or Monroe's motivated sequence; and (5) remembering that because an audience may be moved by both rational and nonrational proofs it is difficult to predict results.

The organizational arena also includes selected special occasions that invite presentational excellence. These occasions may require your building enthusiasm, acknowledging achievements, or paying tribute to a person, idea, or institution. Moreover, our electronic age has increased the likelihood that many of your presentations will be broadcast or taped for replay later. The previous constraints of the public forum have been removed, and its scope, breadth, and power significantly magnified. These changes require the serious consideration of ethical responsibility and societal impact.

The public forum is powerful. It is a seat of power —a place for responsible speakers.

▶ QUESTIONS FOR DISCUSSION AND SKILL DEVELOPMENT

1. Discuss how informative and persuasive speaking are similar in nature. What implications does this have for you as a speaker?

2. Identify the most common types of informative speaking in today's organization. How do these types differ from one another? Which ones would you be most likely to use?

3. How do persuasion's endproducts—changed, reinforced, and shaped attitudes, beliefs or values—differ from one another? Relate these purposes to favorable, neutral, and hostile audiences. Which of these audiences presents the biggest challenge to speakers? Justify your choice. As a representative of an organization, prepare and deliver a speech to a hostile audience.

4. Define by examples spokespeople in public life today. How would you describe their use of persuasive strategies? How do they organize their arguments? What appeals are used to render their arguments acceptable?

5. Identify and describe alternative organizational patterns appropriate to persuasive presentations. When might these patterns be usefully employed? Using Monroe's motivated sequence, identify the steps in a particular speech.

6. Prepare a five- to seven-minute speech to persuade. Select a topic with which you are familiar and in which you believe strongly. After the speech, conduct a survey of the class to determine how successful you were. Try to determine the relative success or failure of the speech. What type of reasoning did you employ? What kinds of evidence did you use? What forms of argumentation? Why?

7. Analyze a special occasion speech you have recently heard. In which category does it belong? How effective was it? Why? In what ways could the speech have been improved? Write a speech of introduction, acceptance, or tribute. What were your concerns?

8. What ethical standards would you apply to public communication? Develop a written rationale for including or excluding certain ethical criteria. How does your ethical code compare with those of Wallace, Alinsky, or Nilsen?

▶ NOTES

1. Peggy Noonan, *What I Saw at the Revolution: A Political Life in the Reagan Era* (New York: Random House, 1990).
2. Ralph Waldo Emerson, *Natural History of Intellect and Other Papers,* vol. 12 (New York: AMS Press, 1979): 91.
3. Marshall McLuhan and Quentin Fiore, *War and Peace in the Global Village* (New York: Bantam Books, 1968).
4. Richard M. Weaver, "Language is Sermonic," in: Richard L. Johannesen, Richard Stricland, and Ralph T. Eubanks, eds., *Essays of Richard M. Weaver on the Nature of Rhetoric* (Baton Rouge, LA: Louisiana State University Press, 1970): 221–224.
5. Raymond E. Nadeau, Carol Jablonski, and Greg H. Gardner, *Speaking Effectively in Public Settings* (Lanham, MD: University Press of America, 1993).
6. Albert J. Vasile and Harold K. Mintz, *Speak With Confidence: A Practical Guide,* 6th ed. (New York: HarperCollins College Publishers, 1993).
7. Richard Saul Wurman, *Information Anxiety* (New York: Doubleday, 1989).
8. Bob Richmond, "Time Not on Side of Information Age," *San Antonio Light,* July 7, 1990, B1.
9. J. Fiala, "Citation Analysis Controls the Information Flood," *Thermochimica Acta* 110 (1987): 11.
10. Connie Koenenn, "The Future is Now," *Washington Post,* February 3, 1989, B5.
11. Michael F. Warlum, "Improving Oral Marketing Presentations in the Technology-Based Company," *IEEE Transactions on Professional Communication* (June 1988): 84.
12. Kathleen Edgerton Kendall, "Do Real People Ever Give Speeches," *Central States Speech Journal* (1974): 233–235.
13. Bruce E. Gronbeck, Raymie E. McKerrow, Douglas Ehninger, and Alan H. Monroe, *Principles and Types of Speech Communication,* 11th ed. (Glenview, IL: Scott, Foresman/Little Brown, 1990).
14. John T. Mallow, "Making Your Point, Not Burying It," *Self* (April 1981): 92.
15. William Safire, "Reagan Betrays a Lack of Homework," *Richmond Times-Dispatch,* June 19, 1981, 14.
16. Gronbeck, McKerrow, Ehninger, and Monroe, *Principles of Speech Communication.*
17. Karl Eller, "Miracle in a Glass: The Free Enterprise System," *Vital Speeches of the Day* (February 1, 1979): 232.
18. Jo Sprague and Douglas Stuart, *The Speaker's Handbook,* 3rd ed. (Fort Worth, TX: Harcourt Brace Jovanovich, 1992): 255.
19. Wurman, *Information Anxiety.*
20. Gerald R. Miller, "On Being Persuaded: Some Basic Distinctions," in: Michael E. Roloff and Gerald R. Miller, eds., *Persuasion: New Directions in Theory and Research* (Beverly Hills, CA: Sage, 1980): 21.
21. Wallace Fotheringham, *Perspectives on Persuasion* (Boston: Allyn and Bacon, 1966).
22. Donald K. Smith, *Man Speaking: A Rhetoric of Public Speech* (New York: Dodd, Mead, 1969): 55.
23. Eugene A. Weinstein, "The Development of Interpersonal Competence," in: D. A. Goslin, ed., *Handbook of Socialization Theory and Research* (Chicago: Rand McNally, 1969): 753.
24. Smith, *Man Speaking, A Rhetoric of Public Speech,* 217–224.
25. Arthur L. Cohen, *Attitude Change and Social Influence* (New York: Basic Books, 1964).
26. Barry R. Schlenker, "Self-Presentation: Managing the Impression of Consistency When Reality Interferes with Self-Enhancement," *Journal of Personality and Social Psychology* (December 1975): 1030–1037.
27. This discussion of the motivated sequence is based in part on information in Gronbeck, McKerrow, Ehninger, and Monroe, *Principles of Speech Communication,* 180–205.
28. John Dewey, *How We Think* (Boston: D. C. Heath, 1910).
29. Gronbeck, McKerrow, Ehninger, and Monroe, *Principles of Speech Communication,* 184–185.
30. Stephen Lucas, *The Art of Public Speaking,* 4th ed. (New York: McGraw-Hill, 1992): 352.

31. Margaret M. Bedrosian, *Speak Like a Pro in Business* (New York: John Wiley & Sons, 1987).

32. Dorothy Leeds, *Powerspeak: The Complete Guide to Persuasive Public Speaking and Presenting* (New York: Prentice Hall, 1988): 99-100.

33. Noonan, *What I Saw at the Rvolution,* 252.

34. Karl R. Wallace, "An Ethical Basis of Communication," in: Charles J. Steward and H. Bruce Kendall, eds., *On Speech and Speakers* (New York: Holt, Rinehart & Winston, 1968): 51–55.

35. Ibid.

36. Ibid., 56–59.

37. Saul D. Alinsky, *Reveille for Radicals* (New York: Vintage Books, 1969): 207.

38. Thomas R. Nilsen, *Ethics of Speech Communication* (Indianapolis, IN: Bobbs-Merrill, 1974): 46.

39. Ibid.

40. Wallace V. Schmidt and Jo-Ann Graham, *The Public Forum, A Transactional Approach to Public Communication* (Sherman Oaks, CA: Alfred Publishing, 1979): 205.

No institution or organization is exempt from change. Change is inevitable and innovation is essential for business and organizational survival. But change and innovation does not have to be something that *happens to* business and organizations; it can be a process that is *managed by* them. Increasingly, the planning of change has become part of the responsibility of management in all contemporary institutions. Peter Drucker observes in *Managing in Turbulent Times* that "all institutions live and perform in two time periods: that of today and that of tomorrow. . . . Managers therefore always have to manage both . . . they must manage for change." Ethics and morality are playing an important part in this changing organizational milieu. Business and professional organizations are accepting a new moral mandate and openly, vocally acknowledging the role of ethics and morality. They are heeding the advice of Cicero in *De Officiis:* "To everyone who proposes to have a good career, moral philosophy is indispensable."

UNIT FOUR

Communication, Action Planning, and Business Ethics

▶ *13   Examines the determinants of change and innovation, focusing on the role communication strategies play in enabling organizations to take advantage of the unforeseen and unforeseeable.*

▶ *14   Defines the new moral mandate being assumed by business and the professions, describing how ethics, values, and morality relate to selected organizational issues and codes of conduct.*

CHAPTER THIRTEEN

13

Change and Innovation

LEARNING OBJECTIVES:

To define change and innovation from a systems perspective, recognizing its importance

To identify and describe the existing forces that create resistance to change and innovation

To discuss the role of managers as leaders and communicators of change and innovation—the skills and abilities necessary to act as change agents

To demonstrate the ability to use necessary information in the planning of change strategy

To develop a general strategic plan for the communication of change and innovation

In today's fast-paced and complex society, change and innovation are no longer choices; they are givens. Recent business history is filled with the skeletons of companies that failed to innovate or even to recognize the need to adapt to obvious change. As uncertainties and interdependencies rise, the past is becoming an increasingly less appropriate guide to the future. More and more, those who have managerial functions in organizations must analyze and predict impending changes and take deliberate action to shape change.

Change and innovation are inevitable facts of organizational life. Technological progress, market fluctuations, hostile takeovers, and new government regulations make change and innovation a certainty. Still, it is incredible that with change swirling all around us many make so little effort to learn about or understand it, or to become part of it. Wendell Johnson notes that "we have not prepared ourselves and are not now preparing our children to live in the here and now, which is to say, to live with swift and accelerating change, to seek it out to our own advantage and to the advantage of others. . . . To live on the soaring curve means to become aware of the reality around us as a process reality and of ourselves as a process too, we ourselves therefore as a process within a complex of processes. Therefore change is expected. The norm is change."[1] And efforts to plan and control change within organizational settings further tend to be fragmented and thwarted by noncommunication and noncollaboration among policymakers.[2]

The consequences of avoiding innovation and change are extremely dangerous. At the most basic level, less innovation means that fewer new, improved products will be available to American consumers in the marketplace. But it has broader economic effects. Without innovative breakthroughs and changes, industry creates fewer jobs. Factories and equipment become obsolete. Productivity growth declines. Adlai Stevenson, as chairman of the Senate subcommittee on science and technology, raised a warning when he said: "This is a rich and resourceful country, but its spirit of adventure and invention may be drying up. Nations fail when that happens."[3] And U.S. industry isn't innovating nearly as well as it should be at a time when innovation has become more important than ever. Listen to James Clark, who left a professorship at Stanford ten years ago to start Silicon Graphics, now a $600 million-a-year computer maker and considered one of the fastest-growing and most innovative companies in the world: "We're losing our creative edge. American industry is on the decline because U.S. managers are too concerned about protecting short-term earnings to innovate."[4] Robert Colton of the National Science Foundation sounds a more hopeful note when he observes, "If you look at the absolute numbers, we're still ahead in productivity, we're still ahead in what is called innovation. The rest of the world is just catching up with us. . . . What we have to do is try to keep ahead."[5] In the face of this growing concern over the need to respond to a changing environment and of the broadened time/space perspective in which it is exercised, the clear moral directive for every modern business or organization is: Learn how to change effectively or die. Change is to be expected, so the question that every business or organization must answer is: What can be done to reduce the trauma, to minimize the dysfunctional features involved in change, and to reduce the errors made in introducing change?

We need to live on the soaring curve of change and embrace it, for to do otherwise means to fear change and to ignore or resist it. Embracing change and innovation implies an openness and responsiveness to proposed changes—changes that could be internally or externally initiated. Embracing change might mean altering an organization's structure, reward systems, operating systems, or control systems. Furthermore, such changes may require unlearning some things before becoming willing to learn a new way of accomplishing goals. It may be necessary to deconstruct one reality or set of operating conditions before constructing a new set of operating conditions. Ultimately, however, people in organizations must be willing to change and accept change—willing to work to create change.

▶ DIMENSIONS OF CHANGE

Organizational change and innovation may be defined as an organization's altering procedures or adopting a new idea or behavior. *Change* intimates a transformation or metamorphosis within the organization. *Innovation* is very similar to change but distinguishable by the criterion of newness: change is the adopting of something different; innovation is the adoption of something new.[6] Still, there is considerable disagreement in the literature concerning what differentiates change from innovation, what constitutes something different and something new. Where should the line between change and innovation be drawn? Perhaps the criterion of newness resides in an organization's adoption of an idea or behavior, regardless of adoption by other organizations, so long as the idea has not previously been used by the adopting organization. Or maybe innovation is "the first or early use of an idea by one of a set of organizations with similar goals."[7] Here, change and innovation will be treated synonymously as necessary components for organizational growth.

Change, a transition from one state, condition, or phase to another, is ongoing. We are products of change, constantly adapting to new environments. Don Fabum, in *Dimensions of Change*, writes:

> What we now call ecology—the study of organisms in relation to their environment— must be the most ancient of sciences. Prehistoric man survived only because he was a superb ecologist. Peering from his hiding place in the bushes around a clearing, or from the opening of his cave, his science was empirical. The laboratory was the place where he lived, the success of his observations could be measured by the fact that he managed to survive through the day.
>
> What the prehistoric ecologist studied was the interface of living systems moving within living systems—the tiger in the bush, the bison on the plain, the edible insect stirring in the rubble of a fallen tree. Today, we might call such vision "halographic" meaning simply that the entire web of living things served as a background against which a figure could be discerned. The figure could be discerned because, within the system, it moved in the field of vision at a rate different than the rest. . . . We select some elements of the pattern and omit the others; the ones we select we call "reality."
>
> Man is, himself, a system moving within a system caught up in, and forming a part of, an intricate web of protoplasm that writes upon the surface of the planet. A pull upon any strand of the web exerts tensions on others.[8]

Change, then, can be viewed from a systems perspective, and research suggests that the more complex a given system is, the faster its rate of change—which creates more complexity. A system facing increasing complexity will either evolve toward a more connected and integrated form, or drift into an increasingly fragmented state. Organizations, when viewed as systems, move over time into higher and more productive states or devolve into lower, less organized, and less effective states.

▶ DETERMINANTS OF CHANGE AND INNOVATION

A useful model for thinking about change and innovation has been proposed by Bennis, Schein, Steele, and Berlew.[9] It is based on observations that behavior in institutional settings is not static, but rather a dynamic balance of forces working in opposite directions within the social-psychological space of institutions. Their scheme of the change process, based on Kurt Lewin's thinking, consists of three stages: (1) *unfreezing*—creating motivation to change, (2) *changing*—developing new responses based on new information, and (3) *refreezing*—stabilizing and integrating the changes. According to this way of looking at change, if it is to occur it must be preceded by an alteration of the present stable equilibrium that supports the organizational system. Once that equilibrium has been upset, the system will be seek out, process, and use information to achieve new perceptions, attitudes, and behaviors. Last, the adopted changes must be integrated and stabilized if they are to endure. There seems to be general agreement that the essential assumptions underlying the change sequence are that problems are perceived and such perceptions lead to search activity that results in a choice for or against change.[10] There is also agreement that rapidly changing environments require that organizations change for continued growth and development.[11]

To accept and manage change effectively requires understanding the major misconceptions that make communicating change problematic. Phillip Clampitt identifies the following common misconceptions or false assumptions that plague the change/innovation process[12]:

▶ *Change is unnatural.* Tradition can help a company maintain high standards of performance. Tradition can also be constraining, so to argue that change is unnatural can be devastating. In effective organizations there exists a healthy tension between the traditions of the past and the beckoning future.[13]

▶ *Change is always disruptive.* Not all changes are resisted. People working closely with one another regularly swap ideas about short cuts and minor changes in procedures. Change is an everyday occurrence and an organizational climate can be fostered that encourages innovations in light of corporate goals.

▶ *Change is always progressive.* There are those who hail every new approach and are constantly in search of the next trend—they like to live on the edge. To these people, newness is more important than merit. But that which is new is not always the best, and passing up one idea does not necessarily indicate a fear of change. Perhaps it is a mark of prudence and thoughtful analysis. Woody Allen—that famous management philosopher—sums up how early you want to be: "Fifteen minutes. Take a movie, for instance. If you get there one hour ahead of time, no one knows where to put you—you're in the middle of the previous show. Come ten minutes late and they won't seat you. Be fifteen minutes early and you have enough time to get popcorn and your choice of seats."[14] The message is that change requires appropriate timing to be progressive.

▶ *Change is always stressful.* Change need not be stressful; it can be seen as a natural part of the job. There are positive changes as well as negative ones, and each has a different effect on the psyche. The critical factor is the personal meaning an individual attaches to the change. Does the change offer hope? Is it beneficial? Is it exciting? These are the salient questions.

▶ *Change indicates that previous practices have been in error.* Many employees believe that changes are initiated because they made errors, were incompetent, or simply made poor decisions. The wise manager must communicate a difficult and seemingly conflicting message: previous practices were appropriate at the time, but changes are needed to meet the challenges of new and perhaps unique circumstances.

► *Real change can be born only out of crisis.* Sometimes crisis is the only vehicle through which change can be accomplished. One survey of 22,000 manufacturing employees found that 63 percent felt a crisis had to flair up before anything was done about a problem.[15] Yet to contend that change can occur only under crisis conditions is to extend the argument too far. Visionary leaders work to persuade others of change before the impending doom of crisis.

Getting beyond these misconceptions helps one to understand the change/innovation process and to foster a spirit for constructive change.

At least since 1958, when James March and Herbert Simon published their book on organizational theory, the problem of organizational innovativeness has been prominent in the literature.[16] It has been prominent partly because of the view that change and innovation are essential for organizational survival. Although survival is given considerable attention, any discussion of the determinants of change and innovation cannot be restricted to this single emphasis, because change and innovation may also occur so that organizations can gain a competitive advantage. The difference between survival and gaining a competitive edge may seem trivial, in that survival in a competitive environment can imply gaining and maintaining a competitive advantage. But there is a real, distinguishable difference between these two kinds of behavior. Changing or innovating for survival implies changing *only* in times of crisis or if other businesses or organizations already functioning in the environment have changed or are about to do so. Organizations, however, may also change as part of their strategy to gain a competitive advantage vis-a-vis their own goals. They may undergo changes to make more money, raise employee motivation, improve job satisfaction, provide consumer protection, reduce ignorance, or eradicate disease.

Manufacturers of steel adopting the oxygen furnace exemplify innovation for survival, and many examples of innovating to gain a competitive advantage could be drawn from the plastics or electronics industries. A hospital might adopt innovations to attract more physicians to its staff, a prison because inmates are near revolt, and a university because of low enrollments—all survival. But another hospital might innovate because one of its physicians has developed a new instrument to fight disease more efficiently, a prison in order to reduce recidivism, or a university because it's interested in applying new learning approaches. Simply put, organizations are complex, goal-seeking units, and in the pursuit of those goals some may be innovative and others may not. So, although some organizations may change or innovate to survive, many do so to gain a competitive edge, to improve performance compared with their own previous success in goal achievement. Change and innovation is a rational process some organizations follow as a means of achieving their goals.

A need for change occurs when an existing procedure is inadequate and a new procedure is desirable. It's the gap between actual and desired performance or procedures that activates decision makers to consider adopting a new technique. The distribution and level of change and innovation is largely determined by demand conditions: demand induces the changes and innovations that satisfy it. Perhaps the word "incentive" rather than "need" or "demand" better describes the reasons organizations change and innovate. Richard Daft and Selwyn Becker advance certain basic propositions relative to the determinants of change and innovation:

► Proposition 1: Organizational innovativeness increases as the incentives for innovation increase.

- ▶ Proposition 2: Organizational innovativeness increases as the efficiency of the organizational mechanisms for developing innovative alternatives increases.
- ▶ Proposition 3: Organizational innovativeness increases as the presence of organizational characteristics enabling adoption increases.[17]

They are arguing that incentives have to be identified before organizational change and innovation can be predicted. Moreover, any given organization must be so structured that innovative alternatives can be developed and implemented. It would seem reasonable that those people charged with the efficient functioning of the organization would be more likely to propose changes or innovations, administrative and technical. Finally, organizations must be capable of adopting changes or innovations, whether small and inexpensive or large, costly, and relatively untried.

For example, John McGovern, CEO and president of Campbell Soup Company, saw the need to change. The red-and-white soup cans and "Campbell Kids" were calling up memories of "M'm! M'm! Good!" for fewer and fewer folks. He identified regional and ethnic marketing as the key attitudes he needed in his organization, and divided Campbell into 50 quasi-independent business units, each responsible for its own profit and loss. Defining the top spots in these independent units as his key leverage positions, he placed marketing-oriented leaders in those spots and gave them autonomy. They produced more than 400 new products between the years 1981 and 1985—with lots of regional and ethnic variations. There's now spicy nacho soup in Texas and California, creole soup in the South, and red-bean soup in Hispanic areas. McGovern identified the required attitudes and orientations, the key leverage positions, and then filled those positions with people with the right skills.[18]

The Campbell Soup case illustrates still another principal determinant of organizational change and innovation—the people who make up the organization. People in organizations must be open to new ideas and the organizations must foster a climate that invites new ideas. Change and innovation "calls for a collection of talents whose confluence in a single individual can only be a statistical freak; even when sought in a collection of people, it requires skill and luck in assemblage . . . the entire process is fraught with anxiety, with the risk of failure, so that in addition to the necessary technical skills the people must have a belief and a commitment, a courage and a persistence that are invulnerable to the inevitable vicissitudes that accompany all innovations."[19]

People deal with information differently and frequently lock themselves into certain patterns of thinking that block their creative abilities. Research on creativity has identified several blocks to creative thought.[20] Roger Von Oech, in *A Whack on the Side of the Head*, lists ten blocks that are frequently observed in organizational settings:

1. *There Is a Right Answer.* There are likely to be many right answers and many ways of reaching them. More importantly, the *right* answer may not be needed at all—just a *good* answer.
2. *That Idea Is Not Logical.* It may not be. That's OK. Logic is fine for the application of ideas, but in the creative phase of management it tends to restrict one's thoughts
3. *We Must Follow the Rules.* There are no rules for being creative. Most revolutionary ideas have disrupted existing principles.
4. *Let's Be Practical.* In other words, stifle your imagination—a sure way to kill a creative idea.

5. *We Should Avoid Ambiguity.* That is, let's look at any situation in the way we always have. No creativity here.

6. *To Err Is Wrong.* To err is to err. Not to err is not to experiment. When you fail, you learn what doesn't work and you get an opportunity to try a new approach. If you are not failing now and then, you are not being very imaginative.

7. *Play Is Frivolous.* Maybe. It is also fun. People are much more creative when they are having fun than when they are "only working."

8. *That's Not My Area.* True. And it is because it is not your area that you have the greatest creativity potential. This is not to say that every one of your creative ideas will be practical. Leave execution up to the experts.

9. *Don't Be Foolish.* Why not? If we never tried anything that might make us look ridiculous, we certainly would not have airplanes, telephones, bicycles. . . .

10. *I'm Not Creative.* Maybe. But one of the worst blocks to our thinking is thinking that we can't be creative.[21]

When we let go of our quest for a right answer, and begin to search for a good answer that meets the needs of the organization, creative ideas emerge and creative solutions to convoluted issues are proposed. Organizations must be designed to encourage individual creativity. Managerial styles must promote active involvement. In this way, the full abilities of organization members will be harnessed, and that, in turn, will lead to greater organizational responsiveness and effectiveness.

Rubbermaid, for example, teaches its people to let ideas flow out of its so-called core competencies. Bud Hellman, who used to run a Rubbermaid subsidiary, was touring one of the company's picnic cooler plants in the late 1980s when he realized he could use its plastic blow-molding technique to make a durable, lightweight, and inexpensive line of office furniture. The result was the WorkManager System which now accounts for 60 percent of Rubbermaid's furniture division sales. Charles Hassel, a member of the product development team observes that "if top management hadn't encouraged us to look at processes and technologies elsewhere in the company, none of this would have ever happened."[22]

So, a major source of organizational innovation is the creative potential of organization members, regardless of position. This frequently requires people letting go of their egos. Lionel Richie wrote and organized the production of the popular song, "We Are the World," inviting music luminaries to cooperate in the record to raise money for starving people in Africa. He posted a sign next to the studio door that said, "Check your ego at the door." His message was clear. The success of the record depended on the cooperation of everyone, not the brilliance of a few. This, likewise, applies to those who wish to embrace change and innovation. Those concerned with the creativity of organization members must emphasize free, open, and psychologically supportive atmospheres that enable creativity and self-actualization to flourish. Consultants agree that the best companies see innovation as a function that needs managing and they recommend a dual approach. First, companies must create cultures where new ideas can thrive and then they must set up systems that will winnow those ideas through development and into the market. A 1991 study of corporate innovation practices by the Arthur D. Little consulting firm reveals, however, that U.S. executives' greatest concern about innovation is not a lack of brilliant scientists and engineers but a "dearth of managers who know how to drive the creative process."[23]

►UNCERTAINTY AND RESISTANCE TO CHANGE

Change and innovation is also associated with the notion of resistance. Change, uncertainty, and resistance usually exist together. No wonder, as Peter Drucker points out, even the most competent management bats only around 0.300 in the game of change and innovation.[24] Change or innovation is a risky business.

Change and innovative activity are associated with general business, market, and technical uncertainties. General business uncertainties are those future decisions affected by such environmental influences as politics, legislation, and economics. Market uncertainty refers to the extent to which the change or innovation will be commercially successful. Technical uncertainty refers to realized standards of performance under various operating conditions for a given expenditure on research and development.[25] There are, however, qualitative differences in uncertainty, and the degrees of uncertainty associated with various types of change and innovation can be identified[26]:

► True uncertainty	fundamental research
	fundamental invention
► Very high degree of uncertainty	major product innovations
	radical process innovations in own establishment or system
► High degree of uncertainty	major product innovations
	radical process innovations in own establishment or system
► Moderate uncertainty	new generations of established products
► Little uncertainty	licensed innovation
	imitation of product innovations
	modification of products and processes
	early adoption of established process
► Very little uncertainty	new model
	product differentiation
	agency for established product innovation
	late adoption of established process
	innovation in own establishment
	minor technical improvements

The degree of uncertainty surrounding change and innovation, therefore, depends on the type of work being carried out. As previously noted, however, timing is everything. Consider, for example, the agreement made between the Western Union Telegraph Company and the newly emerging National Bell group in the late 1870s. The Western Union Telegraph Company had the chance to dominate the nascent telephone business, but in 1879 it signed a contract with the Bell interests that effectively confirmed the Bell group's control of the industry. In any roll of honor for dumb managerial choices, the Western Union settlement surely ranks at the very top. In hindsight it seems a preposterous and costly mistake, but at the time it made perfect sense. By assigning its telephone rights and patents to National Bell, Western Union did what it was most concerned to do—make safe its control over the telegraph. The

▶ THE BIG AND THE BLOATED: IT'S TOUGH BEING NO. 1

By Jennifer Reese

It's the biggest company in the business, the world leader. It's been hobbled by a bloated, slow-moving bureaucracy, overcentralization, and a disdain for ideas—and executives—from anywhere else. In a mature industry, it has had a hard time keeping up with innovative competitors that have made some of its products look like dinosaurs. It has lost touch with customers. Despite a series of restructurings that shrank its work force and capacity, the company shocked Wall Street last year by losing billions. Employee morale is in the dumps.

IBM? Sure, but that litany also describes another preeminent American corporation fallen among the thorns: General Motors, the world's largest industrial company. Says Kim Clark, a professor at Harvard business school: "What you have here are two companies that at one point dominated their industries by producing very large products—main frame computers and big American cars. And they created organizations that were very good at doing that. Then the world changed."

The similarities between the giants are striking. Says Noel Tichy, a professor at the University of Michigan business school: "GM and IBM are both No. 1 companies whose inward-looking cultures kept them from waking up on time." IBM's managers find themselves in a muddle identical to that of GM's top brass: How do you reinvigorate an aging organization? How do you convey to thousands of complacent workers a sense of urgency? How do you cut costs in a company accustomed to operating in comfortable, even luxurious style?

To be fair, IBM is in better shape than the battered auto maker, though it is doing battle in an even more brutally competitive industry. Big Blue seems positively spry compared with GM. And Akers looks like a radical visionary next to GM's chief, Robert Stempel. But what if Akers's reforms fail? What if profits don't pick up, or don't pick up quickly enough? In April, GM's fed-up board removed Stempel as chairman of the executive committee and replaced Lloyd Reuss, Stempel's handpicked No. 2, as president. Could IBM be ripe for a similar shakeup? Not likely. Still, says Michigan's Tichy, "The makeup of the board is different, but the conditions are there for it happening, absolutely."

agreement saw to it that local telephone exchanges served a rather limited area and carried only voice messages—that is, "personal communication." All business messages that went by wire were to go by Western Union's telegraph. Moreover, for 17 years Bell was to pay a 20 percent royalty on the rental income from all leased telephones. Thus, Bell would have all the risk and expense of trying to make a business out of a highly uncertain and commercially unproved technology, while Western Union was freed of a potential competitor and would take a nice cut off the top. At the time, it was a reasonable, and perhaps even excellent, guess. It simply turned out to be wrong.[27] Who could have known that the relations between the telephone and telegraph would not work out as Western Union thought they would?

More recently, Xerox developed the computer mouse—15 years too soon. It sat on the shelf waiting for a market. Apple took it and made it immensely popular.[28] Consider IBM, the most successful commercial company in the world during 1984 and 1985. In those two years IBM made more money than any other organization and was chosen as the "Most Admired" company by *Fortune* magazine. IBM rested on its laurels—a dangerous posture—and got in trouble. CEO John Akers was brought in to spur IBM from its restfulness and he moved quickly to produce change. He designed a new strategy that focused more effort on the midrange product line and transferred a number of people out of office jobs into direct marketing and selling jobs, thus getting more of his talented people out in front of customers. Akers also focused the organization's research and development efforts on fewer projects and made that activity more responsive to marketing. John Akers knows firsthand that change is a *continuous process* for large and small companies alike.[29]

Danny Miller has proposed the "Icarus Paradox," an interesting addendum to our discussion of uncertainty, change, and innovation.[30] He identifies four types of companies: craftspeople, builders, pioneers, and sellers. *Craftspeople* succeed by operating very efficiently and thus undercutting the competition or by producing the highest quality offerings. Examples include Texas Instruments, Caterpillar Tractor, and Marriott Hotels. *Builders* parlay their small operations into robust, rapidly growing, and diversified ones by effecting cost efficiencies or entering promising new businesses. Examples include Litton Industries, General Mills, and Alcoa. *Pioneers* innovate more creatively, more quickly, and more effectively than their competitors and cater to dynamic markets that favor state-of-the-art offerings. Examples include Federal Express Corporation, Apple Computer, and Polaroid Corporation. Finally, *sellers* are image-driven and their major competitive assets are their famous brand names, dependability, and good service. Examples include Procter & Gamble, General Motors, and Kellogg. Miller contends that the very forces that gave strength to these companies—focused tried-and-true strategies, confident leadership, and galvanized corporate cultures—are carried to excess and result in their decline. So the focusing trajectory turns craftspeople into "tinkerers," the venturing trajectory transforms builders into "imperialists," the inventing trajectory converts pioneers into "escapists," and the decoupling trajectory turns sellers into "drifters." Consequently, once the robust, superior organizations evolve into flawed purebreds, they move from "rich character to exaggerated caricature." Just as Icarus of mythology flew so close to the sun with his strong, wax wings and plunged to his death, likewise the success of many outstanding companies potentially leads to complacency, dogma, and ritual. In order for all firms to remain competitive, they must learn to master the "perils of excellence." Martin Smith offers the following management maxim:

> There are no ten best-managed American companies, even when the criteria for selection are rigidly set and observed. The truth is that all companies are fluid over a period of time. Today's winner is tomorrow's failure. Even the very best of companies change styles in response to new management. And management is forever changing.[31]

Change and innovation are also associated with the notion of resistance. Much has been written about resistance to change and the various ways to overcome these problems.[32] Diffusion researchers study and investigate variables that correlate with innovativeness. *Innovativeness* is the degree to which some people in the social system resist and others adapt to innovation and change. People generally prefer the familiar and resist the new. However, *when* people adopt an innovation or change often depends upon personality differences. Everett M. Rogers has identified some of these personality types and associated characteristics.[33]

▶ *Innovators* make up 2.5 percent of the population and may be described as "venturesome." They are eager to try new ideas but are not typical of the larger social system, usually deviating from established norms and rules.

▶ *Early adopters* compose 13.5 percent of the population and may be characterized by the word "respect." They are more innovative than the majority and, possessing knowledge and respect from others in the social system, often serve as opinion leaders and role models.

► The *early majority* are the 34 percent of the population who legitimize change and innovation by adopting just before the average person in the social system. A key word characterizing this group is "deliberate."

► The *late majority* are the 34 percent who adopt just after the average member of the social system. "Skepticism" is characteristic of them, as they are extremely cautious in approaching change and innovation.

► The *final adopters* are the last 16 percent of the population to accept change and innovation. They are highly traditional and quite "suspicious" innovators and change agents.

Change in the organization is thus a very sticky process requiring identification of the intensity, sources, and forces supporting as well as resisting it. Once the relevant variables are identified, a strategy must be developed to promote change and to cope with resistance, remembering that in any situation a number of approaches would probably be equally effective.

The organization's dilemma is to maintain an influx of new ideas and simultaneously to adopt those ideas. The problem is that "high complexity, low formalization, and decentralization have a positive influence on the number of ideas initiated in the organization . . . however, they have a negative influence on the actual adoption and implementation of innovation."[34] Many ideas may be proposed but never adopted because of conflict and disagreement among organization members and because centralized authority and formalized procedures may not sufficiently ensure implementation. Consequently, intervention by outside change agents may be necessary. It is in dealing with this organizational inertia that management and communication consultants can play a part. This will be discussed later in the chapter.

►STRATEGIES FOR CHANGE AND INNOVATION

There have been substantial quantitative changes in organizations with a tendency toward increasing size and a concentration of activity. These changes have been accompanied by qualitative changes in organizational management. The typical industrial enterprise in the U.S. before 1850 was very small, with little need for a full-time organizer or clearly defined administrative, managerial structure. Routine activities were dealt with by the president of the company and long-term plans or decisions were rarely required. However, the rapid growth of the railway system in the latter half of the nineteenth century greatly expanded the potential market for goods and services, and encouraged firms to expand and subdivide their operations. By the end of the century there had developed numerous firms that were multifunctional and vertically integrated. The early twentieth century witnessed the introduction of a multidivisional organizational structure that provided a decentralized solution to the increasingly complex problems of organizing highly diversified firms. This development redefined the organization and institutionalized active consideration of strategic change.

Public enterprises have also expanded. Hospitals have become larger and more specialized, utility companies have started to explore energy alternatives, and colleges/universities have expanded their curricular offerings and programs. In this century we have witnessed the enlargement and expansion of public institutions cognizant of an outside environment and actively seeking to appeal to it.

This rapid pace of activity has fostered a need by organizations to develop a formal innovation/change strategy. Strategy is a look to the future with an associated plan for causing a desired sequence of events to occur. A strategy for change and innovation requires a plan that can prevail over the hazards introduced by the uncertainties associated with change and innovation. This demands that organizations first identify the opportunities for change and innovation, and then give effective leadership to such directions. Here we will discuss various approaches to change and suggest some systemwide strategies for change.

Ronald Lippitt and his associates developed one of the first comprehensive and systematic approaches to change.[35] Their point of view assumed that information exists within the organization that can be translated into corrective actions. Two major principles underlie their "planned" approach: (1) information must be freely and openly shared, and (2) information is helpful only when and if it can be directly translated into action.

Tichy and Hornstein recognize the importance of information and information sources, and proceed to identify four different types of change.[36] *Outside pressure* may be directed toward an organization by a variety of means including strikes, boycotts, mass demonstrations, consumer pressure groups, and governmental legislation. *People change* is directed toward the individuals within the organization with the intent to change the ways in which organizational members behave. It includes such methods as job enrichment, management by objectives, and behavior modification. *Analysis for the top* is directed toward the total organization and concerns providing top leaders with new ideas and persuading them to accept the technological/structural changes. Approaches might include computerized information-processing or the development of new task groups. Lastly, *organizational development* is systems oriented and includes such techniques as team development, confrontation meetings, and survey data feedback.

Sashkin, Morriss, and Horst develop a typology of change using the information gained from the previously identified social agents and further focusing on data application.[37] Acknowledging the prior change processes, they proceed to include three additional factors essential for change.

1. Research, development, and diffusion focuses on innovation, or new research-based information. The emphasis is on the development and diffusion of new knowledge and the communication of data.
2. Social interaction and diffusion gives attention to the communication of data via opinion leaders, gatekeepers, and others. The underlying assumption is that there are key people who are sufficiently influential to get the information to the appropriate sources. The implication is that if a rational sequence is followed and coordinated, the new data will be accepted by the users.
3. Action research serves as a link between action and research to provide additional scientific information on problem solving and change. Emphasis is given to systemwide research that can lead to total organizational action, as opposed to problem-specific solutions.

Change and innovation, when rationally approached, results from conscious decisions to resolve perceived problems and to move the organization to a new tomorrow. The key "leading" questions associated with formulating strategy and planning change are:

- ▶ What is our reason for being?—**mission**
- ▶ Where do we want to go?—**vision**
- ▶ What do we want to accomplish?—**objectives and goals**
- ▶ How will we achieve our objectives and goals?—**strategic actions**[38]

Answering these questions leads to a search activity that results in a choice for or against innovation. Zaltman, Duncan, and Holbeck have developed a useful model that presents a picture of this process of change and innovation (see Exhibit 13-1).[39] Their paradigm extends managers' fields of vision by moving them to higher ground where they can see beyond the horizon. The horizon can, then, be changed with a clearer view of what might lie ahead. As change and innovation become more decisive factors, in competition and survival, the ability to envision situations beyond the horizon becomes an invaluable skill for managers as leaders.

Change/innovation strategies frequently result from a reactive rather than a proactive stance. Organizations encountering a crisis *react*, seeking a self-centered, fault-finding, quick fix to survive for the moment. Other organizations are more

▶ **EXHIBIT 13-1**
Paradigm of Organizational Change and Innovation

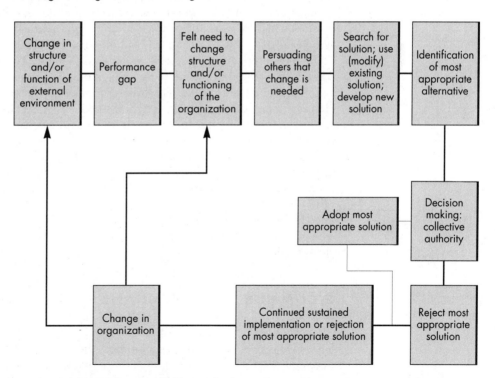

Source: W. Zaltman, M. Duncan, and H. Holbeck, *Innovation and Organization* (New York: John Wiley & Sons, 1973), p. 5. Copyright © 1973 John Wiley & Sons. Reprinted by permission of John Wiley & Sons, Inc.

responsive to change, setting goals and planning actions to maintain their present survival and competitive edge. Then, there are those organizations that take a *proactive* or upstream stance. This upstream approach is described in the following story:

> A man was sitting comfortably on a riverbank when he suddenly saw someone floundering in the water and being swept downstream. He dived into the river, swam out to the person, and pulled him to shore.
>
> No sooner had he completed this rescue, when he saw another person struggling while floating down the river. The man again swam out and was able to rescue the helpless victim.
>
> In the next few minutes, the man had to save two more people adrift in the river. After the second one, he started to walk along the road leading upstream.
>
> At the time, yet another person appeared in the river requiring rescue. A passerby said to the man, "Aren't you going to help him?"
>
> The man replied, "Not this time. I'm going upstream to see whether I can do something about whatever is *causing* all these people to fall into the river."[40]

An upstream or proactive position on organizational change urges all involved to manage performance and actively move toward a set mission and objectives. It encourages expending their efforts most efficiently and promotes long-range planning. Rather than figuratively waiting by the riverbank until a rescue is needed, deliberate actions are taken to promote organizational health and progress. Although the constructive, active intervention of a proactive approach is desirable, some management consultants are working with forward-thinking, transforming organizations to adopt a high-performing posture. Identifying potentials, strategic navigation, managing evaluation, and holistic leadership constitute the elements of this enhanced frame of reference for high-performing work systems. These empowered organizations scan potentials for what might be possible and then strategically navigate along a path for long-range plans. The task is to make both management and labor trailblazers rather than roadblockers to new standards of excellence. Regardless of strategy or approach, change and innovation remain essential factors in meeting individual and organizational goals.

Each of the approaches discussed calls attention to the importance of communication in the change process. The impact of communication in management has been well documented. Here, communication assumes a major part in change/innovation and business/organizational goals. The flow and climate of communication, and the degree of participation in decision making are all variables influencing change and innovation in organizations. To occur, change and innovation must be clearly articulated.

►COMMUNICATION, CHANGE, AND INNOVATION

Artificial intelligence (AI) is the next great frontier in the computer industry. The basic idea is very simple: teach computers the rules by which human experts make decisions. The "knowledge engineers" working on these projects interview acknowledged experts in various areas, trying to understand how they make decisions so this can, in turn, be programmed into a computer. One would suspect the greatest difficulties to be in developing the proper hardware to handle all the complexities, or

► AYE, AI

By Charles Osgood

As you are probably aware by now, Artificial Intelligence (AI) is what the computer whizzes are working on now. Pretty soon, they say, computers will be able to learn from their mistakes, the way people do. Once they have made a mistake, they will absorb it somehow and never make that particular mistake again. This is quite different from us human beings, of course, who keep making exactly the same mistakes over and over again.

The trouble with developing a machine with Artificial Intelligence (AI) based on Human Intelligence (HI), is that Human Intelligence (HI) only accounts for a small part of the progress of our species. It seems to me that Human Stupidity (HS) has also played a key role.

Take Christopher Columbus. On his famous voyage, Columbus had the wrong idea completely about where he was headed. When he got here, he had no idea where he was. Then when he got back home, he had no idea where he had been. But today nobody holds this against him. The world owes a great debt to Columbus's ignorance and intransigence. People tried to talk some sense into him, but he wouldn't listen.

Time and time again, history has demonstrated the value of dumb luck (DL), but until recently nobody has tried to reproduce DL electronically. There is a young man in Geneva, New York, however, who claims to be working on a computer that will play chess badly. In a speech last summer to the Instrument Society of America, Michael Ferris said he would program the computer with a set of human-style excuses. IDMBH ("I did my best, honest!") would include such standard responses as IDKYWIT ("I didn't know you wanted it today.") and TDEI ("The dog erased it.").

Ferris is on to something, I believe. Perhaps the only reason nobody has pursued so obvious a goal as Artificial Stupidity (AS) is that there seems to be such an abundant world supply of the real thing. Ferris should keep at it, though. Someday, a shortage of Human Stupidity and Stubbornness (HSS) may develop and he will be ready with Artificial Stupidity and Stubbornness (ASS) to fill the void.

Source: Charles Osgood, *The Osgood Files* (New York: Fawcett Crest, 1991): 46–47. Reprinted by permission of The Putnam Publishing Group. Copyright © 1991 by Charles Osgood.

---

in translating the experts knowledge into a programming language the computer can understand. However, the real problem has been to get the experts to articulate what they know. Apparently, most experts operate on the basis of an intuition gleaned from years of experience. They know how to make the proper responses but do not always know how they arrived at those responses.[41] A similar dilemma confronts organizations trying to foster a spirit of change and innovation. The desired vision must be clearly communicated to the people in the organization and the daily actions of managers must reflect and reinforce that vision. This requires working through the hierarchical structure, using management group meetings, and being prepared to handle objections and obstacles.[42]

Communicating change and innovation requires multiple techniques. Frequently employed interpersonal interfaces include: (1) the job expectation technique, (2) management by objectives, (3) job enrichment, (4) team building, and (5) organizational development.

The *job expectation technique (JET)* is useful in clarifying the job understanding between managers and their peers and subordinates.[43] JET is a team-building technique that focuses on the clarification of role space and the expectations and obligations of managers and employees. This technique increases shared perceptions about jobs, reduces role conflict and ambiguity, and provides an opportunity for more task-relevant behavior.[44] It allows people to write their own job descriptions, with contributions from the entire management team.

Management by objectives (MBO) attempts to establish a better understanding of personal and organizational goals by increasing communication and shared perceptions between managers and subordinates.[45] MBO is a strategy widely used to reduce role conflict and ambiguity by making goal setting more participative and transactional. The communication between role incumbents is increased so that both individual and organizational goals can be better identified and met. It is a useful system for reviewing performance as it contributes to the overall effectiveness of the organization and the desired career path of workers.

Job enrichment maintains that "if jobs can be shifted or changed in such a way that the job itself provides satisfying sensations, then there is a much more continuous flow of pleasant experiences; and from these will undoubtedly come a higher motivation to achieve job-related goals."[46] The enrichment theory, initiated by Frederick Herzberg, adds both vertical and horizontal activities to a job, thereby providing the whole person with a whole job.[47] It is an approach whereby management can introduce new ways to make tasks both challenging and satisfying. A job diagnostic survey can categorize job characteristics according to people's personal reactions to their work and the work setting, thus determining their readiness to take on "enriched jobs."[48]

Team building is "any planned event with a group of people who have or may have common organization relationships and/or goals which are designed to improve the way in which work gets done by them in some way or another."[49] One of the most effective ways to increase employee satisfaction and motivate employees to produce more is to allow them to participate in decision making—letting them use their talents and skills to the best of their ability and helping managers and supervisors make better decisions. Team building may result in changes in the team's operating procedures or deeper behavioral changes. Team-building efforts are increased when members are given the freedom to discuss the possibilities for change, and when they have an opportunity to identify the organizational constraints within which the team must work.[50] Quality circles represent a new dimension of team building where individuals with similar viewpoints toward tasks and toward one another are placed together.

Finally, *organizational development (OD)* is a process to increase effectiveness by integrating individual desires for growth and development with organizational goals. It is a planned change effort involving the total system over a period of time. The overall effort consists of a "continuing attempt to develop better procedures and a supporting climate for dealing with organizational problems."[51] OD's underlying strategy is to plan and develop a process that will bring about change in the organization's culture. Warren Bennis describes it as "a complex educational strategy intended to change the beliefs, attitudes, values and structure of organizations so that they can better adapt to new technologies, markets, and challenges, and the dizzying rate of change itself."[52] The range of OD intervention strategies include: team building, process consultation, T-groups, encounter groups, and laboratory training.[53]

▶ TYPES AND ROLES OF COMMUNICATION CONSULTANTS

Communication consultants can play a vital role in organizational development and the creative planning of change. Chris Argyris contends that outside agents or "interventionists" are necessary in altering the basic processes.[54] The assumption is that

► THE ILL-INFORMED WALRUS

Anonymous

"How's it going down there?" barked the big walrus from his perch on the highest rock near the shore. He waited for the good word.

Down below, the smaller walruses conferred hastily among themselves. Things weren't going well at all, but none of them wanted to break the news to the Old Man. He was the biggest and wisest walrus in the herd, and he knew his business—but he did hate to hear bad news. And he had such a terrible temper that every walrus in the herd was terrified of his ferocious bark.

"What will we tell him?" whispered Basil, the second-ranking walrus. He well remembered how the Old Man had ranted and raved at him the last time the herd caught less than its quota of herring, and he had no desire to go through that again. Nevertheless, the walruses had noticed for several weeks that the water level in the nearby Arctic bay had been falling consistently, and it had become necessary to travel much farther to catch the dwindling supply of herring. Someone should tell the Old Man; he would probably know what to do. But who? And how?

Finally, Basil spoke up. "Things are going pretty well, Chief," he said. The thought of the receding waterline made his heart feel heavy, but he went on; "As a matter of fact, the beach seems to be getting larger."

The Old Man grunted. "Fine, fine," he said. "That will give us a little more elbow room." He closed his eyes and continued basking in the sun.

The next day brought more trouble. A new herd of walruses moved in down the beach, and with the supply of herring dwindling, this invasion could be dangerous. No one wanted to tell the Old Man, though only he could take the steps necessary to meet this new competition.

Reluctantly, Basil approached the big walrus, who was still sunning himself on the large rock. After some small talk, he said, "By the way, Chief, a new herd of walruses seems to have moved into our territory." The Old Man's eyes snapped open, and he filled his great lungs in preparation for a mighty bellow. But Basil added quickly, "Of course, we don't anticipate any trouble. They don't look like herring eaters. More likely to be interested in minnows. And, as you know, we don't bother with minnows ourselves."

The Old Man let out the air with a long sigh. "Good, Good," he said, "no point in our getting excited over nothing, then, is there?"

Things didn't get better in the weeks that followed. One day, peering down from the large rock, the Old Man noticed that part of his herd seemed to be missing. Summoning Basil, he grunted peevishly, "What's going on, Basil? Where is everybody?"

Poor Basil didn't have the courage to tell the Old Man that many of the younger walruses were leaving every day to joint the new herd. Clearing his throat nervously, he said, "Well Chief, we've been tightening things up a bit. You know, getting rid of some of the dead wood. After all, a herd is only as good as the walruses in it."

"Run a tight ship, I always say," the Old Man grunted. "Glad to hear that everything is going well."

Before long, everyone but Basil had left to join the new herd, and Basil realized that the time had come to tell the Old Man the facts. Terrified, but determined, he flopped up to the large rock. "Chief," he said. "I have bad news. The rest of the herd has left you."

The old walrus was so astonished that he couldn't even work up a good bellow. "Left me?" he cried. "All of them? But why? How could this happen?

"I can't understand it," the old walrus said. "And just when everything was going so well."

Moral: *What you like to hear is not always what you need to hear.*

---

available data exist within the present organization but that there is a blockage in the organizational communication network that prevents adequate dissemination of data and effective problem solving. Consultants with broad and specific expertise can use their skills to solve management problems, to assist in the planning process, and to provide objectivity and perspective.[55] But because consultants cannot be all things to all people, important issues to consider when choosing to use a consultancy service are: (1) generalist versus specialist consulting, (2) process versus content consulting, and (3) diagnostic versus implementation consulting.[56]

Generalist Versus Specialist Consulting

Generalists are diagnosticians who accept assignments on the assumption that there are certain management fundamentals required to run any business successfully. Such fundamentals include strategic planning, organization, marketing, production, financial control, compensation, and communications. Generalists possess knowledge about all of these functional business areas. *Specialists,* on the other hand, believe that we live in a complex world where management knowledge and techniques are changing and advancing rapidly. They are experts in particular areas of business activity and bring their lengthy training and preparation to specific organizational problems. Both types of consultants can be usefully employed. Generalist consultants are more effective on complex problems at the top-management level where a comprehensive diagnosis is necessary before rushing into solutions. Conversely, if it is a clearly defined problem confined to a technical discipline, then a specialist will likely provide far better assistance. Both such consulting services are purchased to meet the organization's needs and then the relationship may be terminated.

Process Versus Content Consulting

Process consultants are the psychiatrists of the consulting trade; *content consultants* are the specialist surgeons. As in the field of psychoanalysis, the nondirective process consultant believes that only the organization can solve the problem, so participants are led through a self-examination and self-healing process where the consultant asks penetrating questions without giving personal evaluation or offering solutions. The organization itself must take the major responsibility for problem identification and solution formulation. A basic assumption is that far greater knowledge for change resides within the organization than within the consultant. In contrast, the content consultant takes direct action to verify the causes of a problem and then writes a report to support a set of specific recommendations. Content consultants believe that they are best able to see the forest despite the trees because they are independent and objective outsiders. Both the process model and the doctor-patient model can be appropriately applied. The process consultant must be highly trained in the fields of psychology, interpersonal communication, and group dynamics, and be extremely adept at raising the right questions at the right time. Good content consultants must be empathetic and willing to involve the organization at frequent intervals throughout the diagnostic and solution stages.

Diagnostic Versus Implementation Consulting

Finally, another way of contrasting different modes of consulting is between those who concentrate on diagnosis and those who focus on implementing change. The *diagnosticians* are adept at producing an X-ray of the problem. They penetrate beneath the symptoms, identify the causes, produce a summary of the real problem(s), and recommend action(s). They often stop at this point, preferring to move on to another analytical project. However, change-oriented *implementation consultants* believe that the organization must be moved off the status quo permanently and this requires their helping the organization actually operationalize their recommendations. These consultants are hands-on people, often specialist technicians involved in computer systems or human resources. They bring to the organization tailor-made solutions or occasionally packaged programs that may be adapted to particular needs. Both approaches are needed to maintain a link between analysis and implementation of change.

We have primarily been examining the role of external consultants. Certainly, many organizations use their own internal consultants to plan for innovation and change. The *Fortune 500* companies have turned increasingly to hiring their own full-time, in-house consultants as members of their corporate staff groups. The advantage to internal consultants is their extensive knowledge of the company and their awareness of the political terrain and the hidden problems that might escape outside eyes. External consultants, however, will never be completely replaced because their independent viewpoint is needed. Together, they effectively facilitate change and innovation by communicating what needs to be said rather than what one might want to hear.

▶ SUMMARY

Charles H. Duell, director of U.S. Patent Office, declared in 1899, "Everything that can be invented has been invented." He was wrong. Change and innovation is swirling all about and too many men and women in leadership positions are so puzzled by the changes that they are failing to prepare for future events. Changes are occurring so rapidly that rigid companies will fail because they will be unable to cope. But this era of kaleidoscopic change can offer unparalleled opportunities. One can have strategies for tomorrow that anticipate the areas in which the greatest changes are likely to occur. And consultants can play a vital role in communicating these new and different opportunities. In an era when competitive advantage is fleeting, when change is constant, and the whole globe is home base, America needs a new vision of success. The ambitious, thoughtful managers who accept the idea that change is inevitable and immediate will, according to Jard DeVille, "get on with business rather than retrenching and holding out until the last round is fired in a futile last stand."[57]

▶ QUESTIONS FOR DISCUSSION AND SKILL DEVELOPMENT

1. Why does change and innovation occur? Identify the problems associated with change and innovation. Which problems do you consider to be the most serious? How might these problems be overcome? How do you respond to change and innovation?

2. List techniques that may be used to communicate change and innovation. Which technique(s) do you consider to be most effective? Why? Can you give examples of where these techniques have been employed?

3. What is the purpose of management/communication consulting in business? When should an organization hire or not hire an external consultant? What type of consultant? What are some of the problems an external consultant might encounter in interpreting and feeding back data to an organization? When would it be best to use someone already in the organization?

4. Interpret the statement, "In one very real sense, evaluation is not the end of the change process, but how the process begins again."

5. Why is it important to change and innovate? What is the status of change and innovation in the U.S.? What American firm(s) do you consider to be the most innovative? Why? What about change and innovation in the public sector? Government? Utility companies? Hospitals? Law enforcement and prisons? Religious institutions? Educational institutions?

1. Wendell Johnson, *Living with Change: The Semantics of Coping* (New York: Harper and Row, 1972): 5, 10.

2. W. G. Bennis, K. D. Benne, and R. Chin, *The Planning of Change* (New York: Holt, Rinehart & Winston, 1969); D. Campbell, *Take the Road to Creativity and Get Off Your Dead End* (Allen, TX: Argus, 1977); P. F. Drucker, *Innovation and Entrepreneurship* (New York: Harper and Row, 1985); and T. E. Harris, "Roadblocks to Change: Executive Behaviors Versus Executive Perceptions" (Paper presented at the Annual Meeting of the Speech Communication Association, Boston, MA, 1987).

3. "Innovation: Has America Lost Its Edge?" *Newsweek,* June 4, 1979, 58.

4. Brian Dumaine, "Closing the Innovation Gap," *Fortune* (December 2, 1991): 56.

5. "Innovation: Has America Lost Its Edge?" 59.

6. Richard Daft and Selwyn Becker, *The Innovative Organization.* (New York: Elsevier North-Holland, 1978); J. Naisbitt and P. Aburdene, *Re-inventing the Corporation: Transforming Your Job and Your Company for the New Information Society* (New York: Warner Books, 1985); and J. Nora, C. Rogers, and R. Stramy, *Transforming the Workplace* (Princeton, NJ: Princeton Research Press, 1986).

7. Selwyn Becker and Thomas Whisler, "The Innovative Organization," *Journal of Business* 40 (1967): 463.

8. Don Fabum, *Dimensions of Change* (Beverly Hills, CA: Glencoe Press, 1971): 14–17.

9. W. G. Bennis, E. G. Schein, F. Steele, and D. Berlew, *Interpersonal Dynamics.* (Homewood, IL: Dorsey Press, 1964): 362–378.

10. E. Huse, *Organization Development and Change* (New York: West Publishing, 1975); R. M. Kanter, *The Change Masters* (New York: Simon & Schuster, 1983); D. A. Nadler and M. L. Tushman, "Organizational Frame Bending: Principles for Managing Reorientation" *Academy of Management Executive* 3 (1989): 194–203; and L. W. Steele, *Innovation in Big Business* (New York: America Elsevier, 1975).

11. R. Foster, *Innovation* (New York: Summit, 1986); P. R. Lawrence and J. W. Lorsch, *Organization and Environment* (Homewood, IL: Richard D. Irwin, 1969); A. D. Meyer and J. B. Goes, "Organizational Assimilation of Innovations: A Multilevel Contextual Analysis," *Academy of Management Journal* 31 (1989): 897–923; and J. A. Morton, *Organizing for Innovation* (New York: McGraw-Hill, 1971).

12. Phillip Clampitt, *Communicating for Managerial Effectiveness* (Newbury Park, CA: Sage, 1991): 179–183.

13. Alan Kantrow, *The Constraints of Corporate Tradition* (New York: Harper and Row, 1984).

14. James Belasco, *Teaching the Elephant to Dance* (New York: Plume, 1991): 64.

15. "Our Bosses Aren't Very Responsive, Most Workers Believe," *The Wall Street Journal,* October 3, 1989, A1.

16. James March and Herbert Simon, *Organizations* (New York: John Wiley & Sons, 1958).

17. Daft and Becker, *Innovative Organization,* 11–14.

18. Bill Saporito, "The Fly in Campbell's Soup," *Fortune* (May 9, 1988): 67–70.

19. Steele, *Innovation in Big Business,* 20.

20. D. L. Bradford and A. R. Cohen, *Managing for Excellence: The Guide for Developing High Performance in Contemporary Organizations* (New York: John Wiley & Sons, 1984); David A. Whetten and Kim S. Cameron, *Developing Managerial Skills* (Glenview, IL: Scott, Foresman, 1984); and G. Egan, *Change Agent Skills A & B* (San Diego, CA: University Associates, 1988).

21. Roger Von Oech, *A Whack on the Side of the Head* (New York: Warner Books, 1983): 9.

22. Dumaine, "Closing the Innovation Gap," 59.

23. Ibid., 57.

24. Peter Drucker, *Managing in Turbulent Times* (New York: Harper and Row, 1980).

25. Neil Kay, *The Innovating Firm* (New York: Macmillan, 1979).

26. C. Freeman, *The Economics of Industrial Innovation* (London: Penguin Books, 1974): 226.

27. George D. Smith, *The Anatomy of a Business Strategy: Bell, Western Electric, and the Origins of the American Telephone Industry* (Baltimore, MD: Johns Hopkins University Press, 1985).

28. "Xerox Rethinks Itself: And This Could Be the Last Time," *Business Week* (February 13, 1987): 90–93, and "Culture Shock at Xerox," *Business Week* (June 22, 1987): 63–67.

29. Carol J. Loomis, "IBM's Big Blues," *Fortune* (January 19, 1987): 34–52; "Big Changes at Big Blue," *Business Week* (November 17, 1986): 152-157; and David Kirkpatrick, "Breaking Up IBM," *Fortune* (July 27, 1992): 44–49.

30. Danny Miller, *The Icarus Paradox* (New York: HarperCollins, 1992).

31. Martin Smith, *Maxims of Management* (Piscataway, NJ: New Century Publishers, 1986): 41.

32. Bennis, Benne, and Chin, *The Planning of Change* (New York: Holt, Rinehart & Winston, 1969); Paul Hersey and Kenneth Blanchard, "The Management of Change," *Training and Development Journal* (June 1980): 80–89; K. E. Haltman, "Identifying and Dealing With Resistance to Change," *Training and Development Journal* (February 1980): 28–33; and R. J. Hermon-Taylor, "Finding Ways of Overcoming Resistance to Change," in: J. M. Pennings, ed., *Organizational Strategy and Change* (San Francisco: Jossey-Bass, 1985): 383–411.

33. Everett M. Rogers, *Diffusion of Innovations* (New York: The Free Press, 1983).

34. Daft and Becker, *Innovative Organization*, 145.

35. R. Lippitt, J. Watson, and B. Westley, *Dynamics of Planned Change* (New York: Harcourt, Brace and World, 1958).

36. N. Tichy and H. Hornstein, "Stand When Your Number Is Called: An Empirical Attempt to Clearly Classify Types of Social Agents," in: Huse, *Organization Development and Change*.

37. M. Sashkin, W. Morriss, and L. Horst, "A Comparison of Social and Organizational Change Models: Information Flow and Data Use Processes," *Psychological Review* 80 (1973): 510–526.

38. Stephen Stumpf and Thomas Mullen, *Taking Charge, Strategic Leadership in the Middle Game* (Englewood Cliffs, NJ: Prentice Hall, 1992): 57.

39. W. Zaltman, M. Duncan, and H. Holbeck, *Innovation and Organization* (New York: John Wiley & Sons, 1973): 5. Copyright © 1973 John Wiley & Sons. Reprinted by permission of John Wiley & Sons, Inc.

40. G. Egan, "People In Systems: A Comprehensive Model for Psychosocial Education and Training," in: D. Larson, ed., *Teaching Psychological Skills: Models for Giving Psychology Away* (Monterey, CA: Brooks/Cole, 1984): 21–43.

41. R. C. Schank, *The Cognitive Computer* (Reading, MA: Addison-Wesley, 1984).

42. M. Dalziel and S. C. Schoonover, *Changing Ways: A Practical Tool for Implementing Change Within Organizations* (New York: AMACOM, 1988).

43. L. Sayles, *Managerial Behavior* (New York: McGraw-Hill, 1964).

44. Warren Bennis, *Changing Organizations* (New York: McGraw-Hill, 1966); I. Doyal and J. Thomas, "Operation KPE: Developing a New Organization," *Journal of Applied Behavioral Science* 4 (1968): 473–506; and Richard Hackman and Greg Oldham, *Work Redesign* (Reading, MA: Addison-Wesley, 1977).

45. A. R. Field, "Managing Creative People," *Success* (October 1988): 85–87; John Humble, *Management by Objectives in Action* (New York: McGraw-Hill, 1970; "The New Breed of Strategic Planner," *Business Week* (September 17, 1984): 62–68; and James Waters and Henry Mintzberg, "Of Strategies Deliberate and Emergent," *Strategic Management Journal* 6 (1985): 257–72.

46. E. Rausch, *Balancing Needs of People and Organizations: The Linking Elements* (Washington, D.C.: Bureau of National Affairs, 1978): 15.

47. K. D. Duncan, M. M. Gruneberg, and D. Wallis, *Changes in Working Life* (New York: John Wiley & Sons, 1980); L. Davis and J. C. Taylor, *Design of Jobs: Selected Readings* (New York: Penguin, 1973); F. Foulkes, *Creating More Meaningful Work* (New York: American Management Association, 1969); C. A. Hanson and D. K. Hanson, "Motivation: Are the Old Theories Still True?" *Supervisory Management* 23 (1978): 14–20; F. Herzberg, *Work and the Nature of Man* (Cleveland: World Publishing, 1966); J. Maher, *New Perspectives on Job Enrichment* (New York: Van Nostrand, Reinhold, 1971); M. Myers, *Every Employee a Manager* (New York: McGraw-Hill, 1970); and H. Rush, *Job Design for Motivation* (New York: The Conference Board, 1971).

48. J. Hackman and G. Oldham, *The Diagnostic Survey: An Instrument for the Diagnosis of Jobs and the Evaluation of Job Redesign Projects. Technical Report No. 4* (New Haven, CT: Yale University, Department of Administrative Sciences, 1974).

49. Johnson, *Living With Change*, 46.

50. D. S. Davidson, "Employee Participation Can Mean Increased Employee Satisfaction," *Supervisory Management* 24 (1979): 34–41; William Dyer, *Team Building: Issues and Alternatives* (Reading, MA: Addison-

Wesley, 1977); and K. Kilmann, "An Organic-Adaptive Organization: The MAPS Method," *Personnel* 51 (1974): 35–47.

51. W. H. Schmidt, *Organizational Frontiers and Human Values* (Belmont, CA: Wadsworth, 1970): 153.

52. Warren Bennis, *Organizational Development: Its Nature, Origins, and Prospects* (Reading, MA: Addison-Wesley, 1969): 10.

53. Huse, *Organizational Development and Change;* Edward Lawler III, *Pay and Organization Development* (Reading, MA: Addison-Wesley, 1981); Gordon Lippitt, *Organizational Renewal: A Holistic Approach to Organizational Development,* 2nd ed. (Englewood Cliffs, NJ: Prentice Hall, 1982); and R. W. Pace, *Organizational Communication: Foundations for Human Resource Development* (Englewood Cliffs, NJ: Prentice Hall, 1983).

54. Chris Argyris, *Intervention Theory and Method* (Reading, MA: Addison-Wesley, 1970).

55. M. Kuhn, *Management Consulting: A Guide to the Profession* (Geneva, Switzerland: International Labor Organization, 1976); Gordon Lippitt and Ronald Lippitt, *The Consulting Process in Action* (La Jolla, CA: University Associates, 1978); and Edgar Schein, *Process Consultation: Its Role in Organization Development* (Reading, MA: Addison-Wesley, 1969).

56. Peter Block, *A Guide to Flawless Consulting* (La Jolla, CA: University Associates, 1981); Henry Boeltinger, "New Directions for Management Consultants," *Conference Board* 12 (March 1975); Don Bowen, "When and How to Use a Consultant: Guidelines for Public Managers," *Public Administration Review* 38 (1978): 21–35; Charles Fergesen, "Concerning the Nature of Human Systems and the Consultant's Role," *Journal of Applied Behavioral Science* 4 (1968): 179–93; Richard Hodgson, "Consulting: A Model for Management Development," *Business Quarterly* 43 (1978): 164–82; Alfred Hunt, *The Management Consultant* (New York: Ronald Press, 1977); David Kolb and Alan Frohman, "An Organization Development Approach to Consulting," *Sloan Management Review* (Fall 1970): 51–65; *Personal Qualifications of Management Consultants* (New York: Association of Consulting Management Engineers, 1971); and Warner Woodworth and Nelson Reed, "Witch Doctors, Messianics, Sorcerers, and OD Consultants: Parallels and Paradigms," *Organizational Dynamics* (Autumn 1979): 164–82.

57. Jard DeVille, "Let's Learn Better Ways to Cope With Social Change," *Training* (February 1980): 76.

CHAPTER FOURTEEN

14

Ethics in Business and the Professions

LEARNING OBJECTIVES:

To understand the nature of ethics and its relationship to business

To understand ethical theories including the teleological and deontological approaches

To explain why a study of business ethics is important

To indicate the importance of whistle blowing to the organization

To describe the ethical dilemmas involved in advertising

To explain the importance of the right to be free from sexual harassment on the job

To demonstrate how mission statements and codes of ethics aid the organization's standards of ethics

To explain the new moral imperative for business

We are surrounded by and concerned with ethical issues nearly every day. Ethical issues form an important part of our lives as we decide whether to follow the strict precepts of the church, deliberately deceive someone we know, or claim an exaggerated deduction on our income taxes. Today, there is a concern among many people that leading an ethical life is not as important as it once was. For instance, a recent study of 6,873 students by the Josephson Institute for Ethics produced the following disturbing findings: 33 percent of high school students admitted to shoplifting during the past 12 months; 18 percent of college students admitted to shoplifting in the same time period; 33 percent of all students said they would lie to get a job; and 40 percent of high school students admitted that they had even lied on the survey itself.[1]

In our business lives, too, we face important ethical questions. Many of these concerns are small and easily settled, but a number of them are complex and difficult to resolve. In a Business Roundtable report on company conduct in America, a group of prominent business leaders called ethics in business "one of the most challenging issues confronting the corporate community in this era."[2] As a present or future member of an American organization, it is important for you to have an understanding of ethics in business and the professions. In this chapter, we examine the nature of ethics, the relationship between business and morality, specific ethical dilemmas that currently exist in business, and ways to establish ethical standards in the organization.

The study of ethics is the study of right and wrong and the morality of the choices that people make. Ethics themselves are values shared by a society and by such collections of people within that society as family, government, and business. People often think that ethics is synonymous with the law. Lester C. Thurow, former dean of the Sloan School of Management at MIT, expressed this belief when he observed that most Americans think that the question "Is it right?" is the same as the question "Is it legal?" Thurow goes on to state, however, that these two questions are not the same.[3] Ethical conduct goes beyond the issue of legality because certain behaviors that may be legal can still be unethical. For example, it may be legal to lie to a close friend about an important issue, yet few would consider this behavior to be ethical. A better way to understand ethics is to associate it with such ideas as character, fairness, and honesty. The person who naturally and consistently displays these attributes would generally be considered an ethical person.[4] One business that emphasizes this connection is the J.C. Penney Company. For more than 75 years, it has considered ethical behavior to be that which conforms to the Golden Rule: "Do unto others as you would have them do unto you."[5] Ethics, then, is a "way of life—an awareness that one is an intrinsic part of a social order, in which the interests of others and one's own interests are inevitably intertwined."[6]

▶ NATURE OF ETHICS

As societies have evolved and progressed, a number of ethical theories have emerged by which to judge moral behavior. Of these theories, two basic approaches to moral reasoning have prevailed.

The *utilitarian* approach states that an action is right if it produces the greatest amount of good for the greatest number of people affected by the action; otherwise, it is wrong. Proponents of utilitarianism argue that, when evaluating an action, one ought to take into account not only the consequences of that action to oneself but its consequences for all those affected by the action, so as to promote the greatest total balance of good over evil. To implement a utilitarian analysis, you must generally follow three steps: (1) determine who will be affected by the action; (2) determine both the positive and negative effects of the action; and, (3) decide which course of action provides the greatest utility.

There are some clear shortcomings to utilitarianism. First, its implementation requires a knowledge of facts, including future positive and negative consequences, that may be difficult to obtain or to know. For example, it is difficult to know how many people are affected if I break a contract with a business partner. Certainly the partner and I are affected; but an indeterminable number of other people who hear about the breaking of the contract may be affected as well because they may be more cautious about entering into future contracts with me or with anyone else. Second, its implementation can lead to injustices. Suppose the management of a company is closing a plant in an economically depressed region. Although the closing may make good sense from an economic—and utilitarian—viewpoint, hundreds of people will be put out of work and the region will become further depressed. Shortcomings such as these that have led some to argue for another ethical theory.[7]

The *deontological* approach holds that an action is morally right or wrong, independent of its consequences—that it is right if it has certain characteristics or is of a certain kind, and is wrong if it has other characteristics or is of another kind. Proponents of deontology deny the utilitarian claim that an action's morality depends on its consequences; they are concerned with the intentions of the person involved, not the consequences of the action. The deontological approach believes that what makes an action right isn't the sum of its consequences but whether it conforms to moral law; that is, it is our duty to do what is morally right regardless of the consequences. Again, let's examine a common example from business to explain this ethical approach. A manager may decide to treat the department's employees in a rude and inconsiderate manner. Even though this approach rarely is successful, he believes it is the best approach for this group of employees at this time. The deontological approach would hold that it is morally wrong to treat employees in this way because it denies them their right to self-respect and dignity—even if this strategy were successful and corporate profits were maximized.

This approach, too, has certain shortcomings. First, it is an imprecise standard. For example, the deontological approach would assume that bribery is immoral and wrong, and therefore, unacceptable because it doesn't conform to moral law. However, it is clear that there are different kinds of bribery and different reasons for bribery. What if the bribery were undertaken to secure the best deal for a client or to save the company from bankruptcy? The standard becomes much less clear given these contingencies. Second, the deontological approach does not offer a framework for resolving conflicts. Although the approach offers a rational basis for rights and duties, it does not offer a methodology for resolving conflicts.[8] The principle of affirmative action provides a common business example of just such a conflict. In order to make up for past injustices in hiring practices, members of minority and other groups are compensated by a relaxing of certain hiring standards that some people believe discriminates against white men. Both compensating the victims of past injustice and refraining from present injustice seem to present a contradiction within the deontological approach.

Despite these shortcomings, both theories can help in the construction of a moral framework by which to make business decisions. Utilitarianism can act as a corporate or personal check on self-interest, and the deontological approach suggests certain limits beyond which we ought not to go, even to maximize the sum total of good. Both are worthy of your interest.

Business ethics refers to rules about how businesses and their employees ought to behave; ethical behavior conforms to these rules but unethical behavior violates them.[9] The CEO of a Scandinavian multinational corporation provides an operational definition of business ethics as he tells his managers to "assume that the decision you are about to make in Timbuktu becomes public knowledge in our home country, the host country, and significant world countries where our company is operating. Assume further that you, as the decision maker, are called upon to defend the decision on television both at home and abroad. If you think you can defend it successfully in these public forums, the probability is high that your decision is ethical."[10] Bowen H. McCoy, managing director of Morgan Stanley and Company, Inc., investment bankers, explained business ethics when he said that "(Business) ethics involves the art of integration and compromise, not blind obedience and conformity. It calls for tolerance of ambiguity; signifies a heightened ability to seek truth that stems from core beliefs and to decide consciously on one's actions in a business context. (Business) ethics deals with free choice among alternatives. In a practical sense . . . it is wrapped up with the integrity and authenticity of the businessman and the business enterprise."[11]

▶RELATIONSHIP BETWEEN BUSINESS AND MORALITY

Business and morality are related in any number of ways that we will discuss throughout this chapter. First, however, you may be wondering why business ethics is important in the first place. Actually, it's very meaningful.

Moral Background of Business

Business is a part of all of our lives. It involves each of us in one way or another. Most people work in business, and all of us purchase goods and services provided by business. Business is not an entity separate from society, but rather an inherent part of our society. Because it is societally based, business is judged like most of us are judged, in terms of our morality. Business actually presupposes a background of morality and could not operate without it. Employers expect their workers to be at work unless unavoidably detained, coworkers expect their colleagues to tell the truth when asked, employees expect management to honor agreements, and people who purchase products expect them to work as advertised. Without these assurances of honesty, business—and by extension, society—would not be able to operate. Richard T. DeGeorge describes this milieu of morality by saying, "Morality is the oil as well as the glue of society, and, therefore, of business. It is only against this background of morality that immorality can be not only possible but profitable. Lying would not succeed if most people were not truthful and did not tend to believe others. A breach of trust requires a background of trust."[12]

In general, then, business is considered to be a moral entity, and there are good reasons why business needs to be considered moral and ethical. Indeed, the issues of ethics and morality have become increasingly important to the public and to government. The concerns of these institutions compel us to observe reasons for business to be highly attentive to ethical concerns. After all, one could argue that corporate profits and shareholders' wealth might be increased if unethical behavior were more acceptable, but experience has shown us that there are two very good and important reasons why organizations need to be ethically responsible.

First, unethical behavior can severely damage the corporation. Issues ranging from insider trading, to check kiting, to overcharging on government contracts, to unauthorized use of alcohol and drugs while on the job have almost destroyed the reputations of many small and large companies. In the past few years, serious ethical questions have adversely affected such major corporations as Union Carbide, General Dynamics, E. F. Hutton, Nestlé, Perrier, and Exxon. The ethical problems faced by these major international corporations only highlight the fact that a company that behaves unethically risks the chance of seriously damaging both the reputation and the very existence of that organization. Indeed, corporate failure is a strong possibility once a company's external image is severely harmed. Unethical behavior has become so important to our nation's corporations that a recent study concluded that over 90 percent of top corporate executives believed the business community was very troubled by ethical problems.[13]

▶ ARE YOU ETHICAL?

By Lowell G. Rein

It is important to understand the significance of ethics to corporate America. It is just as important to understand your own personal ethical standards and to think about what you would do if you were to be placed in a situation where ethics were called into question. The following instrument allows you the opportunity to test yourself about your own business ethics. In the space to the left of each statement, place a "3" if you strongly Agree, a "2" if you Agree, a "1" if you Disagree, and a "0" if you Strongly Disagree. Remember that there are no right or wrong answers and that many of the following situations may fall into a gray area. Check your results when you finish.

_____ 1. Employees should not be expected to inform on their peers for wrong-doings.

_____ 2. There are times when a manager must overlook contract and safety violations to get on with the job.

_____ 3. It is not always possible to keep accurate expense account records; therefore, it is sometimes necessary to give approximate records.

_____ 4. There are times when it is necessary to withhold embarrassing information from one's superior.

_____ 5. We should do what our managers suggest, although we may have doubts about its being the right thing to do.

_____ 6. It is sometimes necessary to conduct personal business on company time.

_____ 7. Sometimes it is good psychology to set goals somewhat above normal if it will help obtain a greater effort from the sales force.

_____ 8. I would quote a "hopeful" shipping date to get the order.

_____ 9. It is proper to use the company WATS line for personal calls as long as it's not in company use.

_____ 10. Management must be goal-oriented; therefore, the end usually justifies the means.

_____ 11. If it takes heavy entertainment and twisting a bit of company policy to win a large contract, I would authorize it.

_____ 12. Exceptions to company policy and procedures are a way of life.

_____ 13. Inventory controls should be designed to report "underages" rather than "overages" in goods received.

_____ 14. Occasional use of the company's copier for personal or community activities is acceptable.

_____ 15. Taking home company property (pencils, paper, tape, etc.) for personal use is an accepted fringe benefit.

_____ TOTAL SCORE

If your total score is:

0–10	You have very high ethical values
11–15	You have high ethical values
16–25	You have average ethical values
26–35	You have low ethical values
36–45	You have very low ethical values

Source: Adapted from Lowell G. Rein, "Is Your (Ethical) Slippage Showing?" *Personnel Journal* (September 1980): 740–742.

Second, and conversely, ethical behavior is actually good for business. The display of fairness, honesty, and high character fosters client/customer trust in the company. Johnson and Johnson, Inc., has established a corporate credo emphasizing the virtues of honesty and integrity, and CEO Ralph Larsen stressed the importance of these qualities to the bottom line of the company when he observed, "The Credo shouldn't be viewed as some kind of social welfare program. It's just plain good business."[14] William D. Smithburg, chairman and CEO of Quaker Oats Company, agreed that good ethics means good business when he wrote, "I know ethical behavior is sound business practice because every day at the Quaker Oats Company I am reminded that we succeed or fail according to the trust consumers have in us."[15] These executives are not alone in their belief that ethics is good for business. The highly respected 1988 study of corporate ethics by Touche Ross and Company found that 63 percent of the respondents believed that high ethical standards strengthen a business's competitive position.[16]

Business of Business

In spite of these good and compelling reasons for business to adhere to a strict code of ethical behavior, there is ample evidence that certain businesses have often been less than interested in ethical standards. Although there is no proof that people are more immoral in their business lives than in their private lives, there is a concern that some businesses are simply uninterested in business ethics. A *U.S. News & World Report*–CNN poll found that the majority of Americans believe dishonesty is more prevalent in business than it was just ten years ago.[17] Another survey indicated that 70 percent of the managers surveyed at Uniroyal Tire Corporation and 59 percent at Pitney Bowes Corporation felt there was pressure in their organizations to compromise personal ethics to achieve corporate goals.[18]

There is an old cliché that "the business of business is business." There are various interpretations of this statement, but usually it is understood to mean that issues such as charity, social welfare, and ethics are not the "business of business." Rather, the cliché argues, business is primarily concerned with the making of profits and the maximizing of shareholder wealth. This is a position with which certain conservative economists agree. Nobel Prize-winning economist Milton Friedman argues that the only social responsibility of business is to increase its profits. He says, "There is one and only one social responsibility of business—to use its resources and engage in activities designed to increase its profits so long as it stays within the rules of the game, which is to say, engages in open and free competition without deception or fraud."[19] The belief that ethics is not the business of business leads some people to conclude that business and ethics just don't mix. They argue that business has its own objectives, and ethical concepts are inappropriate to the business context. They seem to ascribe to the notion that the term "business ethics" is an oxymoron, the rhetorical device that links contradictory words, such as the phrase "cruel kindness."

We hold, however, that the popularity of this point of view is overstated. We believe, in general, that American business is responding to the pressures of the media, the government, and the public to act ethically. This response is signaled in at least three ways. First, the reporting of scandals and the public reaction to these reports has increased significantly. More and more, the least hint of a scandal in business is common knowledge to nearly everyone because of the watchfulness of the press. Second, the formation of populist groups, such as environmentalists and consumerists, has caused business to consider issues other than profits. These groups have grown significantly in the past decade, and they are specifically concerned with values such as the preservation of the planet and with the right of people to adequate information about the goods they purchase. Third, the enacting of codes of conduct and the expressing of corporate concern by business, itself. According to a Bentley College survey of *Fortune 1000* companies, over 40 percent of the respondents are holding ethics workshops and seminars, and about one-third have set up an ethics committee.[20] Businesses, then, are now feeling the need to respond to ethical issues and to weigh ethical concerns in their corporate deliberations.

That does not mean, of course, that all organizations feel this necessity; nor does it mean that very many of our organizations feel the necessity as much as they should.

There is still a lot of important work to be done, and business, in general, does seem to be making a legitimate attempt.

▶ ETHICAL DILEMMAS IN BUSINESS

It is imperative that corporate leaders have an understanding of the important ethical dilemmas that their companies may face in the future, because this understanding will allow them to better develop a system of ethical behavior for those companies. Indeed, they will find it difficult to act on ethical issues if they cannot recognize them. Charles Buckalew agreed when he said, "Recognition of ethical issues is an imperative for acting on them. Unlike other questions where we may decide on an answer without there being any requisite commitment of action, ethical issues necessarily involve commitment and action as part of their resolution."[21]

There are a number of ethical issues common to all areas of business. Here we discuss whistle-blowing and some specific issues that directly affect the customer and the employee in corporate relations.

Whistle-Blowing

This ethical dilemma is similar in some ways to those dilemmas that directly affect the employee of the organization (and will be discussed later in this section), but it is of such importance that we analyze it apart from the other dilemmas. *Whistle-blowing* is the attempt by a current or former employee of an organization to disclose what he or she believes to be wrongdoing in or by the organization. Like blowing a whistle to call attention to a thief, whistle-blowing is an effort to make others aware of practices one considers illegal, unjust, or harmful. Whenever someone goes over the head of immediate supervisors to inform higher management of wrongdoing, the whistle-blowing is considered to be internal to the organization. Whenever someone discloses wrongdoing to outside individuals or groups, such as reporters, public interest groups, or regulatory agencies, the whistle-blowing is considered to be external.[22]

Whistle-blowing is both complex and controversial because it calls into conflict one's loyalty to the corporation and one's responsibility to society. Those employees who blow the whistle obviously believe their social responsibility is more important to them than their corporate loyalty. In effect, this is how it should be, especially if the wrongdoing by business is at all serious. It is now relatively clear that whistle-blowing could have averted the disasters and prevented needless deaths and injuries in the *Challenger* explosion and the toxic gas leak at Union Carbide in Bhopal, India. Engineers in both cases voiced their concerns to upper-level management and were ignored; however, these engineers were reluctant to present their concerns externally.[23] One Union Carbide employee observed that "most of the engineers at Union Carbide think of themselves as part of the company. Besides, if you were identified, that would be the end of your career."[24] This employee refers to a very important issue relevant to the act of whistle-blowing—the repercussions that ultimately face the whistle-blower.

In business, the most widely held view is that whistle-blowing is morally prohibited. There is a large body of evidence that when someone does blow the whistle on

▶ QUESTIONS FOR EXAMINING THE ETHICS OF A BUSINESS DECISION

Any valid discussion of business ethics observes that the trend toward focusing on the social impact of the corporation is an inescapable reality that must be factored into today's managerial decision making. In her Harvard Business Review article, Laura L. Nash presents important questions as a process of ethical inquiry into the larger question, "How do we as a corporation examine our ethical concerns?" Her questions and relevant commentary follow:

1. Have you defined the problem accurately?
   As a first step, defining fully the factual implications of a decision determines to a large degree the quality of one's subsequent moral position.

2. How would you define the problem if you stood on the other side of the fence?
   The purpose of articulating the other side, whose needs are understandably less proximate than operational considerations, is to allow some mechanism whereby calculations of self-interest can be interrupted by a compelling empathy for those who might suffer immediate injury or more annoyance as a result of a corporation's decision.

3. How did this situation occur in the first place?
   As important as deciding the ethics of the situation is the inquiry into its history. Indeed, the history gives a clue to solving the problem.

4. What is your intention in making this decision?
   Despite the fact that intentions are often complex and elusive, a company's intentions do matter. Answering this question makes the executive deliberately analyze the decision-making process.

5. Whom could your decision or action injure?
   Given the limits of knowledge about a new product or policy, who and how many come into contact with it? Could its inadequate disposal affect an entire commu- nity? How might your product be used if it happened to be acquired by a terrorist radical group? To exclude at the outset any policy or decision that might have such results is to reshape the way modern business examines its own morality. So often business formulates questions of injury only after the facts in the form of liability suits.

6. Are you confident that your position will be as valid over a long period of time as it seems now?
   As anyone knows who has had to consider long-range plans and short-term budgets simultaneously, a difference in time frame can change the meaning of a problem significantly. Time alters circumstances, and few corporate value systems are immune to shifts in financial status, external political pressure, and personnel (one survey now places the average U.S. CEO's tenure in office at five years.)

7. Could you disclose without qualm your decision or action to your boss, your CEO, the Board of Directors, your family, or society as a whole?
   The old question, "Would you want your decision to appear on the front page of the New York Times?" still holds. A corporation may maintain that there's really no problem, but a problem does exist if the company is hesitant to disclose important decisions.

These questions are a way to articulate an idea of the responsibilities involved and to lay them open for examination. Whether a decisive policy is also generated or not, there are compelling reasons for holding such discussions. The situations for testing business morality remain complex. But by avoiding theoretical inquiry and limiting the expectations of corporate goodness to a few rules for social behavior that are based on common sense, we can develop an ethic that is appropriate to the language, ideology, and institutional dynamics of business decision making and consensus.

Source: Laura L. Nash, "Excerpts Without the Sermon," Harvard Business Review (November-December 1981).

the company—even for moral reasons and with positive results for the public—he or she is generally ostracized, not only by the management but also by fellow employees. The whistle-blower is seen as a traitor, as someone who has damaged the firm— the working family—to which he or she belongs.[25]

Unfortunately, the law offers these people little protection. Although it is true that a few states, including New York, California, Michigan, Connecticut, and Maine, now have laws intended to protect whistle-blowers, most still uphold statutes or agreements to the contrary.[26] The result is that most employees who blow the whistle, even those who report felonies, are fired or suffer other retaliation. On the federal level, the Occupational Safety and Health Administration (OSHA) has jurisdiction in certain situations when the whistle-blowing concerns health and safety issues; however, these laws are often simply not enforced. A 1981 study indicated that of the 3,100 violations reported to OSHA in 1979, only 16 were litigated and only 270 were settled out of court.[27] Unionized workers would seem to have more protection than others against employers who dismiss at will because most collective-bargaining agreements require just cause for dismissal, but even they have little protection when it comes to whistle-blowing. In fact, arbitrators have tended to agree with employers that whistle-blowing is an act of disloyalty that disrupts business and injures the employer's reputation.[28] Their attitude is best exemplified by the arbitrator who said that one should not "bite the hand that feeds you and insist on staying for future banquets."[29]

The potential whistle-blower, then, faces a clear dilemma. On the one hand, the public may be served well by a disclosure, injuries may be prevented, and lives may even be saved. On the other hand, the whistle-blower may be ostracized by fellow workers and harassed and fired by management. These are the reasons why the issue is so complicated and why whistle-blowers must carefully weigh the ramifications of their actions.

Gene G. James provides a list of factors for whistle-blowers to consider in disclosing wrongdoing if they are to also act prudently and effectively:

1. *Make sure the situation is one that warrants whistle-blowing.* The situation must be one which involves illegal or immoral actions which harm others.

2. *Examine your own motives.* Although the whistle-blower's actions don't need to be praiseworthy to be morally justified, this action can help in deciding whether the situation warrants whistle-blowing.

3. *Verify and document your information.* Information gathered by the whistle-blower should be of a high enough quality to stand up in court or in regulatory hearings. If this isn't possible, the whistle-blower should gather as much information as possible. At times, illegal procedures are necessary when gathering information; in these cases, the situation must be one in which the wrongdoing is so great that this risk is warranted. In general, illegal methods should be avoided unless substantial harm is involved.

4. *Determine the type of wrongdoing involved and to whom it should be reported.* Determining the exact nature of the wrongdoing helps the whistle-blower decide the kind of evidence which is necessary and to whom it should be reported. Usually, illegal wrongdoing needs to be reported to certain legal authorities; legal yet harmful wrongdoing should be reported to a public interest group.

5. *State your allegations in an appropriate way.* Whistle-blowers need to be as specific as possible whenever reporting allegations; technical information, especially, needs to be reported clearly and accurately.

6. *Stick to the facts.* Whistle-blowers need to avoid mud-slinging and report those factual statements known to be true; sticking to the facts also tends to minimize retaliation.

7. *Decide whether the whistle-blowing should be internal or external.* Find out how problems were resolved and how people were treated if they used internal channels in the organization. If they were treated well, use these internal methods; if not, find out which external channels to contact and determine how these agencies have treated whistle-blowers.

8. *Decide whether the whistle-blowing should be open or anonymous.* Document the wrong-doing as thoroughly as possible before deciding to openly or anonymously make a statement. Since anonymity may be difficult to preserve, anticipate what needs to be done if your identity becomes known.

9. *Decide whether current or alumni whistle-blowing is required.* Sometimes it is possible and advisable to quit one's position before blowing the whistle to avoid being fired, being blacklisted, or being the recipient of damaging letters of recommendation. Removing oneself from a job or place, however, is not a substitute for blowing the whistle; these "remedies" only allow a bad situation to continue.

10. *Make sure you follow proper guidelines in reporting the wrongdoing.* Usually, both internal and external channels have guidelines, such as certain forms and specific deadlines, to follow when reporting wrongdoing. To not exactly follow these rules may allow wrongdoers to escape punishment because of a "technicality."

11. *Consult a lawyer.* It is a good idea to consult an attorney before and during the whole process of whistle-blowing. You do need to keep in mind, however, that attorneys are trained to work from a legal framework while decisions to blow the whistle are moral decisions. If you cannot afford an attorney, seek help from the appropriate public interest group.

12. *Anticipate and document retaliation.* One should always anticipate retaliation for reporting wrongdoing. Documentation, including letters and tape recordings of meetings, can help protect the whistle-blower in preventing or redressing retaliation.[30]

Ethics and Customer Relations

Business must also be concerned about its customer relations. This is true because business organizations exist by selling goods and services to people—customers are essential for business. A number of issues exist that are concerned with ethics and customer relations, and these issues have become so important that an entire social program—consumerism—has been created to attend to them. *Consumerism* is the social movement that seeks to augment the rights and powers of buyers in relation to sellers.[31] We examine here the issue of advertising as a representative example of the ongoing relationship between ethics and customer relations.

Advertising is any paid form of nonpersonal presentation of ideas, goods, or services by an identified sponsor. Advertising is a pervasive form of promotion with a significant effect on our American society. In fact, American companies spend more money per person per year on advertising than does any other country in the world, with the result that a person in the U.S. is exposed to between one and two billion advertising messages before reaching the age of 21.[32]

From a moral point of view, advertising is justifiable and permissible if it is not deceptive, misleading, or coercive. Advertising can be abused, but it is not inherently immoral. Perhaps because of its far-reaching effect, the government and public have focused on certain ethical issues concerned with advertising abuses.

The issue of *want creation* by advertisers is one of the most controversial. Critics believe that advertisers actually create a demand for products which the consumer otherwise would not have had. Certain supporters of this advertising practice respond by arguing that it is the quest for instant gratification and not advertising that drives people to exceed their purchasing capabilities. However, Harvard professor John Kenneth Galbraith argues that this abuse is of such concern that the entire activity of advertising has long been regarded with uneasiness and general disapproval by economists. Galbraith believes that in the U.S. the manufacture of consumer demands is as important as, if not more important than, the manufacture of products to satisfy those demands. The same companies that satisfy wants, he claims, also create those wants by advertising, establishing a self-perpetuating cycle of desire and satisfaction. Galbraith summarizes his argument by asking, "Is a new breakfast cereal or detergent so much wanted if so much must be spent to compel in the consumer the sense of want?"[33]

Truth and distortion is another issue of concern among those who believe that abuses can exist in advertising. Some evidence suggests that this issue is among the most frequent complaints about advertising. A study by Raymond A. Bauer and Stephen A. Greyser indicates that distortion and deception are very upsetting to consumers, particularly to those in the higher income brackets.[34] David M. Holley argues that certain businesses, in fact, often enter into deception when their advertising deliberately attempts to mislead the customer by using distorted information as a basis for customer judgment rather than allowing that judgment to be based on accurate beliefs.[35] He suggests that advertising techniques are unethical if they undermine the possibility of a fair and free exchange between buyer and seller; if a customer is led by deceptive advertising (or a sales technique) to buy a product, he or she purchases that product on a false basis. Deception makes it impossible for the free market to satisfy the consumer's needs because the product is not what the consumer intended to buy when the purchase was made. The responsibility to be truthful in advertising generally resides with the company that initiates and directs the advertising. Certainly, any time the decision on advertising is made internally, the company—through the chief operating officer—is ultimately responsible for the content, accuracy, and truth of the advertisement.

Advertising, then, is one of the most important issues involved in any analysis of ethics and customer relations. As consumers, we all need to be on guard for less-than-truthful as well as outright-deceptive advertising practices. As present or future business executives, we must recognize that the ultimate responsibility to be truthful lies with us.

Ethics and Employee Relations

In addition to the obvious connection between ethics and customer relations, business ethics is also concerned with ethics at work—the ethical concerns that an organization has with its employees. Workers, of course, are indispensable to the organization because they provide the productive and decision-making power of business; in essence, workers *are* the organization. The traditional view of the employer–employee relationship held that the employer provided fair wages and the employee provided a satisfactory job performance. This model also held that either side could terminate the "contract" at any time. In the past three decades, a different view of this relationship has emerged and a "new contract" now calls for greater rights of protection for the worker.

We have already examined one of the issues that pertains to these rights of protection—whistle-blowing. Here, we examine another of the most important and representative of the concerns of ethics and employee relations—the right to fair and equitable treatment. Employees have bargained, both individually and collectively, for an expansion of their rights in the area of fair and equitable treatment by the organization. Consequently, organizations today are subject to laws governing such issues as discrimination in hiring and firing, health and safety standards, minimum wages, maximum hours, and the use of child labor. Despite these advances, there is still concern that business acts unethically when it comes to worker rights. David Ewing, professor of organizational behavior at Harvard University, believes that ethics is still an important concern in terms of fair and equitable treatment of workers and he observes, "For nearly two centuries, Americans have enjoyed freedom of press, speech, and assembly, due process of law, privacy, freedom of conscience, and other important rights—in their homes, churches, political forums, and social and cultural life. But Americans have not enjoyed these civil liberties in most companies, government agencies, and other organizations where they work. Once a U.S. citizen steps through the plant or office door at 9 A.M., he or she is nearly rightless until 5 P.M., Monday through Friday."[36] Ewing notes that this analysis is a generalization because many corporations do provide these rights, but he also stresses that there is no guarantee that privileges will survive the next change of chief executive officer in any given organization; he concludes that many basic rights, including the right to privacy and the right to a safe and healthful work environment, are actually rare in a large number of business and public organizations.

One of the most important and most current of these rights is the right to freedom from sexual harassment. The 1991 confirmation hearing of Supreme Court Justice Clarence Thomas provided the forum for testimony of his former staffer, Anita Hill, who said that she had been sexually harassed by Thomas while in his employment. The nation's concern about and awareness of sexual harassment was increased significantly by the furor over her testimony and over what was perceived by many as the hostile and insensitive questioning of Hill by members of the Senate Judiciary Committee.

Sexual harassment is defined by the Equal Employment Opportunity Commission (EEOC) as unwelcomed sexual advances, requests for sexual favors, and other verbal or physical conduct of a sexual nature that takes place under any of the following conditions:

1. Submission is made a condition of the person's employment.
2. Submission to or rejection of such conduct is used as a basis for employment decisions affecting the person, or
3. It unreasonably interferes with the person's work performance or creates an intimidating, hostile, or offensive work environment.[37]

Despite this broad definition, or perhaps because of it, men and women seem to define sexual harassment differently. A 1987 study by the U.S. Merit Systems Protection Board, a federal agency, found that 90 percent of women considered letters and telephone calls of a sexual nature from a supervisor to be sexual harassment but only 76 percent of the men surveyed considered such behavior to be harassment; in the same study, 81 percent of women considered suggestive looks from supervisors to be a form of sexual harassment but only 68 percent of the men believed this constituted harassment.[38] In addition, a survey of 1,200 people conducted by Barbara Gutek found that 67 percent of the men would feel flattered if a colleague of the opposite sex propositioned them, and 63 percent of the women would be offended.[39]

Besides not fully understanding the definition of sexual harassment, many people also still believe that sexual harassment only applies to women. Although it is very true that women are harassed far more often than their male counterparts, it should be made clear that anyone can be sexually harassed and that EEOC guidelines apply to everyone. That was the conclusion of *The Wall Street Journal* which observed that sexual harassment also includes "gay workers harassing others, women harassing men, and subordinates harassing managers."[40]

Unfortunately, sexual harassment is not uncommon in American business. The U.S. Merit Systems Protection Board study found that offensive conduct took the forms of unwanted sexual remarks (cited by 35 percent of women), suggestive looks (28 percent), touching (26 percent), pressure for dates (15 percent), unwanted love letters and telephone calls (12 percent), pressure for sexual favors (6 percent), and actual or attempted rape or assault (1 percent). Men generally suffered the same kinds of harassment, but the incidence was about one-third that of women. Men were also far less apt to talk about it or report it to supervisors.[41]

It should be noted that this survey was conducted four years before the Clarence Thomas Supreme Court confirmation hearings, and harassment charges have climbed steadily since 1988, especially since the hearings. In 1988, for instance, there were approximately 5,000 sexual harassment complaints filed through the EEOC, but by 1992 the number of complaints had doubled to nearly 10,000.[42] A recent study conducted by the National Association for Female Executives (NAFE) found that 50 percent said they have experienced sexual harassment—up seven percentage points from a poll taken immediately after the Thomas confirmation hearings.[43]

The physical, mental, and emotional results of sexual harassment are significant. Carolyn C. Dolecheck and Maynard M. Dolecheck conclude that victims generally suffer from feelings of anger, embarrassment, and helplessness.[44] Other studies indicate that the occupational results for many victims include lowered productivity on the job, greater absenteeism, and even resignations from their positions.[45]

Fortunately, there are ways for organizations to help reduce sexual harassment on the job. Business has been slow to respond to the problem, but many companies have now recognized that they have a critical role to play in the reduction of harassment. They better understand, for example, the concept of "hostile workplace" harassment. *Hostile workplace harassment* refers to any corporate atmosphere that would offend a reasonable person, and this atmosphere is actually much more common than overt harassment actions. Businesses also now understand that they have a financial incentive to help reduce harassment as well. The passage of the Civil Rights Act of 1991 means that victims of sexual harassment can receive punitive and compensatory damages. Attorney Susan M. Benton-Powers clarified the issue by observing, "The (Thomas) hearings made them concerned about the issue. The act raised the concern of the bottom line."[46]

Organizations have also initiated corporate training programs, many of which use role-playing techniques to sensitize employees about harassment. For example, 65,000 of Du Pont's work force have taken a four-hour workshop titled "A Matter of Respect."[47] Other corporations, such as IBM, Conoco, and Knight-Ridder, as well as many colleges and universities, provide similar learning experiences.

Finally, many companies are reevaluating their complaint systems. In the NAFE survey, 46 percent of the women whose companies had taken steps to end harassment since the Thomas hearings said their employers had established a grievance procedure. Many of these new policies call for an independent person within the company, usually a female, to investigate complaints. Palmer and Dodge, a 360-person law firm in Boston, created an ombudsperson to counsel victims and allows employees to file a complaint through an impartial mediator.[48]

Freedom from sexual harassment, then, is an important example of the right to fair and equitable treatment in the work place. Organizations are in the process of understanding that, although sexual harassment may be impossible to eliminate, they can take steps to assure that it is not tolerated when it does take place.

▶ ESTABLISHING ORGANIZATIONAL ETHICS

Although the individual is paramount in terms of ultimately being ethical in business, it is necessary for our organizations to set ethical standards for themselves as a whole. With this in mind, organizations must develop methods for establishing organizational ethics within the corporation. We examine three such procedures: management behaviors, mission statements, and codes of ethics.

Management Behaviors

Management behaviors are critical to the success of any company's program of organizational ethics. If ethics doesn't begin at the front line of management, the chances are that it won't begin at all. Employees must see their managers both promoting ethics and behaving ethically before they will ever feel the necessity to follow suit.

Maynard M. Dolecheck suggests a four-step method for managers to improve ethical behavior in their organizations.[49] First, managers must continually stress ethical behavior. Simply establishing guidelines will not be effective; managers must present the impression that ethical behavior is a part of everyday behavior in the workplace. In part, this is accomplished by talking about ethical concerns, referring to ethical dilemmas, and emphasizing the importance of ethics in everyday business situations. Second, managers must develop realistic goals for their organizations. Goals that are unreachable because of perceived difficulty or because of a lack of resources are likely never to be realized. Especially in the beginning, goals must appear to be plausible to workers; if goals seem unreasonable, employees may not make any effort to accomplish them. Third, managers need to fully discuss the specific areas of work that are most vulnerable to unethical behavior. Discussing potential problem areas with workers is an educational way of heading off problems before they begin. When employees understand both ethical concerns and proper behaviors, they know how management wishes them to act. Fourth, managers must encourage the reporting of unethical activity. This is both the most difficult and the most important step of the method. Unless whistle-blowing is demonstrated to be encouraged, many workers will not participate in the reporting of unethical behavior for fear of retaliation. Managers must constantly show, by their attitudes and their behaviors, that all unethical activities should be reported and acted upon.

Mission Statements and Codes of Ethics

Mission statements and codes of ethics are ways in which organizations can formalize their ethical intent. Specifically, a *mission statement* is a declaration of the means by which an organization is to fulfill its purpose; a *code of ethics* is a published collection of values which is used to guide behavior. These formal statements can range from a brief paragraph to pages in length and represent management's belief that ethical behavior is in the company's long-range best interest. These statements are very common today—most organizations have mission statements and over two-thirds of the major U.S. corporations have codes of ethics.[50]

The *Harvard Business Review* concluded that codes of ethics need to demonstrate at least three features.[51] First, codes should be consistent in both their actual provisions and their overtones. It is important that the code make the same statement in its words and in the meaning the employees will read; an ambiguous statement will confuse the workers and lead to a code that is not likely to be followed. Second, codes should provide both positive and negative guidance. These statements should be as explanatory as possible, and telling all employees what to do as well as what to avoid will better guarantee that they understand the meaning of the code. Third, codes should create a sense of responsibility, not just of caution. If possible, codes of ethics need to indicate what the responsible employee should do in terms of the specific ethical consideration. Cautionary statements tend to be read as indicating that the company isn't fully committed to the particular issue.

▶ NEW MORAL IMPERATIVE FOR BUSINESS

Throughout this chapter, we have seen that ethical and moral issues pervade both society and business. The fact that the society in which we live and the businesses in which we work are intertwined in this way should come as no surprise to anyone. Business, in fact, is a social activity and would not function properly without a set of ethical and moral laws in operation.

There is now a new moral imperative for business. In the past, society demanded little of our organizations when it came to being morally and socially responsible. It was just assumed that it was enough for business to accept an economic responsibility to stockholders and consumers as its primary societal charge. But times have clearly changed, and now the American public is demanding that business assume more of a socially responsible role in our society. The "stakeholders" of our organizations now include not only the shareholders but also the consumers, employees, and general public as well. Richard T. DeGeorge explains his vision of the new moral imperative by observing, "What is clear in the new mandate is that business must now consider the worker, consumer, and the general public as well as the shareholder—and the views and demands of all four—in making decisions. The good of all must be considered. The key to responding positively to this moral requirement is to develop a mechanism for assuming moral responsibility. Business must find structures for doing so."[52]

One way business can continue the process of developing this new moral imperative is to establish a set of principles by which to judge high-ethics organizations. In this way, a framework can be established to educate those companies in need of education, and a model can be created by which to judge all corporations. One such model was developed by Mark Pastin in his study of what he terms "high-profit, high-ethics companies," those organizations that return a high profit to shareholders and do so in a highly ethical corporate atmosphere.[53] The firms studied included Cadbury Schweppes, 3M, Arco, Motorola, Hilby Wilson, Northern Chemical Company, Interwestern Management, and Apple Computer, as well as some smaller companies, several public organizations including a governor's office and a mayor's office, and several semipublic organizations including chambers of commerce and industry associations. The principles generated by the study were the following:

> *Principle 1:* High-ethics firms are at ease interacting with diverse internal and external stakeholder groups. The ground rules of these firms make the good of the stakeholder groups part of the firm's own good.

This principle observes that the high-ethics organization knows that its success depends on many stakeholder groups not ordinarily encompassed in business thinking. It suggests that businesses look at the true stakeholders in the firm and ask whether the firm has any real idea of how its actions look in their eyes. For example, Diesel Engines recognized that clean air was a priority for many of its stakeholder groups and, then adopted a strategy to clean the air and enhance its competitive position at the same time.

> *Principle 2:* High-ethics firms are obsessed with fairness. Their ground rules emphasize that the other person's interests count as much as their own.

The second principle of the study indicates that these organizations waste so little time and energy managing conflict that they appear to be undermanaged. They are able to do this because conflicts are rare where employees feel they are being treated fairly. Hilby Wilson, a land syndication company, succeeds with this attitude. It offers no deal that it would not invest in as an outsider. Its ground rules emphasize putting its own interests on the line before asking anyone else to do so.

> *Principle 3:* In high-ethics firms, responsibility is individual rather than collective, with individuals assuming personal responsibility for actions of the firm. These firms' ground rules mandate that individuals are responsible to themselves.

Principle 3 was the most surprising of the study. Instead of finding that high-ethics firms placed an emphasis on collective responsibility, the study found that the emphasis was placed on the individual worker. High-ethics firms engendered an attitude among their employees that said, "If it happens here, I did it." Jaguar PLC was one of the companies studied that emphasized this individualistic attitude. Two typical comments came from a line worker at Jaguar who said, "I am the emblem man; every emblem you see on a Jaguar is mine." and "That door is crooked; I don't know how that got by me."

> *Principle 4:* The high-ethics firm sees its activities in terms of a purpose. This purpose is a way of operating that members of the firm value. And purpose ties the firm to its environment.

This principle states that the thing that holds high-ethics firms together is purpose, not goals which are future-oriented. The study found that goal-oriented firms don't function as well as purpose-oriented firms which invite members of the firm to see their activities as valuable in themselves and to the world at large. Principle 4 sug-

▶ CAN ETHICS BE TAUGHT? HARVARD GIVES IT THE OLD COLLEGE TRY

By John A. Bryne

A magnificent gift, it raised eyebrows and prompted envy around the world: a $20 million pledge by former Securities & Exchange Commission Chairman John Shad to Harvard Business School to advance the cause of ethics. Along with $10 million from fellow alums, the March, 1987, pledge generated as much controversy as interest.

Some rival deans argued that the subject couldn't be taught in the classroom. Several of Harvard's own professors thought it a nondiscipline, and administrators came to view the pledge as a mixed blessing.

For Thomas R. Piper, a senior associate dean chosen to lead the initiative, the episode has even brought on sleepless nights. "I sometimes woke up at two or three in the morning and said: 'Boy, I wish we didn't get that gift.' We got the gift at a time when we didn't know what in the world to do about ethics. People were expecting an answer, and we didn't have it."

Five years and more than $5 million later, Harvard is still debating the question—and is still taking it on the chin. "What they are offering is a politically correct, cram-down program," says Mark Pastin, director of the Lincoln Center for Ethics in Tempe, AZ. Adds consultant Barbara Ley Toffler, a former Harvard ethics teacher: "They haven't done anything new or innovative."

It doesn't help that the most visible reminder of Shad's gift is the B-school's huge $18 million physical-fitness center named for him. Although none of Shad's pledge went toward the building, it is larger than most B-schools and just across the street from the greater university's athletic complex.

What has changed is the school's commitment. Harvard has recruited a core of four ethics teachers, added courses, and beefed up its research on the topic. Before 1988, it was possible to get a Harvard MBA without any explicit instruction in ethics. The admissions department requires all applicants to write an essay on an ethical dilemma.

Those who gain admission now find that their first class is in a nine-session nongraded "module" dubbed Decision Making & Ethical Values and taught by some of Harvard's most seasoned professors. The school expects to add yet another module in the second year in 1993. It's also a new world for professors who teach traditional business courses. Encouraged by the school, they're integrating ethics into both their classes and research. In the past three years, Harvard has produced 35 case studies in ethics, 15 of which have been written by professors in such fields as accounting and marketing.

Thus far, the student reaction is mixed. "I can't say that I've seen anything significant," says one first-year student about Harvard's attempt to integrate ethics into other courses. "More environmental issues have been introduced into the core courses than ethics." Even those who applaud adding the new module to the curriculum doubt it can alter the values of students. "You can't impart ethics on a student with nine classes," says Christian Johnson, a first-year student at Harvard. "But it was valuable to compare our own sense of ethics with others." Some 150 students are now taking an elective called Moral Dilemmas of Management, up from 100 last year and only 50 two years ago. Nearly 30% of the 806 members of Harvard's class of 1992 have enrolled in one of three key ethics electives.

Yet some critics believe ethics should be treated like any other mainstream subject, with a full-semester, graded course—an approach taken by the University of Virginia's business school. Harvard scoffs at the criticism. "We're not converting sinners," says Piper, "but we're taking young people who have a sense of integrity and trying to get them to connect ethics with business decisions." As for Shad, who has given $5 million and set up a trust fund to cover the remaining $15 million of his pledge, he says he's "very impressed. It's not just a PR program."

The B-school is considering adding a fourth elective in ethics, doing more research on how the issue affects international competition, launching an ethics program for executives, and sponsoring collaborative efforts with other business schools. As long as ethics remains such a hot topic, Piper is likely to endure a few more sleepless nights over it.

Source: John A. Bryne, "Can Ethics Be Taught? Harvard Gives It the Old College Try," *Business Week* (April 6, 1992): 34. Reprinted by special permission. Copyright © 1992 by McGraw-Hill, Inc.

gests that organizations take an honest look at the issue of how many members of the firm view themselves as engaged in work that truly matters. 3M, for example, has innovation as its purpose for existing. Innovation is not a goal although 3M does have goals which reflect its commitment to innovation.

These principles are embodied by organizations that place a high value on ethics in business. They are not answers to all of the problems faced by today's organizations, but they are an important part of the new moral imperative for business.

► SUMMARY

Ethics is the study of right and wrong and the morality of choices made by people. Two of the most important ethical theories that guide our ethical thinking are the utilitarian approach which states that an action is right if it produces the greatest good for the greatest number of people, and the deontological approach which states that an action is right if it has certain characteristics of goodness. Both of these approaches have certain shortcomings, but they are essential to our study of ethics. Business ethics is the study of how businesses and their employees ought to behave.

Many people believe that business is only interested in maximizing shareholder wealth and making profit, and not at all in ethics. A more realistic viewpoint is that business is responding to the pressures of the media, the government, and the public to act ethically.

It is true that ethical dilemmas exist in business, and it is important that corporate leaders understand them. Whistle-blowing is one such dilemma in today's organizations. It is the attempt by an employee or former employee of an organization to disclose what he or she believes to be wrongdoing in or by the organization. The study of whistle-blowing is important because it calls into conflict one's loyalty to the corporation and one's responsibility to society.

Advertising refers to any paid form of nonpersonal presentation of ideas, goods, or services by an identified sponsor, and is a representative example of the relationship between ethics and customer relations in business. The current practices of advertising raise ethical questions in terms of want creation, truth, and distortion.

Sexual harassment refers to unwelcomed sexual advances, requests for sexual favors, and other verbal or physical conduct of a sexual nature, and it is an important ethical concern in many corporations today. Sexual harassment is common in American business today, and the physical, mental, and emotional results of such harassment are significant. Business is now recognizing the scope of this important ethical issue, and many companies are trying to change their hostile work environments by instituting training programs and reevaluating their complaint systems.

Corporations are beginning to set ethical standards for the organization as a whole. Management behaviors, mission statements, and codes of ethics are important ways in which organizations can create these standards.

The new moral imperative observes that organizations must assume more of a socially responsible role. One way in which business can establish this imperative is by creating a set of principles by which to judge high-ethics organizations.

► QUESTIONS FOR DISCUSSION AND SKILL DEVELOPMENT

1. What are the differences between the utilitarian approach and the deontological approach to ethical theory?
2. How is ethical behavior actually good for business?
3. What is whistle-blowing? In what way does the whistle-blower face an ethical dilemma?
4. In what ways and under what circumstances can advertising be considered unethical?
5. How can organizations help reduce sexual harassment in the workplace?
6. What can managers do to improve ethical behavior at work?
7. Are mission statements and codes of ethics effective in improving business ethics?
8. What is the new moral imperative for business?

1. "Raw Data: Significa, Insignifica, Stats, and Facts," *Playboy* (April, 1993): 4.
2. Constance E. Bagley, *Managers and the Legal Environment: Strategies for the 21st Century* (St. Paul, MN: West Publishing, 1991): 1.
3. W. Steve Albrecht, *Ethical Issues in the Practice of Accounting* (Cincinnati, OH: South-Western Publishing, 1992): 170.
4. Ibid.
5. Bagley, *Managers and the Legal Environment*.
6. Robert C. Soloman and Kristine Hanson, *It's a Good Business* (New York: Harper and Row, 1985): 5.
7. Al H. Ringleb, Roger E. Meiners, and Frances L. Edwards, *Managing in the Legal Environment*, 2nd ed. (St. Paul, MN: West Publishing Company, 1993).
8. W. Michael Hoffman and Jennifer Mills Moore, *Business Ethics: Readings and Cases in Corporate Morality*, 2nd ed. (New York: McGraw-Hill, 1990).
9. William H. Cunningham, Ramon J. Aldag, and Christopher M. Swift, *Introduction to Business*, 2nd ed. (Cincinnati, OH: South-Western Publishing Company, 1989): 584.
10. Alden G. Lank, "The Ethical Criterion in Business Decision Making: Optional or Imperative," in: Touche Ross and Co., *Ethics in American Business: A Special Report* (New York: Touche Ross, 1988): 48.
11. Bowen H. McCoy, "Applying the Art of Action-Oriented Decision Making to the Knotty Issues of Everyday Business Life," *Management Review* (July 1983): 20–21.
12. Richard T. DeGeorge, *Business Ethics*, 2nd ed. (New York: Macmillan, 1986): 9.
13. Lank, "Ethical Criterion."
14. Bryan Dumaine, "Leaders of the Most Admired: Corporate Citizenship," *Fortune* (January 29, 1990): 54.
15. Lank, "Ethical Criterion."
16. Touche Ross, *Ethics in American Business*, 48.
17. "A Nation of Liars?" *U.S. News & World Report* (February 23, 1987): 54–61.
18. Samuel C. Certo, Max E. Douglas, and Stewart W. Husted, *Business*, 2nd ed. (Dubuque, IA: Wm. C. Brown, 1987): 68–69.
19. Milton Friedman, *New York Times Magazine* (September 13, 1970).
20. Kenneth Labich, "The New Crisis in Business Ethics," *Fortune* (April 20, 1992): 168.
21. Roy M. Berko, Andrew D. Wolvin, and Ray Curtis, *This Business of Communicating*, 5th ed. (Madison, WI: Brown and Benchmark, 1993): 195.
22. Gene James, "In Defense of Whistle Blowing," in: Hoffman and Moore, *Business Ethics*, 332–333.
23. William M. Pride, Robert J. Hughes, and Jack R. Kapoor, *Business*, 2nd ed. (Boston: Houghton Mifflin, 1988).
24. "Engineers' Duty to Speak Out," *The Nation* (June 28, 1986): 880.
25. DeGeorge, *Business Ethics*.
26. Cunningham, Aldag, and Swift, *Introduction to Business*.
27. Alan F. Westin, *Whistle Blowing!* (New York: McGraw-Hill, 1981).
28. Gene James, "Whistle Blowing: Its Moral Justification," in: Hoffman and Moore, *Business Ethics*.
29. Martin H. Marlin, "Protecting the Whistleblower from Retaliatory Discharge," *University of Michigan Journal of Law Reform* 16 (Winter 1983).
30. James, "Whistle Blowing," 340–342.
31. Philip Kotler, "What Consumerism Means for Marketers," *Harvard Business Review* (May/June 1972): 48–57.
32. Certo, Douglas, and Husted, *Business*, 328.
33. John Kenneth Galbraith, *The Affluent Society* (Boston: Houghton Mifflin 1984).
34. Raymond A. Bauer and Stephen A. Greyser, *Advertising in America: The Consumer View* (Boston: Harvard University School of Business and Administration, 1968).
35. David M. Holley, "A Moral Evaluation of Sales Practices," *Business and Professional Ethics Journal* 5 (1987): 3–21.
36. David Ewing, *Freedom Inside the Organization* (New York: E. P. Dutton, 1977).
37. John A. Reinecke, Gary Dessler, and William F. Schoell, *Introduction to Business: A Contemporary View*, 6th ed. (Boston: Allyn and Bacon, 1989): 230.
38. "Dealing with Sexual Harassment," *Fortune* (November 4, 1991): 145.

39. Ibid., 148.
40. "With Problem More Visible, Firms Crack Down on Sexual Harassment," *The Wall Street Journal,* August 8, 1986, 12.
41. "Dealing with Sexual Harassment," 145.
42. "Getting Serious about Sexual Harassment," *Fortune* (November 9, 1992): 82.
43. Ibid.
44. Carolyn C. Dolecheck and Maynard M. Dolecheck, "Sexual Harassment: A Problem for Small Businesses," *American Journal of Small Business* 7 (1983): 45–50.
45. James Renick, "Sexual Harassment at Work: Why It Happens, What to Do About It," *Personnel Journal* (August 1980): 658–662.
46. "Getting Serious About Sexual Harassment," 78.
47. "Dealing with Sexual Harassment."
48. "Getting Serious About Sexual Harassment," 82.
49. Maynard M. Dolecheck, "Doing Justice to Ethics," *Supervisory Management* (July 10, 1989): 35–39.
50. Hoffman and Moore, *Business Ethics.*
51. Spiro, *Legal Environment of Business.*
52. DeGeorge, *Business Ethics,* 410.
53. Mark Pastin, "Lessons from High-Profit, High-Ethics Companies: An Agenda for Managerial Action," *The Hard Problems of Management: Gaining the Ethics Edge* (San Francisco: Jossey-Bass, 1986).

Epilogue

We have approached the study of business and professional communication in the spirit of a search—hopefully, a deeply personal and rewarding search—for ways to examine and understand various modes of communicating experiences within the context of the modern organization.

"One way to understand communication," writes Jack Gibb, "is to view it as a people process rather than as a language process."[1] And certainly, this is implied in the term "communication," which comes from the Latin root that means common or commonness or to establish a community. It is clear that the term suggests sharing, a meeting of minds—in short, understanding. Communication is a two-way street; messages are sent and received, producing a dynamic rather than a static climate. We communicate not only with spoken and written language, but also with a wide variety of actions, smiles, frowns, gestures, nods, and handshakes as well as shrugs, embraces, pushes, and blows. Nonverbal elements are indeed a significant part of this social process of communication. "Effective" communication implies that an understanding is established, that the message elicits in the receiver the response desired by the sender.

There is much to recommend the study of communication, and particularly communication within organizations. For all of us, a large part of our lives will be spent in organizations, and much of this time will be spent communicating with others. So, being aware of basic principles, organizational theories, the structure of organizations, and the way messages flow and communication impinges upon the organization is important. Equally important is an understanding of the types of communication evidenced in organizations—listening, interpersonal communication, interviewing, group communication, and public communication. These are the communication practices most frequently used in organizations and they largely govern the functioning of organizations.

In the course of this class you have become acquainted with the many variables affecting the communication process and operating within organizations. The text and classroom exercises have exposed you to various modes of communication and

▶ RULES OF THE GAME

1. The game never stops.
2. Players never know all the rules.
3. The game has no referees.
4. The game is tough and hard.
5. All players make mistakes.
6. Choosing not to play is not a superior moral position.
7. You always have choices.
8. You are totally responsible for your performance.
9. Average performance will yield low rewards.
10. Whining does not impress players or change the game.
11. Ignorance, poverty and lack of education must be overcome to be an effective player.
12. You always improve your performance with self discipline, education, and sound decision making.

we hope they've taken you a few steps toward greater effectiveness. Now the task is yours—to work on a personal program to make your communication more viable and purposeful. Good luck.

1. Jack R. Gibb, "Defensive Communication," *Journal of Communication* 11 (1961): 141.

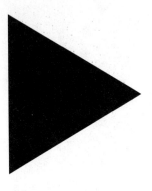

Appendix A: Business Writing

A merican businesses daily generate numerous letters, memos, and reports that are often produced in duplicate and triplicate. Our information society regularly confronts us with millions of bits of information. Magazines, radio, lectures, books, newspapers, television, billboards, conferences, speeches, telephone calls, computers, and more are all bombarding us and acting to inhibit our ability to comprehend. Journalist Edwin Newman expresses the problem well:

> Much written and spoken expression these days is equivalent to the background music that incessantly encroaches on us. . . . it thumps and tinkles away, mechanical without color, inflection, vigor, charm, or distinction. People who work in the presence of background music often tell you, and sometimes with pride, that they don't hear it anymore. The parallel with language is alarming.
>
> Language, then, sets the tone of our society. Since we must speak and read, and spend much of our lives doing so, it seems sensible to get some pleasure and inspiration from these activities. The wisecrack is a wonderful thing, and the colorful phrase, and the flight of fancy. So is the accurate description of a place or an event, and so is the precise formulation of an idea. They brighten the world.[1]

So, if you want your message to penetrate this exploding mass of communication you must be prepared and trained to meet the challenge. Here our concern will be limited to written communication, its importance, dimensions, and basic principles.

▶ IMPORTANCE OF EFFECTIVE WRITTEN COMMUNICATION

Effective written communication in business is necessary for a number of financial, legal, and other practical reasons. When dealing with a supplier or with a customer, the company executive may need to review previous transactions. Without records of prior business dealings, the executive must depend upon his or her memory of the supplier's capabilities or of the customer's needs. When dealing with superiors or subordinates, the executive must remember instructions he or she has given or received. If instructions have not been recorded, the business person must recall the boss's directions and the staff member's duties. Obviously, any executive cannot be expected to remember the details of every company account, conference, or conversation. A spoken message is easily forgotten, but a written message is tangible and acts as a reminder of its very content.

Equally important, every communique sent generates a variety of meanings and impressions. Written messages create impressions about you, the company or organization, the product or service, and your attitude(s) toward the receiver. The nature of these impressions, generated meanings, can significantly affect external and internal relationships and, consequently, the entire operation of the organization.

Finally, the cost of written communication must be considered. An organization spends money on every single piece of written communication sent by any member of that organization. Every letter, memo, or reports costs, in terms of time, paper, and postage to name but a few expenses. Estimates of the cost of a single letter range from less than 5 to more than 12 dollars.[2] So, when you consider that companies may send hundreds of letters each day, the expense involved is truly significant. Effective use of this costly medium, then, is directly related to a company's profitability. Effective letters, memos, and reports reduce the total number of messages needed to communicate and thus directly contribute to greater efficiency.

►DIMENSIONS OF WRITTEN COMMUNICATION

Written, like spoken, communication fundamentally elicits a reaction from a receiver. In the business world, written communication is carried on through letters, memoranda, reports, standardized forms, posters, and company newsletters. There are also company handbooks, guides, and manuals outlining policy. All of these share a few significant characteristics.

Written communication is either direct or indirect; this is to say that it is either aimed at a specific person or persons, or prepared for a broad and often nonspecific audience. A letter or memo, for instance, is written with a specific reader, but a company report or newsletter may be released to the general public.

Another characteristic is that business communication is functional. Business letters are written to initiate or maintain communication with people or groups outside the organization; they give information to, or seek information from, established or potential clients and suppliers. Memoranda carry messages of an instructional nature. The business report is concerned with objectively describing facts and ideas. Its function is limited to transmitting data. All written forms of communication within the business milieu are designed to perform a particular function.

Finally, business writing may be intended for either an internal or external audience. Internal communication is that which is directed to individuals within the organization. It flows along those formal channels that distinguish the hierarchical structure of the organization. External communication is that directed to people outside the organization. The memo is an example of the former; the business letter is an example of the latter.

▶ PRINCIPLES OF BUSINESS WRITING

Communication occurs when an idea is transferred from one person to another. Communication efficiency is the degree to which the idea received matches the idea sent; the greater the agreement, the greater the efficiency. In face-to-face interaction, ideas can be transferred through verbal and nonverbal cues; in written communication the receiver has access to few of the sender's nonverbal messages so the greatest amount of idea transfer is accomplished through the use of language.

Of course written communication consists of words, but writing is more than just words. To put it another way, the meanings derived by the reader from a letter or memo come not only from the words but from other sources as well. For any word to have meaning, the sender and receiver must agree on the idea represented by that word. A word is communicatively efficient when both writer and reader assign to it the same or similar meaning. Well-chosen words are frequently concrete; they produce specific images in the readers mind. Inappropriate words are frequently more general; they express vague images or images not likely to resemble the intended meaning. Abstract words have meanings, but their meanings are numerous, obscure, and difficult to express.

Unusual or abstract words are likely to be communicatively inefficient. To the sender, a word might have a very specific reference, but if the word is unknown to the reader, he or she may assign to it a meaning quite different from that intended by the writer. The original message then becomes distorted, and the receiver responds to the distorted rather than the intended meaning. If you want to communicate with others, you must use symbols understood by others.

Businesses are formally structured, and business relationships are affected by this formality. Business writers seem to believe that "businesslike" is synonymous with "formal," and that "formal" means "stuffy." These writers reason that a business letter must be written in a formal style. To achieve this formal style, the writer feels compelled to use elaborate sentence structure, multisyllabic words, and cryptic terminology. Hence, business chirographers are too frequently verbose, sesquipedelian, pretentious, and incomprehensible (that is, business writers are often wordy, given to using long words, stuffy, and hard to understand).

Unfamiliar, wordy language has been called "doublespeak," "officialese" or "bureaucratese." When used by business and professional people, the language is called "gobbledygook." By any label, it can obscure even the simplest of ideas.

Doublespeak is language that pretends to communicate but really doesn't. It's not a matter of subjects and verbs agreeing; it's a matter of words and facts agreeing. Basic to doublespeak is incongruity: "the incongruity between the word and referent, between seem and be, between the essential function of language—communication—and what doublespeak does—mislead, distort, deceive, inflate, circumvent, obfuscate."[3] William Lutz, chair of the Committee on Public Doublespeak of the National Council of Teachers of English, identifies four kinds of doublespeak. The first is the euphemism used to avoid a harsh, unpleasant, or distasteful reality. A second kind of doublespeak is jargon, the specialized language of a trade, profession, or similar group. A third kind is the bureaucratese used by many people in government. The fourth kind of doublespeak is inflated language designed to make the ordinary seem extraordinary; to make everyday things seem impressive; to give an air of importance to people, situations, or things that would not normally be considered important; to make the simple seem complex. This is why there are no potholes in the streets of Tucson, just "pavement deficiencies." There are no bums, just "nongoal-oriented members of society," and no poor people, just "fiscal underachievers."[4]

One study of government writing revealed a number of common faults in government reports. The discovered faults are also commonly found in business writing and include the following:

▶ *Sentences are too long.* The average sentence length in poor government writing exceeds 65 words per sentence. Average sentence length in good government writing is from 15 to 18 words per sentence.

▶ *There are too many modifications and conditional clauses and phrases.* Such hedging causes suspension of judgment as to the outcome of the sentence, and therefore increases reading difficulty.

▶ *Writers overuse parts of the verb "to be."* They also use too many weak verbs such as "point out," "indicate," or "reveal."

▶ *Repetitious writing is common.* Too many sentences begin the same way, especially with "The."

▶ *Writers make every effort to be impersonal and detached.* An attempt to be impersonal results in too many passive and indirect phrases.

▶ *There is an overabundance of abstract nouns.* Examples of this fault include the overuse of "data," "basis," and "case" which cannot be visualized.

▶ *There is an excess of prepositional phrases.* Samples of government writing show that many officials use at least one prepositional phrase to every four words. Samples from good writing contain only one prepositional phrase to every eleven words.

▶ *Samples indicate an overuse of expletives.* Expletives such as "It is" and "there are" are used too often.

- ▶ *Technical jargon is used rather than plain English.* Technical jargon is used too often when trying to reach a non-technical audience.
- ▶ *The focus is on ideas.* There is a tendency to make ideas the heroes of sentences despite the fact that people find it easier to think in terms of people and things.[5]

The incomprehensible manner in which many government bureaucrats, lawyers, and legislators write has made it increasingly more difficult for intelligent, well-educated people to conduct their daily business. Making a major purchase, filling out government forms such as an Internal Revenue Service income tax report, buying insurance, taking out a loan, making travel arrangements, and so forth, have become frustrating exercises in trying to wrestle with contorted, convoluted, and meaningless English. It took an official act of the president of the United States to curb the pens that had been so busy for so long making our laws and contracts all but impossible to understand. On March 23, 1978, President Jimmy Carter implemented the Plain English movement when he signed Executive Order #12044. It requires that all federal regulations be "written in plain English and understandable to those who must comply with it." This same law has caused businesses to begin to write in plain English and legal contracts are even being written in plain English (requiring some lawyers to go back to school to learn how to write plain English).

Why do we need a federal law requiring the use of simple, understandable English? Consider the following regulation:

> Any holder of this consumer credit contract is subject to all claims and defenses which the debtor could assert against the seller of goods or services obtained pursuant hereto or with the proceeds hereof. Recovery hereunder by the debtor shall not exceed amounts paid by the debtor hereunder.

This is the Federal Trade Commission's "Holder In Due Course" rule, a landmark regulation that took effect in May 1976. Do you understand it? If not, you join millions of other consumers who do not know that when they purchase a defective item on credit they do not have to pay the company which granted them credit. The widespread ignorance of this regulation exists despite the fact that it appears in capital letters on all consumer credit contracts.

Rudolf Flesch, a widely known authority on business writing, presents three basic rules for clear writing:

1. Use nothing but plain English. Writers must be constantly on their guard if they are to successfully adopt a clear, concise, and simple style of writing.
2. Know your reader. Every writer should know who his or her reader is, what the reader wants, and how capable the reader is.
3. Use the right tone. When a government agency is trying to "talk" to an individual, an informal, conversational tone is far more effective. Business writers have more to lose than government writers do when their tone is inappropriate. As citizens, we can take our business elsewhere. In the marketplace the confused business reader can turn to another organization to meet his or her needs.[6]

Do these principles actually work in practice? Consider the following example concerning a Federal Trade Commission case in which a supermarket was supposedly not honoring its advertised sale prices. The supermarket agreed to have a poster displayed in its store to advise the shopper of the store's policy. The copy for the poster, written by FTC and supermarket lawyers, read:

> All items advertised are required by law to be sold at prices no higher than the advertised prices in each Plazamart [not the real name] store, except as specifically noted in this ad. If you have any questions, the store manager will be glad to assist you.
>
> In order to avoid overcharging that might result from incorrect price marking, Plazamart asks each of its customers to inspect the price marked on each item he or she selects to insure that such price is correct, and report instances of merchandise being marked with an incorrect price to store personnel. Plazamart is legally obligated to make available any advertised item at the advertised price during the applicable advertised sale periods regardless of the price marked on any unit of the advertised item. (In the case of coupon offers you must, of course, present the appropriate coupon, or make the minimum purchase in order to receive the advertised price.)
>
> If any checker, when confronted by you with the fact that he is about to ring up, or has rung up, an advertised item at a price higher than the advertised price, refuses to correct the error immediately or to ring up the item at the advertised price, the customer is requested to report the incident to the store manager.

If you were a lawyer or an unhurried shopper who could spend many minutes reading a sign while shopping in a supermarket, this poster might be acceptable. Most people, however, would have had considerable difficulty understanding it in the unlikely event that they had taken the time to decipher it.

When the project was finally placed in the hands of a communicator who writes in plain English, the poster which finally appeared in the supermarket chain read:

To Our Customers

Please check the price of each advertised item you buy against the price in our ad.
If it's more, ask the checker to charge only the price in the ad.
If there's any problem, please let me know. Thank you.
The Manager

This poster, which the FTC commissioned Rudolf Flesch to write, illustrates his three principles of clear writing.[7]

▶ STEPS TO BETTER WRITING

You should regard your writing as a challenge that you'll meet through skill, determination, training, and practice. In *The Elements of Style,* William Strunk, Jr. and E. B. White present a number of suggestions for better writing.[8] Although Strunk and White are primarily addressing literary writing, their advice is equally appropriate for the business writer:

▶ *Place yourself in the background.* This means the message must have a "you" rather than a "me" focus. Concern yourself with your reader's needs, not your own. If you are to hold your reader's attention and cause him or her to do or think what you would like, it is his or her perception of reality which you must address. You must write with an emphasis on your reader and his or her point of view. If you put yourself in your reader's position, you can react to your message as he or she might.

- *Write in a way that comes naturally.* Don't try to write in someone else's style. Communication should fit the writer whether it be a letter, memo, or report.
- *Work from a suitable design.* You should develop a clear, logical, well-structured scheme. It is difficult to write a cogent exposition when no plan has been developed prior to the actual writing. Even shorter messages require an outline of the basic components of the message.
- *Revise and rewrite.* Revision is difficult and time consuming, but necessary. First drafts are usually incomplete or inadequate in some important phase of writing. Essential points can be inadvertently omitted, and others might be insufficiently developed. Grammar and style often need polishing at the very least. Donald Murray notes that "writing is rewriting. . . . rewriting is the difference between the dilettante and the artist, the amateur and the professional. . . . and yet rewriting is one of the writing skills least researched, least examined, least understood, and—usually—least taught."[9] You should include revision as a normal part of your overall writing strategy and consider it to be an opportunity rather than a burden.
- *Be clear.* Write in a style that lends itself to clarity. Sentence structure, word choice, references, mood, and grammar must contribute to the clarity of the message. Do not hesitate to rework a sentence or change a word or a phrase when you recognize ambiguity or confusing language.

Word choice should reflect the characteristics of familiarity, concreteness and conciseness. Once you have identified your target audience, you must use language that is familiar to those readers, but not trite. And don't try to impress your reader with your knowledge of exotic jargon or by using stilted and artificial phrasing.

Clarity and conciseness limits the number of words used to express an idea clearly. Strunk and White admonish that:

> Vigorous writing is concise. A sentence should contain no unnecessary words, a paragraph no unnecessary sentences, for the same reason that a drawing should have no unnecessary lines and a machine no unnecessary parts. This requires not that the writer make all his sentences short, or that he avoid all detail and treat his subjects only in outline, but that every word tell.[10]

What is being asked is that you not waste time and space with needless words. Many words and phrases commonly used in business writing are unnecessary. Avoid terms like:

- *Allow me to say, Allow me to offer*—Why do you need permission?
- *As per*—Stick to one language. You can use your high school Latin elsewhere. Don't write that you've done something, as per request. If the reader requested something be done he or she will remember the request.
- *As you know*—Unless you're a mindreader, you can't possibly have any idea what the reader knows or does not know.
- *As you may know*—Although this phrase does not assume knowledge or imply stupidity, it is unnecessary because you are going to state it anyway.
- *Attached please find, Enclosed please find*—The word "find" suggests that a search will be necessary. Refer to the attached or enclosed material in a sentence: "The enclosed pamphlet gives step-by-step instructions."
- *Await your reply*—You really have no choice. Time must inevitably pass before you will receive an answer.

- ▶ *Beg to inform*—You shouldn't have to beg. Just inform the reader.
- ▶ *Due to the fact that*—This lengthy phrase can be replaced with "because."
- ▶ *Each and every*—This is redundant since "every" includes "each." Instead of "Each and every one of us agree," say, "We agree."
- ▶ *For your information*—The entire letter, memo, or report is for the reader's information.
- ▶ *In the amount of, For the amount of*—Don't say, "We enclose a check in the amount of." Say, "We enclose a check for." Rather than saying "You owe payment for the amount of," say "You owe."
- ▶ *Subsequent to*—"After" is the same.
- ▶ *Thank you again*—One thank you is enough.[11]

These are just a few of many unnecessary terms or phrases that should be omitted from business writing. The problem, however, is widespread and Edwin Newman keenly places it in perspective when he notes:

> A large part of social scientific practice consists of taking clear ideas and making them opaque. . . .
>
> For a social scientist to make obscure what he considers to be unnecessarily clear calls not so much for an imagination as for an appropriate vocabulary in which boundaries are parameters, parts are components, things are not equal but co-equal, signs are indicators, and causes are dependent or exogenous variables (and it may take a regression analysis to find out which). To know oneself is to have self-awareness, communities being studied are target areas, thinking is conceptualization, patterns are configurations, and people do not speak but articulate or verbalize; nor are they injured; they are traumatized.
>
> Once you've caught on to the technique, it's easy. For example, in the social sciences as in business language, inputs and outputs are everywhere.[12]

Audience analysis is essential to good written communication just as it is to good oral communication. An efficient communicator uses symbols that are familiar to the receiver and are defined similarly by both the receiver and the sender. So, the conscientious communicator is aware of audience gender, social and financial status, professional talents, and education. Other information, such as age, interests, and affiliations, is helpful and should be determined whenever possible.

The writer may be addressing one of two audiences: the extraorganizational audience or the intraorganizational audience. Extraorganizational audiences include clients, suppliers, potential and former employees, charitable groups, and the general public. Intraorganizational audiences include all company employees and anyone else directly involved with the operation of the organization.

Beyond identifying the general nature of the receiver of the message, the business writer must carefully evaluate the specific audience. This can involve determining the characteristics of an individual reader, as in the case of a letter or a memorandum, or it can involve determining the characteristics of a number of receivers, as in the case of a report, a company newsletter, or advertising copy.

The following questions can serve as a useful guide in assessing your audience:

- ▶ *What is the extent of the reader's knowledge?* You need to know how much the reader knows about your subject so that you can determine the level of your approach, how much and what types of illustrative material you will use, how much specialized terminology to use, and the level of complexity of the ideas you discuss. Having information about the educational and technical levels of your reader should help you to determine how much he or she knows. Knowledge of your reader's occupation and experience should also be of considerable help.

▶ *What is the reader's attitude toward you and your subject?* You should anticipate how the reader will react to your message and to you as the source of that message. By taking your reader's attitude into account, you will be able to determine which strategies will be most effective in getting your message across.

▶ *What is the reader's relationship to or position in the organization?* When communicating with people outside the organization, an understanding of their relationship to the organization is imperative. Within the organization, you must consider the reader's position in relation to your own, i.e., authority and power. This awareness helps you determine the strategy for eliciting the most appropriate response.

An excellent way to improve your writing is to study examples of good writing. Examine the techniques used by good writers and identify the elements of their writing that make them effective.

▶FORMS OF WRITTEN COMMUNICATION

The most important forms of business writing are the letter, the memorandum, and the report. These are the types of communication which the typical employee is most likely to use, and together they carry the largest volume of messages written by the business communicator.

The *business letter* is the most commonly used vehicle for external communication. It communicates the writer's intended verbal message plus information about the writer and his or her organization. A letter is closely identified with its author—it offers no anonymity.

The letter writer is writing for a single reader, so the message should be tailored to fit the special characteristics of the reader and the situation. The letter writer should respond to this advantage by writing in a unique and creative manner.

The most frequently used format for the business letter is called the *block* format. In this format all but the heading and signature are placed at the left-hand margin. Paragraphs are not indented in this format; rather, they are identified by double-spacing between paragraphs. The *complete block* format is similar to the block format, but the heading and the signature are also placed at the left-hand margin. This format is not as widely used in business letters but is attractive and is gaining acceptance. Finally, a variation on these two formats is the *modified block* format which is similar to the block but has indented paragraphs.

Regardless of which format you choose, all business letters contain the following standard elements:

1. *The letterhead.* This should identify the name of the company and provide its address, telephone number, and, if international, its cable address. In large companies, the name of the department or division should be included. The increasing use of fax machines would also suggest including your fax number.

2. *The heading.* When using letterhead stationary, this is simply the date of writing. When letterhead stationary is not used, the heading will contain the name of the

company, its address, and the date of writing. When writing as a private individual, just the address and date of writing appear in the heading; the writer's name does not appear.

3. *The inside address.* This includes complete information about the destination of the letter: name of reader, his or her title, position, and/or department, and the complete address. The inside address is not simply a formality; frequently the envelop is disposed of after a letter arrives so the inside address becomes the only record for whom the letter was intended.

4. *The salutation.* This part of the letter greets the reader. Whenever you know the reader's name, include it in your salutation rather than using anonymous forms such as "Dear Sir" or "Dear Madam" or "To Whom It May Concern." The correct punctuation for the salutation is a colon. A comma should be used only in letters to personal friends.

5. *The body.* The ideas discussed in the letter are found in the body. Ideas must be well developed and thoughtfully organized. Single spacing should be used within a paragraph; doublespacing should be used between paragraphs.

6. *The signature.* This element contains the complimentary close, the signature, and the signature identification. There are several acceptable phrases for the complimentary close, including " Sincerely," "Sincerely yours," "Cordially," "Respectfully," and "Best regards." The writer's signature adds a personal touch to the letter, and makes the letter official and legal. The signature identification is a legible version of the writer's name and also indicates the writer's position.

The *memorandum* is used when communicating with someone within the organization. Memos can be sent to individuals, departments, sections, or the entire workforce. Memos are normally used to give information or to request instructions.

Clear language is as important to memo writing as it is to letter writing. It is pointless to give instructions if they can't be understood. The rules of clarity, conciseness, and specificity still hold true, but the memo is typically shorter and more informal than the letter. If follows a standard format, but one less rigid than that of the business letter. A memorandum is headed by the date, the name of the intended reader, the name of the writer, and the topic to be considered. The remainder of the page contains the message. Memos are normally typed or done on a wordprocessor. Memos may be handwritten if the writer and the reader have a close working relationship. A vice president may leave a handwritten memo for his or her secretary but the same vice president would send a typed memo to the shipping and receiving department.

A word of caution: memos are so handy and easy to write that they are often overused. Temporary instructions should be given orally, unless they deal with a special occurrence (holiday hours) or with frequent activity (paying employees on Mondays rather than Fridays for the next five months). Permanent changes in procedures or policies should be recorded on memos to be distributed to all employees.

The *report* contains findings—systematically organized facts, generally drawn from surveys and interviews. Most reports are presented to a limited population within an organization. They may be directed to supervisors, coworkers, or to managers of related departments. Reports usually address one of the following topics:

1. the recent developments in a particular field
2. the cause and/or effects of a phenomenon
3. the feasibility of a project

4. organizational or departmental responsibility
5. a description of a process or a mechanism
6. instructions
7. an investigation of the strengths and/or weaknesses of a proposal
8. the collection and/or summary of information for a supervisor
9. a proposal presented to a superior
10. status or progress on a project[13]

The report differs from the letter and the memo in several important ways. The report is considerably longer and far more detailed; its basic function is informational. The letter and the memo, although they can be informational, often deal with advocacy. The report should offer knowledge to someone who is less informed and who is interested primarily in data pertinent to the subject of the report. The report is generally impersonal in style and frequently the product of a committee rather than a single person. The report does not state a position, but objectively presents collected data needed by the decision makers.

▶ SUMMARY

Effective business writing is the result of careful and intelligent planning. The business writer must carefully consider reader characteristics if efficient communication is to occur. The problems associated with business writing can be eliminated by following these steps in preparing the message: (1) develop the proper attitude for writing, (2) emphasize the reader, (3) write in a natural manner, (4) plan the document fully before the writing begins, (5) follow appropriate formats, (6) revise and rewrite, and (7) write clearly. Businesses have a variety of communication needs. Letters, memos, and reports serve many of these needs. Businesses are also formal in nature, and business messages maintain this formality. Formal writing, however, needn't be unintelligible. To use business jargon, the bottom line is this: business writing may not be eloquent literary prose, but the ability to write clearly, cogently, and to the point is a must.

▶ NOTES

1. Edwin Newman, *Strictly Speaking* (Indianapolis, IN: Bobbs-Merrill, 1974): 17.
2. William H. Bonner, *Better Business Writing* (Homewood, IL: Richard D. Irwin, 1974).
3. William Lutz, *Doublespeak* (New York: Harper Perennial, 1990): 2.
4. Ibid.
5. William Dow Boutwell, "Study of Government Reports," *Congressional Record* 88 (1968): A1468.
6. Rudolf Flesch, *How to Write Plain English* (New York: Harper and Row, 1979): 3.
7. Ibid., 29–31.
8. William Strunk, Jr. and E. B. White, *The Elements of Style* (New York: Macmillan, 1959): 56–65.
9. Donald Murray, "Internal Revision: A Process of Discovery," in: Charles R. Cooper and Lee Odell, eds., *Research on Composing* (Urbana, IL: NCTE, 1978): 85–86.
10. Strunk and White, *Elements of Style*, 17.
11. Robert L. Shurter, J. Peter Williamson, and Wayne G. Broehl, Jr., *Business Research and Report Writing* (New York: McGraw-Hill, 1965): 69–72.
12. Newman, *Strictly Speaking*, 146–147.
13. Vincent DiSalvo, *Business and Professional Communication* (Columbus, OH: Charles E. Merrill, 1977): 132.

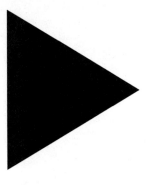

Appendix B: Basics of Parliamentary Procedure

Democracy is our cherished heritage. The use of accepted rules for parliamentary procedure provides the tools to help preserve democracy in all kinds of deliberative assemblies. In an organized society, most arguments are made within deliberative assemblies and decisions are arrived at through prescribed procedures. *Robert's Rules of Order* has become the accepted parliamentary law governing most assemblies. Therefore, knowledge of these rules can make one an active and involved participant. General Henry M. Robert said, "Where there is no law, but every man does what is right in his own eyes, there is the least of real liberty."[1]

Style and rules in meeting procedures have changed to meet the demands of a modern technological society, but the traditional verities of parliamentary procedure still remain as a steadfast framework for effective leadership (see Exhibit B-1 for a partial description of parliamentary motions and their functions).[2] By learning the skills necessary for conducting meetings efficiently, correctly—and with due emphasis on the use of the democratic process in arriving at group decisions—an aspiring leader can better understand the responsibilities consistent with the exercise of leadership and will recognize the need for all members to learn the techniques of human relationships with the group.

▶ ORIGINS AND DEVELOPMENT OF PARLIAMENTARY PROCEDURE

Parliamentary law originally was the name given to the rules and customs for carrying on business in the English Parliament. These rules and customs, as brought to America with the settling of the New World, became the basic substance from which the practice of legislative bodies in the U.S. evolved. Out of early American legislative procedure developed today's rules of order adaptable to the needs and purposes of differing organizations and assemblies.

Thomas Jefferson was the first to define and interpret parliamentary principles for our democratic republic. His 1801 *Manual of Parliamentary Practice* offered a pattern of rules and a measure of uniformity suitable for U.S. legislative processes.

The creation of various political, cultural, scientific, charitable, and religious societies of a nonlegislative nature prompted the need for a more compatible set of procedural principles. The first author who tried to meet the procedural needs of the country's growing number of voluntary societies was Luther S. Cushing. His *Manual of Parliamentary Practice: Rules of Proceedings and Debate in Deliberative Assemblies,* or "Cushing's Manual," was published in 1845 and became an accepted standard. It synthesized earlier efforts and presented a concise, modified body of parliamentary principles adapted for "assemblies of every description, but more especially, for those which are not legislative in their character."

Henry Robert, however, found that considerable confusion still existed regarding material issues of parliamentary practice, so he set out to write a new kind of parliamentary manual "based, in its general principles, upon the rules and practice of Congress, and adapted, in its details to the use of ordinary societies." After considerable time and difficulty in contracting with a publisher, his completed manuscript, titled the *Pocket Manual of Rules of Order for Deliberative Assemblies* (176 pages), was published under the title *Robert's Rules of Order* by S. C. Griggs and Company of Chicago in February 1876. Only a single printing of 4000 copies was made. It met with immediate and enthusiastic acclaim and sold out in only four months. Today, this first edition is considered a rare book. Subsequent editions of *Robert's Rules of Order* expanded and clarified the original parliamentary principles recognized as essential to the operation of the average organization or society. Thus, Robert gave formal direction to a movement toward establishing a more complete common parliamentary law, built upon congressional practice.[3]

Parliamentary procedure is not static and ritualistic but is rather a growing, evolving, constantly developing body of rules that guide the conduct of business. Procedural rules change with changing conditions. The *Sturgis Standard Code of Parliamentary Procedure,* published in 1951, represents a contemporary effort to simplify and modernize the rules of procedure by emphasizing principles rather than technicalities. It is based upon common practice and law and intended for adoption by organizations.[4] Still, the first purpose of parliamentary procedure is to make it easier for people to work together effectively, to aid groups in reaching their goals and carrying out their purposes.

▶ PRINCIPLES AND RULES OF PARLIAMENTARY LAW

> Fundamentally, under the rules of parliamentary law, a deliberative body is a free agent—free to do what it wants to do with the greatest measure of protection to itself and of consideration for the rights of its members.
>
> *Henry M. Robert*

Most of the laws of parliamentary procedure flow naturally from and are a logical application of basic principles. Thus, what appears at first glance to be a technically frustrating exercise in memorizing terminology and rules is actually an example of practically applied reasoning. The leader or member who understands the following principles and applies them thoughtfully will not go far wrong.

Order

Things Must Be Handled One at a Time. This principle means that any organization seeking to make decisions in accordance with parliamentary law will consider one and only one substantive issue at a time. It further means that one and only one mo-

MOTION	PURPOSE	SECOND	DEBATABLE	AMENDABLE	VOTE	INTERRUPTABLE
Principal motions						
Main motion (general)	to introduce business	yes	yes	yes	majority	no
Main motion (specific)						
a. to reconsider	to reconsider previous motion	yes	yes	no	majority	yes
b. to rescind	to nullify previous action	yes	yes	yes	majority or two-thirds	no
c. to take from table	to consider tabled motion	yes	no	no	majority	no
Subsidiary motions						
Lay on the table	to defer action	yes	no	no	majority	no
Call previous question	to stop debate and force vote	yes	no	no	two-thirds	no
Limit/extend debate	to control limit of debate	yes	no	yes	two-thirds	no
Postpone to a certain time	to defer action	yes	yes	yes	majority	no
Refer to committee	to provide for special study	yes	yes	yes	majority	no
Amend	to modify a motion	yes	yes	yes	majority	no
Postpone indefinitely	to suppress action	yes	yes	no	majority	no
Incidental motions						
Rise to point of order	to correct error in procedure	no	no	no	decision by chair	yes
Appeal from decision of chair	to clarify or correct a ruling by the chair	yes	no	no	majority or tie	yes
Suspend rules	to alter existing rules and order of business	yes	no	no	two-thirds	no
Object to consideration	to suppress action on any main motion	no	no	no	two-thirds	yes
Call for division of house	to secure a countable vote from members	no	no	no	majority if chair desires	yes
Close nominations	to stop nomination of officers	yes	no	yes	two-thirds	no
Reopen nominations	to permit additional nominations	yes	no	yes	majority	no
Withdraw a motion	to remove a motion	no	no	no	majority	no
Divide motion	To break down a multipart motion into separate propositions	no	no	yes	majority	no
Request information	to ask for information or make a request for parliamentary inquiry	no	no	no	none	yes
Privileged motions						
Fix time of meeting	to set time of next meeting	yes	no	yes	majority	no
Adjourn	to dismiss meeting	yes	no	yes	majority	no
Take a recess	to dismiss meeting for specific time	yes	no	yes	majority	no
Raise question of privilege	to make a request concerning rights of the assembly	no	no	no	decision of chair	yes
Call for orders of the day	to keep assembly to order of business	no	no	no	none	yes
Special order	to ensure consideration at specified time	yes	yes	yes	two-thirds	no

Source: Henry M. Robert, *Robert's Rules of Order, Newly Revised* (Glenview, IL: Scott, Foresman, 1981).

tion of any type is the immediately pending question and must be disposed of in some way before moving on to the next pending question.

Equality

All Members Have Rqual Rights, Responsibilities, Privileges and Obligations. Parliamentary law, through methods of voting and efforts to equalize opportunities for discussion, acknowledges the equal rights of all members. This principle does not imply that all members have equal abilities, or equal influence, or share equal responsibilities. Indeed, differences do exist among members, but these differences are carefully balanced against a regard for individual rights.

Right of Majority

The Will of the Majority Prevails. Parliamentary law provides the mechanism for finding out what most of the members want to do and then makes their will the policy of the group, for the present. Most organizations in our democratic society make their decisions according to the will of the majority as expressed in a vote at a particular time and place with certain members present and voting. At another time and place, with other members present and voting, the decision might well be different.

Right of Minority

The Rights of the Minority Must Be Protected. The rights of the minority must be protected just as diligently as the rights of those who make up the majority. One of those minority rights is the right to express dissent—to vote against the prevailing side in a counted vote and request that the vote be recorded in the minutes. Equally important is the minority's right to be heard during open debate. In the interest of fairness to all, the majority must be willing to listen to a minority position. Even if only one member dissents, his or her opinions should be permitted a voice and a contrary vote included in the record.

Justice

Meetings Must Be Conducted with Fairness and in Good Faith. The impartiality of the chair is a well-established principle of parliamentary law. The presiding officer must be able to put aside partisan personal beliefs and equally recognize during debate both those who favor and those who oppose a point of view. Equally important, if members are not conversant with parliamentary language, the meaning of a given motion and its effect should be explained clearly by the chair. Parliamentary law is not intended to favor, deceive, or mislead through technical trickery, but rather to ensure understanding and guarantee fairness.[5]

▶ GLOSSARY OF TERMS[6]

Abstain: to refrain from voting
Ad hoc: for this purpose only
Adjourned meeting: continuance of the same meeting held before the next regular meeting

Agenda: details of business listed under the order of business

Amend: to modify or change the wording of a motion

Assembly: members assembled to transact business

Audit: examination and verification of financial records

Ballot: secret vote or method of voting

Board: members elected or appointed to manage organization affairs between meetings

Bylaws: basic rules of governance of an organization

Chair: one selected to preside and conduct business at meetings

Debate: advocacy argument for or against a proposition

Executive session: a misnomer for closed session where only members may attend

General consent: adoption, with no objection, of a motion with no vote taken on it

General orders: business items placed on the agenda

Germane: relevant to the topic under discussion

Informal consideration: method for considering business without the formal rules of debate

Majority: over half the votes cast

Minority: less than half the votes cast

Nomination: formally naming a member for election or appointment to office

Order of business: adopted schedule of business

Precedence: the rank of motions in the order in which action on them will be taken

Question: a stated motion requiring action by the assembly

Quorum: number of members required at a meeting for action taken to be valid

Ratify: to legally approve action taken without a quorum present

Reconsider: to consider the vote a second time on an adopted or rejected motion

Rescind: to annul a previous decision

Revision: to offer a complete new set of bylaws for consideration by the assembly

Rules of order: adopted by the organization, usually those found in its adopted parliamentary authority

Ruling: the official decision of the presiding officer on parliamentary and procedural matters

Seriatim: in a series, one at a time, consideration by section or paragraph

Special order: motion or topic assigned to a certain time on the agenda which interrupts pending business

Standing rules: rules relating to details of administration, not to procedural rules

Substitute: a form of amendment proposed to replace an entire motion or paragraph that must be germane to it

Suspend the rules: a motion permitting the assembly to set aside temporarily its regular order of business in order to consider a specific matter

Table a motion: used to set aside a motion temporarily, in order to consider some other business; unless taken from the table, it kills the motion set aside

Unfinished business: items scheduled but not completed or reached at adjournment of the previous meeting

▶ SUMMARY

Henry M. Robert once said, "Some knowledge of parliamentary law may be justly regarded as a necessary part of the education of every man and woman, every boy and girl."[7] A basic knowledge of parliamentary procedure permits you to be a participative member in a democratic society and enhances your involvement in organizations or assemblies. Such an understanding is basic to leadership and active membership.

1. Henry M. Robert, *Robert's Rules of Order, Newly Revised* (Glenview, IL: Scott, Foresman, 1981): xxxix.

2. *Robert's Rules of Order* has become a classic standard for many organizations, but alternative rules and procedures have been developed to more effectively meet contemporary needs and purposes. See, for example, Riddick-Butcher, *Riddick's Rules of Procedure* (New York: Scribner's Sons, 1985); Hermon Farwell, *Majority Rules* (Pueblo, CO: High Publishers, 1980); and Ray E. Keesey, *Modern Parliamentary Procedure* (Boston: Houghton Mifflin, 1974).

3. Robert, *Robert's Rules of Order, Newly Revised.*

4. Alice F. Sturgis, *Sturgis Standard Code of Parliamentary Procedure.* (New York: McGraw-Hill, 1951). Also see Alice F. Sturgis, *Learning Parliamentary Procedure* (New York: McGraw-Hill, 1953).

5. George Demeter, *Demeter's Manual of Parliamentary Law and Procedure* (Boston: Little Brown, 1969).

6. American Institute of Parliamentarians, *Parliamentary Law and Procedure, Student Workbook* (Dubuque, IA: Kendall Hunt, 1987): 115–116.

7. Cited in a letter from Leo G. Athans, American Institute of Parliamentarians, Fall 1987.

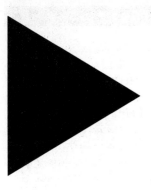

Appendix C: Careers in Communication

The transition from campus to career success is a major transition in your life, and it's only natural and healthy for you to have some anxieties. Where can you find a challenging starting job to use the skills you learned on campus? Where can you find a progressive organization that wants you and will help you reach your career goals? Who will hire you at a salary that lets you live decently and independently. and perhaps pay off some accumulated debts? Will you, in the end, have to settle for an entry job below your expectations?

Fortunately, there are some professional people you can turn to for assistance. Your first visit could be to your college/university placement or career center. Next you might contact alumni or look to national, regional, state, and local professional organizations for assistance (see the sidebox on page C-2). You may also want to visit your state-operated employment development department. There are also private employment agencies. Finally, there are many publications that can assist you, and some of these were noted in Chapter 8 when we discussed selection interviewing.

But more than all such sources combined, you'll have to depend upon yourself. Your career future is in your hands. You should, perhaps more than at any previous time in your life, look to yourself for answers, motivation, and decisions. Your education or training has provided experience in solving problems logically. You have learned how to define a problem, how to break it into manageable components; how to gather and analyze information; how to consider alternative solutions; how to select the best solutions; and finally, how to complete the task by taking some action. The following problem-solving skills come into play primarily as you make decisions about a career prior to starting your actual job search:

- ▶ What are my job interests?
- ▶ What skills do I have to offer?
- ▶ What kind of employer do I want to join?
- ▶ What kind of a job do I want and how would it fit into my lifestyle?

All of these questions and many others are a part of advance career planning. You may already have completed this planning phase and, if so, you're ready to consider some of the types of careers available in communication.

► PROFESSIONAL COMMUNICATION ASSOCIATIONS

Association for Business Communication
Executive Director
Baruch College, 17 Lexington Avenue
New York, NY 10017

International Communication Association
Executive Director
Box 9589
8140 Burnet Road
Austin, TX 78766

International Listening Association
Executive Director
ILA, PO Box 90340
McNeese State University
Lake Charles, LA 70609

Speech Communication Association
Executive Director
5105 Backlick Road, Building E
Annandale, VA 22003

Central States Communication Association*

Eastern Communication Association*

Southern States Communication Association*

Western Communication Association*

*Addresses for these associations change each year as new officers are elected. Check the regularly updated associations directory at your local library.

►SELECTED COMMUNICATION CAREERS

In one sense, communication is a survival skill for any person in any career. The talking–listening interchange is a significant part of business and professional life. Business and professional people spend most of their days in some form of communication: communicating with each other about procedures and problems and relaying information to and receiving it from customers and clients. Success in the business setting is linked to good communication skills. Throughout the text, we have emphasized the importance of communication competencies regardless of career choices. Here, however, we will focus specifically on selected communication careers.

Management

Managers are responsible for planning, coordinating, supervising, and controlling the activities of others. Within the modern organization, there are a number of managerial roles relating to internal communication activities. These include human resource and development specialists, communication analysts, employee representatives, labor relations specialists, and staff consultants. A manager working in internal communication has the following responsibilities:

- Provides consultation, assistance, and guidance to management on matters relating to employee and management communication; coordinates employee communication programs and activities; coordinates publishing of regular employee media; advises, coordinates, and conducts attitudinal and other polls among employees; provides editorial and publishing services; produces, edits, and distributes special publications.
- Develops and maintains informational unit to serve the needs of senior management and the communication department.
- Develops, coordinates, and implements small-group, face-to-face communication programs to facilitate team building, problem identification, and problem solving.[1]

There are also a number of managerial roles relating to external communication activities. The International Communication Association reported the following responsibilities are common among those in external communication positions:

- Is responsible for full range of external public relations activities, from corporate advertising through community, shareholder, financial, and government relations; produces corporate literature, sales promotions, and special publications.
- Directs and coordinates all activity in the development, implementation, and administration of a corporate identification system covering all aspects of visual communication, material, and media.
- Has administrative responsibilities for public relations and development departments.
- Is responsible for internal communication, communication with employees' families, and community relations.
- Plans and directs public information and community relations programs.[2]

External communication roles include public information director, public affairs specialist, public relations supervisor, community relations representative, government relations counselor, press relations coordinator, media relations manager, and field publicity consultant.

Sales/Retailing

Traditionally, the word "sales" carried with it a certain image—the fast-talking, fast-moving person with a ready selection of glib phrases who could "convince an Eskimo to buy an icebox." Today, the expanding area of modern merchandising has changed. Customers need to feel welcome and a salesperson must be able to determine just what they need. Salespeople will use all of their communication skills when giving information to customers and answering their questions. And they must contribute to the impression of a store staffed by interested, friendly people who care about customers' needs and can provide them with merchandise. Communication skills are of primary importance for retail sales.

Mass Media

The mass media arena is particularly open to those with developed communication competencies. Included here are positions in publishing, print journalism, radio, television, advertising, and marketing. People may work as editors, writers, copyright specialists, book designers, reporters, directors, or producers. They are responsible for the development and production of books, magazines, and newspapers. They gather, coordinate, and interpret the news. They electronically mainstream ideas, inform, and entertain. It is a challenging and highly competitive area of activity. Internships and externships, discussed later, can be useful for those interested in entering the media arena.

Social Work

There are many areas of social work that require considerable communication competency. Positions that communicate with government departments, private social agencies, and community groups are but a few. For the social work practitioner the communication effort requires a patient kind of receptive and concerned awareness, an in-depth desire to communicate, and the combined sense of timing and skill necessary to reach the person seeking help. It is the depth and quality of the communication taking place that sets the foundation for the kind of relationship necessary to help people better understand their problems from a new perspective. People in these positions serve as family counselors, drug/alcohol counselors, therapists, adolescent specialists, and career consultants. The field of social work really *is* communication, and there is obviously much that the communication discipline can contribute.

Education

Those seeking a career in education must consider professional certification and advanced degrees. Those with communication backgrounds teach primarily at the secondary level or in junior college, community college, and college and university settings. Job responsibilities include instructional design and development, presentation of educational materials, evaluation of student performance, and individual counseling and guidance. Being flexible and adaptable, thinking critically, solving problems logically, developing a system of values, recognizing the need for continuing education, and seeing the need to become participating members of society— these are the student goals sought by those in education.

Law

A communication background can be excellent preparation for those intending to pursue legal careers. The fundamental nature of the lawyer's work can best be described as that of communication. The personal communication competencies that should characterize the prospective lawyer are: relational competencies, listening competencies, speaking competencies, questioning competencies, decision-making and problem-solving competencies, and competencies in handling conflict. Lawyers must think through, organize, and structure arguments; must ask questions that are precise, clear, and connected; and must recognize and creatively deal with interpersonal, group, and organizational conflicts. Consequently, communication education merits high priority in pre-law preparation and training.

Law Enforcement

Law enforcement officers must be skilled communicators who are able to tolerate stress, resolve problems quickly, and be flexible in difficult interpersonal situations.

They must be skilled in interviewing and able to speak before public and civic groups. In addition, law enforcement requires exceptional listening skills and a genuine sensitivity to cultural diversity. Richard Cheatham and Keith Erickson observe that "communication is vital in law enforcement. Effective communication allows one to minimize misunderstanding and to conduct enforcement duties and responsibilities effectively. Ineffective communication erects unnecessary barriers between those who enforce the law and those protected by it."[3]

Mediator/Arbitrator

Mediation and arbitration, intervention mechanisms that suit many types of conflict, are particularly effective for disputes between people who are involved in ongoing relationships. Management and labor who are dependent upon one another to accomplish organizational goals, neighbors who cannot move out of the neighborhood, and families whose members want to maintain some relationship are all groups of people who need to reach agreement because they must deal with each other in the future. The most effective mediators and arbitrators are people who are good listeners, are patient, and have a tolerance for conflict.

Medicine/Healthcare

Medicine or healthcare is the burgeoning field of the 1990s and will likely continue to be so well into the year 2000. Physicians, technicians, and nurses must be able to communicate effectively with patients; counselors are needed to communicate with the terminally ill and assist in caring for the elderly. Many hospitals, clinics, and wellness centers are using ombudsmen to interface with the administrators, the medical staff, patients, and the community. These people help the healthcare unit heal itself and be responsive to the needs of those it serves.

Research

Research specialists collect and evaluate data from focus group interviews, polls, and surveys. They administer research projects, and organize conferences, symposia, and meetings. Research directors, coordinators, and analysts are found in both the private and public sectors.

Consulting

Consultants help organizations identify problems, evaluate performance, find problem solutions, and implement a wide variety of change activities. They help clients plan, organize, and measure the effectiveness of training programs. Communication consultants work with employees, managers, executives, and key publics. Graduate degrees and extensive work experience are needed for consulting positions.

Speechwriters

We live in a world of talk—talk that influences our lives. Speechwriters are responsible for much of this activity, working in both the political and business spheres, ghostwriting speeches for politicians and executives. Knowledge of rhetoric, speak-

▶ UNDERGRADUATE DEGREES IN COMMUNICATION INCREASE

By James W. Chesebro

Overviews of the health and well-being of the discipline of communication can be particularly useful. A national view of the discipline can be useful when justifying the creation or continuation of communication departments. Or, a national perspective can be important when justifying the creation of new programs, majors, or minors within communication departments. Additionally, a national overview can be helpful when justifying existing or new faculty, adjunct, or teaching assistant positions. Finally, it is frequently necessary to compare the growth and development of the discipline of communication to other disciplines.

Yet, national, comprehensive and reliable views of the discipline of communication are difficult to secure. For fifteen years, the U.S. Department of Education has annually published its compilation of the number of degrees conferred by all academic disciplines. The number of degrees annually awarded by each discipline has been used by the Education Department to compare and contrast disciplines.

The discipline of communication is included in these Education Department tabulations. For example, based upon the number of degrees granted between 1975 through 1985, the Education Department concluded that the discipline of communication was the "sixth" fastest growing of the 30 fields tracked, reporting that the discipline experienced a "122 percent increase" from 1975 through 1985.

The Education Department has recently released its most current compilation of degrees conferred in the discipline of communications. This essay summarizes these results and offers interpretative conclusions regarding the findings.

At the completion of the 1987–1988 academic year, the latest year for which such data are available, the discipline of communication conferred 46,705 bachelor degrees in all areas of communication.

During the last fifteen years, from 1973–74 through 1987–88, the number of bachelor degrees conferred in all areas of the discipline of communication has increased by 173 percent, from 17,096 to 46,705.

On a year-to-year basis, the number of bachelor degrees conferred in all areas of communication has consistently increased. On the average, from 1973–74 through 1987– 88, the number of bachelor degrees conferred in all areas of communication has increased at an annual rate of 7.4 percent. The largest rate of increase of 12.7 percent was recorded from 1981–82 to 1982–83. The lowest rate of increase of 2.3 percent was recorded from 1984–85 to 1985–86.

In terms of the Education Department's classification of the discipline of communication, the five most popular areas for bachelor degrees in communication were: (1) "Com-

munications, general" which includes "speech and rhetorical studies," "communication disorders," "speech teacher education," and "acting and directing," for a total of 21,337 degrees or 45.6 percent of all communication degrees; (2) "Journalism," for a total of 11,060 degrees or 23.6 percent of all communication degrees; (3) "Radio/TV, general," for a total of 5,370 degrees or 11.4 percent of all communication degrees; (4) "Other" which includes degrees in non-Education Department categories, for a total of 2,368 degrees or 5.0 percent; and (5) "Radio/TV technology," for a total of 1,943 degrees or 4.1 percent.

At the completion of the 1987–1988 academic year, the discipline of communication conferred 3,932 masters degrees and 236 Ph.D.s in all areas of communication.

During the last fifteen years, from 1973–74 through 1978–88, the number of masters degrees conferred in all areas of communication increased by 48.9 percent, from 2,640 to 3,932. During the same period, the number of Ph.D.s conferred in all areas of communication increased to 34.8 percent, from 175–236.

In terms of the Education Department's classification of the discipline of communication, the three most popular areas for masters degrees in communication were: (1) "Communications, general" which includes "speech and rhetorical studies," "communication disorders," "speech teacher education," and "acting and directing," for a total of 1,440 degrees or 36.6 percent of all communications degrees; (2) "Journalism," for a total of 1,021 degrees or 25.9 percent of all communication degrees; and (3) "Other" which includes degrees in non-Education Department categories, for a total of 595 degrees or 15.1 percent.

Duplicating the interests of masters degree students, but with a stronger interest in "Communication, general," the three most popular areas for Ph.D.s were (1) "Communications, general" which includes "speech and rhetorical studies," "communication disorders," "speech teacher education," and "acting and directing," for a total of 167 degrees or 70.7 percent of all communication degrees; (2) "Journalism," for a total of 20 degrees or 8.4 percent of all communication degrees; and (3) "Other" which includes degrees in non-Education Department categories, for a total of 16 degrees or 6.7 percent.

Conclusions

Based upon these data, two major conclusions are highlighted here.

1. *In terms of undergraduate students, the discipline of communication has experienced an unusually rapid growth*

when compared to other disciplines. During the last fifteen years, undergraduate students have been attracted to the study of communication, communication courses, and degrees in communication in ever-increasing numbers.

At the same time, a note of caution should be mentioned. Disciplines can gain popularity among undergraduate students, but they can also peak and ultimately decline if measured by the preferences of undergraduate students.

If the last 15 years are examined in five year blocks, the *percentage rate* of increase in bachelor degrees granted in communication has slowed, indicating a relatively modest increase in the number of students being added to the growing pool of students receiving undergraduate degrees in communication. From 1973–74 through 1977–78, the average rate of increase in bachelor degrees granted in all areas of communication was 10.3 percent; from 1978–89 through 1982–83, the average rate of increase was 8.7 percent; and, from 1983–84 through 1987–88, the average rate of increase was 4.6 percent.

It should, however, be noted that for the last fifteen years, without exception, the number of bachelor degrees granted in all areas of communication has increased every year. Additionally, as a percentage of all bachelor degrees granted in all disciplines, the discipline of communication has exerted an increasingly important role. In 1973–74, the discipline of communication awarded 1.8 percent of all bachelor degrees granted by all disciplines. In 1987–88,

the discipline of communication awarded 4.7 percent of all bachelor degrees granted by all disciplines.

2. *The number of masters and Ph.D. degrees granted in communication have not kept pace with the increasing rate of bachelor degrees conferred in communication.* During the last fifteen years, the number of bachelor degrees granted in communication have risen at two to three times the rate of masters and Ph.D. degrees granted in communication.

From a pedagogical perspective, the pool of new instructors with advanced degrees is declining compared to the ever-increasing body of undergraduate students in communication. The disparity between student demand and faculty supply can be met in any number of ways, such as increasing class sizes, reducing the number of courses available, having retired faculty return to teach a limited number of courses, hiring adjuncts with advanced degrees in other disciplines, and so forth. For many, these alternatives may not be satisfying.

An alternative mechanism may be to reinvigorate the masters and Ph.D. programs in the discipline of communication. It may be desirable to devise strategies which more effectively channel outstanding undergraduate students directly into advanced degree programs in communication. The data may also provide a rationale for increasing the total number of masters and Ph.D. programs in the discipline of communication in the U.S.

Source: James W. Chesebro, "Undergraduate Degrees in Communication Increase," *Spectra* (October 1991): 1–2. Used by permission of the Speech Communication Association.

ers and issues, public address, persuasion theory, and audience analysis is critical for those in such careers. The increasing demand for public figures to address concerned constituencies is contributing to a renewed interest in speechwriters.

The career areas explored here are just some of the available opportunities. As you engage in your own search, additional career paths will likely unfold. We hope this brief discussion will assist in your transition to the work world by raising some of the possibilities for careers in communication.

▶ INTERNSHIPS, EXTERNSHIPS AND SHADOWING PROGRAMS

In keeping with procedures established in business, public administration, political science, journalism, and broadcasting, the communication discipline has developed internship programs to provide its majors with practicum opportunities for which academic credit is given. These internships can serve several functions. First, they can integrate theory and research. Second, they can give students practical experience before graduation, allowing them to explore job-related opportunities and establish valuable contacts for future job placement. Finally, they can provide new opportunities for university–community relations.

Community assistantships in communication are similar to internships but designed for graduate students. The development as well as the guidelines and operations of such programs parallel those of communication internships. The major policy difference is that, because of their advanced education and experience, those participating in community assistantships are paid a regular salary. These assistantships have the same value and benefits as internships.

Not all undergraduate or graduate field training need be as formal as intern- or assistantships. Douglass College at Rutgers State University and Ohio University at Athens offer externships—unpaid opportunities for students to spend a week with an alumnus in a career-related area, observing, asking questions, becoming job oriented. Externships offer a number of benefits: students are exposed to their potential career/field of work in a neutral, nonthreatening fashion; alumni interact with students and provide an opportunity to help/share in a non-fundraising manner; valuable contacts are made for both participating students and the college or university. At the graduate level a number of colleges and universities have instituted shadowing programs that operate similarly to externships with the same benefits.

►CAREER EDUCATION AND INTERNSHIPS: A SELECTED BIBLIOGRAPHY

Alexander, E. R. III. "Creating and Maintaining Operative Work Experience Programs: A Student's Perspective." *ACA Bulletin* 22 (April 1975): 26–27.

Amherst College. *The Student Guide to Fellowships and Internships.* New York: E. P. Dutton, 1980.

Argyris, C., and D. A. Schon. *Theory in Practice: Increasing Professional Effectiveness.* San Francisco: Jossey-Bass, 1974.

Arnold, W. "Career Placement in Speech Communication." *ACA Bulletin* 13 (August 1975): 3–16.

Attaway, T. "Career Option Awareness." *ACA Bulletin* 21 (August 1977): 76–79.

Bartoletti, M. D., and E. G. Stark. "Hands-On Mediation Training in a Private-Practice Setting." *ACA Bulletin* 81 (April 1991): 384.

Benjamin, J. B. "Strategies for Finding the Job: Criteria for Selecting a Position." *ACA Bulletin* 34 (October 1980): 84–86.

Benjamin, J. B. and M. L. Williams. "The Development and Administration of an Organizational Communication Internship Program." *Texas Speech Communication Journal* 7 (1981): 7–11.

Berryman-Frank, C. "Communication Instruction in a Lifelong Learning Program. *Communication Education* 31 (October 1982): 349–355.

Blankenship, J. "Skills Required of SCA Members Who Hold Jobs in Business, Industry, Government, and Social Science Settings." *ACA Bulletin* 35 (January 1981): 58–61.

Bowers, J. W., J. Gilchrist, and L. Browning. "A Communication Course for High-Powered Bargainers: Development and Effects." *Communication Education* 29 (January 1980): 10–20.

Braden, W. W. "From the Quill to the Computer: A Traditionalist Examines a Career-Oriented Program." *ACA Bulletin* 27 (January 1979): 28–30.

Calın, D. "Toward an Understanding of Successful Career Placement by Undergraduate Speech Communication Departments." *ACA Bulletin* 30 (October 1979): 46–53.

Calvin, K., and J. Muchmore. "Special Report: Career Education: A Challenge." *Central States Speech Journal* 23 (Spring 1972): 61–63.

Ciofalo, A. "Legitimacy of Internships for Academic Credit Remains Controversial." *The Journalism Educator* 43 (1989): 25.

Conaway, R. N. "A Meta-Perspective on Business Communication Survey Research." *Proceedings of the Association for Business Communication–SW* (1991): 127–134.

Conaway, R. N. "Communication Needs of Business Graduates: What Do Our Publications Reflect?" *Proceedings of the Association for Business Communication–SE* (1989): 103–109.

Courtney, L. W. "Speech in Community Life." *Southern Speech Communication Journal* 15 (March 1950): 219–221.

Dahle, T. "Public Speaking for Public Officials." *Communication Quarterly* 11 (February 1963): 19–20.

DeWine, S., and W. Eadie. "Credentialling Standards for the Communication Specialist." *ACA Bulletin* 29 (August 1979): 16–19.

DiSalvo, V. "A Summary of Current Research Identifying Communication Skills in Various Organizational Contexts." *Communication Education* 29 (1980) 283–290.

DiSalvo, V., D. Larsen, and W. Seiler. "Communication Skills Needed by Persons in Business Organizations." *Communication Education* 25 (November 1976): 269–275.

Downs, C. W. "Internships in Organizational Communication." *ACA Bulletin* 22 (April 1975): 30–32.

Downs, C. W., P. Harper, and G. Hunt. "Internships in Speech Communication." *Communication Education* 25 (November 1966): 276–282.

Duley, J. "Basic Skills for Experiential Learning: What Skills Do Students Need to Make the Most of Experiential Learning Opportunities?" *Papers on Learning and Teaching, No. 75.* East Lansing, MI: Learning and Evaluation Service, Michigan State University, 1978.

Duley, J. *Learning Outcomes: The Measurement and Evaluation of Experiential Education.* Panel Resource Paper #6. Raleigh, NC: National Society for Internships and Experiential Education, 1982.

Erickson, K. V., T. R. Cheatham, and C. Haggard. "A Survey of Police Communication Training." *Communication Education* 25 (November 1976): 299–306.

Femmel, R. "Why Not Make Internships Mandatory for Everyone?" *Journalism Educator* (October 1978).

Fisher, M. A. "Developing Diversity: Bringing More Minorities into Advancement Through Internships." *Currents* 18 (April 1991): 14.

Fitch-Hauser, M., and S. B. Padgett. "Long Distance Supervision of Internships." *ACA Bulletin* 75 (January 1991): 68.

Fry, R. W. *Internships.* Hawthorne, NJ: Career Press, 1988.

Gartrell, R. B. "Career Education and the Communication Profession: A Central States Impact Survey." *Central States Speech Journal* 27 (Summer 1976): 155–157.

Gaske, P. C., C. R. Lassater, and J. A. Stewart. "Speech Communication and Public Relations: Problems and Prospects." *ACA Bulletin* 26 (1978): 37–38.

Goetzinger, C., and M. Valentine. "Business and Professional Communications Training Programs." *Communication Quarterly* 11 (November 1963): 10–11.

Graduate Group. *Internships in Law, Politics and Medicine.* West Hartford, CT: The Group, 1985.

Gross, L. *The Internship Experience.* Prospect Heights, IL: Waveland Press, 1981.

Hall, J. "Panel—A Resource for Internship Development." *ACA Bulletin* 49 (August 1984): 76–77.

Hanna, M. S. "Speech Communication Training Needs in the Business Community." *Central States Speech Journal* 29 (Fall 1978): 163–172.

Hanson, J. "Internships and the Individual: Suggestions for Implementing (or Improving) an Internship Program." *Communication Education* 33 (1984): 53–61.

Harper, N. L. "Promoting the Department to Outside Agencies: What Do Communication Students Know and What Can They Do?" *ACA Bulletin* 39 (1982) 8–13.

Harper, P., R. Bates, and J. Hughey. "Extension Programs in Speech Communication: Departmental Involvement and the Reward System." *ACA Bulletin* 39 (January 1982): 52–58.

Harris, T. E., and D. T. Thomlison. "Career-Bound Communication Education: A Needs Analysis." *Central States Speech Journal* 34 (Winter 1983): 260–267.

Haskins, W. A. "Internships in Communication." *Journal of the Wisconsin Communication Association* 10 (1980).

Heath, R. L. "Corporate Advocacy: An Application of Speech Communication Perspectives and Skills." *Communication Education* 29 (September 1980): 370–377.

Heath, R. L. "Employer Images of Speech Communication Majors: A Question of Employability." *ACA Bulletin* 15 (1976): 14–17.

Heathington, M. "The Importance of Oral Communication." *College Education* 44 (1982): 570–574.

Hellweg, S., and R. Falcione. *Internships in the Communication Arts and Sciences.* Phoenix: Gorsuch Scarishrick Publishers, 1985.

Hendrix, J. "Recycling a Traditional Speech Communication Program for Non-Academic Career Preparation." *ACA Bulletin* 27 (January 1979): 26–27.

Hite, R. "A Career Alternative for Communication Professionals: Education and Training in the Health Care Field." *ACA Bulletin* 18 (October 1976): 10–13.

Holley, D. "A Survey of Communication Majors After Graduation: Implications for More Realistic Career Counseling." *ACA Bulletin* 34 (October 1980): 49–54.

Hollingsworth, P. "The Case for Interns." *Folio* (June 1990): 131–132.

Hollwitz, J., and E. Matthiesen. "Communication and Productivity: A Rationale for Speech Education in Industry." *ACA Bulletin* 38 (October 1981): 45–48.

Huseman, R. C. "Work Experience Programs for Speech Communication Students: A Time for Increased Emphasis." *ACA Bulletin* 12 (April 1975): 21–22.

Hutchings, P., and A. Wutzdorff. *Knowing and Doing: Learning Through Experience. New Directions for Teaching and Learning, No. 35.* San Francisco: Jossey-Bass, 1988.

Hyre, J. M. Jr,. and A. W. Owens. "Interns: The Ivory Tower at Work." *Communication Education* 33 (October 1984): 371–376.

Internships: The Guide to On-the-Job Training Opportunities for Students and Adults, 12th ed. Princeton, NJ: Peterson's Guides, 1992.

Isenhart, M. W. "An Investigation of the Interface Between Corporate Leadership Needs and the Outward Bound Experience." *Communication Education* 32 (January 1983): 123–129.

Jamieson, K., and A. Wolvin. "Non-Teaching Careers in Communication: Implications for the Speech Communication Curriculum." *Communication Education* 25 (November 1976): 283–291.

Jenks, C. L., and C. J. Murphy. *A Sampler of Experiential Courses*. San Francisco: Far West Laboratory for Educational Research and Development, 1981.

Jobst, K. *1987 Internships: 35,000 On-the-Job Training Opportunities for College Students and Adults*. Cincinnati, OH: Writer's Digest Books, 1987.

Jobst, K. *1988 Internships: 38,000 On-the-Job Training Opportunities for College Students and Adults*. Cincinnati, OH: Writer's Digest Books, 1987.

Jobst, K. *1989 Internships: 38,000 On-the-Job Training Opportunities for College Students and Adults*. Cincinnati, OH: Writer's Digest Books, 1988.

Jobst, K., and B. C. Rushing. *1990 Internships: 38,000 On-the-Job Training Opportunities for Students and Adults*. Cincinnati, OH: Writer's Digest Books, 1989.

Johnson, E. "Groups with a Future: In a New Communication System." *Journal of Communication* 5 (Fall 1955): 89–101.

Johnson, J. "Training and Development: A Career Alternative." *ACA Bulletin* 50 (October 1984): 45–49.

Kaupins, G. E. "Ideas for Integrating Organization Behavior into Internships." *Organizational Behavior Teaching Review* 14 (1990): 39.

Keenan, K. L. "Student Internships in Undergraduate Advertising Education." *Journalism Educator* 47 (1992): 48.

Keeton, M., and Tate, J. *New Directions for Experiential Learning: Learning by Experience—What, Why, How, No. 1*, San Francisco: Jossey-Bass, 1978.

Kendall, J. C. *A Guide to Environmental Internships: How Environmental Organizations Can Utilize Internships Effectively*. Raleigh, NC: National Society for Internships and Experiential Education, 1984.

Kessler, M. "Communicating Within and Without: The Work of Communication Specialists in American Corporations." *ACA Bulletin* 35 (January 1981): 45–50.

Kolb, D., and R. Fry. "Toward an Applied Theory of Experiential Learning." In: C. Cooper, ed. *Theories of Group Process*. New York: John Wiley & Sons, 1975.

Konsky, C. "Internships in Speech Communication: A National Survey and Commentary." *ACA Bulletin* 41 (August 1982): 39–51.

Konsky, C. "Practical Guide to Development and Administration of an Internship Program: Issues, Procedures, Forms. *ACA Bulletin* 22 (October 1977): 15–28.

MacDaniels, J. "Designing Communication Curricula for Job Success." *ACA Bulletin* 34 (October 1980): 49–54.

Matlon, R. J. "Bridging the Gap Between Communication Education and Legal Education." *Communication Education* 31 (January 1982): 39–53.

McBath, J. "Career Development and Speech Communication." *ACA Bulletin* 26 (October 1978): 34–36.

McCroskey, J. C. "Applied Graduate Education: An Alternative for the Future." *Communication Education* 28 (September 1979): 353–358.

Meister, J. E., and N. L. Reinsch, Jr. "Communication Training in Manufacturing Firms." *Communication Education* 27 (September 1978): 235–244.

Metro United Way. *Metro United Way Internship Program*. Louisville, KY: Metro United Way, 1985.

Mier, D. "Learning the Art of Management Through the Art of Oral Reading." *Communication Education* 32 (July 1983): 293–301.

Migliore, S. A. *The National Directory of Internships*. Raleigh, NC: National Society for Internships and Experiential Education, 1987.

Moore, D. T. *Students at Work: Identifying Learning in Internship Settings*. Occasional Paper #5. Raleigh, NC: National Society for Internships and Experiential Education, 1982.

Morse, B., and R. Vogel. "How Can the Speech Communication Discipline Best Meet the Needs of the Vocational Student." *ACA Bulletin* 21 (August 1977): 76–79.

Muchmore, J. "The Community College and Career Communications: An Unlimited Opportunity." *ACA Bulletin* 13 (August 1975): 60–62.

Muchmore, J., and K. Galvin. "A Report of the Task Force on Career Competencies in Oral Communication Skills for Community College Students Seeking Immediate Entry Into the Work Force." *Communication Education* 32 (1983): 207–220.

Newman, G. "Teaching the Basic Speech Course With Career Orientation: An Affirmative Case." *ACA Bulletin* 13 (August 1975): 45–46.

Oritz, J. "The Community Service Class at the Small College: A Medium for Discovery." *ACA Bulletin* 54 (October 1985): 65–66.

O'Connell, S., and R. L. Minker. "The Role of Faculty in Career Counseling: Can You Wear Another Hat?" *ACA Bulletin* 35 (1981): 51–53.

Parker, C. A. "Cooperative Education for Speech Majors." *ACA Bulletin* 22 (October 1977): 15–28.

Patton, P. L. "Testing the Water: A Survey on HRD Internships." *Training and Development Journal* 42 (October 1988): 48.

Penrose, J. M. "A Survey of the Perceived Importance of Business Communication and Other Business-Related Abilities." *Journal of Business Communication* 13 (1976): 17–24.

Permaul, J. S. *Monitoring and Supporting Experiential Learning*. Panel Paper #5. Raleigh, NC: National Society for Internships and Experiential Education, 1982.

Permaul, J. S., and M. B. Miko. *Documentation and Evaluation of Sponsored Experiential Learning*. Princeton, NJ: CAEL Educational Testing Service, 1976.

Piersal, D. "Responsibility for Career Training." *ACA Bulletin* 6 (January 1974): 22–24.

Porterfield, C. "The Work Experience Program in the Department of Speech at Appalachian State University." *ACA Bulletin* 22 (April 1975): 28–29.

Pound, G. "Dual Responsibility: Career Training and General Education." *ACA Bulletin* 6 (January 1974): 27–29.

Renetzky, A., and G. Schachter. *Directory of Internships, Work Experience Programs and On-the-Job Training Opportunities*. Thousand Oaks, CA: Ready Reference Press, 1976.

Richmond, V., and J. Daly. "Extension Eduction: An Almost Inexhaustible Job Market for Communication Graduates." *ACA Bulletin* 11 (January 1975): 6–8.

Romano, B. "A 'Communi-Site-Ed' Approach to Basic Speech." *ACA Bulletin* 15 (January 1976): 21–23.

Ruiz, J., and S. Vandermeer. "Internships: High Returns on Low Investments—The Benefits of Internships Can Be Realized by Both Individuals and Local Governments." *Public Management* 71 (1989): 16.

Rushing, B. C. *1990 Internships: 35,000 On-the-Job Training Opportunites for All Types of Careers*. Cincinnati, OH: Writer's Digest Books, 1990.

Rushing, B. C. *1991 Internships: 50,000 On-the-Job Training Opportunities for Students and Adults*. Princeton, NJ: Peterson's Guides, 1991.

Sanborn, G. A. "Business Internships." *ACA Bulletin* 22 (April 1975): 23–25.

Schmidt, W. V. "Trainers: Who They Are, What They Think." *Training* (1979): 18.

Schuelke, F. D. "Types of Positions Available in Business and Government for the Graduate in Communication." *ACA Bulletin* 18 (1976): 14–16.

Scott, A., and V. Bowen. "Publishers and Students Favor Summer Internship Plan." *Journalism Quarterly* 26 (June 1949): 197–199.

Scott, M. E. "Internships Add Value to College Recruitment." *Personnel Journal* 71 (April 1992): 59.

Sexton, R. F. *Dimensions of Experimental Education.* Washington, D.C.: National Center for Public Service Internship Programs, 1976.

Simmons, G. "Serendipity of Summer Internships." *Journalism Quarterly* 33 (Fall 1956): 517–520.

Smith, D. *Great Careers: The Fourth of July Guide to Careers.* Garrett Park, MD: Garrett Park Press, 1990.

Spicer, C. "Identifying the Communication Specialist: Implications for Career Education." *Communication Education* 28 (May 1979): 188–198.

Spivey, C., S. Mitchell, R. Jones, and R. Berko. "A Basic Speech Communication Course for Community College Technical Career Students: A Structural Design." *Communication Quarterly* 23 (Summer 1975): 15–18.

Student Guide to Co-Op/Internships. ERIC ED 196 477. Bloomington, IN: Education Resources Information Center, 1980.

Student Interns in the Public Sector. ERIC ED 154 663. Bloomington, IN: Education Resources Information Center, 1976.

Town, M., and L. Meeks. "The Non-Traditional College Student: Continuing Education Programs." *ACA Bulletin* 49 (August 1984): 71–72.

Trent, J. S., and J. D. Trent. "Public Relations Education: An Opportunity for Speech Communication." *Communication Education* 25 (November 1976): 292–298.

Twiname-Dungan, M., and B. Schnettler. "College Interns: School and Agency Partnership." *Journal of Volunteer Administration* (1985): 11–22.

Wasylik, J., L. Sussman, and R. Leri. "Communication Training as Perceived by Training Personnel." *Communication Quarterly* 24 (Winter 1976): 32–44.

Weitzel, A. R. "Teaching Career Communication." *ACA Bulletin* 38 (October 1981): 58-61.

Weitzel, A. R., and Paul Gaske. "An Appraisal of Communication Career-Related Research." *Communication Education* 33 (April 1984): 181–194.

Where to Look: A Sourcebook on Undergraduate Internships. ERIC ED 129 173. Bloomington, IN: Education Resources Information Center, 1976.

Whiterabbit, J. "Internships: Education and Practical Experience in the Workplace." *Winds of Change* 7 (Winter 1992): 49.

Wilson, G. L. "Internship Programs: Managing a Communication Learning Laboratory." *ACA Bulletin* 31 (January 1980): 60–61.

Witham, M., and T. Stanton. *Prefield Preparation: What, Why, How.* Panel Resource Paper #4. Raleigh, NC: National Society for Internships and Experiential Education, 1979.

Wolvin, A. D. "New Directions for Careers in Communication." *ACA Bulletin* 35 (January 1981): 54–57.

Wood, J. "Implementing a Field Approach in Teaching Communication Skills." *ACA Bulletin* 36 (April 1981): 47–55.

▶ SUMMARY

The transition from campus to a career role of responsibility may continue for a number of years. It often takes the recent graduate a few months or longer to land the best entry-level job available, and then a much longer time to earn a position with authority and meaning. Most starting jobs can and should be considered internships to the more responsible positions that lie ahead. You probably won't feel you have really arrived as far as your career is concerned until you have:

1. Earned a position important enough to give you a strong feeling of accomplishment and identity.

2. Held down a position that has some degree of responsibility and influence within the organization.

3. Moved up in your organization to the level where you are making sufficient income to live the lifestyle you had in mind when you started.

This will take time—of course, most graduates don't move into such positions as quickly as they would like. But with experience, training, and continued education, you can build a positive image of someone ready for and capable of assuming responsibility. Be patient and your dreams will be realized.

▶ NOTES

1. C. Petrice, E. Thompson, D. Rogers, and G. Goldhaber, *Report of the Ad Hoc Committee on Manpower Resources* (Report presented to a meeting of Division IV of the International Communication Association, Chicago, 1975).

2. Ibid.

3. T. Richard Cheatham and Keith V. Erickson, *The Police Officer's Guide to Better Communication* (Glenview, IL: Scott, Foresman, 1984): 3–4.

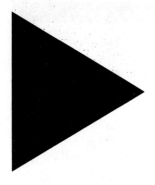

Indexes

Subject Index